Preface

The law relating to or affecting social work practice seems to be in a constant state of flux. A large number of changes have taken place in the period since the second edition was published and even as this preface is being written there are intimations of further significant changes[1] quite apart from those which are already likely, some of which are anticipated in the final chapter of the text. Changes have involved not only changes in law, but also changes in the policy and practice background, for example the development of Getting it Right for Every Child, the development of a variety of themes following on from the *Changing Lives* Report, for example personalisation, and the increasing amount of joint working undertaken by social work and other agencies. Guidance in many areas has been revised (though often leaving a variety of different guidance on the same topic which is not always easy to reconcile).

The rationale for the text continues to be to include a broad selection of topics which comprise the core of the subject and to offer some pointers to more in depth coverage elsewhere. The main aim is to enable the reader to gain an understanding of the legal framework within which social work is practised in Scotland, and to facilitate the acquisition or review of specific legal knowledge necessary to make sense of most day-to-day social work practice. I have also sought to refer, to a more limited extent, to guidance on the implementation of various statutes in order to better explain what the law might mean in practice and also because failure to comply with guidance may be a basis for challenging decisions and actions taken by social workers.

A secondary aim is to provide one text which covers the most commonly encountered areas of law for social workers in Scotland in a way which will serve as a ready reference. Often there is confusion about what is law, what is policy, what are procedures, and what is the status of each, and so another aim is to clarify the law and its status and thus distinguish the law from policy and procedures.

I am very grateful to Frances for (amongst many other things) reading the text and making many helpful suggestions, the responsibility for any errors and infelicities in expression remains, of course, mine. Thanks

1 '38,000 council workers facing a switch to NHS', *The Herald*, 2 February 2011, discussing plans to transfer staff providing community care services to the NHS.

are also due to Veronica and Madeleine for their support and understanding. I also owe a debt to Janet Fabb, it was a pleasure working with her on the first two editions and some of her perspective, I hope, remains in this edition.

I have attempted to state the law and practice issues as at January 2011, though changes due to take place in February and April 2011 have been anticipated and some changes taking place further into the future are also identified.

Where I refer to particular sections of Acts of Parliament I have referred only to the section of the original or principal Act. Readers should be aware that in many cases the provisions of the original Act will have been subsequently amended; for the sake of simplicity I have not referred to the amending legislation.

Tom Guthrie
February 2011

A note on finding law

It has become easier to access legal materials via the internet in the last couple of years.

All new legislation, as well as legislation dating back to 1988 and some older legislation can be found at www.legislation.gov.uk. This site gives access not only to Acts of Parliament, but also to statutory instruments. Older legislation has been updated to some extent, but unfortunately not all amendments are incorporated into the legislation here, though they are noted.

More recent English cases, as well as High Court and Court of Session cases, are often cited using neutral citation, which identifies the year the court and the case number, for example [2010] CSOH 1 – case number 1 in the Outer House of the Court of Session in 2010. Aside from CSOH, other abbreviations which will be found in the text are CSIH – Court of Session Inner House; EWCA Civ – Court of Appeal (England & Wales) Civil Division; EWHC (Admin) – High Court (England & Wales) Administrative Court; and, EWHC (Fam) – High Court (England & Wales) Family Division. The British and Irish Legal Information Institute maintains a database of judgements (www.bailii.org) and Scottish judgements are available via www.scotcourts.gov.uk.

Social Work Law in Scotland

Third Edition

Tom Guthrie
Professor of Private Law, University of Glasgow

Bloomsbury Professional

Bloomsbury Professional Limited, Maxwelton House, 41–43 Boltro Road, Haywards Heath, West Sussex, RH16 1BJ

A CIP Catalogue record for this book is available from the British Library.

ISBN: 978 184766 165 4

Typeset by Phoenix Photosetting, Chatham, Kent
Printed and bound in Great Britain by
CPI Group (UK) Ltd, Croydon, CR0 4YY

Contents

Preface v
Table of cases xi
Table of statutes xxv
Table of statutory instruments xxxv
Table of guidance, circulars, etc xli
Tables of international materials li
Further reading liii
Abbreviations lvii

Chapter 1 The Scottish legal context of social work **1**
Introduction 1
The functions of law in society 4
Law and social problems 5
The distinctive character of Scots law 6
Formal sources of law 7
Rights, powers and duties 11
Legal personnel 13
Civil court system and procedures 16
Criminal court system and procedures 19
Evidence 27
Children's hearings 34
Tribunals 34
Challenging local authority decisions 34
Legal aid 36
Human rights 38
The Social Work (Scotland) Act 1968 42
The Children (Scotland) Act 1995 45
Further statutory changes 46
Exclusions from social work services 46

Chapter 2 General law relevant to social work **49**
Introduction 49
Housing 50
Debt recovery 68
Discrimination 74
Information, confidentiality and sharing 84
Education 107

Chapter 3 Children and their families **109**
The responsibilities, rights and powers of parents and children 109
Legally recognised relationships 119
Adoption 125
Occupancy rights 140
Measures directed at domestic violence 142

Chapter 4 Local authority services to children **147**
Introduction 147
Getting it right for every child 148
The core components of GIRFEC 149
Services for children in need 152
Children 'looked after' by the local authority 167
Placement of looked after children 179
Private fostering 190
Secure accommodation 192
Parental responsibilities orders 196
After-care 196
Challenging decisions 199

Chapter 5 Children in need of supervision or emergency protection **201**
Introduction 201
Overriding principles governing decisions by the court or hearing 205
Children in need of compulsory measures of supervision 206
Schedule 1 Offences 213
Offences against children under the age of 17 years to which special provisions apply 213
Referrals from the court system 235
Court orders sending children to local authority accommodation 236
Emergency protection of children 237
Exclusion orders 245
Short-term refuges 247
Human rights 248
Appendix 253

Chapter 6 Community care **257**
Background 257
What are community care services? 259
Assessment 261

Key principles in single shared assessment 264
Provision of services 266
Charging for services 274
Challenging decisions 280

Chapter 7 Incapacity **283**
Background 283
Local authority functions and relevant organisations 286
The meaning of 'Incapacity' 287
Principles governing intervention in the lives of adults with incapacity 289
Mechanisms for taking decisions on behalf of an adult provided by the 2000 Act 293
Provision of services to adults with incapacity 312

Chapter 8 Mental health **317**
Introduction 317
Local authority duties 323
Compulsory treatment 326
Suspension of detention 344
Nurse's power to detain 345
Medical treatment 345
Social circumstances reports 348

Chapter 9 Adult support and protection **351**
Introduction 351
The principles 352
The duty to investigate 352
Local authority powers 354

Chapter 10 Offenders **361**
Law and crime 361
Sentencing: objectives and criteria 371
Non-custodial disposals 372
Alternatives to prosecution 390
Compensation for criminal injuries 392
Custodial disposals 393
Release from prison and detention 397
Management of offenders 405
Mentally disordered offenders 408
Rehabilitation of offenders 413
Victims 413

Chapter 11 Professional regulation, responsibility and accountability **415**
Introduction 415
Registration and regulation 416
The legal framework for liability and accountability 423
Breach of duty 427
Judicial review: further examples 434
Employers' liability for and to social workers 438
Conclusion 441

Chapter 12 Changes **443**
Chapter 5 443
Chapter 8 450
Chapter 10 451

Index **459**

Table of Cases

References are to Paragraph Number

A

A v East Sussex County Council [2010] EWCA Civ 743, [2010] 2 FLR 1596, [2011] 1 FCR 116 .... 11.10
A v Essex County Council [2003] EWCA Civ 1848, [2004] 1 WLR 1881, [2004] 1 FLR 749, [2004] 1 FCR 660 .... 11.11
A v G 1996 SCLR 787, 1996 SLT (Sh Ct) 123, Sh Ct 1.44
A v Kennedy (Reporter to Children's Panel, Strathclyde Region) 1993 SC 131, 1993 SLT 1188, 1993 SCLR 107, IH 5.8
A County Council v MB, JB, A Residential Home [2010] EWHC 2508 (COP) 7.19
A's Guardian, Applicant 2007 SLT (Sh Ct) 24 .... 7.4
AD & OD v United Kingdom (Application No 28680/06) (2010) 51 EHRR 8, [2010] 2 FLR 1, ECHR 11.10
AD & OH v Bury Metropolitan Borough Council. *See* D v Bury Metropolitan Borough Council; H v Bury Metropolitan Borough Council
Advocate (HM) v Hood 1987 SCCR 63, HCJ 10.25
Advocate (Lord) v Scotsman Publications Ltd 1989 SC (HL) 122, 1989 SLT 705, HL 2.29
Akbarali v Brent London Borough Council; Abdullah v Shropshire County Council; Shabpar v Barnet London Borough Council; Shah (Jitendra) v Barnet London Borough Council; Barnet London Borough Council v Shah [1983] 2 AC 309, [1983] 2 WLR 16, [1983] 1 All ER 226, (1983) 127 SJ 36, (19893) 81 LGR 305, (1983) 133 NLJ 61, HL 6.14
Al-Ameri v Kensington and Chelsea Royal London Borough Council [2004] UKHL 4, [2004] 2 AC 159, [2004] 2 WLR 354, [2004] 1 All ER 1104 .... 2.9
Argyll and Bute Council v Scottish Public Services Ombudsman [2007] CSOH 168 .... 6.8, 6.13
AS v Poor Sisters of Nazareth. *See* Bowden v Poor Sisters of Nazareth & Ors; Whitton v Poor Sisters of Nazareth & Ors
Austin v Commissioner of Police of the Metropolis [2009] UKHL 5, [2009] AC 564, [2009] 2 WLR 372, [2009] 3 All ER 455, HL 7.19
Authority Reporter v S. *See* Knox v S and the Lord Advocate; Ritchie v L and the Lord Advocate

B

B v A. *See* B, Petitioner

B v Croydon Health Authority; *sub nom* LB v Croydon Health Authority [1995] Fam 133, [1995] 2 WLR 294, [1995] 1 All ER 683, [1995] 1 FLR 470, [1995] 1 FCR 662, [1995] PIQR P145, [1995] Fam Law 244, (1995) 144 NLJR 1696, CA 8.9
B v Croydon Health Authority [1995] 1 FCR 332, QBD 8.9
B v Harris 1990 SLT 208; *sub nom* C v Harris 1989 SC 278, 1989 SCLR 644 .... 5.8
B v Kennedy 1987 SC 247, 1987 SLT 765, 2 Div 5.8
B v Sister Bernard Mary Murray (No 2). *See* Bowden v Poor Sisters of Nazareth & Ors; Whitton v Poor Sisters of Nazareth & Ors
B Reading Borough Council & Ors [2007] EWCA Civ 1313, [2008] 1 FLR 797; *sub nom* L and another v Reading Borough Council and others [2008] 1 FCR 295.. 11.10
B, Applicant 2005 SLT (Sh Ct) 95 .... 7.11
B, Petitioner 1993 SLT 455, 1992 SCCR 596; *sub nom* B v A 1993 SC 232... 10.44
Barrett v Enfield London Borough Council [2001] 2 AC 550, [1999] 3 WLR 79, [1999] 3 All ER 193, HL.. 11.10
Beattie v Dunbar (Mental Health Officer) 2006 SCLR 777, Sh Ct .8.17
Bernard v Enfield London Borough Council [2002] EWHC 2282 (Admin), [2003] HLR 111, [2003] LGR 423 .... 1.65, 2.3
Birmingham City Council v Ali [2009] UKHL 36, [2009] 1 WLR 1506, [2009] 4 All ER 161, HL.. 2.10
BJ v Proudfoot, Children's Reporter for Stirling and the Lord Advocate [2010] CSIH 85 .... 5.16
Bowden v Poor Sisters of Nazareth & Ors; Whitton v Poor Sisters of Nazareth & Ors [2008] UKHL 32, 2008 SLT 561, 2008 SCLR 547; *sub nom* AS v Poor Sisters of Nazareth; B v Sister Bernard Mary Murray (No 2) [2007] CSIH 39, 2007 SC 688, 2007 SLT 605 .... 11.7
Britton v Britton's Curator Bonis 1996 SLT 1272, 1992 SCLR 947, Ct of Sess (OH).. 7.1
Bury Metropolitan Council v D; D (Unborn Baby) (Birth Plan: Future Harm), Re [2009] EWHC 446 (Fam), [2009] All ER (D) 266 (Mar) 5.36
Byrd v Wither 1991 SLT 206 .... 5.8

C

C v Harris. *See* B v Harris
C (Sexual Abuse: Disclosure to Landlord), Re [2002] EWHC 234 (Fam), [2002] 2 FCR 385.. 2.32
Caparo Industries pic v Dickman [1990] 2 AC 605, [1990] 2 WLR 358, [1990] 1 All ER 568, [1990] BCC 164, [1990] BCLC 273, [1990] ECC 313, (1990) 134 SJ 494, HL.. 11.7
City of Edinburgh Council v D (2010) 30 September, Edinburgh Sh Ct.. 7.3
City of Edinburgh Council v Z 2005 SLT (Sh Ct) 7 .... 7.4
Clarke and Powell v Eley (IMI) Kynoch Ltd [1983] ICR 165, [1982] IRLR 482, EAT 2.22

Coco v AN Clark (Engineers) Ltd [1969] RPC 41, [1968] FSR 415, ChD 2.29
Constanda v M 1997 SC 217, 1997 SLT 1396, 1997 SCLR 510, 1 Div 5.8, 5.15
Conway v Glasgow City Council 1999 SCLR 248, Glasgow Sh Ct .2.4
Cooke v Telford 2005 SCLR 367, Sh Ct 7.4, 7.7, 7.9
Council of Civil Service Unions v Minister for the Civil Service [1985] AC 374, [1984] 1 WLR 1174, [1984] 3 All ER 935, [1985] ICR 14, [1985] IRLR 28, (1984) 128 SJ 837, (1985) 82 LS Gaz 437, HL .. 11.14
Covezzi & Morselli v Italy (2004) 38 EHRR 28, ECHR 4.14, 5.36
Crossan v South Lanarkshire Council [2006] CSOH 28, 2006 SLT 441 .... 4.5, 4.6
Cunningham v M 2005 SLT (Sh Ct) 73 .... 5.8

D

D v Bury Metropolitan Borough Council; H v Bury Metropolitan Borough Council [2006] EWCA Civ 1, [2006] Fam 348, [2006] 2 FLR 147, [2006] 1 FCR 148 .... 11.10
D v East Berkshire Community Health NHS Trust; K v Dewsbury Healthcare NHS Trust; K v Oldham NHS Trust [2005] UKHL 23, 83 BMLR 66, [2005] 2 All ER 443, [2005] 2 AC 373, [2005] 2 WLR 993, [2005] 2 FLR 284 .... 11.10
D v H 2004 Fam LR 41 .... 3.7
D v Kelly 1995 SLT 1220 .... 5.8
D v Kennedy 1988 SLT 55 .... 5.8
D v NSPCC [1978] AC 171, [1977] 2 WLR 201, [1977] 1 All ER 587, (1977) FLR Rep 181, HL 1.44
D v Strathclyde Regional Council 1991 SCLR 185, Sh Ct 5.16
Davers v Butler 1994 SCLR 717, Sh Ct 1.44
DC, Application in Relation to (2010) 22 October, Glasgow Sh Ct 7.9
Di Mascio v MHTS (2008) 4 August, Glasgow Sh Ct 8.17
Docherty (Anne) (2005) 8 February, Glasgow Sh Ct 7.10, 7.18
Donoghue v Stevenson [1932] AC 562, 1932 SC (HL) 31, HL 1.9
Dorset Yacht Co Ltd v Home Office [1970] AC 1004, [1970] 2 WLR 1140, [1970] 2 All ER 294 .... 11.11
Durant v Financial Services Authority [2003] EWCA Civ 1746, [2004] FSR 28, [2004] IP & T 814 .... 2.30
Dyer v Watson; K v HM Advocate [2002] UKPC D1, 2002 SCCR 220, 2002 SC (PC) 89, 2002 SLT 229 .... 1.31

E

E v E 2004 Fam LR 115 .... 3.7
EB, Application in Respect of (2005) 1 December, Glasgow Sh Ct 7.9
Errico v Italy, Application number 29768/05, (2009) 24 February, ECHR 5.36
ES's Application [2007] NIQB 58 .... 5.23

F

F v Kennedy (Reporter To Children's Panel, Strathclyde Region) (No 2) 1993 SLT 1284, 1992 SCLR 750, Ct of Sess (IH), 2 Div 1.48
F v Wirral Metropolitan Borough Council and Liverpool City Council [1991] Fam 69, [1991] 2 WLR 1132, [1991] 2 All ER 648, CA 4.11
Fairlie v Perth and Kinross Healthcare NHS Trust 2004 SLT 1200, Ct of Sess (OH) 11.10
FB, Applicant, (2005) 17 May, Glasgow Sh Ct 7.4
Ferguson v P 1989 SLT 681, 1989 SC 231, 1989 SCLR 525 .... 5.15
Ferguson v S 1992 SCLR 866, Ct of Sess (IH), Extra Div 5.8
Ferguson v S 1993 SC 564, 1993 SCLR 712, Ct of Sess (IH) 1.56
Fife Council v X, (2005) 22 December, Kirkcaldy Sh Ct 7.3, 7.4
Finlayson, Applicant 1989 SCLR 601, Edinburgh Sh Ct 3.2, 5.8

G

G v E, A Local Authority, F [2010] EWHC 621 (Fam), [2010] 2 FLR 294, [2010] All ER (D) 120 (Apr), Ct of Protection 7.19
G v Scanlon 1999 SLT 707, 1999 SC 226, 2000 SCLR 1, Ct of Sess, Extra Div 5.8
G, Applicant 2009 SLT (Sh Ct) 122 .... 7.4
Gardiner (1869) 7 M 1130 .... 7.1
Gaskin v United Kingdom (Application No 10454/83) (1990) 12 EHRR 36, [1990] 1 FLR 167, ECHR 2.28, 4.20
Gillick v West Norfolk and Wisbech Area Health Authority and the DHSS [1986] AC 112, [1985] 3 WLR 830, [1985] 3 All ER 402, [1986] Crim LR 113, (1985) 135 NLJ 1055, (1985) 82 LS Gaz 3531, HL 3.5
Gorrie v Marist Brothers 2002 SCLR 436, Dumfries Sh Ct 11.7
Grainger v Nicholson [2010] IRLR 4, EAT 2.21
Green v Argyll & Bute Council (2002) 28 February (unreported), Ct of Sess (OH) 11.16
Guyan v Guyan 2001 Hous LR 99 .... 3.30
Guzzardi v Italy (1981) 3 EHRR 333, ECHR 7.19

H

H v Lees, D v Orr 1994 SLT 908, 1993 JC 238, 1993 SCCR 900 .... 5.8
H v McGregor 1973 SC 95, 1973 SLT 110, 2 Div 5.19
H v Sweeney 1982 JC 70,1983 SLT 48, 1982 SCCR 161, HCJ 1.12
H and L v A Council and B Council [2010] EWHC 466 (Admin), [2010] All ER (D) 127 (Mar), QBD 2.31
Hamilton v Scott 1987 SCCR 188, HCJ 10.13
Hardie v Hardie 1993 SCLR 60, Sh Ct 3.13
Harris v F 1991 SLT 242, 1991 SCLR 124 .... 5.8, 5.15
Harrison v Surrey County Council. *See* T (A Minor) v Surrey County Council
Hastie v SCRC 2006 SLT (Sh Ct) 14 .... 11.3

Hatton v Sutherland, Barber v Somerset County Council, Jones v Sandwell Metropolitan Borough Council, Bishop v Baker Refractories Ltd [2002] EWCA Civ 76, [2002] 2 All ER 1, [2002] ICR 613 .... 11.16
Henderson (Gordon) v MHTS (2010) 23 July, Edinburgh Sh Ct 8.20
HL v United Kingdom (2005) 40 EHRR 32, ECHR 7.19
Houston, Applicant 1996 SCLR 943, (1996) 32 BMLR 93, Sh Ct 3.2
Hughes' Tutrix v Glasgow District Council 1982 SLT (Sh Ct) 70 .... 2.3
Humberside County Council v B [1993] 1 FLR 257, [1993] 1 FCR 613, FD 5.23
Humphries v X and Y. *See* Humphries, Petitioner
Humphries, Petitioner; *sub nom* Humphries v X and Y 1982 SC 79, 1982 SLT 481 .... 5.15

J

J v Fife Council 2007 SLT 85 .... 11.7
JA and SY, Children's Hearing Appeal, (2010) 3 November, Dumbarton Sh Ct 5.8
JD v East Berkshire Community Health NHS Trust [2005] UKHL 23. *See* D v East Berkshire Community Health NHS Trust
JE v DE (By His Litigation Friend The Official Solicitor), Surrey County Council And EW [2006] EWHC 3459 (Fam), [2007] 2 FLR 1150, (2007) 10 CCLR 149, FD 1.65, 7.19
JG v Mental Health Tribunal for Scotland (2010) 14 October, Glasgow Sh Ct 8.17
JL v Kennedy (1995) 6 March (unreported) Ct of Sess (IH) 5.19
Johansen v Norway (1997) 23 EHRR 33 .... 5.36

K

K v Authority Reporter 2009 SLT 1019, Ct of Sess (IH) 5.11
K v Kennedy 1993 SLT 1281, 1992 SCLR 386 .... 1.48
K and F, Applicants 2002 SCLR 769, Edinburgh Sh Ct 5.23, 5.35
K & T v Finland (2003) 36 EHRR 18, ECHR 5.36
Kelly, Petitioner 1985 SC 333 .... 2.8
Kelly v Monklands District Council 1986 SLT 169 .... 1.59, 2.12
Kennedy v A 1993 SLT 1134 .... 5.8
Kennedy v B 1992 SCLR 55, Ct of Sess (IH), 2 Div 5.15
Kennedy v M 1989 SLT 687, 1989 SCLR 769 .... 5.15
Kennedy v M 1995 SLT 717, 1995 SCLR 88, Ct of Sess (IH) 5.19
Kennedy v R's Curator ad litem 1993 SLT 295, 1992 SC 300, 1992 SCLR 546 .... 5.8
Kennedy v S 1986 SC 43, 1986 SLT 679, 2 Div 5.8
Khaliq v HM Advocate 1984 JC 23, 1984 SLT 137, 1983 SCCR 483 ... 9.1
Kirkham v Anderton [1990] 2 QB 283, [1990] 2 WLR 987, [1990] 3 All ER 246, (1990) 140 NLJ 209, CA 11.11
Kirkham v Chief Constable of the Greater Manchester Police. *See* Kirkham v Anderton

Knox v S and the Lord Advocate; Ritchie v L and the Lord Advocate [2010] CSIH 45; sub nom Authority Reporter v S 2010 SLT 765.. 5.8, 5.35, 12.17
Koca v Secretary of State for the Home Department 2005 SC 487, 2005 SLT 838, Ct of Sess (IH)...... 8.17
Koniarska v United Kingdom, (Application no 33670/96), decision 12th October 2000, ECHR...... 1.65, 4.35

L

L v Birmingham City Council. *See* YL v Birmingham City Council
L v Kennedy (1995) 6 March (unreported) Ct of Sess (IH)...... 1.43
L, Petitioner 1996 SCLR 538...... 7.1
L, Petitioners (No 1) 1993 SLT 1310; sub nom L v Kennedy 1993 SCLR 693, 1 Div...... 5.19
L, Petitioners (No 2) 1993 SLT 1342...... 5.19
Lambert v Cardiff City Council [2007] EWHC 869 (QB), [2007] 3 FCR 148, 97 BMLR 101...... 11.7, 11.11
Laurie v Mental Health Tribunal for Scotland (2007) 30 August, Paisley Sh Ct...... 8.17
Law Hospital NHS Trust v Lord Advocate 1996 SC 301, 1996 SLT 848, [1996] 2 FLR 407, [1996] Fam Law 670, IH...... 7.1
Lawrence v Pembrokeshire County Council [2007] EWCA Civ 446, [2007] 2 FLR 705, [2007] 2 FCR 329, 96 BMLR 158...... 11.10
LB v Croydon Health Authority. *See* B v Croydon Health Authority
LC (Mrs) (2005) 19 May, Glasgow Sh Ct...... 7.9
Lee v Leeds City Council [2002] EWCA Civ 06, [2002] 1 WLR 1448, [2002] 1 EGLR 103, [2002] HLR 367...... 2.3
Lewisham London Borough Council v Lewisham Juvenile Court Justices [1980] AC 273, [1979] 2 WLR 513, [1979] 2 All ER 297, (1979) 123 SJ 270, (1979) 77 LGR 469, HL...... 4.11
Lindsay v Murphy 2010 GWD 29–604...... 3.15
Lister v Hesley Hall Ltd [2001] UKHL 22, [2002] 1 AC 215, [2001] 2 WLR 1311, [2001] 2 All ER 769,HL...... 11.7
LM v Mental Health Tribunal for Scotland (2010) 31 August, Glasgow Sh Ct...... 8.15, 8.16
Local Authority, A v A; sub nom A and C (Equality and Human Rights Commission Intervening), Re [2010] EWHC 978 (Fam), [2010] 2 FLR 1363, FD and Ct of Protection...... 7.19
Local Authority, A v A and anor [2010] EWHC 1549 (Fam), [2011] All ER (D) 205 (Jan), COP...... 7.3
Local Authority, A v DL, RL & ML [2010] EWHC 2675 (Fam), [2010] All ER (D) 280 (Oct)...... 7.1
Lothian Health Board v M 2007 SCLR 478, Airdrie Sh Ct...... 7.21

M

M (A Minor) v Newham London Borough Council [1994] 2 WLR 554, [1994] 4 All ER 602, [1994] 1 FLR 431, 92 LGR 427, (1994) 144 NLJ 357, CA...... 11.11

M v C 2002 SLT (Sh Ct) 82 .... 3.7
M v Dumfries and Galloway Regional Council 1991 SCLR 481, Dumfries Sh Ct 4.11, 5.23
M v Irvine 2005 Fam LR 113 .... 5.8
M v Kennedy 1993 SLT 431, 1991 SCLR 898 .... 5.14
M v Kennedy 1995 SLT 123, 1995 SCLR 15 .... 5.19
M v M, AW139/06 .... 7.6
M v Scottish Children's Reporter for Renfrewshire [2009] CSIH 49 .... 5.8
M v McClafferty [2007] CSIH 88 .... 5.8
M v McGregor 1982 SLT 41 .... 5.8
M v Orr. *See* McD v Orr
M, Applicant 2007 SLT (Sh Ct) 207 .... 7.4
M, Applicant 2009 GWD 24–394 .... 7.7, 7.9
M, Applicant 2009 SLT (Sh Ct) 185 .... 7.19
M (C) v Kennedy 1996 SLT 434, 1 Div 5.15
M and M v Glasgow Corporation 1976 SLT (Sh Ct) 45 .... 11.11
McArdle v City of Glasgow District Council 1989 SCLR 19, Glasgow Sh Ct 2.3
McCafferry v McCafferty 1986 SC 178, 1986 SLT 650, 2 Div 3.34
McCulloch v HMA [2005] HCJAC 120, 2005 SCCR 775, HCJA 10.44
McD v Orr; sub nom M v Orr 1995 SLT 26, 1994 SCCR 645 .... 5.8
McGlennan v McKinnon 1998 SLT 494, 1998 SCCR 285, HCJ 10.33
McGregor v H 1983 SLT 626 .... 5.8
McGregor v K 1981 SC 328, 1982 SLT 293 .... 5.8
McGregor v L 1981 SLT 194 .... 5.8
MacGregor v South Lanarkshire District Council 2001 SC 502 .... 1.59, 6.5, 6.8
McMichael v United Kingdom (1995) 20 EHRR 205, ECHR 1.65
Maddock (Helen) v Devon County Council [2003] EWHC 3494 (QB) 2.32
MAK & RK v United Kingdom (2010) 51 EHRR 14, ECHR 11.10
Merrin v S 1987 SLT 193 .... 5.8
Merthyr Tydfil County Borough Council v C [2010] EWHC 62 (QB), [2010] 1 FLR 1640, [2010] 1 FCR 441 .... 11.11
MIG and MEG, Re [2010] EWHC 785 (Fam) (2010) 15 April, (unreported), FD 7.19
Mitchell v Glasgow City Council [2009] UKHL 11 [2009] AC 874, [2009] 2 WLR 481, [2009] 3 All ER 205, HL 2.31, 11.7
Mitchell v H 2000 SC 334 .... 5.9
MM (an adult), Re; Local Authority X v MM (By the Official Solicitor) and KM [2007] EWHC 2003 (Fam), [2009] 1 FLR 443, [2008] 3 FCR 788 .... 7.3, 7.4
Morgan v Morgan & Kyle & Carrick DC 2000 Hous LR 90 .... 3.29
Morrison v Stirling District Council 1996 Hous L R 5, Ct of Sess (OH) 2.3
Mosley v News Group Newspapers Ltd. [2008] EWHC 687 (QB), [2008] All ER (D) 135 (Apr) 2.29
Muldoon, Applicant 2005 SCLR 611, Glasgow Sh Ct 7.4, 7.19

Murray v Express Newspapers plc [2008] EWCA Civ 446, [2008] 3 WLR 1360; *sub nom* Murray v Big Pictures (UK) Ltd [2008] 2 FLR 599, CA 2.29
Murray v Big Pictures (UK) Ltd. *See* Murray v Express Newspapers plc

N

North Ayrshire Council v M 2004 SCLR 956, Kilmarnock Sh Ct 7.9
North Lanarkshire Council v Crossan 2007 SLT (Sh Ct) 169 .... 2.16
NXS v London Borough of Camden [2009] EWHC 1786 (QB), [2010] 1 FLR 100, [2009] All ER (D) 178 (Jul) 11.10

O

O v Rae (Reporter To Children's Panel, Wigtown District) 1993 SLT 570, 1992 SCLR 318, Ct of Sess (IH) 1 Div 5.14
Olsson v Sweden (1988) 11 EHRR 72, ECHR 5.36
Olsson v Sweden (No 2) (1994) 17 EHRR 134, ECHR 4.14
O'Neill v Gilhooley 2007 Fam LR 15 .... 3.13
Osman v UK (2000) 29 EHRR 245, ECHR 1.65, 2.31

P

P v Kennedy 1995 SLT 476, 1995 SCLR 1 .... 5.15
P v Reporter 2008 SLT (Sh Ct) 85 .... 5.13
P v Tayside Regional Council 1989 SC 38 .... 2.28, 2.32
P v Tayside Regional Council 1989 SCLR 165, Ct of Sess (OH) 1.44
P, C & S v United Kingdom (2002) 35 EHRR 31, ECHR 5.36
Palmer v Tees Health Authority [2000] PIQR P1, [1999] Lloyd's Rep Med 351, [2000] PNLR 87, (2000) 2 LGLR 69, CA 2.31
Peebles v MacPhail 1990 SLT 245, 1989 SCCR 410, HCJ 5.8
Petition of East Lothian Council for a Permanence Order (2010) 30th July, Haddington Sh Ct 3.21
Pierce v Doncaster Metropolitan Council [2007] EWHC 2968 (QB), [2008] 1 FLR 922, [2008] 1 FCR 122, 100 BMLR 76 .... 11.10
Pratley v Surrey County Council [2003] EWCA Civ 1067, [2004] ICR 159, [2003] IRLR 794, [2004] PIQR 252 .... 11.16
Principal Reporter v K [2010] CSIH 5, 2010 SC 328, 2010 SLT 308 .... 3.7, 5.11, 5.16
Public Guardian, Application for Directions by (2010) 30 June, Glasgow Sh Ct 7.6

R

R, Petitioner; *sub nom* R v Kennedy 1993 SLT 910, 1993 SCLR 623, Ct of Sess (IH) 5.14
R v Avon County Council, ex parte Crabtree (1994) 22 March (unreported), QBD 11.12
R v Avon County Council, ex parte Hills (1995) 27 HLR 411, [1995] EGCS 41, QBD 4.8

R v Avon County Council, ex parte M [1994] 2 FCR 259, [1994] 2 FLR 1006, [1995] Fam Law 66, QBD 4.46, 11.15
R v Barnet London Borough Council, ex parte Shah. *See* Akbarali v Brent London Borough Council
R v Bedfordshire County Council, ex parte C; R v Hertfordshire County Council ex parte B [1987] 1 FLR 239, (1987) 85 LGR 218, (1987) 17 Fam Law 55, 151 JP 202, QBD 11.14
R v Birmingham City Council, ex parte A (A Minor) [1997] 2 FLR 841, [1997] 2 FCR 357, FD 11.8
R v Bristol City Council ex parte Penfold (1997–98) 1 CCLR 315, [1998] COD 210, QBD 6.4
R v Chief Constable of North Wales Police, ex parte AB; *sub nom* R v Chief Constable of North Wales Police, ex parte Thorpe [1999] QB 396, [1998] 3 WLR 57, [1998] 3 All ER 310, [1998] 2 FLR 571, [1998] 3 FCR 371, [1998] Fam Law 529, (1998) 95(17) LSG 29, CA 2.32
R v Chief Constable of North Wales Police, ex parte Thorpe. *See* R v Chief Constable of North Wales Police, ex parte AB
R v Devon County Council, ex parte L [1991] 2 FLR 541, [1991] Fam Law 369, [1991] COD 205, (1991) 155 LG Rev 784, [1991] FCR 784, (1992) 4 Admin LR 99, QBD 2.31, 2.32
R v Dorset County Council, ex parte Beeson [2002] EWCA Civ 1812, [2004] LGR 92, CA; [2001] EWHC Admin 986, [2002] HLR 368 .... 6.12
R v East Sussex CC, ex parte T; *sub nom* T (A Minor), Re [1998] AC 714, [1998] 2 WLR 884, [1998] 2 All ER 769, [1998] 2 FCR 221, (1998) 10 Admin LR 453, [1998] Ed CR 206, [1998] ELR 251, [1998] CCL Rep 352, (1998) 42 BMLR 173, (1998) 148 NLJ 781, (1998) 95(24) LSG 33, (1998) 142 SJLB 179, HL 6.5
R v Gloucestershire County Council, ex parte Barry; R v Lancashire County Council, ex parte Royal Association for Disability and Rehabilitation [1997] AC 584, [1997] 2 WLR 459, [1997] 2 All ER 1, (1997) 36 BMLR 92, (1997) 9 Admin LR 209, (1997) 1 CCL Rep 40, [1997] COD 304, (1997) 147 NLJ 453, (1997) 94(14) LSG 25, (1997) 141 SJLB 91, HL; [1996] 4 All ER 421, (1997) 36 BMLR 69, (1997) 9 Admin LR 69, (1997) 1 CCL Rep 19, [1996] COD 387, (1996) 93(33) LSG 25, (1996) 140 SJLB 177, CA 6.5, 6.8
R v Gloucestershire County Council, ex parte RADAR (1997–98) 1 CCLR 476, [1996] COD 253,QBD 6.5
R v Grant 2000 SLT 372 .... 5.8
R v Harrow London Borough Council, ex parte D [1990] Fam 133, [1989] 3 WLR 1239, [1990] 3 All ER 12, [1990] 1 FLR 79, CA... 11.13, 11.14
R v Hereford and Worcester Councy Council, ex parte D [1992] 1 FLR 448, [1992] Fam Law 238, [1992] 1 FCR 497, (1992) 156 LG Rev 644, QBD 11.12
R v Hertfordshire County Council, ex parte B. *See* R v Bedfordshire County Council, ex parte C

R v Kennedy. *See* R, Petitioner
R v Kingston-upon-Thames Royal Borough Council, ex parte T [1994] 1 FLR 798, [1994] 1 FCR 232, [1994] Fam Law 375, [1993] COD 470, FD 4.5, 4.46
R v Lewisham London Borough Council, ex parte P [1991] 1 WLR 308, [1991] 3 All ER 529, 89 LGR 610, [1991] 2 FLR 185, [1991] Fam Law 316, [1991] COD 286, [1991] FCR 684, (1991) 155 LG Rev 804, ... QBD11.12
R v Local Authority in the Midlands, A, Ex parte LM [2000] 1 FLR 612, [2000] 1 FCR 736, QBD 2.32
R v London Borough of Bexley, ex parte B (1995) 31 July (unreported) QBD 4.6
R v London Borough of Ealing, ex parte Leaman (1984) Times, 10 February, QBD 11.15
R v London Borough of Islington, ex parte Rixon [1997] ELR 66, (1996) 32 BMLR 136, (1997) 1 CCLR 119, (1996) Times, 17 April, QBD 4.46, 6.5
R v London Borough of Wandsworth, ex parte P [1989] 1 FLR 387, [1989] Fam Law 185, 87 LGR 370, [1989] COD 262, (1989) 153 LG Rev 550, (1989) 153 JPN 803, QBD 11.12
R v North Yorkshire County Council, ex parte Hargreaves (1995) 26 BMLR 121, (1997) 1 CCL Rep 104, QBD 4.46, 6.2
R v Royal County of Berkshire ex parte P (1997) 33 BMLR 71, (1996) Times, August 15, QBD 6.4
R v Waveney District Council, ex parte Bowers [1983] QB 238, [1982] 3 WLR 661, [1982] 3 All ER 727, (1982) 126 SJ 657, (1982) 80 LGR 721, [1983] 15 HLR 118, (1982) 79 LS Gaz 1413, CA........ 2.8
R (A) v Hertfordshire County Council [2001] EWCA Civ 2113, [2001] BLGR 435, [2001] ELR 666........ 2.32
R (A) v London Borough of Croydon [2008] EWCA Civ 1445, [2009] 1 FCR 317, [2009] 1 FLR 1324........ 4.10
R (A) v National Probation Service [2003] EWHC 2910 (Admin), [2003] All ER (D) 241 (Nov)........ 2.32
R (AM) v Birmingham City Council [2009] EWHC 688 (Admin), (2009) 12 CCLR 407, [2009] All ER (D) 68 (Jul)........ 2.27
R (B) v Cornwall County Council [2009] EWHC 491 (Admin), [2009] All ER (D) 244 (Jun)........ 6.2, 6.4, 6.12
R (Boyejo) v Barnet London Borough Council; R (Smith) v Portsmouth Borough Council [2009] EWHC 3261 (Admin), [2009] All ER (D) 169 (Dec)........ 2.27, 6.15
R (Brown) v Secretary of State for Work and Pensions [2008] EWHC 3158 (Admin), [2009] PTSR 1506, [2008] All ER (D) 208 (Dec)........ 2.27
R (G) v Barnet London Borough Council [2003] UKHL 57, [2003] 3 FCR 419, [2004] 1 All ER 97, [2004] 2 AC 208, [2003] 3 WLR 1194, [2004] 1 FLR 454........ 4.5
R (G) v London Borough of Southwark [2009] UKHL 26, [2009] 1 WLR 1299, [2009] 3 All ER 189, [2009] 2 FLR 380, [2009] 2 FCR 459........ 4.10

R (G) v Nottingham City Council and Nottingham University Hospital [2008] EWHC 400 (Admin), [2008] 1 FLR 1668, [2008] 3 FCR 568 ..... 5.36
R (H) v Secretary of State for Health [2005] UKHL 60, [2006] AC 441, [2005] 4 All ER 1311, 86 BMLR 71 ..... 7.21
R (L) v Nottinghamshire County Council [2007] EWHC 2364 (Admin), [2007] All ER (D) 158 (Sep) 4.10
R (M) v London Borough of Hammersmith and Fulham; R (Hertfordshire County Council) v London Borough of Hammersmith and Fulham [2010] EWHC 562 (Admin), 116 BMLR 46, [2010] All ER (D) 218 (Mar) 6.14
R (Macdonald) v Royal Borough of Kensington and Chelsea [2010] EWCA Civ 1109, [2010] All ER (D) 138 (Oct) 6.7
R (Savva) v Royal Borough of Kensington and Chelsea [2010] EWCA Civ 1209, [2010] All ER (D) 271 (Oct) 6.8, 6.10
R (W) v Lambeth London Borough Council [2002] EWCA Civ 613, [2002] 2 All ER 901, [2002] 2 FLR 327, [2002] 2 FCR 289 ..... 4.8
Renfrew District Council v Gray 1987 SLT (ShCt) 70 ..... 2.3
RK & AK v United Kingdom (2009) 48 EHRR 29, [2009] 1 FLR 274, ECHR 11.10
Robb (Judith) v Dundee City Council 2002 SC 301, 2002 SLT 853, Ex Div 2.3
Robbins v Mitchell, (2007) 14 May, Airdrie Sh Ct 8.17
Roberton v Roberton 1999 SLT 38, 1 Div 3.34
Robertson (Mary) v Fife Council [2002] UKHL 35, 2003 SCLR 39, 68 BMLR 229 ..... 6.8

S

S v County of San Diego (1993) 16 Cal App 4th 887 ..... 11.12
S v HM Advocate 1989 SLT 469; *sub nom* Stallard v HM Advocate 1989 SCCR 248 ..... 3.8
S v Kennedy 1987 SC 247, 1987 SLT 765, 2 Div 5.15
S v Kennedy 1996 SCLR 34 ..... 5.8, 5.15
S v Miller 2001 SLT 485 ..... 1.65
S v Miller 2001 SC 977 ..... 5.13
S v N 2002 SLT 589 ..... 5.8
SA (Vulnerable Adult with Capacity: Marriage), Re [2005] EWHC 2942 (Fam), [2006] 1 FLR 867, [2007] 2 FCR 563 ..... 7.1
Savage v South Essex Partnership NHS Foundation Trust & Anor [2007] EWCA Civ 1375, [2008] 1 WLR 1667, (2007) 100 BMLR 98 ..... 1.65
Scottish Ministers v MHTS, Re JK [2009] CSIH 9, 2009 SCLR 224 ..... 8.17
Scottish Public Services Ombudsman Case 200701327: Renfrewshire Council 11.9
Shtukaturov v Russia [2008] ECHR 44009/05, [2008] MHLR 238, ECHR 7.19, 7.20
Sloan v B 1991 SLT 530 ..... 5.12, 5.15
Soutar v McAuley, 31st March 2010, Dundee Sh Ct 3.30, 3.31

Stallard v HM Advocate. *See* S v HM Advocate
Stewart v Lockhart 1991 SLT 835, 1990 SCCR 390, HCJ 10.1
Stewart v Thain 1981 JC 13, 1981 SLT (Notes) 2, HCJ 5.8
Storck v Germany (Application No 61603/00) (2006) 43 EHRR 96, ECHR 7.19
Summers v Salford Corporation [1943] AC 283, 59 TLR 78, [1943] 1 All ER 68, HL 2.3
Swift v Westham Central Mission (1984) 6 June (unreported) QBD 11.11

T

T (A Minor), Re. *See* R v East Sussex CC, ex parte T
T (A Minor) v Surrey County Council; *sub nom* Harrison v Surrey County Council [1994] 4 All ER 577, [1994] 2 FCR 1269, (1994) 144 NLJR 319, (1994) 158 LG Rev 1021, QBD 11.11
T (Accommodation by Local Authority), Re [1995] 1 FLR 159, [1995] 1 FCR 518, [1995] Fam Law 125, QBD 4.10, 4.46
Tagro v Cafane [1991] 1 WLR 378, [1991] 2 All ER 235, [1991] 1 EGLR 279, 23 HLR 250, CA 2.4
Tarasoff v Regents of the University of California (1976) 17 Cal 3d 425, California Supreme Ct 2.31
TH, HH & AI (2008) 8 February, Glasgow Sh Ct 7.8, 7.9
Todd v Clapperton 2009 CSOH 112, 2009 SC 112, 2009 SLT 837, 2009 Hous LR 48 .... 2.3
Treasure v McGrath 2006 Fam LR 100 .... 3.7

V

V v F 1991 SCLR 225, Edinburgh Sh Ct 3.2
Vicar of Writtle v Essex County Council (1979) 77 LGR 656, QBD 11.11
W (A Minor) (Medical Treatment), Re [1992] 3 WLR 758, [1992] 4 All ER 627, [1993] 1 FLR 1, CA 3.2
W v Egdell [1989] 2 WLR 689, [1989] 1 All ER 1089, (1989) 133 SJ 570 .... 2.31
W v Egdell [1990] Ch 359, [1990] 2 WLR 471, [1990] 1 All ER 835, (1990) 134 SJ 286, CA 2.29
W v Essex County Council [1999] Fam 90, [1998] 3 WLR 534, [1998] 3 All ER 111, [1998] 2 FLR 278, [1998] 2 FCR 269, [1998] PIQR P346, [1998] Fam Law 455, (1998) 95(20) LSG 33, CA 11.11
W v Essex County Council [2001] 2 AC 592, [2000] 2 WLR 601, [2000] 2 All ER 237, [2000] 1 FCR 568, [2000] 1 FLR 657, HL 11.11
W v United Kingdom (1987) 10 EHRR 29, ECHR 4.15
W v Westminster City Council [2005] EWHC 102 (QB) , [2005] 4 All ER 96, [2005] All ER (D) 144 (Feb) 2.32
Walker v C (No 2) 2003 SLT 293 .... 5.15
Walker v Northumberland County Council [1995] 1 All ER 737, [1995] ICR 702, [1995] IRLR 35, [1995] PIQR P521, (1994) 144 NLJ Rep 1659, QBD 11.16

Wilson v Nithsdale District Council 1992 SLT 1131, Ct of Sess (OH).. 2.12
Wincentzen v Monklands District Council 1988 SLT 259, Ct of Sess... 2.7
Windram, Applicant 2009 Fam LR 157 .... 3.15

X

X v BBC [2005] CSOH 80, 2005 SLT 796, 2005 SCLR 740............ 2.31, 10.4
X v Hounslow London Borough Council [2009] EWCA Civ 286, [2009] 2 FLR 262, [2009] 3 FCR 266 .... 11.11
X (Emergency Protection Orders), Re [2006] EWHC 510 (Fam), [2006] 2 FLR 701, [2007] 1 FCR 551 .... 5.23
X (Minors) v Bedfordshire County Council, M (A Minor) v Newham London Borough Council; E (a Minor) v Dorset County Coucil; Christmas v Hampshire County Council; Keating v Bromley County Council [1995] 2 AC 633, [1995] 3 WLR 152, [1995] 3 All ER 353, [1995] 2 FLR 276, [1995] 3 FCR 337, (1995) 7 Admin LR 705, [1995] Fam Law 537, (1995) 145 NLJR 993, HL.... 11.10, 11.13
X Council v B (Emergency Protection Orders) [2004] EWHC 2015 (Fam), [2005] 1 FLR 341, [2007] 1 FCR 512.......... 5.23

Y

YL v Birmingham City Council [2007] UKHL 27, [2008] 1 AC 95, [2007] 3 All ER 957, [2007] HLR 651, [2007] NPC 75.......... 1.65
Yule v South Lanarkshire Council 1999 SCLR 985, (1999) 2 CCL Rep 394, Ct of Sess (OH).......... 6.12
YW v Office of the Public Guardian, (2010) 25 June, Peterhead Sh Ct.... 7.12

Z

Z v United Kingdom (2001) 34 EHRR 97, ECHR 11.10
Z v United Kingdom (Application No 29392/95) (2002) 34 EHRR 3, [2001] 2 FLR 612, (2001) 10 BHRC 384, ECHR 1.65, 5.34

Table of Statutes

References are to Paragraph Number

Adoption and Children (Scotland) Act 2007 ..... 1.70, 1.71, 3.17
ch 6 ..... 3.17
ss 1–3 ..... 3.17
s 1(3) 3.17
6 ..... 3.17
10 ..... 3.28
11 ..... 3.28
14 ..... 3.20
(1) 3.18, 3.24
(3) 3.18
(4)(a)–(d) 3.18
(6), (7) 3.18
15 ..... 3.20
16 ..... 3.20
18 ..... 3.25
19 ..... 3.25
ss 20–24 ..... 3.24
s 24(4)–(7) 3.20
29 ..... 3.19
30 ..... 3.19
(1) 3.19
(7) 3.19
31 ..... 3.21
(11) 3.21
(12) 3.25
(14) 3.25
32 ..... 3.2, 3.20
35 ..... 3.17
36 ..... 3.25
38 ..... 2.30
71 ..... 3.26
75 ..... 3.25
81 ..... 3.23
82 ..... 3.23
83 ..... 3.23
84 ..... 3.23
89 ..... 3.23

Adoption and Children (Scotland) Act 2007 – *contd*
s 106 ..... 3.22
119(1) 3.2

Adult Support and Protection (Scotland) Act 2007 ... 1.9, 1.71, 7.2, 8.13, 8.14, 9.1, 9.2, 9.4, 9.8, 11.11
s 1 ..... 9.2
2 ..... 9.2
3 ..... 9.3
4 ..... 9.3
5 ..... 2.31, 9.1
6 ..... 9.3
ss 7–9 ..... 9.5
s 10 ..... 2.31, 9.6
ss 11–34 ..... 9.7
s 12 ..... 9.7
15 ..... 9.7
20 ..... 9.7
35(3), (4) 9.8
42 ..... 9.1
43 ..... 9.1
53(1) 9.3

Adults with Incapacity (Scotland) Act 2000 ..... 1.9, 1.18, 1.71, 6.11. 7.1, 7.2, 7.3, 7.5, 7.6, 7.14, 7.20, 8.5, 8.12, 9.1, 9.8, 11.3
s 1(2)–(5) 7.4
(6) 7.3
15(3)(b) 7.6
16 ..... 7.6
(6) 7.17
19(1) 7.6
(2)(c) 7.6

Adults with Incapacity (Scotland) Act 2000 – *contd*
s 19(3) ... 7.6
20(1) ... 7.6
(2)(a)–(e) ... 7.6
22 ... 7.6
23 ... 7.6
37(1) ... 7.13
47(1A) ... 7.15
48 ... 7.15
50(5)–(8) ... 7.16
53(14) ... 7.17
57(1)–(4) ... 7.8
(5), (6) ... 7.9
58(1) ... 7.3
(a), (b) ... 7.9
(3), (4) ... 7.9
(5) ... 7.7
59(1)(a) ... 7.9
(4), (5) ... 7.9
62 ... 7.7
(1)(a) ... 7.9
(6) ... 7.7
64(1) ... 7.9
(2) ... 7.17
70 ... 7.10
73(1)–(4) ... 7.10
87(1) ... 7.3
Age of Legal Capacity (Scotland) Act 1991 ... 3.1, 3.2, 3.3, 5.7
ss 1–3 ... 3.2
Antisocial Behaviour etc (Scotland) Act 2004
Pt 9 ... 5.17
Carers (Recognition and Services) Act 1995 ... 6.2
Child Support Act 1991 ... 3.16
Children Act 1989 ... 1.9, 1.70, 4.4, 4.11
s 3(5) ... 4.11
17 ... 1.9
(11) ... 4.4
22 ... 1.9
23 ... 1.9
23A–24D ... 1.9
43 ... 1.9
44 ... 1.9

Children Act 1989 – *contd*
Sch 2 ... 1.9
para 5 ... 5.28
Children and Young Persons Act 1933
Sch 1 ... 4.34
Children and Young Persons (Scotland) Act 1937
s 12 ... 5.8, 5.37
(1) ... 5.8
15 ... 5.8, 5.37
22 ... 5.8, 5.37
33 ... 5.8, 5.37
Children (Scotland) Act 1995 ... 1.9, 1.63, 1.66, 1.70, 3.1, 3.5, 4.1, 4.4, 4.5, 4.10, 4.11, 4.14, 5.1, 5.11, 5.12, 5.13, 5.19, 5.22, 5.32, 6.2, 8.17, 12.7, 12.17
Pt I (ss 1–15) ... 1.70
Pt II (ss 16–93) ... 1.57, 1.70
Pt II, Chs 2, 3, 4 ... 4.21
Pt IV (ss 99–105) ... 1.70
s 1 ... 3.2, 3.4
(2)(b) ... 3.2
s 2 ... 3.2, 3.5, 5.13
(7) ... 4.11
3 ... 5.8
4A ... 3.6
5 ... 3.6, 4.11, 4.16
6 ... 3.3, 3.4
7 ... 3.6
11 ... 3.6, 3.7, 3.25, 4.11, 4.16, 5.8, 5.20
(3)–(5) ... 3.7
(5) ... 4.11
(7B)–(7D) ... 3.7
(11) ... 3.7
12 ... 3.7, 3.13
16 ... 1.9, 3.3
(1) ... 5.2
(2) ... 5.4
(3) ... 5.5
(4) ... 5.4

Children (Scotland) Act 1995 – *contd*
s 17 .... 1.9, 2.19, 4.14
(1)(c) 4.19
(3)(b)–(d) 4.15
(6)........................ 4.13
19 .... 4.1
20 .... 4.1
21 .... 4.7
22 .... 1.9, 1.72, 4.1, 4.3, 4.8, 5.28
(1)........................ 8.12
(2)........................ 4.8
(3)........................ 4.5
23 .... 4.6
(3)(b) 4.6, 4.12
24 .... 4.6
(1)(b) 4.6
25 .... 4.10, 4.13, 4.18, 4.22, 4.34, 12.7
(6)........................ 4.11
26 .... 4.10
27 .... 4.9
ss 29–30........................ 1.9, 3.3
s 29(1), (2)........................ 4.42, 4.43
30 .... 4.42
38(1)(a) 5.32
43 .... 5.11
45 .... 5.11
(1)(a) 3.3
(2)........................ 5.11
(4), (5) 4.39
(7)........................ 4.39
46 .... 5.11
49 .... 5.20
51 .... 5.19
(1)(a) 12.16
(5)(c)(iii) 5.19
(11)........................ 5.19
52(2)........................ 5.8
53(1)........................ 2.31, 5.7
(b) 4.11
54 .... 3.7, 3.25, 5.20
55 .... 1.9, 5.7
56 .... 5.9
(4)(1)(a)........................ 5.9
(b) 5.9
57 .... 1.9, 5.23
(1), (2)........................ 5.23

Children (Scotland) Act 1995 – *contd*
s 57(4)........................ 5.24
(6)........................ 5.25
58 .... 5.24
59 .... 5.26
(2)........................ 5.26
60(1)........................ 5.25
(3)–(5) 5.26
(7), (8) 5.26
(10)........................ 5.26
(12), (13) 5.26
61 .... 5.27
64 .... 5.12
65 .... 5.14
(2)........................ 5.26
66 .... 5.14
(2)........................ 5.14
(6)........................ 4.35
67 .... 5.14
(1)........................ 4.39
(3)........................ 4.35
68 .... 5.15
(3)(b) 5.15
(11)........................ 4.35
(12)........................ 5.15
68A........................ 5.15
68B........................ 5.15
69(1)–(11) 5.14
(3)........................ 5.26
(11)........................ 4.35
70 .... 5.16
(7)........................ 5.16
(9)–(17) 5.16
(10)........................ 4.36
71 .... 5.16
71A........................ 5.16
73 .... 5.18
(4)(c)(v)........................ 3.22
(8), (9) 3.22
(12)........................ 5.18
(13)........................ 3.22
(13A)........................ 3.22
(14)........................ 3.22
ss 76–80........................ 5.28
s 76(2), (3) 5.29
(9)........................ 5.29
(11)........................ 5.29
77 .... 5.30

Children (Scotland) Act 1995 – *contd*
s 78 .... 5.30
79(1).... 5.31
85 .... 5.19
90 .... 3.2, 5.7, 5.24
93(1).... 4.1
(2)(a), (b).... 3.2, 4.1
(4)(a) 4.4
Children's Hearings (Scotland) Act 2011.... 12.2, 12.3, 12.5, 12.6, 12.7, 12.12, 12.15
s 52 .... 12.4
54 .... 12.4
54(b).... 12.4
60 .... 12.3
60(3).... 12.3
61 .... 12.3
67 .... 12.7
73(3), (4) 12.8
79(9)(a) 12.9
81(3).... 12.9
83(4)–(6) 12.10
ss 86, 87.... 12.11
s 90 .... 12.11
111(3).... 12.12
117 .... 12.12
121 .... 12.13
ss 123, 124.... 12.13
125, 126.... 12.14
s 140 .... 12.14
144–148 .... 12.15
154 .... 12.16
157 .... 12.16
160 .... 12.9
161 .... 12.14
162 .... 12.16
186 .... 12.5, 12.11
Chronically Sick and Disabled Persons Act 1970.... 1.9, 2.3, 4.5, 4.6, 6.2, 6.3, 6.4, 6.5, 6.6, 6.7, 11.15
s 2 .... 2.3, 6.4, 6.5, 6.7, 6.8
(1).... 4.6
(e) 2.3
Civic Government (Scotland) Act 1982
s 52 .... 5.8
52A.... 5.8
Civil Evidence (Scotland) Act 1988.... 1.48
Civil Partnerships Act 2004 .. 3.14, 3.32
s 101 .... 3.29
Community Care and Health (Scotland) Act 2002 ... 1.9, 1.71, 6.2
s 1 .... 6.13
(1).... 6.13
Sch 1 .... 6.13
Criminal Justice (Scotland) Act 2003
s 14 .... 10.73
ss 16, 17.... 10.74
s 21 .... 10.4
40 .... 10.51
50 .... 10.31
Criminal Justice and Licensing (Scotland) Act 2010
s 3 .... 10.8
17 .... 12.35
52 .... 3.1, 5.8
64 .... 5.21
Criminal Law (Consolidation) (Scotland) Act 1995
Pt I (ss 1–17).... 5.8, 5.37
ss 1–3.... 5.8
s 4(6).... 10.4
Criminal Procedure (Scotland) Act 1995.... 8.12
Pt III.... 1.36
s 24(5)(d).... 10.4
41 .... 3.2
42 .... 3.2
(7), (8) 10.7
43 .... 5.21
44 .... 10.44, 10.59
(1).... 5.21
(3).... 4.13, 5.21
ss 48, 49.... 5.20
s 51 .... 5.21
(1)(a)(i).... 4.40

Criminal Procedure (Scotland) Act 1995 – *contd*
ss 52B–52J 10.63
52K–52S 10.63
53–53D 10.64
54–57 .... 10.69
57A–57D 10.64
s 58 .... 10.67
59 .... 10.65
ss 59A–60A 10.66
s 60B 10.67
65 .... 1.33
69(6), (7) 10.36
101(9)–(11) 10.36
116(9)–(11) 10.36
118(7) 10.8
189(7) 10.8
196 .... 10.8
197 .... 10.8
201 .... 10.4
(3) 10.4
203 .... 10.4
204(2) 10.4
205 .... 4.40
206 .... 10.42
207(4) 10.4
208 .... 4.40, 10.44
209(2) 10.4
210A 10.4, 10.56
210B 10.55, 10.56
210E 10.55
214(4) 10.15
219(1)(b) 10.15
226B 10.16
227 .... 10.11
227a(1) 12.21
227M(2) 12.26
227P(2), (3) 12.27
227Q(3) 12.28
ss 227R–227T 12.29
s 227U(6) 12.30
227V(6) 12.12.31
227W(2) 12.32
227ZC(7), (8) 12.34
ss 227ZE–227ZK 12.34
s 228 .... 10.21
(1) 10.19
(b) 10.4

Criminal Procedure (Scotland) Act 1995 – *contd*
s 229(4)(a) 10.19
229A 10.4
s 234A–234K 10.32
234A 10.33
234B(3)(b) 10.4
ss 235–237 .... 10.18
s 235(1) 10.17
(4) 10.17, 10.18
238(1) 10.25
(2)(c) 10.4
245A 10.31
246(1) 10.10
(2), (3) 10.9
ss 249–253 .... 10.29
s 254A(11A) 10.4
259 .... 1.53
302A 10.37
303ZB 10.38
Sch 1 .... 4.34, 5.37
Sch 4 .... 10.70
Sch 7 .... 10.18
Curators Act 1585 .... 7.1
Custodial Sentences and Weapons (Scotland) Act 2007 .... 12.35
Data Protection Act 1984 .... 1.44
Data Protection Act 1998 .... 2.28, 2.30, 2.31, 2.32
s 1(1) 2.30
(d) 2.30
2 .... 2.30
7(4)–(6) 2.30
(8) 2.30
(10) 2.30
10 .... 2.30
13 .... 2.30
14 .... 2.30
66 .... 2.30, 3.3
68(1)(c) 2.30
Schs 2, 3 .... 2.30, 2.31, 2.32
Sch 12 .... 2.30
Debt Arrangement and Attachment (Scotland) Act 2002 .... 2.14
Sch 2 .... 2.15

Debtors (Scotland) Act 1987. 2.14
s 5 ... 2.14
(5) ... 2.14
Disability Discrimination Act 1995 ... 2.27
Disabled Persons (Services, Consultation and Representation) Act 1986 ... 1.60, 6.2
s 4 ... 6.4
8 ... 6.6, 6.7
Disability Discrimination Act 1995
s 18B ... 2.23
49A ... 2.27
Divorce (Scotland) Act 1976 ... 3.10
s 2 ... 3.11
Education (Additional Support for Learning (Scotland) Act 2004 ... 5.1, 5.37
s 1(1), (1A), (1B) ... 4.17
2 ... 4.17
ss 9–11 ... 4.17
12, 13 ... 4.17
Education (Scotland) Act 1980
s 28ff ... 2.33
30 ... 2.33, 3.2
31 ... 3.2, 4.42
Electoral Administration Act 2006
s 17 ... 3.2
Environmental Protection Act 1990
s 82 ... 2.3
Equality Act 2010 ... 2.20, 2.23, 2.27
s 1(1) ... 2.20
ss 4–12 ... 2.21
s 6(1) ... 2.21
13 ... 2.22
(2), (3) ... 2.25
19 ... 2.22
(2)(d) ... 2.25
20 ... 2.23
22 ... 2.23
29 ... 2.24
(6) ... 2.24
Equality Act 2010 – *contd*
s 149 ... 6.15
Sch 1 ... 2.21
Sch 3, para 1 ... 2.25
Family Law (Scotland) Act 1985
s 1 ... 3.2, 3.3
Family Law (Scotland) Act 2006 ... 3.15
s 23 ... 3.6
25 ... 3.15
ss 28, 29 ... 3.15
Foster Children (Scotland) Act 1984 ... 4.34
s 7 ... 4.34
Health and Safety at Work etc Act 1974 ... 11.16
Health and Social Care Act 2008
s 145 ... 1.65
Health and Social Services and Social Security Adjudications Act 1983
s 23 ... 6.12
Homelessness etc (Scotland) Act 2003 ... 2.5
s 4 ... 2.7
11 ... 2.4
Housing (Homeless Persons) Act 1977 ... 2.5, 2.7
Housing (Scotland) Act 1987 .. 2.6
Pt II ... 2.5
s 24(3)(b), (bb) ... 2.6
27(2)(iii) ... 2.9
28(2) ... 2.7
ss 135–137 ... 2.6
Housing (Scotland) Act 1988
ss 36, 37 ... 2.4
Housing (Scotland) Act 2001
ss 27, 28 ... 2.3
s 30 ... 2.3
Sch 4 ... 2.3
Housing (Scotland) Act 2006
s 13 ... 2.3
14(1) ... 2.3
ss 17–19 ... 2.3
s 22 ... 2.3
24(1) ... 2.3

Housing (Scotland) Act 2006 – *contd*
s 27 .... 2.3
52 .... 2.3
(2)(a) 2.3
53 .... 2.3
ss 74–97 .... 2.3
s 92 .... 2.3
Human Rights Act 1998........ 1.65, 2.29, 11.8
s 6 .... 1.65, 3.3, 11.10
(1)................................ 11.7
(3)(b) 1.65
s 7 .... 1.65, 3.3, 11.8
(5)................................ 11.7
Interpretation Act 1978
Sch 1 .... 4.11
Immigration and Asylum Act 1999
s 115(9)............................. 1.72
120 .... 1.72
122(5)............................. 1.72
Law Reform (Miscellaneous Provisions) (Scotland) Act 1990
s 7(1)................................ 7.6
Law Reform (Parent and Child) (Scotland) Act 1986
s 3 .... 4.11
Local Government (Scotland) Acts 1.10
Local Government etc (Scotland) Act 1973
s 29 .... 3.2
Local Government etc (Scotland) Act 1994.............. 1.66
s 45 .... 1.66
180 .... 1.66
Sch 14.............................. 1.66
Management of Offenders (Scotland) Act 2005 ...... 1.71, 10.60
s 1(2)(a) 2.31
10 .... 2.31
(1)............................. 10.62
Marriage (Scotland) Act 1977
s 1.................................... 3.2
Matrimonial Homes (Family Protection) (Scotland) Act 1981 .... 2.6, 2.7, 3.14, 3.15, 3.29, 3.32, 3.35
Matrimonial Proceedings (Children) Act 1958
s 11 .... 3.13
Mental Capacity Act 2005 .... 1.9
s 1(1).............................. 7.3
(5).............................. 7.4
ss 24–26 .... 7.4
Mental Health Act 1983........ 1.9
Mental Health (Care and Treatment) Scotland Act 2003.................. 1.9, 1.60, 1.71, 1.72, 4.4, 4.34, 5.1, 5.37, 6.2, 6.3, 6.4, 7.20, 8.1, 8.2, 8.5, 8.6, 8.8, 8.9, 8.11, 8.12, 9.1, 9.8, 12.18
Pt 5.................................. 8.16
Pt 6.................................. 8.16
s 1(3)................................ 8.10
(3)(d) 8.17
(4)–(7) 8.10
2 .... 8.10
(4)................................ 8.10
ss 25–27 .... 8.12
30, 31 .... 8.12
s 33 .... 8.13
35 .... 8.13
41, 42 .... 8.22
45 .... 8.16
50 .... 8.16
53, 54 .... 8.22
ss 57–60............................ 8.17
s 60(1).............................. 8.17
(2)(b) 8.17
61 .... 8.17
64(4)(a)(i)....................... 8.17
(5).............................. 8.17
(7), (8) 8.17
96 .... 8.17
98 .... 8.17
ss 112–115........................ 8.21
s 120 .... 8.21
ss 127–129........................ 8.22

Mental Health (Care and Treatment) Scotland Act 2003 – *contd*
s 227(1) 8.12
228 .... 8.12
231(1) 10.63
232(2) 8.25
(b)(iii) 10.63
234 .... 8.24
ss 237–243 .... 8.24
250–253 .... 8.6
s 255(1)–(4) 8.17
(6) 8.17
s 257 .... 8.6
275 .... 8.10
(1), (2) 8.24
276 .... 8.10
(7), (8) 8.24
291 .... 8.15
ss 293–295 .... 8.14
s 299 .... 8.23
320 .... 8.16, 8.20
328 .... 7.3
(1) 8.8
329(1) 8.9
Mental Health (Scotland) Act 1984 .... 7.1
Misuse of Drugs Act 1971 .... 5.8
National Assistance Act 1948
s 22(1) 6.12
National Health Service and Community Care Act 1990 .... 1.9, 1.67, 6.1, 6.2
Nationality, Immigration and Asylum Act 2002
s 54 .... 1.72
Sch 3 .... 1.72
Prescription and Limitation (Scotland) Act 1973
s 17 .... 11.7
19A 11.7
Prisoners and Criminal Proceedings (Scotland) Act 1993
s 3 .... 10.50
12AB 10.52
Prohibition of Female Genital Mutilation (Scotland) Act 2005 .... 5.8
Protection from Abuse (Scotland) Act 2001 .... 3.38
s 7 .... 2.6
Protection from Harassment Act 1997 .... 3.37
Protection of Children (Scotland) Act 2003 .... 11.5
Protection of Children and Prevention of Sexual Offences (Scotland) Act 2005
s 1 .... 5.8
ss 9–12 .... 5.8
Protection of Vulnerable Groups (Scotland) Act 2007 .... 1.9
ss 2, 3 .... 11.5
ss 7, 8 .... 11.5
s 8 .... 11.5
10 .... 11.5
95 .... 11.5
97(1) 11.5
Schs 1–3 .... 11.5
Public Services Reform (Scotland) Act 2010
Pt 5, ch 4 .... 11.3
s 44 .... 1.60
47 .... 11.3
52 .... 1.60
59 .... 11.3
Sch 12 .... 11.3
Race Relations Act 1968 .... 2.20
Race Relations Act 1976
s 71(1) 2.27
Regulation of Care (Scotland) Act 2001 .... 1.71
Pt 2 .... 11.3
s 2 .... 11.3
(28) 8.12
7 .... 11.3
Rehabilitation of Offenders Act 1974 .... 10.72
Rent (Scotland) Act 1984
ss 22, 23 .... 2.4
Representation of the People Act 1983
ss 1, 2 .... 3.2
Safeguarding Vulnerable Groups Act 2006 .... 1.9

Scotland Act 1998
ss 29, 30 .... 1.9
Schs 4, 5 .... 1.9
Sex Discrimination Act 1975
s76A 2.27
Sexual Offences Act 2003 ..... 10.61
Sexual Offences (Scotland) Act 2009 .... 5.8, 5.37
Pt 1 .... 12.7
Pts 4, 5 .... 12.7
ss 5–9 .... 5.8
s 18–20 .... 5.8
ss 21–26 .... 5.8
s 28–30 .... 5.8
ss 31–37 .... 5.8
42–45 .... 5.8
s 42 .... 5.8
43(6) 5.8
Sheriff Courts (Scotland) Act 1971
s36B(3) 2.14
Social Work (Scotland) Act 1968 .... 1.1, 1.8, 1.9, 1.10, 1.57, 1.60, 1.66, 5.6, 5.12, 5.19, 6.2, 6.3, 6.11, 10.4
Pt III 1.57
Pt IV 1.69
s 5 .... 1.9
12 .... 1.10, 1.67, 1.72, 2.3, 2.19, 6.3, 6.4

Social Work (Scotland) Act 1968 – *contd*
s 12(1) 6.3, 8.12
(2A) 1.72
(6) 1.67, 6.4
12A 1.9, 1.67
(1) 6.4, 8.12
(b) 6.7
(4) 6.5
(5) 6.4
12AA(2)(b) 6.7
12AB 6.6
12B(1) 6.10
(5) 6.10
13A 1.72, 8.12
13B 1.72, 8.12
13ZA 6.11, 7.18
14 .... 1.67, 8.12
27 .... 1.68
(1)(a) 10.4
(b)(i)–(vi) 10.4
(c) 10.47
31 .... 1.57
86 .... 6.14
87 .... 6.12
(1A) 6.12
(3) 6.12
94(1) 1.67, 6.3
Vulnerable Witnesses (Scotland) Act 2004 .... 1.56
s 24 .... 1.46

Table of Statutory Instruments

References are to Paragraph Number

Act of Adjoumal (Criminal Procedure Rules) 1996, SI 1996/513
ch 22 .... 1.56
Act of Sederunt (Child Care and Maintenance Rules) 1997, SI 1997/291
ch 3 .... 5.4
ch 3, pt V 5.28
ch 3, pt VII 5.15
r 3.5 .... 5.4
Act of Sederunt (Sheriff Court Ordinary Cause Rules) 1993, SI 1993/1956
r 33.22 .... 3.13
Act of Sederunt (Sheriff Court Rules Amendment) (Adoption and Children (Scotland) Act 2007) 2009, SSI 2009/284 .... 3.25
r 25 .... 3.27
Act of Sederunt (Summary Applications, Statutory Applications and Appeals etc Rules) 1999, SI 1999/929
r 3.16.8 .... 7.9
Adoption and Children (Scotland) Act 2007 (Commencement No 4, Transitional and Savings Provisions) Order 2009, SSI 2009/267
arts 13–15 .... 4.41
Adoption Agencies (Scotland) Regulations 2009, SSI 2009/154
regs 3–6 .... 3.17
reg 6(3) 3.18
(5) 3.19

Adoption Agencies (Scotland) Regulations 2009 – *contd*
reg 7 .... 3.19
(1) 3.19
8 .... 3.19
(6) 3.19
(c) 3.19
regs 9, 10 .... 3.19
reg 16 .... 3.21, 3.24
17 .... 3.23
18 .... 3.24
20 .... 3.21, 3.23
21 .... 3.23, 3.24
22 .... 3.22
24(3) 3.24
(5) 3.24
25 .... 3.24
Sch 1, Pt 1 .... 3.19
Schs 2, 3 .... 3.24
Adoption (Disclosure of Information and Medical Information about Natural Parents) (Scotland) Regulations 2009, SSI 2009/268 ... 2.30, 3.27
Adoption Support and Allowances (Scotland) Regulations 2009, SSI 2009/152 .... 3.28
reg 6 .... 3.28
regs 10–17 .... 3.26
Adoptions with a Foreign Element (Scotland) Regulations 2009, SSI 2009/183 .... 3.17
Adult Support and Protection (Scotland) Act 2007 (Restriction on the Authorisation of Council Officers) Order 2008, SSI 2008/306 .... 9.4

Adults with Incapacity (Conditions and Circumstances Applicable to Three Year Medical Treatment Certificates) (Scotland) Regulations 2005, SSI 2005/100....... 7.15
Adults with Incapacity (Management of Residents' Finances) (No 2) (Scotland) Regulations 2003, SSI 2003/266....... 7.13
Adults with Incapacity (Medical Treatment Certificates) (Scotland) Regulations 2007, SSI 2007/104 .... 7.15
Adults with Incapacity (Reports in Relation to Guardianship and Intervention Orders) (Scotland) Regulations 2002, SSI 2002/96
Sch 2 .... 7.8
Adults with Incapacity (Specified Medical Treatments)(Scotland) Regulations 2002, SSI 2001/275 .... 7.15
Arrangements to Look After Children (Scotland) Regulations 1996, SI 1996/3262
reg 19(1) 11.12
Charging Orders (Residential Accommodation)(Scotland) Order 1993, SI 1993/1511 .... 6.11
Children's Hearings (Legal Representation) (Scotland) Rules 2002, SSI 2002/63
r 3 .... 5.13
rr 3A, 3B 5.13
Children's Hearings (Scotland) Rules 1996, SI 1996/3261 .... 1.9, 5.11
r 4 .... 5.12
Children's Hearings (Scotland) Rules 1996 – *contd*
r 6 .... 5.14
11 .... 5.13
12 .... 5.11
20 .... 5.14
(6) 5.16
Civil Legal Aid (Scotland) Regulations 2002, SSI 2002/494
reg 18 .... 1.63
Community Care (Deferred payment of Accommodation Costs) (Scotland) Regulations 2002, SSI 2002/266....... 12.6
Community Care (Direct Payments)(Scotland) Regulations 2003, SSI 2003/243
regs 2, 3 .... 6.10
Criminal Procedure (Scotland) Act 1995 Compensation Offer (Maximum Amount) Order 2008, SSI 2008/7 .... 10.37
Data Protection (Subject Access Modification) (Social Work) Order 2000, SI 2000/415
art 4 .... 2.30
5(1) 2.30
(3), (4) 2.30
6 .... 2.30
7 .... 2.30
(2) 2.30
Sch 1, Pt 2 .... 2.30
Emergency Child Protection Measures (Scotland) Regulations 1996, SI 1996/3258
regs 3, 4 .... 5.27
reg 8 .... 5.27
Equality Act 2010 (Disability) Regulations 2010, SI 2010/2128 .... 2.21

Foster Children (Private Fostering) (Scotland) Regulations 1985, SI 1985/1798 .... 4.34
Home Detention Curfew (Amendment of Specified Days) (Scotland) Order 2008, SSI 2008/126 .... 10.52
Home Detention Curfew Licence (Prescribed Standard Conditions) (Scotland)(No 2) Order 2008, SSI 2008/125 .... 10.52
Homeless Persons (Provision of Non-Permanent Accommodation) (Scotland) Regulations 2010, SSI 2010/2 .... 2.10
Homeless Persons (Unsuitable Accommodation) (Scotland) Order 2004, SSI 2004/489
reg 2(3) 2.5
3 .... 2.5
Housing (Scotland) Act 2006 (Scheme of Assistance) Regulations 2008, SSI 2008/406 .... 2.3
Intensive Support and Monitoring (Scotland) Regulations 2008, SSI 2008/75 .... 5.16
Looked After Children (Scotland) Regulations 2009, SI 2009/120 .... 4.23
reg 3 .... 4.15
4 .... 4.15
(5) 4.21
5 .... 4.15
7 .... 5.16
8 .... 4.15
(1) 4.22
(2) 4.10, 4.22
10(1), (2) 4.23
(3)(b) 4.23
11(2) 4.23
13 .... 4.31
Looked After Children (Scotland) Regulations 2009 – *contd*
reg 14 .... 4.18
15, 16 .... 4.33
regs 18–20 .... 4.25
22–24 .... 4.26
reg 25(1), (2) 4.26
27(2) 4.27
(g) 4.27
29 .... 4.31
30 .... 4.18
31, 32 .... 4.33
33 .... 4.23
34 .... 4.31
36(1) 4.29
37 .... 4.30
40 .... 4.31
41 .... 4.30
(4) 4.31
regs 42, 43 .... 4.20
regs 44–46 .... 4.32
reg 45(3)(a) 4.18
Sch 1 .... 4.15
para 10 .... 4.15
Sch 2, Pts I, II 4.15
Sch 4 .... 4.27
Sch 6 .... 4.26
Mental Health (Advance Statements) (Prescribed Class of Persons) (Scotland) (No 2) Regulations 2004, SSI 2004/429 .... 8.24
Mental Health (Class of Nurse) (Scotland) Regulations 2005, SSI 2005/446, reg 2 .... 8.23
Mental Health (Conflict of Interest) (No 2) Regulations 2005, SSI 2005/380 .... 8.17
Mental Health (Medical treatment subject to safeguards) (Section 234) (Scotland) Regulations 2005, SSI 2005/291 .... 8.24

Mental Health (Medical treatment subject to safeguards) (Section 237) (Scotland) Regula-tions 2005, SSI 2005/292......... 8.24
Mental Health (Social Circumstances Reports) (Scotland) Regulations 2005, SSI2005/310
reg 2.................................. 8.25
Mental Health Tribunal for Scotland (Practice and Procedure)(No 2) Rules 2005, SSI 2005/519....... 1.9
National Assistance (Assessment of Resources) Regulations 1992, SI 1992/2977 .... 6.12
Notice to Local Authorities (Scotland) Regulations 2008, SSI 2008/324....... 2.4
Parental Responsibilities and Parental Rights Agreements (Scotland) Regulations 1996, SI 1996/2549 .... 3.6
Parental Responsibilities and Parental Rights Agreements (Scotland) Amendment Regulations 2006, SSI 2006/255 .... 3.6
Prescription as 'Persons in Need' (Persons subject to Immigration Control) (Scotland) Order 1997, SI 1997/2452................ 1.67
Prisons and Young Offenders Institutions (Scotland) Rules 2006, SSI 2006/94.................................. 10.45
Protection of Vulnerable Groups (Scotland) Act 2007 (Prescribed Services) (Protected Adults) Regulations 2010 , SSI 2010/161
reg 5.................................. 11.5
Recovery of Expenditure for the Provision of Social Care Services (Scotland) Regulations 2010, SSI 2010/72 .... 6.14
Refuges for Children (Scotland) Regulations 1996, SI 1996/3259....... 5.32
Regulation of Care (Requirements as to Care Services) (Scotland) Regulations 2002, SSI 2002/114....................... 11.3
Residential Establishments – Child Care (Scotland) Regulations 1996, SI 1996/3256 .... 4.28
Rules of the Court of Session 1994
r 49.23.............................. 3.13
Schools General (Scotland) Regulations 1975, SI 1975/1135
regs 4 .... 2.33
4A.................................... 2.33
Secure Accommodation (Scotland) Regulations 1996, SI 1996/3255....... 4.28
regs 4, 5 .... 4.35
reg 6.................................. 4.37
(1) 4.36
7.................................. 4.38
(1) 4.36
8.................................. 4.38
9(1)(b)......................... 4.36
(2)(a)......................... 4.39
(e)......................... 4.39
regs 10–12 .... 5.16
13–15 .... 4.40
Secure Tenants (Right to Repair) (Scotland) Regulations 2002, SSI 2002/316 .... 2.3
Small Claims (Scotland) Order 1988, SI 1988/1999........ 2.14
Small Claims (Scotland) Amendment Order 2007, SSI 2007/496...... 2.14

Social Security (Claims and Payments) Regulations 1987, SI 1987/1968
reg 33 .... 7.1
Social Work (Scotland) Act 1968 (Choice of Accommodation) Directions 1993
para 3 .... 6.7
Support and Assistance for Young People Leaving Care (Scotland) Regulations 2003, SSI 2003/608 .... 4.42, 4.44
reg 2(1) 4.43
Victim Notification (Prescribed Offences) (Scotland) Order 2004, SSI 2004/411 .... 10.74
Victim Statements (Prescribed Offences) (No 2) (Scotland) Order 2009, SSI 2009/71 .... 10.73

Table of Guidance, Circulars, etc

References are to Paragraph Number

Adults with Incapacity (Scotland) Act 2000: Revised Code of Practice for Persons Authorised under Intervention Orders and Guardians (2008)
  para 2.13 .... 7.1
Audit Scotland, Dealing with offending by young people (2002)
  paras 147–148.................... 5.16
BASW, Code of Ethics for Social Work (2002) 1.10, 11.1
  para 4.17 .... 2.28
Birmingham Safeguarding Children Board, Serious Case Review In respect of the Death of a Child: Case Number 14, April 2010.............................. 2.32
Circulars
  CCD8/2001 Guidance on Single Shared Assessment of Community Care Needs, Scottish Executive.................. 6.5
    para 4............................ 6.5
    para 19.......................... 6.5
  CCD2/2003 Community Care and Health (Scotland) Act 2002: New Statutory Rights for Carers: Guidance, Scottish Executive
    para 9.3.......................... 6.6
  CCD5/2003 Free Personal and Nursing Care – Consolidated Guidance, ... 6.13

Circulars – *contd*
  CCD8/2003/ Choice of Accommodation – Discharge from Hospital, Scottish Executive.................. 6.7
  Circular CCD5/2004 Single Shared Assessment Indicator of Relative Need 6.8
  CCD8/2004 Guidance on Care Management in Community Care, Scottish Executive Circular 6.5, 6.7
    annex 1 para 11 .... 6.7
    annex 1, paras 33–35..... 6.9
  CCD13/2004 Deferred Payments and Other Funding Arrangements which Allow Care Home Residents to Delay Selling Their Homes, ... 6.12
  CCD5/2007 Scottish Executive: Guidance for Local Authorities (March 2007): Provision of community care services to adults with incapacity.............. 7.19
    paras 23–24 .... 6.11
  CCD7/2007 Self-Directed Support – New National Guidance 6.2
  CCD3/2008 National Minimum Standards for Assessment and Care Planning for Adults, Scottish Executive 6.5

Circulars – *contd*
CCD1/2010 Guidance and Directions for Self Arrangers of Free Personal and Nursing Care
Appendix – Personal Care and Nursing Care (Self Arrangers) (Scotland) Directions 2009 .... 6.13
CCD3/2010 Guidance on the Recovery of Expenditure on Accommodation and Services Under Section 86 of the Social Work (Scotland) Act 1968 – Ordinary Residence, ... 6.14
CCD4/2010 .... 6.12
JD 1/2007 Integrated Practice Guidance for Staff Involved in the Home Leave Process, Scottish Executive 10.57
SWSG1/1989 Code on Confidentiality of Social Work Records, Scottish Office
paras 11, 12 .... 2.28
SWSG11/91 Community Care in Scotland: Assessment and Care Management, Scottish Office 6.5
para 5.8 .... 6.9
para 22.1 .... 6.9
SWSG5/93 Scottish Office 6.7
SWSG15/93 Community Care: Health and Social Services and Social Security Adjudications Act 1983 (HASSASSA): Sections 21–24: Orders and Guidance 6.12

Circulars – *contd*
SWSG10/98 Community Care Needs of Frail Elderly People – Integrating Professional Assessment and Care Management, Scottish Office 6.5
Commission for Racial Equality (Scotland)
Code of Practice on the Duty to Promote Race Equality in Scotland (2002)
para 2.9 .... 2.27
para 3.6 .... 2.27
Duty to Promote Race Equality: A guide for public authorities in Scotland (2002)
p 11 .... 2.27
Convention of Scottish Local Authorities – Charging Guidance for Non-residential Social Care Services 09/10 (October 2010) 6.12
Crown Office and Procurator Fiscal Service, Prosecution Code (2001) 1.12
DCA, Data Sharing: Legal Guidance for the Public Sector (2004) 2.28
DCFS, Working Together to Safeguard Children: A guide to inter-agency working to safeguard and promote the welfare of children (2010)
paras 1.28–1.29 .... 5.23
Department of Health
Care management and assessment. Manager's Guide (1991) 6.5
Care management and assessment. Practitioner's Guide (1991): 6.2, 6.5

Circulars – *contd*
Caring for People, Community Care in the Next Decade and Beyond: Policy Guidance (1990)........ 6.5
Disability Rights Commission
Code of Practice: Rights of Access: services to the public, public authority functions, private clubs and premises (2006),
para 11.8........................ 2.24
ch 19............................ 2.3
Duty to Promote Disability Equality: Statutory Guidance (2006)
paras 1.5–1.11 .... 2.27
para 2.7.......................... 2.27
para 2.32........................ 2.27
para 5.16–5.19............... 2.27
Guidance on matters to be taken into account in determining questions relating to the definition of disability (2006): 2.21
Disclosure Scotland, Protecting Vulnerable Groups Scheme Guidance for individuals, organisations and personal employers (June 2010)
ch 2, paras 79–83.............. 11.5
Equal Opportunities Commission (Scotland), Gender Equality Duty Code of Practice Scotland (2007)
para 1.26.......................... 2.27
ch 5.................................. 2.27
H M Government, Information sharing: Guidance for practitioners and managers (2008)
para 3.15.......................... 2.28
para 3.19.......................... 2.31
para 3.36.......................... 2.31
Information Commissioner's Office
Data Protection Act 1998 – Legal Guidance
para 2.3.......................... 2.30
para 3.1.5................. 2.31, 2.32
Data Protection Good Practice Note: Data sharing between different local authority departments (2008)........................ 2.28
Data Protection Technical Guidance Note: Subject access requests and social services records (2008)............ 2.30
Mental Health (Care and Treatment)(Scotland) Act 2003 (Qualifications, experience and training of approved medical practitioners) Directions 2005.............................. 8.3
Mental Health (Care and Treatment) (Scotland) Act 2003 (Requirements for continuing appointment as mental health officers) Direction 2006: 8.2
Mental Health (Care and Treatment) (Scotland) Act 2003 (Requirements for appointment as mental health officers) Direction 2009 .... 8.2
Mental Welfare Commission, Adults with Incapacity Act: When to Invoke the Act
pp 11, 12.......................... 7.20
Multi Agency, Public Protection Arrangements: Extension of Management of Offenders (Scotland) Act 2005 to Restricted Patients: Health Service Guidance.......................... 10.62

National Care Standards 11.3
Adoption agencies
standard 23.1 .... 3.19
Foster care and family placement services
standard 6.4 .... 4.26
standard 11.1 .... 4.26
National Objectives for Social Work Services in the Criminal Justice System (2004) 10.2, 10.19, 10. 10.42
National Outcomes and Standards for Social Work Services in the Criminal Justice System: Community Payback Orders Practice Guidance (2010)........... 12.20
ch 14 .... 12.33
para 11.8 .... 12.31
National Outcomes and Standards for Social Work Services in the Criminal Justice System: Criminal Justice Social Work Reports And Court-Based Services Practice Guidance (2010).............. 12.19
para 6.36 .... 12.19
National Standard Eligibility Criteria and Waiting Times for the Personal and Nursing Care of Older People – Guidance (October 2009)............ 6.8, 6.13
para 7.1 .... 6.8
paras 9.4–9.5...................... 6.8
Revised Guidance on Charging for Residential Accommodation (April 2010) 6.12
Scottish Children's Reporter Administration, A Study of Children Subject to Child Protection Orders in Edinburgh 2006/2007 (2008)........................... 5.26
Scottish Commission for the Regulation of Care, Private Fostering: the unknown arrangement (2010)............................ 4.34
Scottish Executive
Adults with Incapacity (Scotland) Act 2000: Code of Practice for Managers of Authorised Establishments under Part 4 of the Act (SE/2003/177)............................ 7.13
Children and Young People: Child Protection Committees (2005)
paras 3.1–3.14 .... 5.1
para 4.6......................... 5.1
paras 4.10–4.14 .... 5.1
Choice of Accommodation – Discharge from Hospital Circular CCD8/2003/ 6.7
Code of Guidance on Homelessness (2005).. 2.5, 2.6, 2.7, 2.8
paras 6.7, 6.8 .... 2.8
para 7.2......................... 2.7
para 8.16....................... 2.9
para 9.57....................... 2.10
para 11.2....................... 2.10
Community Care Services for People with a Sensory Impairment: Policy and Practice Guidance, (2007)....... 6.2
Data Sharing: Legal Guidance for the Scottish Public Sector (2004)....................... 2.28
For Scotland's Children: Better indicated Children's Services (2001)
p 33.............................. 4.4

Scottish Executive – *contd*
Framework for Social Work Education in Scotland (2003) 1.1
Getting it Right for Every Child Consultation Pack on the Review of the Children's Hearings System (2004) 4.1, 4.2
Guidance for Local Authorities (March 2007): Provision of community care services to adults with incapacity, Circular CCD5/2007 .... 7.19
paras 23–24 .... 6.11
Guidance on Local Authority Accountability Antisocial Behaviour etc. (Scotland) Act 2004 .... 5.16
para 42 .... 5.16
Guidance on Parenting Orders (2005)
para 39 .... 5.17
Integrated Practice Guidance for Staff Involved in the Home Leave Process, Circular JD 1/2007 .... 10.57
Its everyone's job to make sure I'm alright
para 7.4 .... 2.32
para 8.55 .... 2.32
Mental Health (Care and Treatment) (Scotland) Act 2003: Code of Practice (2005) 8.1
vol 1, ch 6, paras 44–89 .. 8.24
vol 1, ch 11 .... 8.25
para 16 .... 8.25
vol 2, ch 1, para 16 .... 8.16
vol 2, ch 3
paras 49, 50 .... 8.17
para 55 .... 8.17
paras 56, 57 .... 8.17

Scottish Executive – *contd*
Mental Health (Care and Treatment) (Scotland) Act 2003: Code of Practice (2005) – *contd*
vol 2, ch 3 – *contd*
para 61 .... 8.17
para 63 .... 8.17
vol 2, p 123, para 13 ...... 8.19
vol 2, ch 5
para 33 .... 8.19
para 55 .... 8.19
vol 2, ch 6 .... 8.21
vol 3, pt 1, ch 5, paras 32–44 .... 10.64
National Objectives for Social Work Services in the Criminal Justice System: Standards – Probation (2004) 10.20
National Objectives for Social Work Services in the Criminal Justice System: Standards – Social Enquiry Reports and Associated Court Services (2004) 10.4
para 5.6 .... 10.4
ch 8 .... 10.3
Protecting Children and Young People: Child Protection Committees (2005) 5.1
Self-Directed Support – New National Guidance, Circular CCD7/2007 .... 6.2
Sharing Information About Children at Risk: A Guide to Good Practice (2003)
para 8 .... 2.31
para 9 .... 2.28
Single Shared Assessment Indicator of Relative Need, Circular CCD5/2004 .... 6.8

Scottish Executive – *contd*
Supporting Young People Leaving Care in Scotland: Regulations and Guidance on Services for Young People Ceasing to be Looked After by Local Authorities (2004) 4.42
Scottish Executive/SPS/ADSW, ICM Practice Guidance Manual 2007 .... 10.45
Scottish Government
A Guide to Getting it Right for Every Child (2008), Section 4: Getting it right for every child: the approach in practice 4.7
p 12 .... 4.2
p 20 .... 4.2
p 25 .... 4.2
Adult Support And Protection (Scotland) Act 2007 Code Of Practice For Local Authorities And Practitioners Exercising Functions Under Part 1 Of The Act (2008, as amended 2009)
ch 8, para 8 .... 2.31
Adults with Incapacity (Scotland) Act 2000 Code of Practice – Access to Funds (2008) 7.12
Adults with Incapacity (Scotland) Act 2000: Code of Practice for Continuing and Welfare Attorneys (2008) 7.6

Scottish Government – *contd*
Adults with Incapacity (Scotland) Act 2000: Code of Practice for Local Authorities Exercising Functions under the 2000 Act (2008)
p 8 .... 7.4
paras 6.1–6.16 .... 7.11
paras 6.30–6.42 .... 7.8
paras 6.33–6.37 .... 7.9
para 6.50 .... 7.10
paras 6.52–6.66 .... 7.10
para 6.62 .... 7.10
paras 7.15–7.42 .... 7.8
paras 7.23–7.33 .... 7.9
ch 4 .... 6.11
ch 8 .... 7.2, 7.10
ch 9 .... 7.2
annex 1 .... 6.11
Adults with Incapacity (Scotland) Act 2000: Code of Practice (Second Edition) for practitioners authorised to carry out medical treatment or research under part 5 of the act (2007) 7.14
Adults with Incapacity (Scotland) Act 2000: Communication and Assessing Capacity: A guide for social work and healthcare staff (2008)
ch1, para 3 .... 7.1
ch1, para 4 .... 7.3
Adults with Incapacity (Scotland) Act 2000: Revised Code of Practice for persons authorised under intervention orders and guardians (2008)
chs 2, 3 .... 7.11
ch 4 .... 7.8
chs 5, 6 .... 7.10

Scottish Government – *contd*
Code of Practice For Local Authorities and Practitioners Exercising Functions Under Part 1 of the Act (revised 2009)..... 9.8
ch 1, para 2–7............... 9.2
ch 1, para 8–12............. 9.3
ch 3, paras 2–8 .... 9.3
ch 4............................... 9.3
chs 5–7 .... 9.5
ch 6, para 8................... 9.5
ch 8............................... 9.6
ch 8, para 14................. 9.6
ch 9............................... 9.7
ch 9, para 7................... 9.7
ch 10............................. 9.7
ch 10, para 10............... 9.7
ch 11............................. 9.7
ch 11, para 9................. 9.7
ch 13............................. 9.1
Consultation on Public Sector Equality Duty Specific Duties (2009): 2.20
Framework for Parenting Orders in Scotland (2007)....................... 5.17
Getting it right for every child: Guidance on the Child's or Young Person's Plan (2007).. 4.2, 4.5, 4.8
section 5 .... 4.5
Guidance for Local Authorities on Regulation 5 of the Homeless Persons (Provision of Non-Permanent Accommodation)(Scotland) Regulations 2010 (2010)...................... 2.5, 2.10
Guidance on Looked After Children (Scotland) Regulations 2009 and the adoption and Children (Scotland) Act 2007 (2010) LAC...3.17, 4.1, 4.11

Scottish Government – *contd*
Guidance on Looked After Children (Scotland) Regulations 2009 and the adoption and Children (Scotland) Act 2007 (2010) LAC – *contd*
p 21, 22......................... 4.15
pp 24–26........................ 4.15
pp 28, 29........................ 4.15
p 33............................... 4.16
p 34, 35......................... 4.17
pp 38–43........................ 4.19
p 43............................... 4.21
pp 47–49........................ 5.16
pp 50–56........................ 4.22
p 65............................... 4.23
pp 71–72........................ 4.33
pp 75–81........................ 4.25
pp 79, 80........................ 4.26
pp 83–105...................... 4.26
p 83............................... 4.26
pp 89, 90........................ 4.26
pp 91–93........................ 4.26
p 98............................... 4.26
pp 105–109.................... 4.27
p 107............................. 4.27
pp 110–112.................... 4.33
pp 113, 114.................... 4.27
pp 116–125.............. 4.29, 4.30
p 116............................. 4.29
p 119............................. 4.29
pp 121–122.................... 4.29
p 122............................. 4.32
pp 126–128.................... 4.20
p 130............................. 4.32
pp 133–139.................... 4.32
pp 142–145.................... 4.24
p 155........................ 3.17, 4.15
p 156............................. 3.18
pp 158–160.................... 3.17
pp 163–167.................... 3.19
pp 169–174.................... 3.19
p 185............................. 3.23
pp 200–213.................... 3.28
pp 214–218.................... 3.26

Scottish Government – *contd*
MAPPA Guidance (version 4, April 2008), Cir-cular CEL 19(2008) 10.62
Pt 3, para 3 .... 10.62
Annex 4 .... 10.62
Memorandum of Procedure on Restricted Patients (2010) 10.65
Modifying local connection provisions in homelessness legislation (2006) 2.9
National Guidance for Child Protection in Scotland: draft for public consultation (2010) 5.1
paras 38–44 .... 5.23
para 39 .... 5.1
paras 154–156 .... 5.1
paras 160–175 .... 5.1
para 240 .... 5.1
paras 426–609 .... 5.23
National Outcomes and Standards for Social Work Services in the Criminal Justice System 10.2
p 5 .... 10.2
National Outcomes and Standards For Social Work Services in the Criminal Justice System: Criminal Justice Social Work Reports and Court-based Services Practice Guidance (2010) 10.2, 10.4
National Training Framework for Care Management: Practitioner's Guide: March 2006 .... 6.7
part 4 – care planning.... 6.7

Scottish Government – *contd*
Section 11 Statutory Guidance (2009), Scottish Government, Statutory Guidance for Local Authorities on Preventing Homelessness (2009) 2.5
Self-Directed Support: A National Strategy for Scotland (2010) 6.10
para 2.3 .... 6.8
Statutory Guidance for Local Authorities on Preventing Homelessness (2009). 2.12
Statutory Guidance for meeting the best interests of children facing homelessness (2010) 2.5
Supporting children's learning code of practice, revised edition (2010) 4.17
pp 19–20 .... 4.17
pp 113–120 .... 4.17
ch 5 .... 4.17
Scottish Office
Circular SWSG5/93 .... 6.7
Code on Confidentiality of Social Work Records, Circular SWSG1/1989
paras 11, 12 .... 2.28
Protecting Children: A shared responsibility (1998)
para 3.5 .... 5.1
para 4.1 .... 2.31
Scottish Social Services Council
Code of Practice for Social Service Workers 11.1, 11.2
Code of Practice for Social Service Workers (2002) 1.10

Scottish Social Services Council – *contd*
Code of Practice for Social Service Workers (2009)
para 2.3 .... 2.28
Rules for Social Work Training (2003)
r 6(d)(ii) 1.1
Scottish Social Services Council (Registration) Rules 2009B 11.2
r 2(1) 11.2
Social Work Inspection Agency, On the record – getting it right: Effective management of social work recording (2010) .. 11.4
Social Work (Representations Procedure) (Scotland) Directions 1996............ 1.60
Social Work Services Inspectorate, Helping the Court Decide (1996)
para 9.10 .... 10.4
Social Work Services Inspectorate and Mental Welfare Commission, Investigations into Scottish Borders Council and NHS Borders Services for People with Learning Disabilities: Joint Statement from the Mental Welfare Commission and the Social Work Services Inspectorate, April 2004 2.32
Standards in Social Work Education 1.1
Stationery Office
Children (Scotland) Act 1995 Regulations and Guidance: Volume I, Support and Protection for Children and their Families (1997)
ch 1
para 16....................... 4.5
para 29....................... 4.5
ch 6 .... 4.6
para 5......................... 4.6
ch 7 .... 5.22, 5.28
para 2......................... 4.1
para 5......................... 5.23
paras 13–74 .... 5.7
para 17....................... 5.7
para 29....................... 5.7
ch 8 .... 5.32
Children (Scotland) Act 1995 Regulations and Guidance: Volume 2, Children Looked After by Local Authorities................ 4.1
ch 1
para 121 .... 4.11
Children (Scotland) Act 1995 Regulations and Guidance: Volume 3, Adoption and Parental Responsibilities Orders 4.1

Table of International Materials

References are to Paragraph Number

European Convention on Human Rights 1.9, 1.65, 2.29, 3.3, 5.1, 11.7, 11.10, 11.17

Art 2 .... 1.65, 2.31, 6.15

3 .... 1.65, 1.72, 4.5, 5.33, 5.34, 11.10

5 .... 1.65, 5.16, 7.1, 7.18, 7.19, 7.21, 7.22

(1) 7.18

(d) 4.35

(e) 7.18

(4) 7.18

European Convention on Human Rights – *contd*

Art 6 .... 1.65, 5.16, 5.33, 5.35, 7.1, 11.10

(1) 1.31

8 .... 1.65, 2.3, 2.28, 2.29, 2.31, 2.32, 4.5, 4.14, 4.15, 4.19, 5.33, 5.34, 5.36, 7.1, 11.10

(1), (2) 5.36

10 .... 2.29

United Nations Convention on the Rights of the Child 1.70

Further Reading

CHAPTER 1

Braye, S & Preston-Shoot, M, *Practising Social Work Law* (3rd edn, 2009, Palgrave Macmillan) chs 1 & 2

Roche, J, 'Legal values and Social Work Values', in Davis, R & Gordon J (eds) *Social Work and the Law in Scotland* (2nd edn, 2011, Palgrave Macmillan)

CHAPTER 2

Clark, C & McGhee, J, *Private and Confidential? Handling Personal Information in the Social and Health Services* (2008, Policy Press)

CPAG, *CPAG Welfare Benefits and Tax Credits Handbook* (revised annually)

Scottish Executive, *Code of Guidance on Homelessness* (2005)

Scottish Government, *Statutory Guidance for Local Authorities on Preventing Homelessness* (2009)

Scottish Government, *Statutory Guidance for Meeting the Best Interests of Children Facing Homelessness* (2010).

CHAPTERS 3–5

Choudry, S & Herring, J, *European Human Rights and Family Law* (2010, Hart Publishing)

Cleland, A & Sutherland, E (eds), *Children's Rights in Scotland* (2nd edn, 2009, W Green)

Cleland, A, *Child Abuse, Child Protection & the Law* (2008, W Green)

Munro, E, *Effective Child Protection* (2nd edn, 2008, Sage)

Scottish Executive, *Supporting Young People Leaving Care in Scotland: Regulations and Guidance on Services for Young People Ceasing to be Looked after by Local Authorities* (2004).

Scottish Government, *A Guide to Getting it Right for Every Child* (2008)

Scottish Government, *Getting it Right for Every Child: Guidance on the Child's or Young Person's Plan* (2007)

Scottish Government, *Guidance on Looked after Children (Scotland) Regulations 2009 and the Adoption and Children (Scotland) Act 2007* (2010)

Scottish Government, *National Guidance for Child Protection in Scotland* (2010)

Scottish Government, *Supporting Children's Learning Code of Practice*, revised edition, 2010

Thomson, J M, *Family Law in Scotland* (5th edn, 2006, Bloomsbury Professional)

CHAPTER 6

Clements, L & Thompson, P, *Community Care and the Law* (4th edn)

Glasby, J & Littlechild, R, *Direct Payments and Personal Budgets: Putting Personalisation into Practice* (2nd edn)

McDonald, A *Understanding Community Care: A Guide for Social Workers* (2nd edn)

Oliver, M & Sapey, B, *Social Work with Disabled People* (3rd edn, 2006, Palgrave Macmillan)

Phillips, J, Ray, M & Marshall, M, *Social Work with Older People* (4th edn, 2006, Palgrave Macmillan)

Scottish Executive, *Self-Directed Support – New National Guidance*, Circular CCD7/2007

Scottish Executive: *Guidance for Local Authorities (March 2007): Provision of Community Care Services to Adults with Incapacity*, Circular CCD5/2007

CHAPTER 7

Patrick, H, *Mental Health, Incapacity and the Law in Scotland* (2006, Bloomsbury Professional)

Scottish Executive, *Adults with Incapacity (Scotland) Act 2000: Code of Practice for Managers of Authorised Establishments under Part 4 of the Act* (2003)

Scottish Government, *Adults with Incapacity (Scotland) Act 2000 Code of Practice – Access to Funds* (2008).

Scottish Government, *Adults with Incapacity (Scotland) Act 2000: Code of Practice for Local Authorities Exercising Functions under the 2000 Act* (2008)

Scottish Government, *Adults with Incapacity (Scotland) Act 2000: Communication and Assessing Capacity: A Guide for Social Work and Healthcare Staff* (2008)

Scottish Government, *Adults with Incapacity (Scotland) Act 2000: Code of Practice for Continuing and Welfare Attorneys* (2008)

Scottish Government, *Adults with Incapacity (Scotland) Act 2000: Revised Code of Practice for Persons Authorised under Intervention Orders and Guardians* (2008)

Scottish Government, *Adults with Incapacity (Scotland) Act 2000: Code of Practice (Second Edition) for Practitioners Authorised to Carry out Medical Treatment or Research under Part 5 of the Act* (2007).

Ward, A, *Adult Incapacity* (2003, W Green)

CHAPTER 8

Hothersall, S, Mass-Lowit, M & Golightly, M *Social Work and Mental Health in Scotland* (2008, Learning Matters)

McManus, J & Lindsay, D, *Mental Health and Scots Law in Practice* (2005, W Green)

Patrick, H, *Mental Health, Incapacity and the Law in Scotland* (2006, Bloomsbury Professional)

Scottish Executive, *Mental Health (Care and Treatment) (Scotland) Act 2003: Code of Practice* (2005)

CHAPTER 9

Patrick, H & Smith, N, *Adult Protection and the Law in Scotland* (2009, Bloomsbury Professional)

Scottish Government, *Code of Practice for Local Authorities and Practitioners Exercising Functions under Part 1 of the Act* (revised 2009)

CHAPTER 10

McNeill, F & Whyte, B, *Reducing Reoffending: Social Work and Community Justice in Scotland* (2007, Willan Publishing)

Moore, G and Whyte, B, Moore and Wood's *Social Work and Criminal Law in Scotland* (3rd edn, 1998, Mercat)

Scottish Government, *National Outcomes and Standards for Social Work Services in the Criminal Justice System: CRIMINAL JUSTICE SOCIAL WORK REPORTS AND COURT-BASED SERVICES PRACTICE GUIDANCE* (2010)

Scottish Government, *National Outcomes and Standards for Social Work Services in the Criminal Justice System* (2010)

CHAPTER 12

Scottish Government, *National Outcomes and Standards for Social Work Services in the Criminal Justice System: COMMUNITY PAYBACK ORDERS PRACTICE GUIDANCE* (2010)

Abbreviations

CASE REPORTS

AC	Appeal Cases
All ER	All England Law Reports
BMLR	Butterworths Medico-Legal Reports
EHRR	European Human Rights Reports
Fam	Family Law Division
FCR	Family Court Reporter
FLR	Family Law Reports
IRLR	Industrial Relations Law Reports
JC	Justiciary Cases
LGR	Local Government Reports
QB	Queen's Bench Division
SC	Session Cases
SCCR	Scottish Criminal Case Reports
SCLR	Scottish Civil Law Reports
SLT	Scots Law Times
SLT (Sh Ct)	Scots Law Times (Sheriff Court)

STATUTES

the 1968 Act	the Social Work (Scotland) Act 1968
the 1970 Act	the Chronically Sick and Disabled Persons Act 1970
the 1981 Act	the Matrimonial Homes (Family Protection)(Scotland) Act 1981
the 1985 Act	the Family Law (Scotland) Act 1985
the 1986 Act	the Disabled Persons (Services, Consultation and Representation) Act 1986
the 1987 Act	the Housing (Scotland) Act 1987
the 1991 Act	the Age of Legal Capacity (Scotland) Act 1991
the 1995 Act	the Children (Scotland) Act 1995
the 2000 Act	the Adults with Incapacity (Scotland) Act 2000
the 2003 Act	the Mental Health (Care and Treatment) Scotland Act 2003
the 2007 Act	the Adult Support and Protection (Scotland) Act 2007

OTHER

ASBO	Antisocial Behaviour Order
BASW	British Association of Social Workers
CA	Court of Appeal
CAO	Child Assessment Order
CICA	Criminal Injuries Compensation Authority
CPAG	Child Poverty Action Group
CPO	Child Protection Order
CSO	Community Service Order
CTO	Compulsory Treatment Order
DAS	Debt Arrangement Scheme
DCSF	Department for Children, Schools and Families
DMP	Designated Medical Practitioner
ECtHR	European Court of Human Rights
EDC	Emergency Detention Certificates
HC	House of Commons Papers
HDC	Home Detention Curfew
HL	House of Lords
IH	Inner House
JP	Justice of the Peace
MAPPP	Multi Agency Public Protection Partnership
MAPPA	Multi Agency Public Protection Arrangements
MHO	Mental Health Officer
MHT	Mental Health Tribunal
MWC	Mental Welfare Commission
OH	Outer House
RMO	Responsible Medical Officer
SCR	Social Circumstances Report
SCRC	Scottish Commission for the Regulation of Care
SCSWIS	Social Care and Social Work Improvement Scotland
SSSC	Scottish Social Services Council
STDC	Short Term Detention Certificates
SWIA	Social Work Inspection Agency

Chapter 1

The Scottish legal context of social work

INTRODUCTION

1.1 Most social work in Scotland is practised within the context of local authority departments, many of which bear the name social work or social service department. This text will concentrate on this framework and for simplicity's sake refer to these settings as social work departments, except where special reference is made to the voluntary or private sector. There is a legal dimension to all of the work undertaken by social workers employed by the local authority.

Social workers are **obliged** to perform some functions and **permitted** to perform others by the laws passed by Parliament (either the UK or the Scottish Parliament) and arising out of court cases. They also have specified **powers** and **duties** which are defined by the law and derive much of their authority from the law. People who come into contact with social workers employed by the local authority have specified **rights** and **responsibilities** which are based in law. The contact between these people and the social worker is therefore driven by the law and without a knowledge of that law the social worker cannot function competently and the service user may also forfeit various legal entitlements.

Social workers need to be able to recognise and make use of this legal dimension in social work practice. Social workers occupy a privileged and unique position in relation to people who have legal needs. Here is an opportunity for social workers to assist in enhancing quality of life by sharing their understanding of the law and the legislative framework with service users who may be in crisis and so temporarily unable to make sense of their circumstances, who may be unfamiliar with the legal system, and/or who may be without the necessary social skills to navigate in legal waters.

Further opportunities arise for social workers through direct involvement with offenders and ex-offenders. The retention of the probation service functions under the auspices of social work departments has provided the continuing recognition that social work values, knowledge, and skills are most appropriate in dealing with this service user population.

Social work law has not in general proved an attractive area of specialisation for solicitors,[1] and so there is an additional incentive and requirement for social workers to share their awareness and understanding of the legal dimension of their work both with service users and with other professionals. We are not advocating that social workers become second-rate lawyers but that they use their knowledge of law to inform their practice and contribute to the facilitating of shared social work goals. A study of the law relating to social work also contributes to an understanding of the variety of acceptable roles which are appropriate for social workers. In view of society's ambiguous relationship with social workers, these roles are often contradictory and ambivalent. They include investigator, assessor, supervisor, witness, conciliator, reporter, facilitator, liaison, advisor, guide, support, broker, enabler, teacher, mediator and advocate.[2] Social workers may be in a position to help to identify and enforce the rights of vulnerable service users and/or they may be in the position of enforcing service users' compliance with the law. These roles will be explored in more depth subsequently.

The importance of a thorough grounding in the law relevant to social work practice cannot be sufficiently emphasised. This point is made in several places in the *Standards in Social Work Education* which set out the knowledge, skills and competences to be demonstrated by newly graduated social workers.[3] In addition to requirements which imply an underpinning understanding of the law these set out more specific requirements, for example, the requirement to understand 'social worker roles as statutory agents with duties and responsibilities to protect the public and uphold the law'[4] and the 'nature of legal authority, the application of legislation in practice, statutory responsibility and conflicts between statute policy and

1 See, for example, Scottish Government, *Limited Review of the Mental Health (Care and Treatment) (Scotland) Act 2003* (2009), noting (at p 57) that 'Mental health law is not currently an area of law which attracts a broad interest from within the profession'.

2 These last four interventive roles are discussed in B Compton and B Galaway *Social Work Processes* (6th edn, 1999), pp 309–312.

3 These are set out in Scottish Executive, *The Framework for Social Work Education in Scotland* (2003) and form the basis of approval of programmes leading to a social work degree by the Scottish Social Services Council (SSSC) (see SSSC, Rules for Social Work Training 2003, r 6(d)(ii)).

4 Scottish Executive, *The Framework for Social Work Education in Scotland* (2003), p 34.

practice.'[5] Graduating social workers also need to be able to 'assess and evaluate needs, strengths, risks and options taking account of legal ... duties',[6] 'revise and regularly update their own knowledge of relevant legislation...',[7] and 'assess human situations taking account of a number of factors including ... legislation.'[8]

Three things should be made clear at the start about the operation of law. The first is that the law does not necessarily specify a precise course of action to be followed in given circumstances. In most cases there is room for considerable discretion in applying the law, though once it is applied there may be precise procedures to be followed (a good example of this is the law relating to child protection orders).[9] The way in which discretion is to be exercised in these areas may be the subject of guidance from various sources or may be the subject of departmental policies. In such areas knowledge of the guidance and policies is essential, but the underlying legal framework must not be ignored.

Secondly, there are areas of social work which are not covered specifically or in detail by legislation (for example, much work with elderly people) and which are simply covered by the general (and very vague) obligation to promote social welfare and assist those in need contained in the Social Work (Scotland) Act 1968 (see para 1.67 below).

Third, legal rules are not self applying. In other words, legal rules have to be put into action by individuals and organisations. This has the consequence that these individuals and organisations have to interpret the law and that they also have to interpret the world to decide whether the circumstances they see are circumstances to which a particular legal rule applies. For example, are the circumstances of a child's life such as to qualify him/her as a 'child in need' in terms of the Children (Scotland) Act 1995?

This means that there is discretion in applying the legal rules, individuals and organisations can decide both how to apply the law and also when to apply it.

One final general comment needs to be made about the language of the law and the language of social work. The occasional incompatibility of these two is characteristic of the nature and value base of each. Legal language can seem obscure, arcane and even offensive with its insist-

5 Ibid, p 37.
6 Ibid, p 28.
7 Ibid, p 36.
8 Ibid, p 28.
9 See paras 5.22–5.26.

ence on false generics (such as the use of the pronoun 'he' to represent both sexes) while social work language can seem politically correct and driven by the dominant ideology of the day. We have attempted to use language which is representative of each discipline in an effort to find a language understandable to both.

THE FUNCTIONS OF LAW IN SOCIETY

1.2 Although there has been some dispute about the need for law to regulate society much of that debate is, in fact, about the precise form of law or about its appropriateness as a means of resolving social problems. There is in reality broad agreement about the need for some system of universal rules to regulate the operation of society.[10] Since social workers' interventions are so inextricably entwined with the functions of law, it is imperative that they understand and appreciate these functions. The principal functions of law can be said to be:[11]

(a) Social control

1.3 It does this through the enforcement of criminal law and the provision of mechanisms to allow private individuals to resolve their disputes (principally the civil courts). The former of these is sometimes seen, simplistically and erroneously, as the sole or main function of law.

(b) Constitution of law-making and law-enforcing bodies

1.4 The law also provides for the make up and procedure of the UK and Scottish Parliaments and the court system. As part of this process individuals may be given certain rights and protections, such as the right of access to legal representation for court appearances.

10 The Russian anarchist Kropotkin, for example, noted that 'No society is possible without certain principles of morality generally recognised': *Revolutionary Pamphlets* (1970), p 73.

11 These functions can be formulated in various ways, for an alternative see Braye, S & Preston-Shoot, M, *Practising Social Work Law* (3rd edn, 2009), pp 24–34.

(c) Enabling function

1.5 At a very basic level it is sometimes argued that law, by guaranteeing peace, enables people to carry on with their lives. However, it also makes much more specific provision to allow people to make arrangements which will be legally recognised and enforced, such as adoption, contracts and appointment of attorneys.

(d) Promotion of social welfare

1.6 Law is used as a tool for the promotion of social welfare (or at least the policies of various governments which are said to be directed towards this end). Clearly, law cannot do this by itself but rather it provides the framework of organisations, such as local authority social work departments, to do so, gives them powers and duties (as it confers these on the employees of social work departments), and confers rights, such as to benefits and as to certain types of assessment, on individuals.

LAW AND SOCIAL PROBLEMS

1.7 Social problems are not necessarily amenable to purely legal solutions. However, when the legal solution facilitates the potential resolution of a social problem then the use of such means can be justified and the failure to use such means would be inexcusable.

On a broader level there are difficulties in successfully using purely legal means to resolve social problems. One illustration is the failure of anti-discrimination legislation to secure equal pay[12] and employment prospects for women. Legal intervention can bring about benefits and improvements and may, perhaps, perform a function in changing attitudes or raising awareness of issues, but it is often not on its own able to provide a complete resolution of the problem to which it is addressed.

In approaching the resolution of either collective or individual problems in society there may be a conflict between the values of law and those of

12 See, most recently, Office for National Statistics, *2009 Annual Survey of Hours and Earnings*, p 4.

social work.[13] This apparent conflict cannot, however, obscure the reality that practice takes place in a framework of law nor that the discretion inherent in the application of the law permits its application to be mediated by social work values.

THE DISTINCTIVE CHARACTER OF SCOTS LAW

1.8 The Scottish legal system had, at least until 1707, a different history from the legal system in the rest of the UK. One of the consequences of this is that the structure of the court system in Scotland is quite different from that in England, Wales and Northern Ireland. There were also significant differences in substantive law, and these continued after 1707. Despite the existence of a single parliament within the UK, separate and different provision continued to be made for Scotland in many areas, one example being the Social Work (Scotland) Act 1968 which, in contradistinction to the position in England and Wales, incorporated probation services within generic social work departments and introduced a distinctive means of dealing with the cases of children through the system of children's hearings. Despite this, it is not true to suggest that all the law which applies in Scotland differs from that which applies in other parts of the UK. At the other end of the scale there are areas of law where the law is the same throughout the UK, obvious example are the benefits system, the law relating to rights in employment, the law regarding discrimination and the rules about driving. There is, finally, a third category of law. In this category there are similarities between the law in Scotland and the law in the rest of the UK. These differences may be in the substance of the law, in other words what the law says might be slightly different, or the law might be the same but the source of the law is different. The creation of the (new) Scottish Parliament in 1999 has not really changed this pattern. The period since 1999 has seen a large number of Acts of the Scottish Parliament (asps) concerned with the services provided by social work departments. Reflecting the pattern above most of these have made separate provision, but there are also provisions which mirror developments in England and Wales, for example in relation to the protection of vulnerable groups and the extension of carer's rights to assessment.

13 See, for example. Preston-Shoot, M *et al*, 'Working Together in Social Work Law', (1998) *Journal of Social Welfare and Family Law*, 137; Braye, S and Preston-Shoot, M, 'The Role of Law in Welfare Reform: Critical Perspectives on the Relationship between Law and Social Work Practice', (2006) 15 *International Journal of Social Welfare* 19.

In some cases, for example in relation to civil partnerships, the Scottish Parliament has permitted the UK Parliament to legislate for Scotland in an area within the competence of the Edinburgh parliament. Table 1 on the next page sets out some of the areas of law relevant to social work practice where there are similarities and differences between Scotland and England and Wales. There are also more general areas of difference, for example large parts of criminal law[14] are different as between Scotland and the rest of the UK.

FORMAL SOURCES OF LAW

1.9 Formal sources of law are the actual statements of the law, as opposed to textbooks or commentaries on the law. The main formal sources of law as it affects social workers are Acts of Parliament (either the UK or the Scottish Parliament) (statutes), such as the Children (Scotland) Act 1995 and the Mental Health (Care and Treatment) (Scotland) Act 2003; delegated legislation (usually in the form of statutory instruments or Scottish statutory instruments), such as the regulations governing the care and placement of looked after children;[15] and case law, that is the law derived from decisions made by courts.

As we noted in a previous section, one of the functions of law is the promotion of social welfare, and this has resulted in a fairly substantial volume of legislation. This growth in legislation was given further impetus by the creation of the new Scottish Parliament in 1999. Any legislation passed by the Scottish Parliament must be compliant with the European Convention on Human Rights and the Scottish Parliament has power to legislate in any area not reserved to the UK Parliament. The areas reserved to the UK Parliament include:[16] data protection, nationality and immigration, consumer protection, social security (excluding support provided under the Social Work (Scotland) Act 1968, the Chronically Sick and Disabled Persons Act 1970 and the Children (Scotland) Act 1995), employment, and equal opportunities (including anti-discrimination legislation). From this list it should be clear that the Scottish Parliament has the power to legislate in most areas related to social work practice. Most of the law we will be discussing in the remainder of

14 Eg there is no crime of manslaughter in Scotland (it is culpable homicide) nor is there breaking and entering in Scotland, this is theft by housebreaking.

15 See ch 4.

16 The powers of the Scottish Parliament are set out in the Scotland Act 1998, sections 29 & 30 and Schedules 4 & 5.

Area	Scottish Provision	E & W provision	Similarities/differences
Mental Health	Mental Health (Care and Treatment) (Scotland) Act 2003	Mental Health Act 1983	Significant differences in content, processes and terminology. For example there is no set of principles set out in the 1983 Act, instead these are in a Code of Practice, and nearest relatives can still make applications for detention.
Adults with Incapacity	Adults with Incapacity (Scotland) Act 2000	Mental Capacity Act 2005	Significant differences in content, processes and terminology. For example the 2005 Act contains safeguards relating to deprivation of liberty not found in the 2000 Act and the appointees able to take decisions on behalf of adults are described in the 2005 Act as 'deputies.'
Looked after children	Children (Scotland) Act 1995, ss 16 & 17	Children Act 1989, ss 22 & 23	Some similarities, but also some differences
Emergency protection of children	Children (Scotland) Act 1995, s 55 (Child Assessment Order (CAO)) & s 57 (Child Protection Order)	Children Act 1989, s 43 (CAO) & s 44 (Emergency Protection Order)	Similarities in grounds for action and making of orders, but differences in procedure in obtaining order and subsequent to granting of order
Children in need of compulsory measures	Children (Scotland) Act 1995	Children Act 1989	Procedures entirely different, in E & W application made to court for care order or supervision order, limited court involvement in Scotland (aside from determining existence of grounds of referral & appeals) – dealt with by children's hearings

Area	**Scottish Provision**	**E & W provision**	**Similarities/differences**
Children in need	Children (Scotland) Act 1995, s 22	Children Act 1989, s 17	Very similar, though powers in E & W set out more fully in schedule 2 of 1989 Act
Aftercare	Children (Scotland) Act 1995, ss 29–30 (& regulations)	Children Act 1989, ss 23A – 24D	Similar, but not identical
Free personal care	Community Care and Health (Scotland) Act 2002	No equivalent	
Community Care Assessments & services	Social Work (Scotland) Act 1968 & Chronically Sick and Disabled Persons Act 1970	NHS & Community Care Act 1990 & Chronically Sick and Disabled Persons Act 1970	Provisions virtually identical except that statutory basis in Scotland is slightly different (1990 Act inserted new provisions, eg section 12A into 1968 Act)
Adult Protection	Adult Support and Protection (Scotland) Act 2007	No equivalent	
Vulnerable groups	Protection of Vulnerable Groups (Scotland) Act 2007	Safeguarding Vulnerable Groups Act 2006	Following from Bichard Report[17] these provide for vetting and barring of people working with children and other vulnerable groups – procedures and administrative bodies differ between Scotland and E & W.

17 *The Bichard Inquiry Report* (2004), 2003–4 HC 653.

this book is derived from statute. The precise mechanism for the passing of an Act of Parliament need not concern us here,[18] but Acts are often preceded by consultation documents produced by the government setting out its intentions as to legislation which allow for comment from interested parties on the proposals before they are finalised.

For a variety of reasons statutes often omit detailed regulations. The power to make these is usually delegated to a government minister or in the Scottish context to the Scottish Ministers. Even though the power to legislate is delegated, any delegated legislation made has the same legal effect as an Act of Parliament. Examples of delegated legislation are the rules regulating the conduct of children's hearings[19] and those regulating procedure at the Mental Health Tribunal.[20] These rules can be changed more rapidly than Acts in response to increased awareness of their potential implications. The power to make more detailed rules may be delegated to other bodies. Thus the power to make procedural rules for civil court cases such as adoption cases has been delegated to the Court of Session. Statutes may also provide for the Scottish Ministers to issue guidance, such as the guidance issued on the Children (Scotland) Act 1995[21] and the general power to issue guidance conferred by the Social Work (Scotland) Act 1968.[22]

Acts of Parliament do not necessarily or usually become part of the law as soon as they are passed. Instead, an Act will usually provide that it is to be brought into force (that is, become part of the law) by orders made by the appropriate Minister; consequently, different sections of the Act may be brought into force at different times. One example of this is the Children (Scotland) Act 1995. Part of this came into force in November 1995, other provisions came into force in November 1996 and virtually all of the remainder in April 1997. Acts are also subject to amendment and (total or partial) repeal, for example the Social Work (Scotland) Act 1968 in its current form is very different from the Act passed in 1968.

Case law may offer a definitive interpretation of the provisions of an Act of Parliament, such as, for example, the grounds for compulsory meas-

18 And differs as between the UK and Scottish Parliaments.

19 The Children's Hearings (Scotland) Rules 1996, SI 1996/3261.

20 Mental Health Tribunal for Scotland (Practice and Procedure) (No 2) Rules 2005, SSI 2005/519.

21 Extensive guidance has been issued on a range of topics and in a variety of forms. It will be discussed in the text as appropriate.

22 Social Work (Scotland) Act 1968, s 5.

ures of supervision. It is also the source of legal rules in some areas, for example the law relating to liability for negligence.[23]

RIGHTS, POWERS AND DUTIES

1.10 As we indicated at the beginning of this chapter, most social workers work for local authorities. It is particularly important for workers in this setting to understand the statutory basis for most of their work. What we mean by this is that local authorities, social work departments and individual workers all owe their existence, their powers and their duties to Acts of Parliament. Were it not for the Local Government (Scotland) Acts local authorities would not exist and would have no powers. Were it not, for example, for the Social Work (Scotland) Act 1968 they would have no duty to provide reports for courts.

The notions of rights, powers and duties merit some further discussion. Duties[24] are obligations imposed on authorities and workers to act. There are different types of duty imposed on social workers. They may be subject to ethical, moral or professional duties,[25] but they, and their employers, also have legal duties. Legal duties are requirements to act (they might be seen as orders to do something). Some of these duties are very general and impose rather vague obligations on local authorities and workers. The classic example of this is section 12 of the 1968 Act, which begins by stating that 'it shall be the duty of every local authority to promote social welfare by making available advice, guidance and assistance on such a scale as may be appropriate for their area'. This is arguably so broad that it confers a general power on local authorities to provide services. Other duties are much more specific and will confer rights on specific individuals enabling them to enforce these duties. For example, the local authority has a duty to assess the needs of a person with possible need for community care services. If the authority failed or refused to carry out an assessment that person could go to court to obtain an order forcing it to do so. The more general duties imposed on local authorities are more difficult to enforce because it is more difficult to argue that they impose specific duties towards (and confer specific rights on) specific individuals. In many cases a duty will arise only where certain prior conditions have been fulfilled. For example, a specific duty to provide a service may arise only fol-

23 Usually seen as being based on *Donoghue v Stevenson* 1932 SC (HL) 31, apocryphally credited with giving rise to the phrase 'gie's a slug of your ginger'.
24 Duties are sometimes referred to as responsibilities or obligations.
25 For example those set out in Scottish Social Services Council, *Code of Practice for Social Service Workers* (2002) and BASW, *Code of Ethics for Social Work* (2002).

lowing an assessment and the making of a judgement about need. Not all duties imposed on social workers are imposed by statute or by a statute specific to local authorities, for example duties to exercise reasonable care in the performance of their work derive from case law. Duties imposed by law can sometimes conflict with other types of duty to a service user and with service users' expectations.[26]

Powers are authorisations to act. They may give the authority or worker the ability or capacity to do something, but do not require that it is done. An example is the power to apply for a child protection order. This discretionary nature of powers means that their use is not determined by the law, but is, rather, informed by the professional judgment of those entitled to exercise them. One consequence of the statutory basis of social work is that local authorities and social workers only have the powers conferred on them by statute or implied by duties imposed on them and any attempt to exercise powers beyond these would be unlawful. The law would describe such an attempt as acting *ultra vires*, that is, beyond the powers conferred by statute.[27]

Legal rights usually refer to entitlements conferred on individuals which they can enforce through the legal system. Some of these rights are general, such as the right to defend yourself against attack; others involve specific claims against individuals or organisations. Examples of this second category are the right to claim damages from someone who has injured you, the right to benefits and the right not to be unfairly dismissed. In many cases the rights exist because of a duty imposed on someone else. Most rights in the context of social work involve service users' rights. Some of these are seen in the duties noted above, such as the right to an assessment, but there are others, for example the right of access to social work records.

As we have seen, use of powers depends on the exercise of judgment by workers. In some cases duties may arise only after the exercise of judgment: for example, as we will see[28], a duty to provide services to a disabled person arises only after judgments have been made about the needs of that person and what services should be provided to meet these needs. Decisions involving judgment are described in law as discretionary and the discretion enjoyed by workers is not unrestrained: their decisions can be challenged in a variety of ways, including by judicial

26 See, for example, Shardlow, S, 'Confidentiality, Accountability and the Boundaries of Client-worker Relationships' in Hugman and Smith (eds) *Ethical Issues in Social Work* (1985).

27 Though the powers conferred on local authorities are very wide.

28 See ch 6.

review (see para 1.59 below and chapter 11). Workers may also have to take account of guidance issued by government or by their employers in exercising their discretion.

LEGAL PERSONNEL

(1) Solicitors and advocates

1.11 The basic division within the legal profession is between solicitors and advocates (the latter are sometimes referred to as counsel). Solicitors are the most numerous. They have direct contact with their clients and may practice in all areas of the law, as is common in smaller towns, or specialise in a particular area of law. The Law Society of Scotland, the solicitors' professional body, publishes a directory of firms indicating the areas of work which they will undertake. Often social workers develop a local knowledge of solicitors who have a particular interest in social welfare, mental health law family law, and/or criminal law which can prove useful to service users.

Advocates specialise in court appearance and in giving advice on complex matters of law. Advocates have no direct contact or relationship with their ultimate client: the relationship is managed by the client's solicitors. Historically, advocates had an exclusive right to appear in the higher courts (that is the High Court, the Court of Session and the Supreme Court) but there are now provisions to allow solicitors to appear in these courts. Solicitor-advocates, as these are described, are solicitors who have passed a test of competence and fulfilled certain other requirements to allow them to represent people in the High Court or in the Court of Session. Complaints about members of the legal profession in Scotland are dealt with through the Scottish Legal Complaints Commission.

(2) Procurators fiscal and the system of public prosecution

1.12 Prosecutions for crimes and offences in Scotland have for a long time been undertaken by a public prosecutor, this function is now carried out by the Crown Office Procurator Fiscal Service. The system is headed by the Lord Advocate who advises the Scottish government on matters of law generally, as well as being the head of the system of prosecution. The Lord Advocate is assisted by the Solicitor General. Together they are known as 'the Law Officers'. Below these two are a number of Advocates Depute, also referred to as Crown

Counsel, though this term also includes the Law Officers. Advocates Depute are advocates who are appointed to the position usually for a relatively short period of time. Solicitor-advocates and senior members of the fiscal service may now also be appointed to act as Crown Counsel. In practice, most of the work in the prosecution system is done by procurators fiscal and procurators fiscal depute who are the local representatives of the public prosecution service. These are full-time permanent civil servants and there will be a procurator fiscal in each sheriff court. The administration of the system of prosecution is the responsibility of the Crown Office Procurator Fiscal Service.

Where someone has been apprehended on suspicion of having committed a crime, or where a serious crime has been committed, the matter will be reported to the procurator fiscal. The fiscal is, legally, in charge of the investigation of the crime and can direct the police in their conduct of the investigation. In most cases, however, little or no further investigation will be necessary, and the fiscal simply has to decide how to process the report, that is, to decide whether to prosecute or not.

In cases where prosecution will take place in a summary court (for an explanation of this see para 1.26 below), the decision is entirely one for the fiscal, operating under the guidance of a book of regulations issued by the Lord Advocate. It is the fiscal's decision whether to prosecute or not, which court to prosecute in, and if no prosecution is to take place, whether simply to let the matter drop or to take some form of action which falls broadly into the category of diversion.

In more serious cases, where the crime/offence might be prosecuted before a solemn court (for an explanation of this see para 1.26 below), the fiscal must report the case to the Crown Office and the decision on how to proceed will be made by a senior advocate depute in cases which will be prosecuted in the High Court. For cases which will be tried in the sheriff solemn court the decision will be taken by a member of staff in the Crown Office.[29]

In deciding whether to prosecute a fiscal will take account of two main factors – whether there is sufficient admissible evidence and the public interest. The latter involves consideration of a variety of matters including the nature and gravity of the offence, the impact of the offence on the victim, the ages of the accused and the victim, mitigating circumstances, the risk of further offending and public concern.[30]

29 See *Renton & Brown's Criminal Procedure* (6th edn), 3–03.
30 Crown Office and Procurator Fiscal Service, *Prosecution Code* (2001).

Despite the history of public prosecution in Scotland, it is still technically possible for an individual to pursue a private prosecution. Such private prosecutions require the consent of either the Lord Advocate or of the High Court. There were only two cases in the twentieth century in which a private prosecution was allowed to proceed.[31]

Prosecutions in the sheriff and district courts will normally be undertaken by the fiscal or a depute. In the High Court the prosecutor will be one of the Law Officers or an Advocate Depute.

In cases where there is sufficient evidence to proceed to prosecution the fiscal may, instead of prosecuting, administer a warning. Before this can be done there must be sufficient evidence to justify proceedings and the case must not be so trivial as to merit no action. Fiscals also have the power in certain types of cases to offer an individual the option of paying a fixed penalty or the option of paying compensation to the victim as an alternative to prosecution. Finally, there are a number of diversion schemes in operation where individuals are diverted to social work assistance in place of prosecution. These options are considered in paras 10.35–10.40.

As well as being a prosecutor the fiscal is also responsible for investigating all sudden and suspicious deaths and suicides.

(3) Judges

1.13 Justice of the Peace (JP) courts are most often presided over by one or more lay justices of the peace. These are people who have no legal training but have been appointed to act as justices. They will be guided as to the law by the clerk to the court. The practice as to the number of justices sitting to hear a case varies between different areas. There are also, in Glasgow, a number of stipendiary magistrates who sit in the JP court. They are legally qualified and sit alone to hear cases. They have greater sentencing powers than lay justices. Sheriff courts are staffed by sheriffs who are legally qualified, most having been advocates. Finally, there are the judges who preside both in the Court of Session and in the High Court. They are all legally qualified and are variously described as Lords of Session, Lord Commissioners of Justiciary and Senators of the College of Justice. How they are described depends on which role they are fulfilling.

31 The more famous being the so-called 'Glasgow rape case' of the early 1980s, *H v Sweeney* 1983 SLT 48.

(4) Clerks of court

1.14 Sheriff clerks are responsible for the running of sheriff courts, recording of proceedings (though not shorthand note-taking), arranging for reports, arranging (in consultation with the procurator fiscal) the court timetable, maintenance of records, collection of fines, and the organisation and distribution of social enquiry reports. This last task will involve co-operation with the social worker(s) attached to the court, who will make arrangements with the appropriate social work area office for the report to be provided. Each sheriff court will have a sheriff clerk who will be assisted by deputes. The JP and High Courts have clerks who broadly perform the same function for them as sheriff clerks do for the sheriff court.

(5) Sheriff officers and messengers-at-arms

1.15 Sheriff officers are officers of court who must fulfil certain requirements (for example having completed a period of training and passed specified examinations) and hold a warrant from the sheriff principal to act. They are not directly employed by the court system but rather are court officers in the sense that they are authorised to do certain things by virtue of their warrant and are accountable to court for their actions. Sheriff officers are used to serve summonses and citations in civil cases, to carry out the enforcement of civil judgments, such as evictions and warrant sales, and to serve witness citations for the defence in criminal cases. Messengers-at-arms perform similar functions in relation to actions in the Court of Session.

(6) Miscellaneous

1.16 As well as those noted above there is a variety of other people involved in the operation of the court system. These include ushers and bar officers who assist in the actual functioning of the courts, directing people to the right court and maintaining order in court.

CIVIL COURT SYSTEM AND PROCEDURES

1.17 The civil court system basically deals with all cases which do not involve the commission of a crime or offence and which are not dealt with by a special body, such as an employment tribunal, mental health tribunal or children's hearing. Examples of the sorts of case it deals with are given below. Before going on to look at the various courts in the civil court system some explanation of the distinction between courts of first instance and courts of appeal is necessary. Courts of first instance are the courts at which trials take place and in which civil cases are initially disposed of. Appeal courts deal only or mainly with appeals from the decisions of courts of first instance.

(1) Sheriff court

1.18 Scotland is divided up into six sheriffdoms, five of which (the exception being Glasgow and Strathkelvin) are then subdivided into sheriff court districts, each of which has a sheriff court building. Each sheriffdom is staffed by a sheriff principal and a number of sheriffs. The precise organisation of the court will depend on the level of business; in rural areas, for example, the court may sit only on one day a week or as necessary to deal with the business.

The sheriff civil court involves a sheriff sitting alone to deal with cases at first instance. It cannot deal with some matters; the main exclusions being judicial review (see para 1.59 below). On the other hand, there are certain matters that can only be dealt with at the sheriff court, for example eviction and actions for sums of money less than £5,000.

The sheriff civil court deals with such matters as adoption, proofs on reference from children's hearings, divorce, applications under the Adults with Incapacity (Scotland) Act 2000 and (accounting for most of its business) small debt actions.

Decisions of the sheriff can be appealed to the sheriff principal and then to the Inner House of the Court of Session or direct to the Inner House. The ability to appeal to the Inner House is subject to some restrictions.

(2) Court of Session

1.19 The Court of Session sits only in Edinburgh. It is divided into an Outer House, which consists of judges sitting alone to deal with cases at first instance, and an Inner House. The Inner House is divided into two divisions (usually three judges sit in a case) and deals primarily with appeals from the Outer House and from the sheriff court and sheriff principal. The Inner House is also a court of first instance for a variety of applications under companies legislation and other specialised forms of procedure. Appeals arising from the children's hearing system may end up in the Inner House.

(3) Supreme Court

1.20 This operates only as a court of appeal. In cases originating in the sheriff court the appeal must be concerned with a question of law rather than a factual dispute. It replaced the House of Lords as the final appeal court in October 2009.

(4) Procedures

(a) Small claims procedure

1.21 This type of procedure is designed to provide a simple and inexpensive form of action which can be easily used by members of the public. It can be used to recover money up to £3,000 or for the recovery of property up to that value. Most cases in practice are of the former type and may be actions to recover debts (most commonly) or actions to recover damages.

There is no provision for legal aid in this process (see para 1.61 ff below) as the intention is that private individuals will be able to conduct cases themselves. There is, however, provision allowing either party to be represented at any hearing by any other person. Where that person is not a solicitor the sheriff must be satisfied that the person is a 'suitable person'.

(b) Summary cause procedure

1.22 Summary cause procedure, again a simplified form of procedure, is similar to small claims procedure. It is the appropriate means of recovering sums of money between £3,000 and £5,000; it is also used for actions for eviction.[32]

(c) Ordinary procedure

1.23 This form of procedure is used in the sheriff court. It is appropriate for claims in excess of £5,000 and for other types of case, including divorces not covered by the 'do-it-yourself procedure.[33] Procedure in the Court of Session is similar to ordinary procedure. Unlike small claims and summary cause procedure, this type of procedure is based

32 See also para 2.4.
33 See para 3.11.

on extensive written pleadings (essentially the claims and counter-claims made by the parties to the court action).

(d) Special procedures

1.24 A variety of types of case of interest to social workers have their own special forms of procedure. These include proof of grounds of referral to a children's hearing, appeals from hearing decisions and adoption. The procedures will be explained in more detail when we look at these areas.

(5) Standard of proof

1.25 The standard of proof in civil cases is proof on the balance of probabilities. Generally, then, the person initiating the case must satisfy the court that his/her version of events is more probable than that put forward by the other party. The nature of the evidence used to establish this standard is considered in paras 1.39–1.56 below.

CRIMINAL COURT SYSTEM AND PROCEDURES

1.26 Within the criminal court system there is a distinction between solemn and summary courts. The essential distinction between these is that in summary courts the judge(s) takes the decision on guilt or innocence, whereas in solemn courts this is done by a jury of 15. There are also some differences in the procedure followed in the different types of court. These will be considered more fully below.

(1) JP courts

1.27 Justice of the Peace (JP) courts replaced District Courts[34] and are administered by the Scottish Courts Service rather than by the local authority. As noted above, the JP court will normally be presided over by one or more JPs with legal advice from the clerk of court.

The sorts of cases the JP court can deal with are restricted. It cannot deal with housebreaking cases, serious assaults, forgery, theft and fraud cases where the amount involved is more than £2,500, and cases involving the prosecution of children under 16.

34 The process was completed between 2008 and 2010.

The sentencing powers of the court are limited to a fine of up to level 4 on the standard scale (currently £2,500) and up to 60 days' imprisonment. Where the court is presided over by a stipendiary magistrate it has the same sentencing powers as the sheriff summary court. As always in this chapter, references to sentencing powers are to the maximum sentence that can be imposed in the absence of a specific statutory provision restricting or enhancing the power in respect of particular crimes or offences.

(2) Sheriff summary court

1.28 The sheriff summary court is held in the same buildings and staffed by the same personnel as the sheriff civil court.

The sentencing powers of this court are, currently, a fine of £10,000 and custodial sentence of up to 12 months. The sheriff summary court deals with over half of all criminal cases.

(3) Sheriff solemn court

1.29 The sheriff solemn court deals with slightly more serious cases and this is reflected in its sentencing power. The sheriff sitting in this court can impose an unlimited fine and a custodial sentence of up to 5 years. In cases where the sheriff considers that these sentencing powers are inadequate the case can be remitted to the High Court for sentence. This happens very rarely in practice. The sheriff solemn court deals with about 3–4% of criminal cases.

(4) High Court of Justiciary

1.30 Although this has the same personnel as the Court of Session it sits not only in Edinburgh but also at locations throughout Scotland, and is, for example, in almost permanent session in Glasgow. The High Court is the only court which can deal with certain crimes, the most notable being murder and rape. The High Court deals with around 1% of criminal cases.

(5) High Court as court of appeal

1.31 The High Court has always operated as a court of appeal from summary courts. For this purpose it sits in Edinburgh and is presided over by three judges or, if the appeal is only about sentence, two judges.

Since 1926 it has also operated in the same format as the Court of Criminal Appeal to deal with appeals from solemn courts. It is possible to make a further reference to the Supreme Court in cases involving devolution issues.[35]

(6) Procedures

(a) Summary procedure

1.32 Summary procedure is initiated by the service of a document known as a 'complaint' on the accused. The complaint will contain brief details of the alleged offence, including the time and date. This narration of events is known as 'the libel'. Attached to the complaint will be a notice of previous convictions, if relevant, where the offence is a statutory offence there will be a notice of penalties setting out the possible penalties on conviction and, where the offence is one of a list of sexual offences (including rape and indecent assault), a notice covering certain matters, including that the defence may only be conducted by a lawyer.

On the first appearance of the accused, either from custody or on the date specified for the hearing on the citation accompanying the complaint, the plea will be taken. Proceedings in criminal cases are known as 'diets', and this diet is sometimes referred to as 'the pleading diet'. If the accused pleads guilty the court may proceed to sentence, or may defer sentence for reports or for the accused to be of good behaviour. If the accused pleads not guilty a date will be set for trial.

If the accused pleads not guilty there will be an intermediate diet called before the trial diet. The purpose of this diet is to assess the state of preparation on both sides, the number of witnesses required for trial by the prosecution and defence, to establish if the accused intends to maintain the plea of not guilty, and to supervise the extent to which the prosecution and defence have fulfilled their duty to identify and agree uncontroversial evidence. The reason for introducing this intermediate diet was to try to reduce the number of people pleading not guilty at the first diet and changing the plea to guilty at the trial. Procedure at the trial is considered below.

35 Devolution issues relate to whether an official or the Scottish government or Parliament has acted competently, for example whether their actions contravene the European Convention on Human Rights. One example is *Dyer v Watson* 2002 SC(PC) 89 where a delay in prosecution was held to infringe the rights of the accused under Article 6(1) of the Convention.

(b) Solemn procedure

1.33 The accused's first appearance will be on petition. The petition will specify the preliminary form of the charge against him/her. This first hearing will take the form of a judicial examination in front of the sheriff in the sheriff's chambers. The fiscal may ask questions at this stage and a transcript of the questions and any answers may be read out at any subsequent trial. After examination the accused may be committed for further examination, in which case he/she will appear before the sheriff again, or may be committed for trial (sometimes described as being 'fully committed'), and may be released on bail or kept in custody.

Once the accused has been committed for trial an indictment will be served on him/her (assuming that the case is proceeding). The indictment will contain the final version of the charge against the accused, will specify a date for the trial and will have attached to it, as appropriate, a notice of previous convictions, as well as a list of the prosecution witnesses and of any productions (that is, any physical evidence such as photographs or weapons) the prosecution intend to present at the trial. It will also, where the offence is one of a list of sexual offences (including rape and indecent assault), have attached a notice covering certain matters, including that the defence may only be conducted by a lawyer.

If the accused is kept in custody the indictment must be served within 80 days. If he or she is to be tried in the High Court the preliminary hearing must start within 110 days, and the trial within 140 days. Where trial is to be in the sheriff court the trial must start within 110 days. In all cases these periods start with the date of full committal and it is possible to apply to have them extended. If there is no extension the effect is that the accused is to be released on bail.[36] If the accused is at liberty the trial must start within 12 months of the first appearance on petition, and where the trial is to be in the High Court the preliminary hearing must take place within 11 months. In cases tried at the sheriff court there will a first diet at least ten days before the trial diet. The function of this is similar to that of the intermediate diet in summary proceedings. If the case is to be tried in the High Court there will be a preliminary diet covering similar ground.

36 Criminal Procedure (Scotland) Act 1995, s 65.

(c) Procedure at trial

1.34 Around 90% of criminal cases do not go to trial. The accused simply pleads guilty and is sentenced. Although the accused has a right to defend him/herself[37] in those cases that go to trial, legal representation can greatly assist the accused's case and make sure it is properly presented.

Procedure at trial is similar in solemn and summary procedure, the chief differences being due to the presence of the jury in solemn procedure. The main stages are:

(a) Presentation of the prosecution evidence. There are no opening statements in Scottish trials of the sort which might be familiar from American films or television. The prosecution simply call their first witness and the trial proceeds from there. Each witness will be examined by the prosecution (this initial questioning is known as the examination-in-chief); he/she will then be cross-examined by the defence and then, if necessary, be re-examined by the prosecution.
(b) At the end of the prosecution case the defence may move that the charges be dropped on the ground that there is no case to answer, in other words that the prosecution has not produced sufficient evidence to find the accused guilty.
(c) If this motion is rejected the defence will then present their evidence in the same way as the prosecution. There is, of course, no need for the defence to give evidence, or, more particularly, for the accused to give evidence, though failure to give evidence may be commented on by the prosecution and the judge. It is up to the prosecution to prove their case beyond reasonable doubt.
(d) Following the defence case both sides, prosecution first, will make their concluding speeches. In summary cases these are addressed to the judge(s), in solemn cases to the jury.
(e) In solemn cases the judge will then address the jury explaining their function, the standard of proof which the prosecution must meet and any relevant legal points. The judge will usually also highlight some of the significant points of evidence, although the jurors must decide on their own recollection of the evidence. After this the jury will retire to consider its verdict, a process which is widely recognised to be far from scientific.

37 Except in respect of trials for certain sexual offences.

(f) The judge or jury will then reach a verdict. The verdict may be guilty, not guilty or not proven. This last is a Scottish curiosity and appears to mean 'we rather suspect that you are guilty, but the evidence has not persuaded us beyond a reasonable doubt'. There have been campaigns to abolish this verdict but they have so far been unsuccessful.[38] The campaign seems in part to be based on the notion that criminal proceedings are concerned with establishing guilt or innocence in some objective sense corresponding to the truth of what actually happened. This, however, is not the case:

> It is sometimes maintained that the object of leading evidence in a criminal trial is, or should be, the elucidation of the truth. That statement, however, requires considerable qualification. First, the matter to be elucidated is not the whole truth about all the circumstances of the events narrated in the libel, but only the question of whether the Crown has proved beyond reasonable doubt that the accused committed the crime charged against him. While a verdict of 'guilty' answers that question in the affirmative, a verdict of 'not guilty' or 'not proven' only means that the question has not been so answered: it is not a determination of the accused's innocence. And whatever the verdict, it may not reflect the truth.[39]

(g) Following a guilty verdict the court will move on to sentence. Sentence may be deferred either for reports or for some other reason, for example, for the accused to show that he/she can be of good behaviour or for repayment of a sum of money dishonestly obtained. In some cases the judge must obtain a criminal justice social work[40] report before sentencing, for example, when considering a custodial disposal for an offender not previously sentenced to custody or for an offender under 21. Before sentence is passed the accused's solicitor or counsel will normally make a plea in mitigation, the purpose of which is to attempt to influence the sentencer to be lenient.

38 Objections to the verdict are not new: in 1827 Sir Walter Scott described it as 'that bastard verdict': J G Wilson *Not Proven* (1960), p 7. For a review of the verdict and these campaigns see House of Commons Library Standard Note SN/HA/2710, *The 'not proven' verdict in Scotland.*

39 Scottish Law Commission *Evidence: Report on Hearsay in Civil Proceedings* HC 177 1994–95, para 2.14.

40 These replaced social enquiry reports as from 1st February 2011.

(d) Standard of proof

1.35 As we have noted the standard of proof in criminal cases is proof beyond reasonable doubt. This is more exacting than the standard in civil cases and requires the prosecution to produce evidence which does not leave any reasonable doubt in the mind of the judge (in summary cases) or the jury (in solemn cases) as to the guilt of the accused. This standard of proof is also relevant in hearings before the sheriff to establish a referral to a children's hearing on offence grounds.[41] The nature of the evidence which can be used to establish this standard is considered in paras 1.39 to 1.56 below.

(e) Bail[42]

1.36 Bail may be applied for on any appearance in court and refusal of bail can be the subject of an application for review on the grounds of changed circumstances or new evidence or can be appealed against. It is also possible to seek review of any conditions attached to the grant of bail. There are no non-bailable offences. Bail is to be granted, subject to two exceptions, except where there is a good reason to refuse bail having regard to the public interest and to other, specified, factors. These factors, which can be the grounds for refusing bail, include substantial risk of absconding, substantial risk of further offending and substantial risk of interference with witnesses. The two exceptions, where bail is only to be granted where there are exceptional circumstances justifying bail, are cases where the accused is facing charges:

(a) of violent or sexual offences and has a previous conviction on indictment for such an offence; or
(b) of drug trafficking and has a previous conviction on indictment for such an offence.

An individual may be released on bail both before conviction and after conviction but before sentence; he/she may also be released pending the outcome of an appeal against a custodial sentence.

If bail is granted the person released on bail will be subject to a number of standard conditions set out in Part III of the Criminal Procedure (Scotland) Act 1995. The main conditions are:

41 See para 5.15.
42 Most people who are not kept in custody after a court hearing will not be on bail. They will be released simply on agreeing to attend the next hearing.

(a) a requirement to appear at all court diets;
(b) a requirement not to commit further offences;
(c) a requirement not to interfere with witnesses;
(d) a requirement to be available for the purposes of enabling enquiries or reports to be made to assist the court's disposition of the case. This would include, for example, a criminal justice social work report requested by a court prior to sentencing.

The court may attach other conditions to the granting of bail as appropriate, these can include a requirement for remote monitoring. Generally speaking, lodging of a sum of money in court by way of guaranteeing future appearances is not required unless there are special circumstances.

It is important to note that breach of any of the bail conditions, except committing another offence while on bail, is itself a criminal offence. So, for example, if a person on bail refused to make her/himself available to a social worker in connection with the compilation of a report, that would be breaching one of the conditions of bail and committing a further offence. Where an offence is committed while on bail, that breach of bail conditions is to be reflected in the sentence imposed for that offence.

(f) Appeals

1.37 Appeals can be made against both conviction and sentence, and the prosecution have a right of appeal against sentence either on a point of law or if the sentence, or a condition attached to it,[43] is considered to be too lenient. An offender who wishes to appeal must obtain leave to appeal from the High Court. Offenders can also appeal against sentence or conviction by way of bill of suspension where a miscarriage of justice is claimed. If the appeal is against sentence, the sentence must be shown to be unreasonable. The court can increase as well as decrease the sentence on appeal. The Scottish Criminal Cases Review Commission has the power to review cases and to refer cases back to the High Court where this is in the interests of justice, or where there has been a miscarriage of justice.

(g) Accelerated diets

1.38 There is provision for accelerated diets to take place. This would happen when an accused who has pled not guilty changes his/

43 Such as a condition in a probation or community payback order.

her plea to guilty, sometimes after some negotiation of the charges with the prosecution, and wishes the matter dealt with before the date set for the trial diet.

EVIDENCE

1.39 In normal circumstances, individuals make use of a wide range of information in order to arrive at conclusions. For example, we use physical evidence, things which can be directly perceived, we use information from other people, and we use information about the reported comments of other people. When it comes to taking decisions in court, however, the range of evidence which can be use is restricted. More specifically, if evidence is to be accepted by a court it must be:

(1) relevant; and
(2) admissible.

(1) Relevant evidence

1.40 Relevant evidence is simply evidence which is relevant to proving the matter before the court. Evidence of other matters, such as the past history of the parties or of the accused in a criminal case, are not generally relevant and will not be allowed to be led in evidence. In other words, there must be some logical link between the evidence and the matter before the court.

(2) Admissible evidence

1.41 This is evidence which is not excluded by some rule of law, that is evidence which will be admissible provided it does not run foul of one of the exclusions provided for by the law. Some of these exclusions are:

(a) Hearsay evidence

1.42 This is considered more fully below.

(b) Evidence obtained improperly

1.43 One example of this is evidence that the police have obtained illegally in a criminal case, for example by carrying out a search without a necessary warrant or procuring a confession through violence or the threat of violence. The exclusion also applies in civil cases and, of course, in cases involving children. One area where this has been an issue is in cases where the courts have taken the view that social workers and police have not acted properly in obtaining evidence of child abuse. The courts may then take the view that such evidence cannot be relied on (though this may be a question of credibility rather than admissibility) and the referral to a children's hearing based on that evidence is discharged.[44]

(c) Evidence protected by privilege

1.44 In certain circumstances the relationship between two parties may be privileged, with the result that information passing between them is privileged and disclosure of this information cannot be required by the court. The main example of this is the solicitor/client relationship. This, indeed, seems to be the only clearly established case, and it is apparent that privilege does not apply to communications between a social worker and service user. English courts have recognised a 'public interest privilege'. In one case it was held that this allowed the NSPCC to refuse to disclose the identity of someone who had made an allegation of child abuse to the NSPCC.[45] The view of courts in Scotland is that there is no such concept as 'public interest privilege': instead, information will be protected by confidentiality. This was certainly the view expressed in a case where an adoptive parent sought access to social work records concerning the adopted child. It was said that:

> '... [I]f a case arose in Scotland in which a party sought to recover from the RSSPCC [now Children 1st] the name of an informer, it would only be in exceptional circumstances that such a motion would be granted. This would not be because public interest privilege is extended to the RSSPCC, but because the nature of the work of that body is such that their claim to confidentiality would be awarded a high degree of protection.'[46]

Such information is not, of course, required to be revealed under the Data Protection Act 1998.[47]

44 This is essentially what seems to have happened in *L v Kennedy* (6 March 1995, unreported) IH.

45 *D v NSPCC* [1978] AC 171.

46 *P v Tayside Regional Council* 1989 SCLR 165 at 168. See also *Davers v Butler* 1994 SCLR 717; *A v G* 1996 SCLR 787.

47 See ch 2, para 2.30.

(d) Opinion evidence

1.45 In general, witnesses are not allowed to express opinions in giving evidence. The main exception to this rule is in respect of expert witnesses, who are permitted to make statements of their opinions about facts which they may or may not have observed for themselves. Social workers may be called upon to act as expert witnesses in their areas of competence and expertise. Such expert evidence, it should be noted, does not supplant the court: the court has to take its decision on the basis of the whole evidence presented to it, which frequently involves competing opinions expressed by experts. Of course, it is often not possible to question a non-expert witness without seeking expressions of opinion, for example as to whether a car was being driven fast, or as to whether someone appeared to be upset, and it has been argued that identification evidence is, in fact, opinion evidence.[48] There seems to be no clear rule of law explaining to what extent non-experts can state opinions.

(3) A competent witness

1.46 Previously a witness had to be competent, ie, legally permitted to give evidence, in the sense that he/she understood the notion of giving evidence and could clearly understand and explain what he/she has seen/heard. In practice, the assumption was that everyone was a competent witness unless they were excluded by a rule of law. There was no exclusion of children from giving evidence, and the evidence of children as young as 3½ and 4 has been heard in criminal cases. This requirement for witnesses to be competent was removed by the Vulnerable Witnesses (Scotland) Act 2004 which provides[49] that the evidence of anyone called as a witness is not inadmissible solely because he/she does not understand his/her duty to give truthful evidence or the difference between truth or lies. Because of this courts are prohibited from taking steps to establish understanding of either of these matters.

(4) Hearsay evidence

1.47 The hearsay rule has been defined as providing that:

48 See, for example, F Raitt *Evidence: Principles, Policy and Practice* (2008), 4–01 to 4–03.

49 In section 24.

> Any assertion other than one made by a person while giving oral evidence in the proceedings is inadmissible as evidence of any fact or opinion asserted.[50]

In other words, any statement made by a third party and reported to court by a witness is not admissible as evidence that what is claimed in the statement actually happened. It is only admissible as evidence of the fact that the statement was made. Assume, for example, that X said to Y 'I saw Ramon Mercador killing Trotsky'. If Y was subsequently called as a witness in the trial of Mercador and repeated the statement made by X, that would only be evidence that the statement was made: it would not be evidence, admissible by the court, that Mercador killed Trotsky. There are, however, some exceptions to the general rule where hearsay evidence is treated as admissible evidence of the facts contained in the second hand statement. The main exceptions are:

(a) Civil cases

1.48 As a result of the Civil Evidence (Scotland) Act 1988, the hearsay rule was abolished for all civil proceedings in Scotland. This includes all proof hearings on grounds of referral to a children's hearing except where the ground of referral is that the child has committed an offence. The case of *F v Kennedy (No 2)*[51] illustrates the effect of this provision. At a proof hearing a child witness, J, was called to give evidence. In addition, evidence was given of statements which J had made on previous occasions. These statements were not put to J when he was giving evidence and he was not asked about them. They were reported by other witnesses as hearsay evidence. The child's father challenged the decision to admit J's hearsay evidence, arguing that proceeding in this way was at odds with the best evidence rule which would require J to give all of his evidence in court. The challenge was rejected. The Inner House of the Court of Session took the view that 'the fact that the maker of the statement has given oral evidence does not prevent hearsay evidence being given of what he has said upon another occasion.' They then continued: '... there may well be occasions where it will be difficult to take the whole of a child's evidence in court. It may therefore be important for the sheriff to be able to rely to

50 Cross on *Evidence* (7th edn, London, 1990, by the late Sir Rupert Cross and C Tapper) at p 509, quoted in Scottish Law Commission, *Evidence: Report on Hearsay Evidence in Criminal Proceedings* (Scot Law Com No 149), para 3.2.
51 1993 SLT 1284.

some extent at least on hearsay evidence of what the child has said on other occasions.'[52] In one case, hearsay evidence in the form of a statement made to the police was accepted by the sheriff even though the statement was retracted by the witness when she appeared before him.[53]

(b) Res gestae

1.49 Where statements are made as part of the events which are claimed to constitute an offence, they will be admissible, even though the identity of the maker of the statement is unknown. One of the standard texts on evidence suggests that two obvious examples of statements forming part of the *res gestae* would be the screams and protests of a rape victim and the use of nicknames in an unguarded moment by members of a team of hooded armed robbers.[54]

(c) Confessions

1.50 Confessions made by an accused either to the police or to someone else are admissible evidence.

(d) Previous inconsistent statements

1.51 Where a witness departs from a previous statement, for example if a footballer originally told police that he had been head butted but in the witness box suggests that the head contact was accidental, the previous statement is admissible to attack the credibility of the witness and the evidence being given.

(e) Statements made by someone who can no longer give evidence

1.52 One example of this is a statement by someone who has died since the statement was made.

52 1993 SLT 1284 at 1287F–H.
53 *K v Kennedy* 1993 SLT 1281.
54 F Raitt *Evidence: Principles, Policy and Practice* (2008), para 11.20.

(f) *Criminal cases*

1.53 Under the Criminal Procedure (Scotland) Act 1995[55] hearsay evidence can be admitted in criminal trials as evidence of any matter stated in that evidence in a number of circumstances including cases where the person making the statement cannot be found, is dead or unfit or unable to give evidence, has been authorised not to give evidence on the grounds that to do so might incriminate him/her, or refuses to give evidence.

(5) Corroboration

1.54 Corroboration requires that each fact essential to proving a case is supported by two pieces of evidence. The two pieces of evidence need not be statements by eye witnesses, but may be physical evidence, for example fingerprints, or medical evidence, or circumstantial evidence. The requirement for corroboration no longer applies in civil cases, though the existence of corroboration will strengthen a case. Corroboration is still required in criminal cases (and in proof hearings on referrals from a children's hearings where the grounds of referral involve commission of an offence) and in such cases there are two things which must be established by corroborated evidence: that the crime was committed and that the accused (or the child) committed it.

(6) Deciding on the evidence

1.55 Once all the relevant admissible evidence has been led, the court (or, in solemn cases, the jury) has to arrive at a decision on the case. In order to do this it will have to decide whether the evidence led discharges the burden of proof imposed on the parties involved in the case before it. In criminal cases it will have to decide whether the prosecution have proved their case beyond a reasonable doubt; in civil cases whether the pursuer has established his/her case on the balance of probabilities. In arriving at its decision the court will have to weigh up the evidence before it. Doing this involves the court looking at whether the evidence was direct or circumstantial, the sufficiency of any corroboration, the coherence of the evidence and, perhaps most importantly assessing the credibility of the evidence. This last matter is often of crucial importance because there will often be directly contradictory evidence before the court. In such cases the decision as

55 Section 259.

to who is a credible witness will have an important bearing on the outcome of the case.

(7) Children and vulnerable adults giving evidence

1.56 The Vulnerable Witnesses (Scotland) Act 2004 makes provision for protecting vulnerable witnesses. It applies both to children (ie those under 16) and other vulnerable witnesses. A person other than a child will be a vulnerable witness if there is a significant risk that the quality of the evidence he or she will give will be diminished by reason of mental disorder or fear or distress in connection with giving evidence at the trial.

In criminal cases, there are five ways in which the giving of evidence by a child or vulnerable adult who is called to give evidence can be made less stressful and the child can be given some degree of protection.[56]

(a) In appropriate cases, the witness can be permitted to give evidence via a live video link. A court faced with a request to allow this has to take into account the possible effect on the witness if the application is not granted and whether the witness will be better able to give evidence if the application is granted. Relevant considerations include the age and maturity of the witness, the nature of the evidence he/she is likely to give, and the relationship, if any, between the witness and the accused.
(b) A screen can be placed so as to conceal the accused from the witness giving evidence. The same considerations apply to granting an application for this as apply to the permitting of live video evidence.
(c) An application can be made to allow the evidence of the witness to be taken on commission, with the proceedings being videotaped.
(d) Use of a supporter.
(e) Giving evidence in chief in the form of a prior statement.

In civil cases, including most referrals from a children's hearing, the provisions discussed above regarding hearsay in civil cases mean that the child need not be present at all, instead his her evidence may be given in the form of hearsay either by a witness or in the form of a videotaped interview.[57] In addition, special arrangements can be made in respect of court proceedings related to children's hearings (eg proof

56 Act of Adjournal (Criminal Procedure Rules) 1996, SI 1996/513, ch 22.
57 As happened in *Ferguson v S*, 1993 SCLR 712.

hearings in the sheriff court), the special measures available are those listed at (a) – (d) above.

CHILDREN'S HEARINGS

1.57 The system of children's hearings was introduced by the Social Work (Scotland) Act 1968 to deal with a whole range of cases relating to children which were formerly dealt with in a variety of different courts. These include offences committed by children, children beyond parental control, children against whom offences may have been committed and children who truant. The relevant provisions (Part III, with the exception of s 31) of the 1968 Act have been repealed and replaced by provisions in Part II of the Children (Scotland) Act 1995. Children's hearings are considered in greater detail in chapter 5.

TRIBUNALS

1.58 Tribunals have been set up to adjudicate in a wide variety of areas affected by state intervention. Examples are social security and child support tribunals, mental health tribunals and employment tribunals. Procedure and the rules of representation before tribunals are generally much more relaxed than those before courts. This opens up greater possibilities for representation by non-lawyers, for example, of claimants before social security tribunals. This is particularly important as there is evidence to suggest that claimants who are represented have a greater chance of success than those who are not.

CHALLENGING LOCAL AUTHORITY DECISIONS

(1) Judicial Review

1.59 Judicial review is a procedure by which decisions of many public bodies may be challenged. It differs from appeal in that the right to seek review exists without the express statutory provision which is needed to create a right of appeal; indeed the courts have sometimes reviewed decisions in spite of specific statutory provisions excluding their jurisdiction. This makes review particularly useful in cases where there is no provision for appeal against a decision.

There are, however, two major drawbacks to using judicial review to challenge decisions. The first of these is that actions for judicial review can be dealt with only by the Court of Session in Edinburgh.

This is not as much of a problem as it used to be following the introduction of a simpler and quicker form of procedure, though it makes the process more expensive than it would otherwise be. The second drawback is that review can be sought only on restricted grounds. To succeed the applicant must be able to show that the person or body taking the decision acted outwith their powers (that is, *ultra vires*), acted unreasonably, or did not comply with the requirements of natural justice. In taking its decision the court can also take into account human rights issues.[58] (For examples and further discussion, see chapter 11).

Despite these drawbacks judicial review has been a valuable remedy in certain areas. One has been its use by people who have been refused accommodation under the homelessness legislation, made necessary because there is no statutory provision for appeal against a local authority decision to refuse housing. One example is the case of *Kelly v Monklands District Council*.[59] In this case a 16-year-old girl left home because of violence inflicted by her father. She had nowhere to stay and had attempted suicide. She applied for housing as a homeless person. One of the cases in which an authority is bound to provide housing is if the applicant is vulnerable. The local authority decided that Ms Kelly was not vulnerable despite a report from the social work department to the contrary. The court decided that the authority had acted unreasonably in arriving at its conclusion on vulnerability and in not taking proper account of the report from the social work department. The council was ordered to house Ms Kelly.[60]

Another use, though not pursued as commonly in Scotland, is use of judicial review to challenge community care assessments and decisions about service provision.[61]

(2) Complaints procedure

1.60 Local authorities must have a complaints procedure to deal with representations (including complaints) about the authority's performance, or lack of performance, of their obligations under the 1968 Act and various other pieces of legislation, such as the Disabled Persons (Services, Consultation and Representation) Act 1986 and the Mental Health (Care and Treatment) (Scotland) Act 2003. There is no national representations procedure: rather,

58 See part 15 below.
59 1986 SLT 169.
60 See also ch 2, paras 2.5 to 2.13. There have been some changes to law and guidance since this case was decided.
61 See, for example, *MacGregor v South Lanarkshire District Council* 2001 SC 502.

each authority will have developed its own within the context of directions issued to local authorities. In broad outline, these directions require a three-stage process. Initially an attempt is to be made resolve the complaint informally without proceeding to the formal process. If this fails an investigation is carried out by an officer of the local authority. If the service user is dissatisfied with the outcome of this, there is a right to have the complaint considered by a review committee which must include at least one person independent of the local authority.[62] If the person making the complaint is not happy with the outcome of this process a complaint can be made to the Scottish Public Services Ombudsman or the outcome can be challenged by judicial review. Such a challenge can also be made to the decision of the Ombudsman.

In addition to the local authority complaints procedure all service providers whose services are registered[63] with the Scottish Commission for the Regulation of Care must, as a condition of such registration, have a complaints procedure. In addition complaints about such services can also be made to the Commission through its complaints procedure. This means that an individual whose services are arranged through the local authority but provided by a body external to the authority may have a choice of three different complaints procedure. As a result of this complexity (and lack of clarity) the Scottish Government is currently reviewing complaints procedures.[64]

LEGAL AID

1.61 Legal aid in Scotland is administered by the Scottish Legal Aid Board. There are three types of legal aid: legal advice and assistance; civil legal aid; and criminal legal aid.

(1) Legal advice and assistance

1.62 This is a means tested scheme which provides free advice and assistance to applicants who qualify on the basis of a means test. Above

62 The Social Work (Representations Procedure) (Scotland) Directions 1996.

63 The process of registration is considered in ch 11. In April 2011 the Commission will be replaced by a body with an expanded role having the title Social Care and Social Work Improvement Scotland, Public Services Reform (Scotland) Act 2010, ss 44 & 52.

64 Scottish Government, *Scrutiny Improvement: Government Response To Action Group Reports*, May 2009.

the qualifying level for free assistance there is a sliding scale for contribution up to the point where full payment must be made. People in receipt of income support or income-based jobseeker's allowance qualify automatically on income grounds, but may be ineligible through their ownership of capital above the permitted limit. The decision as to entitlement is made by the solicitor who is approached for advice.

Legal advice and assistance covers advice about any matter of Scots law, civil or criminal. With very limited exceptions, it only covers assistance short of representation before a court or tribunal, one such exception is representation before the Mental Health Tribunal where assistance by way of representation is available.

(2) Civil legal aid

1.63 Civil legal aid is available to raise or defend actions in the civil courts. Once again it is means tested, and again those in receipt of income support or income-based jobseeker's allowance qualify automatically on income grounds. As with legal advice and assistance there is a sliding scale of contributions above the level of free entitlement, up to the point where the applicant is not entitled to any assistance.

This is the type of legal aid that would be appropriate for actions under the Children (Scotland) Act 1995, for example proof hearings in the sheriff court, and for adoption proceedings.

In urgent cases a solicitor may be able to act before a decision is made on the application for legal aid.[65] This might be necessary, for example, to allow a woman to obtain an interim exclusion order excluding a violent spouse from the family home.

Children are entitled to apply for legal aid in their own right, and their eligibility is determined on the basis of their resources rather than that of other members of their family.

(3) Criminal legal aid

1.64 The operation of this scheme depends on whether the prosecution is solemn or summary and on whether or not the first appearance in court is made from custody. Applications for legal aid in solemn cases are decided by the court while applications in summary cases go

65 Civil Legal Aid (Scotland) Regulations 2002, SSI 2002/494, reg 18.

to the Board. The granting of legal aid is almost automatic in solemn cases. The only ground for refusal is that the accused could pay for his/her defence without undue hardship. Where an accused appears in court from custody that person is entitled to be represented by the duty solicitor assigned to that court.

HUMAN RIGHTS

1.65 The European Convention on Human Rights was signed shortly after the Second World War. In form it prevents states from undertaking certain types of activity, though, as we will see it may require positive action by the state and/or local authorities, and grants individuals certain rights, for example the right to respect for family life. Until 2000 complaints that rights under the Convention had been violated involved taking a case to the European Court of Human Rights (ECtHR) in Strasbourg, a process which could be time consuming.[66] However, the Human Rights Act 1998 which came into effect in 2000 provided the possibility of direct action being taken against local authorities (and other public authorities) for failing to act consistently with the rights which the Convention provides for. More specifically, section 6 provides: 'It is unlawful for a public authority to act in a way which is incompatible with a Convention right' and section 7 allows individuals to take proceedings against public authorities[67] and also to rely on their Convention Rights in any proceedings brought against them. The right conferred by these sections would allow an individual to seek damages from a local authority or to seek an interdict ordering them to stop any action which is incompatible with a Convention right. In addition to the direct rights conferred by the 1998 Act, and in a related development, convention rights are now considered in judicial review actions.

The rights conferred by the European Convention will be considered more fully in the context of consideration of the substantive law later in

66 One example is *McMichael v United Kingdom* ((1995) 20 EHRR 205) which concerned procedures in children's hearings. The complaint was made in 1989 and a decision made by the court in 1995.

67 A public authority includes, as well as courts and tribunals, 'any person certain of whose functions are functions of a public nature', Human Rights Act 1998, s 6(3)(b). The definition has been extended to include private sector providers of accommodation, together with nursing, personal care or personal support, as a care home service where this accommodation is provided by arrangement with a local authority, Health and Social Care Act 2008, s 145. This extension was to avoid perceived unfairness in that decisions of local authorities about care homes (for example closure) could be challenged under the Human Rights Act, but those of private providers could not, see *L v Birmingham City Council* [2007] UKHL 27.

this text, but there are some general points which set the context consideration of individual rights. Rights conferred by the Convention may be absolute or relative. An example of an absolute provision is the prohibition on torture contained in Article 3 of the Convention. In contrast, other provisions envisage a balancing of rights. For example Article 8 provides that everyone has the right to 'respect for his private and family life, his home and his correspondence'. It then goes on to provide, however, that these rights may be interfered with provided that this interference is in accordance with the law and is necessary in a democratic society to achieve one of a number of objectives, for example the protection of the rights and freedoms of others. A second general point is that some of the rights are expressed in such a way as to prohibit certain types of behaviour. For example, Article 3 mentioned above provides that; '[n]o one shall be subjected to torture or to inhuman or degrading treatment or punishment.' On the face of it this would seem to impose only a negative obligation on public bodies not to subject people to such forms of treatment. However, the ECtHR has taken the view that such obligations go beyond this and impose a positive obligation on public bodies to act when they are (or should be) aware that people are being subjected by others to such treatment, with the objective of such intervention being to bring the treatment to an end.[68]

Finally, the main convention rights which are likely to be relevant to social work practice are those set out in Articles 2, 3, 5, 6 and 8. Article 2 provides for a right to life, this may at least be a relevant consideration in considering whether to warn relevant authorities of knowledge of a risk to another.[69] Article 3 has been discussed above and may have some application in, for example, cases of suspected child abuse. Article 5 provides that no one is to be deprived of his or her liberty except in a limited number of cases (for example, convicted criminals and detention of those who are of 'unsound mind') and in accordance with procedures established by law. This article may be relevant in considering whether processes involving detention of mentally ill patients or placement of adults with incapacity is compliant with their convention rights. Article 6 provides that civil rights and obligations are to be determined by an independent and impartial body and provides a number of other safeguards. Finally, Article 8 has been mentioned above and might come into play, for example in relation to the removal of a child from his or her family or the closure of residential accommodation. These rights, whether they are qualified or not, and examples of cases concerning alleged breaches are set out in the table on the following page.

68 See, for example, Z *v United Kingdom* (2002) 34 EHRR 3.
69 See, for example, *Osman v UK* (2000) 29 EHRR 245.

Article	Text of Article	Qualified right?	Examples
2	Everyone's right to life shall be protected by law. No one shall be deprived of his life intentionally save in the execution of a sentence of a court following his conviction of a crime for which this penalty is provided by law.	Yes	*Osman*[70]: '…article 2 of the Convention may also imply in certain well-defined circumstances a positive obligation on the authorities to take preventive operational measures to protect an individual whose life is at risk from the criminal acts of another individual.' *Savage*:[71] Duty to take steps to avoid risk of harm to suicidal detained patient because of knowledge of immediate risk to her life.
3	No one shall be subjected to torture or to inhuman or degrading treatment or punishment.	No	*Z*:[72] Duty to take action where local authority knew or should have known that treatment of children amounted to inhuman and degrading treatment.

70 *Osman v United Kingdom* (1998) 29 EHRR 245.
71 *Savage v South Essex Partnership NHS Foundation Trust & Anor* [2007] EWCA Civ 1375.
72 Z *v United Kingdom* (2002) 34 EHRR 3.

Article	Text of Article	Qualified right?	Examples
5	Everyone has the right to liberty and security of person. No one shall be deprived of his liberty save in the following cases and in accordance with a procedure prescribed by law: (a) the lawful detention of a person after conviction by a competent court; (d) the detention of a minor by lawful order for the purpose of educational supervision or his lawful detention for the purpose of bringing him before the competent legal authority; (e) the lawful detention of persons for the prevention of the spreading of infectious diseases, of persons of unsound mind, alcoholics or drug addicts or vagrants.	No	*JE*:[73] Placement of incapable adult in care home which not permitted to leave to stay elsewhere amounted to deprivation of liberty *Koniarska*:[74] Placement of child in secure accommodation where she received (some) education fell within paragraph (d) as being for the 'purpose of educational supervision', this purpose was not restricted to school attendance

73 *JE v DE* [2006] EWHC 3459 (Fam).
74 *Koniarska v United Kingdom,* Application no. 33670/96, decision 12 October 2000.

Article	Text of Article	Qualified right?	Examples
6	In the determination of his civil rights and obligations or of any criminal charge against him, everyone is entitled to a fair and public hearing within a reasonable time by an independent and impartial tribunal established by law.	Yes[75]	*S*:[76] Lack of provision of legal aid for children's hearings breached Art. 6. *McMichael*:[77] Failure to provide parents with social background reports for children's hearing breached Art. 6.
8	Everyone has the right to respect for his private and family life, his home and his correspondence.	Yes	*Bernard*:[78] Failure to provide suitable accommodation which meant that mobility impaired woman could not access toilet or leave room in which she slept breached Art. 8 rights.

THE SOCIAL WORK (SCOTLAND) ACT 1968

(1) Introduction

1.66 The Social Work (Scotland) Act 1968 (the 1968 Act) grew out of two developments. The first was a trend towards generic social work based on the view that social work with all types of people has a common base of values and skills. The second was the recommendation of the Kilbrandon Report[79] for the setting up of a social education department to provide support for the children's hearings which the report proposed. These two developments were brought together in the White Paper *Social Work and the Community*[80] which formed the basis for the 1968 Act.

75 In relation to publicity of hearing.
76 *S v Miller* 2001 SLT 485.
77 *McMichael v United Kingdom* (1995) 20 EHRR 205.
78 *Bernard v Enfield London Borough Council* [2002] EWHC 2282 (Admin).
79 *Children and Young Persons* Cmnd 2306 (1964).
80 Cmnd 3065 (1966).

The 1968 Act was one of the core pieces of legislation, providing much of the framework for the activities of social workers employed by local authorities, as well as setting down specific duties and specific procedures that have to be followed in particular circumstances. Although most of the provisions relating to children have been replaced by the Children (Scotland) Act 1995, the basic provisions of the 1968 Act regarding the overall duties and powers of social workers remain in place and it is worth undertaking a brief survey of the Act at this point. It must be remembered, of course, that the 1968 Act is only one of a large number of statutes conferring duties and powers on social workers.

The major contribution of the 1968 Act, as far as provision of social work services is concerned, was to draw all of the disparate services provided by local authorities into one department under one overall director and with a council committee responsible for its oversight. Although councils must still appoint a chief social work officer there is no longer any requirement to have a separate social work committee.[81]

(2) Persons in need and assessments

1.67 In keeping with the interventionist tenor of the times, section 12 of the 1968 Act imposes an overall duty to 'promote social welfare' by making available advice, guidance and assistance and securing the provision of facilities, including residential accommodation.

This section also allows the provision of assistance in cash or kind in certain circumstances. This type of assistance can be provided in an emergency to a 'person in need' (see below) aged 18 or over where doing so would avoid greater cost to the local authority either in the provision of some other service, such as the direct provision of accommodation, or at some future date because of aggravation of the person's need. Social work departments have their own policies and practices in relation to the giving of section 12 assistance. It should be noted that it is not intended to operate as an alternative to the benefits system: indeed consideration must be given to the person's eligibility for assistance from any other statutory body and the availability of that assistance before a payment is made. Section 12 payments can be made conditional on repayment.

81 Social Work Scotland Act 1968 as amended by Local Government etc (Scotland) Act 1994, ss 45, 180 and Sch 14.

Various interpretations in different authorities and within authorities have led to enormous variation in the use of section 12. Strategies which have encompassed the promotional use of these funds and those which have used the funds for preventative services have come and gone over the years. The bureaucratic hierarchical structures of social work departments have also been reflected in the policies of departments regarding the amounts of section 12 money which can be dispensed to the public by various grades of staff. For example, many basic grade social workers can dispense only limited sums without authorisation from a higher grade member of staff.

Section 14 deals with the provision of domiciliary services (usually referred to as home helps) for households including a person in need or an expectant mother, and also the provision of laundry services in such cases.

As we have seen these provisions refer to persons in need, defined in the 1968 Act as being persons who:

(a) are in need of care and attention arising out of infirmity, youth or age; or
(b) suffer from illness or mental disorder or are substantially handicapped by any deformity or disability; or
(c) being persons prescribed by the Scottish Ministers who have asked for assistance, are, in the opinion of a local authority, persons to whom the local authority may appropriately make available the services and facilities provided by them under the 1968 Act.[82]

In addition, for the purposes of section 12 only, the definition is extended to include those in need as a result of drug or alcohol dependence and release from prison or other form of detention.[83]

Section 12A of the Act, added by the National Health Service and Community Care Act 1990, requires the authority to carry out an assessment of need before providing community care services. This provision is considered more fully in chapter 6.

82 Social Work (Scotland) Act 1968, s 94(1). This power has only been used once: Prescription as 'Persons in Need' (Persons subject to Immigration Control) (Scotland) Order 1997, SI 1997/2452.
83 Social Work (Scotland) Act 1968, s 12(6).

(3) Reports and supervision of offenders

1.68 Section 27 deals with the responsibilities of the social work department in relation to the provision of reports to criminal courts and the provision of supervision to probationers and those released from custody on licence. Chapter 10, paras 10.4, 10.19–10.24 and 10.51, look at this area in more detail.

(4) Residential establishments

1.69 Part IV of the Act deals with the provision of residential establishments by local authorities. The system of registration with the local authority of other residential establishments, for example private residential homes for persons who are elderly which was created by the 1968 Act has now been replaced by a system of registration for services (including those provided by a local authority) with the Scottish Commission for the Regulation of Care.[84]

THE CHILDREN (SCOTLAND) ACT 1995

1.70 The years between the passing of the Children Act 1989, which made major changes to child care law in England and Wales, and the Children (Scotland) Act 1995 were relatively tumultuous ones for child care in Scotland. Initially, the view had been that unlike the position in England and Wales, Scotland did not require a major overhaul of child care law. Many events, including ones in Orkney,[85] Fife[86] and Ayrshire, provided the impetus and the ammunition to thoroughly take stock, adapt some initiatives from south of the border and move beyond those innovations to others designed to take child care law in Scotland into the next millennium. Additionally, a paradigm shift occurred which is seen in the move from parental rights to parental responsibilities and children's rights holding a central position and which reflects the significance of the United Nations *Convention on the Rights of the Child.*

The 1995 Act does not codify the law relating to children and so other provisions, for example in the Adoption and Children (Scotland) Act 2007, remain relevant.

84 Though this is now subject to change, see ch 11.
85 See the Clyde Report, *The Report of the Inquiry into the Removal of Children from Orkney in February 1991* (1992).
86 Kearney, B, *The Report of the Inquiry into Child Care Policies in Fife* (1992).

Part I (sections 1–15) sets out the private law and law in relation to parental responsibilities. Part II (sections 16–93) covers the duties of local authorities to children in their area (chapter 1), provisions for children's hearings and child protection (chapters 2 and 3), and arrangements for parental responsibilities orders (chapter 4). Part IV (sections 99–105) sets out miscellaneous provisions.

FURTHER STATUTORY CHANGES

1.71 Particularly since the establishment of the Scottish parliament a large amount of legislation has come into force which affects social work practice. Some of this applies to both adults and children, for example the Mental Health (Care and Treatment) (Scotland) Act 2003, which deals with provision of services for, and compulsory treatment of, individuals with a mental disorder. Others are more specifically directed at services for adults, for example the Adults with Incapacity (Scotland) Act 2000, which provides a framework for taking decisions on behalf of adults who cannot do this for themselves, the Adult Support and Protection (Scotland) Act 2007, imposing a duty to investigate cases where vulnerable adults may be suffering abuse, and the Community Care and Health (Scotland) Act 2002, mandating closer working between local authorities and the NHS and providing for (limited) free personal care for the elderly. Still other legislation has been concerned with offenders (the Management of Offenders (Scotland) Act 2005) and with regulation of services and the profession (Regulation of Care (Scotland) Act 2001). Further legislation has been concerned with children, for example the Adoption and Children (Scotland) Act 2007 which, as well as amending the law of adoption in Scotland paved the way for a change in the regulatory regime for looked after children.

EXCLUSIONS FROM SOCIAL WORK SERVICES

1.72 Following the introduction of new system of Asylum support in legislation in 1999 a number of groups of people were excluded from entitlement to the provision of certain social work services. For those who have made a claim for asylum support is instead provided through the National Asylum Support Service. Three main groups are affected by these rules and the scope of the exclusions differs as between these groups. The first group[87] comprises people who are subject to immigra-

87 Immigration and Asylum Act 1999, ss 115(9) & 120. The exclusions are given effect to in the Social Work (Scotland) Act 1968, ss 12(2A), 13A and 13B.

tion control, for example those who require leave (permission) to enter and remain in the UK and those who have been given leave to enter the subject to a condition that they will not have recourse to public funds. For this group the exclusion extends to services under section 12 of Social Work (Scotland) Act 1968 (including community care) where need for these arises solely because of destitution or the physical effects of destitution, but the exclusion does not extend to other services which the authority might provide.

The second group[88] includes former asylum seekers who have been refused permission to stay in the UK and who have not co-operated with their removal from the UK, those who are recognised as refugees in other EEA state (and who can therefore reside there), and those, other than asylum seekers, who are in the UK in breach of immigration controls (for example by overstaying the period for which they were allowed to enter the UK). For this group most services provided by a local authority are excluded, except that in appropriate cases powers and/or duties under the Mental Health (Care and Treatment) (Scotland) Act 2003 will have to be exercised and/or performed and services may have to be provided to avoid breach of Art 3 of the European Convention on Human Rights.

The final group[89] excluded from service provision are the dependent children of asylum seekers, though children travelling independently are entitled to services in the same way as any other child. This exclusion relates to services provided under section 22 of the Children (Scotland) Act 1995.[90]

88 Nationality, Immigration and Asylum Act 2002, s 54 & Sch 3.
89 Immigration and Asylum Act 1999, s 122(5).
90 See paras 4.3 to 4.5.

Chapter 2

General law relevant to social work

INTRODUCTION

2.1 As well as a knowledge of what has been described as professional law, namely, that law which is central to the professional activities of a social worker, social workers also need to have some knowledge of other areas of law in order to be able to assist service users with some of the problems and concerns they may have. This chapter is intended to give a brief outline of the law in the areas of housing, discrimination, debt, access to information and education. The coverage is not exhaustive and we have attempted to give further references where more detail may be found. It may also be the case that where a service user has a problem in these areas counsel to seek qualified legal advice, perhaps under the legal advice and assistance scheme, would be warranted. The first edition of this text contained a section on welfare benefits. It has been omitted from this edition (as from the second edition) for a number of reasons, but mainly because of the frequent changes in benefits and because in the space available it was not possible to give proper coverage of the topic. References to various benefits will still be found at various stages in the text as appropriate. This omission is not to deny or undervalue the indisputable link between material deprivation and a range of other factors which bring people to social workers and one which can not be ignored. It therefore follows that a basic understanding of the benefits system is a crucial component in a social worker's repertoire.[1] Social workers have no legal mandate to become involved in benefits matters other than in pursuing the general obligation to promote social welfare, but notions of good practice suggest that until material needs are addressed, other needs are less accessible. In some social work departments there is an expectation that benefits checks will be carried out for new service users.

1 See, for example, CPAG *Welfare Benefits and Tax Credits Handbook*, revised and republished annually as well as various benefits calculators, for example, *Benefits adviser* operated by the Department of Work and Pensions (https://www.dwpe-services.direct.gov.uk/portal/page/portal/ba/lp) and that operated by Glasgow City Council (http://www.glasgow.gov.uk/en/Residents/GettingAdvice/WelfareRights/Benefits/Calculators/).

HOUSING

2.2 Housing problems experienced by social work service users are not always limited to the bricks and mortar. The typology of problems identified by Gill Stewart and John Stewart[2] provides an excellent framework for making sense of and exploring these problems: ones arising from changing personal relationships and family patterns, these can include problems of access to suitable housing; ones which initially seem to be individually based but relate more to how society views specific groups of service users, for example 'problem families' from 'difficult' areas; and ones which are rooted directly in the quality of the housing either in terms of physical condition of the housing or changes in its suitability deriving from changes in the occupiers, for example old age or disability. The links between housing problems and other problems which seriously detract from service users' quality of life, such as health and parenting, are undeniable. These links provide the rationale and urgency for social workers to 'think housing'[3] when assessing.

(1) Housing condition

2.3 Owner-occupiers are responsible[4] for maintaining the condition of their housing though they can access advice from local authorities and may, in limited circumstances, have access to assistance in the form of a grant, particularly in cases where the work to the house involves adapting it in light of disability.[5]

Where someone rents his or her accommodation, certain obligations are imposed on all landlords, whether in the private or public sector, to repair rented houses. In this context the public sector consists mainly of houses let by local authorities and by housing associations.

There is a general common law duty imposed on landlords to keep premises wind and water tight and in a proper tenantable condition. An example of breach of this duty is *McArdle v City of Glasgow*

2 G and J Stewart *Social Work and Housing* (1993), p 22.
3 *Social Work and Housing*, p 21.
4 In most cases they will have legal obligation to do so imposed under the terms of the mortgage used to purchase the property.
5 There may also be an entitlement to assistance if adaptation of the home is required under the terms of the Chronically Sick and Disabled Persons Act 1970, see para 6.4.

District Council[6] where a tenant successfully sued the landlord for damages for loss arising as a result of chronic dampness in the flat.

There are also a number of statutory obligations relating to repairs imposed on landlords, the precise content of which depends on whether the tenancy is in the private or public sector. As will be seen the obligations are similar, but not identical.

For most private sector tenancies the landlord is responsible for ensuring that premises reach a standard described as the 'repairing standard.' This duty has two components:[7]

(a) The premises must meet this standard at the start of the tenancy and the landlord has an obligation to inspect the premises before the start of the tenancy to identify any work which needs to be done.[8] The scope of this first component is not entirely clear, under previous legislation the view was taken that the landlord's duty could be breached by the presence of latent defects, that is, defects which would not necessarily be discovered by inspection.[9] It remains to be seen whether the same view will be taken under the current legislation.

(b) The premises must continue to meet the repairing standard during the currency of the tenancy. The landlord's duty to carry out work to ensure that this is the case is only triggered by notification to the landlord of the need for work (or the landlord becoming aware of this need) and any work must be carried out within a reasonable time of the landlord being notified (or becoming aware). The landlord's obligation to repair does not extend to damage caused by improper use of the premises by the tenant or to destruction or damage caused by fire, storm or flood.

The 'repairing standard' has a number of components:[10]

(a) The house must be wind and watertight and in all respects suitable for human habitation. 'If the state of repair of a house is such that by ordinary user [ie occupation] damage may naturally be caused to the occupier, either in respect of personal injury to life or limb or injury to health, then the house is not in all respects reasonably fit for human habitation.'[11] It is not necessary for the whole of

6 1989 SCLR 19.
7 Housing (Scotland) Act 2006, s 14(1).
8 Housing (Scotland) Act 2006, s 19.
9 *Todd v Clapperton* 2009 SLT 837.
10 Housing (Scotland) Act 2006, s 13.
11 *Summers v Salford Corporation* [1943] AC 283, per Lord Atkin at 289.

the house to be affected by the defects, a defect in any part of the house which could cause injury or injury to health in normal use will be enough to render the whole house unfit for human habitation.[12]

(b) The structure and exterior of the house, including any drains and external pipes, must be in a reasonable state of repair (taking into account the age of the house and the locality) and in proper working order.

(c) The water, gas and electricity supply, heating system, sanitation and water heater must be in proper working order and in a reasonable state of repair.

(d) Any fixtures, fittings and appliances (for example cookers or washing machines) supplied by the landlord must be working and in a reasonable state of repair and any furnishings provided by the landlord must be safe to use.

(e) There must be satisfactory smoke detectors and fire alarms in the house.

The landlord's obligations cannot be contracted out of by the terms of the lease without the agreement of landlord, tenant and the sheriff,[13] and tenants must be provided with information about the landlord's obligations.

If the landlord does not fulfil her/his obligations to maintain and repair the house the tenant can apply to the private rented housing panel (prhp)[14] which may make a repairing standard enforcement order requiring the landlord to carry out work so that the obligations are met.[15] In addition, the prhp may make a rent relief order reducing the amount of rent payable during the period that the landlord was in breach of her/his obligations.[16]

In the public sector the landlord's obligation is similar,[17] though less detailed (in part reflecting the fact that most public sector tenancies are

12 For example in *Morrison v Stirling District Council* 1996 Hous LR 5, even though some rooms in the house, including the kitchen, living room and a bedroom, were not affected by severe dampness, the severe dampness in other rooms rendered the whole house unfit for human habitation.

13 Housing (Scotland) Act 2006, ss 17 & 18.

14 Housing (Scotland) Act 2006, s 22; http://www.prhpscotland.gov.uk.

15 Housing (Scotland) Act 2006, s 24(1).

16 Housing (Scotland) Act 2006, s 27. The maximum reduction is 90%. At common law it was possible to seek an abatement of rent and in some cases the condition of the house would be so bad that a 100% abatement was applied, see *Renfrew District Council v Gray* 1987 SLT (Sh Ct) 70.

17 Housing (Scotland) Act 2001, s 27 & sch 4.

unfurnished). The landlord must inspect the house prior to the start of the tenancy and must ensure that:

(a) the house is wind and watertight and in all respects fit for human habitation at the start of the tenancy; and
(b) the house in such a condition throughout the tenancy, this duty to carry out work during the tenancy being triggered by notice to the landlord.

Public sector tenants also have limited powers to have repairs carried out themselves if their landlord fails to do them and to recover the costs and a small compensation payment from the landlord. This power arises only in respect of a limited list of repairs, including blocked drains, loss of electrical power and insecure doors and windows, and then only if the landlord fails to carry out repairs within a specified time after being notified (usually one day).[18]

In both public and private sector tenancies, where the landlord is responsible for the maintenance and repair of the premises he/she must take reasonable care in carrying out this responsibility so as to prevent danger to people coming into the premises. *Hughes' Tutrix v Glasgow District Council*[19] is an example where a mother successfully sued for damages for her daughter who was injured on a defective toilet bowl. Tenants may also be able to take action against a landlord if the state of the property amounts to a statutory nuisance, essentially where it is no longer tolerable to live there because of the condition of the property.[20]

In addition to the statutory and common law responsibilities other obligations may be imposed on the landlord in the lease of the property. If the landlord fails in carrying out any of their repairing obligations the tenant has a number of remedies. In addition to the rights set out above, the tenant may, unless this is excluded by the lease, withhold his/her rent or may take legal action against the landlord for damages or for an order requiring the landlord to meet his/her obligations. Where the tenant withholds rent all of the arrears of rent must be repaid when the landlord fixes the defect.[21]

Councils also have power to take action against properties which are in disrepair or which are dangerous to health. They may, of

18 Secure Tenants (Right to Repair) (Scotland) Regulations 2002, SSI 2002/316.
19 1995 SCLR 393.
20 Environmental Protection Act 1990, s 82. The prospects for success may be limited: *Robb v Dundee City Council* 2002 SC 301.
21 Subject to what is said about reduction of rent above.

course, be reluctant to use these powers where they own the property.

In addition to these specific statutory provisions about housing condition, the condition of a house may be such that the rights of the occupier under Article 8 of the European Convention on Human Rights are being infringed.[22] If the state of the house is so bad as to infringe these rights then the local authority will be in breach of its obligation to act compatibly with the Convention if it does not take action to ensure that the infringement of rights is brought to an end. Where the authority does not provide the housing itself, the duty will only arise where it is, or ought to be, aware of the conditions in which the occupier is living.

The unsuitability of accommodation may derive, not from the physical condition of the premises, but from changes in the tenant, for example disability making it impossible to access all or part of the house. In such cases the tenant will have the right to apply to the landlord for permission to carry out alterations to the house to make it more suitable.[23] The landlord is not to refuse consent unreasonably and will have to take account of the prohibition on discriminating on the grounds of disability in reaching a decision.[24] In public sector tenancies any work can be carried out with the landlord's consent and the tenant may be entitled to compensation for improvements to the house.[25] In the private sector the works which can be carried out are those which the tenant considers necessary for the accommodation, welfare or employment of any disabled person who occupies or intends to occupy the house as his or her sole or main residence.[26] The scope of these provisions means that the alterations need not be restricted to, for example, making the accommodation accessible to someone with a mobility impairment, but also extending or adapting the accommodation to enable a carer to live there. Some assistance may be available to the tenant in carrying out any work under the Scottish Government's Care and Repair initiative, and this may include access to grants.[27] Assistance may also be available under the Chronically Sick and Disabled Per-

22 See, for example, *Lee v Leeds City Council* [2002] EWCA Civ 06, *Bernard v London Borough of Enfield* [2002] EWHC 2282 Admin.

23 Housing (Scotland) Act 2001, s 28, Housing (Scotland) Act 2006, s 52.

24 Disability Rights Commission, *Code of Practice: Rights of Access: Services to the Public, Public Authority Functions, Private Clubs and Premises* (2006), ch 19.

25 Housing (Scotland) Act 2001, s 30.

26 Housing (Scotland) Act 2006, s 52(2)(a), factors which may be considered by the landlord in deciding whether to give consent are set out in s 53.

27 Housing (Scotland) Act 2006, s 92, see generally ss 74–97; Housing (Scotland) Act 2006 (Scheme of Assistance) Regulations 2008, SSI 2008/406.

sons Act 1970, section 2 of which provides that the local authority must, providing other requirements are met,[28] provide assistance in arranging for the carrying out of adaptations to a person's home or the provision of any additional facilities 'designed to secure his greater safety, comfort or security.'[29]

Social workers have limited mandatory duties in relation to people whose assessed needs relate to the condition of their accommodation other than under the general umbrella of the duty to promote social welfare contained in section 12 of the Social Work (Scotland) Act 1968. However, a social worker may be well placed to advise the service user what legal obligations fall to the landlord and what remedies fall to the tenant.

Using the legal knowledge available to inform social work practice can contribute to the empowerment of the service user in arranging, for example, for repairs to be completed. It may well be agreed that the social worker becomes actively involved taking on the role of liaison or advocate with the housing authority, while continuing to support the service user through what may well be experienced as a very stressful situation.

(2) Eviction

2.4 Most tenants enjoy some statutory protection against eviction. This takes two forms, first the landlord cannot remove the tenant without first obtaining an order from the sheriff court, and the tenant will need to be given some form of notice that an application for such an order is to be made. These requirements are discussed more fully below. The other form of protection is a restriction on the grounds on which a sheriff can make an order to remove a tenant from rented property. The nature of this last form of protection will depend on the nature of the tenancy which the tenant has. In the private sector tenants may have an assured tenancy, a short assured tenancy[30] or may be what are described a common law tenants. This last group includes tenants of resident landlords or of educational establishments, and they enjoy very limited protection, the landlord does not have to establish any

28 See para 6.4.
29 Chronically Sick and Disabled Persons Act 1970, s 2(1)(e).
30 A short assured tenancy is a tenancy for a fixed period of 6 months or more and the tenant must be served a notice that the tenancy is a short assured tenancy prior to the commencement of the tenancy.

particular grounds to remove such tenants. Short assured tenants also enjoy limited protection, it is sufficient to evict such tenants that the period of the lease has expired (provided the landlord has satisfied certain procedural requirements). A further group which enjoys very limited protection against removal (either in the private or public sectors) are those who live in hostel accommodation.[31] Public sector tenants will normally have a Scottish secure tenancy, though in some cases they may have a short Scottish secure tenancy. The latter type of tenancy enjoys less protection (the tenant can be evicted simply on the basis that the period of the let has expired) and can only be used in limited circumstances. Examples are temporary lets to intentionally homeless people with priority need and cases where the tenant, or somebody living with them, is subject to an Antisocial Behaviour Order (ASBO). It is possible for the short tenancy to be converted into an ordinary secure tenancy. A secure tenancy can be converted into a short secure tenancy if the tenant or anyone living with them is made subject to an ASBO.

Where a tenant has an assured tenancy or a secure tenancy the effect is that the court will grant an order for possession only on certain restricted grounds, such as non-payment of rent or causing a nuisance to neighbours. In the private sector, some of these grounds are mandatory, that is, the sheriff must grant an order for eviction if the ground is established. One example is if the tenant owes 3 months' rent arrears both at the time when the notice of proceedings was given and at the date of the court hearing.

Before a landlord can start proceedings to remove a tenant it will be necessary to serve certain notices on the tenant. There are statutory forms for such notices which require, for example, that they contain advice on possible sources of advice and assistance for the tenant, there are also certain required periods of notice, the minimum period of notice which can be given is 28 days, and in many cases it must be longer than this. If the notices served do not comply with these requirements then they cannot be relied on in court proceedings for eviction. The forms are:

(a) Common law tenants must be served with a notice to quit.
(b) Assured and short assured tenants must always be served with a notice of intention to raise an action for possession, and in most cases will also have to be served with a notice to quit.

31 *Conway v Glasgow City Council* 1999 SCLR 248.

(c) In the public sector a notice of intention to start proceedings must be served not only on the tenant, but also on any 'qualifying occupier.' Qualifying occupiers include any member of the tenant's family aged 16 or over and any lodger living in the accommodation with the consent of the landlord. It is not clear what effect failure to serve a notice on a qualifying occupier is once an order for removal has been granted.
(d) In all cases the landlord (other than a local authority landlord) must notify the local authority of the raising of proceedings against the tenant.[32]

In many cases the sheriff has the power to adjourn the hearing. This power might be used, for example, to allow payment of arrears of rent or to allow a 'bad neighbour' to mend his/her ways. It is an offence for a private sector landlord to evict someone without following the correct legal procedure or to harass a tenant into leaving accommodation.[33] In both cases the tenant has a right to damages assessed on the difference in value between the house without the tenant and its value with a sitting tenant.[34] This can amount to a substantial sum.[35]

If possible, the social worker should help the service user identify the type of tenancy or facilitate the service user getting this information from a specialist agency or solicitor. This will, of course, influence which set of statutory procedures and protections apply. The process of possible eviction is potentially extremely stressful and if a social worker is involved with the person/family threatened with eviction there are a number of things which may prove helpful in diminishing unnecessary stress. For example, it may help the person/family to learn that the notice means that there are at least 28 days before the council (or other landlord) can apply to the sheriff for an order for recovery of possession (an eviction order) and that they cannot be removed until there has been a hearing and the sheriff has issued such an order. If the notice to quit is not in the statutory form designed for this purpose, then the service user may be helped by learning that it is invalid.

So, the social worker should advise the service user not to leave his/her home unless alternative accommodation is already available and he/she wants to leave; to get legal advice under the legal advice and assistance

32 Homelessness etc (Scotland) Act 2003, s 11, Notice to Local Authorities (Scotland) Regulations 2008, SSI 2008/324.
33 Rent (Scotland) Act 1984, ss 22 and 23.
34 Housing (Scotland) Act 1988, ss 36 and 37.
35 In *Tagro v Cafane* [1991] 2 All ER 235 damages were assessed at £31,000.

scheme;[36] and to attend the court hearing and/or arrange for an application to be made to the court on their behalf. Tenants who attend the hearing or are represented at the hearing are less likely to be evicted.

The social worker may determine that it would be appropriate to negotiate with the service user to act as an advocate on his/her behalf to the housing authority or the sheriff court. The service user may require the social worker to act as liaison with other agencies for a limited period until his/her level of coping has been restored.

(3) Homelessness

2.5 Homelessness is a significant problem both in Britain as a whole and in Scotland. There are a variety of reasons for this, including the decline in the private rented sector and the decline in the number of public sector houses available for rent. The number of young people leaving local authority care who become homeless should be of particular concern to social workers.

Until 1978 the duty to provide for those who became homeless rested on social work departments. In 1977 the Housing (Homeless Persons) Act was passed and this transferred the responsibility to housing authorities. The law is now contained in Part II of the Housing (Scotland) Act 1987 (the 1987 Act)[37] and the Homelessness etc (Scotland) Act 2003 which operate in conjunction with a code of guidance (the Code) issued to local authorities by the Scottish Government.[38]

The Code is not binding on authorities or on the courts, but it may be taken into account in any proceedings for judicial review of a decision taken by a local authority in this area. The Code emphasises the importance of considering the individual circumstances of each case.

36 See para 1.62. Social workers may become involved with those who are threatened with eviction as a result of the obligation placed on landlords to notify the local authority of possession proceedings.

37 As amended by the Housing (Scotland) Act 2001 and the Homelessness etc (Scotland) Act 2003.

38 Scottish Executive, *Code of Guidance on Homelessness* (2005), supplemented by: Scottish Government, *Section 11 Statutory Guidance* (2009), Scottish Government, *Statutory Guidance for Local Authorities on Preventing Homelessness* (2009), Scottish Government, *Guidance for Local Authorities on Regulation 5 of the Homeless Persons (Provision of Non-Permanent Accommodation) (Scotland) Regulations 2010* (2010), and Scottish Government, *Statutory Guidance for Meeting the Best Interests of Children Facing Homelessness* (2010).

When someone who claims to be homeless approaches a housing authority for assistance the first obligation on the authority is to carry out initial inquiries.[39] These may involve a request for information from the social work department. The code suggests that these inquiries should be completed in 28 days. The inquiries are directed towards answering four questions:

(a) Is the applicant homeless or threatened with homelessness?
(b) Is the applicant in this position intentionally?
(c) Does the applicant have priority need?
(d) Does the applicant have a local connection with the authority dealing with the application?

If the authority has reason to believe that the applicant is homeless, the authority must provide temporary accommodation while these inquiries are being carried out. Where the person being provided with such accommodation has family commitments, this accommodation cannot be unsuitable.[40] Examples of features which would make accommodation unsuitable are that it is outwith the local authority area, it has inadequate toilet or washing facilities, there are no adequate cooking facilities, there is not 24 hour access to the accommodation, there is no ready access to health or educational provision, or the accommodation is not suitable for occupation by children.[41] However, where accommodation is suitable for children an applicant can be placed in accommodation which is otherwise unsuitable if:

(a) he or she expresses a wish to go there (eg for family reasons) despite the availability of suitable accommodation, or
(b) the accommodation is either a women's refuge or local authority accommodation where health, childcare or family welfare services are provided to the household.[42]

39 The text below should be read in conjunction with the flow diagram in Figure 1.
40 The Homeless Persons (Unsuitable Accommodation) (Scotland) Order 2004, SSI 2004/489. The term 'family commitments' includes an applicant who is, or who has a partner who is, pregnant or who has dependent children living with them or who might reasonably be expected to live with them, reg 2(2).
41 The Homeless Persons (Unsuitable Accommodation) (Scotland) Order 2004, SSI 2004/489, reg 2(3).
42 The Homeless Persons (Unsuitable Accommodation) (Scotland) Order 2004, SSI 2004/489, reg 3.

(a) Is the applicant homeless or threatened with homelessness?

2.6 A person is homeless for the purpose of the 1987 Act if one of the following three conditions is satisfied:

(a) *If there is no accommodation in Great Britain that he/she is legally entitled to occupy together with his/her family or any other person it is reasonable for him/her to live with.* This means, for example, that if a family unit has no accommodation that they can occupy together then they will be homeless. The reference to another person with whom it is reasonable for an applicant to live could extend to a carer, and the applicant would be regarded as homeless if there was no accommodation which could be occupied together with the carer.

(b) *If accommodation is available, but it is not reasonable for him/her to continue living there.* Local housing conditions will be relevant in considering whether it is reasonable for an applicant to continue to live in the accommodation. The Code gives the following as examples of accommodation in which it would not be reasonable for a person to remain: housing which is below the tolerable standard (for example, it is badly affected by damp, or has no bath/shower, is structurally unstable, or has an outside toilet), though reasonableness might depend on why the accommodation is below the tolerable standard; bed and breakfast accommodation; short-stay hostel accommodation; accommodation where there is external violence, including racial or other harassment; where continued occupation would pose a substantial risk to health (including mental health); or accommodation which is impracticable for the applicant to occupy because of his or her impairment(s). The Code also makes the point that possession of an order under the Matrimonial Homes (Family Protection) (Scotland) Act 1981 guaranteeing occupation or an interdict against abuse or harassment is not by itself be enough to make continued occupation reasonable.[43]

(c) *If accommodation is available to him/her but* one of the following conditions also applies:
    (i) he/she cannot gain entry to the property; or

43 See paras 3.29, 3.33 to 3.36.

(ii) occupying the property would probably lead to abuse,[44] or threats of abuse whether or not from someone who has previously shared accommodation with the applicant, wherever that sharing may have taken place; or

(iii) the accommodation is a houseboat or mobile home but there is no mooring or pitching place available, or

(iv) it is overcrowded as defined in the Housing (Scotland) Act 1987[45] and may endanger the health of the occupants; or

(v) the accommodation is temporary accommodation and before the applicant moved into it the local authority had a duty under the homelessness legislation to provide him/her with permanent accommodation.

A person is threatened with homelessness if he/she is likely to become homeless within the next two months.

(b) Is the applicant in this position intentionally?

2.7 For an applicant to be intentionally homeless the following conditions must be satisfied:

(a) The applicant must deliberately have done or failed to do something as a result of which occupation of available accommodation ceased. An example is deliberate failure to pay rent or a mortgage resulting in eviction.[46] There must be a clear causal connection between the act or omission on the part of the applicant and the homelessness. It must be the applicant who is responsible for the deliberate act or omission. The actions of one member of a family which might lead to that person being regarded as intentionally homeless do not necessarily mean that if another member of the family applies for housing that other family member will be so regarded, particularly if the applicant had not been aware of or had not acquiesced in the other person's actions, for example non-payment of rent.

44 Abuse in this context includes violence, harassment, threatening conduct, and any other conduct giving rise, or likely to give rise, to physical or mental injury, fear, alarm or distress, Housing (Scotland) Act 1987, s 24(3)(b) & (bb), Protection from Abuse (Scotland) Act 2001, s 7.

45 Sections 135–137. This consists of a room standard which is contravened if two people of opposite sexes over ten who are not married have to share accommodation and a space standard which provides, for example, that a three-room house is overcrowded if more than five people over ten live there.

46 Though the Code indicates that where failure is due to real personal or financial difficulties this should not result in a finding of intentional homelessness.

(b) It must be reasonable to have expected the applicant to remain in the accommodation. The considerations as to reasonableness discussed above apply also here.

(c) The applicant must have been aware of the consequences of his/her action, so an act done in ignorance of a relevant fact will not be significant. *Wincentzen v Monklands District Council*[47] illustrates this. In this case a young woman left home temporarily despite her father's warning, which she did not believe, that she would not be allowed to return. When she returned her father refused her access to the house. The Court of Session decided that she was not intentionally homeless as when she left she had acted in good faith and in ignorance of the relevant fact that her father meant what he said.

The Code suggests that a victim of domestic violence should never be regarded as intentionally homeless, nor should failure to exercise occupancy rights under the Matrimonial Homes (Family Protection) (Scotland) Act 1981 on its own be taken to indicate intentional homelessness. The Code also notes that in considering applications by young people the local authority should consider the position sensitively, given that failed tenancies are common when young people first leave home, and should not automatically consider a young person who has left home because of a clash of lifestyle with her/his parents as intentionally homeless. Finally the Code notes that: 'Whether or not someone is found to be intentionally homeless the local authority should seek to find solutions to the person's homelessness and offer support to address any difficulties that they face.'[48]

The same considerations are relevant in deciding whether someone threatened with homelessness is in that position intentionally. The status of intentionally homeless is not immutable: it can be reviewed as circumstances change and time passes

The concept of intentional homelessness was one of the compromises accepted during the passing of the 1977 Act. It was designed to reduce the demands for housing on local authorities by giving them a ground for refusing permanent accommodation. At the time of writing legislation is on the statute book, but not yet in force, which would make inquiring into intentionality optional.[49]

47 1988 SLT 259.

48 Scottish Executive, *Code of Guidance on Homelessness* (2005), para 7.2.

49 Homelessness etc (Scotland) Act 2003, s 4, amending Housing (Scotland) Act 1987, s 28(2).

(c) Does the applicant have priority need?

2.8 There are nine categories of applicant with priority need:

(a) Those who have dependent children, that is, children under the age of 16 or those under the age of 19 undergoing full-time education or training or who are unable to support themselves. The children must either be residing with the applicant or it must be reasonable to expect them to reside together. This last proviso ensures that families split up in temporary accommodation will not therefore be deprived of priority status. The Code stresses that the normal expectation is that families would stay together under the same roof.[50]

(b) Those whose homelessness or threatened homelessness is due to an emergency, such as flood, fire or other disaster.

(c) Those who are vulnerable as a result of:
    (i) old age;
    (ii) mental illness;
    (iii) personality disorder;
    (iv) learning disability;
    (v) physical disability;
    (vi) chronic ill health;
    (vii) having suffered a miscarriage or undergone an abortion;
    (viii) having been discharged from a hospital, a prison or any part of the regular armed forces of the Crown; or
    (viiii) other special reason.

    In making a determination as to whether a person is vulnerable the definition offered by the Code must be taken to account. This states that: 'A person is considered vulnerable when they are less able to fend for themselves so that they may suffer in a situation where another homeless person would be able to cope without suffering.'[51] In determining whether an applicant is vulnerable the department taking that decision may seek advice from others, including the social work department, and must take any advice it receives into account in arriving at its decision.[52]

(d) Anyone with whom a person described in (a) or (c) might reasonably be expected to reside.

50 Though, of course, there may be good reasons for families being separated.

51 Para 6.7. This reflects the definition offered by Waller, L J in *R v Waveney District Council, ex p Bowers* [1983] QB 238 at 244H to 245A, quoted with approval, for example, in *Kelly, Petitioner* 1985 SC 333.

52 *Code of Guidance*, para 6.8; *Kelly, Petitioner* 1985 SC 333.

(e) Those who are pregnant or who reside with a pregnant woman.
(f) Those aged 16 or 17.
(g) Those aged 18 to 20 who are either at risk of sexual or financial exploitation or serious misuse of drugs, alcohol or volatile substances because of the conditions in which they are living or who were looked after at any time after reaching school leaving age but are no longer looked after.
(h) Someone who runs the risk of violence or is likely to be a victim of harassment because of religion, sexual orientation or ethnic or national origins.
(i) Someone who runs the risk of domestic abuse.

Priority need is to be abolished in 2012 and in the run up to this local authorities are working towards the aim of providing housing to everyone who is unintentionally homeless by increasing the proportion of applicants assessed as having priority need.

(d) Does the applicant have a local connection with the authority dealing with the application?

2.9 A local connection is a connection arising from voluntary residence,[53] from employment, from family connections or from other special circumstances.[54] The issue of local connection is relevant only if the applicant is in priority need and is not intentionally homeless. The question is: does the applicant have a local connection with the authority processing his/her application? If the answer is yes, then that authority must comply with the housing duty set out below. If the answer is no, a further question arises: does the applicant have a local connection with another area in Great Britain? If the answer to this is yes, the applicant's case can be notified to the authority for that area, but only if there would be no risk of domestic abuse to the applicant if housed by this second authority. Should no local con-

53 An asylum seeker placed by the National Asylum Support Service would not be considered to be living in the area where he or she is placed as a result of his/her own choice: Housing (Scotland) Act 1987, s 27(2)(iii), see *Al-Ameri v Kensington and Chelsea Royal London Borough Council* [2004] UKHL 159. A consultation has taken place on modifying the local connection requirement, but so far no action has been taken, see Scottish Government, *Modifying Local Connection Provisions in Homelessness Legislation* (2006).

54 The Code suggests that this might include the need to continue education or medical treatment in the area, para 8.16.

nection exist with another area, the duties outlined below fall on the council receiving the application.

If the notified authority accepts that there is a local connection and no risk of domestic abuse, the obligation to secure housing devolves on it. If this is not accepted the duty remains with the notifying authority, which, in any event, has a duty to provide temporary housing while this decision is made. Note that the legislation refers to a local connection in Great Britain: a local connection in Northern Ireland would therefore be irrelevant.

(e) Local authority duties

2.10 Once the authority has carried out its investigation and answered these questions it must notify the applicant of its decision and the reasons for it. The notification must be clear and contain a full explanation of the reasons for the decision and of what happens next.[55] Regardless of the decision the authority will have a duty to provide some form of assistance to the applicant. The nature of that assistance will depend on how the questions have been answered:

(a) The authority has a duty to take reasonable steps to ensure that accommodation does not cease to become available to the applicant where he/she has priority need and is threatened with homelessness but this is not intentional. For other categories of those threatened with homelessness the authority has a duty to provide advice and assistance.

(b) It has a duty to secure that permanent accommodation[56] becomes available to an applicant who has priority need and is not intentionally homeless. This obligation is only to secure the provision of accommodation: the actual provision may be done by someone other than the housing authority[57]. Any accommodation

55 Code of Guidance, para 11.2.

56 In other words usually a Scottish secure tenancy or an assured tenancy, though in some cases the duty can be fulfilled by providing a short assured tenancy, or, in some cases, the level of housing support required by the applicant may make permanent accommodation inappropriate. See Homeless Persons (Provision of Non-Permanent Accommodation) (Scotland) Regulations 2010, SSI 2010/2; Scottish Government, *Guidance for Local Authorities on Regulation 5 of the Homeless Persons (Provision of Non-Permanent Accommodation) (Scotland) Regulations 2010* (2010). Where an applicant is determined to be homeless because of the condition /size of his/her current accommodation the local authority can leave him/her in that accommodation for a short (but not indefinite) period while alternative accommodation is secured, *Birmingham City Council v Ali* [2009] UKHL 36.

57 In some cases the housing authority will control no housing stock of its own.

provided must not be overcrowded, must not pose a threat to the health of the occupants, must meet any special needs of the applicant or a person who might reasonably be expected to live with her/him and must be reasonable for the applicant to occupy. The Code notes that technically the local authority's obligation could be met by making a single offer of accommodation which satisfied these requirements, but advises that a homeless applicant should be treated in the same way as any other applicant for local authority housing in terms of entitlement to offers.[58]

(c) In cases not covered by (b) the local authority has a duty to secure the provision of accommodation for the applicant for such a period as will give the applicant a reasonable opportunity to secure permanent accommodation, and to provide her/him with advice and assistance in attempting to secure accommodation. The Code indicates that what a 'reasonable opportunity' means will depend, at least to some extent, on the characteristics of the applicant. It also indicates that where advice and assistance have been offered but it has not been possible to identify a housing option for the applicant, then she/he cannot be deemed to have had a reasonable opportunity to secure accommodation.

(f) Challenging decisions

2.11 There is no statutory provision for appeal against any of the decisions a local authority may take in processing an application by someone who is homeless or threatened with homelessness. Instead, there is a right to have the decision reviewed within the local authority. Aside from these arrangements, the only way of challenging these decisions is by seeking judicial review of them in the Court of Session.[59]

(g) The social work role

2.12 The Morris Committee emphasised that homelessness was an area in which 'there is an overwhelming need for effective co-operation between the two services [social work and housing]'.[60] The importance

58 Para. 9.57.
59 See para 1.59.
60 *Housing and Social Work: A Joint Approach* (1975, SDD), para 8.2.

of co-operation is further stressed in the code of guidance which identifies a role for social work in, for example, the initial inquiries, in preventing arrears and evictions, and in providing support for rehoused families.

Since housing is a perpetually scarce resource and housing authorities are normally organised following the rules of large bureaucracies, it may well be justified and acceptable to both service user and social worker for the social worker to take an active role in assisting the service user with an application and in being supportive throughout the process. Prevention of homelessness is clearly preferable to dealing with the trauma associated with having already lost one's home, and a thorough assessment while co-operating with housing authorities is clearly the key in this respect. There is specific guidance on preventing homelessness, though there is little direct mention of the social work role in this.[61] In addition, social workers may become involved at the stage where a client is threatened with eviction.[62]

Accommodation provided, particularly temporary accommodation, can prove to be an additional source of anxiety and stress for people and so further warrant the involvement of a social worker. Particular difficulties for families centre on 'first, access to mainstream services particularly education, health services and social security benefits; and secondly, personal health and safety'.[63]

Through the provision of a comprehensive initial inquiry report, the social worker may provide relevant information highlighting the factors which are significant in determining the service user's eligibility. Some of these include availability of suitable accommodation, reasons for threatened homelessness or homelessness, responsibility for dependent persons, presence of persons vulnerable through various risks, emergency conditions, pregnancy, and local connection. In light of the decision in *Kelly v Monklands District Council*[64] that housing authorities must take social

61 Scottish Government, *Statutory Guidance for Local Authorities on Preventing Homelessness* (2009).

62 Though a report in 2005 (Communities Scotland, *Thematic study: Evictions in Practice*) said little about social work involvement and concluded that: 'In many cases, joint working between housing management and arrears staff and services such as housing benefit, homelessness, support and social work services happened too infrequently and too late to prevent eviction.'(p 4).

63 G and J Stewart *Social Work and Housing* (1993), p 87.

64 1986 SLT169. See also *Wilson v Nithsdale District Council* 1992 SLT 1131.

work reports and information into account in deciding on an application, social workers clearly can play an important part in the process by providing information about and advocating for a service user.

(h) Conclusion

2.13 It should be noted that the statutory framework guiding housing authorities is just that: a framework- it is therefore clearly the case that local authorities retain considerable discretion. Some authorities will simply provide the bare minimum: others will go beyond their strict statutory obligations and provide a more generous service for homeless people. For this reason knowledge of how the policy is operated by particular authorities is of as much practical importance as an understanding of the legal framework.

DEBT RECOVERY

(1) Court actions

2.14 Generally speaking, the process of debt recovery must be initiated by court action. In the vast majority of cases the action will be raised in the sheriff court and will take the form of a small claims action or a summary cause action. The former is available where the sum involved is less than £3,000, the latter for sums between £3,000 and £5,000.

Apart from the financial limits there are a number of other differences between small claims and summary causes, principally:

(a) Legal aid is available in summary causes, but not in small claims, although assistance for these can be obtained through the legal advice and assistance scheme.
(b) Procedure in court is intended to be much more informal in small claims cases.
(c) The summons in a small claim can be served by the sheriff clerk, while a summary cause summons must be served by a solicitor or sheriff officer.
(d) An individual can be represented by someone other than a solicitor at all stages in a small claim. Such representation is possible only at the first, largely formal, hearing of a summary cause.
(e) There is a restriction on the amount of expenses that can be awarded against the unsuccessful party in small claims. Currently the position is that, provided the defender has defended the action

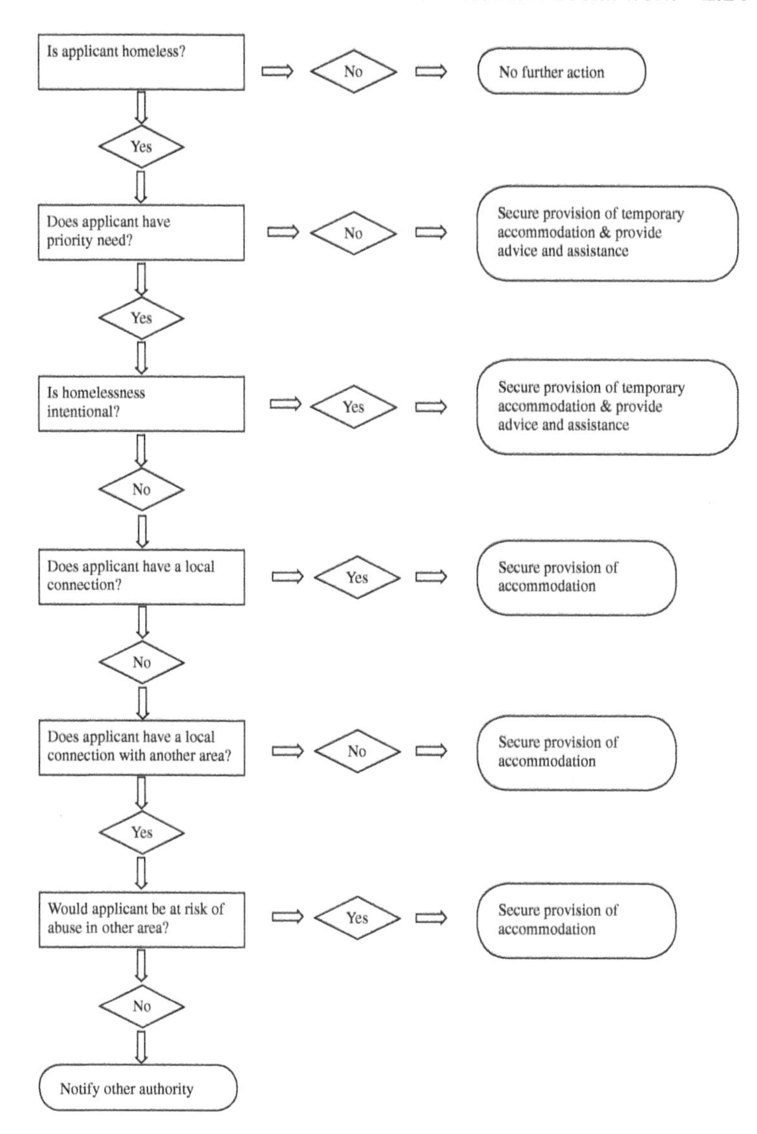

Fig 1 Homelessness flow diagram

and has acted reasonably and in good faith, no expenses can be awarded where the claim is for less than £200, and above that there are ceilings on the expenses that can be awarded against the unsuccessful party depending on the size of the claim.[65]

Once a creditor has initiated action there are four courses of action open to the debtor. He/she can:

(a) defend the action. This would be appropriate if there was a dispute about the amount owed or the quality of goods or services supplied. In order to defend the action the relevant form attached to the summons should be returned to court by the date specified there. Failure to return this form, indicating an intention to defend, will allow the creditor to obtain a judgment in his/her favour simply by means of a written minute without the need to turn up in court on the appointed day;
(b) apply for a time to pay direction permitting payment by instalments or as a lump sum at some future date. Again, the relevant form must be returned to court with details of the proposal for repayment;
(c) do nothing. The result of this is that the creditor will get a judgment (decree) in his/her favour which will require payment of the whole amount, plus any legal expenses and interest, which is payable upon the service of an extract decree. In this situation, subject to certain limitations, the debtor can apply to the court for a time to pay order, which has the same effect as a time to pay direction. A time to pay order cannot be granted once notice of auction of attached items has been given;[66]
(d) pay the debt. If the debtor has already received a summons he/she will be liable for the creditor's legal expenses.

Even following the granting of a decree for payment of money to the creditor, the creditor may still decide to write off the debt if there is no realistic hope of payment. Once a decree for the payment of money has been granted in favour of a creditor and he/she decides to pursue repayment, there are a number of courses of action (collectively known as 'diligence') open to the creditor if payment is still not forthcoming. The main forms of diligence are attachment; arrestment; and arrestment

65 Sheriff Courts (Scotland) Act 1971, s 36B(3); Small Claims (Scotland) Order 1988, SI 1988/1999, as amended by SSI 2007/496. The restriction on expenses does not apply to appeals.
66 Debtors (Scotland) Act 1987, s 5(5). On attachment see below.

of earnings.[67] Even after the creditor has embarked on one of these it is still possible to return to court and seek a time to pay order, such an application can be made after a charge has been served (as a precursor to attachment) or after an arrestment has been executed.[68]

(2) Attachment

2.15 There are two types of attachment, depending on whether the goods to be attached are found in a dwellinghouse. If they are not in a dwellinghouse the process involves three stages. First, a charge (or demand for payment) will be served on the debtor, before the creditor does this the debtor must be provided with a debt advice and information package. Second, if payment of the debt is still not made, an attachment will take place. This involves the listing and valuation of the debtor's possessions. There is a short list of items excluded from attachment (which therefore cannot be sold by a creditor) which consists mainly of tools of the trade. The debtor can seek to have individual items removed from the attachment. The debtor can also redeem items which have been attached by paying the value given to them. The final stage is sale of the possessions by auction. Any goods not sold are passed to the creditor and the debtor is credited with the value given to them when they were listed plus the sum raised by the sale.

Where the debtor's property is located in a dwellinghouse a different procedure must be followed. An attachment can only take place if an order (an exceptional attachment order) has been granted by the sheriff. Before granting such an order the sheriff must be satisfied that there are exceptional circumstances (relevant factors include failed attempts to negotiate a settlement and prior use of an arrestment) and must consider whether money advice has been given to the debtor. Thereafter the procedure is similar to that outlined above, except that there is a longer list of excluded items including: clothing, books required for education, medical aids or equipment, toys, and certain items of furniture.[69] The sale must take place away from the house and after attachment an application can be made to stop the auction of goods on the grounds that it would be unduly harsh in the circumstances.

67 These are largely regulated by the Debtors (Scotland) Act 1987 and the Debt Arrangement and Attachment (Scotland) Act 2002.

68 Debtors (Scotland) Act 1987, s 5.

69 Debt Arrangement and Attachment (Scotland) Act 2002, sch 2.

(3) Arrestment

2.16 Arrestment involves the freezing of assets belonging to or owed to the debtor, but which for the time being are in the hands of a third party. A common example would be money in a bank account.[70] The effect of an arrestment is to prevent the third party dealing in any way with the property. In order for the debtor to have it released he/she must raise a separate action known as an action of furthcoming. The effect of this is to order the third party to hand over to the creditor assets to the value owed by the debtor.

(4) Arrestment of earnings

2.17 Arrestment of earnings involves an order to the debtor's employer to pay a part of the debtor's pay to the creditor. The order lasts until the debt is paid. There are statutory restrictions on the amount which can be deducted. There are two forms of arrestment of earnings: the earnings arrestment which covers ordinary debts and arrears of maintenance (that is, payments of periodical allowance or aliment); and current maintenance arrestment to enforce current maintenance payments.

(5) Debt Arrangement[71]

2.18 At the same time as attachments replaced poinding and sale, provision was made to allow debtors to apply for approval of a debt payment programme. This will, in effect, consolidate all of their debts and prevent diligence being carried out against them whilst it is in force and whilst the debtor complies with its terms. The first stage is that the debtor consults a money adviser. The adviser then seeks to negotiate a debt payment programme with the creditors. This can then be presented to the Debt Arrangement Scheme (DAS) Administrator for approval. Normally the scheme will need the agreement of all of the creditors (though creditors who do not respond will be treated as having agreed), though the Administrator (who is a civil servant) has the power to dispense with the consent of creditors in certain circumstances. Where a creditor or creditors object to the proposed payment programme the

70 This can include any welfare benefits paid into an account, *North Lanarkshire Council v Crossan* 2007 SLT (Sh Ct) 169.

71 Further information on this process can be found at: http://www.moneyscotland.gov.uk.

Administrator can apply to the sheriff, who has power to approve the programme. In general, regardless of the approval process, the programme can only be approved if it is fair and reasonable. In deciding this, the following factors will be relevant: the total debt, the period of repayment, the comments of the money adviser, the extent of creditors consent and the availability of an asset (for example a house or car) which could be sold to repay the debt.

Once the programme is approved the debtor (or the debtor's employer) will make payments to a payment distributor, who will then distribute the money to creditors as provided for by the programme. Once the programme is approved creditors cannot carry out any diligence against the debtor, nor, in general must they offer the debtor more credit. The debtor also is subject to certain restrictions, they must:

(a) make all payments under a programme as they fall due;
(b) pay a continuing liability when due for payment; continuing liabilities include rent/mortgage payments, utilities bills and hire purchase instalments;
(c) except for a continuing liability, make no payment to a creditor taking part in a programme other than a payment under the programme;
(d) not, except under limited circumstances, apply for or obtain credit;
(e) notify the money adviser for a programme of a change of address or material change of circumstances; and
(f) within 10 days after receipt by the debtor of a written request from the money adviser for the programme, supply the adviser with such information or evidence as the adviser may request in respect of the income, assets or liabilities of the debtor.

It is possible to apply for the programme to be amended, and once the programme is completed the money adviser must be informed of this by the payment distributor and must in turn inform the DAS Administrator.

(6) Social work contribution

2.19 Increasingly people are finding themselves in debt. It is useful to distinguish between debt which is the result of inability to keep up with and pay for essentials like rent and fuel and debt which is associated with non-essential purchases and commitments. Sometimes the usual coping mechanisms fail. Some people panic and find themselves in a state of crisis. Many go to citizens' advice bureaux and some go to the social work department. Under section 12 of the Social Work

(Scotland) Act 1968, social workers are enabled, through the duty to promote social welfare and power to provide small amounts of money, to become involved with people in debt.[72]

Social workers are ideally placed to advise service users about the process of debt recovery: reminding them, for example, that they may be eligible for legal aid; that they must return the summons to the court if they intend to defend the debt action; that they may apply for time to make payment toward the debt; that they may be subject to diligence (attachment and sale of their property or arrestment of assets or earnings); that only certain items of property are liable to be attached; that any surplus money raised in a sale belongs to them; and that only a limited amount of money may be arrested from their earnings.

Social workers may well provide support for families suffering from the stress of these procedures. If the debtor is eligible,[73] it may be possible for the social work department to provide material assistance as well. Families who have defaulted on the payment of rent or mortgages may need advice and guidance about alternative accommodation.[74] Debtors may also be entitled to benefit, about which a social worker might advise them.

DISCRIMINATION

(1) Introduction

2.20 Legislation on discrimination started with the Race Relations Act 1968. This depended on both parties agreeing to the resolution of any dispute and was widely seen as being ineffective. Chronologically legislation was then passed dealing with equal pay, sex discrimination, race discrimination (repealing the 1968 Act), disability discrimination, discrimination on the grounds of race and ethnic or national origin, discrimination on the grounds of gender reassignment, discrimination on the grounds of religious or other belief, discrimination on the grounds of sexual orientation and discrimination in employment on the grounds of age. This legislation covers discrimination in employment and other areas, for example provision of goods and services, though in respect

72 The duties to children and families under s 17 of the Children (Scotland) Act 1995 may also be relevant here. See ch 4.

73 See para 1.67.

74 The requirement to notify the local authority of actions for repossession of rented and mortgaged properties should be noted, see para 2.4.

of some areas not all protected characteristics are protected. For example in respect of services and public functions no protection is offered against discrimination on the basis of marriage and civil partnership or on the grounds of age, at least as far as treatment of someone aged under 18 is concerned. Local authorities have both general and specific duties under this legislation and these are considered more fully below.

In 2007 the three bodies charged with overseeing the implementation of the legislation, the Equal Opportunities Commission, the Commission for Racial Equality and the Disability Rights Commission, were replaced by the Equality and Human Rights Commission. The Equality Act 2010, most of which came into effect in October 2010, repealed most of the previous legislation and replaced it with a single framework covering discrimination on any ground. In addition to consolidating the current law it made some changes including imposing a duty[75] on local authorities:

> when making decisions of a strategic nature about how to exercise its functions, [to] have due regard to the desirability of exercising them in a way that is designed to reduce the inequalities of outcome which result from socio-economic disadvantage.

The Act also envisages changes in the specific duties which would be imposed on local authorities in relation to discrimination.[76]

The following paragraphs will discuss, in outline, the law in relation to discrimination other than disability discrimination, which is considered later in the chapter.

(2) Protected characteristics

2.21 The Equality Act 2010 makes it illegal to discriminate against individuals on the basis of one of nine 'protected characteristics.' These protected characteristics are:[77]

(a) Age.
(b) Disability. A disability is any physical or mental impairment having a substantial and long-lasting effect on the ability of a

75 S 1(1), though following the change of government in May 2010 this section will not be implemented.

76 See, for example, Scottish Government, *Consultation on Public Sector Equality Duty Specific Duties* (2009). These changes will be implemented in April 2011. The current duties are explained below and are broadly similar to those introduced by the 2010 Act.

77 Equality Act 2010, ss 4–12.

person to carry out normal day-to-day activities.[78] Day-to-day activities are activities which fall into that category for a particular individual rather than being an abstract set of day-to-day activities undertaken by a notional 'normal' person. Therefore, for example, the day-to-day activities undertaken by a deep sea diver will be very different from those of a social work student. The definition given above is supplemented by others, mainly contained in the first Schedule to the Act. 'Long-term' generally means lasting 12 months or more and an impairment is regarded as affecting the ability to carry out 'day-to-day' activities if it affects, for example, mobility, manual dexterity, speech or perception of physical danger. Regulations provide an additional definition of 'disabled', for example, excluding most drug addictions, disfigurement caused by tattoos and hay fever, but providing that in a case of a child under six the impairment is to be assessed in the context of activities that a child over six would undertake.[79] This means that a very young child is not to be prejudiced just because the child is too young to participate in most of the activities which are used in judging whether a person is disabled. People with progressive diseases, such as multiple sclerosis or HIV infection are to be treated as disabled for the purposes of the Act.[80]

(c) Gender reassignment.

(d) Marriage and civil partnership.

(e) Pregnancy and maternity.

(f) Race. This includes not only discrimination on the ground of race, but also on the grounds of colour, nationality[81] or ethnic or national origin.

(g) Religion and belief. This includes not only religion and religious belief, but also any similar philosophical belief and any lack of

78 Equality Act 2010, s 6(1). This definition of disability has been criticised for being medicalised and inconsistent with individual's perception of themselves as disabled, see Pearson, C & Watson, N, 'Tackling Disability in the United Kingdom: The United Kingdom Disability Discrimination Act', (2007) 25 *Journal of Law & Policy* 25. For a broader discussion of disability see Thomas, C 'How is disability understood? An examination of sociological approaches', (2004) 19 *Disability and Society* 569 and Oliver, M, *Understanding Disability, From Theory to Practice*, (2nd edn, 2009).

79 Equality Act 2010 (Disability) Regulations 2010, SI 2010/2128. See also DRC, *Guidance on matters to be taken into account in determining questions relating to the definition of disability* (2006).

80 Equality Act 2010, Sch 1.

81 Nationality is not connected with citizenship, it is possible to make a claim that you were discriminated against on the grounds that you were Scottish under this provision.

religion It is not entirely clear what will qualify as a 'philosophical belief', but it has been suggested that:[82]

(i) The belief must be genuinely held.
(ii) It must be a belief and not an opinion or viewpoint based on the present state of information available.
(iii) It must be a belief as to a weighty and substantial aspect of human life and behaviour.
(iv) It must attain a certain level of cogency, seriousness, cohesion and importance.
(v) It must be worthy of respect in a democratic society, be not incompatible with human dignity and not conflict with the fundamental rights of others.

A belief in man-made climate change was considered to be a philosophical belief in the case in which these guidelines were suggested, and it was also suggested that Pacifism and vegetarianism might also qualify and that: 'belief in the political philosophies of Socialism, Marxism, Communism or free-market Capitalism might qualify.'[83]

(h) Sex.
(i) Sexual orientation. This is defined as orientation towards: persons of the same sex, persons of the opposite sex and towards people of both the same sex and the opposite sex.

(3) What does discrimination involve?

2.22 The legislation prohibits both direct and indirect discrimination. Direct discrimination simply involves treating some less favourably because of a protected characteristic,[84] eg because they are black or because they are female. This definition is wide enough to provide protection to people who are discriminated against because of their association with a person who has the protected characteristic or because a person is wrongly thought to have the protected characteristic.[85] Indirect discrimination exists where the same provision, criterion or practice is applied to everyone, but in practice this has the effect of discriminating against someone who has a protected characteristic (excluding pregnancy and maternity). For example, a requirement that all social workers are over 2 metres in height could apply equally to all aspiring social

82 *Grainger v Nicholson* [2009] UKEAT 0219_09_0311.
83 At para 28.
84 Equality Act 2010, s 13.
85 Equality Act 2010, Explanatory Notes, para 59, the example given of association is a carer.

workers, but would discriminate (at least) against female applicants since a smaller proportion of females than males are likely to meet the requirement. The statutory definition of indirect discrimination provides that a person (A) discriminates against another (B) if A applies to B a provision, criterion or practice which is discriminatory in relation to a relevant protected characteristic of B's:[86] It then provides that:

> a provision, criterion or practice is discriminatory in relation to a relevant protected characteristic of B's if—
>
> (a) A applies, or would apply, it to persons with whom B does not share the characteristic,
> (b) it puts, or would put, persons with whom B shares the characteristic at a particular disadvantage when compared with persons with whom B does not share it,
> (c) it puts, or would put, B at that disadvantage, and
> (d) A cannot show it to be a proportionate means of achieving a legitimate aim.

An example of indirect discrimination is a case where employers had agreed with a trade union that part-time workers would be made redundant first. This was found to amount to indirect discrimination. The reason for this was that the proportion of women who could meet the requirement for avoiding redundancy, full-time employment, was considerably less than the proportion of men who could comply.[87]

The discrimination which is prohibited is discrimination in any aspect of employment as well as discrimination in the provision of goods and services, including services provided by local authorities, provision of premises (either by sale or by renting) and provision of education. Separate provision based on race also amounts to discrimination.

(4) The duty to make reasonable adjustments

2.23 In respect of disability the law provides additional protection in that it imposes on employers, as well as the providers of services (considered below), a duty to make reasonable adjustments.

Where a disabled employee would be put at a substantial disadvantage as compared to someone without a disability by an employer's provision, criterion or practice (for example, as to timing of the working day or methods of working), a physical feature of the employer's premises

86 Equality Act 2010, s 19.
87 *Clarke and Powell v Eley (IMI) Kynoch Ltd* [1982] IRLR 482.

or failure to provide an auxiliary aid place a disabled employee the employer is obliged to make adjustments to the provision, criterion or practice or premises or to provide the auxiliary aid.[88] The duty is to take such steps as are reasonable to have to take to avoid the disadvantage.

There is no specific guidance in the Equality Act 2010 on what factors are relevant in determining whether it is reasonable to take certain steps.[89] The previous legislation suggested the following factors:[90]

(a) the extent to which the disadvantage will be prevented by the adjustment;
(b) the practicability of the adjustment;
(c) the costs and disruption to the employer;
(d) the extent of the employer's financial and other resources;
(e) the availability of financial or other assistance to the employer; and
(f) the nature and size of the employer's undertaking.

Examples of steps which might be taken are adjustments to premises, providing a reader or interpreter, or altering the hours worked by the employee. Finally, this duty to make adjustments applies in respect of job applicants who are known to the prospective employer to be disabled.

(5) Provision of services

2.24 As far as providers of services are concerned (and this includes local authorities), several duties are imposed:[91]

(a) Not to discriminate by not providing a service.
(b) Not to discriminate either on the terms on which a service is provided, by terminating the services or by subjecting a person to any other detriment in the provision of the service.
(c) Not to harass[92] or victimise a person requiring a service by not providing it or by acting in any of the ways set out in (b).
(d) To make reasonable adjustments.

88 Equality Act 2010, s 20.
89 There is provision for regulations to be made covering this, none have so far been made, Equality Act 2010, s 22.
90 Disability Discrimination Act 1995, s 18B.
91 Equality Act 2010, s 29.
92 For the purposes of harassment neither sexual orientation or religion or belief are protected characteristics.

Finally, it is unlawful for local authorities (and other public bodies) to do anything that constitutes discrimination, harassment or victimisation in carrying out their functions where these do not involve provision of a service to the public or a section of the public.[93] Local authorities and other public bodies also have a duty to make reasonable adjustments. This duty applies to all 'persons' exercising a public function. Private companies may, therefore, also be covered when their functions are of a public nature, for example a company running a private prison.[94]

(6) When can discrimination be justified?

2.25 In some cases discrimination on the basis of one of the protected characteristics considered above may be permissible. Both direct and indirect discrimination can be justified if it can be shown that it is a proportionate means of achieving a legitimate aim.[95] In the case of employment discrimination this would be justified if having a particular characteristic is an occupational requirement in the sense that it is necessary for the performance of the job.[96]

Examples where discrimination may be justified may include: special treatment of women in connection with pregnancy or childbirth; entertainment (where particular characteristics are required to play a role); and provision of personal social or welfare services where this can best be done by a member of a particular sex or racial group.[97] This would allow the appointment of someone of a particular racial group and sex to provide social work services to a particular group. In addition discrimination on the grounds of religious belief may be justified where the person or organisation discriminating is doing so on the basis of their own religious belief.

Finally, more favourable treatment for disabled people is permitted.[98]

93 Equality Act 2010, s 29(6).
94 This is the example given in Disability Rights Commission, *Code of Practice: Rights of Access: Services to the Public, Public Authority Functions, Private Clubs and Premises* (2006), para 11.8.
95 Equality Act 2010, ss 13(2), 19(2)(d).
96 Equality Act 2010, sch 3, para 1.
97 These are derived from previous legislation, but would still seem to be applicable.
98 Equality Act 2010, s 13(3).

(7) Enforcement of Rights

2.26 The Equality and Human Rights Commission can give advice and/or assistance to people bringing cases alleging discrimination. In addition it can carry out formal investigations into particular bodies or areas of provision and if it finds discrimination it can serve a non-discrimination notice requiring an end to discrimination, if the notice is not complied with it can ultimately be enforced through the court system. Finally, it has the sole right to enforce provisions concerning discrimination in advertising, pressure to discriminate and instructions/inducements to discriminate.

In general, individuals can enforce their rights relating to employment are enforced through the Employment Tribunal system and other rights are enforced through the court system, in Scotland this means initially in the sheriff court.

(8) Local authority duties[99]

2.27 Local authorities have a general duty to have due regard to the need to eliminate discrimination and to promote equality when carrying out their functions. This is required in respect of race discrimination, sex discrimination and disability discrimination. The local authority must, in carrying out its functions, have due regard to:

1. The need to eliminate unlawful racial discrimination and to the need to promote equality of opportunity and good relations between persons of different racial groups.[100] Promoting equality of opportunity and good relations between different racial groups involves promoting 'communities that respect their differences, and, secure in the knowledge that they have equal rights and opportunities, pool their talents and energies to achieve common goals.'[101]

99 This section describes the law at the time of writing (February 2011), the relevant provisions of the Equality Act 2010 are not due to come into effect until April 2011. In general terms the local authority duties are similar to those described here except that they now extend to all the protected characteristics and not just sex, race and disability. A revised Code of Practice is due to be published in April 2011.

100 Race Relations Act 1976, s 71(1).

101 Commission for Racial Equality (Scotland), *The Duty to Promote Race Equality: A Guide for Public Authorities in Scotland* (2002), p 11.

2. The need to eliminate unlawful discrimination and harassment and to promote equality of opportunity between men and women.[102]
3. In the context of disability to:[103]
   (a) promote equality of opportunity[104] between disabled persons and other persons;
   (b) eliminate unlawful discrimination;
   (c) eliminate harassment related to disabilities;
   (d) promote positive attitudes towards disabled people;
   (e) encourage participation by disabled people in public life; and
   (f) take steps to take account of a disabled person's disabilities even if it involves treating the disabled person more favourably.

The general duty imposed in respect of disability, unlike the other two duties, may require positive discrimination in favour of people affected by disabilities. Local authorities are required to take a proactive approach to the elimination of discrimination and the promotion of equality in the areas of gender and disability.[105] The duty will still apply to local authorities even where its functions are carried out in practice by private or voluntary organisations,[106] even though such organisations are not directly bound by the general duty.[107]

Having 'due regard' means that the weight given to promoting equality should be proportionate to its relevance to a particular function. It is noted in the statutory guidance on the duty that the small size of an ethnic minority population in a particular local authority area does not mean that race equality is less important. It is not acceptable to seek to

102 Sex Discrimination Act 1975, s 76A.
103 Disability Discrimination Act 1995, s 49A.
104 This is defined as meaning that 'disabled people should have full opportunities and choices to improve the quality of their lives, and be respected and included as equal members of society.' Disability Rights Commission, *The Duty to Promote Disability Equality: Statutory Guidance* (2006), para 2.7, see also paras 1.5 to 1.11.
105 Equal Opportunities Commission (Scotland), *Gender Equality Duty Code of Practice Scotland* (2007), para 1.26, Disability Rights Commission, *The Duty to Promote Disability Equality: Statutory Guidance* (2006), para 2.32.
106 Commission for Racial Equality (Scotland), *Code of Practice on the Duty to Promote Race Equality in Scotland* (2002), para 2.9.
107 Commission for Racial Equality (Scotland), *Code of Practice on the Duty to Promote Race Equality in Scotland* (2002), para 2.9, Equal Opportunities Commission (Scotland), *Gender Equality Duty Code of Practice Scotland* (2007), ch 5, Disability Rights Commission, *The Duty to Promote Disability Equality: Statutory Guidance* (2006), paras 5.16 to 5.19.

avoid any of the general duties on resource grounds,[108] and in carrying out the duties local authorities must not just look at the future, but also at existing and past decisions and actions to ensure that these are consistent with its duties. The following guidance has been given in respect of defining what a local authority has to do to fulfil its duty to have regard under the Disability Discrimination Act 1995:[109]

(a) those in the public authority who have to take decisions that do or might affect disabled people must be made aware of their duty to have due regard to the identified goals, and this must be more than a mere general awareness;[110]
(b) the 'due regard' duty must be fulfilled before and at the time that a particular policy that will or might affect disabled people is being considered by the public authority in question;
(c) the duty must be exercised in substance, with rigour and with an open mind, it has to be integrated within the discharge of the public functions of the authority and is not a question of 'ticking boxes It is good practice for the policy or decision maker to make reference to the provision and any code or other non – statutory guidance …';
(d) the duty is a non – delegable duty which will always remain on the public authority charged with it;
(e) the duty is a continuing one; and
(f) it is good practice for those exercising public functions in public authorities to keep an adequate record showing that they had actually considered their disability equality duties and pondered relevant questions. Proper record – keeping encourages transparency and will discipline those carrying out.

It has also been held that in fulfilling the duty to have regard to what is important is the substance of decision making, rather than the form, so lack of a specific mention of consideration of the duties or failure to carry out an impact assessment will not matter if, in substance, the duty has been complied with.[111]

As well the general duties, local authorities have specific duties to produce and implement equality schemes in each of the three areas,

108 Commission for Racial Equality (Scotland), *Code of Practice on the Duty to Promote Race Equality in Scotland* (2002), para 3.6.

109 *R (on the application of Brown) v Secretary of State for Work and Pensions* [2008] EWHC 3158 (Admin), paras 90–96.

110 *R (Boyejo) v Barnet London Borough Council* [2009] EWHC 3261 (Admin).

111 *R (on the application of Brown) v Secretary of State for Work and Pensions* [2008] EWHC 3158 (Admin), *R (on the application of AM) v Birmingham City Council* [2009] EWHC 688 (Admin).

although authorities may produce an overall single equality scheme covering all of them. One of the functions of these schemes is to allow local authorities to set out the arrangements which they will put in place to meet their general duties. In each case there are statutory requirements as to content, but local authorities may add to these in their schemes.

INFORMATION, CONFIDENTIALITY AND SHARING

2.28 One of the requirements of the Code of Practice for social workers in Scotland is that confidential information is respected.[112] Confidentiality, it is said, is an important factor in enabling clients 'to engage confidently and honestly',[113] but what, exactly, is involved in 'confidentiality'. At one extreme it might be taken to mean that information shared by a client with his or her social worker, or information about a client, must never be disclosed to anyone else, at least without the client's informed consent, indeed, this might be the expectation of the service user when the information is disclosed. However, it is unlikely that confidentiality can imply this absolute protection of information,[114] at the most basic level information may have to be shared with others in order to ensure that a client receives a service. Clark notes that:

> The client's information is often widely distributed without his full understanding, and including content that he supposed was to remain private. What is happening therefore is that the professional and the agency are transmitting information that the client naively imagines is to remain private, not out of negligence or malice, but in order to serve the client's interests: the infringement of confidentiality is thus justified by the professional's legitimate purposes.[115]

Indeed, there may in some cases be a positive expectation that information will be shared, both without the client's consent and in cases where

112 Scottish Social Services Council, *Code of Practice for Social Service Workers* (2009), para 2.3, which refers to 'Respecting confidential information and clearly explaining agency policies about confidentiality to services users and carers'.

113 Scottish Executive, *Sharing Information About Children at Risk: A Guide to Good Practice* (2003), para 9.

114 And it has certainly never been the case that the law takes this view.

115 Clark, C, 'Confidentiality, trust and truthfulness in professional relationships', in Clark, C & McGhee, J, *Private and Confidential? Handling Personal Information in the Social and Health Services*, (Policy Press, 2008), at 39. It may be, in fact, that such sharing does not amount to infringement of confidentiality if confidentiality is seen as permitting some sharing rather than as imposing a complete ban on any sharing of information.

it would be difficult to argue in any sense that the information sharing is in his or her interests.

Clark's comment also raises the issue of the parties to the confidential information and it has been suggested that the relationship is between the agency and the client and therefore that information can be shared within the agency, but not, subject to what is said below, outwith it.[116]

The need to share information is recognised indirectly in the Code of Practice in its reference to 'agency policies' about confidentiality, but more fully in the *BASW Code of Ethics* and in the Scottish Office Guidance on the confidentiality of social work records.[117] This last recognises that information will need, as a matter of course, to be shared with others in the social work department. In addition to these codes and guidance which largely *permit* disclosure in certain circumstances, there are some cases where disclosure and information sharing is expected or required, some of these are considered below.

Confidentiality extends beyond clients to third parties who provide information to the social work department.[118] Where this information is, at least in part, about the third party, or might serve to identify him or her, then he or she will have a right to have the information and his or her identity treated as confidential. This does not mean that it may not be disclosed, in some cases it may be, and there are statutory provisions to the effect that certain types of informant do not enjoy protection from disclosure of information.

A final aspect of information about a client is the right of the client to see information held about him or her by the social work department. There is specific statutory provision regarding this, which is discussed below. In addition to this provision, there will also, in certain cases, be a right to access information which flows from Article 8 of the European

116 See H M Government, *Information sharing: Guidance for Practitioners and Managers* (2008), para 3.15; see also Scottish Office, Code on Confidentiality of Social Work Records, Circular SWSG1/1989, para 12. In addition, the Information Commissioner suggests that 'if one local authority department passes personal information to another department, this will not be a disclosure of personal information as defined by the [Data Protection] Act' – though the Data Protection Principles must still be adhered to. Information Commissioner's Office, Data Protection Good Practice Note: *Data Sharing Between Different Local Authority Departments* (2008).

117 BASW, *Code of Ethics*, para 4.17; Scottish Office, *Code on Confidentiality of Social Work Records*, Circular SWSG1/1989, paras 11 & 12.

118 For example someone providing information about suspected child abuse, see *P v Tayside Regional Council* 1989 SC 38 at 42.

Convention on Human Rights.[119] This is illustrated in *Gaskin v United Kingdom*.[120] Mr Gaskin had, as a child, been taken into care by Liverpool City Council. He remained in its care between 1960 and 1977, during which time he was in a variety of placements. He subsequently sought access to the case records held by the Council covering his period in care. A combination of government guidance and legal action prevented release of most of this material and Mr Gaskin eventually took his case to the European Court of Human Rights, claiming a breach of Article 8 of the European Convention on Human Rights.[121] The court accepted the view of the European Commission of Human Rights[122] that 'respect for private life requires that everyone should be able to establish details of their identity as individual human beings and that in principle they should not be obstructed by the authorities from obtaining such very basic information without specific justification'.[123] In conclusion it indicated that people in Gaskin's position have 'a vital interest ... protected by the Convention, in receiving the information necessary to know and to understand their childhood and early development', though this had to be balanced against the importance of confidentiality 'for receiving objective and reliable information, and that such confidentiality can also be necessary for the protection of third persons'.[124]

Having set the scene we will now consider the legal bases for protection of personal information, the common law of confidence and the Data Protection Act 1998, going on to consider cases in which there is an expectation of, or a legal requirement for, the sharing of information.[125]

119 As we will see below this can also form the basis for protecting private information about an individual.

120 (1990) 12 EHRR 36.

121 Although Art 8 is phrased negatively to prevent infringement of rights it has been interpreted as creating positive obligations on the part of government and local government.

122 Under the procedure which existed at this time cases were first considered by the Commission.

123 At para 39.

124 At para 49. One of the difficulties was that at the time Gaskin sought access to the records there was no independent body which could adjudicate on these competing interests if the local authority refused access to information.

125 See also Scottish Executive, *Data Sharing: Legal Guidance for the Scottish Public Sector* (2004), based on DCA, *Data Sharing: Legal Guidance for the Public Sector* (2004).

(1) Breach of Confidence

2.29 As well as protecting sensitive commercial information the law of breach of confidence protects personal information about individuals. In its traditional form there were three elements which had to be established before breach of confidence could be shown, these elements therefore also set out the conditions under which information would be treated as confidential.[126] The first of these is that the information is confidential, in essence this means that it is private information rather than information which is public knowledge. It is not essential that only the person passing on the information and the recipient of the information know the content of the information – if its circulation is restricted it will still be confidential. For example, a client may disclose details of an illness to a social worker, the fact that details of the illness are also known to the client's family and to medical staff providing treatment does not mean that the information is not confidential. The second requirement is that the information is disclosed in circumstances which can be seen as imposing an obligation of confidence. Such an obligation could arise from an express statement that the information is to be kept confidential (eg 'don't tell anyone else') or, more commonly, from the relationship between the person passing on the information and its recipient. There is no doubt that the relationship between social worker and client is one which imposes such an obligation of confidence, the same will also be true of the relationship between the worker and those, aside from the client, to whom he or she speaks in the course of performing his or her duties, for example compiling a criminal justice social work report or a Social Circumstances Report.[127] The third and final requirement is that disclosure is likely to cause some loss or harm to the person who is the subject of the information. It is not necessary that this harm is financial, it could be emotional harm or loss of reputation or esteem, indeed, in many cases protection of information has been granted without any clear quantification of the damage that has been or would be caused by disclosure. It seems to have been assumed that disclosure of the information will inevitably be detrimental.

Partly under the influence of the introduction of the European Convention on Human Rights into UK law by the Human Rights Act 1998, the

126 Set out, for example, in *Coco v A N Clark (Engineers) Ltd* [1968] FSR 415.

127 Though, for reasons explained immediately below, it doesn't really matter that this relationship gives rise to a duty of confidence.

law of confidentiality has developed from this traditional formulation.[128] It is no longer necessary for a relationship to exist between the original source of the information and the person receiving it who then passes it on to a third party. Instead the law has developed to protect any private or personal information and any information about which there is a reasonable expectation of privacy.[129]

Where breach of confidence is established the injured party may be entitled to seek damages, though this may be little consolation if the information is by then in the public domain. Alternatively, he or she may, in advance of the information being disclosed, take action to prevent such disclosure by obtaining an interdict.

The availability of these remedies does not, however, mean that disclosure of confidential information is always prohibited. We will discuss specific requirements for and expectations about information sharing below, but it has always been the case that there will be some circumstances in which it is permissible to share confidential information. One example is *W v Edgell.*[130] This concerned the disclosure of a report on a psychiatric patient to hospital authorities and to the Home Office. The patient, W, was seeking a review of his case by a mental health review tribunal, with a view to discharge or transfer to a regional secure unit from the secure hospital where he was detained. There were two reports favourable to the transfer, which had in the past been refused by the Home Office. The prisoner's solicitors sought a third report from Dr Egdell, who concluded that, for reasons not explored in the other reports, W was still highly dangerous. In light of this report the application to the review tribunal was withdrawn. Some time later, Dr Egdell spoke to the assistant medical director of the secure hospital who had not seen the report but indicated that he would welcome sight of it. W's solicitors refused permission for a copy to be forwarded, but Dr Egdell sent on a copy anyway and on his insistence a copy was sent to the Home Office. W raised a breach of confidence action.

The Court of Appeal took the view that there are two public interests to be balanced: the public interest in confidentiality and the public

128 The relevant article is Article 8, though there is a tension between this and Article 10, which protects freedom of speech. Signs of this development can be seen before the Human Rights Act was passed, see, for example, *Lord Advocate v Scotsman Publications Ltd.* 1989 SC (HL) 122.

129 See, for example, *Murray v Express Newspapers* plc [2008] EWCA Civ 446, *Mosley v News Group Newspapers Ltd* [2008] EWHC 687 (QB).

130 [1990] 1 All ER 835.

interest in disclosure of the information to the relevant authorities. In this case the latter won.

> The suppression of the material contained in his [Dr Egdell's] report would have deprived both the hospital and the Secretary of State of vital information, directly relevant to questions of public safety.[131]

> There is one consideration which in my judgment ... weighs the balance of public interest decisively in favour of disclosure. It may be shortly put. Where a man has committed multiple killings under the disability of serious mental illness, decisions which may lead directly or indirectly to his release from hospital should not be made unless a responsible authority is properly able to make an informed judgment that the risk of repetition is so small as to be acceptable. A consultant psychiatrist who becomes aware, even in the course of a confidential relationship, of information which leads him ... to fear that such decisions may be made on the basis of inadequate information and with a real risk of consequent danger to the public is entitled to take such steps as are reasonable in all the circumstances to communicate the grounds of his concern to the responsible authorities.[132]

Other, perhaps more mundane, exceptions might be implied by the public interest to allow disclosure in the proper performance of social worker's duties (for example, in a case conference) or where they are providing a report which they are legally obliged to complete (such as a criminal justice social work report or a social background report).

(2) Data Protection

2.30 The Data Protection Act 1998 covers the processing of personal data as well as giving those whose data is held and used by organisations (data subjects[133]) certain rights. 'Personal Data'

131 At 846f, *per* Sir Stephen Brown P.

132 [1990] 1 All ER 835 at 852j-853b, *per* Bingham LJ. Note that the public interest sanctions disclosure to the responsible authorities. Where the public interest justifies disclosure it will also usually limit the scope of disclosure. If a service user were to express a real threat to harm a third party confidence could be breached to the extent of informing the police, not ringing the *Daily Record*.

133 Someone can be a data subject both in the sense that information is about them and in the sense that they can be identified as the source of information about someone else, Data Protection Act 1998, s 1(1).

is defined broadly and covers information which is kept by local authorities in carrying out their social work functions.[134] The requirement that data is 'personal data' has been interpreted to mean that the mere fact that a person is named in a document is not enough to make that document personal data relating to the named individual. In *Durant v Financial Services Authority*[135] it was held that 'mere mention of the data subject in a document ... does not necessarily amount to his personal data'.[136] Instead:

> Whether it does so in any particular instance depends on where it falls in a continuum of relevance or proximity to the data subject as distinct, say, from transactions or matters in which he may have been involved to a greater or lesser degree.

The court identified two factors that might be helpful in deciding whether data is personal data:

(a) If the information is biographical in a significant sense, that is, going beyond the recording of the individual's involvement in a matter or an event that has no personal connotations, in other words, an event in respect of which his or her privacy could not be said to be compromised.
(b) How focussed is the information on the individual? It should have the individual as its focus rather than, for example, some other person with whom he or she may have been involved or some transaction or event in which he or she may have figured or have had an interest.

In short, the court said, personal data is information that affects the individual's privacy, whether in his or her personal or family life, business or professional capacity.

Edwards and Rodrigues suggest one effect of this approach:

> In the context of children it might conceivably be highly restrictive – for example, in a social work report compiled on child A, it is possible that a brief mention of child B, A's sibling, might not

134 This information falls within the definition of an 'accessible public record', Data Protection Act 1998, ss 1(1)(d) & 68(1)(c), sch 12.
135 [2003] EWCA Civ 1746.
136 Per Auld, LJ, at para 28.

be regarded *ab initio* as personal data, thus restricting B's rights of access to this data, as well as other data protection rights.[137]

Personal data is not restricted to 'facts' about individuals, but also includes expressions of opinion and indications of intentions in relation to the data subject and the Act covers not only data kept and processed electronically, but also manual records.

'Processing' is widely defined and it has been said that 'it is difficult to imagine any action involving data which doesn't amount to processing'.[138] The statutory definition specifically includes such actions as collecting data, organising it, consultation or use of the data and disclosure of the data.

All personal data is subject to the data protection principles set out in the box below and there are, in addition, specific conditions to be met to permit the processing of data. These conditions depend on whether or not the personal data falls into the category of sensitive personal data. For personal data, *one* of a number of conditions must be met before it can be processed. These conditions include:[139]

1. The data subject has consented to the processing.
2. The processing is necessary to protect the interests of the data subject.
3. The processing is necessary for the exercise of functions conferred on any person by any legislation.[140]
4. The processing is necessary for the purpose of legitimate interests pursued by the person holding the data.

137 Edwards, L & Rodrigues, R, 'The right to privacy and confidentiality for children: the law and current challenges', in Clark, C & McGhee, J, *Private and Confidential? Handling Personal Information in the Social and Health Services*, (Policy Press, 2008), at 94. Given the reference to privacy interests in *Durant* it seems at least arguable (as conceded in the quotation) that, depending on the extent of information about B, B's privacy interests would be engaged in such a case.

138 Information Commissioners Office, *Data Protection Act 1998 – Legal Guidance*, para 2.3.

139 Data Protection Act 1998, sch 2.

140 This would cover a range of processing by local authorities for the purpose of carrying out their functions.

The Data Protection Principles

1. Personal data shall be processed fairly and lawfully and must not be processed unless one of the conditions which permits processing is met [see text].
2. Personal data should be obtained only for one or more specified and lawful purpose, and shall not be processed in a way incompatible with the purpose(s) for which it is collected.
3. Personal data should be adequate, relevant and not excessive as judged against the purpose(s) for which it is processed.
4. Personal data should be accurate and, if necessary, kept up to date.
5. Personal data should not be kept for longer than is necessary for the purpose(s) for which it is being processed.
6. Personal data should be processed in accordance with the rights of data subjects.
7. Appropriate measures, both technical and organisational, are to be taken to prevent unauthorised or unlawful processing and accidental loss of, or damage to, personal data.
8. Transfer of data outside the European Economic Area is restricted.

A different set of conditions applies to sensitive personal data, which includes data about physical or mental health, sexual life, commission or alleged commission of an offence and any proceedings in relation to an offence or an alleged offence.[141] The conditions for processing such data, one of which must apply, include that the processing is:[142]

1. taking place with the *explicit* consent of the data subject (note that this goes beyond the condition required for processing personal data and requires explicit rather than implicit consent);
2. necessary to protect the vital interests of the data subject or another person where either the data subject cannot consent or it would be unreasonable to expect consent to be obtained;

141 Data Protection Act 1998, s 2.
142 Data Protection Act 1998, sch 3.

3. necessary to protect the vital interests of someone other than the data subject where his or her consent to processing is being withheld unreasonably;
4. necessary for the purposes of or in relation to legal proceedings;
5. necessary for the exercise of functions conferred on any person by any legislation.

As well as regulating the use of personal data the 1998 Act also confers an access right on data subjects.[143] This access right can be exercised by a child, provided that he or she has a general understanding of what it means to exercise the right.[144] An access request can be made by a data subject to an organisation which he or she thinks may hold data concerning him or her. Any such requests must be responded to promptly and, in any case, within 40 days.[145] The access right has three components:

1. A right to be informed whether any personal data about a data subject is being processed by or on behalf of the organisation (Right 1).
2. If data is being processed, a right to a description of the personal data, the purposes of processing and any recipient(s) to whom data may be disclosed (Right 2).
3. A right to have a copy of the data in an intelligible form together with information as to the source of the data (Right 3).

Access rights are subject to some restrictions which effectively mean that certain types of information may not be disclosed by the organisation holding the data. Some of these restrictions are specific to certain types of information, and we will consider the limitations applying to social work records below. In respect of all types of data, however, there is a restriction on disclosure where the data affects third parties. This provides that where an access request cannot be complied with without disclosing information about

143 See Information Commissioner's Office, *Data Protection Technical Guidance Note: Subject access requests and social services records* (2008). There are also special rules about access to adoption records, see Adoption and Children (Scotland) act 2007, s 38, Adoption (Disclosure of Information and Medical Information about Natural Parents) (Scotland) regulations 2009, SSI 2009/268.

144 Data Protection Act 1998, s 66, children aged 12 or over are presumed to have such an understanding.

145 Data Protection Act 1998, s 7(8) & (10).

another individual who can be identified from the information[146] then the request need not be complied with unless either the third party has consented to disclosure of the information or it would be reasonable in all the circumstances to disclose the information without such consent.[147] A number of factors are to be taken into account in deciding whether it is reasonable to disclose information without consent, these are: any duty of confidentiality owed by the organisation holding the data to the third party, any steps taken to seek consent, the capacity of the third party to give consent and any express refusal of consent.[148] This exception is limited. It only prevents disclosure of information regarding the third party. If the third party does not consent (and the decision is taken that it would not be reasonable to disclose without consent) then the organisation must still disclose any other information held about the person making the access request that does not identify the third party and which is not subject to any other restrictions on disclosure. A further limitation is that it does not apply in the case of social work records where the third party is a social work employee.[149]

Specific restrictions affecting social work records provide that that information is not to be disclosed:

1. Where disclosure would be likely to prejudice the carrying out of social work by reason of the fact that serious harm to the physical or mental health or condition of the applicant for access or any other person would be likely to be caused.[150]
2. Where information is supplied to court by a social work department, the court may be entitled to withhold the information in whole or in part, the effect of this is that the decision of a court to withhold information cannot be bypassed by seeking direct access to the social work record.[151]

146 This includes identifying the individual as the source of information, Data Protection Act 1998, s 7(5).

147 Data Protection Act 1998, s 7(4).

148 Data Protection Act 1998, s 7(6).

149 Data Protection (Subject Access Modification) (Social Work) Order 2000, SI 2000/415, art 7(2).

150 Data Protection (Subject Access Modification) (Social Work) Order 2000, SI 2000/415, art 5(1).

151 Data Protection (Subject Access Modification) (Social Work) Order 2000, SI 2000/415, art 4 and Sch 1, pt 2.

3. Information provided to the social work department by the Reporter can only be disclosed if the Reporter certifies that the exception set out in 1 above does not apply to the information.[152]
4. Where someone having parental responsibilities for a child under the age of 16 applies to see that person's record, there are restrictions on the information that can be disclosed to them. Information is not to be disclosed:[153]
   (a) where it was provided by the person under 16 in the expectation that it would not be disclosed to the person making the request;
   (b) where it resulted from an examination or investigation of the person aged under 16 and he or she consented to this examination or investigation in the expectation that the outcome would not be disclosed to the person making the request; and,
   (c) where the person aged under 16 has specifically indicated that the information should not be disclosed. Similar restrictions apply where an application is made by a guardian in respect of information held about an adult with incapacity.[154]
5. Where information derives from a health professional, unless the appropriate health professional has been consulted as to whether disclosure would be likely to cause serious harm to the physical or mental health or condition of the person to whom the information elates or another person.[155] If the health professional certifies that this is the case then the information is not to be disclosed.[156]

In addition to access rights, data subjects have other rights under the 1998 Act, including the right to seek to have changes made to information held about them,[157] a right to prevent processing of personal data which would cause damage or distress[158] and a right to seek damages if loss is caused by misuse of information about them.[159]

152 Data Protection (Subject Access Modification) (Social Work) Order 2000, SI 2000/415, art 6.
153 Data Protection (Subject Access Modification) (Social Work) Order 2000, SI 2000/415, art 5(3), (4).
154 Data Protection (Subject Access Modification) (Social Work) Order 2000, SI 2000/415, art 5(3), (4).
155 Data Protection (Subject Access Modification) (Health) Order 2000, SI 2000/413, art 6.
156 Data Protection (Subject Access Modification) (Health) Order 2000, SI 2000/413, art 7.
157 Data Protection Act 1998, s 14.
158 Data Protection Act 1998, s 10.
159 Data Protection Act 1998, s 13.

(3) Sharing Information

2.31 It will be clear from the discussion above that the description of information as confidential or the fact that it is personal data covered by the Data Protection Act 1998 does not mean that it cannot be shared with other people or organisations. The requirements for processing personal data (including disclosure to others) listed above, for example, make this clear. There is no doubt that information can be shared if the person who provides the information (and, where appropriate, the person to whom it relates, where these are different) consents. Good practice suggests that where information is being sought or gathered from a client or from a third party the boundaries of confidentiality and any possible sharing of information should be made clear.[160] There can, however, be problems with consent. In some cases these may arise from the inability of the client to consent, for example because the client is a child or as a result of incapacity or mental illness. Youth, incapacity or illness in themselves do not mean that a person is unable to understand what is involved in giving consent in particular cases and careful consideration will need to be given to capacity to consent in the specific context and of the possible difficulties or disadvantages of seeking consent.[161] In cases where the client is unable to consent there may be others who can consent on his or her behalf, for example a parent, attorney or guardian. Where there is no one who can consent decisions on information sharing will have to be taken on the basis of other considerations.

There will be circumstances in which it is inappropriate to seek consent, for example where it would put the person whose consent is sought at risk or where seeking consent would result in unnecessary delay in taking emergency action.[162] Seeking consent will

160 For example, H M Government, *Information Sharing: Guidance for Practitioners and Managers* (2008) suggests that: 'Obtaining explicit consent for information sharing is best practice and ideally should be obtained at the start of the involvement …' (para 3.19). The view of the Information Commissioner is that 'consent is not particularly easy to achieve', and that reliance should be placed on the other conditions which permit processing and are set out in schs 2 & 3 of the Data Protection Act 1998, see Information Commissioners Office, *Data:Protection Act 1998 – Legal Guidance*, para 3.1.5.

161 See Hughes, J & Louw, S, 'Confidentiality and Cognitive Impairment: Professional and Philosophical Ethics ', (2002) 31 *Age and Ageing* 147.

162 See H M Government, *Information Sharing: Guidance for Practitioners and Managers* (2008), para 3.36.

also be unnecessary and inappropriate where information sharing is required either as a matter of policy and guidance or as a result of a statutory requirement.

Consent may also, in some cases, rather than being express, be implied from the circumstances and the actions of the client (that is, be implicit rather than explicit consent). For example where information is being obtained for the purposes of securing provision of a service to the client from a third party some of the information will have to be shared with the third party provider and the continued involvement of the client in working towards service provision can be taken as providing implied consent for any necessary information to be shared with the service provider.[163]

Refusal of consent (or inability to consent) does not mean that information cannot be shared. We have already seen this in respect of personal data protected by the Data Protection Act 1998, where consent is only one of a number of conditions which can justify sharing. The possibility of sharing without consent also exists under the law relating to breach of confidence, we have already seen this in relation to *W v Edgell*, where it was also suggested that:

> In my view, a doctor called on, as Dr Egdell was, to examine a patient such as W owes a duty not only to his patient but also a duty to the public. His duty to the public would require him, in my opinion, to place before the proper authorities the result of his examination if, in his opinion, the public interest so required. This would be so, in my opinion, whether or not the patient instructed him not to do so.[164]

This suggests that there will be some cases where there is in fact an expectation that information will be shared or a legal requirement to share it rather than there simply being an option of disclosing information without breaching either confidence or the provisions of the 1998 Act. The following is a non-exhaustive list of examples of this:

163 Though note the apparent restriction mentioned above in respect of sensitive personal data where explicit consent is required.

164 *W v Egdell* [1989] 1 All ER 1089, *per* Scott, J at 1104.

1. In cases where a child may be at risk of harm, *Protecting Children: A shared responsibility*[165] instructs that 'Any person who believes that a child is being abused, or is at risk, should tell the social work service, the police or the reporter about their concerns'. Where these circumstances mean that the child is considered to be in need of compulsory measures of supervision the social work department must inform the Reporter.[166] In addition, there is some case law suggesting that local authorities may have positive duties to pass on concerns about an individual who is a risk to children, though it not always clear whether what is being referred to is a legal duty or a professional duty. These cases are discussed more fully below.
2. In carrying out various types of assessment, for example a single shared assessment or an assessment in preparation of a child or young person's plan.
3. Where required by statutory provision, for example:
   (a) The Adult Support and Protection (Scotland) Act 2007[167] empowers council officers to require production of records relating to vulnerable adults and requires co-operation with investigations being carried out by the local authority, which by implication will include sharing information.[168]
   (b) The Protection of Vulnerable Groups (Scotland) Act 2007 requires the passing on of information about an individual if he or she has been dismissed or transferred for one of a specified number of reasons.

165 Scottish Office, 1998, at para 4.1. See also *Sharing Information about Children at Risk: A Guide to Good Practice* (Scottish Executive, 2004): 'If there is reasonable concern that a child may be at risk of harm this will always override a professional or agency requirement to keep information confidential', para 8. Though note, for example, Swain's conclusion that 'social workers (as with other helping professions) do not have a strong track record for accurate prediction of harm', Swain, P A, 'A Camel's Nose Under the Tent? Some Australian Perspectives on Confidentiality and Social Work Practice', (2006) 13 BJSW 91, at 98.

166 Children (Scotland) Act 1995, s 53(1).

167 S 10.

168 Adult Support and Protection (Scotland) Act 2007, s 5. See also Adult Support And Protection (Scotland) Act 2007 *Code Of Practice For Local Authorities And Practitioners Exercising Functions Under Part 1 Of The Act*, (Scottish Government, 2008, as amended 2009), ch 8, para 8: 'Whilst confidentiality is important, it is not an absolute right. Co-operation in sharing information is necessary to enable a council to undertake the required inquiries and investigations'.

(c) The duty to cooperate in the management of certain offenders (through Multi-Agency Public Protection Arrangements) includes a duty to share information.[169]

4. In presenting reports to tribunals or to courts, for example reports associated with applications for Compulsory Treatment Orders, Social Background Reports and criminal justice social work reports.[170]

A final example of cases where there may be an expectation that information may be shared is where there might be considered to be a duty to warn. The best known example of this is *Tarasoff v Regents of the University of California.*[171] In *Tarasoff* the family of a young woman sought compensation from a psychologist, Moore, who had failed to warn their daughter, Tatiana, of the potential danger posed to her by one of his patients. The patient, Poddar, had confided in Moore his intention of killing a young woman who could easily have been identified as Tatiana. Moore notified the campus police and Poddar was briefly detained. A few weeks later, Poddar murdered Tatiana. One basis of the claim by the family was the existence of a duty to warn potential victims whose life or safety was at risk.[172] The Supreme Court of California concluded that:

> '[O]nce a therapist does in fact determine, or under applicable professional standards reasonably should have determined, that a patient poses a serious danger of violence to others, he bears a duty to exercise reasonable care to protect the foreseeable victim of the danger.'[173]

The *Tarasoff* decision has had a varied subsequent career in the US[174] and does not yet seem to have been applied to social workers. One suggested difficulty which might arise in extending the rationale to social workers is establishing their diagnostic competence to decide when someone poses a serious threat to another person.

Is there such a duty to warn or to take further action in the UK? In *Osman v United Kingdom*[175] the father of a pupil at a school in London

169 Management of Offenders (Scotland) Act 2005, ss 1(2)(a) & 10.

170 The status of information contained in Social Enquiry Reports is considered in *X v BBC* [2005] CSOH 80, see also para 10.4.

171 (1976) 17 Cal 3d 425.

172 The other basis was a failure in a duty to control or to commit Poddar.

173 (1976) 17 Cal 3d 425 at 439.

174 See, for example, Herbert, P & Young, K, '*Tarasoff* at Twenty-five', (2002) 30 *Journal of the American Academy of Psychiatry and the Law* 275.

175 (2000) 29 EHRR 245.

was killed and his son injured by a teacher from the school. The teacher had formed what was described as 'an attachment' to the boy and there had been a large number of incidents over a long period prior to the shooting. The dead man's widow sued the police for negligence claiming that they had a duty of care which had been breached. She was unsuccessful and then went to the European Court of Human Rights claiming infringement of rights under articles 2 and 8 of the European Convention on Human Rights. The Court took the view that Article 2 imposed a positive duty to protect life but that:

> where there is an allegation that the authorities have violated their positive obligation to protect the right to life in the context of their above-mentioned duty to prevent and suppress offences against the person, it must be established to its satisfaction that the authorities knew or ought to have known at the time of the existence of a real and immediate risk to the life of an identified individual or individuals from the criminal acts of a third party and that they failed to take measures within the scope of their powers which, judged reasonably, might have been expected to avoid that risk.[176]

On the basis of the factual background to the case the Court concluded that the police in this case did not have the required degree of knowledge of the danger to Mr Osman's life to require action to be taken. The same conclusion was reached in respect to the positive obligation arising under Article 8 of the European Convention on Human Rights. From the requirement that there is knowledge of a 'real and immediate risk' it follows that the standard for imposing a positive duty to take action will be high and that the circumstances in which it will be met will be very limited.[177]

The *Osman* decision is not the only possible basis for a duty to warn being in existence. In a number of cases the court has referred to a duty on the part of professionals to warn. One of these is, as we have seen, *W v Edgell.*[178]

176 At para 116.

177 No duty was found to exist in *Mitchell v Glasgow City Council* [2009] UKHL 11, where a local authority landlord had failed to warn a tenant of action taken against a neighbour who was likely to blame the tenant for his predicament and who in the past had threatened the tenant. See also Gavaghan, C, 'Dangerous Patients and Duties to Warn: a European Human Rights Perspective', (2007) 14 *European Journal of Health Law* 113.

178 *Per* Scott, J, *W v Egdell* [1989] 1 All ER 1089 at 1104.

A further example is *R v Devon County Council, Ex parte L*,[179] which involved a man against whom allegations of child sexual abuse had been made. Although he was not prosecuted, members of a social services department warned women with whom he subsequently lived of the allegations of child abuse and of the possibility that their children would be placed on the child protection register if he continued living with them. An attempt by the man to stop this course of conduct was unsuccessful:

> In my judgment, social workers, in the discharge of the local authority's statutory obligation to protect the welfare of children, in this case, were under a duty to inform the two mothers and the one grandmother in this case that they believed that the applicant was an abuser, if they honestly believed on reasonable grounds that he was an abuser.[180]

Finally, in *H & L v A Council & B Council*[181] one of the plaintiffs (H) was a convicted sex offender. The A Council had concluded that he was a risk to children and proposed, amongst other actions, to take a decision on whether to disclose this to organisations with whom H might work in the future based on an assessment of risk to children from H's work with the organisation. H challenged this decision, but the court took the view that:

> the policy adumbrated in the decision letter represented the minimum permissible response to the situation with which ACC was faced. Anything less would have been open to legitimate criticism as constituting a failure of the duty of ACC towards children within the area.[182]

It is, as has been noticed above, not clear whether the reference here is to a legal duty or a professional duty. It is at least the latter, though it is suggested that in extreme cases, where the test set out in *Osman* is met, that there may also be a legal duty, but that these cases will be very few. Such a legal duty to warn or to take further action, despite what was said in *Edgell*, is likely to be owed only to specific individuals rather than to groups or to the public at large.[183]

179 [1991] 2 FLR 541.

180 At 557.

181 [2010] EWHC 466 (Admin).

182 At para 47, though other proposed actions of, and requirements imposed by, the councils were considered to be excessive.

183 See, for example, *Palmer v Tees Health Authority* [2000] PIQR P1.

(4) Conclusion

2.32 There is increasing emphasis in social work on joint working and information sharing as well as criticism of failures to share information which have resulted in deaths or serious harm,[184] though in some cases these criticisms have also reflected inadequate recording, failure to carry out proper assessments and failure to properly analyse information.[185] Some of the difficulties in information sharing may derive from differing professional perspectives[186] and suggestions have been made that reluctance to share information may be due to the complexity of the law as well as to a possible belief that where information sharing is not specifically required by statute this means that no information can be shared[187] or a mistaken belief that the Data Protection Act 1998 means that information cannot be shared.

Despite the encouragement of data sharing it is not possible to offer precise guidance on when information may or may not be shared, largely because these decisions depend on discretion and on professional judgement, often the judgements will involve assessments of risk, which may also mean that decisions are influenced by prevailing cultures of risk. In other words the decision as to whether a particular level of risk is high enough to warrant disclosure will depend on what level of risk is considered to be acceptable. As *6 et al* point out:

> Where decision makers face a genuine dilemma, no legal clarification, however extensive, can provide substantive algorithms that will lead to a single correct decision. Instead, frontline practitioners need

184 See, for example, the inquiries referred to in Scottish Executive: *Its Everyone's Job to Make Sure I'm Alright*, at para 7.4, para 8.55 highlights the need for better information sharing; Social Work Services Inspectorate and Mental Welfare Commission, *Investigations into Scottish Borders Council and NHS Borders Services for People with Learning Disabilities: Joint Statement from the Mental Welfare Commission and the Social Work Services Inspectorate*, April 2004; Birmingham Safeguarding Children Board, *Serious Case Review in respect of the Death of a Child: Case Number 14*, April 2010.

185 Eg Social Work Services Inspectorate and Mental Welfare Commission, *Investigations into Scottish Borders Council and NHS Borders Services for People with Learning Disabilities: Joint Statement from the Mental Welfare Commission and the Social Work Services Inspectorate*, April 2004. On analysis, see Helm, D, *Analysis and Getting it Right for Every Child: A Discussion Paper* (2009).

186 Eg Richardson, S & Asthana, S, 'Inter-agency Information Sharing in Health and Social Care Services: The Role of Professional Culture', (2006) 36 *British Journal of Social Work* 657; Pinkney, L *et al*, 'Voices from the frontline: social work practitioners' perceptions of multi-agency working in adult protection in England and Wales', (2008) 10 *Journal of Adult Protection* 12.

187 Thomas, R & Walport, M, *Data Sharing Review Report* (2008), paras 5.28–5.29.

tools and skills to increase their confidence in exercising professional judgement.[188]

All that can be offered are some general propositions which seem to reflect current law. The starting point is that confidentiality does not have the implication that the information is to be kept absolutely private. Although there is a public interest in confidentiality there is equally a public interest in disclosure without consent in certain circumstances. Although it is impossible to describe precisely when the public interest comes into play, it is possible to offer some guidance:

1. Information will have to be disclosed where this is required for court or other legal proceedings, this includes not only criminal cases where information may be required in the form of a criminal justice social work report,[189] but also various tribunals, for example Children's Hearings and Mental Health Tribunals, and civil cases, for example the reports prepared in connection with adoption hearings. There may also be other cases where a court may order production of information as part of court proceedings. One example is *P v Tayside Regional Council*[190] where an adoptive parent successfully sought access to the local authority's records regarding an adopted child as part of a court action based on her claim that she had contracted hepatitis B from the child.
2. Information may be disclosed where there is a clear risk to an identified individual, either the client or someone else. As we have seen, in some cases there may be a legal duty to warn or take other actions, but even where the high threshold for this is not met it is likely that it will still be legally permissible to disclose information.
3. Disclosure may also take place where there is a significant risk to members of the public or to particular sections of the public. Most of the case law relates to children and the view has been taken that such disclosure should only be made where there is a 'pressing need' for such disclosure, these cases are discussed briefly below.
4. Finally, although there appears to be no case law specifically on this point, it appears that sharing of information will be permit-

188 6, P *et al*, 'Information-sharing dilemmas in public services: using frameworks from risk management', (2010) 38 *Policy & Politics* 465.

189 Though see para 10.4 for ways in which circulation of information can be restricted.

190 1989 SC 38.

ted where this might broadly be regarded as in the interests of the client, for example to obtain services for him or her.[191]

Although only mentioned in relation to 3 above, it might be said that both 2 and 3 represent cases where there is a pressing need to disclose information in view of the risk to others. The concept of pressing need derives from *R v Chief Constable of North Wales Police, Ex p AB*.[192] After their release from custodial sentences for sexual offences involving children, a husband and wife were staying on a caravan park. Shortly before Easter, and after discussions with the offenders who had undertaken to move but did not, the police disclosed to the owner of the caravan park the couple's background (by way of showing the owner press coverage regarding them). A concern about risk to children who were likely to arrive at the caravan park for the holidays prompted the disclosure, which the couple then sought to challenge. In the Court of Appeal the view was taken that that there was a pressing need for disclosure in this case. The same test has been applied in the following circumstances:

1. Disclosure (to new partners who had children) of allegations of sexual abuse against an individual was considered to be justified. Despite the individual's denials, social workers had a reasonable belief that he was a child sex abuser.[193]
2. A disclosure to an education department of allegations of child abuse involving a person who supplied school transport was not considered to be justified by a pressing need and the local authority making the disclosure had not considered whether there was a pressing need to do so.[194]
3. A limited disclosure to a tenant's landlord of findings of sexual abuse involving the tenant was authorised, it was likely that families with children would stay nearby in other accommodation rented from the landlord. The findings had been made in care proceedings and the tenant had no convictions for sexual offences.[195]
4. An intention to disclose a conviction to a sheltered housing provider was not justified as it had been taken on the basis of a presumption of disclosure and without balancing the need for

191 Though Clark notes that in some cases the interests of the client (and/or the working relationship with the client) may require a certain amount of economy with the truth: Clark. C, 'Confidentiality, Trust and Truthfulness in Professional Relationships', in Clark, C & McGhee, J, *Private and Confidential? Handling Personal Information in the Social and Health Services*, (Policy Press, 2008).

192 [1999] QB 396, *per* Lord Woolf at 428B-C. In addition to the cases cited below, see also *R(A) v Hertfordshire County Council* [2001] EWCA Civ 2113.

193 *R v Devon County Council, Ex parte L* [1991] 2 FLR 541, see also above.

194 *R v Local Authority in the Midlands, Ex p LM* [2000] 1 FLR 612.

195 *Re C (Sexual Abuse: Disclosure to Landlord)* [2002] 2 FCR 385.

disclosure with the released prisoner's rights or the potential harm that might flow from disclosure. The decision could be revisited and disclosure made if there was a pressing need for it.[196]

5. Disclosure of concerns about a student's suitability to be a social worker to the university where she was undertaking her degree programme were considered to be justified. It was noted that it is 'a matter of public interest that persons who are not suited to do so should not become social workers.'[197]

What does it mean to say that there is a pressing need and what factors and requirements have to be taken into account in taking the decision? Each decision must be taken on its own merits rather than simply applying a blanket policy. In principle as a matter of good practice the person concerned should be informed about the intended disclosure,[198] though there may be good reasons for not doing so in individual cases. In addition, account needs to be taken of the position of the subject of the disclosure, for example the possibility of disclosure leading to harassment which impedes rehabilitation and of the danger of driving offenders underground.[199] Finally there are three factors which have been judicially suggested, particularly in the context of allegations of child sex abuse, though they may clearly be useful in other cases:[200]

(a) The disclosing organisations belief in the truth of the allegations – the more convinced it is the more pressing the need for the disclosure. The belief, it goes without saying, needs to be based on sound evidence and assessment.

(b) The nature of the legitimate interest of the third party in receiving the information. Where the recipient is a local authority with a statutory duty to protect children then the need will be more pressing than if disclosure is to others. A more pressing need might also arise in the case where the recipient is the parent of a child who may be at risk.

(c) The degree of risk posed by the person if the disclosure is not made, this will require some decision as to what level of risk is

196 *R(A) v National Probation Service* [2003] EWHC 2910 (Admin).

197 *Maddock v Devon County Council* [2003] EWHC 3494 (QB), para 71.

198 For example, *Maddock v Devon County Council* [2003] EWHC 3494 (QB), paras 54 & 68.

199 *R v Chief Constable of North Wales Police, Ex p AB* [1999] QB 396, *per* Lord Woolf at 420A-C. In fact in this case the couple had gone to ground between the first court hearing and the appeal hearing – it should be noted that this was before sex offender notification was required.

200 In *R v Local Authority in the Midlands, Ex p LM*, [2000] 1 FLR 612, applied in *Re C (Sexual Abuse: Disclosure to Landlord)* [2002] 2 FCR 385.

acceptable and will need to take account of time that has passed since allegations were made.

In addition to these guidelines derived from judicial decision, the Scottish Government has also run a Sex Offender Community Disclosure Pilot in the Tayside police area. This allowed the parents of children to seek information from the police as to whether anyone who had access to their children was a registered sex offender or posed a risk to the child. Following evaluation of this project[201] it has been continued on Tayside and extended (in February 2011) to the Grampian police area.

As well as these types of cases where disclosure can take place without consent it is always possible to disclose information with the consent of the person who is the subject of that information. Consent can, as we have noted, be problematic.[202] There may be issues about capacity to consent, capacity to understand the range of possible sharing which might occur or the occasions on which sharing might happen, understanding the details of what sharing involves, the duration of consent and whether consent has to be obtained whenever information is obtained or shared or whether one consent is enough to cover all occasions in the future (leading back to the question of how long it can last). In addition, there will be some circumstances in which consent should not be sought.[203]

Regardless of the basis on which information is shared the decision to share information does not necessarily imply that all information about an individual is shared, instead the principle of proportionality applies – only that information should be shared which is necessary for the purposes to be achieved by the sharing of information. There should also be clarity about the reliability of the information, inappropriate sharing of unreliable information or information which has not been checked may infringe the client's rights to a private life under Article 8 of the European Convention on Human Rights.[204] Anyone sharing information should be satisfied as to the security of the information once it is shared and as to the uses to be made of the information after it has been shared.

201 Chan, V *et al*, *Evaluation of the Sex Offender Community Disclosure Pilot* (2010).

202 The view of the Information Commissioner is that 'consent is not particularly easy to achieve', and that reliance should be placed on the other conditions which permit processing and are set out in schs 2 & 3 of the Data Protection Act 1998, see Information Commissioners Office, *Data Protection Act 1998 – Legal Guidance*, para 3.1.5.

203 See above.

204 *W v Westminster City Council* [2005] EWHC 102 (QB).

Returning to the points made at the beginning of this section and the question of what we mean by confidentiality and what duties follow from that, the position is well summarised by Swain:[205]

> No social worker can give a guarantee that information imparted within a supposedly 'confidential' relationship or interview will not at some point have to be disclosed—whether by statutory direction, through perceived risk to others or duty of care concerns, or as a necessary outcome of skilled intervention within the service network or agency. All, in truth, the worker can attempt to guarantee is that client communications will be respected within the limits of law and current perceptions of what constitutes 'good practice'—but will clients perceive this as equating to treating their information 'confidentially'?

EDUCATION

2.33 This section is intended to deal briefly with the rights and duties of parents and discipline in schools. The principal right that parents have in relation to education is the right, subject to availability of places, to choose the school where their child will be educated.[206] The principal duty of parents is to ensure that their child receives a suitable education while of school age.[207] This may be done at home, or by sending the child to an independent school or, most commonly, to a local authority school. Failure to meet this responsibility can result in an attendance order being served requiring the child to attend a specific school, or in prosecution of the parents. Successful prosecution may result in the parents being fined. The child may be referred to the reporter for the children's hearing as being in need of compulsory measures of supervision if he/she fails to attend school regularly without a reasonable excuse.[208]

A child may no longer be subjected to corporal punishment in school, but may be disciplined in other ways, for example, by being given additional homework or a verbal reprimand. In serious cases the child may be excluded from school. If this happens the parents must be notified right

205 Swain, P A, 'A Camel's Nose Under the Tent? Some Australian Perspectives on Confidentiality and Social Work Practice', (2006) 13 BJSW 91, at 99.
206 Education (Scotland) Act 1980, s 28 ff.
207 Education (Scotland) Act 1980, s 30.
208 See para 5.8.

away and there is a right of appeal against the exclusion and against any conditions imposed on the child's re-attendance at school.[209]

Provision for children who require additional support is discussed in para 4.17 below.

209 Schools General (Scotland) Regulations 1975, SI 1975/1135, regs 4 & 4A.

Chapter 3

Children and their families

THE RESPONSIBILITIES, RIGHTS AND POWERS OF PARENTS AND CHILDREN

(1) Introduction

3.1 This section starts with an attempt to explain the powers and rights that a child has at different stages of his/her life. Powers are concerned with the ability or capacity of children to enter into legal transactions, for example contracts, and to give legally effective agreement, such as the giving of consent to medical treatment. Rights are concerned with the child's rights to make choices about his/her life, for example choices about friends, about religious beliefs and about where to stay. The extent of a child's rights is closely connected with the extent of the responsibilities and rights enjoyed by his or her parent(s): the child's power to control his/her own life grows with the decline of the parents' role. For this reason we will also consider the responsibilities and rights of parents and the major changes brought about by the Children (Scotland) Act 1995 (the 1995 Act).

The age of majority, the age at which, technically, one is fully an adult, is 18 in Scotland. There are other age limits relevant for other purposes.[1] For example, at the age of 16 one can marry and enter into other legal transactions (see below). Sixteen is also the age at which compulsory education finishes and below which children can be referred to a children's hearing and be the subject of actions seeking parental responsibilities or rights (see below). Children under the age of eight[2] cannot be guilty of a criminal offence or be referred to a children's hearing on the ground that they have committed an offence.

Below the age of 18 the historically important division was between pupils and minors. Pupils are boys under 14 and girls under 12, minors are those between those ages and 18. Pupils had very restricted powers

1 See table below.

2 Though there is currently legislation which would raise this 12, Criminal Justice and Licensing (Scotland) Act 2010, s 52, which is not yet (February 2011) in force.

and were subject to the control and guidance of their tutor, normally their parent. Minors had slightly greater powers, for example to enter contracts and to consent to some types of medical treatment, and acted with the concurrence of a curator, again usually the parent. Where a child had two parents in the legal sense (see below), both were tutor/curator of the child.

The Age of Legal Capacity (Scotland) Act 1991 made some changes to this position. In particular, it made changes which affect the capacity of children and it abolished tutors and curators, creating instead the position of guardian who, in relation to children under the age of 16, was to have the powers of a tutor. The first of these developments is discussed in more detail below, but it should be noted that although the distinction between pupils and minors is generally no longer relevant as far as the powers or capacity of children is concerned it is still relevant as far as children's rights are concerned.

Knowledge and an understanding of the law in this area should prove invaluable to social workers and young persons in such situations as leaving care and planning for independent living; entering into contractual arrangements, for example with online retailers; and being on home supervision and perhaps in conflict with parents or being looked after by the local authority and needing to know what rights and responsibilities are relevant.

(2) Legal capacity of children

3.2 The Age of Legal Capacity (Scotland) Act 1991 (the 1991 Act) sets out the rules about the capacity of children. In terms of this Act the important age is 16[3]. Below this age, subject to the exceptions noted below, children have no capacity to enter into what the 1991 Act calls 'transactions'. The term 'transactions' includes contractual agreements, the giving of any consent having legal effect (for example, consent to medical treatment), and the bringing or defending of any legal action in a civil court. It describes, in other words, actions which will have legal consequences for the child. The main exceptions are:[4]

(a) Children under 16 may enter into transactions of a kind normally entered into by children of the child in question's age and circumstances,[5] provided the terms of the transaction are reason-

3 The implications of other ages are set out in Table 1.
4 Age of Legal Capacity (Scotland) Act 1991, s 2.
5 For example purchase of small items, payment for leisure facilities.

able. Note that the comparison here is with other children of the same age and circumstances, and the focus is not on the capacity of the individual child.

(b) Children over the age of 12 have the power to make wills.

(c) A child under 16 may consent to any surgical, medical or dental procedure or treatment[6] where, in the opinion of the medical practitioner attending him or her, the child is capable of understanding the nature and possible consequences of the procedure or treatment. Here the focus is on the specific capacity of the individual child.

(d) Children over 12 have the power to consent (or withhold consent) to adoption and freeing for adoption.

(e) A child under 16 has the capacity to instruct a solicitor in respect of a civil law matter, provided that the child has a general understanding of what it means to instruct a solicitor. Such children also have capacity to sue and defend in civil court actions.

Children over the age of 16 have full legal capacity in respect of the matters covered by the Act. Sixteen and 17 year olds enjoy some additional protection in that before their 21st birthday they can challenge any transactions entered into at those ages on the grounds that the transaction was prejudicial.

As we have noted, a child can now give effective consent to medical treatment if capable of understanding the nature and possible consequences of the treatment, with the judgment as to ability to understand being made by the doctor or dentist treating the child. This capacity is also regarded as extending to refusing medical treatment,[7] though in England the view has been taken that the parents of a child can overrule his/her refusal of treatment.[8]

A problem might arise where the child is unable to consent and the parents refuse to consent to therapeutic treatment. In such cases treatment may be authorised by the general welfare principle extending to children. There is also the possibility of applying to court for permission for treatment under section 11 of the 1995 Act. Failure on the part of the parent to consent to therapeutic treatment may also give

6 This would include consenting to the prescribing of contraceptives.

7 See Norrie's annotation to s 90 of the Children (Scotland) Act 1995; see also *Houston, Applicant* 1996 SCLR 943 and annotation.

8 *Re W (a minor) (medical treatment)* [1992] 4 All ER 627 at 639j-640a. See also *V v F* 1991 SCLR 225 and comment thereon.

rise to a referral to a children's hearing on the ground of lack of parental care.[9] In emergency cases treatment can be given without consent.

Table 1

Age	Consequences
8 or over	can be prosecuted for criminal offence (Criminal Procedure (Scotland) Act 1995, s 41)[10]
12 or over	can make a will (1991 Act, s 2) deemed to understand what is involved in instructing a solicitor (1991 Act, s 2) must consent to adoption (Adoption and Children (Scotland) Act 2007, s 32)
Under 16	although can be prosecuted for crime will normally be referred to children's hearing (Criminal Procedure (Scotland) Act 1995, s 42) can only enter into transactions of type which children of that age and circumstances would commonly enter into, provided that transaction reasonable (1991 Act, s 2) can only consent to medical treatment if practitioner given treatment considers her/him to be capable of understanding the nature & possible consequences of the treatment (1991 Act, s 2) can instruct solicitor in relation to civil matter if has general understanding of what it means to do so – can also raise civil action (1991 Act, s 2) parent has duty to ensure that child attends school or is otherwise provided with efficient education (Education (Scotland) Act 1980, ss 30 & 31)
16 or over	can marry (Marriage (Scotland) act 1977, s 1) parental responsibilities and rights aside from responsibility to provide guidance cease (1995 Act, ss 1 & 2) can only be referred to a children's hearing if already subject to supervision requirement (1995 Act, s 93(2)(b)) capacity to enter into any transaction (ie contracts & consent to medical treatment), though transactions at age 16 & 17 may, subject to limitations, be set aside if prejudicial – application to set aside can be made up to 21 (1991 Act, ss 1 & 3)

9 *Finlayson, Applicant* 1989 SCLR 601. See para 5.8.

10 Though there is currently legislation which would raise this 12, Criminal Justice and Licensing (Scotland) Act 2010, s 52, which is not yet (February 2011) in force.

Age	Consequences
Under 18	subject to parental responsibility to provide advice (1995 Act, s 1(2)(b)) covered by child welfare provisions of Children (Scotland) Act 1995, eg provision of accommodation, provision of services to children (1995 Act, s 93(2)(a)) can be referred to children's hearing if subject to existing supervision requirement (1995 Act, s 93(2)(b)) can be subject of adoption order (Adoption and Children (Scotland) Act 2007, s 119(1)) right to financial support from parent (Family Law (Scotland) Act 1985, s 1)
18 or over	no longer any parental responsibilities/rights (though if in education/training can claim support) (1995 Act, s 1(2)(b); Family Law (Scotland) Act 1985, s 1) able to vote & stand for parliament/local government (Local Government (Scotland) Act 1973, s 29; Representation of the People Act 1983, ss 1 & 2; Electoral Administration Act 2006, s 17)

1991 Act = Age of Legal Capacity (Scotland) Act 1991
1995 Act = Children (Scotland) Act 1995

(3) Children's rights

3.3 As children get older the responsibilities and rights of their parents diminish, and the rights of the child to manage his/her affairs and take decisions about his/her life increase. Where the exercise of rights involves doing things which have legal consequences for the child the rules in the Age of Legal Capacity (Scotland) Act 1991 explained above apply. In the absence of a coherent list, rights conferred on children at various ages are found scattered through other law and legislation, examples are:

(a) the right to a share of a parent's moveable estate on death of the parent;
(b) the right to be supported by a parent up to the age of 18 (or up to 25 if in education or training), this right extends to give a claim against the biological father even if he has no parental responsibilities or rights, and a claim can also be made against anyone who has accepted a child into her/his family;[11]

11 Family Law (Scotland) Act 1985, s 1.

(c) a right of access to personal information kept about him/her provided that they 'have a general understanding of what it means to exercise' the access right,[12] children aged 12 or over are deemed to have such an understanding;
(d) the right to have her/his views taken into account when a major decision is being taken about her/his life;[13]
(e) the right to have her/his views taken into account in a variety of court and other proceedings;[14]
(f) the right to attend a children's hearing concerning her/him;[15] and
(g) the right of children who have been looked after to be provided with certain aftercare services.[16]

In addition, children may be able to rely on the rights protected under various articles of the European Convention on Human Rights and exercise the right given to sue local authorities under the Human Rights Act 1998.[17]

(4) Parental responsibilities

3.4 Parents have responsibilities to their children, and the legal emphasis is on these responsibilities rather than the rights that parents have. The responsibilities of a parent to a child under 16 are:[18]

(a) to safeguard and promote the health, development and welfare of the child;
(b) to provide direction to the child appropriate to his/her age (which implies that as the child gets older the responsibility to direct lessens);
(c) in cases where the child is not living with the parent (for example, because the parents are separated or divorced) the parent has to maintain regular contact and 'personal relations' with the child;
(d) to act as the child's legal representative, for example, in relation to entering contracts and managing property. As we have seen above, when the child gets older the capacity to do these things is acquired.

12 Data Protection Act 1998, s 66.
13 Children (Scotland) Act 1995, s 6.
14 For example, Children (Scotland) Act 1995, s 16.
15 Children (Scotland) Act 1995, s 45(1)(a).
16 Children (Scotland) Act 1995, ss 29 & 30.
17 Sections 6 & 7.
18 Children (Scotland) Act 1995, s 1.

For children of 16 and 17, the parent has a responsibility to provide guidance appropriate to the child's age, though the right to give such guidance expires on the child's 16th birthday. In all cases the responsibilities are to be fulfilled only where this is practicable and in the interests of the child. Fulfilment will also be subject to any court orders about parental responsibilities.

These responsibilities replace any analogous duties imposed by common law, so that the duties of a parent are as described in the 1995 Act and in other statutory provisions, for example, as to aliment and ensuring that children are provided with education, as well as any duties imposed by common law which are not analogous to those listed above.

There is one further provision of the 1995 Act to be considered under this heading. This is the duty to 'have regard to' the views of the child in taking any major decision involving the exercise of parental responsibilities and rights. The age of the child is relevant to this process and children of 12 and over are deemed to be capable of forming a view. It is not clear what decisions will be major decisions, though presumably an objective standard will be invoked; nor is it clear how a child could enforce this provision and prevent an action in respect of which his/her views had not been sought. Perhaps the only remedy would be for the child to seek an order in relation to parental responsibilities or rights. Finally, the requirement is only to have regard to what the child wants and does not extend to a requirement to do what the child wants.[19]

(5) Parental rights

3.5 Parents have certain legal rights which are conferred on them for the express purpose of enabling them to fulfil their parental responsibilities. This reflects some views expressed in relation to parental rights before the 1995 Act was passed. For example, Lord Scarman in the case of *Gillick v West Norfolk and Wisbech Area Health Authority* said: 'The principle is that parental right or power of control of the person and property of the child exists primarily to enable the parent to discharge his duty of maintenance, protection and education until [the child] reaches such an age as to be able to look after himself and make his own decisions'.[20]

Parents have the right:[21]

19 1995 Act, s 6.
20 [1985] 3 All ER 402 at 421d.
21 1995 Act, s 2.

(a) to have their children living with them or to regulate their residence;
(b) to control, direct or guide their children's upbringing in a manner appropriate to the age of the child;
(c) to maintain direct contact on a regular basis with any child who is not living with them and to maintain personal relations with the child;
(d) to act as their children's legal representative.

These rights supersede any analogous common law rights held by parents. One of the rights encompassed in (d) above is the right to manage any property belonging to a child. In doing this a parent must act as a reasonable and prudent person acting on his/her own behalf would act. Parents still have other rights conferred by statute, such as the right to attend a children's hearing involving their child. The rights listed above apply until the child reaches the age of 16.

Where more than one person has parental rights in respect of a child they may exercise their rights independently of each other. For example, if the parents are separated, the mother can take any decision about the child without consulting the father. Clearly this is one scenario which may well augur conflict and in which social workers may find themselves involved.

(6) Who holds parental responsibilities and rights?

3.6 The mother of a child holds parental responsibilities and rights automatically, as does the father of the child, if he was married to the mother either at the time of conception of the child or subsequently.

Aside from this, the biological father does not automatically have responsibilities and rights, but can acquire these in one of three ways. He can enter into an agreement with the mother of the child (providing she has not been deprived of any responsibilities or rights). To be effective this agreement must be in a prescribed form and be registered in the Books of Council and Session.[22] Alternatively, he could apply to court for an order in respect of parental responsibilities and rights under sec-

22 Parental Responsibilities and Parental Rights Agreements (Scotland) Regulations 1996, SI 1996/2549, as amended by the Parental Responsibilities and Parental Rights Agreements (Scotland) Amendment Regulations 2006, SSI 2006/255. Similar provisions apply to the acquisition of responsibilities and rights by a female parent other than the birth mother, 1995 Act, s 4A.

tion 11 of the 1995 Act. Other people may come to hold responsibilities and rights as a result of such an order or as a result of another type of court order, for example, a permanence order. Finally, in the case of a child whose birth is registered after 4 May 2006 a biological father will have parental responsibilities and rights if he is registered as the father on the child's birth certificate.[23]

Parents holding parental responsibilities and rights can appoint a guardian to take over those rights and responsibilities after their death.[24]

Where someone without responsibilities and rights has care or control of a child, that person has the responsibility of doing what is reasonable in the circumstances to safeguard the child's health, development and welfare. Included within this is the power to consent to medical treatment where the child is unable to and the person does not know that the parent would refuse consent to treatment. These powers are not conferred on teachers, but would apply where a child is under the care and control of a foster parent or, possibly, a social worker.[25]

(7) Court orders and parental responsibilities[26]

3.7 Anyone claiming an interest can, under section 11 of the 1995 Act, apply to court for an order relating to parental responsibilities and rights.[27] This includes the child concerned, but local authorities are specifically excluded.[28] An application for an order can also be made by anyone holding parental responsibilities and rights, as well as by someone who previously held them but has lost them, provided they were not lost in a number of specified ways. Application for an order can be made even though an adoption order in respect of a child has been made, and an order can be made in other proceedings without application by any of the parties if the court considers that the order should be made.[29] Restrictions on the ability to apply for an order under section 11 exist once a permanence order has been made in respect of a child, of the orders listed later only a specific issues order can be applied for. It

23 Family Law (Scotland) Act 2006, s 23.
24 1995 Act, s 7.
25 1995 Act, s 5.
26 1995 Act, s 11.
27 The right to attend a children's hearing relating to a child is not a parental responsibility/right and therefore cannot be conferred by a court order, *Principal Reporter v K* [2010] CSIH 5.
28 1995 Act, s 11(5).
29 1995 Act, s 11(3) & (4).

also appears that a child can make an application for an order regulating contact with a sibling.[30]

The 1995 Act provides a non-exclusive list of the types of order that may be sought:

(a) an order depriving someone of some or all rights or responsibilities;
(b) an order imposing responsibilities and conferring rights;
(c) a residence order specifying where a child is to live;
(d) a contact order, regulating personal relations and direct contact with someone with whom the child is not living;
(e) a specific issue order which is designed to regulate any specific issue which has arisen with respect to parental responsibilities, for example, a question about medical treatment;
(f) an interdict preventing some action in exercise of parental responsibilities and rights.[31]

The application for such an order can be made in a legal action intended to resolve that particular issue or it can form an incidental part of any other proceedings, such as a divorce action.

In making any of these orders:

(a) The court must regard the welfare of the child as its paramount consideration.
(b) The court must not make any order about parental responsibilities or rights unless it considers that making the order would be better for the child than making no order at all. This emphasises a strategy of minimum intervention.
(c) The child involved must be given an opportunity to indicate if he/she wishes to express a view about any order and if the child does wish to express a view he/she must be given an opportunity to do so and the court must have regard to any views expressed before making an order. In order to allow this to happen, a child must be notified of applications for orders dealing with responsibilities and rights and on the notification there is a form which the child can return indicating whether he/she wishes to express a view. If the child does, the form allows him/her to nominate someone to communicate his/her views to the court or to write to the judge expressing his/her views. The procedural rules also envisage the

30 *E v E* 2004 Fam LR 115, though see *D v H* 2004 Fam LR 41.

31 Though it may be that the same effect can be achieved through a specific issue order. In *M v C* 2002 SLT (Sh Ct) 82 a specific issue order was granted to prevent the child's mother from changing the child's surname.

judge either speaking to the child directly or sending someone to speak to the child on his/her behalf.

(d) Consideration must be given to the need to protect the child from any abuse or risk of abuse which might affect her/him. 'Abuse' is defined widely and includes violence, harassment, threatening conduct and any other conduct giving rise to, or likely to give rise to, physical or mental injury, fear alarm or distress, as well as domestic abuse and abuse of a person other than the child.[32]

(e) The court will need to consider whether two people would have to co-operate with one another as respects matters affecting the child.[33] The underlying consideration is whether the two (or more) people who have to co-operate would be able to do so.[34]

If, during the course of a hearing on an application for an order under section 11, the judge considers that any of the non-offence grounds of referral to a children's hearing exist, the judge may refer the case of the child to the reporter.[35] The effect of an order conferring parental rights on one person is not, automatically, to remove them from another person having parental rights. For example, if the court were to make a residence order in favour of a wife that would not automatically deprive the husband of the right to have the child living with him. Deprivation of rights occurs only where the court expressly takes them away from someone who previously enjoyed them.[36]

LEGALLY RECOGNISED RELATIONSHIPS

(1) Marriage

3.8 Before two people can get married certain requirements must be fulfilled. Both parties must be over 16, must be of sound mind, must be single, must not be within the forbidden degrees of relationship and one must be male and the other female. If these requirements are met the parties will generally go through a regular marriage, that is, a religious ceremony or civil wedding. In the past it was possible to have a legally recognised marriage without such a ceremony, but this is no longer possible. Reference is sometimes made to 'common law' marriages. These situations, where, for example, a man is referred to as

32 1995 Act, s 11(7B) & 7(C).
33 1995 Act, s 11(7D).
34 See *Treasure v McGrath* 2006 Fam LR 100.
35 1995 Act, ss 12 & 54.
36 1995 Act, s 11(11).

being a woman's common law husband, usually amount simply to cohabitation and do not give rise to the legal consequences which follow from a proper marriage. The father of a child who is actually married to the mother will have parental responsibilities and rights in respect of that child, whereas the 'common law' husband who fathers a child will not automatically have parental responsibilities and rights and will have to acquire these in one of the ways set out above.

After marriage the parties have a mutual obligation of financial support and an obligation to live together as husband and wife. Marriage also provides rights of inheritance or succession to the spouse and children. A wife need not take the surname of her husband. Even while married and living together, a husband may be charged and convicted of raping his wife. In the case deciding this the earlier view that, in agreeing to the marriage, a wife was giving blanket consent to sexual intercourse with her husband was rejected.[37]

(a) Separation

3.9 It is possible to obtain a formal judicial separation requiring the parties to a marriage to live apart but not releasing them from the other obligations of marriage. So, for example, the couple will still be required to support one another financially and the commission of adultery while separated will still be acceptable as a ground for evidencing the irretrievable breakdown of the marriage. In general any separation will be informal, as will any arrangements for aliment or for residence and contact regarding any children. If such informal arrangements are impossible it may be necessary to take action in the sheriff court to regulate these matters.

(b) Divorce

3.10 The Divorce (Scotland) Act 1976 introduced a single ground for divorce in Scotland: 'irretrievable breakdown of the marriage'. In some ways this simply amounted to a restatement of the previously existing grounds of divorce, since they, together with two new grounds based on non-cohabitation, were to be evidence of breakdown.

The four grounds evidencing an irretrievable breakdown are:

37 *S v HM Advocate* 1989 SLT 469.

(a) adultery;
(b) behaviour – where the defender 'has behaved ... in such a way that the pursuer cannot reasonably be expected to cohabit with the defender'. This ground would cover violence by the defender, drunkenness or unnatural, excessive or insufficient sexual demands;
(c) one years' non-cohabitation with consent – where the parties have not lived together as husband and wife for one year and the defender consents to the divorce;
(d) two years' non-cohabitation – here the defender's consent is not required.

(c) Divorce procedure

3.11 Provided that one of these grounds can be established, a spouse may seek a divorce at any time following the marriage ceremony. Most cases are now dealt with in the sheriff court. There are two types of procedure by which a divorce can be obtained: ordinary and simplified. The ordinary procedure is similar to that involved in an ordinary court action, for example, in a claim for compensation following a road accident. If, during a divorce action, it appears to the court that there is a reasonable prospect of reconciliation between the parties, the court has to continue[38] the action to enable attempts to be made to effect a reconciliation.[39]

The simplified procedure amounts essentially to a do-it-yourself divorce. It is available only where the divorce is based on non-cohabitation, there are no children of the marriage under 16, and no financial provisions are being sought. An application is completed and returned to the clerk of the court (either the sheriff court or Court of Session) who notifies the other party. If there is no dispute, a decree of divorce will arrive through the post after a short while.

(d) Financial provision on divorce

3.12 There are two types of financial provision to be considered on divorce – provision for children and provision for the other spouse. The first of these generally takes the form of a continuing payment of aliment. In the second case, the statutory guidelines which now exist

38 Effectively stop any further procedure.
39 Divorce (Scotland) Act 1976, s 2.

encourage 'clean break' settlements. ie settlements where there is no continuing payment to an ex-spouse, rather payment is a lump sum at the time of divorce. In most cases these financial provisions will be agreed between the parties, if not there are statutory rules governing the settlement. As between spouses these essentially involve equal sharing of resources. In arriving at its decision the court has to take into account a number of factors including, for example, any economic advantage obtained by one spouse from the contributions of the other or any economic disadvantage suffered by one in the interests of the other. This would allow the courts to compensate a wife for giving up her career to allow the husband to pursue his.

(e) Arrangements for children

3.13 There are children involved in a significant proportion of divorces and normally the arrangements for bringing up the children will be agreed between the parties. Even if they are, the court is obliged to consider whether to exercise its power to make an order about parental responsibilities or rights or to exercise its power to refer the case to the reporter because it appears to it that one of the grounds of referral is satisfied in respect of a child of the marriage under 16. If it concludes that it should exercise one of these powers the judgment in the divorce action can be postponed if it is necessary to obtain more information before exercising the power.[40] This can include obtaining a report from the social work department.[41] In addition where an order in relation to parental responsibilities and rights is in issue the case may, at any stage, be referred for mediation.[42]

Social workers required to produce such a report will need to complete exhaustive inquiries about the backgrounds and parenting capacities of parents in the form of a matrimonial proceedings report. This will be used by the judge, in conjunction with other information, to make decisions about the arrangements for children. In situations where the court deems it necessary, social workers will be required to supervise the contact visits for children. Some of the most stressful experiences for parents and children arise over contact arrangements and visits. The verdict of research is clear: children who continue to have

40 1995 Act, s 12.

41 Matrimonial Proceedings (Children) Act 1958, s 11; see *Hardie v Hardie* 1993 SCLR 60, *O'Neill v Gilhooley* 2007 Fam LR 15.

42 Act of Sederunt (Sheriff Court Ordinary Cause Rules) 1993, SI 1993/1956, r 33.22; Rules of the Court of Session 1994, r 49.23.

close, loving relationships with both parents are least likely to exhibit the worst effects of the divorce and a social worker's attention to alleviating barriers to parental contact may contribute enormously to minimising these effects.

(2) Civil Partnerships

3.14 These were introduced by the Civil Partnerships Act 2004, which came into force during 2005 and allows same sex couples to formalise their relationship. Before this can take place the parties must meet certain criteria: they must be aged 16 or over, they must be of the same sex (though this requirement can be fulfilled if one has a gender recognition certificate which in most cases will mean that that they are recognised as being the other gender from their biological birth gender), they must not be within the forbidden degrees of relationship, and they must be legally free to enter the partnership, ie they must not still be married or in another civil partnership. The ceremony must be preceded, as in the case of marriage, by notice given to the Registrar, which is then published.

The effect of a civil partnership is to put the couple legally in the same position as husband and wife, for example:

(a) A partner (including a non-entitled partner) can take advantage of the provisions of the Matrimonial Homes (Family Protection) (Scotland) Act 1981.
(b) Partners have legal rights in succession.
(c) There are rights to financial provision on dissolution of the partnership.
(d) A partner will have the same benefits and pension entitlements as a husband/wife would have.
(e) Discrimination on the grounds that someone has entered a civil partnership is illegal in the same way that discrimination against people on the grounds that they are married is illegal.

The partnership can be dissolved on the same grounds as apply in the case of divorce, with an additional ground that an interim gender recognition certificate has been granted to one of the partners. The consequence of this is, of course, that the partners will no longer be legally regarded as being of the same sex and therefore civil partnership is no longer appropriate. Where dissolution proceedings are started, as with divorce proceedings, the court must, in cases where it appears that there are real prospects of reconciliation, continue the case to allow efforts to be made to effect a reconciliation.

(3) Cohabitation

3.15 Historically, simple cohabitation created no legal relationship between the parties[43] and had few legal consequences. The position was changed by the Family Law (Scotland) Act 2006 which conferred certain rights on cohabitants. These rights are, however, limited and it seems clear that the limitations resulted from a desire on the part of the Scottish Parliament to avoid putting cohabitants in the same legal position as husband and wife (or civil partners) no matter the length and nature of the relationship.[44] In order to enjoy these rights the cohabitants must be living together as husband and wife or as civil partners, and it is up to the court to which application is made for the exercise of the rights to determine whether there is cohabitation, taking into account factors such as its length, the nature of the relationship and financial arrangements.[45] The main rights granted to cohabitants are, first a right to apply to the court for financial provision on termination of the cohabitation based on economic advantage obtained or economic disadvantage suffered during the cohabitation.[46] The second right is a right to apply to court for financial provision on the death of a cohabitant, though this is only available where some or all of the cohabitant's estate has not been disposed of by a will.[47] Other consequences of cohabitation may be possible effects on any benefit claimed, and the entitlement of cohabitants to apply for occupancy rights under the Matrimonial Homes (Family Protection) (Scotland) Act 1981.

(4) Child support

3.16 In addition to the arrangements covered above, there are likely to be situations where a child's parents have separated and the non-residential parent is not paying aliment for the child. Since the Child Support Act 1991 came into force in April 1993 it has been possible for the residential parent to apply to the Child Support Agency for a maintenance assessment, any payment may be made direct to the parent seeking support or may be made via the agency which will collect and enforce if

43 Though it could, if other conditions were fulfilled, result in legal recognition by the courts that the cohabitants were married, this possibility no longer exists.

44 For the background see T Guthrie & H Hiram, 'Property and cohabitation: understanding the Family Law (Scotland) Act 2006', 2007 *Edinburgh Law Review* 208.

45 Family Law (Scotland) Act 2006, s 25.

46 Family Law (Scotland) Act 2006, s 28, for a successful application see *Lindsay v Murphy* 2010 GWD 29–604.

47 Family Law (Scotland) Act 2006, s 29, see, for example, *Windram, Applicant* 2009 Fam LR 157.

so required. Decisions of the Child Support Agency may be appealed and are reviewed by the Child Support Appeal Tribunal.

ADOPTION

(1) Introduction

3.17 Adoption is a process by which a new legal relationship of parent and child is created. In cases where the application is made by one partner in a couple, where the other partner is the parent of the child adopted, the order will not affect any parental responsibilities and rights held by that parent. In other cases the effect of an adoption order is to extinguish any pre-existing parental responsibilities and rights.[48] Any parent who loses rights as a result of the making of an adoption order can, however, still apply for contact, and it is possible for an adoption order to specifically provide for continued contact between the child and his/her birth parents.[49] In broad terms, as far as the law is concerned, the relationship between the child and the adoptive parent(s) is the same as that with his/her original parent(s). Adoption law is now contained in the Adoption and Children (Scotland) Act 2007 (the 2007 Act), supplemented by a variety of regulations and by guidance.[50] The 2007 Act was passed after a review of adoption law in Scotland which recommended substantial changes.[51]

Around one third of all adoptions involve someone who is related to the child, mainly involving step-parent adoptions. The remaining adoptions are arranged by adoption agencies. All local authorities are adoption agencies, and there is also a number of independent adoption societies approved by the Scottish Ministers.[52] Local authorities must provide an adoption service[53] which will include provision of arrangements for assessing children for adoption, assessing prospective adopters, placing children for adoption, providing information about adoption and providing adoption support services. This last includes the provision of counselling, guidance and other appropriate assistance. Specific groups are identified

48 Adoption and Children (Scotland) Act 2007, s 35.

49 See LAC Guidance, pp 158–160.

50 Scottish Government, *Guidance on Looked after Children (Scotland) Regulations 2009 and the Adoption and Children (Scotland) Act 2007* (2010) (LAC Guidance).

51 Adoption Policy Review Group, *Adoption: Better choices for our children* (2005).

52 All must be registered as adoption services with the Scottish Commission for the Regulation of Care, see ch 11.

53 Adoption and Children (Scotland) Act 2007, ss 1–3.

as intended beneficiaries of the adoption service, including adopted children, adopters and the birth parents and siblings of adopted children.[54] In providing the adoption service the local authority can ask for assistance from other agencies, including other local authorities and Health Boards.[55] Local authorities must also prepare and publish a plan for the provision of adoption services, and this can either be done as a self-standing plan or it may form part of the authority's children's services plan.

Slightly different rules apply to related adoptions and to those arranged by an adoption agency. These differences will be considered as appropriate. One of the differences is that adoption agencies must appoint an adoption panel.[56] The functions of this panel are to make recommendations to the agency as to the suitability of prospective adopters, the suitability of a particular placement for adoption, whether adoption is in the child's best interests, whether application should be made for a permanence order including authority for the child to be adopted, and whether there should be continued contact between the child and his/her parents. The agency must take a decision on any recommendation made by the panel within 14 days of the recommendation. Although it must take the panel's recommendation into account, the agency is not bound by it, but if the recommendation is not followed the reasons for this must be recorded in writing. The panel must have at least six members, including a medical adviser and a legal adviser, with the quorum for any meeting of the panel being at least three, excluding these advisers. In some cases, the panel must include, or have received advice from the legal adviser, these cases include recommendations as to whether adoption is in the best interests of the child or a recommendation that application is made for a permanence order. In addition to its specified functions in relation to adoption, the agency can also refer other matters to the panel (eg adoption support plans) for advice, and the guidance suggests that:[57]

> It would be in the spirit of the 2007 Act and also good practice … that all cases where children cannot return home and need a secure family placement should be treated similarly and be referred to the adoption panel for consideration of the plan for permanence.

Special rules apply to inter-country adoptions and these are not considered here. Adoption agencies may be involved in assessing the suitabil-

54 Adoption and Children (Scotland) Act 2007, s 1(3).

55 Adoption and Children (Scotland) Act 2007, s 6. In general such requests can only be refused if agreeing would be incompatible with the functions of the body to which the request is made or would prejudice the body's performance of its functions.

56 Adoption Agencies (Scotland) Regulations 2009, SSI 2009/154, regs 3–6.

57 LAC Guidance, p 155.

ity of prospective adopters who intend to adopt from abroad, and once a child is in Scotland with prospective adopters, they and the child will be monitored by the local authority until the adoption order is granted.[58]

(2) The welfare of the child

3.18 The paramount consideration in all decisions relating to the adoption of a child, whether the decision is taken by an adoption agency or a court, is the need to safeguard and promote the welfare of the child throughout his/her life.[59] Those involved in decision making must also take into account the views of the child (children over 12 are deemed mature enough to form a view), the child's religious persuasion, racial origin and cultural and linguistic background, the value of a stable family unit[60] in the development of the child and the likely effect on the child throughout his/her life of making an adoption order.[61] Before making any arrangement for adoption, agencies must also consider whether adoption is the option which is likely to best meet the needs of the child or whether there is some practicable alternative which would be better.[62] This last will include ensuring that 'all possibilities of retaining the child with their family network have been checked.'[63] Adoption panels, as part of their advisory function, must, if they are recommending that adoption is in the best interests of the child, produce a written report on their consideration of alternatives to adoption.[64]

(3) Who can adopt?

3.19 There are certain restrictions affecting the ability to adopt. A single individual wishing to adopt must be aged 21 or over and is subject to the further condition that he/she is either:[65]

58 Adoption and Children (Scotland) Act 2007, ch 6, The Adoptions with a Foreign Element (Scotland) Regulations 2009, SSI 2009/183; see also http://www.scotland.gov.uk/Topics/People/Young-People/children-families/17972/Intercountry.

59 Adoption and Children (Scotland) Act 2007, s 14(3), LAC Guidance, p 154.

60 This implies, of course, that the adopters can provide such a stable unit, see LAC Guidance, p 157.

61 Adoption and Children (Scotland) Act 2007, s 14(1), (4)(a)–(d).

62 Adoption and Children (Scotland) Act 2007, s 14(6), (7).

63 LAC Guidance, p 156.

64 Adoption Agencies (Scotland) Regulations 2009, SSI 2009/154, reg 6(3).

65 Adoption and Children (Scotland) Act 2007, s 30.

(a) single; or
(b) married to, or in a civil partnership with, the natural parent (provided he/she is aged 18 or over) of the child (provided he or she has parental responsibilities and rights); or
(c) married or in a civil partnership but either separated or the other partner either cannot be found or is incapable of making an application for health reasons; or
(d) living with someone as husband and wife or as civil partners and the other partner is incapable of applying because of ill-health.

Where a single applicant is the mother or father of the child, the other parent (in the sense of a parent having parental responsibilities or rights) must either be dead, have disappeared, there must be some other reason justifying his/her exclusion, or there must be no other parent in terms of the legislation governing fertility treatment.[66]

Couples can adopt if they are either married or in a civil partnership or alternatively if they are living together as if they were married or in a civil partnership in 'an enduring family relationship.'[67] In addition, neither of the couple must be a parent of the child and both must be aged 21 or over.

In all cases the adopter(s) must be domiciled in the United Kingdom and have lived in the United Kingdom for at least a year before the application for adoption is made.

Aside from the above there are no **legal** restrictions on ability to adopt. Agencies are obliged to prepare and make available the criteria to be used in deciding whether to assess someone as a prospective adopter[68] and may impose restrictions as a matter of policy, but these will need to be clearly expressed and legally justifiable.[69] They may, for example, refuse to consider smokers as adopters of children under 5.

Adoptive parents for children placed by an adoption agency must be approved by the adoption agency. The process of approval involves a lengthy and detailed investigation of the prospective adopters, their family circumstances and their motives for wishing to adopt, which is likely to be protracted over a period of months. The information

66 Adoption and Children (Scotland) Act 2007, s 30(1) & (7).
67 Adoption and Children (Scotland) Act 2007, s 29. The guidance notes that 'Finding ways of testing and articulating this will be helpful in considering *any* relationships – simply stating that people have been married for a number of years can no longer be taken as a guarantee of this', p 167, emphasis added.
68 Adoption Agencies (Scotland) Regulations 2009, SSI 2009/154, reg 7(1).
69 LAC Guidance, p 163.

required is set out in the Adoption Agencies (Scotland) Regulations 2009,[70] though the guidance notes that good practice goes beyond these requirements, informed by reports into cases where good care has not been provided by adopters.[71] The assessment should be completed within 6 months of the date of the application to be considered as adopters.[72] On completion of the investigation a report is prepared, a copy of which is provided to the prospective adopters and it is then considered by the adoption panel who will advise on suitability.[73] The prospective adopters must be allowed to meet the adoption panel before a recommendation is made.[74] A decision maker in the local authority then has to make a decision based on the recommendation within 28 days.[75] If the decision is that the applicant is not suitable then he/she can seek a review of the decision, which will be undertaken by a differently constituted adoption panel from that making the original recommendation.[76] The decision on any recommendation following review should be taken by a different decision maker. Once adopters have been approved the approval will need to be reviewed either if there has been no placement of a child with them within two years or where a child has been placed for adoption but no application for adoption has been made and the authority considers that a review is needed.[77] After the initial review there is no provision for further review of approval if no placement is made, though the guidance suggests that this should take place every two years (noting that it will be extremely unusual for no placement to be made with an adopter).

(4) Who can be adopted?

3.20 Anyone under the age of 18 who is not, and has never been, married or been in a civil partnership can be adopted. An adoption order can also be made in respect of someone aged 18 if the adoption application

70 Adoption Agencies (Scotland) Regulations 2009, SSI 2009/154, sch 1, pt 1.
71 LAC Guidance, p 166.
72 Adoption Agencies (Scotland) Regulations 2009, SSI 2009/154, reg 7; LAC Guidance, pp 164–167, *National Care Standards: Adoption Agencies*, standard 23.1.
73 Adoption Agencies (Scotland) Regulations 2009, SSI 2009/154, reg 8. The LAC Guidance (pp 169–171) suggests that the recommendation made by the panel should also comment on the range and number of children for whom the adopters might be suitable and on possible support needs.
74 Adoption Agencies (Scotland) Regulations 2009, SSI 2009/154, reg 6(5).
75 Adoption Agencies (Scotland) Regulations 2009, SSI 2009/154, reg 8(6).
76 Adoption Agencies (Scotland) Regulations 2009, SSI 2009/154, regs 8(6)(c) & 9.
77 Adoption Agencies (Scotland) Regulations 2009, SSI 2009/154, reg 10; LAC Guidance, pp 171–174.

was made before his/her 18th birthday.[78] There are, however, certain requirements as to residence with the proposed adopters before an adoption order can be granted. These are:[79]

(a) Where the prospective adopter is the child's parent, step-parent or a relative or where the placement has been made by an adoption agency, the child must have had a home with the adopters for at least 13 weeks prior to the adoption and be at least 19 weeks old.
(b) In other cases, the child must have had a home with the adopters for 12 months.

Before making the order the court must also be satisfied that the local authority (where the placement is not by an adoption agency) or the adoption agency has had sufficient opportunity to see the child with the adopters in their home environment. This requirement may prolong the periods set out above.[80]

Children aged 12 or over must consent to adoption and their consent can be dispensed with only if they are incapable of giving it.[81] In addition, the court must have regard to the views of the child regarding the adoption (taking account of his/her age and maturity), so the views of children under 12 are also relevant to the adoption decision.[82]

(5) Rights of the child's parents

3.21 The parents of the child usually have to consent to the adoption, unless a permanence order giving authority for adoption has previously been made in respect of the child. There is also provision for parental consent to be dispensed with in the following cases:

(a) if the parent is dead, cannot be found or is incapable of giving consent;
(b) if the parent is unable to discharge parental responsibilities and rights satisfactorily and this is likely to continue;
(c) if the parent has no parental responsibilities and rights because a permanence order has been made and is unlikely to have these imposed or granted;

78 Adoption and Children (Scotland) Act 2007, s 24(4)–(7).
79 Adoption and Children (Scotland) Act 2007, s 15.
80 Adoption and Children (Scotland) Act 2007, s 16.
81 Adoption and Children (Scotland) Act 2007, s 32.
82 Adoption and Children (Scotland) Act 2007, s 14.

(d) if the welfare of the child otherwise requires that consent is dispensed with.[83]

The consent of the child's mother to adoption (or to freeing for adoption) is ineffective if it is given within 6 weeks of the birth of the child.[84]

Once a decision has been made by an adoption agency that adoption is in the best interests of the child, the parents of the child must be notified of this. Once the agency proposes to make arrangements for adoption of the child the parent(s) must be provided with certain information and asked if they agree with the decision.[85] If they do not reply within 28 days, or they indicate that they disagree with the decision, the agency must apply for a permanence order.[86] Where parental agreement is initially given and is then withdrawn the case is to be treated from the date of withdrawal as one where consent is unlikely to be forthcoming.

(6) Children subject to supervision requirements

3.22 Where an agency intends to place a child who is subject to a supervision requirement for adoption it must refer this to the reporter who will then organise a hearing to consider the matter. The hearing will then prepare a report to be considered by the court which will have to take the decision on the application for an adoption order.[87]

(7) Permanence Orders

3.23 Permanence orders replaced both the process of freeing a child for adoption and parental responsibilities orders. Both of these were criticised by the Adoption Policy Review Group.[88] The freeing process because, for example, of the lengthy delays experienced in practice, the lack of provision for contact with birth parents and the lack of any way back after a freeing order had been granted. Parental responsibilities orders were criticised for being all or nothing, parents lost all paren-

83 Adoption and Children (Scotland) Act 2007, s 31. On the last ground see *Petition of East Lothian Council for a Permanence Order*, Haddington Sheriff Court, 30 July 2010.

84 Adoption and Children (Scotland) Act 2007, s 31(11).

85 Adoption Agencies (Scotland) Regulations 2009, SSI 2009/154, reg 16.

86 Adoption Agencies (Scotland) Regulations 2009, SSI 2009/154, reg 20.

87 1995 Act, s 73(4)(c)(v), (8), (9), (13), (13A) and (14); Adoption and Children (Scotland) Act 2007, s 106; Adoption Agencies (Scotland) Regulations 2009, SSI 2009/154, reg 22.

88 Adoption Policy Review Group, *Adoption: Better Choices for our Children* (2005), paras 5.5–5.11.

tal responsibilities and rights, and because the transfer was to the local authority rather than to substitute parents. The review recommended replacement of both with permanence orders.

Para 3.24 below sets out some cases in which the local authority is required to apply for a permanence order as part of the process of placing a child for adoption, but the order may also be used in other circumstances to give permanency to arrangements made for looked after children, for example in a long term fostering placement. Where the authority decides to apply for a permanence order similar procedures for notification of parents and obtaining their consent, and for action if consent is refused or the parents do not reply, apply as in the case of notifications of an intention to make arrangements for adoption.[89]

Application for the order is made to the sheriff court and the process will involve the appointment of a curator ad litem, and, in cases where the application includes seeking authority for the child to be adopted or where the child is aged 12 or above, a reporting officer. These have functions similar to the equivalents appointed as part of the adoption application process.[90] The order can only be granted if any child aged 12 or over consents (unless he/she is incapable of consenting) and:[91]

(a) the court considers that making the order is better for the child than not making it;
(b) the court has had regard to the paramount consideration of safeguarding and promoting the welfare of the child throughout his/her childhood;
(c) the court has had regard to the views of the child, the likely effect of making the order and the child's religious persuasion, racial origin and cultural and linguistic background;
(d) the court is satisfied that no one with the parental right to regulate the child's residence or, if there is such a person, that residence with that person is, or is likely to be, seriously detrimental to the welfare of the child.

Any permanence order must contain certain mandatory provisions, these are:[92]

89 Adoption Agencies (Scotland) Regulations 2009, SSI 2009/154, regs 17, 20 & 21. See para 3.24 below. See Petition by Aberdeenshire Council for a Permanence Order relating to CW, Banff Sheriff Court, 6 December 2010, Petition of East Lothian Council for a Permanence Order in respect of KAH, Haddington Sheriff Court, 20 January 2011.
90 See para 3.25 below.
91 Adoption and Children (Scotland) Act 2007, s 84.
92 Adoption and Children (Scotland) Act 2007, s 81.

(a) A transfer to the local authority of the responsibility to provide guidance to the child.
(b) A transfer to the local authority of the right to regulate the residence of the child.

In addition, the order can also contain ancillary provisions which can include vesting in the local authority or in someone else (eg a foster carer) any or all of the other parental responsibilities and rights or extinguishing parental responsibilities or rights held by anyone.[93]

Finally, the order may also grant authority for the child to be adopted. Before such authority can be granted as part of the order the court must be satisfied that the child has been placed, or is likely to be placed, for adoption, that it would be better to grant the order than not to grant it and that the child's parents have either consented or their consent can be dispensed with on grounds similar to those which apply in the case of consent to adoption.[94]

Special provisions apply where the local authority intends to apply for a permanence order in respect of the child who is subject to a supervision requirement.[95] The case must be referred to the Reporter and an advice hearing held. The view of the hearing that an application should not be made does not, however, prevent the local authority from going ahead with it. If the court making a permanence order considers that supervision of the child is no longer required it can terminate the supervision requirement.[96]

Once a permanence order has been made it can be varied or revoked, and will be revoked if an adoption order is made. Variation can involve adding authority for a child to be adopted to an existing order.

(8) Placement with proposed adopters

3.24 Placement of children for adoption by an adoption agency will be the culmination of a number of decisions. Where the child is looked after there will have been a decision that the best way of securing permanency for the child is by pursuing adoption. A decision will have been made that adoption is in the best interests of the child, following consideration of this matter and a recommendation by the adoption

93 Adoption and Children (Scotland) Act 2007, s 82.
94 Adoption and Children (Scotland) Act 2007, s 83, see para 3.21 above.
95 The guidance notes that most children for whom an application is made will fall into this category, LAC Guidance, p 185.
96 Adoption and Children (Scotland) Act 2007, s 89.

panel. Consideration of whether adoption is in the child's best interests may reach the conclusion that it is not and in that case steps will need to be taken to pursue alternatives which are considered to be in his/her best interests, these alternatives may have to be secured by a permanence order. Finally, there will need to be a decision to make arrangements for adoption and placement of the child with an adopter, again following consideration and recommendation by the adoption panel.

If a decision is taken that adoption is in the best interests of a child, notification must be given to the child's parents[97] and others, including the child (if it is considered that he/she will understand the effect of the decision), and, if considered to be, in the child's best interests, parents not holding parental responsibilities and/or rights.[98]

When a decision that adoption is in the interests of the child has been made and an agency proposes to make arrangements for the adoption of the child, the child's parents (or guardians) must be provided with specific information about this in the form of a memorandum.[99] The agency must then take reasonable steps to ensure that anyone provided with this information signs and returns a certificate confirming that they have read and understood the memorandum[100] and a form indicating whether or not they consent to the arrangements being made.[101] If the agency is aware that there are parents who do not have parental rights and/or responsibilities it must seek to obtain information about such parents and if possible find out if they intend to seek parental responsibilities or rights or to enter into a parental responsibility and rights agreement.

If the parent does not consent to the making of arrangements for adoption, or if they do not respond to the notification, the procedure that follows depends on whether the adoption agency is the local authority or an independent adoption service. If it is the latter, it must refer the case to the local authority for the area in which the child lives. If it is a local authority, or if a case is so referred to the local authority, the authority must then make an application for a permanence order with authority for the child to be adopted and which vests certain parental responsibili-

97 For these purposes if they hold any parental responsibilities and /or rights or have had these removed by a permanence order. The requirement also extends to guardians.

98 Adoption and Children (Scotland) Act 2007, s 14(1).

99 Adoption Agencies (Scotland) Regulations 2009, SSI 2009/154, reg 16.

100 In the form set out in sch 2 to the Adoption Agencies (Scotland) Regulations 2009, SSI 2009/154.

101 In the form set out in sch 3 to the Adoption Agencies (Scotland) Regulations 2009, SSI 2009/154.

ties and rights in the local authority.[102] The requirement to apply for a permanence order does not apply where an application has been made for an adoption order.

Placement with a specific adopter cannot be made unless the agency is satisfied that the specific placement is in the child's best interests and has complied with a number of further requirements, including obtaining reports on the health of the child and adopter(s), interviewing the adopter(s) and passing a report to an adoption panel which must then make a recommendation which will be followed by a decision made by the agency.[103] The consent of the child's parent(s) to the placement should also be sought.

Placements must be notified to the child's parents and to a variety of others, for example, the education authority and health board for the area where the prospective adopter stays.[104] The child must also be visited within 1 week of the placement and thereafter whenever necessary to supervise the child's welfare. Written reports of the meetings must be prepared.[105] A child who has been placed for adoption cannot be removed from that placement, by a parent or anyone else, in any of the following circumstances:[106]

(a) Where the parent has consented to adoption as noted above.
(b) Where the child is looked after by the local authority.
(c) Where the child has had a home for five years with prospective adopters who give notice of an intention to adopt or apply to adopt.

(9) Adoption procedure

3.25 The main feature of the adoption process in court is the emphasis on confidentiality. There are strict limits on those allowed to see the court papers which must be sealed at the end of the case. Any court hearings must be held in private unless the court directs otherwise and this is unlikely.

102 Adoption Agencies (Scotland) Regulations 2009, SSI 2009/154, reg 21. These are the responsibilities to safeguard and promote the child's health, development and welfare, to provide guidance to the child and to act as the child's legal representative, and the rights to control, direct or guide, in a manner appropriate to the stage of development of the child, the child's upbringing and to act as his/her legal representative.
103 Adoption Agencies (Scotland) Regulations 2009, SSI 2009/154, reg 18.
104 Adoption Agencies (Scotland) Regulations 2009, SSI 2009/154, reg 24(3) & (5).
105 Adoption Agencies (Scotland) Regulations 2009, SSI 2009/154, reg 25.
106 Adoption and Children (Scotland) Act 2007, ss 20–24.

If the child has not been placed for adoption by an adoption agency, the local authority must be informed of the intention to adopt.[107] Before an adoption order can be granted in such cases a report must be produced by the local authority.[108] The report will cover such matters as the suitability of the applicant and any matters relevant to the effect of the adoption on the safeguarding and promotion of the child's welfare; relevant matters would include the occupations of the adopters and their ability to look after the child. In addition, the report must comment on the feelings and wishes of the child. Finally, the report must confirm that the placement has not been made contrary to section 75 of the Adoption and Children (Scotland) Act 2007, which permits placements to be made only by an adoption agency, unless the proposed adopter is a relative of the child. Where the placement has been made by an adoption agency it must provide a report covering all of these matters.

Once the relevant reports have been obtained, the petition for adoption can be lodged in court and in virtually all cases the court will be the sheriff court.[109] Along with the petition the report mentioned above will be lodged, together with evidence as to the health of the proposed adopters.

Once the petition is lodged a curator ad litem and reporting officer will be appointed. In sheriff court cases these two posts can be combined if the sheriff considers this to be appropriate. The individual appointed may be drawn from a panel maintained by the local authority, and if this is done and the adoption order is granted the authority will pay his/her fees.

The duty of the curator ad litem is to protect the interests of the child in the proceedings and to produce a report to the court. The functions of the curator are dealt with at length in the court rules. Briefly, they are to protect the child's interests; to ascertain whether the facts stated in the petition are correct; to establish whether the adoption is likely to safeguard and promote the welfare of the child; and to establish the reasons for adoption.

Reporting officers' duties are principally to witness the parents' consent to the adoption and to ensure that they understand the effects of adoption.

107 Adoption and Children (Scotland) Act 2007, s 18.
108 Adoption and Children (Scotland) Act 2007, s 19.
109 The rules for this are set out in the Act of Sederunt (Sheriff Court Rules Amendment) (Adoption and Children (Scotland) Act 2007) 2009, SSI 2009/284.

Following receipt of the reports a pre-proof hearing will be held, to establish whether the proof can proceed on the date set for it. The child's parent may appear at the proof hearing and object to the granting of the order[110] and in such a case it will be necessary to ascertain whether the consent of the parent can be dispensed with.

At the end of the proceedings a number of options are open to the court. The decision is subject to the considerations discussed above. The options are:

(a) to refuse the order;
(b) to grant the order as sought;
(c) to exercise its general powers under section 11 of the 1995 Act to make an order in respect of parental responsibilities or rights;
(d) if it considers that any of the grounds of referral, except commission of an offence by the child, is satisfied in respect of the child, to refer the case to the reporter who must then investigate and decide whether the child is in need of supervision. If the reporter decides that this is the case a hearing must be arranged.[111]

The court has the power to terminate a supervision requirement if it considers that, as a result of its order, compulsory supervision is no longer necessary.[112] Once an adoption order is made it will be recorded in the Adopted Children's Register kept in the General Register Office for Scotland in Edinburgh.

(10) Adoption allowances[113]

3.26 Adoption agencies are now enabled to pay adoption allowances. These are paid, for example:

(a) where payment is necessary to ensure that the adopter(s) can look after the child;
(b) where it is desirable to place a child with siblings or with a child who has previously shared his/her home;

110 Though in some cases they may need leave from the court to do this, Adoption and Children (Scotland) Act 2007, s 31(12) & (14).
111 Children (Scotland) Act 1995, s 54.
112 Adoption and Children (Scotland) Act 2007, s 36.
113 Adoption and Children (Scotland) Act 2007, s 71; Adoption Support and Allowances (Scotland) Regulations 2009, SSI 2009/152, regs 10–17, LAC Guidance, pp 214–218.

(c) where the child needs special care requiring additional spending because of disability or emotional or behavioural difficulties or the consequences of past abuse or neglect.

The amount of the allowance is determined after considering the resources available to the adopters, the financial needs of the adopters (excluding the costs incurred in respect of the child) and the financial needs of the child. Where an adopter had previously looked after the child as a foster or kinship carer and had received a fee element in addition to any allowance, this can be paid for a period of two years after the adoption.

(11) Access to adoption records

3.27 As we have noted, the making of an adoption order is recorded in the Adopted Children Register. In addition, the Registrar General must keep other registers and information linking the Adopted Children Register with a child's original birth certificate. Once an adopted child reaches the age of 16 he/she is entitled to access to these records. On application the Registrar General must advise the child of the availability of counselling. Counselling is optional but if it is requested it will be provided by an adoption agency if it made the original placement; otherwise it will be provided by the local authority for the area where the child resides. The adopted person is also entitled to access his/her local authority records (and may be given access to these if under 16 and the authority thinks it appropriate to give access) and the court adoption records.[114]

(12) Adoption support services[115]

3.28 Local authorities have a clear and enhanced duty to provide adoption support services to a range of individuals, including children who may be adopted, children and older people who have been adopted, adopters and prospective adopters, and the birth parents of adopted children. These services are wide-ranging and include the provision of

114 Adoption (Disclosure of Information and Medical Information about Natural Parents) (Scotland) Regulations 2009, SSI 2009/268; Act of Sederunt (Sheriff Court Rules Amendment) (Adoption and Children (Scotland) Act 2007) 2009, SSI 2009/284, r 25.

115 Adoption Support and Allowances (Scotland) Regulations 2009, SSI 2009/152; LAC Guidance, pp 200–213.

counselling, provision of guidance about adoption and the provision of any other assistance which is considered appropriate in the circumstances.[116] Although, as discussed below, the process of providing support will be triggered by a request, the guidance makes it clear that at certain key points in the process the local authority will have to consider the need for an adoption support plan.

In most cases the authority must, on request, carry out an assessment of the need for support services, and, normally, services are only to be provided following an assessment. Services can be provided without assessment in cases where support is required as a matter of urgency,[117] and a limited range of services, for example assessment of prospective adopters, can be provided simply on request.

The assessment must take into account the needs of the person who is being assessed, the needs of any adopted child and a variety of other environmental and family factors.[118] Those being assessed must be given notice of the proposed decision following assessment and have the opportunity to make representations before a final decision is made. The form of provision will depend on whether it is intended to provide services for a member of a relevant family. A relevant family is one which includes a child who has been placed for adoption or adopted, the person who has adopted the child or with whom he/she has been placed, and any other children in the household. Where the person being assessed is in a relevant family then an adoption support plan will need to be prepared setting out services to be provided and a draft of this plan will have to be sent to those concerned for comment before a final decision is made. A support plan is, by default, required for each member of the relevant family, but it is possible for the members of the family (aged 12 or over) to agree that a single plan should be prepared covering the whole family. Once made, anyone being provided with services can seek a review of the plan and the local authority must, in any case, review it from time to time, and the guidance indicates that local authority procedures should set out both the frequency of and the procedures for such reviews.

116 Adoption and Children (Scotland) Act 2007, s 10.
117 Adoption and Children (Scotland) Act 2007, s 11.
118 Adoption Support and Allowances (Scotland) Regulations 2009, SSI 2009/152, reg 6.

OCCUPANCY RIGHTS

(1) Introduction

3.29 Under the previous law the only person with a legal right to occupy a home was the person who was the owner or tenant of the property, or who enjoyed some other permission from the owner to occupy it. The difficulty in this was that the ownership or tenancy of the family home was usually taken in the name of the husband alone, with the consequence that the wife had no legally recognised right of occupation. She could therefore be ejected from the family home and had no legal power to prevent this or to resume occupation after it had happened.

The Matrimonial Homes (Family Protection) (Scotland) Act 1981 provides a partial remedy for this. It does this by defining the spouse who is the owner or tenant of the family home (referred to in the Act as the matrimonial home) as an 'entitled spouse' and the other spouse as a 'non-entitled spouse', and by granting all non-entitled spouses what is referred to as an 'occupancy right' in the family home.[119]

The precise content of this occupancy right depends on whether or not the non-entitled spouse is in occupation of the matrimonial home. If she is in occupation the right is to remain in occupation and to have free access to the home: if not the right is to be allowed to enter and occupy the matrimonial home. Should access be refused or should the non-entitled spouse be excluded from the home the occupancy right can only be enforced by application to court.

The situation noted above, where the title to the matrimonial home was in the name of only one of the spouses is now rarer, it is much commoner now for the title to be taken in the names of both husband and wife. Where this is the case both have property rights, including occupancy rights, in the home regardless of the 1981 Act.

Wherever occupancy rights exist either spouse can apply to court for an order enforcing the rights, restricting the occupancy rights of the other spouse, regulating the exercise of the other spouses occupancy rights, or protecting the occupancy rights of the spouse applying for the order.

119 Similar rights apply in the case of civil partnerships, Civil Partnerships Act 2004, s 101. Where an entitled spouse ceases to be entitled, for example because he is ejected from a tenancy, then the non-entitled spouse will lose her occupancy right since this is dependent on the existence of an entitled spouse, *Morgan v Morgan & Kyle & Carrick DC* 2000 Hous LR 90.

Either spouse may also apply for an exclusion order excluding the other spouse from the matrimonial home.

The non-entitled spouse will lose the benefit of the occupancy right if he/she has ceased cohabitation for two years and during that period did not occupy the matrimonial home.

(2) Transfer of Tenancy

3.30 Where one spouse is the legal tenant of the matrimonial home, and therefore the entitled spouse, the non-entitled spouse may apply to court for the tenancy to be transferred to them. Before granting such an order the court must consider all the circumstances[120] of the case and in particular: the conduct of the spouses; the respective needs and resources of the spouses; the needs of any children;[121] the extent of any business use of the home by one of the spouses; and any offer by the entitled spouse to provide accommodation for the non-entitled spouse.

(3) Cohabiting Couples

3.31 In the case of a man and a woman living together as if man and wife or a same sex couple living together as if they were civil partners there is also the possibility that one has a title to the shared home and the other does not. In such cases the non-entitled partner may apply to court for the grant of occupancy rights. This grant may be made for up to six months, but is renewable for further six month periods. Where such an order is in force the provisions set out above in relation to occupancy rights, exclusion orders and transfer of tenancy apply to the non-entitled partner.[122] It is also possible that both partners here are 'entitled' in which case the provisions about occupancy rights and exclusion order will apply to both.

120 For example, which of the parties would be the less troublesome neighbour, *Soutar v McAuley*, Dundee Sh Ct, 31 March 2010.

121 See *Guyan v Guyan* 2001 Hous LR 99, noting that in balancing the interests of adults and children, children have to come first. In this case the spouse with care of children obtained the tenancy.

122 See *Soutar v McAuley*, Dundee Sh Ct, 31 March 2010 for a case involving parties living together as if civil partners.

MEASURES DIRECTED AT DOMESTIC VIOLENCE

(1) Introduction

3.32 As well as providing some protection for non-entitled partners, the 1981 Act also contained a number of measures directed at providing protection against domestic violence. These originally extended only to spouses and to cohabitants living as if husband and wife, but similar provision is now made in the Civil Partnership Act 2004 for civil partners and for those living as if they were civil partners.

(2) Exclusion Orders

3.33 A spouse or a civil partner or a cohabitant holding an order conferring occupancy rights[123] can apply to court for an exclusion order suspending the occupancy rights of the other partner. This can be done **both** where there is an entitled and non-entitled partner **and** where the title to the property is held in common and both partners are effectively entitled partners. It is now clear that the partner applying for the exclusion order need not be in occupation of the matrimonial home when the application is made.

There are two requirements to be fulfilled before the court can grant the order. Firstly, the order must be necessary to protect the applicant or any child of the family from actual or threatened conduct of the other partner which would be detrimental to their physical or mental health. Secondly, the court must not make an order if it would be unjustified or unreasonable to do so.

(a) Need for Protection

3.34 In the first place making the order must be necessary. The implication is that there must be no other remedy, for example an interdict,[124] which will provide the necessary protection. On the other hand it does not mean that an applicant must proceed in stages, first of all seeking interdict and then, if that is unsuccessful, applying for an exclusion order.

123 For ease of explanation these will be collectively referred to as partners.

124 The behaviour involved may be such that it is difficult to frame an interdict to prevent it, *Roberton v Roberton* 1999 SLT 38.

The threat must come from some conduct on the part of the other partner, the provision will therefore not cover the case where the upset arises simply from the desire of the other partner to remain in the home despite the break-up of the relationship. Finally it should be noted that actual physical injury need not have occurred for an order to be granted, similarly, there is no need for the behaviour to be violent or notably offensive, in one case the conduct was characterised as involving imposition of the husband's aspirations for reconciliation in such a way as to continuously upset and distress his wife.[125]

The courts have formulated four relevant questions to be considered in deciding on this type of application. They are:

(a) What is the nature and quality of the alleged conduct?
(b) Is the court satisfied that the conduct is likely to be repeated if cohabitation continues?
(c) Has the conduct been, or, if repeated would it be, injurious to the physical or mental health of the applicant spouse or any child of the family?
(d) If so, is the order sought necessary for the future protection of the physical or mental health of the applicant or child?[126]

(b) Unjustified or Unreasonable

3.35 In deciding on whether granting the order would be unjustified or unreasonable the Act directs the court to consider a number of factors. These include the conduct of the parties, the respective needs and resources of the parties, the needs of any children, and the offer by an entitled partner to make accommodation available to the non-entitled partner. In the specific case of tied housing where there is a requirement that the non-applicant partner reside there the courts must consider that requirement and the possible consequences of making an exclusion order in deciding whether or not it is unjustified or unreasonable to make the order.

When the court makes an exclusion order it must also, if requested to do so by the applicant, grant a warrant for the ejection of the other partner from the home and/or an interdict preventing the other partner from entering the matrimonial home without the permission of the partner applying for the order. The court may also grant an interdict prohibiting the other partner from entering or remaining in a specified area in the vicinity of the matrimonial home.

125 *Roberton v Roberton* 1999 SLT 38.
126 *McCafferty v McCafferty* 1986 SLT 650.

Pending the grant of a full exclusion order the court may make an interim (temporary) order, this may only be done if the non-applicant partner has been afforded an opportunity of being heard or represented before the court prior to the order being made.

(3) Interdicts

3.36 In general terms an interdict is a court order ordering an individual to desist from a course of conduct which is causing or is likely to cause injury (whether physical, mental or financial) or detriment to another. One legal text notes that 'on general principle, interdict is available to prohibit any act which amounts to an invasion, or a threat of invasion, of the legal rights of the party seeking interdict.' Normally breach of the terms of an interdict is a civil matter and will only be punished if the person who has obtained the interdict takes proceedings to bring the offender before the court. If this is done the offender can be punished since they are effectively guilty of contempt of court. Specific provision is made in relation to interdicts in cases involving domestic violence, though the terminology varies depending on the nature of the relationship. The ability to apply for an interdict exists even where parties are living together and in such cases does not depend on having or exercising an occupancy right.

The first category are matrimonial interdicts. A matrimonial interdict is one which either:

(a) restrains or prohibits any conduct of one spouse towards the other spouse or a child of the family; or
(b) prohibits a spouse from entering or remaining in:
   (i) a matrimonial home (an interdict to prevent this can only be granted if the person against whom it is sought is the subject of an exclusion order excluding them from the matrimonial home or where the court has refused leave to exercise occupancy rights);
   (ii) any other residence occupied by the applicant spouse;
   (iii) any place of work of the applicant spouse;
   (iv) any school attended by a child in the permanent or temporary care of the applicant spouse.

The court can attach a power of arrest to the interdict which gives the police the power to arrest the person subject to the interdict if there is reasonable cause to suspect that a breach of the interdict has taken place. There are two circumstances in which the power of arrest must be attached to a matrimonial interdict:

(a) where the interdict is ancillary to an exclusion order or interim exclusion order;

(b) where the non-applicant spouse has had the opportunity of being heard or represented before the court, and attaching the power of arrest is necessary to protect the applicant from a risk of abuse in breach of the interdict.

A matrimonial interdict with a power of arrest attached must be notified to the non-applicant spouse and the Chief Constable.

The power of arrest is to the effect that a constable *may* arrest if breach of the interdict is suspected and it is considered that there would be a risk of abuse or further abuse if the person breaching the interdict were not arrested. Once the spouse has been arrested he must be detained until charged with an offence arising from the circumstances of the arrest. If he is not so charged he must be brought before the sheriff and if the sheriff is satisfied that there is a *prima facie* breach of interdict, and that there will, if detention is not ordered, be a substantial risk of abuse or further abuse in breach of the interdict he/she may order further detention for up to two days.

Similar provisions to those set out in relation to married couples exist for civil partners. Where partners are living together as husband and wife or as civil partners it is still possible to obtain an interdict, referred to as a domestic interdict. This is available on the same terms as a matrimonial interdict except that an interdict prohibiting entry to the family home may only be granted if it is ancillary to an exclusion order or if an order granting or extending occupancy rights is recalled.

(4) Protection from Harassment Act 1997

3.37 This allows a victim of harassment to claim damages for any injury suffered because of the harassment or to seek either an interdict or a non-harassment order to prevent future harassment. Breach of a non-harassment order will be a criminal offence.

(5) Protection from Abuse (Scotland) Act 2001

3.38 A person who is applying for, or who has obtained, an interdict for the purpose of protection against abuse may apply to the court for a power of arrest to be attached to the interdict under this Act. The court must attach a power of arrest to the interdict if satisfied that:

(a) the interdicted person has been given an opportunity to be heard by, or represented before, the court; and
(b) attaching the power of arrest is necessary to protect the applicant from a risk of abuse in breach of the interdict.

Abuse includes violence, harassment, threatening conduct, and any other conduct giving rise, or likely to give rise, to physical or mental injury, fear, alarm or distress and conduct includes speech and presence in a specified place or area.

The court must specify a date of expiry for the power of arrest which must be not later than three years after the date when the power is attached. Procedures on breach of an interdict containing a power of arrest are as set out above in relation to matrimonial interdicts.

Chapter 4

Local authority services to children

INTRODUCTION

4.1 One of the major changes in emphasis introduced in the Children (Scotland) Act 1995 (the 1995 Act) was the importance placed on providing services to promote the welfare of children and their families and to ensure that children are brought up by their families. The provision of services is not to be seen negatively as being concerned only with preventing care being taken over by the local authority, but positively as enabling children to achieve and maintain a reasonable standard of development. This is expressed in a duty to provide services to promote welfare,[1] a duty to plan the provision of services for children[2] and a duty to publish information about these services.[3]

The focus of service provision in the 1995 Act is not on children generally, but on children in need, many of whom may also potentially be in need of protection or at risk. There is no explicit link between the categories of children at risk and children in need, though the guidance issued under the 1995 Act does say:

> ... the Act introduces various powers enabling authorities to provide a range of different types of support for children and their families. The effective use of those powers will help to avoid situations which could lead to children being subjected to abuse and may thus avert the need for child protection intervention.[4]

1 Children (Scotland) Act 1995 (the 1995 Act), s 22.

2 1995 Act, s 19.

3 1995 Act, s 20.

4 *The Children (Scotland) Act 1995 Regulations and Guidance: Volume I, Support and Protection for Children and their Families* (1997), ch 7, para 2. The other two volumes, both published by the Stationery Office in 1997, are volume 2 on Children Looked After by Local Authorities and volume 3 on Adoption and Parental Responsibilities Orders. Volume 2 was replaced in 2010 by Scottish Government, *Guidance on Looked After Children (Scotland) Regulations 2009 and the Adoption and Children (Scotland) Act 2007* (2010) (LAC Guidance). In future the two remaining volumes will be referred to as '*Guidance*' with the relevant volume number.

There is some evidence, however, that priority is given to children who are at risk rather than simply being in need. Recent research, for example, concluded that being in need could sometimes be used to justify provision of services to children and their families, but that it was more common for this to be justified on the basis that the child was at risk.[5]

Other changes introduced by the 1995 Act were a changed view of the role of accommodation provided by a local authority. It is seen as part of promoting the welfare of children and a resource to support the upbringing of a child by his/her family, and a change in terminology so that children are no longer 'in care', but are being 'looked after' by the local authority. This second change was made as an attempt to remove the stigma attached to being labelled as in care as well as incorporating the notion of partnership with parents and was accompanied by a clarification of which groups of children are to be regarded as looked after.

In considering these provisions below, three definitions should be remembered. The first is that for the purpose of these provisions a child is a person under 18;[6] the second is that the term 'family' extends not only to someone with parental responsibility, but also to any person with whom the child has been living;[7] and the third is that a 'relevant person' is anyone holding parental responsibilities or parental rights or anyone who ordinarily has charge of or control over a child (unless this is in the course of their employment).[8]

Finally, statutory provision in this area is supplemented by regulations, directions from central government and by local procedures. An important element of current provision is the implementation of *Getting it Right for Every Child* (GIRFEC), and the main elements of this will be considered before looking at the relevant statutory provisions.

GETTING IT RIGHT FOR EVERY CHILD

4.2 Getting it Right for Every Child (GIRFEC) had its genesis in a review of the children's hearing system,[9] but developed into an approach concerned with all children. There are 10 core components of the

5 Tisdall, K & Plows, V, *Children in Need; Examining its use in practice and reflecting on its currency for proposed policy changes* (University of Edinburgh, 2007), pp 61–62 & 70.

6 1995 Act, s 93(2)(a).

7 1995 Act, s 93(1).

8 1995 Act, s 93(2)(b).

9 Scottish Executive, *Getting it Right for Every Child: Consultation Pack on the Review of the Children's Hearings System* (2004).

GIRFEC approach, set out in the box below. In addition, the approach identifies a number of objectives for children, which are for them to be successful learners, confident individuals, effective contributors and responsible citizens.

The Core Components of GIRFEC

- A focus on improving outcomes for children, young people and their families based on a shared understanding of well-being.
- A common approach to gaining consent and to sharing information where appropriate.
- An integral role for children, young people and families in assessment, planning and intervention.
- A co-ordinated and unified approach to identifying concerns, assessing needs, agreeing actions and outcomes, based on the Well-being Indicators.[10]
- Streamlined planning, assessment and decision-making processes that lead to the right help at the right time.
- Consistent high standards of co-operation, joint working and communication where more than one agency needs to be involved, locally and across Scotland.
- A Lead Professional to co-ordinate and monitor multi-agency activity where necessary.
- Maximising the skilled workforce within universal services to address needs and risks at the earliest possible time.
- A confident and competent workforce across all services for children, young people and their families.
- The capacity to share demographic, assessment, and planning information electronically within and across agency boundaries through the national eCare programme[11] where appropriate.

The approach is based on progressive support for children and families based on an assessment of their needs against these objectives with a focus, where appropriate, on inter-agency working. This starts with the

10 See below.
11 A Scotland-wide network for data sharing.

support provided by universal services such as education and health and moves on up in a spiral from there, encompassing more focused intervention, compulsory if necessary, directed at supporting the achievement by the child of the objectives noted above. This is represented in the material prepared as part of GIRFEC in the graphic reproduced as Figure 1 below, starting in the centre with 'normal' support and moving out to more intensive support. In a slide show[12] setting out GIRFEC it is noted that: 'In GIRFEC there are **no thresholds** – but depending on need, action should be taken'.

Figure 1[13]

12 Available here: http://www.scotland.gov.uk/Topics/People/Young-People/childrens services/girfec/Practitioners/ToolsResources/GIRFECMay09.

13 See Scottish Government, *A Guide to Getting it Right for Every Child* (2008), Section 4: Getting it right for every child: the approach in practice, p 20.

Figure 2[14]

Assessment under GIRFEC makes use of a number of tools, including the well-being indicators, ie the extent to which the child is safe, healthy, achieving, nurtured, active, respected, responsible and included (see Figure 2) and the My World Triangle[15] (Figure 3), which is used to provide focus on the information which is required about the child and her/his environment. There is also guidance on producing a children's or young person's plan.[16]

14 See Scottish Government, *A Guide to Getting it Right for Every Child* (2008), Section 2: Getting it right for every child: the approach, p 12.

15 See Scottish Government, *A Guide to Getting it Right for Every Child* (2008), Section 4: Getting it right for every child: the approach in practice, p 25.

16 Scottish Government, *Getting it Right for Every Child: Guidance on the Child's or Young Person's Plan* (2007).

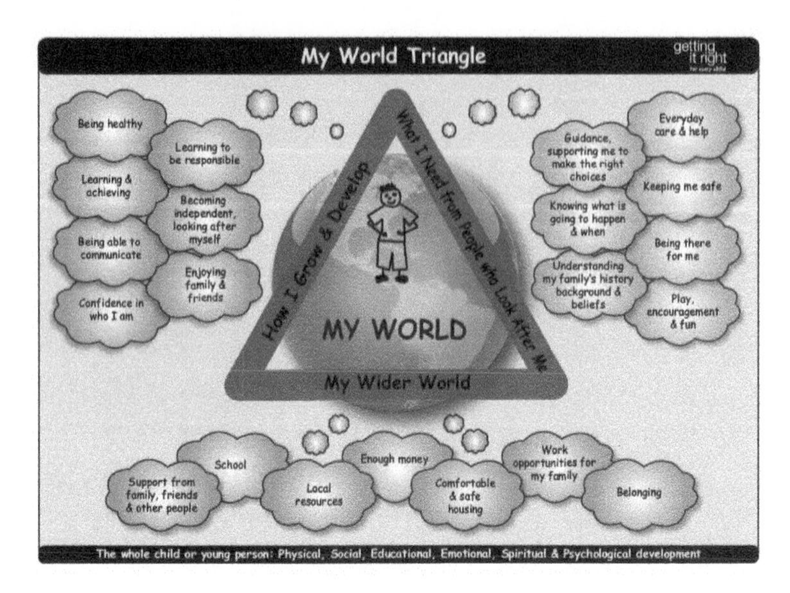

Figure 3

SERVICES FOR CHILDREN IN NEED

(1) Promoting welfare

4.3 Two main duties are imposed on local authorities. They must, first, safeguard and promote the welfare of children in need living in their area. Second, they must promote the upbringing of such children by their families, provided that this is consistent with safeguarding and promoting the children's welfare. Both of these duties are to be fulfilled by providing services to children which are of an appropriate type and at an appropriate level.[17]

This general statement of local authority duties raises a number of questions. When is a child 'in need? How is the decision about provision of services taken? Are there special provisions for particular groups of children? Can the social work department call on others for help? What sort of services can be provided? How can decisions be challenged? These questions are addressed below.

17 1995 Act, s 22.

(2) Children in need

4.4 A child will be considered in need if he/she is in need of care and attention for one of the following reasons:[18]

(a) The child is unlikely to achieve or maintain or have the opportunity to achieve or maintain a reasonable standard of health or development unless services are provided.
(b) His/her health or development is likely to be significantly impaired or further impaired unless services are provided.
(c) The child is disabled. In this context 'disabled' means chronically sick or disabled or suffering from a mental disorder as defined in the Mental Health (Care and Treatment)(Scotland) Act 2003.
(d) The child is adversely affected by the disability of another member of his/her family. This could be a sibling or a parent.

This definition is almost identical to that contained in the Children Act 1989, in which context it has been described as 'rather broad and indeterminate, except in so far as it is clear that we are dealing with a restricted category of children'.[19] More definition is given in England and Wales of some of the terms. 'Development', for example, is defined to include 'physical, intellectual, emotional, and social development'.[20] No further definition is offered either in the 1995 Act or in the guidance issued on it. This means that a great deal of discretion is left to local authorities to define their own terms for implementation of these provisions. For example, when is a child 'in need of care and attention', what amounts to significant impairment and what is a reasonable standard? It is clear that in practice there is considerable variation amongst practitioners as to the definition of 'a child in need' as well as variation in the extent to which the term 'in need' is used in practice.[21] One thing, however, is clear: the definition looks not only to past and present disadvantage, but also to possible future disadvantage. In this respect, the 1995 Act has clearly taken into account the link established in research between poverty and deprivation.

18 1995 Act. s 93(4)(a). See para 1.72 for children excluded from secure provisions.
19 A Bainham, *Children – The Modern Law* (3rd edn, 2005, Family Law), p 422.
20 Children Act 1989, s 17(11).
21 Tisdall, K & Plows, V, *Children in Need; Examining its use in practice and reflecting on its currency for proposed policy changes* (University of Edinburgh, 2007), pp 61–62 & 70. The Report, *For Scotland's Children: Better Indicated Children's Services* (Scottish Executive, 2001) noted (at p 33) that:' There is a general problem in that, although local authorities have a statutory responsibility in relation to Children in Need, no one has defined exactly which groups fall within the category of 'Children in Need'. There is certainly no common understanding of which groups we are actually talking about'.

(3) Assessment

4.5 Although the original legislation says little or nothing about assessment, it is clear from the guidance which accompanied the original implementation of the 1995 Act that children who may be in need must be assessed to establish what needs they might have and whether it is necessary for the local authority to provide services to the child and/or the child's family. The point is made in the guidance that the assessment necessary, in terms of scope and depth, will differ as between different children, notes that where assessments are being carried out for different purposes they should as far as possible be combined, and recommends the guidance on community care assessments as a model. In the process of assessment the local authority has considerable discretion and it is clear that the resources available to the authority are a relevant factor both in the assessment of needs and in the decision as to provision of services.[22]

There is no right to have an assessment carried out, nor is there any statutory trigger for such an assessment. Where a child's parent requests an assessment or where a problem has been identified, either by a social worker or by others, which requires assessment, then an assessment should be carried out.[23] More recent guidance now suggests that the purpose of the assessment is the production of a child's or young persons plan.[24] There should be such a plan '[w]henever a child or young person, family or professional thinks a plan would help to identify and meet needs.' Creation of such a plan will require some degree of assessment. The assessment should take place making use of the tools provided under the GIRFEC approach.

Different cases will call for assessments of differing complexity involving varying groups of professionals. Where a number of different professionals is involved one will need to be designated as Lead Professional. In some cases a simple, brief assessment carried out by the social work department will be all that is required, in other cases those involved with the child's health and education will also need to participate and the process of assessment will be more complex. The creation of the plan will require a contribution from all agencies involved with the child

22 See *Crossan v South Lanarkshire Council* [2006] CSOH 28.
23 *Guidance*, vol. 1, ch 1, para 16.
24 Scottish Executive, *Guidance on the Child's or Young Person's Plan*, 2007.

as well as from the child and from his/her family.[25] The information to be recorded in the plan should include: concerns or matters to be tackled; partners to the child's or young person's plan; summary of analysis of the child's or young person's circumstances; desired outcomes and milestones for achievement; what should be done to improve a child's circumstances; agreed action to be taken; resources to be provided; contingency plans; monitoring, review and lead professional arrangements; child's or young person's view (and those of parents/carers): and, any compulsory measures considered to be necessary.[26] Assessments of the child may need to be carried out for purposes other than the provision of services under the 1995 Act, for example to establish if the child needs the provision of services under the Chronically Sick and Disabled Persons Act 1970.

Where different types of assessments need to be carried out they should, as far as possible, be conducted at the same time. Regardless of the form of the assessment, it should include an assessment of risk to the child as well as the needs of the child and family. This points to the fact that children in need may also be at risk and that an assessment, and indeed the initial referral triggering the assessment, may indicate the need to take some appropriate child protection measures.

At the end of the assessment the social worker will have to reach a conclusion as to the needs of the child and his/her family. The decision about needs is one for the professional judgment of the worker, operating, of course, within the policies and procedures of the local authority. A further decision then has to be taken about which services are to be provided to meet the identified needs of the child and family. This process, like the assessment, should involve the family fully in the spirit of partnership and empowering practice. As with all these sorts of decisions the question arises whether there is a clear right or entitlement to services once needs have been identified and whether the local authority has discretion, particularly as to whether resources can be considered. The vagueness of the definition of 'in need', referred to above, and the reference to providing 'appropriate' services leaves considerable discretion to the local authority. The second edition of this text explained that:[27]

25 It should be noted that quite apart from guidance it is clear that parents have a right to be involved in meetings where decisions are taken about their children by virtue of Art 8 of the European Convention on Human Rights, subject to protecting the rights and welfare of the child.

26 Scottish Government, *Getting it Right for Every Child: Guidance on the Child's or Young Person's Plan* (2007), section 5.

27 At p 112.

More specifically, the guidance says:

> 'Once a need has been identified, the local authority should consider whether assistance is appropriate, and if so should plan with the family how best to meet this need *within the resources and services available*.'[28]

This seems to indicate that resources are a relevant consideration in deciding whether to meet needs,[29] though it should be borne in mind that in some cases the need will be so great and clear that a refusal to provide services will be regarded by the courts as unreasonable and so be open to challenge.

Since this was written, some guidance has been offered by the Scottish courts on the nature of the duty owed towards children in need. This decision[30] interpreted the duty towards children in need to be a general duty owed towards the class of 'children in need' rather than as conferring rights on, or imposing a duty towards, an individual child. The consequence of this is that a child who has been assessed as needing the provision of a particular service will, subject to what is said below, have no right to that service, nor will the local authority have a legally enforceable duty to provide it. Support for the court's conclusion came from English case law[31] and from the terms of the 1995 Act, particularly the provision in section 22(3) which confers a *discretion* to provide services to an individual child.

There will be cases, as we said in the second edition, in which a child's need will be so substantial that a refusal to provide services would be open to challenge as unreasonable. A further limit is that in some cases the circumstances of a child's life might be such that his/her rights under Article 8 of the European Convention on Human Rights (or, in an extreme case, Article 3) are being infringed. In such cases the local authority will have a duty to take action to prevent continued infringement.

28 *Guidance*, vol 1, ch 1, para 29, emphasis added.

29 See also *R v Kingston-upon-Thames Royal Borough Council, ex parte T* [1994] 1FLR798.

30 *Crossan v South Lanarkshire Council* [2006] CSOH 28.

31 *R (on the application of G) v Barnet London Borough Council* [2003] UKHL 57.

(4) Children and disability

4.6 Special provision is made for children affected by disability.[32] A child may be affected by disability either because the child is disabled or because he/she is affected by the disability of another family member. In general, services provided to such children under the local authority's obligation to promote welfare are to be designed to give the child the opportunity to lead as normal a life as possible and to minimise the effect of the disability.

As well as the obligation to provide services the local authority has specific assessment duties in respect of children affected by disability. The parent or guardian of such a child can request an assessment of the child or of the disabled family member[33] and it is hoped that the family's singular understanding of the needs of the child will be fully appreciated and represented. Although only the parent or guardian has the statutory right to request an assessment, the guidance makes it clear that it is good practice to carry out an assessment if requested to do so by a child affected by disability. A request for assessment can also be made by a Mental Health Officer who is involved with the child.[34] The guidance also goes into more detail on the assessment process and suggests that the policy and practice guidance on community care assessment are possible further sources of guidance.

The purpose of the assessment is to identify the needs of the child and so to help the local authority in carrying out its duties as regards provision of services both to minimise the effect of the disability and give the child the chance to lead as normal a life as possible and, more generally, to promote the welfare of the child. Although the 1995 Act restricts assessments to identifying needs flowing from disability, the guidance goes further and suggests, correctly in view of the general requirement to assess before providing services, that the assessment should 'consider whether services available for children in need … should be provided to meet the child's wider needs, in addition to those attributable to his or her disability'.[35]

32 1995 Act, s 23; *Guidance,* vol 1, ch 6.
33 1995 Act, s 23.
34 1995 Act, s 23(3)(b).
35 *Guidance,* vol 1, ch 6, para 5.

A final element of the assessment process is that, where a disabled child is being assessed, the child's carer[36] can request an assessment of his/her ability to provide or to continue to provide care for the child.[37] The outcome of the assessment of the carer must be taken into account in taking decisions about service provision.

Once the assessments have been carried out a decision will need to be made about the provision of services for the child and his/her family. If the local authority decides that the child has a specific need for a service, however, then, subject to what is said below about the Chronically Sick and Disabled Persons Act 1970, the 1995 Act does not require the local authority to provide that service or give the child an enforceable right to it.[38]

Duties to disabled children under the 1995 Act are superimposed on other duties owed to people with disabilities, and the relationship between these provisions is unclear. It has been said that 'the statutory provisions are unnecessarily difficult to unravel, and are complex and obscure in an area where clarity and simplicity are appropriate'.[39] Other duties owed by local authorities are considered in chapter 6, but there is one specific statutory provision which should be briefly examined here. Section 2(1) of the Chronically Sick and Disabled Persons Act 1970 imposes a duty on the local authority to provide certain services (which are listed in the subsection) to certain classes of disabled people if it is satisfied that this is necessary to meet their needs. Important consequences follow from this. The first is that disabled children to whom a duty arises under the 1995 Act are one of the classes to which this section applies. The second is that once a decision has been made that the child's needs call for the provision of a service, then that service must be provided. This contrasts with the position under the 1995 Act. Third, even though a specific request for assessment for services under the 1970 Act is not made by the child or his/her parent/guardian, the local authority must be alive to the possibility of duties arising under it. If it fails to consider it and carry out an appropriate assessment considering services under the 1970 Act, any decision on provision of services could be illegal.[40] If the local authority decides after assessment that the

36 Defined as a person who 'provides or intends to provide a substantial amount of care on a regular basis' for the child: 1995 Act, s 24(l)(b). Volunteer carers operating as part of a voluntary organisation and employed carers are excluded.

37 1995 Act, s 24.

38 *Crossan v South Lanarkshire Council* [2006] CSOH 28.

39 *R v London Borough of Bexley, ex parte B* (31 July 1995, unreported) QB.

40 *R v London Borough of Bexley, ex parte B* (31 July 1995, unreported) QB.

child's needs call for the provision of a specific service then, in contrast to the position under the 1995 Act, that service must be provided.

Where a child is affected by the disability of an adult in his/her family, the local authority's duties to adults affected by disability must also be considered.

(5) Assistance from other bodies

4.7 In carrying out its duties a local authority may request assistance from another local authority, a health board or an NHS trust. These bodies must comply with this request unless doing so would either be incompatible with their own statutory or other duties or would prejudice the discharge of any of their functions.[41] The inclusion of this section is significant in recognising the pivotal nature of collaboration and co-operation amongst agencies which has so evidently been at the root of difficulties in service provision in the past. Getting it Right for Every Child in particular stresses the need for joint working and the involvement, where appropriate, of different services in providing support for a child.

(6) Provision of services

4.8 If services are to be provided, then the outcome of the assessment process will be a care plan agreed with the family, which should be in the form of a child or young person's plan.[42] This plan should be a written document and its implementation will have to be monitored and reviewed.[43] Service provision under the plan may include the provision of services by the local authority, provision by other agencies, or provision of self-directed support.[44]

In providing services the local authority must take account of a number of factors. First it must act in partnership with families and pursue the duty to promote the upbringing of the child in his/her own family. Secondly, the local authority must listen to the child and take into account his/her views. Thirdly, it must 'have regard so far as practicable to each child's religious persuasion, racial origin and cultural and linguistic

41 1995 Act, s 21.

42 See also the specific plan requirements where a child is looked after (see para 4.15 below).

43 Scottish Executive, *Guidance on the Child's or Young Person's Plan*, 2007.

44 See para 6.10.

background'.[45] Finally, for a child away from home, the local authority must promote the child's contact with his/her family.

It is important to remember that the duty to promote welfare is laid at the door not only of the social work department, but is a duty owed by the council as a whole. Because of this, all the services of the local authority should be considered when it comes to identifying and meeting needs, and services provided by the housing and education departments will be particularly relevant.

The relationship between services for children and families and other services provided by the local authority is not entirely clear. When a local authority requests help from an outside body, that body is entitled to refuse if complying with the request would be inconsistent with its statutory duties or detrimental to the performance of these duties. Does the same apply within the same local authority? One area where this may arise is in respect of housing and families who are intentionally homeless. If a family with children approaches the housing department of a local authority to ask for housing as homeless persons they will usually need to be given temporary accommodation. The housing department will then have to decide if it has an obligation to secure the provision of permanent accommodation for the family. This obligation will arise only if the applicant is in priority need and is not intentionally homeless. Because there are children involved, the family will be in priority need, but if they were evicted because of non-payment of rent or anti-social behaviour they may be regarded as intentionally homeless. An approach might then be made to the social work department for assistance and it, in turn, might approach the housing department seeking the provision of accommodation, since it now seems to be clear that the services provided to children under section 22 of the 1995 Act can include providing housing for children and their families.[46] Can the housing department, though part of the same authority, refuse? Given what has been said above about the nature of the duty to provide services the answer would appear to be that there is no automatic duty owed to a particular child and his/her family to provide housing.

A final point on the relationship between housing and social work services is that it has been suggested that before a local authority takes a decision which may result in duties being owed to children and families it must consider these potential obligations, and that failure to do this

45 1995 Act, s 22(2).
46 *R (on the application of W) v Lambeth London Borough Council* [2002] EWCA Civ 613.

will leave the decision open to legal challenge.[47] This suggests that local authorities, before taking a decision to implement or enforce eviction, will have to consider that they will have a potential duty to accommodate the family under the 1995 Act.

(7) Day care and after-school services

4.9 Appropriate day care services must be provided for children in need who are under five and have not started school, and after-school/school holiday services must be provided for children in need who are at school.[48] Authorities are empowered to provide these services to other children.

(8) Provision of accommodation to children

4.10 A local authority has a duty to provide accommodation to any child who appears to require it for one of the following reasons:[49]

(a) no one has parental responsibility for the child;
(b) the child is lost or abandoned; or,
(c) the person caring for the child is prevented temporarily or permanently from providing suitable accommodation and care.

This last criterion has been interpreted widely by the courts in England and Wales, taking the view that the carer will be unable to provide suitable accommodation, where the child's carer is seriously ill or unable to control the child, the child has assaulted her/his carer or where the child is not prepared to be accommodated by the carer.[50]

Before providing accommodation the authority must have regard to the views of the child, if she/he wishes to express a view, taking into account the child's age and maturity,[51] and as far as having regard to the child's views is practicable. There is no requirement to comply with or follow the views expressed by the child and in the English courts there has been some discussion about whether a child aged 16 or over can be

47 *R v Avon County Council, ex parte Hills* (1995) 27 HLR411.
48 1995 Act, s 27.
49 1995 Act, s 25. In considering what a child requires reference should be made to future as well as current needs: *Re T (Accommodation by Local Authority)* [1995] 1 FLR 159. Unlike some other duties imposed under the 1995 Act, the duty to accommodate is enforceable by individual children, *R (on the application of A) v London Borough of Croydon* [2008] EWCA Civ 1445.
50 See, for example, *R(L) v Nottinghamshire CC* [2007] EWHC 2364 (Admin).
51 Children aged 12 or over are deemed to have sufficient maturity to express a view.

forced to accept accommodation, the prevailing view appears to be that she/he cannot.[52]

Local authorities also have the power under section 25 of the 1995 Act to provide accommodation to any other child and to anyone between 18 and 21.

A child can be accommodated in a variety of settings:[53]

(a) with a family, relative or other suitable person, but a family consisting of the people who have parental responsibilities for the child or people with whom the child has been living are excluded, so the child cannot be accommodated with them;
(b) in a residential establishment;
(c) by the authority making other arrangements that appear to be appropriate.

A child cannot be cared for by his/her parents while being accommodated by the local authority.[54] The consequence of this would appear to be that the local authority cannot fulfil its obligation to accommodate a child by providing accommodation for the child and his/her family. There is, of course, no reason why this accommodation cannot be provided under the authority's duties and powers towards children in need.

The provision of accommodation for a child by the local authority is likely to be one of the most stressful events in the lives of all concerned. The social worker's role in these situations can often be contradictory. At its crudest and simplest, there is often a conflict of interest amongst the child, the family and the local authority at the point of accommodation being provided and the child being looked after by the local authority and the resulting tensions must be carefully managed. Social workers will be hard pressed systematically to make assessments, negotiate decision-making and marshall appropriate resources while remaining open to the feelings of all those involved in the process, including themselves.

(9) Rights to object to provision of accommodation

4.11 A child cannot be accommodated against the objection of a person who **both**:[55]

52 *R(G) v London Borough of Southwark* [2009] UKHL 26.
53 1995 Act, s 26. Placements need not be in Scotland.
54 Looked After Children (Scotland) Regulations 2009 (the 'LAC Regs') SI 2009/120, reg 8(2).
55 1995 Act, s 25(6).

(a) holds parental responsibilities and the parental rights to have the child living with him/her and to control, direct or guide the child; **and**

(b) is willing to provide or arrange the provision of accommodation for the child.

Such a person can remove the child from accommodation provided by the local authority at any time. This power to object to the provision of accommodation and to remove the child is subject to two limitations. In the first place it will not arise where accommodation is being provided to a child of 16 or over who agrees to be provided with accommodation[56] or where a person holding a residence order in respect of the child agrees to the provision of accommodation. Secondly, 14 days' notice must be given of the intended removal once the child has been being accommodated for 6 months.[57]

Where a child is being provided with accommodation, his/her plan, which should be agreed with the child's parents, should contain an express agreement about the ending of the provision of accommodation and may say something about the need to give notice before a child is removed. This agreement, of course, does not override the parent's right to remove the child, though some parents may feel, wrongly, that because they have entered into a written agreement they are bound by it and cannot exercise their rights.

The right of parents to remove children who are being provided with accommodation gives rise to two problems. First, who is to judge whether the parent is qualified to remove the child? It will have to be established that the parent holds responsibilities and the relevant rights, and it should be remembered that unmarried fathers will often not hold these. It will also have to be established that the parent is willing and able to provide accommodation for the child. Does this mean that if, in the judgment of the local authority, the parent is unable to provide accommodation then the parent has no right to take the child? What criteria might be used in arriving at that decision? Is the nature and suitability of the accommodation relevant? It is notable that the 1995 Act refers only to providing 'accommodation' and makes no reference to the suitability of the accommodation. If the local authority was of

56 It might be argued that the provision that children over the age of 16 cannot be removed against their will is redundant, since there can be no one with the parental rights needed to remove the child once the child is 16: see s 2(7) of the 1995 Act.

57 The notice requirement is not part of the Children Act 1989. The reason for this is that the view was taken that retaining the notice requirement blurred the distinction between voluntary and compulsory care.

the opinion that the accommodation was not suitable, then its objection might come under the heading of the second problem, namely what is to be done when the parent demands that children are returned but the local authority does not think that it is in the interests of the child to comply with this?

In *M v Dumfries and Galloway Regional Council*[58] it was decided that if a local authority considered it not to be in the child's best interests to be returned to the parents it could refuse to do this. If the parents objected, they would have to go to court to seek an order for delivery of the child. Such an application was to be treated as an application under section 3 of the Law Reform (Parent and Child) (Scotland) Act 1986 (the 1986 Act), which meant that the court could not grant it unless it was satisfied that it was in the best interests of the child to do so. The authority of this decision has been doubted[59] on the grounds that the 1986 Act did not allow local authorities to rely on it, being purely a private law provision which could only be relied on by individuals. This seems to have been confirmed by the express provision in section 11(5) of the 1995 Act excluding local authorities from applying for orders relating to parental responsibilities or rights. It is debatable whether the local authority was in fact 'relying' on the 1986 Act and whether the 1995 Act overrules the decision. However, the precedent set is undesirable for the different reason that it appears to allow the local authority to override the safeguards for parents and children built into the procedures which allow it to exercise compulsory powers over a child.[60] What options then are open to the local authority in this situation?

(a) The local authority could apply for a child protection order if it considered that the conditions for this were fulfilled, or it could refer the case to the reporter if it considered that the child was in need of compulsory measures of supervision. Indeed, if it thought the child was in need of such measures it would have a duty to make the referral.[61] These powers would not help, however, where instant action was needed as they both take time.

(b) Any foster carer with whom the child had been placed or any individual social worker might be able to rely on section 5 of the 1995 Act. This states that:

58 1991 SCLR 481.

59 See K Norrie The Children (Scotland) Act 1995 (2nd edn, 2004), commentary on s 11 of the 1995 Act and *City of Edinburgh Council v M* 1996 SCLR 779.

60 See Professor Thomson's commentary on *M v Dumfries and Galloway Regional Council* 1991 SCLR 481.

61 1995 Act, s 53(l)(b).

> … it shall be the responsibility of a person who has attained the age of sixteen and who has care or control of a child under that age, but in relation to him either has no parental responsibilities or rights or does not have the parental responsibility [to safeguard or promote the child's health, development or welfare], to do what is reasonable in all the circumstances to safeguard the child's health, development and welfare; and in fulfilling his responsibility … the person may … [subject to certain conditions] give consent to any surgical, medical or dental treatment or procedure…

This could be supplemented by the duty of the authority to safeguard and promote the welfare of children whom it is looking after. There is some support for the view that the equivalent English provision would allow the local authority to refuse to hand over a child, at least temporarily, while some other measures were taken.[62] Indeed, while this provision was going through Parliament reference was made to the use of the provision to refuse to hand over a child to an inebriated parent.[63] It was also suggested that unless a social worker's decision to refuse to return a child to his/her parent was 'wholly unreasonable' the social worker would be protected by this provision.[64] No similar debate took place during the passage of section 5 of the 1995 Act; indeed the section was seen as being entirely a private law matter, and the provisions as to medical treatment were described as concerning 'private law' and not dealing with 'public intervention on behalf of the child'.[65] For this reason it might be difficult to argue that section 5 gives powers to social workers and foster carers. The relevant part of the original guidance noted that:

62 Children Act 1989, s 3(5). See eg A Bainham *Children: The Modern Law* (3rd edn, 2005), p 433. It should be noted that there is some authority for the view that the right of the parent to remove is unrestricted: *London Borough of Lewisham v Lewisham Juvenile Court Justices* [1979] 2 All ER297, though this was decided before the 1989 and 1995 Acts and also contains a reference to a 'moral duty' which authorities may consider they have to keep a child temporarily rather than return him/her to an unsuitable parent (Lord Salmon at p 306H). The wording of the English legislation is slightly different from that of the 1995 Act, referring only to a 'person' which can include a corporate body such as a local authority: Interpretation Act 1978, Sch 1.

63 By David Mellor (HC Standing Committee B, 18 May 1989, col 148) and by the Lord Chancellor (HL, vol 505, cols 370–371).

64 HC Standing Committee B, 18 May 1989, col 152.

65 By Lord James Douglas-Hamilton, HC Special Standing Committee, 23 February 1995, col 279.

> Carers will need advice on how to handle those occasional cases in which it may be necessary for the social worker to seek an emergency order to prevent an inappropriate or unplanned removal where this would be likely to cause significant harm to the child (for example, a drunk parent coming to 'collect' his or her child in the middle of the night).[66]

This does not really deal with the question of the legal basis for retaining a child until such an emergency order is obtained and it is suggested, notwithstanding the terms of the debate in Parliament, that section 5 of the 1995 Act does empower social workers and foster carers to refuse to return a child, but only temporarily while other action is taken to protect the child.

Even if we are wrong and no protection is offered by section 5 of the 1995 Act, it would be unlikely that a claim against the worker by the parent(s) for interference with the exercise of their rights would succeed.[67]

(c) The police could be called and asked to exercise their emergency powers to protect children.[68]

(10) Assistance in cash or kind

4.12 The services provided by the local authority to children in need may be in kind or, in exceptional circumstances, in cash.[69] If assistance is provided in this way it may be unconditional or subject to repayment, in whole or in part, either of the cash sum or of the value of the benefit in kind. No repayment can be required of anyone receiving income support, working families' tax credit, child tax credit (subject to some exceptions), income based jobseeker's allowance or employment and support allowance, and any requirement to repay can be made only after full consideration of the means of the child and his/her parent(s).

66 *Guidance vol 2,* ch l. para 121. There is no specific coverage of this in the LAC Guidance.

67 See *F v Wirral Metropolitan Borough Council* [1991] Fam 69.

68 1995 Act, s 61(5).

69 1995 Act, s 22(3)(b).

CHILDREN 'LOOKED AFTER' BY THE LOCAL AUTHORITY

(1) Who is looked after?[70]

4.13 Children defined as being looked after by the local authority are:

(a) children being provided with accommodation under section 25 of the 1995 Act;
(b) children subject to a supervision requirement made by a children's hearing, even if they are staying at home;
(c) children subject to a variety of authorisations or warrants issued under the 1995 Act, for example, a child protection order, a child assessment order, a warrant for apprehension and/or detention issued by a hearing or sheriff court, or a parental responsibilities order. These children are looked after only if the order or warrant imposes responsibilities on the local authority. The local authority will have responsibilities in virtually every case where such a warrant or order is made. One exception might be where a child protection order is made in favour of someone who is not an employee of the local authority;
(d) children sentenced to detention by the sheriff summary court;[71]
(e) children in respect of whom a permanence order has been made; or
(f) children subject to an order made elsewhere in the UK under which the local authority has responsibility for her/him, eg a care order made in England or Wales.

Although these children are all being looked after by the local authority it is important to remember that, with the exception of those children in respect of whom a parental responsibilities order[72] or a permanence order extinguishing parental responsibility and rights has been made, the child's parent(s) retain parental responsibilities and rights in respect of the child. In some cases, of course, these rights will be limited, as where the sheriff, in making a child protection order, or a children's hearing, in making a supervision requirement, regulate contact between the child and his/her parent(s), or, by definition, in cases where a permanence order has been made, though the extent to which parental respon-

70 1995 Act, s 17(6).
71 Criminal Procedure (Scotland) Act 1995, s 44(3).
72 Such orders can no longer be made and any orders in existence in September 2009 are now deemed to be permanence orders, see para 4.41 below.

sibilities and rights have been lost by the parents will depend on the precise terms of the order.

(2) Statutory duties[73]

4.14 In terms of the 1995 Act the local authority has a number of duties towards children who are being looked after. These duties are supplemented by further obligations contained in regulations which are further explained in guidance. The regulations and guidance will be dealt with below. The duties directly imposed by the 1995 Act are:

(a) To safeguard and promote the welfare of the child. This is to be the paramount concern of the local authority and includes the duty to provide advice and assistance to prepare the child for when he/she is no longer looked after by the local authority.
(b) To make use of such services for children being looked after by their parents as appear to be reasonable.
(c) To take steps to promote regular contact and personal relations between the child and anyone having parental responsibilities in respect of the child. These steps must only be taken so far as the authority considers them to be practicable and appropriate in light of its paramount duty. A duty to take active steps to promote contact and to avoid arrangements which inhibit or prevent contact arises also under Article 8 of the European Convention on Human Rights.[74] This duty, like that under the 1995 Act, may be limited by the need to consider and protect the child's interests.[75]
(d) To seek the views of the child, his/her parents, any non-parent holding parental rights and anyone else considered to be relevant (eg a sibling) before taking any decision with respect to a child that the authority is looking after or proposing to look after. The authority must obtain these views only as far as is reasonably practicable.
(e) To take the views of the child into account before making a decision.
(f) To take the views of those others identified in (d) above into account as far as it has been possible to obtain them.
(g) To take the child's religious persuasion, racial origin, culture and language into account before taking a decision.

73 1995 Act, s 17.
74 See, for example, *Olsson v Sweden (No 2)* (1994) 17 EHRR 134.
75 *Covezzi & Morselli v Italy* (2004) EHRR 28.

Authorities may act inconsistently with these duties only where they consider that this is necessary to protect members of the public from serious harm.

(3) Regulations and guidance: assessment and care plans

4.15 A local authority must obtain certain information about and then carry out an assessment of any child who is about to be or who becomes looked after.[76] The assessment is then to be used as the basis for preparing a care plan (the 'child's plan') for the child.[77] The objective of the assessment is to identify the needs of, and any problems facing, the child and his/her family, to identify how these might be addressed and to identify any strengths within the family which can be built on.[78]

In preparing the plan the local authority must, as far as reasonably practicable, obtain certain information set out in the box below.[79] This is the minimum information which is required, additional information needed will depend on the circumstances of the child and his/her family. In addition the authority must obtain a written assessment of the child's health and of her/his need for healthcare.

Information to be obtained by the local authority in respect of a child to be or being looked after by them

1. Name, sex, date and place of birth and present address of the child, their parents and any relevant person.
2. Nationality, race, religion and language.
3. Physical description.
4. Present legal status of the child, including any statutory responsibility the local authority has for the child.
5. Why consideration is to be given to the child being looked after by the local authority.
6. Previous history of involvement of the child with any local authority or other relevant organisation.

76 LAC Regs, regs 3 & 4.
77 LAC Regs, reg 5.
78 LAC Guidance, p 21.
79 LAC Regs, Sch 1.

7	Details of any brothers and sisters, including their dates of birth, addresses and any details in respect of their being looked after by a local authority.
8	The extent of contact with members of the child's family and any other significant person who does not live in the same household as the child.
9	The child's health history, current state of health and development and existing arrangements for their medical and dental care.
10	The child's education history and current arrangements for provision of education.
11	Personality and social development.
12	Interests and recreational activities.

After the information has been obtained the local authority must carry out an assessment of the child. What the assessment is to cover for all children is set out in the box below.[80] In making the assessment the local authority must seek and take account of the views of:

(a) the child;
(b) the child's parents;
(c) anyone else with parental responsibilities/rights in relation to the child; and
(d) anyone else the local authority considers to be appropriate.

The guidance stresses the need for the active involvement of the child. his/her parents and any other carer in the process of assessment.[81]

Where the child is to be placed away from home a number of additional matters must form part of the assessment:

(a) there must be an assessment of contact arrangements with the child's family and others and whether changes need to be made to them;
(b) where the placement will be in a residential establishment there must be an assessment whether that placement is appropriate;
(c) where more than one child is to be looked after, the assessment must take into account the need to ensure, where this is practicable and appropriate, that they are placed together or, at least, close together.

80 LAC Regs, reg 4.
81 LAC Guidance, p 22. This involvement is also required by Article 8 of the European Convention on Human Rights, see, eg *W v United Kingdom* (1987) 10 EHRR 29.

As the matter which must be considered indicate, the assessment will look both at the immediate needs of the child (which will be the initial focus of the assessment) and his/her longer term needs. As regards the latter, the guidance indicates that:[82]

> From the outset in every case, there should be active consideration of the purpose of a child becoming looked after and of the possible outcomes. In its broadest interpretation, 'permanence planning', should cover all options, with the aim of a stable living situation for a child and one which meets his or her needs for consistent, sustainable positive relationships, normally within a family setting.[83]

The assessment should be recorded in writing and discussed with the child, parents and any carer.[84]

Matters to be covered in assessment of child

(a) the child's immediate needs and how those needs can be met;
(b) the child's long term needs and how those needs can be met;
(c) proposals for safeguarding and promoting the child's welfare;
(d) proposals for making sustainable and long term arrangements for the care of the child;
(e) the nature of the services proposed for the child in the immediate and long term with particular regard to the information specified in Schedule 1[85];
(f) alternative courses of action including the possibility of making an arrangement in accordance with regulation 8 or approving a person as a kinship carer;
(g) whether the local authority should seek a change in the child's legal status;
(h) the arrangements which require to be made for the time when the child will no longer be looked after by the local authority;
(i) the existing health arrangements for the child and whether there is a need to change such arrangements taking into account the information specified in paragraph 9 of Schedule 1;

82 LAC Guidance, p 24.
83 The LAC Guidance also suggests that the local authorities adoption panel may have a role in giving advice on plans for permanence for looked after children not involving adoption, LAC Guidance, p 155.
84 LAC Guidance, p 25.
85 This is the informaion set out in the list above.

(j) having regard to the information specified in paragraph 10 of Schedule 1, the child's educational needs, the proposals for meeting those needs, and the proposals for achieving continuity in the child's education;
(k) the child's religious persuasion and the need for the child to continue to be brought up in accordance with their religious persuasion; and
(l) any other matter relating to the welfare of the child either in the immediate or long term as appears to the local authority to be relevant.

After completing the assessment the local authority then has to produce a child's plan for the child.[86] In preparing this plan it must consult, so far as reasonably practicable and consistent with the interests of the child with:

(a) the child, taking account of his age and maturity;
(b) the child's parents;
(c) anyone with (or who has had, to the knowledge of the authority) parental responsibilities or rights in respect of the child;
(d) anyone who has, or who the authority is aware has had, charge of or control over the child; and
(e) anyone else the authority considers appropriate.

The plan as finally formulated must include the matters required by the LAC Regulations and set out in the box below:

Contents of the child's plan

The child's plan must include:

(a) The assessments and the findings flowing from this;
(b) Arrangements concerning the matters specified in Part I of Schedule 2 of the LAC Regulations, ie:
    (i) The local authority's immediate and longer-term plans for the child.

86 Used with a specific meaning distinct from the more general child's plan under GIRFEC (see LAC Guidance, p 26). References to a child's plan in the context of looked after children are to this plan.

- (ii) Details of any services to be provided to meet the care, education and health needs of the child.
- (iii) The respective responsibilities of:
  - (A) the local authority;
  - (B) the child;
  - (C) any person with parental responsibilities for the child;
  - (D) any foster carer or kinship carer of the child;
  - (E) the designated manager of that establishment who is responsible for the care of the child whilst in that establishment where the child has been placed in a residential establishment; and
  - (F) any other relevant person.

(c) In each case where the local authority are considering placing or have placed the child with a kinship carer, with a foster carer or in a residential establishment arrangements concerning the matters specified in Part II of Schedule 2 of the LAC Regulations, ie:

- (i) The type of accommodation to be provided and its address together with the name of any person who will be responsible for the child at that accommodation on behalf of the local authority.
- (ii) The contribution the child's parents or any other person will make to the child's day to day care.
- (iii) The arrangements for involving those persons and the child in decision making.
- (iv) The arrangements for contact between the child and any of the categories of persons mentioned in section 17(3)(b) to (d) of the 1995 Act and, if appropriate, the reasons why contact with such a person would not be reasonably practicable or would be inconsistent with the child's welfare.
- (v) The expected duration of arrangements and the steps which should be taken in bringing the arrangements to an end including arrangements for the return of the child to their parents or other suitable person.

(d) The nature of services proposed for any person to ensure the arrangements concerning the matters specified in Part I or II of Schedule 2 are met;

(e) The health assessment referred of the child referred to above.

Once the plan is agreed a copy must be provided to the child if, having regard to his age and maturity, the authority considers that he is capable of understanding the meaning and effect of the plan. A copy must normally also be provided to the child's parent and to any person with parental responsibilities or rights in respect of the child, though this will not apply if the authority is of the view that, taking into account its duties towards looked after children and the terms of any order warrant or authorisation affecting the child, it would not be in the child's best interests for a copy of the child's plan to be given to someone in one of these classes. In practice the plan should, as far as possible be agreed with the child and his/her parent(s) and this should be confirmed by signature of the plan. Where there are disagreements about the plan these should be recorded in writing.[87]

The plan should set out clearly what needs to be done in order to meet the objectives set out in the plan.[88] This covers actions by the local authority and other agencies and actions by the child and his/her family or carer. It should also set out how long it is expected that the child will be looked after. The plan will need to be regularly monitored and reviewed.

(4) Health care

4.16 As we have seen, the local authority must obtain an assessment of the health of a looked after child and of the child's need for healthcare. Following from this the child's plan must set out any services required to meet the child's health needs, which will include ensuring adequate health care for the child. When the child stays at home the parents will retain parental responsibilities and rights which give them control over medical care of a young child, unless, of course, there is a supervision requirement or other order requiring medical assessment or treatment. As children get older they acquire the ability to consent to treatment themselves, and the authority will have to work with these children.

Where the child is placed away from home the local authority should act as a good parent would in relation to the health of children placed away from home. This does not confer on the authority any powers of consent. Instead, it is suggested that the authority should obtain the consent of the parents to allow it to seek and obtain any immunisations and treatment recommended for the child, in the form of a general medical consent form.[89] If consent is withheld or no agreement is reached, the

87 *LAC Guidance*, p 28.
88 *LAC Guidance*, p 29.
89 *LAC Guidance*, p 33.

authority does not have the power to authorise treatment, though it may be possible to seek a child protection or child assessment order, to refer the case to the reporter or to get a doctor or other medical professional to apply to court for an order relating to parental rights to allow the treatment to be given[90] (since local authorities will no longer be able to apply for such orders). In cases where no agreement is reached (but not in cases where there is opposition to the treatment) the provisions of section 5 of the 1995 Act may be useful. This allows someone who has care or control of a child to consent to medical treatment in fulfilment of the obligation to do what is reasonable to safeguard the child's health, development and welfare, which would seem to include local authority workers who have care or control of children as part of their job, as well as foster carers (see the discussion above). This consent can be given only if the child is unable to consent and if the person consenting is ignorant of the fact that the child's parents would refuse consent.[91]

(5) Education

4.17 The guidance on looked after children explains that:[92]

> Children who are looked after should have the same opportunities as all other children for education, including further and higher education, and access to other opportunities for development. They should also receive additional help, encouragement and support to address special educational needs or compensate for previous disadvantage and gaps in educational provision.

The reference to additional support is apposite as local authorities have a duty to provide additional support for children who have additional support needs. A child will have such additional support needs where:

> for whatever reason, the child or young person is, or is likely to be, unable without the provision of additional support to benefit from school education provided or to be provided for the child or young person.[93]

Looked after children are considered to have such additional support needs simply because they are looked after, at least until it is established

90 1995 Act, s 11.

91 See the *LAC Guidance*, suggesting, at p 33, that foster carers should be discouraged from consenting to major treatment where this is not urgent.

92 *LAC Guidance*, p34.

93 Education (Additional Support for learning (Scotland) Act 2004, s 1(1), Scottish Government, *Supporting Children's Learning Code of Practice*, revised edition, 2010.

that they do not.[94] If a child has additional support needs then the local authority has a duty to provide the additional support required to meet the identified needs and keep this provision under review. The support may be provided by the school or the wider education department, but it may also involve services from other parts of the council, or from further afield, for example from another local authority where it provides a specific type of educational provision required by a child. In addition, the authority has an obligation to carry out an assessment of a child if requested to do so by a child's parent or by a young person (or, if the young person lacks capacity, by his/her parent), and must also have its own arrangements for identifying children with additional support needs and the specific needs of any child so identified.

In many cases the additional support needs will be dealt with through the preparation of an individual educational plan, but in some cases a co-ordinated support plan will be required. A co-ordinated support plan will be needed where a child has additional support needs:[95]

(a) which arise from one or more complex factors or multiple factors: the former are factors which are likely to have a significant effect on the child's education, the latter will arise where there is more than one factor which contributes to the additional support needs;
(b) which are likely to continue for more than a year; and,
(c) which require significant additional support to be provided both by the education authority and by either another agency or the local authority exercising functions other than education.

In the period leading up to a child with additional support needs leaving school the education authority must seek information from other agencies and, on the basis of that, then pass on information to other agencies as to the date on which the child or young person is expected to cease receiving school education and such other information as the authority considers appropriate about the child or young person and his/her additional support needs.[96]

94 Education (Additional Support for Learning) (Scotland) Act s 1(1A) & (1B); LAC Guidance, p 35; Scottish Government, *Supporting Children's Learning Code of Practice*, revised edition, 2010, pp 19–20.

95 Education (Additional Support for Learning) (Scotland) Act s 2 & 9–11; Scottish Government, *Supporting Children's Learning Code of Practice*, revised edition, 2010, ch 5.

96 Education (Additional Support for Learning) (Scotland) Act ss 12 &13; Scottish Government, *Supporting Children's Learning Code of Practice*, revised edition, 2010, pp 113–120. Where a child is looked after this will overlap with the authority's aftercare duties, see paras 4.42 to 4.45 below.

(6) Respite care

4.18 Children who are provided with short periods of care away from home in order to provide respite for their families will qualify as looked after children as they are being provided with accommodation under section 25 of the 1995 Act during these short periods of respite care. Periods of respite can occur relatively frequently and it would clearly be problematic if each short period of respite was treated as being a new episode of the child coming to be looked after and therefore setting in motion the processes described above. Because of this, a series of planned short-term placements will be treated as a single placement and the regulations will apply as if what was involved was a single placement. There are certain restrictions on this: the individual placements must not be for longer than four weeks and the total duration of the series of placements must not exceed one hundred and twenty days in the course of one year.[97]

There is one modification of the regulations as they apply to such deemed single placements. The first review is to take place within three months of the date of the first placement and reviews should thereafter take place at least every six months.[98]

(7) Contact with the child's family[99]

4.19 In the case of children placed away from home, the local authority must bear in mind its obligation to 'promote, on a regular basis, personal relations and direct contact' between the child and his/her family.[100] This obligation is limited by the requirement that the contact is practicable and appropriate, as well as by the need to safeguard the welfare of the child. Reasons for any restriction on contact should be clearly recorded. Contact may, of course, be restricted under the terms of any court order or supervision requirement in terms of which the child is being looked after, and the arrangements made by the social work department must comply with the terms of the order or requirement. The child's wishes in respect of contact must also be taken into account. Where the child has siblings who are placed in a different set-

97 LAC Regs, regs14 & 30.
98 LAC Regs, reg 45(3)(a).
99 See *LAC Guidance*, pp 38–43.
100 1995 Act, s 17(1)(c), such an obligation is also implied by Article 8 of the European Convention on Human Rights, requiring active steps to be taken to maintain contact unless this is against the interests of the child.

ting from the child consideration will need to be given to ensuring contact between the siblings.

Most children looked after by the local authority and placed away from home will be returning to their parent(s) and families to live and so the requirement to encourage and facilitate meaningful contact arrangements works to provide a sound basis for the preparation for a return home.

(8) Records

4.20 Records must be kept in relation to any looked after child.[101] This record should include any child's plan, any reports about the welfare of the child, any documentation associated with review of a child's case and details of any placements.[102] The guidance indicates the importance of these records for children later on in life when they may wish to exercise their right to access these records.[103] It suggests that it is important that records include:

- a chronology of significant events in the child's life to which all relevant services contribute;
- consistent recording of all staff contacts with children and families, including details of when the child has been seen;
- decisions taken and reasons for these;
- a distinction made between facts and opinions;
- outcomes of interventions; and
- details of the child's views.

Where the child has been placed in accommodation by the local authority the records are to be kept for 100 years from the birth of the child, or if the child dies before his/her 18th birthday, for 25 years from the date of death.[104] There is no duration set out for looked after children who have not been placed by the local authority, eg those looked after because on home supervision, but the guidance suggests that it would be good practice to retain such records for at least 30 years following the child's 18th birthday.[105]

101 See *LAC Guidance*, pp 126–128.
102 LAC Regs, reg 42.
103 See also the comments in *Gaskin v UK* quoted above at para 2.28.
104 LAC Regs, reg 43.
105 *LAC Guidance*, p 128.

PLACEMENT OF LOOKED AFTER CHILDREN

(1) Introduction

4.21 Looked after children can be accommodated in a variety of settings. In some cases the setting will be regulated by the terms of a supervision requirement made by a children's hearing in respect of the child.[106] Where a placement is made by a children's hearing, that placement will not be subject to the arrangements and regulations discussed here. Otherwise, arrangements will have to be made by a local authority to arrange for the care of children who are looked after and this can be done by arranging foster care, kinship care and residential care. In some cases, authorities will have to find accommodation in an emergency, for example if a child is removed from home on a child protection order. Below we will consider the specific rules applying to each type of care, considering general requirements applying to more than one of them at the end.

One general restriction is that placements are subject to the terms of any supervision requirement made by a children's hearing, any permanence order, or any order, authorisation or warrant granted under Part II, Chapters 2, 3 and 4 of the Children Scotland Act 1995. The main warrants, orders and authorisations that this covers are warrants issued by a children's hearing to obtain the attendance of a child, child protection authorisations and orders, child assessment orders, warrants to keep a child when a hearing is unable to determine his/her case, and exclusion orders. In addition, the authority may not return the child to anyone from whose care he or she was removed by virtue of any order, authorisation or warrant.

Where siblings are to be looked after, they should be placed together if this is appropriate and practical, or in placements as near to each other as is appropriate and practicable.[107] This recognizes that it will not always be in the interests of a child to be placed with his or her siblings.

(2) Care by parents

4.22 A looked after child can be cared for by her or his parents or by someone having parental rights *and* responsibilities in relation to him[108] unless he or she is being provided with accommodation under section

106 See para 5.16.
107 LAC Regs, reg 4(5); *LAC Guidance*, p 43.
108 LAC Regs, reg 8(1).

25 of the 1995 Act, at least as long as the conditions giving rise to the local authority duty to accommodate continue to exist.[109] Children who are looked after because they are subject to a supervision requirement which involves them living at home form the largest group of looked after children who are cared for by their parents.[110]

(3) Kinship care

4.23 Kinship care provides a means for a looked after child to be cared for by someone the child knows or by a member of his/her family. The LAC Regulations only apply where children who are looked after by the local authority are provided with kinship care. They do not apply to informal arrangements made by the child's parent(s), though such arrangements may be subject to regulation as private fostering.[111] Two classes of person can be approved as kinship carers in respect of a child: someone who is related to the child by blood, marriage or civil partnership or someone who is known to the child and with whom the child has a pre-existing relationship.[112]

In order to approve such an individual as a kinship carer the local authority must first, as far as reasonably practicable, obtain specified information about him/her, including full personal details, details of those in his/her household, his/her religious persuasion and ability to care for a child of any particular religious persuasion, racial origin or cultural or linguistic background, his/her capacity to care for his/her own other children, his/her motivation and references.[113] On the basis of this information the local authority then has to carry out an assessment of the suitability of the individual to care for a child and decide whether to approve him as a kinship carer.[114] There is no formal process for approving kinship carers set out in the LAC Regulations, though the guidance suggests that local authorities[115] should consider using a process similar to that involved in approval of foster carers. Approval will be as a kinship carer for a specific child.

109 LAC Regs, reg 8(2).
110 See *LAC Guidance*, pp 50–56.
111 See para 4.34 below.
112 LAC Regs, reg 10(1) & (2).
113 LAC Regs, reg 10(3)(b). The *LAC Guidance* suggests that these referees should be visited, p 65.
114 LAC Regs, reg 10(3)(b).
115 Or registered fostering services.

Before making a placement with an approved kinship carer the local authority must be satisfied that:[116]

(a) the placement is in the best interests of the child;
(b) the placement of the child with the particular kinship carer is in the best interests of the child:
(c) the kinship carer is a suitable person[117] to care for the child, based on the local authority's assessment of him;
(d) the local authority has taken into account all the information available to it which is relevant to performing its duties towards looked after children;
(e) the kinship carer has entered into a kinship carer agreement with the local authority regulating his relationship with the authority; and
(f) the kinship carer has entered into a kinship placement agreement with the local authority, setting out the responsibilities of the carer and the local authority in respect of the particular placement.

Kinship care is also subject to the regulations as to notification, review, short-term placements, termination and records which are considered below. Kinship carers caring for looked after children should be paid an allowance by the local authority.[118] At least until 2011 this will be on the same basis as payment of allowances to foster carers, though normally excluding any fee element.[119] The kinship carer agreement should set out the support and training which the carer is to be given.

(4) Foster care

4.24 Local authorities can provide a fostering service[120] themselves and/or enter into an arrangement with a registered fostering service to provide these services.[121] In some cases the local authority will place most children with its own service and make occasional use of the registered service.

116 LAC Regs, reg 11(2).
117 See also para 11.5.
118 LAC Regs, reg 33.
119 This is part of the Concordat between the Scottish Government and the Convention of Scottish Local Authorities covering 2008–9 to 2010–11.
120 Which will need to be registered, para 11.3.
121 *LAC Guidance*, pp 142–145.

(a) Fostering panels[122]

4.25 Fostering panels carry out various functions in relation to arrangements for children to be cared for by foster carers. A panel must consist of at least six members, with a quorum for any meeting of at least three. Local authorities (or registered fostering services[123]) must appoint medical advisers to provide advice to the panel and may appoint a legal adviser, though in many cases legal advice will be provided by the legal services department of the authority. The functions of the fostering panel include consideration of the case of every foster carer and proposed foster carer referred to it by the local authority.[124] It must also make recommendations on:

(a) whether a prospective foster carer is, or existing foster carers continue to be, suitable to be foster carers;
(b) the suitability of a prospective foster carer for a particular child, any child, or certain categories of child;
(c) the maximum number of children a particular foster carer may have in his home at any one time.

The panel also has other functions noted in passing below.

(b) Approval and review of foster carers[125]

4.26 There is no longer any legal restriction on who can act as a foster carer. Prospective foster carers will initiate the process of formal approval by completing an application form, though it is likely that there will have been previous contact with the local authority. After the application has been made the local authority must carry out an assessment of the applicant, which must normally be completed within 6 months of the application.[126] On completion of the assessment a report will be prepared containing a recommendation. The report should be shared with the applicants and they should be asked to identify any elements of the report with which they disagree.[127] This report will then go to the fostering panel, and the guidance indicates that the applicants should be

122 LAC Regs, regs 18 to 20; *LAC Guidance*, pp 75–81.
123 In general the regulations discussed in this section apply equally to local authorities and to registered fostering services unless this is made clear in the text.
124 Prospective foster carers must be given the opportunity to meet the panel.
125 *LAC Guidance*, pp 83–105.
126 *LAC Guidance*, p 83; *National Care Standards: Foster Care and Family Placement Services*, standard 6.4.
127 *LAC Guidance*, p 89.

invited to meet the panel.[128] The panel will then make a recommendation to the local authority, though the final decision on the prospective carer is made by the local authority.[129] In making the decision that a prospective foster carer is suitable to be approved as a foster carer the local authority must be satisfied that he has been interviewed by or on behalf of the authority and that he is a suitable person with whom to place a child or children.

Approval may be restricted to a particular child or children, or to certain categories of children (for example those over a certain age), or it may be unrestricted, approving the foster carer for all children.[130] It may also limit the number of children which a foster carer may have in his home at any one time.

Once a foster carer is approved, he or she must enter into a foster carer agreement with the local authority which will cover the support, including financial support, and training to be given by the local authority, complaints procedures, procedures for placement, confidentiality obligations and the foster carer's obligation not to use corporal punishment on any child.[131]

After approval the regulations require that a foster carer's suitability must be reviewed, initially within twelve months of approval and then at least every three years.[132]

Anyone approved as a foster carer can seek a review of the terms of that approval. Review can also be requested of a decision not to approve a person as a foster carer, to vary the terms of an approval after review or to terminate approval after review. Where review of a decision is sought the case must be referred to a fostering panel which is constituted differently from the panel involved in the original decision. Once the review panel has made a recommendation the local authority must take a decision, which should be taken by someone other than the person who took

128 *LAC Guidance*, p 90; there is no statutory requirement for this.

129 LAC Regs, reg 22. The person taking the decision is designated as the Agency Decision Maker, *LAC Guidance*, p 79.

130 LAC Regs, reg 22. The *LAC Guidance* indicates that: 'It is unlikely that foster carers will be given completely open approval for any child for any duration.' (p 80).

131 LAC Regs, reg 24 & Sch 6.

132 LAC Regs, reg 25(1)&(2). More frequent, annual review is required by the *National Care Standards: Foster Care and Family Placement Services*, standard 11.1, providing that: 'each year the agency reviews your performance and the quality of care that you provide and a review meeting is held with your supervising social worker.' The *LAC Guidance* (p 98) indicates the frequency with which Disclosure Scotland (see para 11.5) and health checks should be undertaken.

the decision under review. There is no further review of this decision provided for in the regulations.

A foster carer who has already been approved by one local authority can be approved by another authority without going through the whole approval process.[133] This is described as derivative approval.

(c) Foster care: arranging a placement[134]

4.27 A child can only be placed in foster care with an approved foster carer and proposed placements will be considered by the fostering panel.[135] Before making an individual placement the local authority must be satisfied that:[136]

(a) the placement is in the best interests of the child;
(b) the placement of the child with the particular foster carer is in the best interests of the child:
(c) it has taken into account all the information available to it which is relevant to performing its duties towards looked after children;
(d) it has given full consideration to the possibility of arranging for the child to be cared for by his parents or by a kinship carer
(e) the foster carer has entered into a foster carer agreement with the local authority regulating their relationship with the authority;
(f) the foster carer has entered into a foster placement agreement[137] with the local authority, setting out the responsibilities of the carer and the local authority in respect of the particular placement; and
(g) the terms of the foster carer's approval are consistent with the placement.

Placements with a foster carers it are subject to the provisions about notification, review, short-term placements, termination and records considered below. Foster carers will be paid an allowance by the local authority, and this allowance should ensure that:[138]

133 LAC Regs, reg 23, *LAC Guidance*, pp 91–93.
134 *LAC Guidance*, pp 105–109.
135 The exception is an emergency placement, discussed below.
136 LAC Regs, reg 27(2).
137 LAC Regs, reg 27(2)(g), sch 4. This should set out specific requirements for the child and be discussed with the child and his/her parents as well as the foster carer(s), LAC Guidance, p 107.
138 *LAC Guidance*, p 113, also noting that: 'Foster carers are … charged with providing not just basic care but optimum care for looked after children'.

children are offered high quality physical care and provision, and also that they have the opportunities to fill some of the gaps in experience that are often found in looked after children

The level of the allowance will be set by the local authority.[139] Local authorities may also pay a fee to foster carers over and above any allowances.[140]

(e) Residential care

4.28 A looked after child may be placed in residential care. Such placements are partly regulated by the LAC Regulations, but also by separate regulations, which impose specific duties as regards some aspects of residential care.[141] The managers of the residential establishment must ensure that the child:

(a) receives an efficient and adequate education;
(b) is, as far as possible, able to attend such religious services and religious instruction as might be appropriate;
(c) is able to maintain hygiene; and
(d) receives medical treatment is available.

(f) Emergency placements not involving a residential establishment[142]

4.29 It is preferable for placements to be planned, but this is not always possible and the local authority will sometimes have to find accommodation for a child in an emergency.[143]

An emergency placement can be made initially for up to three working days.[144] This can be with an approved foster carer, someone who is approved as a kinship carer in relation to the child, or any person who is known to and who has a pre-existing relationship with the child. Before making the placement, the authority must be satisfied that it is

139 The fostering network recommends minimum levels of allowance, www.fostering.net.
140 *LAC Guidance*, p 114.
141 Residential Establishments – Child Care (Scotland) Regulations 1996, SI 1996/3256; Secure Accommodation (Scotland) Regulations 1996, SI 1996/3255.
142 LAC Guidance, pp 116–125.
143 Though the *LAC Guidance* also suggests that where a family's situation is deteriorating efforts should be made to identify people who could assist in an emergency, p 116.
144 LAC Regs, reg 36(1).

the most suitable way of meeting the child's needs. The carer must agree to comply with certain duties, including a duty to care for the child as if she or he were a member of the carer's own family and in a safe and appropriate manner, to allow visiting by the local authority or someone authorised by the authority, to allow the child to be removed if the placement is terminated, to keep information obtained in their role as a carer confidential, and to allow contact with the child's family. The carer must be provided with information about the child's background and health and emotional development. Where the placement is not with someone who is an approved carer the local authority must carry out certain other tasks, including visiting the address at which the child will stay.[145]

A review of the child's case must be held within three working days of the placement to determine if the placement is still in the best interests of the child.[146] After the review the local authority may conclude that the placement is no longer in the interests of the child, in which case alternative arrangements will need to be made, or it might be the case that the emergency has passed. On the other hand, if the placement continues to be in the best interests of the child the local authority can allow the placement to continue for a further period of up to twelve weeks from the end of the original three day period, with a further review within six weeks of that date. If it does this it must then, unless this has already been done, carry out a full assessment and prepare a child's plan for the child.

An emergency placement cannot be continued beyond this twelve-week period unless it becomes, effectively, either a kinship care placement or a foster care placement, having followed the procedures which require to be followed for such placements. Where the original placement is with someone known to the child and who has a pre-existing relationship with him but who is not an approved carer, the placement can only continue if that person is approved as a kinship carer for the child and the procedure involved in making arrangements for kinship care is carried out.

(g) Emergency placements in residential establishments[147]

4.30 Before placing a child in a residential establishment the local authority must be satisfied that this is the most suitable way of meeting

145 *LAC Guidance*, p 119.
146 See *LAC Guidance*, pp 121–122.
147 LAC Regs, regs 37 & 41; *LAC Guidance*, pp 116–125.

the child's needs, and it must have given full consideration to the possibility of other forms of emergency placement.

The initial emergency placement will be for up to three days. Within that period the placement must be reviewed. The child can continue in the placement if the review concludes that it continues to be in the child's best interests. If the placement continues, the local authority must, if this has not already been done, carry out a full assessment of the child and prepare a child's plan for him/her, supply the information to the managers of the residential establishment which is required for such placements and enter into the required agreements and make any necessary notifications.

(h) Common provisions: notification

4.31 Once an arrangement has been made for a child to be cared for in foster care, kinship care, a residential establishment or by way of an emergency placement which has been extended, the local authority is responsible for making a number of notifications as soon as this is reasonably practicable. These notifications must be in writing and give particulars of the placement:[148]

(a) In cases where the child is placed in the area of another local authority that other authority must be notified.
(b) The health board for the area where the child is placed must be notified.
(c) Any person having any parental rights or responsibilities in relation to the child must be notified. For all placements aside from placement in kinship care the child's parents must also be notified. These notification requirements are subject to three exceptions:
    (i) where the person to be notified has already received a written copy of the child's plan, though this exception does not apply to notifications of extended emergency placements not involving a residential establishment;
    (ii) no notice is to be given where the authority considers, in light of its overall duties to looked after children, that it would not be in the best interests of the child for notification to be made;
    (iii) where the child is subject to a permanence order, a supervision requirement or another warrant or order which specifies

148 LAC Regs 13, 29, 34, 40 & 41(4).

that the whereabouts of the child should not be disclosed to a particular person.

(i) Common provisions: visits and reviews[149]

4.32 Local authorities have a duty to carry out visits to children for whom *they* have arranged care,[150] subject to the following exceptions:

(a) looked after children cared for by their parents or someone with parental responsibilities and rights;
(b) where children have been placed in foster care on behalf of the local authority by a registered fostering service;
(c) in the first three days of an emergency visit.

The first visit should take place within one week of the placement being made and is a visit to the child and his carer. Further visits must take place at least every three months, and additional visits are to be made where requested by the child or carer, at any other times where the authority considers that a visit is necessary and appropriate to safeguard and promote the welfare of the child and on any occasion where the local authority considers it necessary to give support and assistance to a foster carer or kinship carer for the purpose of safeguarding and promoting the welfare of the child. Written reports of these visits must be produced and must be considered at any review.

Regular reviews of all looked after children must take place. The focus of these reviews[151] is the same regardless of the nature of the child's placement, though there are differences in the frequency of reviews. As part of the review process the views of the child, his carers, and anyone with parental responsibilities or rights in relation to the child need to be sought and taken account of. The child's needs, both in the short and in the long term need to be assessed as does how these are being met. The assessment will also have to consider whether the child's welfare is being safeguarded and promoted, the child's development, whether current accommodation is suitable for the child and, finally, the child's educational needs and whether these are being met. Reports of placement visits must also be considered as part of the review. Reviews should be chaired by someone without direct day-to-day responsibility for the case.[152]

149 LAC Regs, regs 44 to 46.
150 Ie these duties do not extend to cases where a placement has been made by a children's hearing, see *LAC Guidance*, pp 137–139.
151 *LAC Guidance*, pp 133–134.
152 *LAC Guidance*, p 134.

If a child is being cared for by his/her parent(s) of a child or by someone who has parental rights and responsibilities the frequency of review is to be agreed with the carer. If agreement cannot be reached then an initial review must take place within six weeks of the placement being made with further reviews every twelve months, though the guidance indicates that in practice the agreed reviews should be more frequent than this, at least in the initial stages.[153]

Where a placement is with a foster or kinship carer or in a residential establishment the normal position is that the first review will take place within six weeks of the start of the placement with a further review within three months of that review and further reviews every six months. Different time limits apply where the placement is not continuous, but involves a number of short placements, typically cases involving respite care. The first review in such cases must take place within three months of the start of the placement, with subsequent reviews every six months. In cases where an emergency placement has been extended the first review under the general provisions for review must take place within three months of the start of the placement, with subsequent reviews every six months.

The time limits set out for reviews are maxima, in practice reviews may be, and may need to be, to be more frequent than this.[154] After a child has been placed away from home by the local authority and has not returned home after six months then any review after this 'should consider whether a plan for permanency away from birth parents is required.'[155]

In addition to these scheduled reviews, further reviews must be carried out before a decision by the local authority to refer the case of a child to the Principal Reporter, before the local authority applies for a permanence order in respect of the child and, if practicable in the circumstances, when a children's hearing is convened to consider the case of a looked after child.

(5) Records

4.33 Records of approved kinship carers and foster carers with whom a child has been placed as well as for perspective kinship and

153 *LAC Guidance*, p 130.
154 *LAC Guidance*, p 122.
155 *LAC Guidance*, p 135, see also pp 135–137.

foster carers.[156] Case records should be retained until the death of the carer or if later a period of 25 years. In the case of kinship carers this will date from the date when the placement was terminated[157] and for foster carers or prospective foster carers the date on which their approval was terminated.[158] The regulations make no provision as to how long the records of prospective kinship carers should be retained, though the guidance suggests that they are treated in the same way as prospective foster carers.[159]

PRIVATE FOSTERING

4.34 It is possible for fostering to be arranged privately and for situations which are legally defined as private fostering to arise without any necessary intention on the part of those involved.

Private fostering is regulated by the Foster Children (Scotland) Act 1984 and by the Foster Children (Private Fostering) (Scotland) Regulations 1985.[160] These will apply in general to any situation where a child under the age of 16 is placed by her/his parents for a period which is intended to or does exceed 27 days 'with someone who is neither a guardian appointed to the child (eg in a parent's will) or who is not a relative of the child'.[161] In this context, relative means a grandparent, brother, sister, uncle or aunt and covers relatives both of the full and of the half blood.

Where it is intended to place a child in private fostering, at least 2 weeks' notice must be given to the local authority, unless in an emergency, where notification must be made with one week of the placement. On receipt of the notification the local authority must carry out certain investigations:

(a) obtaining a statement as to the child's health and that of the foster carer;

156 LAC Regs, regs 15 & 31; *LAC Guidance*, pp 71–72 & 110–112. This notes that although there is no mention of foster carers who have not had a child placed with them, it is good practice to treat them in the same way as carers who have had a child placed with them, p110.
157 LAC Regs, reg 16.
158 LAC Regs, reg 32.
159 *LAC Guidance*, p 72.
160 SI 1985/1798.
161 There are some exceptions to this covering, for example, children at boarding school, children in hospital, children placed for adoption, placements by a children's hearing and compulsory detention under the Mental Health (Care and Treatment)(Scotland) Act 2003.

(b) to find out as far as possible, bearing in mind the age and understanding of the child, his/her wishes and feelings in relation to the proposed placement;
(c) to interview the proposed foster parents and satisfy itself as to the suitability of the foster home.

The purpose of these is to allow the authority to satisfy itself that the placement will not be detrimental to the child's welfare and to decide whether the placement is appropriate to the child's needs.

The decision as to whether the placement is appropriate must be communicated to those involved, and the authority may seek to have changes made, or impose conditions on the foster carer, to make the placement more appropriate or better able to promote the welfare of the child. If necessary the authority can prohibit the placement if it considers that it would be detrimental to the child.

Certain types of person cannot act as foster parents.[162] These include: people convicted of Schedule 1 offences;[163] anyone who has previously had a foster child removed from his/her care; anyone who has had a child removed from his/her care under a supervision requirement; and anyone whose parental responsibilities and rights have been transferred to the local authority by a parental responsibilities order.

Once a placement has been made the authority must visit the child within 7 days, then every 3 months for the first year and subsequently every 6 months. Other visits may be made as the authority thinks necessary. If, as a result of these visits, the authority considers that the placement is no longer in the child's interests it must notify the foster parents of this.

The local authority can apply to the sheriff court, or where the child is in imminent danger to a justice of the peace, for an order removing the child to a place of safety if the child is kept, or is about to be kept, by any person who is unfit to have his/her care, by anyone who falls into one of the categories prohibited from being a foster parent, or in any premises or environment likely to be detrimental to the child.

If a foster carer refuses to allow a visit either to the child or to inspect the premises, this is to be regarded as establishing that there is reasonable cause to suspect that the child is being so treated or neglected that he/she is suffering or is likely to suffer significant harm for the purpose of an application for a child assessment order. The place of safety order

162 Foster Children (Scotland) Act 1984, s 7.
163 Ie Schedule 1 to the Children and Young Persons Act 1933 and Schedule 1 to the Criminal Procedure (Scotland) Act 1995.

will apply until other arrangements can be made for the child, and any child removed from private fostering is to be treated as requiring accommodation under section 25 of the 1995 Act.

Officially at least there are very few private fostering arrangements in Scotland, only 16 reported in 2008–9. The Care Commission considers that this is an underestimate, and that applying equivalent rates to those reported in England and Wales would suggest that there may be between 460 and 600 such placements.[164]

SECURE ACCOMMODATION

(1) Introduction

4.35 Children may be placed in secure accommodation provided by a local authority in a variety of ways. The placement may be a condition of a supervision requirement made by a children's hearing; it may be a condition of a warrant or order to take or keep a child in a place of safety made by a hearing or a court;[165] a child being looked after by the local authority may be placed in secure accommodation; or a child detained under an order made by a criminal court may be placed in secure accommodation.

Regardless of the method of placement the manager of the secure accommodation must promote and safeguard the welfare of the child and make sure that the child is provided with whatever education, provision for his/her development and control as is conducive to his/her interests.[166] The period for which a child is kept in secure accommodation must not exceed a total of 72 hours in any 28-day period unless the secure placement has been authorised by a court or a hearing.[167] The European Convention on Human Rights indicates that a child is to be deprived of his/her liberty only in two cases.[168] The first of these is for the purpose of bringing him before the competent legal authority, the second is for the purposes of educational supervision. Secure accommodation as described here is likely to be covered by one or other of these, in relation to the latter it has been said that:[169]

164 Scottish Commission for the Regulation of Care, *Private Fostering: the unknown arrangement* (2010).
165 1995 Act, ss 66(6), 67(3), 68(11), 69(11).
166 Secure Accommodation (Scotland) Regulations 1996, SI 1996/3255, reg 4.
167 Ibid, reg 5.
168 Art 5(1)(d).
169 *Koniarska v United Kingdom*, Application no. 33670/96, 12 October 2000.

The Court considers that, in the context of the detention of minors, the words 'educational supervision' must not be equated rigidly with notions of classroom teaching. In particular, in the present context of a young person in local authority care, educational supervision must embrace many aspects of the exercise, by the local authority, of parental rights for the benefit and protection of the person concerned.

(2) Rules applying to all placements

4.36 Certain rules apply to all placements in secure accommodation which are made by the local authority. The chief social work officer of the local authority and the person in charge of the secure accommodation must be satisfied that **either**:

(a) the child has previously absconded and is likely to abscond unless kept in secure accommodation and if the child absconds his/her mental, physical or moral welfare will' be at risk. Examples of this would be a child subject to a supervision order requiring that the child stays in a residential establishment who absconds, or a child being provided with accommodation by the local authority through a foster placement who continually runs away; **or**
(b) the child is likely to injure him/herself or someone else unless kept in secure accommodation.

The chief social work officer for the authority must also be satisfied that the placement is in the best interests of the child.[170]

(3) Children subject to supervision requirements[171]

4.37 Children who are subject to a supervision requirement which does not contain a condition requiring residence in secure accommodation may still be placed in such accommodation. If this is done the relevant person and the reporter must be told about it 'forthwith', and the child must also be told in a way which is appropriate to his/her age and understanding. Within 24 hours, regardless of whether the child is still in secure accommodation, a full report must be made to the reporter, and a review hearing to consider the supervision requirement must be held within 72 hours of the original placement in secure accommodation.

170 Ibid, regs 6(1), 7(1) and 9(l)(b); 1995 Act, s 70(10).
171 SI 1996/3255, reg 6.

(4) Children being looked after[172]

4.38 Children who are being looked after by being provided with accommodation by the local authority or because a parental responsibilities order or permanence order has been made in respect of them may be placed in secure accommodation. This can only happen if, in addition to the general requirements outlined above, the chief social work officer and the person in charge of the secure accommodation are both satisfied that the child is in need of compulsory measures of supervision. Once the child has been put in secure accommodation the relevant person and the reporter must be informed 'forthwith', and within 24 hours a full report must be made to the reporter.

The reporter then has to decide what to do, and the decision must be taken within 72 hours of placement in secure accommodation. There are two possible decisions. It might be decided that no hearing is necessary, in which case the child would have to be released from secure accommodation. As a complement to this decision the reporter can refer the child's case to the local authority for advice, guidance and assistance provided by virtue of the local authority's duties to children and families, The second option is to refer the case of the child to a hearing, which is possible only if the reporter thinks the child is in need of compulsory measures of supervision. The hearing must take place within 72 hours, though an extra 24 hours is allowed if the hearing cannot take place or the reporter cannot state the grounds for referral within 72 hours.

(5) Children in a place of safety

4.39 Children may be taken to a place of safety under a warrant or order made by a hearing or a sheriff. Even if the order does not impose a condition requiring placement in secure accommodation such children can still, in general, be placed there. The main exceptions to this are children taken to a place of safety under a child assessment order or a child protection order.

If such a placement is made the relevant person and the reporter must be informed. The procedure then depends on the type of warrant or order to which the child is subject. If the order was issued by a hearing either to secure the attendance of the child at a hearing to consider the child's

172 Ibid, regs 7 and 8.

case or because the child did not turn up to this hearing,[173] a hearing must be arranged, if possible on the next working day.[174] If the warrant was issued by the sheriff to extend a warrant issued by the hearing[175] an application must be made to the sheriff within 72 hours.[176] In all other cases a hearing must be convened within 72 hours of the child being placed in secure accommodation.

(6) Children detained by order made by a criminal court[177]

4.40 The criminal courts (with the exception of the district court) may remand children to residential accommodation provided by the local authority. For example, a child found guilty in the sheriff summary court may be detained in residential accommodation for up to 12 months. Subject to the exceptions considered below, such children may be placed in secure accommodation if the general rules noted above apply. Once a child has been placed in secure accommodation he/she must not be kept there for longer than the person in charge and the chief social work officer consider necessary. In addition, the cases of such children must be reviewed within 7 days of the placement (even if the child is no longer in secure accommodation) and then at least every 3 months or more often if this is necessary in light of the progress made by the child. As part of this review the views of a Secure Placement Review Panel, which must include one person independent of the local authority, must be obtained. The secure placement is to continue after review only if the person in charge and the chief social work officer consider that it is in the best interests of the child. The main exceptions to these requirements are:

(a) children remanded to secure accommodation by the court before trial or sentence.[178] Such children must be kept in secure accommodation;
(b) children sentenced for murder or after conviction on indictment. The conditions for the detention of such children are specified by the Scottish Ministers.[179]

173 1995 Act, s 45(4) or (5).
174 SI 1996/3255, reg 9(2)(a) and 1995 Act, s 45(7).
175 1995 Act, s 67(1).
176 SI 1996/3255, reg 9(2)(e).
177 Ibid, regs 13–15.
178 See s 51(l)(a)(i) of the Criminal Procedure (Scotland) Act 1995.
179 Criminal Procedure (Scotland) Act 1995, ss 205 and 208.

PARENTAL RESPONSIBILITIES ORDERS

4.41 The effect of parental responsibilities orders was to transfer parental responsibilities for a child to the local authority. It is no longer possible to apply for such orders as they have been replaced by permanence orders. Any parental responsibilities orders in existence when the law was changed in September 2009 are effectively deemed to be permanence orders.[180]

AFTER-CARE

(1) Powers and duties

4.42 Local authorities have certain powers and duties to provide assistance to young people who have been looked after by them. In order to qualify, the young person must have been looked after on his/her 16th birthday[181] or later and must no longer be looked after. The duty is to provide guidance and assistance (including financial assistance) to people between the ages of 16 and 19 unless the local authority is satisfied that the guidance or assistance is not needed for the welfare of the person involved.[182]

The powers are:

(a) to provide guidance and assistance (including financial assistance) if asked to do so by someone aged between 19 and 21;[183]

(b) to provide financial support to people aged 16-21 to help with education, training or employment costs or with accommodation/maintenance associated with the education/training/employment. The authority can continue to provide support past the 21st birthday of the person concerned if their education/training continues.[184]

180 The Adoption and Children (Scotland) Act 2007 (Commencement No. 4, Transitional and Savings Provisions) Order 2009, SSI 2009/267, arts 13–15.

181 The statutory formulation is 'at the time he ceased to be of school age.' School age is defined in the Education (Scotland) Act 1980, s 31.

182 1995 Act, s 29(1).

183 1995 Act, s 29(2).

184 1995 Act, s 30.

Regulations impose more specific duties on local authorities towards children and young people who are either about to stop being looked after or have been looked after until fairly recently.[185]

(2) Who is covered?

4.43 The regulations identify four categories of young people:[186]

(a) Currently looked after = those still being looked after who are aged 16 or 17.
(b) Compulsorily supported person = those aged 16–18 who were being looked after when they were of school leaving age. Local authorities have duties towards this group under section 29(1) of the Children (Scotland) Act 1995.
(c) Prospective supported persons = those aged 19 and 20 who were being looked after when they were of school leaving age and who have applied to the local authority to provide them services under the power the local authority has to provide assistance to this group under section 29(2) of the Children (Scotland) Act 1995.
(d) Discretionarily supported person = those aged 19 and 20 who were being looked after when they were of school leaving age and who are receiving services from the local authority under the power the local authority has to provide assistance to this group under section 29(2) of the Children (Scotland) Act 1995.

(3) Pathway assessments

4.44 The pathway assessment has to be carried out in respect of the first 3 groups set out above to assess their need for provision of services. The assessment must include the views of the young person involved (referred to as their pathway views) and should include the following matters:[187]

185 Support and Assistance for Young People Leaving Care (Scotland) Regulations 2003, SSI 2003/608, supported by Scottish Executive, *Supporting Young People Leaving Care in Scotland: Regulations and Guidance on Services for Young People Ceasing to be Looked After by Local Authorities* (2004).
186 Support and Assistance for Young People Leaving Care (Scotland) Regulations 2003, SSI 2003/608, reg 2(1).
187 The Support and Assistance of Young People Leaving Care (Scotland) Regulations 2003.

(a) The young person's emotional state, day to day activities, personal safety, influences on the young person and the young person's personal identity.
(b) The young person's family relationships, their children, other caring responsibilities, life story, friends, and other significant people in their life.
(c) The young person's general health (including any mental health needs), contact with health services, medical conditions and disabilities, activities that might affect the young person's health, and emotional and mental well being.
(d) The young person's future plans for study, training or work, schooling (including support needs), skills and experience, qualifications and certificates, and training and work.
(e) The young person's accommodation arrangements, practical living skills, accommodation options for the future, and support required for living.
(f) The young person's sources of income, outgoings, savings and debts, requirement for financial support, and budgeting skills.
(g) The young person's knowledge of their rights and legal entitlements, involvements in legal proceedings, including criminal proceedings as a victim, witness, or alleged perpetrator.

(4) Pathway plan

4.45 Following the assessment a pathway plan must be completed for compulsorily supported persons and may be produced for currently looked after persons. In addition a plan must be prepared for all discretionarily supported persons.

In the preparation of the plan the authority has to appoint a pathway co-ordinator who will be involved in the preparation of the assessment, the plan, any review of the plan and will also have the responsibility of providing support to the young person and co-ordinating provision of services. The young person may also appoint someone, the young person's supporter, to assist them through this process.

The identity of the pathway co-ordinator, the timetable for the assessment and the list of who are to be consulted all have to be agreed with the young person. All stages of the assessment, obtaining of views and preparation of the plan need to be documented in writing, and the young person has the right to attend at and participate in meetings where the assessment is being considered. Once the plan is complete, the young person has a right of appeal to a nominated local authority officer against decision on the provision or nature of services and support.

The plan must be reviewed at least every six months and a review can be triggered at any time by the young person, the review co-ordinator, or the local authority.

One thing which can be provided under a plan is regular financial assistance. This is relevant because 16 and 17-year olds no longer have an entitlement to social security benefits. The regulations provide that such financial assistance can be provided to 16 and 17-year olds, at a level no less than the social security payments they would previously have been entitled to, subject to two conditions:

(a) They must have been looked after *and* accommodated by the local authority for at least 13 weeks in total after reaching the age of 14. In calculating this period short periods of respite care are to be discounted.
(b) They must not be living at home.

These specific provisions cover regular financial payments, one off payments can also, of course, be made to any of the young people covered by the regulations.

The local authority must also, if necessary, assist the young person to obtain suitable accommodation or help to stay in such accommodation.

Obligations in relation to plans and assessment are summarised below:

Category of young person	*Pathway views*	*Pathway assessment*	*Pathway plan*	*Pathway co-ordinator*
Currently supported	Yes	Yes	Possibly	Possibly
Compulsorily supported	Yes	Yes	Yes	Yes
Prospective supported	Yes	Yes	No	No
Discretionarily supported	No	No	Yes	Yes

CHALLENGING DECISIONS

4.46 Children or their families may be unhappy about decisions made about the provision of services or other decisions taken by the local authority in exercising its powers and duties. Decisions taken can be challenged using the complaints and representations procedure set up under the 1968 Act.

It may also be possible to challenge decisions by seeking judicial review of the decision. The challenge will generally be on the grounds that the local authority has exercised the considerable discretion conferred on it in an unreasonable way, though the very extent of the discretion may make challenges difficult. Grounds for a challenge might include a failure to take proper account of procedures laid out in the guidance[188] or a failure to follow a decision or recommendation resulting from pursuing the complaints procedure,[189] unless proper consideration has been given before doing this.[190] In light of the comments made above about the relevance of resources to decisions involving service provision, it will be difficult, but not impossible, to challenge a refusal to provide services on resource grounds. Generally, no challenge by way of judicial review will be possible until the complaints procedure has been exhausted.[191]

Complaints about council actions can also be made to the Scottish Public Services Ombudsman.

188 *R v North Yorkshire County Council, ex parte Hargreaves* (1995) 26 BMLR 121; *R v London Borough of Islington, ex parte Rixon* (1997) 1CCLR 119.
189 *R v Avon County Council, ex parte M* [1994] 2 FCR 259.
190 *Re T (Accommodation by Local Authority)* [1995] 1 FLR 159.
191 *R v Kingston-upon-Thames Royal Borough Council, ex parte T* [1994] 1 FLR 798.

Chapter 5

Children in need of supervision or emergency protection

INTRODUCTION

5.1 There is no field in social work practice which has a higher public profile, which is subject to such intense scrutiny and which engenders more anxiety for those involved than child care and, in particular, child protection. Changing public attitudes and views about what characterises good enough parenting, the rights and responsibilities of parents, the rights of children, the justification for state intervention into family life, and the need to protect children have each contributed to the ongoing debate about the most appropriate role for social workers. The intricacies of the dynamic operating amongst social work departments, other professionals involved with the children, the children's hearings and the courts further complicate an understanding of the duties and responsibilities of social workers.

Local authority activities in this area are carried out subject to a variety of legal provisions as well as a substantial amount of guidance. In terms of law there is statutory provision, principally in the form of the Children (Scotland) Act 1995 (the 1995 Act) and regulations made under it which provide some of the framework and procedures for supporting children and their families,[1] and, in addition, there are requirements derived from the European Convention on Human Rights,[2] and, indirectly, from the developing law about liability for negligence in decisions about child protection.[3] Guidance plays an important role in this area, both in terms of setting the general context through the Getting it Right for Every Child (GIRFEC) approach,[4] with its emphasis on

1 See also ch 4. Other statutory powers and duties may also be relevant in the context of children at risk or in need of protection, for example the Education (Additional Support for Learning) (Scotland) Act 2004 and the Mental Health (Care and Treatment) (Scotland) Act 2003.
2 See paras 5.33 to 5.36 below.
3 See para 11.10
4 See para 4.2.

coordination and cooperation between agencies and in setting outcomes for children, but also in more specific guidance on particular areas, for example, child protection.[5]

One aspect of the guidance on child protection involves a non-statutory system of child protection committees and a child protection register.

Child protection committees[6] incorporate representatives of a variety of agencies and the core membership of these committees should include representatives from local authority social work services, local authority education services, community services, housing services, health services, services in relation to drugs and alcohol, police, procurator fiscal, Scottish Children's Reporter Administration, the armed services where there is a significant local presence, the independent education service where this is a significant local presence, and the voluntary sector.[7] Each committee will have a chair, who should be experienced in inter-agency work and child protection and a lead officer responsible for implementing the core functions of the committee.[8] The committee has a variety of functions including:

(a) providing of information to the public, including raising awareness of child protection issues;
(b) development and review of inter-agency child protection policies;
(c) ensuring that all agencies have their own up-to-date policies and procedures;
(d) having mechanisms for assuring the quality of practice and procedures;
(e) promoting good practice;
(f) promoting and delivering training; and
(g) strategic planning for child protection work.[9]

Local authorities are required have child protection registers, a formal list of names of children where there are concerns about the possibility

5 See: http://www.scotland.gov.uk/about/ED/CnF/00017834/page2114553360.aspx.

6 Scottish Government, *National Guidance for Child Protection in Scotland* (2010) paras 129 to 159.

7 *Children and Young People: Child Protection Committees* (Scottish Executive, 2005), para 4.6. The new National Guidance does not specify membership in such a detailed way.

8 Scottish Government, *National Guidance for Child Protection in Scotland* (2010), paras 134–136.

9 Scottish Government, *National Guidance for Child Protection in Scotland* (2010), paras 140–159.

of future abuse and where a child protection plan has been agreed. The requirements for placing a child on the register are that the child is at risk of serious harm and that their welfare was considered to require an interagency child protection plan.[10] In this context harm involves ill-treatment of the child or impairment of his/her health and development and the significance of the harm is to be determined by comparing the child's health and development with what might reasonably be expected of a similar child.[11]

The guidance sets out a process for dealing with concerns about children summarised in the diagram on the following page. This process envisages, in appropriate cases, that decision making and investigation will be a joint activity potentially involving a variety of agencies. Decisions, for example to place a child on the child protection register or to refer the case to the Reporter, would normally be taken at a multi-agency child protection case conference, though in some cases there may be no need for joint working or action will need to be taken in an emergency. Where there is a child protection plan in place for he child this will be put into effect and monitored by a core group of professionals.

Having described some of the guidance, the main focus here will be on the statutory provisions set out in the Children (Scotland) Act 1995, though the Children's Hearings (Scotland) Act 2011, which will make some changes to the system described below, as well as restating some of the current law. The main changes are to a limited extent referred to in the text at the appropriate point and described in more detail in the final chapter.

10 Scottish Government, *National Guidance for Child Protection in Scotland* (2010) paras 55–56. Placement will follow a decision of a child protection case conference. The general ground for placing a child on the Register replaced the previous list of criteria for doing this. In the previous approach a child could only be placed on the Register if he/she met a particular criteria of harm: physical injury, sexual abuse, non-organic failure to thrive, emotional abuse or physical neglect. See Scottish Office, *Protecting Children – A Shared Responsibility* (1998) para 3.5.

11 Scottish Government, *National Guidance for Child Protection in Scotland* (2010), paras 39–44.

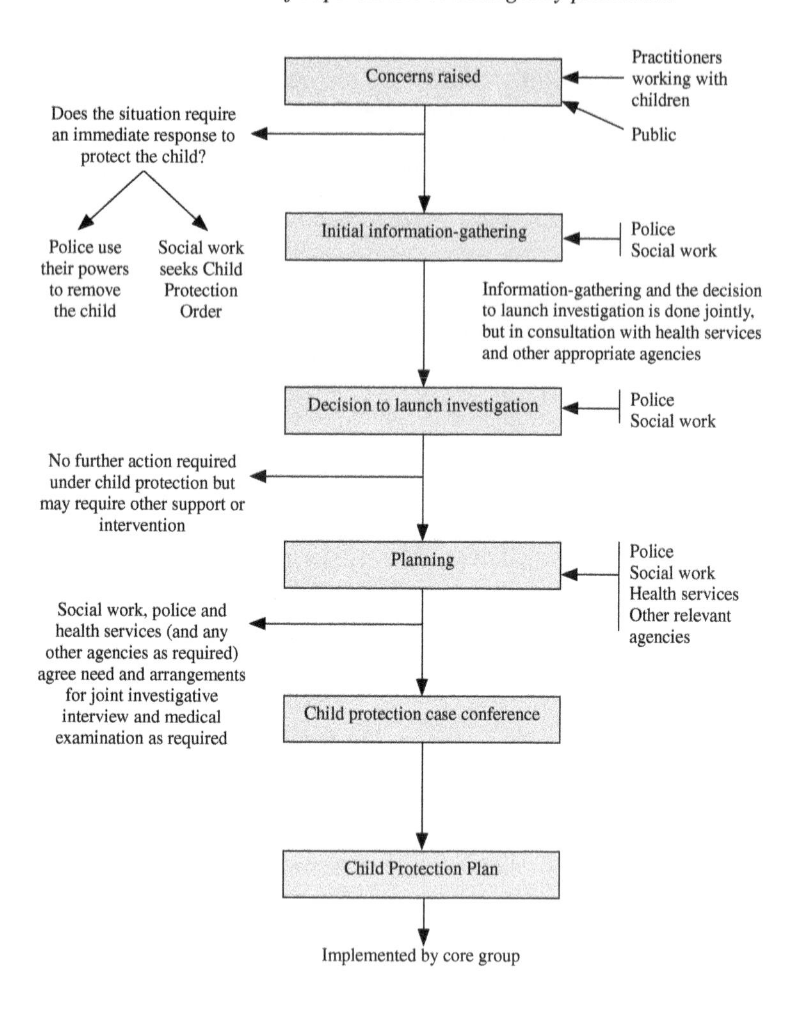

Fig 1: Diagram from Scottish Government, *National Guidance for Child Protection in Scotland* (2010), p 103

OVERRIDING PRINCIPLES GOVERNING DECISIONS BY THE COURT OR HEARING

5.2 When a court or a children's hearing is considering a case involving a child they must pay attention to three principles set out in the 1995 Act.[12]

(a) Principle I

5.3 The overriding principle governing decisions by the courts and by hearings, which applies to all cases, is that the paramount consideration must be the welfare of the child throughout his/her childhood (referred to as the 'welfare principle'). This differs from the standard in adoption where the reference is to the whole of the child's life.

(b) Principle II

5.4 In some cases the court or hearing must give the child the opportunity to express his/her views and take those views into consideration before a decision is made (the 'right to be heard' principle).[13] The situations in which this must be done are:[14]

(1) Cases where a children's hearing is:
   - (a) considering whether to make a supervision requirement or reviewing such a requirement;
   - (b) considering whether to grant a warrant to apprehend and detain a child or to grant a warrant to detain a child where consideration of a case by the hearing is continued to seek further information. Note that this requirement does not apply when the hearing is deciding whether to continue a child protection order;
   - (c) meeting to provide advice to the sheriff who is deciding an application to vary or discharge a child protection order;[15]
   - (d) drawing up a report in connection with a proposed permanence order, adoption or placement for adoption.

12 1995 Act, s 16(1).

13 1995 Act, s 16(2). The procedural rules are in the Act of Sederunt (Child Care and Maintenance Rules) 1997, SI 1997/291, ch 3, especially r 3.5.

14 1995 Act, s 16(4).

15 See para 5.26.

(2) Cases where the sheriff is considering:
- (a) whether to make, vary or discharge a child assessment order or an exclusion order;
- (b) whether to vary or discharge a child protection order, but not when considering whether to make a child protection order;
- (c) whether to grant a warrant for the continued detention of the child;
- (d) whether to substitute his/her own disposal of the case for that of the hearing on a successful appeal against a supervision requirement;
- (e) any appeal against the decision of a children's hearing.

A child of any age can have a view but it is presumed that children over the age of 12 will have a view which must be considered. Social workers and others will need to work in close partnership with a child to ascertain if the child has a view and further if the child wants that view expressed. It is in precisely this sort of situation that the child may be full of ambivalence and/or conflict. A child may confuse the right to be heard with the right to obtain whatever he/she wants.

(c) Principle III

5.5 Finally, in the cases covered by (1)(a) and (b) and (2)(a)-(d) above the hearing or sheriff must not make a requirement or order unless they consider that it would be better for the child to make the requirement or order than to make none (a principle of minimum intervention or 'no order' applies).[16]

These three principles are sometimes referred to as the 'overarching principles'.

CHILDREN IN NEED OF COMPULSORY MEASURES OF SUPERVISION

(1) Introduction

5.6 The Social Work (Scotland) Act 1968 (the 1968 Act), following on from the report of the Kilbrandon Committee, introduced a new way of dealing with what were described as 'children in need of compulsory measures of care' (now described as 'children in need of compulsory

16 1995 Act, s 16(3).

measures of supervision'). This category covered all of the groups of children who would previously have been dealt with in different ways through the court system and whose behaviour the Kilbrandon Committee regarded as being symptomatic of some social or family dislocation. The Kilbrandon Committee concluded that:[17]

> In terms of the treatment measures to be applied, the children appearing before the courts, whatever the precise circumstances in which they do so, show basic similarity of underlying situation. The distinguishing factor is their common need for special measures of education and training, the normal upbringing process for whatever reason having failed or fallen short.

These children are now dealt with by way of referral to the reporter to the children's hearing who, after an initial investigation, decides whether or not the case should go on to a hearing. The courts are only involved in cases where there is a dispute about the grounds for taking action in respect of a child and as the forum for dealing with appeals against decisions of the hearing. In law anyone can refer a case to the reporter if that individual is of the view that a child may be in need of compulsory measures of supervision, so that, for example, a concerned neighbour could report suspicions of child abuse. In practice, however, the overwhelming majority of referrals (around 90% in 2009/10) come from the police, followed by the social work department, the procurator fiscal and educational sources.

In spite of changes, the children's hearing system and the Kilbrandon philosophy have continued to take centre stage in child care law.[18]

(2) Duties of the social work department[19]

5.7 When a social work department receives a report suggesting that a child may be in need of compulsory supervision, it has a duty to investigate the report unless it is satisfied that no inquiry is necessary, for example because they already have extensive information relating to the child. If it concludes, with or without an investigation, that compulsory measures may be needed in respect of the child, the department must pass on whatever information it has about the child to the reporter. In cases where this investigation is being thwarted local authorities can

17 *Children and Young Persons* Cmnd 2306 (1964), para 252.
18 For example, the Policy Memorandum for the Children's Hearings (Scotland) Bill states that: 'It is right that the Children's Hearings system evolves to adapt to these changes without losing the vision and philosophy of Kilbrandon', (para 14).
19 1995 Act, s 53(1).

apply for an assessment order.[20] The purpose of these orders is to allow an assessment of the health, development and treatment of the child. The application for the order is made to the sheriff who may grant an order if all of the following conditions are satisfied:

(a) the local authority has reasonable cause to suspect that the child is being so treated or neglected that the child is suffering or is likely to suffer significant harm;
(b) an assessment is needed to establish whether there is reasonable cause to believe that the child is being so treated or neglected;
(c) an assessment is unlikely to be carried out or carried out satisfactorily without an order being granted.

Although the grounds for the order refer to suspicion of risk to the child, the guidance on the use of the order suggests that every effort should be made to find out whether the child is in fact at risk before an application is made for an order.[21] Clear evidence will also be needed that the parents are acting unreasonably and in relation to the nature of the risk to the child. The need for arranging assessment in advance is stressed. This is so that it can take place quickly if an order is granted and is especially important given the short life of the order.[22]

The order will specify the date on which the assessment of the child is to begin and is effective for a period of 7 days starting with this date. It requires anyone in a position to produce the child to do so and to permit the assessment authorised by the order and may allow the child to be taken to and kept at a specified place to be assessed. Where an order is made allowing the child to be taken to a specified place, the sheriff may also regulate contact between the child and any other person for the duration of the child assessment order. If, when an application for an assessment order is made, the sheriff considers that the grounds for granting a child protection order are established[23] the sheriff must make such an order.

In making an order the sheriff is subject to the overriding principles set out in section 2 above, including the obligation to seek the views of the child. This requirement may avert a potential problem where an assessment order is made but the child has capacity, in terms of the Age of Legal Capacity (Scotland) Act 1991, to consent to medical treatment and, by implication, to refuse treatment. Section 90 of the 1995 Act expressly

20 1995 Act, s 55.
21 *Guidance,* vol 1, ch 7, para 17.
22 *Guidance,* vol 1, ch 7, paras 13–74.
23 See para 5.23.

provides that examinations or treatment under certain provisions of the Act are not to be carried out unless the child consents. Child assessment orders are not covered by this specific provision. Two interpretations of this are possible. One is that, since Parliament did not provide that the child's agreement is necessary, as it did in other cases, there is no need for the child to consent to assessment under an assessment order and such assessment can be carried out against the wishes of the child. The preferable view is that section 90 does extend to child assessment orders and that a child assessment order does not affect the ability of the child to refuse consent to medical examination or treatment under the 1991 Act.[24] The requirement to take the child's views into account may mean that in practice no order will be made if the child would refuse the assessment.

Two final issues in respect of assessment orders are the short duration of the order and the vagueness of the grounds for making an order. What is 'reasonable cause', how does reasonable cause to 'suspect' differ from reasonable cause to 'believe', and what is 'significant' harm?[25] These terms are not clarified in the Guidance.

Another duty of the social work department is to provide reports on children who have been referred to a hearing. The production of a report for a child referred to a hearing (normally referred to as a 'social background report') can give rise to both opportunities and problems for the social worker. If the child and/or family are known to the social worker or social work department, then more comprehensive material may be available in the compilation of the report. The social worker is well placed to provide information about the children's hearing system, procedures and possible outcomes to the child and family while also collecting and analysing data about the people and situations involved. The report is to be completed before the hearing and the child/family may not accept that the grounds of referral apply and may be unwilling to participate in the preparation of the report. In such cases they cannot be forced to assist, though the social worker may try to persuade them that some level of co-operation is in their interest.

There may also be conflict over the identity of the client. Is it the hearing or is it the child and family with whom the social worker may have to work if the child is placed on supervision? The legal answer is probably that the client is the hearing, much as in the preparation of criminal

24 See HC Official Report Special Standing Committee (Children (Scotland) Bill) 7 March 1995, col 516, see also *Guidance*, vol 1, ch 7, para 29. It is made clear that the child's consent is required in the Childrens Hearings (Scotland) Act 2011, s 186, though this is not yet (February 2011) in force.

25 See below, para 5.23.

justice social work reports the court is considered to be the client. If a hearing is to be held reports provided to the reporter will be sent to the child's parent(s) (or other relevant person) as well as, in some cases, to the child.[26]

Finally, the department has a number of responsibilities in terms of providing supervision for children when this is required by a hearing, and for carrying out reviews of the cases of children subject to supervision requirements.

(3) When is a child in need of compulsory measures of supervision?

5.8 A child may be in need of compulsory measures of supervision if one of the conditions listed below applies to the child. It is for the children's hearing to decide, if the child is referred to them on one of these grounds, whether he/she is in need of compulsory measures of supervision. The conditions, which are contained in section 52(2) of the 1995 Act, are:[27]

(a) *The child is beyond the control of any relevant person.* The term 'relevant person' is used in several places in the 1995 Act and covers parents enjoying parental responsibilities or rights; anyone in whom parental responsibilities or rights are vested either under the 1995 Act (for example, someone who has had them conferred on him/her by an order under section 11)[28] or because of a permanence order; and anyone who ordinarily has charge of or control over the child[29] even though he/she enjoys no parental responsibilities or rights. In relation to this last what is required is *de facto* care and possession of the child rather than any legal status or right,[30] and a person can still have care and control if that is the usual position, even if this care and control has been lost temporarily.[31] In general terms it is not enough that a person is simply considered to be significant in the life of the child.[32] A parent, normally the biological father, or anyone else who has been granted only a contact order does not, by virtue of this, have any parental responsibilities

26 See below, para 5.13.
27 These will be reordered and restated with some changes if the Children's Hearings (Scotland) Act 2011 is bought into force. See ch 12.
28 See paras 3.4–3.7.
29 Unless this is the result of his/her employment.
30 *S v N* 2002 SLT 589. In this case foster carers with whom the child had been placed 7 months earlier were held to qualify as relevant persons.
31 *M v Irvine* 2005 Fam LR 113.
32 *M v Irvine* 2005 Fam LR 113.

and rights so as to qualify as a relevant person.[33] However, despite this, it has been held in the context of rights to attend a hearing that the definition of relevant person must be read so as to include someone having a right to contact by virtue of a contact order.[34]

(b) *The child is falling into bad associations or is exposed to moral danger.* Thomson suggests that this ground might exist where the child's parents or friends were prostitutes, drug addicts or alcoholics.[35] Most of the reported cases involve (actual or possible) sexual conduct towards the child or in his/her presence. One example is of the father of the friend of a 6 year old girl shining a torch on her naked private parts.[36] Another case involved a child (K) living with a married couple. K was the child of the husband and another female child who was living with the couple and with whom the husband had been having sexual intercourse since before she was 15. Despite any evidence of any sexual conduct by the husband towards K it was considered on the evidence that the past conduct of the husband towards K's mother 'could carry forward with implications for K amounting to moral danger.'[37]

(c) *The child is likely to suffer unnecessarily or to be impaired seriously in his/her health or development due to lack of parental care.* The question here is whether the consequences of the care being provided by the parent(s) are likely to result in harm to a child, regardless of the intention of the parents.[38] Lack of parental care may exist even where the parents act with the best of motives, even if the child appears to be well looked after, and regardless of whether blame should be attached to the parents.[39] For example, this ground was held to be established in a case where the parents of a haemophiliac child were unwilling to give consent to treatment using Factor VIII, even though the court accepted that the parents were concerned parents and that their refusal to consent to this treatment arose from a fear that the child might become HIV

33 *Knox v S* [2010] CSIH 45.

34 *Knox v S* [2010] CSIH 45. This extends beyond parents to other having rights to contact by virtue of a contact order, *Children's Hearing Appeal JA and SY*, Dumbarton Sheriff Court, 3 November 2010 (grandmother). See also Pricipal Report UK [2010] UKSC 56 and para 5.36.

35 J M Thomson *Family Law in Scotland* (5th edn, 2006, Bloomsbury Professional), p 381.

36 *Harris v F* 1991 SLT 242; see also *B v Kennedy* 1987 SLT 765, *Constanda v M* 1997 SC 217.

37 *G v Scanlon* 1999 SC 226, at 234G.

38 In one case the sheriff took the view that the children's mother had acted 'out of the best of motives', *R v Grant*, 2000 SLT 372.

39 *D v Kelly* 1995 SLT 1220.

positive as a result of the treatment.[40] Another example is a case where the children were described by the sheriff as well nourished and clean, but on two occasions they had effectively been thrown out of the house and left to fend for themselves. In both instances there were long delays before their absence was reported to the police by their father.[41] This ground can apply even where the child has never actually ever been in the care of the parents.[42] It can involve excessive restriction and supervision of the child as well as the opposite.[43]

It was also held to exist in where children's parents were convinced that their children had an autistic spectrum disorder, insisted on them attending an inappropriate special school and refused access to the children for assessment.[44] A further example involved failure on the part of a mother to recognise the risk posed to her child by a partner with a history of abusing children. Additional factors here were the partner's failure to complete a programme to address his behaviour and the mother's lack of honesty about her relationship with the partner.[45]

It has been said that the test for determining whether this ground is satisfied is:[46]

> whether a reasonable person looking to the circumstances of the particular case would consider that this child is likely to be caused unnecessary suffering or serious impairment to her health or development through lack of parental care on the part of this mother?

In the case in which this test was formulated, failure by a mother to visit a child in hospital for 5 months was not sufficient to establish likely lack of care where the mother had serious medical problems and lived far from the hospital.

'Likely' in this context is not to be regarded as equivalent in meaning to 'probably' or to 'more likely than not', but indicates that there must be a significant or substantial risk of the harm set out in the definition occurring.[47] Judgement about likelihood must be

40 *Finlayson, Applicant* 1989 SCLR 601.
41 *Kennedy v S* 1986 SLT 679.
42 *McGregor v L* 1981 SLT 194.
43 *D v Kelly* 1995 SLT 1221, it was considered sufficient that lack of care was likely to occur based on the known habits of the carers.
44 *R v Grant* 2000 SLT 372.
45 *M v Scottish Children's Reporter for Renfrewshire* [2009] CSIH 49.
46 *M v McGregor* 1982 SLT 41, at 43.
47 *M v McClafferty* [2007] CSIH 88.

based either on a risk assessment or on clear evidence from which an inference about the likelihood of harm could be drawn. There is a need to consider the past and to draw inferences about what is likely in the future based on inductive reasoning from past events and other information about the character of those involved.

(d) *A Schedule 1 offence has been committed in respect of the child.* Schedule 1 offences are mainly assaults and sexual offences committed against children, they are set out briefly in the box below.[48] It is not necessary that the alleged offence is committed against the child in Scotland,[49] nor is it necessary that the alleged offender is identified – the point is that the child has been the victim of such an offence.[50]

SCHEDULE 1 OFFENCES

OFFENCES AGAINST CHILDREN UNDER THE AGE OF 17 YEARS TO WHICH SPECIAL PROVISIONS APPLY

1. Any offence under Part I of the Criminal Law (Consolidation) (Scotland) Act 1995.
2. Any offence under section 18 (rape of a young child) or 28 (having intercourse with an older child) of the Sexual Offences (Scotland) Act 2009.
3. Any offence under section 19 (sexual assault on a young child by penetration) or 29 (engaging in penetrative sexual activity with or towards an older child) of that Act.
4. Any offence under section 20 (sexual assault on a young child) or 30 (engaging in sexual activity with or towards an older child) of that Act.
5. Any offence under section 42 of that Act (sexual abuse of trust) towards a child under the age of 17 years but only if the condition set out in section 43(6) of that Act is fulfilled.
6. Any offence under section 12, 15, 22 or 33 of the Children and Young Persons (Scotland) Act 1937.

48 The list here takes account of changes introduced by the Sexual Offences (Scotland) Act 2009 which came into force on 1 December 2010. A fuller explanation of some of these is given in the Appendix to this chapter.

49 *S v Kennedy* 1996 SCLR 34, otherwise offences committed whilst on holiday overseas would not be relevant, for example.

50 *McGregor v K* 1982 SLT 293.

7. Any offence under the Prohibition of Female Genital Mutilation (Scotland) Act 2005 where the person mutilated or, as the case may be, proposed to be mutilated, is a child under the age of 17 years.
8. Any offence under section 52 or 52A of the Civic Government (Scotland) Act 1982 in relation to an indecent photograph of a child under the age of 17 years.
9. Any offence under section 1, 9, 10, 11 or 12 of the Protection of Children and Prevention of Sexual Offences (Scotland) Act 2005 in respect of a child under the age of 17 years.
10. Any other offence involving bodily injury to a child under the age of 17 years.
11. Any offence involving the use of lewd, indecent or libidinous practice or behaviour towards a child under the age of 17 years.
12. Any offence under section 5 (coercing a person into being present during a sexual activity), 6 (coercing a person into looking at a sexual image), 7 (communicating indecently etc), 8 (sexual exposure) or 9 (voyeurism) of the Sexual Offences (Scotland) Act 2009 towards a child under the age of 17 years.
13. Any offence under any of sections 21 to 26 or 31 to 37 of that Act (certain sexual offences relating to children).

One example of a Schedule 1 offence is section 12(1) of the Children and Young Persons (Scotland) Act 1937 which creates a number of offences to do with child neglect, one of them being neglect likely to cause unnecessary suffering or injury to the child's health. In one case[51] a 9 month old baby was left alone in the house for a short period of time by his mother who was very drunk. She was convicted of this offence and appealed. The appeal court held that for this offence to be committed the behaviour had to be wilful, in the sense of being deliberate and intentional; there had to be neglect in the form of failing to do '... what a reasonable parent, in all the circumstances, would regard as necessary to provide proper care and attention to the child';[52] and there must be some evidence that there was a substantial risk to the child. Here the court was not satisfied that the third requirement was met. Their view, which was also applied in the case of

51 *H v Lees, D v Orr* 1994 SLT 908. See also *McD v Orr* 1994 SCCR 645, dealing with a case of abandonment under the same provision.
52 *H v Lees* 1994 SLT 908 at 913H.

a 15 year old girl left alone in the house for an evening,[53] was that leaving a child alone in the house did not automatically mean that the offence had been committed.

Parents still have the right to use force on their children by way of punishment, provided that the force falls within the bounds of reasonable chastisement. Whether or not what a parent does falls within these boundaries will depend on the facts of each case, with the courts taking into account whether the parent lost his/her temper, the parent's intention, the blameworthiness of the child's conduct and the degree of force used.[54] Reasonable chastisement will not provide the grounds for a referral to a hearing under this subsection,[55] though if a child is struck deliberately without any justification (such as reasonable chastisement) or other exonerating factor this will constitute a ground of referral.[56]

(e) *The child is, or is likely to become a member of the same household as a child against whom a Schedule 1 offence has been committed.* The most notable feature of this ground is the broad approach that has been taken by the courts to the interpretation of 'household'. Their general view is that it is not necessary for all the members of the household to be living together, or even living at the same place at the same time. In *Kennedy v R's Curator ad litem*[57] it was said that:

> The important question … is whether the ties of affection and regular contact which hold the parties together as a group of persons still continue.

Two cases illustrate the breadth of the interpretation of the term. In the first, the child who had been the victim of the offence was staying with foster parents separated from his family, his sister was regarded as being in the same household as the fostered child.[58] The term 'household' was 'plainly intended to connote a family unit or something akin to a family unit – a group of persons held together by a particular kind of tie who normally live together, even if individual members of the group may be temporarily sepa-

53 *H v Lees, D v Orr* 1994 SLT 908.

54 See *Stewart v Thain* 1981 SLT (Notes) 2; *Peebles v MacPhail* 1990 SLT 245; *B v Harris* 1990 SLT 208; and *Byrd v Wither* 1991 SLT 206.

55 *B v Harris* 1990 SLT 208.

56 *Kennedy v A* 1993 SLT 1134.

57 1992 SC 300, at 307.

58 *McGregor v H* 1983 SLT 626. See also *Cunningham v M* 2005 SLT (Sh Ct) 73.

rated from it'.[59] In the second,[60] the child who was referred under this ground was born 8½ years after the death of a previous child as the result of a Schedule 1 offence; he was still regarded as being a member of the same household as that child. A household was still considered to exist even if one or more members were separated from it permanently where, as here, there was continuity in the form of the parents of the two children and of an elder sister who had been part of the household when the child died.

(f) *The child is, or is likely to become, a member of the same household as a person who has committed a Schedule I offence.* The same extended definition of 'household' applies here, though where there is no evidence that a child normally lives with the offender this ground may not be established.[61] If the child stops living with the offender by the time of the proof hearing there will need to be clear evidence that the household relationship has broken down to avoid the ground being established.[62]

(g) *The child is, or is likely to become a member of the same household as a person who has been the victim of an offence under sections 1 to 3 of the Criminal Law (Consolidation) (Scotland) Act 1995.* The offences referred to here involve incest or cases of intercourse between a child and a person in a position of trust.[63]

(h) *The child has failed to attend school regularly without a reasonable excuse.* A child suspended from school cannot be referred under this ground unless, possibly, the exclusion from school was made necessary by his/her behaviour.[64]

(i) *The child has committed an offence.* This follows from the provision that no child under the age of 16 is to be prosecuted except on the instructions of the Lord Advocate which may relate to an individual case or may be general regarding the types of case where children should be prosecuted. If a child under 16 is prosecuted this may be done only in the High Court or in the sheriff court. Generally, children will be prosecuted only in a limited number of cases, for example, if they have committed serious crimes or offences, such as murder, rape, or robbery if aged 15 or over, they

59 1983 SLT 626 at 628.

60 *A v Kennedy* 1993 SLT 1188.

61 *Ferguson v S* 1992 SCLR 866.

62 *Kennedy v R's Curator ad litem* 1993 SLT 295.

63 Section 3, which involved intercourse between a child and a person in a position of trust, was repealed in December 2010. The replacement offence is set out in s 42 of the Sexual Offences (Scotland) Act 2009. As will be seen above an offence under s 42 of a Schedule 1 offence.

64 *D v Kennedy* 1988 SLT 55.

have committed an offence which can be punished by disqualification and it is in the public interest to obtain this.[65] This ground of referral is available only in respect of children over the age of 8,[66] which is the age of criminal responsibility in Scots law.[67] For this condition to be established the higher standard of proof used in criminal law applies.

(j) *The child has misused alcohol or any drug.* The term 'drug' covers all kinds of drugs, not only those which are controlled under the Misuse of Drugs Act 1971. This means that a child could fulfil this condition if, for example, he/she was addicted to cough bottle.[68]

(k) *The child has misused any volatile substance by inhaling it, other than for medicinal purposes.* This would cover glue sniffing and inhaling butane gas, for example.

(l) *The child is being provided with accommodation by a local authority or is subject to a parental responsibilities order and special measures are needed in order to supervise the child properly either in his/her interest or in the interests of others.* This mainly applies to children who are considered to be in need of secure accommodation.

(m) *The child has been made subject to an antisocial behaviour order or interim antisocial behaviour order and in making that order the sheriff has also made an order requiring the Reporter to refer the child to a hearing.* Once the case is referred to a hearing it will then be up to the hearing to decide whether to either impose a supervision requirement or to change an existing requirement.

The table below shows the percentage of referrals to the reporter on the various grounds set out above in the periods 1998/9 and 2009/10. There have been clear changes in the nature of referrals over that period, though the absolute number of referrals has declined, from a total of 55,197 in 1998/9 to 42,532 in 2009/10.

Ground	a	b	c	d	e	f	g	h	i	j	k	L
1998/9	5.7	3.2	15	11.6	2.6	1.4	0.01	7.3	51.1	1.6	0.2	0.03
2009/10	9.2	5.6	33.9	39.2	2.7	1.3	0.03	4.8	23.5	2.6	0.04	0.07

65 Lord Advocate's Guidelines to Chief Constables – Reporting to Procurator Fiscal of Offences Alleged to have been Committed by Children (November 2010).

66 Though there is currently legislation which would raise this 12, Criminal Justice and Licensing (Scotland) Act 2010, s 52, which is not yet (February 2011) in force.

67 *Merrin v S* 1987 SLT 193.

68 See, for example, Darboe M *et al*, 'The Abuse of Dextromethorphan-based Cough Syrup: A Pilot Study of the Community of Waynesboro, Pennsylvania', *Adolescence* 1996; 31:633–44.

(4) Investigation by the reporter[69]

5.9 Once the reporter receives information about a child he/she must carry out an initial investigation. Anyone can give information about children who may be in need of compulsory supervision to the reporter, and the police have particular duties to report offences committed by children to the reporter and to report other cases where they have reasonable cause to believe that a child may need supervision. As part of this initial investigation the reporter may request information from the local authority. This is sometimes referred to as requesting a 'social background report', though there is an argument that this term should be restricted to reports produced once a referral has been made.

At the end of this investigation the reporter may reach one of two decisions. The first is that no hearing is necessary in respect of the child. Where this decision is made the child may be referred to the local authority for provision of advice, guidance or assistance on a voluntary basis.[70] A decision not to refer to a hearing may be taken because the child is already subject to a supervision requirement or because the reporter does not consider that compulsory measures of supervision are necessary. If the reporter decides that a hearing is not necessary a hearing cannot subsequently be arranged based only on the information on which this decision was taken. Between 80 and 90% of cases are not referred to a hearing.

The second possibility is for the reporter to arrange a hearing to consider the child's case. A hearing must only be arranged if the reporter considers that the child is in need of compulsory measures of supervision (and, of course, that one of the conditions explained above exists). Once a hearing has been arranged, the reporter will request a social background report on the child from the local authority and the authority has a duty to provide this. If the information originally given to the reporter came from the police or a local authority then, whatever decision the reporter reaches, he/she must notify the police or the local authority, whichever was the original source of the information.[71]

A hearing will have the power to deal with the case of a child referred to it if it had power to do so at the date of the referral by the Reporter, even if the child subsequently moves.[72]

69 1995 Act, s 56.

70 1995 Act, s 56(4)(b). Debate has raged about the meaning of 'voluntary' in this context as well as an erroneous presumption that use of this type of supervision keeps a child 'out of the system'.

71 1995 Act, s 56(4)(1)(a).

72 *Mitchell v H* 2000 SC 334.

(5) Children's panel

5.10 The children's panel is composed of volunteers from the community who have completed training to equip them to undertake the role. These panel lists are maintained for each local authority area. The children's hearing which is convened to consider the case of a child deemed by the reporter to be in need of compulsory measures of supervision is composed of three of these lay members chosen from the larger children's panel. At least one woman and one man must be present and one member will act as chair.

(6) Who can attend a hearing?[73]

5.11 Conduct of hearings is governed partly by the 1995 Act and partly by the Children's Hearings (Scotland) Rules 1996 ('Hearings Rules').[74]

The child who is the subject of the referral has both a right and an obligation to attend. If the child does not attend, a warrant can be issued to apprehend the child and this will authorise detention in a place of safety until a hearing is convened. Attendance by the child at the hearing can be excused in two cases. First, if the hearing is considering a referral concerning a Schedule 1 offence and it considers that the child's presence is not necessary for the just hearing of the case. Secondly, in any other case where the hearing considers that it would be detrimental to the interests of the child to be present.[75] These provisions allow the hearing to excuse attendance: they do not allow the hearing to exclude the child, who can still attend if wishing to do so.

The 'relevant person' (see para 5.8(a) above) also has the right and obligation to attend the hearing, though this obligation can be dispensed with if it would be unreasonable to require attendance or if this attendance is not necessary to allow the hearing to dispose of the case. The right to attend a children's hearing is not itself a parental responsibility or right, and therefore it is not possible to apply to court for grant of this specific right,[76] though it will flow from the imposition/grant of any parental responsibility or right. Despite the obligation to attend, the rele-

73 1995 Act, s 45.
74 SI 1996/3261.
75 1995 Act, s 45(2).
76 *Principal Reporter v K* [2010] CSIH 5, noting that in any event a court would have to be persuaded on the merits before imposing/conferring responsibilities/rights.

vant person can be excluded from the hearing for as long as is necessary in the interest of the child. Exclusion can take place where the hearing is satisfied that this is necessary in order to obtain the views of the child or where the presence of the excluded person is causing the child distress or is likely to cause distress. Social workers will be all too familiar with the family interview scenario in which a parent will answer for the child and it is not until the child is seen on his/her own that sometimes there is the opportunity for the child to speak freely. Where a person is excluded the chair must explain to that person the substance of what took place in his/her absence.[77] The child's father also has a right of attendance if he does not fall within the definition of 'relevant person', and provided that he is living with the child's mother.[78] The child and relevant person are entitled to be represented and this representative has a right to attend.[79] If any person who has a right to attend is in the custody of a constable, prison officer or such official, then that person also has a right to attend. If a safeguarder has been appointed, then that individual is entitled to be present throughout the hearing.

Other people normally attend but have no right of attendance, like the social worker who prepared the social background report. The social worker usually clarifies and updates the contents of the report if necessary, identifies appropriate resources, and when appropriate encourages the child and family to participate in the hearing which may be an unfamiliar system where there is a power imbalance. Members of the press are entitled to attend, but may be excluded on grounds similar to those for exclusion of a relevant person, the important difference being that there is no obligation to explain to the press what happened during the exclusion. Other than these, the chair of the hearing can permit others to attend like people training to become members of the children's panel or social workers, subject to the proviso that the number of persons attending is kept to a minimum.[80]

(7) Business meetings[81]

5.12 The practice of holding a business meeting outwith the presence of the child and parents to discuss aspects of the running of the

77 1995 Act, s 46.
78 Hearings Rules, r 12.
79 Though strictly he/she has no powers to *represent* them at the hearing. See also para 5.13 below.
80 1995 Act, s 43.
81 1995 Act, s 64 and Hearings Rules, r 4.

hearing was recognised as legitimate in the case of *Sloan v B*,[82] even though there was no express provision for such meetings in the Social Work (Scotland) Act 1968. These meetings were given formal recognition in the 1995 Act. They can be arranged by the reporter and the child and relevant person have to be informed that the meeting will take place and of the purpose of the meeting. They can then make written representations to the reporter which will be passed on to the business meeting. The business meeting can decide a number of procedural matters and can give the reporter instructions about how his/her functions should be carried out in connection with the referral. It can, for example, decide whether or not to inform the child or the relevant person about being excused attendance at the hearing. The obvious problem which these meetings may raise for the child and family are concerns about decisions being (all but) reached in advance of the hearing.

(8) Legal Representation and Access to Reports

5.13 Although regulations made under the 1995 Act provide for the child's parent or relevant person to be provided with a copy of any report going to the hearing, there is no statutory provision for the child to be given access to such a report. The regulations require that the reports are provided three days before the date of the hearing and any additional reports for an adjourned hearing must be provided at least three days before the date of the adjourned hearing.[83] In the course of *S v Miller*[84] the Principal Reporter indicated that the intention was to start providing these reports to children. The scheme currently in operation is that children over 12 automatically get the reports. Children between 8 and 12 can get them if they wish to see them. There is provision for those writing reports to indicate on a separate sheet information which they feel would be detrimental to the child. This separate sheet is not disclosed. The child is also provided with a leaflet '*Having Your Say*'[85] on which to express his/her views.

Although hearings have had, since the 1995 Act, an obligation to consider whether a safeguarder should be appointed to protect and secure the rights of the child, there was, until recently no right to assisted legal representation. It was, of course always possible to bring a solicitor (or another representative, such as a lay advocate) along to the hearing, but

82 1991 SLT 530.
83 *P v Reporter* 2008 SLT (Sh Ct) 85.
84 2001 SC 977.
85 Which sets out a number of questions for the child to consider.

there was no legal aid to pay for this. As a result of *S v Miller* this has changed and initially provision was made for a legal representative to be appointed for a child by a business meeting prior to a hearing (or at a subsequent hearing). This can be done either:[86]

(a) where despite the entitlement of the child to be accompanied by a representative under rule 11 of the Children's Hearings (Scotland) Rules1996,[87] legal representation is required to allow the child to effectively participate at the Hearing; or
(b) the child may be made subject to a supervision requirement with a requirement to reside in secure accommodation.

This right to representation has now been extended to relevant persons. A legal representative can be appointed by a business meeting prior to a hearing (or at a subsequent hearing) where:[88]

(a) it may be necessary to make a supervision requirement (or review a supervision requirement) which includes a requirement:
    (i) that the child who is the subject of a children's hearing reside at any place, where such a requirement would result in the child no longer residing with the relevant person;
    (ii) regulating the relevant person's contact with the child; or
    (iii) affecting the relevant person's parental rights under section 2 of the Act; and
(b) despite the entitlement of the relevant person to be accompanied by a representative under rule 11 of the Children's Hearings (Scotland) Rules1996,[89] legal representation is required to enable the relevant person to effectively participate at the Hearing.

It is provided that a relevant person's ability to participate effectively may be affected by:[90]

(a) the complexity of the case, including the points of law in issue;
(b) the nature of the issues involved;
(c) the ability of the individual, with the assistance of a representative under rule 11 of the 1996 Rules, to consider and challenge any document or information before the Hearing;

86 Children's Hearings (Legal Representation) (Scotland) Rules 2002, SSI 2002/63, r 3.
87 SI 1996/3261.
88 Children's Hearings (Legal Representation) (Scotland) Rules 2002, SSI 2002/63, r 3A.
89 SI 1996/3261.
90 Children's Hearings (Legal Representation) (Scotland) Rules 2002, SSI 2002/63, r 3B; see also the considerations noted in *K v Authority Reporter* 2009 SLT 1019.

(d) the ability of the individual, with the assistance of a representative under rule 11 of the 1996 Rules, to present their views in an effective manner.

Legal representatives are drawn from a panel and financial provision is made by the local authority.[91]

(9) Procedure at the hearing[92]

5.14 The hearing starts with the chair explaining the grounds of referral to those present and finding out if the grounds of referral are accepted by the child and the relevant person. If the grounds are not accepted the hearing can either discharge the referral or instruct the reporter to apply to the sheriff for a finding that the grounds are established.[93] This procedure is also followed if the child is not capable of understanding the explanation given (for example, because the child is very young) or if the child has not in fact understood the explanation. If the grounds are accepted in part the hearing can either proceed on the basis of those grounds accepted or proceed as if the grounds were not accepted. The hearing is also obliged to consider if it is necessary to appoint a safeguarder to protect and secure the interests of the child and the reasons for making any appointment must be stated in writing by the chair of the hearing. If a safeguarder is appointed he/she must produce a report which will be considered by the hearing. If the appointment is made at the beginning of the hearing it will presumably be necessary to continue the hearing for further investigation, as described below, in order to allow the preparation of the report.

If the grounds of referral are accepted, or if they are established after a proof hearing before the sheriff, the hearing moves on to consider the case. This takes the form of a discussion involving all of the participants (except those excused attendance or excluded). The discussion is not limited to the grounds of referral. Anything which is relevant to a consideration of the case can be taken into account,[94] the sole possible exception being allegations which have been found not to be established by the sheriff at a proof hearing.[95] Hearings have the task of investigating the case as far as is necessary for a complete consideration of what is in the child's best interests, and this includes taking account of

91 Though this will change. The Children's Hearings (Scotland) Act makes provision for legal representation to be provided under the legal aid scheme.

92 1995 Act, s 65 and Hearings Rules, r 20.

93 See para 5.15 below.

94 *O v Rae* 1993 SLT 570.

95 *M v Kennedy* 1991 SCLR 898.

information which is not included in the grounds of referral which were accepted or established. Indeed, it has been decided that the hearing can consider allegations which were deleted from the grounds of referral which were then accepted by the child or relevant person at the proof hearing[96] as well as information which may disclose grounds of referral additional to those established at a proof hearing or accepted by the child or relevant person.[97] There is no need for the hearing to seek to have these additional grounds accepted or established before they can be taken into account. Overall, then, once consideration of a child's case has been triggered by the acceptance or establishment of any ground of referral, the hearing can consider any relevant information, by which is meant information relevant to the issue of what should be done in the child's best interests.

The views of the child have to be considered by the hearing before reaching a decision. His/her views can be conveyed to the hearing by the child or his/her representative in person, by the child in writing or by any safeguarder. When the child is notified of the hearing, that notification will ask the child if he/she wishes to express his/her views to the hearing and give an opportunity to state those views in writing to the reporter at that stage.[98] If the child is already subject to a supervision requirement that requirement must be reviewed in the course of the hearing. In an ideal world, the relatively informal atmosphere of a children's hearing would prove to be an environment in which all participants, including the child and relevant persons or parents would contribute fully and freely. In practice, the structures may be experienced as intimidating and/or individual's attitudes towards authority may be such that the inherent power imbalances are insurmountable. Here, the social worker who has established good working relationships with the child and others may work to facilitate their full participation. Research published in 1998 suggested that the chair of the hearing made the largest number of contributions and that although children made a high proportion of contributions 'very few asked questions or initiated discussion and what they said was frequently short or monosyllabic (with 76% of their contributions being one line or less of typed text).'[99]

After the discussion the hearing reaches a decision. Three decisions are possible: to discharge the referral; to make a supervision requirement;

96 *O v Rae* 1993 SLT 570.

97 *R, Petitioner* 1993 SLT 910.

98 Hearings Rules, r 6.

99 Hallett, C *et al*, *The Evaluation of Children's Hearings in Scotland: Deciding in Children's Interests* (1998).

or to continue the case for further investigation.[100] This further investigation may require the child to go to a clinic, hospital or anywhere else for investigation and to stay there for up to 22 days. The child can be kept in a place of safety during this period if the hearing is satisfied either that keeping the child there is necessary in the interests of promoting or safeguarding the interests of the child, or that there is reason to believe that the child will not attend on the next hearing date. A child can be kept in a place of safety for only 22 days.[101] Once the further investigation is completed a decision must be made to impose a supervision requirement or to discharge the referral.

A note of the decision and of the reasons for the decision (which must be clear, unambiguous and intelligible to the person receiving them) is sent to the child and the relevant person, It may sometimes be appropriate for the social worker to spend time with the child and family following the hearing's decision to clarify the meaning of the decision, to discuss the practicalities and to make arrangements for future contacts. Hearings can be fraught with tension and may even contribute toward the precipitation of a crisis in the family, and so the intervention of a social worker may be welcomed and necessary.

If the hearing is unable to dispose of the case it can grant a warrant to find the child or to keep him/her in a place of safety for up to 22 days.[102] Conditions can be attached regarding medical treatment or examination and about contact with other people. This type of warrant can be issued only where either there is reason to believe that a child will not attend a future hearing (or comply with a condition requiring attendance for further investigation), or where it is necessary to keep the child in a place of safety in order to safeguard or promote his/her welfare.[103] The warrant can be renewed by the hearing subject to a maximum of 66 days and can be further renewed by the sheriff without any upper limit of time.[104] One instance where use of this power would be appropriate is where the grounds of referral are denied, the case goes to a proof hearing and the proof hearing is delayed pending a criminal trial. In this sort of case, the hearing will be unable to dispose of the referral until after the proof hearing has taken place.

100 1995 Act, s 69(1).
101 1995 Act, s 69(2)–(11).
102 1995 Act, s 66.
103 1995 Act, s 66(2).
104 1995 Act, s 67.

(10) Proof hearings[105]

5.15 The hearing before the sheriff must take place within 28 days of the application being made by the Reporter. The sheriff has to consider whether or not to appoint a safeguarder to look after the interests of the child in the proceedings. Any safeguarder who was appointed by the children's hearing will continue through the court hearing. The safeguarder must make a report to the court if he/she does not intend to appear in person at the court hearing, and may make a report in other circumstances. The report may contain recommendations.[106]

In general, the proof hearing will take place in the sheriff court that covers the geographical area of the children's hearing. The exception to this is where the ground of referral is commission of an offence by the child, in which case the proof hearing will take place in the sheriff court which would have had jurisdiction in any prosecution of the crime.[107] The child can be represented by someone other than a qualified lawyer and can be excused attendance on the same grounds as at a children's hearing.

After hearing evidence[108] and considering the terms of any safeguarder's report, the sheriff may find the grounds not established and discharge the referral. Alternatively, the sheriff may find the grounds established and the matter will be referred back to the hearing for consideration and disposal. If the ground is that the child has committed an offence, the sheriff must be satisfied beyond reasonable doubt that the child has committed the offence; in other cases the sheriff must simply be satisfied that the ground is established on the balance of probabilities.[109] In making a finding, the sheriff may make deletions from the statement of facts in the grounds of referral, but cannot amend it.[110] Where the ground of referral is that a Schedule 1 offence has been committed by a

105 1995 Act, s 68. The procedural rules are in the Act of Sederunt (Child Care and Maintenance Rules) 1997, SI 1997/291, ch 3, pt VII.

106 *Kennedy v M* 1989 SLT 687.

107 The sheriff court needs to have geographical jurisdiction, it does not need to have jurisdiction to try the particular type of offence in a criminal trial, *Walker v C (No 2)* 2003 SLT 293, the crime involved in this case was rape which the sheriff has no jurisdiction to try.

108 There are restrictions on certain types of evidence or questioning at the proof hearing where the grounds of referral involve sexual abuse of the child, 1995 Act, ss 68A & 68B.

109 1995 Act, s 68(3)(b). See *S v Kennedy* 1987 SLT 765; *Harris v F* 1991 SLT 242. The higher standard of proof cannot be avoided by a referral of what is really an offence on one of the other grounds: *Constanda v M* 1997 SC 217.

110 *S v Kennedy* 1996 SCLR 34.

named individual, the court hearing on establishing the ground of referral should not, unless there are exceptional circumstances, be adjourned pending the outcome of any criminal trial.[111] Evidence at the proof hearing should not be restricted because of the possible trial of the alleged perpetrator.[112] An acquittal of a Schedule 1 offence in criminal proceedings does not indicate that a supervision requirement which was made on the basis that the offence was established as a ground of referral should automatically be terminated.[113] Where the evidence establishes that a Schedule 1 offence has been committed, but the sheriff is unable to decide which Schedule 1 offence, the ground of referral should be held to be established.[114]

It is also clear now that the sheriff should not, in most cases, rule on any procedural objections without hearing the evidence first. The only exceptions are where the objections, if successful, would mean that the grounds of referral could never be established.[115] An example of this would be a case where the referral was of a child under 8 accused of an offence.

If, during the course of the hearing, the child and the relevant person accept the grounds of referral, the sheriff has to stop the hearing and deem the grounds to be established. Where only the relevant person accepts the grounds the sheriff can either do this or hear the evidence if satisfied that this should be done.

If grounds of referral are established and the case referred back to the hearing for disposal, the sheriff may issue a warrant for the child's detention if it is likely that the child would run away before the hearing or if detention is in the child's own interests (for example, if the ground of referral was commission of a Schedule 1 offence against the child). Such detention may last, at most, 3 days.[116]

111 *Humphries, Petitioner* 1982 SLT 481; *Ferguson v P* 1989 SCLR 525.

112 *P v Kennedy* 1995 SCLR 1.

113 *Kennedy v B* 1992 SCLR 55. The main reason for this is the difference in standard of proof. The evidence may be such that the sheriff taking the proof hearing is satisfied on the balance of probabilities that the offence was committed. That same evidence may not satisfy a criminal court beyond a reasonable doubt. In *Kennedy v B* it was noted that acquittal in a criminal trial was a factor to be taken into account in determining whether a supervision requirement was still necessary.

114 *M v Kennedy* 1996 SLT 434.

115 *Sloan v B* 1991 SLT 530.

116 1995 Act, s 68(12).

(11) Supervision requirements[117]

5.16 The 1995 Act abolished the distinction between residential and non-residential supervision requirements. There is now only one type of supervision requirement which can contain a wide variety of conditions, including a condition specifying where the child is to stay, requiring medical examination or treatment, or regulating contact between the child and any other person. It is also possible for the hearing, when it is making a requirement, to fix a time for its review.[118] Before a condition can be imposed requiring the child to stay in a residential establishment, with an approved foster carer, with a kinship carer or with anyone who is not a relevant person, the hearing must have considered a report from the local authority which deals with the needs of the child and the suitability of the proposed placement to meet those needs. The report will also need to confirm that such a placement would be in the best interests of the child.[119]

The supervision requirement can also involve placement in secure accommodation[120] or a movement restriction order,[121] providing that one of two conditions are met:[122]

(a) that the child has previously absconded, is likely to abscond again and if the child does, this will put his/her physical, mental or moral welfare at risk; or
(b) that the child is likely to injure him/herself or someone else unless kept in secure accommodation.

The local authority can make a recommendation that the child be placed in secure accommodation only if these two conditions are met and if it is in the child's best interests to be placed and kept in secure accommodation.[123] Before any child is placed in secure accommodation a full assessment of his/her needs must be made and any placement will normally include screening procedures within the social work department. For example, a screening group may be set up which may include a senior psychologist, a senior person from the child care section and the head of the establishment. A requirement with a condition

117 1995 Act, s 70.
118 1995 Act, s 70(7).
119 Hearings Rules, r 20(6); LAC Regs, reg 7; LAC Guidance, pp 47–49.
120 Making secure accommodation a condition in a supervision requirement, and the associated procedures, has been held to be compliant with Articles 5 and 6 of the European Convention on Human Rights, *BJ v Proudfoot* [2010] CSIH 85.
121 See Intensive Support and Monitoring (Scotland) Regulations 2008, SSI 2008/75.
122 1995 Act, s 70(9)–(17).
123 Secure Accommodation (Scotland) Regulations 1996, SI 1996/3255, reg 10.

that the child be kept in secure accommodation must be reviewed within 3 months,[124] and a child kept in secure accommodation can require a review of the condition if he/she has not been placed in secure accommodation for 6 weeks.[125]

Supervision requirements impose limits on the parental rights and responsibilities of the parents of the child, not least because a child who is subject to a requirement is treated as a child being looked after by the local authority. A requirement to stay away from home clearly suspends the right to have the child staying with the parent(s). This requirement also affects the exercise of the responsibility or right to maintain contact and personal relations: the requirement may make express provision about contact as one of its conditions or the question of contact may be left to the discretion of the local authority.[126] Despite the effective suspension of some responsibilities and rights under the terms of the supervision requirement a court may still impose responsibilities even where these would be of no effect because of the existence of the supervision requirement. However, making a contact order would be inappropriate if this would conflict with the terms of a supervision requirement.[127]

Once a supervision requirement has been made, the main duty of the local authority is to give effect to its requirements. Where it provides that the child is to stay at a specified address other than residential accommodation or a foster placement, the authority has to visit the child to make sure that he/she is staying there and that the conditions of the requirement are being fulfilled.[128]

In all cases the local authority must refer the case back to the reporter if the conditions of the requirement are not being complied with, for example, if a fostering placement breaks down or the child cannot be placed in the specified residential establishment. The child also becomes a child being looked after by the local authority, which imposes on the authority all the duties which exist in respect of such children.[129] Social workers would probably take a different view in seeing these duties as important but seeing the actual contact with the child and family members, foster family members, residential workers and other professionals

124 Secure Accommodation (Scotland) Regulations 1996, SI 1996/3255, reg 11.
125 Secure Accommodation (Scotland) Regulations 1996, SI 1996/3255, reg 12.
126 The requirement must be clear enough so that the intention of the hearing can be understood: In *D v Strathclyde Regional Council* 1991 SCLR 185 the view was taken that the form in which the condition was expressed left some doubt as to whether the hearing intended that there should be contact or that contact should be terminated.
127 *Principal Reporter v K* [2010] CSIH 5.
128 1995 Act, s 71.
129 See ch 4.

as the core of work with the opportunities to engage with the child and significant others to effect change for the better.

Although s. 71 of the Children (Scotland) Act 1995 imposes a duty on local authorities to give effect to the requirements of a supervision requirement, until January 2005 there was no formal mechanism for making sure that this happened and also considerable evidence that supervision requirements were not being supervised and implemented.[130] The Antisocial Behaviour etc (Scotland) Act 2004 introduced provisions which provide a power by which duties imposed on a local authority by a supervision requirement can be clearly specified and a process through which these duties can be enforced in the event of non-compliance.[131]

Where duties on the local authority are clearly identified and there are concerns that these may not be fulfilled it may be appropriate for the hearing to exercise its power to set a review date so that the compliance of the authority with the requirement can be monitored. In any event, where at a review of a supervision requirement it appears that the authority is in breach of a duty imposed on it, the hearing can direct the Reporter to give the local authority notice of an intention to apply to the sheriff principal for an order requiring the authority to perform the duty. The hearing has discretion on whether to direct the service of the notice. The guidance suggests that the Reporter should only be required to take this step where there is a specific failure that, if left unchecked, would have a serious impact on the young person.[132] The notice gives the authority 21 days to respond. After this period has passed the hearing will meet again to consider the response and decide whether to authorise the Reporter to apply to the Sheriff Principal for an enforcement order. Once authorised, the Reporter then has to decide whether to make the application. In taking this decision any lack of resources on the part of the authority must not be taken into account. The application is made direct to the sheriff principal who has the power to order to authority to perform its duty.[133]

130 For example, Audit Scotland, *Dealing with Offending by Young People*, (2002), paras 147–148.

131 1995 Act, ss 71 & 1A.

132 *Guidance on Local Authority Accountability Antisocial Behaviour etc. (Scotland) Act 2004*, para 42.

133 See generally, Scottish Executive, *Guidance on Local Authority Accountability Antisocial Behaviour etc. (Scotland) Act 2004.*

(12) Parenting Orders

5.17 A children's hearing, whether considering a referral for the first time or conducting a review of an existing supervision requirement, can require the Reporter to consider for him/herself whether to apply for a parenting order.[134] Before doing this the hearing must consider that such an order might be appropriate. The requirement must set out the parent in respect of whom the application is to be made and the ground on which the application might be made, ie is the hearing of the opinion that the behaviour condition, the conduct condition or the welfare condition for making such an order exists in relation to the child (see box). The Reporter is not obliged to apply for an order and must consider the matter before making a decision as to whether to apply. As part of this consideration the Reporter may request a report from the local authority which it is obliged to provide.

> The *behaviour condition* is satisfied if the child has engaged in antisocial conduct and making the order is desirable in the interests of preventing further such behaviour.
>
> The *conduct* condition is satisfied if the child has engaged in criminal conduct and making the order is desirable in the interests of preventing further such conduct.
>
> The *welfare* condition is that making the order is desirable in the interests of improving the welfare of the child.

The Guidance notes that:[135]

> Parenting orders are not intended to address behaviour that is merely different, or behaviour that is the result of a medical or developmental condition or a mental disorder and should not be used to promote the harassment of individuals or groups for behaviour that results from being of a different race or religion

134 A parenting order imposes certain requirements on the parents of the child. See Antisocial Behaviour etc (Scotland) Act 2004, pt 9, Scottish Government, *A Framework for Parenting Orders in Scotland* (2007).

135 Scottish Executive, *Guidance on Parenting Orders* (2005), para 39.

(13) Duration and review of supervision requirements[136]

5.18 The guiding principle is that the supervision requirement should last no longer than is necessary in the interests of promoting or safeguarding the welfare of the child. Once a requirement is made there are several means through which it can come to be reviewed. The child or the relevant person can require a review 3 months after the requirement was made or 3 months after any previous review. Reviews can be initiated at any time by the local authority if it is satisfied that the requirement ought to be ended or varied; that a condition of the requirement is not being complied with; or that the best interests of the child would be served either by placing the child for adoption or the authority intends to apply for a permanence order. The special provisions for reviews of children required to reside in secure accommodation are noted above.[137]

If the requirement will expire within 3 months, the reporter must arrange a hearing. The requirement will expire automatically on the 18th birthday of the child or after 1 year from the date on which the order was made or last continued. The reporter must therefore arrange a hearing both once the child reaches the age of 17 years and 9 months and once 9 months have elapsed from the making of the order or the last review.

At the review hearing the case can be continued for further investigation, the requirement can be terminated or the requirement can be varied, for example, by adding to or altering the conditions attached to the requirement. Where the hearing is considering a requirement which is to lapse within 3 months, it has a specific obligation to consider whether, if the requirement is terminated, the child will still require supervision or guidance. If the decision is that such guidance or supervision is necessary it must be provided by the local authority, but only to the extent that the child is willing to accept it.[138]

Since the child who is the subject of a supervision requirement is treated as being looked after by the local authority the review requirements set down for children being looked after apply to him/her.[139]

136 1995 Act, s 73.
137 See para 5.16.
138 1995, s 73(12).
139 See ch 4.

(14) Rights of appeal[140]

5.19 There is a right of appeal to the sheriff against any decision of the children's hearing. Legal aid is available for this. The appeal must be made within 3 weeks of the decision and if it concerns a supervision requirement made by the hearing, an application can be made to the hearing asking it to suspend the requirement pending the appeal. Although the 1995 Act suggests that any decision can be appealed against, it will not be possible to appeal against decisions which involve procedural steps. An example of this is the decision to instruct the reporter to apply to the sheriff for a finding that the grounds of referral are established. Appeal will therefore usually be possible only against those decisions involving a final disposal of the case.[141]

Exceptionally, it is possible to appeal against a warrant issued by the hearing to find a child or to keep that child in a place of safety. Where the appeal is against a warrant, it must be dealt with within 3 days or the warrant will lapse.

At the appeal the sheriff will hear evidence and may question anyone who has compiled a report for the hearing and seek a further report. If the appeal is unsuccessful the decision of the hearing stands. If the appeal is successful the sheriff has a number of options, depending on the decision which is being appealed:

(a) where a warrant is appealed against, the warrant will be recalled;
(b) where the appeal is against a condition attached to a supervision requirement which means that the child has to stay in secure accommodation, the condition will be removed from the requirement;
(c) in other cases the sheriff can either:
  (i) send the case back to the hearing for reconsideration with a note of the reasons for his/her decision;
  (ii) discharge the referral; or
  (iii) impose a supervision requirement in terms that the sheriff thinks appropriate to replace the requirement made by the hearing. This provision seems to conflict with the ethos of the hearings system that decisions about what steps to take are best taken after discussion in the relatively informal setting of the hearing.[142]

140 1995 Act, s 51.
141 *H v McGregor* 1973 SLT 110.
142 1995 Act, 51(5)(c)(iii).

The appeal is to be allowed if, in the words of the 1995 Act, the sheriff is satisfied that the decision of the children's hearing is not justified in all the circumstances of the case. No further indication is given as to the grounds of appeal, but it is clear that it includes procedural irregularities at the hearing.[143] If an appeal to the sheriff results in the sheriff ordering that the case is remitted to a hearing for reconsideration, such a hearing need not be arranged if the sheriff's decision is itself being appealed.[144] In such cases care must be taken not to act in a way which might cause difficulty if the appeal was successful. There is a right of appeal from any decision of the sheriff to the sheriff principal or to the Court of Session, and if the initial appeal is made to the sheriff principal his/her decision can be appealed to the Court of Session. This right of appeal covers not only the decision of the sheriff in an appeal from a decision of the hearing, but also other decisions made by the sheriff, for example, a finding that the grounds of referral are established. Once an appeal has been lodged, the original decision of the sheriff need not be implemented pending the outcome of the appeal. If this appeal is successful the case will be sent back to the sheriff with instructions as to disposal.

Even though an unsuccessful appeal has been made against a finding that grounds of referral are established, it is still possible at a later stage to re-open the question of the existence of these grounds. Under the 1968 Act this was possible in exceptional cases through application to the *nobile officium* of the Court of Session, as happened in the Ayrshire cases.[145] The 1995 Act introduced a procedure allowing an application to be made for a review of a finding that grounds of referral were established.[146] This review can take place both where the grounds were found to be established by the sheriff against the opposition of the child and/or relevant person and where the grounds were deemed by the sheriff to be established following acceptance by the child and/or relevant person as described above. Either the child or a relevant person may make the application, and it must be based on the following grounds:

143 *M v Kennedy* 1995 SCLR 15. In *W v Schaffer* 2001 SLT (Sh Ct) 86, at 87, it was said that the task of the sheriff was 'to see if there has been some procedural irregularity in the conduct of the case; to see whether the hearing has failed to give proper, or any, consideration to a relevant factor in the case; and in general to consider whether the decision reached by the hearing can be characterised as one which could not, upon any reasonable view, be regarded as being justified in all the circumstances of the case.

144 *Kennedy v M* 1995 SCLR 88.

145 *L, Petitioners (No 1)* 1993 SLT 1310; *L, Petitioners (No 2)* 1993 SLT 1342; see also *JL v Kennedy* (6 March 1995, unreported) IH.

146 1995 Act, s 85

(a) there is evidence which might have had material effect on the outcome of the proof hearing which was not considered by the sheriff;
(b) the evidence would have been admissible at the proof hearing and is likely to be credible and reliable; and
(c) there is a reasonable explanation for the failure to bring this evidence to the proof hearing.

If these three conditions are met the sheriff will consider the new evidence. There are three possible outcomes. First, the sheriff may be satisfied that none of the original grounds of referral are established and that no other grounds are established. If so, the supervision requirement will be terminated either immediately or on a date fixed by the sheriff. The question of whether the child will need some supervision and guidance after the ending of the supervision requirement must be considered by the sheriff and he/she may direct the local authority to provide such guidance or supervision. The social work department must comply with this direction, except where a child is old enough to understand the supervision or guidance being offered and refuses it. Where the requirement is not to be terminated immediately the sheriff can vary conditions in the requirement. Secondly, the sheriff may be satisfied that none of the original grounds of referral are satisfied but that the evidence establishes some other ground which was not the subject of the original proof hearing. If so, the sheriff may find that ground established and remit the case back to the hearing for disposal. Finally, if one of the grounds of referral at the original proof hearing is established the sheriff may refer the case back to the hearing for disposal or can take no action. The decision of the sheriff can be appealed to the sheriff principal and then to the Court of Session or direct to the Court of Session.[147]

REFERRALS FROM THE COURT SYSTEM

5.20 A child under the age of 16 not subject to a supervision requirement who pleads or is found guilty in a criminal court may be referred to a hearing for advice or for disposal. After considering the advice of the hearing the court may refer the case to it for disposal. Where a child under 16 who is subject to a supervision requirement pleads or is found guilty the High Court may, and sheriff and JP courts must, ask the reporter to arrange a hearing to consider the case and give advice on the treatment of the child. On receipt of the advice the case can be referred back to the hearing for disposal.[148]

147 1995 Act, s 51(11).
148 1995 Act, s 49. There are some limited exceptions to the power to refer to a hearing.

Summary courts can also refer cases of people between 16 and 17½ to a hearing for advice if they plead or are found guilty. After receiving the advice the case can be referred to a hearing for disposal. None of these provisions apply in cases where there is a fixed penalty, for example, murder or for certain minor traffic offences.[149]

If a court convicts someone of a Schedule 1 offence it may refer the child who was the victim of the offence or a child who is or is likely to become a member of the same household as the offender to the reporter.[150]

If, during the course of a variety of court hearings, including actions for divorce, actions under section 11 of the 1995 Act in relation to parental rights and responsibilities, adoption proceedings or proceedings relating to permanence orders, it appears to the judge that any of the non-offence grounds of referral to a children's hearing exist in respect of a child involved in the hearing, the judge may refer the case of the child to the reporter. The reporter must then investigate and decide whether a hearing is necessary. If a hearing is arranged, the ground of referral found to exist by the judge is regarded as being established.[151]

COURT ORDERS SENDING CHILDREN TO LOCAL AUTHORITY ACCOMMODATION

5.21 Children remanded in custody by criminal courts are to be remanded to the care of a local authority. It is no longer possible to remand a child aged 14 or 15 to a remand centre or prison or to a young offenders institution.[152]

Where a child is convicted in a summary court he/she may, provided someone over 21 could have been imprisoned by the court, be sentenced to detention for up to 1 year with the place and conditions of detention to be decided by the local authority.[153] A child so sentenced is to be treated as subject to a supervision requirement.[154]

A child who has been arrested and not liberated is to be detained in a place of safety unless the child is so unruly that he/she cannot be so

149 Criminal Procedure (Scotland) Act 1995, s 49.
150 Criminal Procedure (Scotland) Act 1995, s 48.
151 1995 Act, s 54.
152 Criminal Procedure (Scotland) Act 1995, s 51, amended by Criminal Justice and Licensing (Scotland) Act 2010, s 64.
153 Criminal Procedure (Scotland) Act 1995, s 44(1).
154 Criminal Procedure (Scotland) Act 1995, s 44(3). One consequence is that he/she will be a looked after child.

detained, it is impractical to detain the child in a place of safety, or it is inadvisable to detain him/her in a place of safety because of his/her health or mental or bodily condition.[155] In common with others detained the child must be brought to court on the next lawful day.

Social work involvement includes the negotiation for the most appropriate resource for the child. Detention of a child through court proceedings may be experienced as especially traumatic by the child and family and so there may be a need for a social worker to become further involved with them, for example, in supporting them through the court process, in clarifying the meaning and implications of any order made, and in making practical arrangements for visits.

EMERGENCY PROTECTION OF CHILDREN[156]

5.22 The 1995 Act introduced an entirely new means of protecting children in an emergency by way of the child protection order (CPO) which is granted by the sheriff.

(1) Grounds for application[157]

5.23 Like the place of safety order which it replaced, anyone can apply to the sheriff for a child protection order,[158] which the sheriff may grant provided that the following conditions are met:[159]

(a) the sheriff has reasonable grounds to believe that the child either:
   (i) is being so treated or neglected that he/she is suffering significant harm; or
   (ii) will suffer significant harm if not removed to and kept in a place of safety or if he/she does not remain in the place where presently accommodated; and

155 Criminal Procedure (Scotland) Act 1995, s 43.

156 See *Guidance,* vol 1, ch 7.

157 1995 Act, s 57.

158 Though in practice around 90% of applications are made by social workers.

159 1995 Act, s 57(1). There is only one reported Scottish case on the granting of a child protection order or the processes leading up to it: *K and F, Applicants* 2002 SCLR 769. There is extensive guidance on the grounds for making an order in relation to the equivalent order in England and Wales, the emergency protection order: see *X Council v B (emergency protection orders)* [2004] EWHC 2015 (Fam), [2007] 1 FCR 512; *Re X (emergency protection orders)* [2006] EWHC 510 (Fam), [2007] 1 FCR 551 both referred to in *ES's Application* [2007] NIQB 58. See also the discussion of the human rights aspects of removal of children in paras 5.33–5.36 below.

(b) a CPO is necessary to protect the child from the actual or anticipated harm.

There is no further explanation or definition of when harm will be 'significant' – the *Guidance* has this to say:[160]

> It will, therefore, be a matter for the judgment of those concerned with determining the outcome of applications to consider whether the degree of harm to which the child is believed to have been subjected or is suspected of having been subjected (or is likely to be subjected) is significant. Those contemplating an application for an order or authorisation will need to make a judgment based on as much information as can be obtained about the child and his or her family, They must be satisfied that they can demonstrate to a sheriff … that the criteria for granting the particular Order … are met.

This is consistent with the view expressed in one English case that significant harm was harm which was 'considerable, noteworthy or important.'[161] Guidance in England and Wales sets out the considerations in the box on the next page as relevant to significant harm.[162]

The reference in the grounds to a child suffering harm if removed from the place where currently resident would allow the granting of an order, for example, for a baby to remain in hospital if it would be dangerous to go home or in the situation that arose in *M v Dumfries and Galloway Regional Council*[163] where a child disclosed abuse by her father while in the voluntary care of the local authority and the authority wished to keep her in care.

As well as these general grounds there is a further set of grounds which can be used only by a local authority to apply for a CPO.[164] These are that the authority:

(a) has reasonable grounds to suspect that a child is being or will be so treated or neglected that he/she is suffering or will suffer significant harm;

160 *Guidance*, Vol. 1, ch 7, para 5.

161 *Humberside County Council v B* [1993] 1 FLR 257.

162 See also Scottish Government, *National Guidance for Child Protection in Scotland: draft for public consultation* (2010), paras 38–44, 426–609. Research published in 2006 indicated that few local authorities offered guidance on what was meant by significant harm, Francis, J, *et al*, *Protecting Children in Scotland: An Investigation of Risk Assessment and Inter-agency Collaboration in the Use of Child Protection Orders* (2006), paras 4.9–4.17.

163 1991 SCLR 481.

164 1995 Act, s 57(2). There is an overlap between these grounds and the grounds for applying for a child assessment order, though the criteria for a CPO impose a slightly higher standard.

(b) is either making inquiries or having inquiries made to allow it to decide if it needs to do anything to safeguard the child's welfare; and

(c) has reasonable cause to believe that access to the child is needed as a matter of urgency, but that it is being unreasonably denied and this is preventing it from completing its inquiries.

DCSF, Working Together to Safeguard Children: A guide to inter-agency working to safeguard and promote the welfare of children (2010), paras 1.28–1.29

There are no absolute criteria on which to rely when judging what constitutes significant harm. Consideration of the severity of ill-treatment may include the degree and the extent of physical harm, the duration and frequency of abuse and neglect, the extent of pre-meditation, and the presence or degree of threat, coercion, sadism and bizarre or unusual elements. Each of these elements has been associated with more severe effects on the child, and/or relatively greater difficulty in helping the child overcome the adverse impact of the maltreatment. Sometimes, a single traumatic event may constitute significant harm, for example, a violent assault, suffocation or poisoning. More often, significant harm is a compilation of significant events, both acute and long-standing, which interrupt, change or damage the child's physical and psychological development. Some children live in family and social circumstances where their health and development are neglected. For them, it is the corrosiveness of long-term emotional, physical or sexual abuse that causes impairment to the extent of constituting significant harm. In each case, it is necessary to consider any maltreatment alongside the child's own assessment of his or her safety and welfare, the family's strengths and supports8, as well as an assessment of the likelihood and capacity for change and improvements in parenting and the care of children and young people

To understand and identify significant harm, it is necessary to consider:

- the nature of harm, in terms of maltreatment or failure to provide adequate care;
- the impact on the child's health and development;
- the child's development within the context of their family and wider environment;

- any special needs, such as a medical condition, communication impairment or
- disability, that may affect the child's development and care within the family;
- the capacity of parents to meet adequately the child's needs; and
- the wider and environmental family context.

Social workers and their managers take decisions about children believed to be at such a degree of risk of significant harm that they must urgently be protected, in some cases by removal from their homes. The power to intervene so intrusively in the private lives of families is the subject of much debate and misunderstanding. The quality of information processing, decision-making and the interaction skills of the social workers all contribute toward a child being believed to be in need of protection and set the scene conducively for future work towards either the child's return home or placement in a permanent alternative. The unresolved societal conflicts about the role of social workers are perhaps most clearly seen in the consideration and use of CPOs. Although the overriding principles of obtaining the views of the child and seeking the most minimal intervention do not pertain legally to the making of a CPO, good practice would suggest that they are still relevant.[165]

There is evidence that practitioners consider that the introduction of the CPO has increased the level of scrutiny which is given to applications as compared to the place of safety orders which the child protection order replaced. There also appears to be more emphasis on preparation of applications and it appears that few applications are refused.[166] Guidance indicates that social work departments will need to clarify who will have responsibility for preparing CPO applications, whether the legal department of the authority[167] is involved or not; how social workers will be prepared for going before a sheriff; and what the procedure will

165 As do the requirements of the European Convention on Human Rights, see para 5.33–5.36.

166 Francis, J, *et al*, *Protecting Children in Scotland: An Investigation of Risk Assessment and Inter-agency Collaboration in the Use of Child Protection Orders* (2006), paras 4.18–4.21.

167 The research reported in Francis, J, *et al*, *Protecting Children in Scotland: An Investigation of Risk Assessment and Inter-agency Collaboration in the Use of Child Protection Orders* (2006) suggested a fairly even split between authorities where application was made by legal services, where it was made by social work and where the application was jointly made, para 3.15.

be if and when the order is granted. The appearance before the sheriff is not a full proof hearing although the social worker will have to convince the sheriff of the necessity for such an order by providing supporting evidence in the application, in supplementary documents and in discussion with the sheriff. This will require preparation and confidence on the part of the social worker.

(2) Effect of the order

5.24 The order can, at the discretion of the sheriff, contain one or more of these requirements or authorisations:[168]

(a) a requirement addressed to whoever is in a position to produce the child to do so;
(b) authorisation for removal of the child to a place of safety and to keep the child there;
(c) authorisation to prevent the removal of the child;
(d) a provision that the location of the place of safety should not be disclosed to a particular person or group of people.

In addition the sheriff has to consider whether to attach directions to the CPO concerned with regulating contact with the child and this would include prohibiting contact. A second type of direction, concerned with the exercise or fulfilment of any parental right or responsibility, can be made only if it is applied for, and application should be made only where the direction is necessary to safeguard and promote the welfare of the child.[169] This type of direction can cover examination and treatment of the child or any assessment or interview, though if the child has capacity he/she can refuse any examination or treatment.[170]

Once an order is made, the reporter must be notified.

(3) Implementation

5.25 Once an order is made, it must be implemented only if the person who applied for the order has a reasonable belief that this is necessary to safeguard or promote the child's welfare.[171] In any event, an attempt must be made to implement the order within 24 hours of it being

168 1995 Act, s 57(4).
169 1995 Act, s 58.
170 1995 Act, s 90.
171 1995 Act, s 57(6).

made: otherwise the order will lapse.[172] Note that this only requires an attempt to implement the order. An unsuccessful attempt will continue the order in force.[173] This requirement does not apply where the order is to keep the child in the place where he/she is already resident. A child taken to a place of safety is owed the same duties by the local authority as a child being looked after by it.

(4) How long does the CPO last and what happens next?

5.26 There are a variety of possible routes that can be followed after a CPO has been implemented and which may result either in discharge of the CPO or in other measures being taken in respect of the child.

(a) *Discharge by the reporter.* The CPO can be discharged by the reporter if, on the basis of new information or of a change in circumstances, the reporter considers that the conditions for making a CPO are no longer satisfied. In taking that decision the reporter must have regard to the welfare of the child. Conditions and directions attached to the CPO can also be varied by the reporter on the same grounds.[174] These powers can be exercised only (i) if no initial children's hearing has been arranged, and (ii) before the beginning of any hearing before the sheriff of an application to set aside or vary the CPO.[175] If this power is exercised both the applicant for the CPO and the sheriff who granted it must be notified.[176]

(b) *Arranging an initial hearing.*[177] If the CPO is not discharged and if the reporter has not been notified of an application to set aside or vary the CPO, an initial meeting of the children's hearing must be arranged to consider the case of the child. This meeting must take place on the second working day after implementation of the CPO. Where the CPO authorises removal of the child to a place of safety implementation occurs when this is actually done. When the CPO prevents removal it is deemed to be implemented on the day it is made. The purpose of this initial hearing is solely to con-

172 1995 Act, s 60(1).

173 Where this happens there is no clear statutory provision for the duration of the order, though it could be brought to an end by the Reporter as described below. Once in force the Children's Hearings (Scotland) Act 2011 will set a maximum direction for orders. See ch 12.

174 1995 Act, s 69(3).

175 1995 Act, s 60(4).

176 1995 Act, s 60(3) & (5).

177 1995 Act, s 59.

sider whether to continue the CPO.[178] Continuation can be ordered only where this is in the interests of the child and where the hearing is satisfied that the grounds for making a CPO are established. This latter requirement presumably means that it must be satisfied that the grounds exist on the day when it meets to consider the case. Where the hearing continues a CPO its terms can be varied and it will be continued to a further hearing arranged to consider the child's case, which must take place on the eighth working day after implementation of the CPO.[179] This hearing will take the same format as any other hearing to consider the case of a child referred to it, and the CPO will lapse at the beginning of this hearing, so that if the hearing wishes to continue the case and keep the child in a place of safety other powers must be used.

The CPO will lapse if not continued by the initial hearing and also, presumably, if the hearing is not held on the second working day. If the CPO is continued by the initial hearing, the reporter still has to exercise his/her discretion in deciding whether to refer the child to the second hearing. If the decision is taken not to proceed with such a referral the CPO will lapse.

There is an appeal to the sheriff within 2 working days against the continuation of a CPO by the hearing,[180] and the reporter, on being notified of such an appeal, may arrange a hearing to give advice to the sheriff. The time limits and powers of the sheriff in dealing with the appeal are the same as those when dealing with an application to set aside or vary the order.

(c) *Application to vary or set aside the order.* Such an application can be made by the child, anyone having parental rights, a relevant person or the person who applied for the order.[181] The application is made to the sheriff and must be made before the initial hearing, arranged as described above, has begun.[182] The reporter is notified of the application and can arrange an optional hearing to

178 1995 Act, s 59(2).

179 1995 Act, s 65(2). A study conducted by the Scottish Children's Reporter Administration suggested that in the cases of nearly all children removed from home under a CPO a supervision requirement was made (or an existing requirement varied) at this hearing. In addition, after three months only 10% of the children involved in the study had returned home. Scottish Children's Reporter Administration, *A Study of Children Subject to Child Protection Orders in Edinburgh 2006/2007* (2008).

180 1995 Act, s 60(8).

181 1995 Act, s 60(7).

182 1995 Act, s 60(8).

give advice to the sheriff.[183] The application must be disposed of by the sheriff within 3 working days.[184] Although it is not clearly stated the CPO would, presumably, lapse if this time limit was not complied with. After hearing evidence, at which stage the reporter has the right to make representations, the sheriff has to decide if the conditions for making a CPO are satisfied or if any direction attached to the CPO should be varied. In the latter case the sheriff can make any necessary modification. If the conditions for making a CPO are not satisfied the CPO is recalled.[185] If the conditions are satisfied the sheriff has 4 options which may be taken:[186]

(i) the order can be confirmed or varied;
(ii) any direction attached to the CPO can be confirmed or varied;
(iii) a new direction can be attached to the CPO;
(iv) the order may be continued in force until the beginning of the second children's hearing described in (b) above, that is, the hearing which takes place on the eighth working day.

(5) Emergency protection when there is no time to apply to the sheriff[187]

5.27 In emergencies, authorisation to remove a child or to keep him/her in a particular place can be granted by a justice of the peace. This is possible, in the words of the 1995 Act, where 'it is not practicable in the circumstances to apply to the sheriff for a CPO or for the sheriff to consider such an application'. The authorisation can be granted on either of the sets of grounds set out above for granting a CPO, but only if the order granted would probably have contained authorisation to remove the child to a place of safety or authorisation to prevent the child's removal. As well as authorising removal or retention of the child, the authorisation issued by the JP may require production of the child by whoever is in a position to do this. The authorisation must be implemented as soon as reasonably practicable[188] and in any event will lapse 12 hours from the time it was made if no arrangements have been made to prevent removal of the child or if he/she has not been or is not

183 1995 Act, s 60(10).
184 1995 Act, s 60(8).
185 1995 Act, s 60(13).
186 1995 Act, s 60(12).
187 1995 Act, s 61.
188 Emergency Child Protection Measures (Scotland) Regulations 1996, SI 1996/3258, reg 4.

being taken to a place of safety. Otherwise the authorisation will lapse 24 hours after being granted or, if this is earlier, when there is a disposal of an application for a CPO.

Police constables have the power to take a child to a place of safety if they have reasonable cause to believe that the conditions for making a CPO are satisfied; that it is not practicable to apply for a CPO or to have the application considered by a sheriff; and that it is necessary to remove the child to a place of safety to protect him/her from significant harm or significant further harm. A child can be kept in the place of safety for 24 hours unless an application for a CPO is disposed of earlier.

If either of these emergency measures is taken the reporter must be informed.[189] Both of these types of emergency action will terminate if the reporter forms the view that the grounds for them no longer exist or that it is no longer in the child's best interests to be kept in the place of safety. At all times the general principle is that a child should not be detained unnecessarily in a place of safety and the reporter has broad powers to liberate or discharge a child, for example, when there is a change of circumstances.

EXCLUSION ORDERS[190]

5.28 The traditional approach to the emergency protection of children involved the removal of children from the danger. The 1995 Act introduced the possibility of removing the alleged source of the danger and leaving the child at home. This is done by way of exclusion orders which are, to some extent, based on the exclusion orders provided for in the Matrimonial Homes (Family Protection) (Scotland) Act 1981. One significant difference is that these exclusion orders can be applied for only by the local authority. There are issues about where the excluded person will live;[191] what financial provisions might be made available; and significantly about the principle of excluding a person who is only just alleged to have been the cause of a child suffering. These concerns

189 Emergency Child Protection Measures (Scotland) Regulations 1996, SI 1996/3258, regs 3 & 8.

190 1995 Act, ss 76 to 80. See *Guidance,* vol 1, ch 7. The procedural rules are in the Act of Sederunt (Child Care and Maintenance Rules) 1997, SI 1997/291, ch 3, Pt V.

191 The Children Act 1989 makes specific provision for assisting someone who has left accommodation to protect a child: Sch 2, para 5. It could be argued that the same sort of assistance could be provided by the local authority in Scotland under the terms of s 22 of the 1995 Act, given that a service can be provided to another member of the child's family if it will safeguard and promote the child's welfare.

may be reduced given that the person accused has the opportunity to appear and be represented at court hearings. Many social workers and others have long held the view based on their experience, research and their value base that removing a child from his/her home environment and primary carer just at a time of trauma and stress is illogical, enormously damaging and counterproductive in both the short and long term. In spite of what may prove to be insurmountable practical and civil rights problems, these orders provide the possibility to consider an alternative which may prove to be much more in keeping with the three overriding principles of the paramountcy of the child's welfare, the child's right to be heard and that no order should be made if this would be better for the child.

(1) When can an exclusion order be made?

5.29 Exclusion orders can be made if these three conditions exist:[192]

(a) the child has suffered, is suffering or is likely to suffer significant harm as a result of any actual conduct by the person named in the application for the order (who is referred to as the 'named person'), or conduct by this named person which is threatened or reasonably apprehended;

(b) the order is necessary to protect the child regardless of whether he/she is living in the family home and would better safeguard the child's welfare than removal from the family home;

and

(c) the application identifies someone who is capable of looking after the child and any other family members left in the family home properly (the 'appropriate person').

No final exclusion order can be made until the named person has been given an opportunity to be heard by the sheriff, but until this is done an interim order can be made and this order has the same effect as a final one.[193]

Even if the grounds are made out, the sheriff still has to take account of the overriding principles set out above before making an order and must also not make an order if doing so would be unreasonable and unjustified.[194] This has two aspects. First, the order may be unreasonable and unjustified in all the circumstances of the case. The sheriff must, in par-

192 1995 Act, s 76(2).
193 1995 Act, s 76(3).
194 1995 Act, s 76(9) and (11).

ticular, look at the conduct of members of the child's family; the needs and resources of members of that family; and the extent to which the family home and anything in it is used in connection with a trade, business or profession. The second aspect to be considered is the possible consequences of making an order if the home involved is an agricultural tenancy or tied accommodation.

If the sheriff dealing with an application for an exclusion order thinks that the conditions for granting a CPO have been established he/she may instead of making an exclusion order make a CPO.

(2) The effect of an order[195]

5.30 The effect of an exclusion order is to exclude the named person from the family home, which he/she can enter only with the permission of the local authority. Additional orders can be attached to the exclusion order, for example, a warrant to eject the named person; an interdict preventing this named person from entering the home or entering the vicinity of the home; an interdict preventing the named person from taking any step in respect of the child; and an order regulating contact between the child and the named person. The power of arrest can be attached to these orders.[196]

(3) How long does the order last?

5.31 The exclusion order will last for 6 months.[197]

SHORT-TERM REFUGES

5.32 Local authorities can provide short-term refuges for children (who for this purpose are those under 18) who appear to them to be at risk.[198] The provision of accommodation is triggered by a request from the child and can be either in a residential establishment or with a foster family approved for the purpose. Refuge can be provided for up to 7 days, or up to 14 days if the authority has been unable to find a respon-

195 1995 Act, s 77.
196 1995 Act, s 78.
197 1995 Act, s 79(1).
198 1995 Act, s 38(1)(a). It appears that there is only one such refuge operating in Scotland, run by the Aberlour Childcare Trust.

sible person in relation to the child and has no suitable accommodation for the child. The main categories of 'responsible person' are the child's parent; a non-parent with parental responsibilities; someone who ordinarily has charge or control of the child; a local authority looking after the child; and anyone providing accommodation for the child under the 1995 Act.

The local authority must notify the 'authorised officer' of the fact that the child is being provided with refuge, of the child's name, of his/her last permanent address, of the address of any responsible person and of a contact telephone number. Notification must be made as soon as reasonably practicable and at the latest within 24 hours of providing refuge. An 'authorised officer' is a police officer identified by the Chief Constable for the purposes of these provisions. The local authority may approve residential establishments run by others for the purpose of providing refuge. If refuge is provided in one of these establishments, the local authority and the authorised officer must be notified as soon as practicable and, in any event, within 24 hours.

As soon as reasonably practicable after providing refuge, or being notified of the provision of refuge by an approved establishment, the local authority must notify the responsible person and the local authority in which the child had his/her last permanent address.

This provision permits social work departments to listen to and respond more appropriately to the views of children who are saying they are at risk and can no longer stay in the place where they believe themselves to be in danger. It provides the time for the social worker to complete a full assessment of the child and his/her whole situation with a view to ensuring as high a quality of life for the child as possible. While, clearly, there may be occasions when children's motivations for claiming to be at risk may be questionable, at least with the possibility of short-term refuge, children who are genuinely at risk can be accommodated.[199]

HUMAN RIGHTS

5.33 Some human rights issues which affect child protection have already been mentioned and this section will briefly explore some other issues, focusing particularly on Articles 3, 6 and 8 of the European Convention on Human Rights (ECHR) and some of the principles that can

199 See also *Guidance*, vol 1, ch 8; Refuges for Children (Scotland) Regulations 1996, SI 1996/3259.

be derived from the interpretation of these by the European Court of Human Rights (ECtHR).

(1) Article 3

5.34 Article 3 of the ECHR states that:

> No one shall be subjected to torture or to inhuman or degrading treatment or punishment

This clearly imposes a duty on states not to treat individuals in this way, but it goes beyond this to impose a duty on states and on government organisations, including local authorities, to act to prevent further infringement of an individual's rights when they become aware of such infringement. In a European Court of Human Rights case concerning children the point was put in this way:

> [States are required] to take measures designed to ensure that individuals within their jurisdiction are not subjected to torture or inhuman or degrading treatment, including such ill-treatment administered by private individuals. These measures should provide effective protection, in particular, of children and other vulnerable persons and include reasonable steps to prevent ill-treatment of which the authorities had or ought to have had knowledge.[200]

What this means for local authorities is that they will have a duty to intervene when a child's treatment meets the threshold of torture or inhuman and degrading treatment, provided that they were aware, or ought to have been aware of this. If it is (or ought to be) so aware, then it must take reasonable steps to prevent the continued infringement of the child's rights, it is not required to guarantee against harm to children. In order for the duty to arise under Article 3 the threshold is high, though it can be met. In the case from which the quotation was taken the threshold was considered to be reached and exceeded: the children were poorly fed, lived in extremely poor home conditions and had little supervision. If the treatment of the children does not amount to a breach of Article 3 rights then it may still amount to a breach of their rights under Article 8 which will also require positive action by a local authority. It is clear, however, that not all neglect or mistreatment of children will involve infringement of their rights under Article 8.

200 *Z v United Kingdom* (2002) 34 EHRR 3, at para 73.

(2) Article 6

5.35 Article 6 of the ECHR provides that:

> In the determination of his civil rights and obligations … everyone is entitled to a fair and public hearing within a reasonable time by an independent and impartial tribunal established by law.

Issues of a fair hearing have arisen in respect to procedure before the children's hearing. This has resulted in the introduction of legal representation in some cases[201] as well as the decision that individuals who hold a contact order permitting contact with a child, but who do not have any parental responsibilities or rights and don't have day to day care of the child, should be permitted to attend a children's hearing. The reason for this is that any supervision requirement may regulate the contact the child has with any other person and so may suspend the contact provided for by the contact order. As the rights to contact are civil rights, the hearing would then be determining the civil rights of the holder of the contact order. If the holder were not permitted to attend then he/she would not get a fair trial in the determination of these civil rights.[202] A further issue about Article 6 is whether the procedure for obtaining a CPO is compliant with this Article. The procedure involves application to the sheriff without notice to the child or his/her parents (though they may, in fact be aware of the intention to apply for the order). However, Article 6 does not require that a decision is always taken by a process and by a tribunal which allows a party to be present and be represented, as long as such a decision can be reviewed by a body and through a process which is does allow this. Since there is a right to seek recall of a CPO before the sheriff with full legal representation, the process as a whole complies with Article 6.[203]

(3) Article 8

5.36 Article 8 of the ECHR states that:

> 1. Everyone has the right to respect for his private and family life, his home and his correspondence.
>
> 2. There shall be no interference by a public authority with the exercise of this right except such as is in accordance with the law

201 See para 5.13 above.
202 *Knox v S* [2010] CSIH 45. See also Principal Reporter UK [2010] UKSC 56.
203 See *K and F, Applicants* 2002 SCLR 769.

> and is necessary in a democratic society in the interests of national security, public safety or the economic well-being of the country, for the prevention of disorder or crime, for the protection of health or morals, or for the protection of the rights and freedoms of others.

The second paragraph of the Article clearly indicates that interference with family life can be justified in certain circumstances, the most relevant exception in the case of children is likely to be 'the protection of the rights and freedoms of others.' There will in many cases be a balance to be struck between the interests of the child and those of the parents and it has been said that in carrying out this balancing:

> [T]he Court will attach particular importance to the best interests of the child, which depending on their nature and seriousness, may override those of the parent. In particular…the parent cannot be entitled under Article 8 of the Convention to have such measures taken as would harm the interests of the child.[204]

Any removal of a child from his or her family will involve an interference with family life and this interference will have to be, first of all, in accordance with law, in other words following the procedures prescribed for removal of a child, ie by applying for a child protection order or making use of one of the other ways of authorising this.[205] In addition, the decision to remove must be justified by 'sufficiently weighty considerations in favour of the child.'[206] In light of ECtHR decisions it will be particularly difficult to justify the removal of a newly born child, especially where he/she is or will be in hospital and under supervision, though there may be cases where this can be justified, for example where there is likely to be a risk to the child from the actions of the mother as soon as he/she is born.[207] The conclusion that action to remove a child is necessary must follow on from a proper assessment and consideration of the alternatives,[208] though it is clear that, given the circumstances, this assessment need not be exhaustive.

After a child has been removed (and while a child is being looked after away from home) there will be a duty, so far as this is consistent with the interests of the child, to promote contact between the child and his/her family, including parents and siblings, though there is a limit to the extent to which children can be forced into such contact. This obligation

204 *Johansen v Norway* (1997) 23 EHRR 33, para 78.

205 See part 6(5) above. In *R(G) v Nottingham City Council* [2008] EWHC 1152 (Admin) a child was removed without following the correct procedures.

206 *Olsson v Sweden* (1988) 11 EHRR 72.

207 *Bury Metropolitan Council v D* [2009] EWHC 446 (Fam).

208 *P, C & s v United Kingdom* (2002) 35 EHRR 31.

implies that the placement of children should not make contact practically impossible and is related to the view frequently expressed by the ECtHR that the objective if possible, should be reunification of the child with his/her family.[209]

As well as conferring substantive rights on children and their families, Article 8 also confers procedural rights, and, in particular a right to be involved in decision making about the child.[210] This right extends even to the decision making process involved in emergency removal of children, though this may not always be possible[211] or desirable.[212]

209 On these points see *K & T v Finland* (2003) 36 EHRR 18.

210 *W v United Kingdom* (1987) 10 EHRR 29.

211 *K & T v Finland* (2003) 36 EHRR 18.

212 For example, see *Covezzi and Morselli v Italy* (2004) 38 EHRR 28, where involvement of parents was undesirable because of their close links with alleged abusers. See also *Errico v Italy*, Application number 29768/05, 24 February 2009, *Bury Metropolitan Council v D* [2009] EWHC 446 (Fam).

APPENDIX

Offences under Schedule 1 of the Criminal Procedure (Scotland) Act 1995 – some further explanation

5.37 NB These offences qualify as Schedule 1 offences only if they are committed against a person under the age of 17.

(a) *Any offence under Part 1 of the Criminal Law (Consolidation) (Scotland) Act 1995*. These offences include:
   (1) procuring for the purposes of prostitution or unlawful intercourse;
   (2) procuring by the use of threats, intimidation or false pretences, or using drugs to facilitate unlawful intercourse;
   (3) a group of offences related to incest. These offences include sexual intercourse within the forbidden degrees of relationship; intercourse with a step-child under 21 or who has lived in the same household as the step-parent while under 18; and intercourse by a person in a position of trust (for example, a foster parent) with someone under 16 living in the same household as him or her;
   (4) intercourse with a girl under 13;
   (5) unlawful detention in a brothel or for the purposes of having unlawful intercourse;
   (6) permitting a girl under 16 to use premises for the purposes of unlawful sexual intercourse;
   (7) causing or encouraging the seduction or prostitution of, unlawful intercourse with, or indecent assault on, a girl under 16;
   (8) allowing a child between the ages of 4 and 16 to reside in or frequent a brothel;
   (9) the commission or procuring of a homosexual act; (i) otherwise than in private; (ii) without the consent of both parties; (iii) with a person under 18.

(b) *Any offence under ss 12, 15, 22 or 33 of the Children and Young Persons (Scotland) Act 1937.*
   (1) Section 12 makes it an offence for someone over 16 having parental responsibility for or custody, care or charge of a child to ill-treat, abandon, or expose the child in a manner likely to cause unnecessary suffering or injury to the health (including mental health) of the child. Procuring the commission of any of these acts is also an offence. Aside from any other circumstances where it might be established, neglect is deemed to take place in two cases. First, where the

person legally liable to maintain a child has failed to provide or procure the provision of (for example, by obtaining available benefits) adequate food, clothing or medical aid for the child. Secondly, where the death of a child is caused by suffocation (other than that involving a foreign body) and the child at the time of death was sharing a bed with someone over the age of 16 who was under the influence of drink when he or she went to bed.

(2) Section 15 makes it an offence to cause or allow a child to beg or be used for begging.

(3) Section 22 deals with the situation where a child under 7 is left in a room with an improperly guarded open grate fire without reasonable precautions being taken against the risk of burning or scalding. An offence is committed if the child is killed or suffers serious injury.

(4) Section 33 makes it an offence to allow a child under 16 to take part in a performance where his or her life or limb is endangered.

Introduction to Chapters 6 to 9

The following four chapters all concern law, primarily based on statute, which relates to adult service provision (though the law on mental health also covers children). They are dealt with separately, but there are clear links between them[213] and there may be cases where there is a question about which legislative framework is most appropriate to be considered in relation to promoting the welfare of an individual service user. For example it may be possible to consider intervention either under the Adults with Incapacity (Scotland) Act 2000 (considered in chapter 7) or under the Mental Health (Care and Treatment) (Scotland) Act 2003 (considered in chapter 8) and it may, as well, be appropriate to consider provision of services under the general banner of community care (perhaps supplemented by the specific obligations contained in the 2003 Act). A further linkage is the obligation to carry out investigations imposed by the 2000 Act which then provides no tools for doing this in the face of resistance from those who might be investigated, it may in some cases then be possible to make use of the tools provided by the Adult Support and Protection (Scotland) Act 2007 (considered in chapter 9) to carry out the investigation, though the 2007 Act does not provide for any specific course of action to be taken following the conclusion of an investigation or other temporary intervention, and consideration will then have to be given to powers under the 2000 or 2003 Act or under the community care legislation.

A further feature of the legislation in this area is that it does not always fit together very well and there are overlaps and gaps between the various statutory provisions, these are not considered in detail in the text, but similar difficulties have prompted an attempt in England and Wales to make adult social care law more coherent. There is no sign of such a move in Scotland.

213 See Scottish Government, Comparison of the Adult Support and Protection (Scotland) Act 2007 (ASP) with the Adults with Incapacity (Scotland) Act 2000 (AWI) and the Mental Health (Care and Treatment) (Scotland) Act 2003, (2009).

Chapter 6

Community care

BACKGROUND

6.1 Community care in the contemporary sense was introduced by the National Health Service and Community Care Act 1990 and associated guidance, regulations and financial transfers. Its introduction followed a number of reports, particularly *Community Care: Agenda for Action* (the Griffiths Report) and the government White Paper *Caring for People.*[1] A variety of impulses contributed to the introduction of this legislation. One was the feeling that provision for people in need was service-led rather than needs-led, that is, that services were being provided on the basis of what was available rather than what the user needed. Another was that changes in the benefits system allowing payments to be made for private residential care had led to spiralling costs.

According to *Caring for People,* the objectives of the new system were:[2]

(a) to promote the development of domiciliary, day and respite services to enable people to live in their own homes wherever feasible and sensible;
(b) to ensure that service providers made practical support for carers a high priority;
(c) to make proper assessment of need and good case management the cornerstone of high quality care;
(d) to promote the development of a flourishing independent sector alongside good quality public services;
(e) to clarify the responsibilities of agencies and so make it easier to hold them to account for their performance; and
(f) to secure better value for taxpayers' money by introducing a new funding structure for social care.

Following the views expressed by Griffiths, the White Paper identified local authorities as the lead agency in provision of community care with the remit to organise and co-ordinate the provision of packages

1 Cm 849 (1989). For a brief history see McDonald, A, *Understanding Community Care: A guide for Social Workers* (2nd edn, 2006), ch 2.
2 Para 1.11.

of care for persons in need. The overall system was initially sometimes described as care management,[3] since after the assessment has taken place and a service package (care plan) has been agreed, the social worker manages that care plan. This may involve purchasing from and monitoring a range of providers. This highlights the potential difficulties inherent in the situation when the local authority has a duty to provide various services and is also the body responsible for upholding the rights of users. From a practical point of view the following were the main immediate consequences of community care:

(a) assessments of need had to be carried out before services were provided;
(b) a split between purchasers of services and providers of services was encouraged;
(c) a mixed economy of care was to be encouraged; and
(d) the responsibility of paying for people in residential care was transferred from the Department of Social Security to local authorities, with an associated transfer of resources.

Since the introduction of community care by the 1990 Act, there has been a number of developments both legal and in practice and implementation. Legal changes include greater recognition for carers, the introduction of free personal and nursing care in Scotland and specific provision for those suffering from a mental disorder.[4] Changes in practice and implementation include the fulfillment of the planned development of a 'mixed economy' of care, with much direct service provision being undertaken by private or third sector organisations, the development of the personalisation agenda, the introduction of single shared assessments and increased emphasis on self-directed support.

(1) Legal framework

6.2 Although community care was introduced by the NHS and Community Care Act 1990 this operated in Scotland to amend the Social Work (Scotland) Act 1968, and so the principal legislation in Scotland is the 1968 Act. There are, however, a number of other pieces of legislation which have to be read along with, or which amend, the provisions of the 1968 Act. These include the Chronically Sick and Disabled Per-

3 Though this term now has a much more specific meaning, see below para 6.7.
4 See ch 8.

sons Act 1970,[5] the Disabled Persons (Services, Consultation and Representation) Act 1986, the Carers (Recognition and Services) Act 1995,[6] the Community Care and Health (Scotland) Act 2002,[7] and the Mental Health (Care and Treatment)(Scotland) Act 2003. In addition, work carried out to assess a need for community care services may identify concerns which in turn may raise questions about whether an adult has full capacity or whether he or she is vulnerable. Further, where children are involved, either being disabled themselves or being affected by the disability of an adult member of their family, the Children (Scotland) Act 1995 may also be relevant. The legislation in this area is not always consistent and can be difficult to piece together, in England and Wales it has been said that the statutory framework is 'inadequate, incomprehensible and outdated'.[8] The same could be said of legislation in Scotland.

As well as these statutory provisions there is a large amount of guidance. Some of this dates back to the introduction of community care,[9] but there has been a constant flow of further guidance, sometime general, sometimes directed at particular groups[10] or particular types of provision.[11] This guidance, of course, does not have the force of law, but if the decision of a local authority about provision of community care services is challenged the court may look at whether the authority has followed guidance and, if it has not, may set aside the authority's decision on this ground.[12]

WHAT ARE COMMUNITY CARE SERVICES?

6.3 The term 'community care services' covers a wide range of services, the definition set out in the Social Work (Scotland) Act 1968 includes the following:

5 Which gives a list of services which may have to be provided after assessment, these are considered more fully below. The Act was only extended to Scotland in 1972.
6 Extending carers rights to assessment.
7 Introducing free personal and nursing care.
8 Law Commission, *10th Programme of Law Reform*, Law Comm No 311 (2008), p 10.
9 For example, Department of Health, *Care Management and Assessment: Practitioner's Guide* (1991).
10 For example, Scottish Executive, *Community Care Services for People with a Sensory Impairment: Policy and Practice Guidance*, (2007).
11 For example, Scottish Executive, *Self-Directed Support – New National Guidance*, Circular CCD7/2007.
12 For example *R v North Yorkshire Council v Hargreaves* (1994) 26 BMLR 121 and, more recently, *R(B) v Cornwall County Council* [2009] EWHC 491 (Admin).

(a) provision of residential accommodation with nursing care for people who appear to be in need of such accommodation by reason of infirmity, age, illness or mental disorder, dependency on drugs or alcohol or being substantially handicapped by any deformity or disability;
(b) arrangements for the prevention of illness, the care of persons suffering from illness and after-care of such persons[13];
(c) provision of domiciliary services[14] for a person in need,[15] or an expectant mother, or someone who is lying-in;
(d) provision of laundry services for households for which domiciliary services are being or can be provided;
(e) payments to defray the costs of parents, relatives or others visiting a child who is being looked after or of an adult who is either in the care of the local authority or receiving assistance from them – payments can only be made where justified and where making the trip would otherwise result in undue hardship;
(f) payments to allow for attendance at the funeral of a child who had been looked after or an adult who had been either in the care of the local authority or receiving assistance from them;
(g) burying or cremating the body of anyone who, immediately before her/his death, was either in the care of the local authority, receiving assistance from the authority or was a looked after child;
(h) certain services provided under the Mental Health (Care and Treatment) (Scotland) Act 2003;[16]
(i) any services provided under section 12(1) of the Social Work (Scotland) Act 1968, this subsection enables provision of a wide range of services, including provision of facilities and accommodation by imposing a very general duty on the local authority to promote social welfare and enabling it to pursue this objective by providing assistance in cash or in kind.

Partly because of the provision noted in (i) above, the scope of 'community care services' is potentially wide, though it is likely to exclude services which are provided by local authorities under or as a result of other enactments which make specific provision for these services or their provision. For example, services provided as a result of an assessment

13 Excluding health services, such as medical care or health visiting.
14 This provision used to refer to home helps and the services here are services provided in the service user's home which are designed to enable her/him to maintain an independent existence for as long as possible.
15 A person will be in need if he or she in need of care and attention arising out of infirmity, youth or age; or suffers from illness or mental disorder or is substantially handicapped by any deformity or disability, Social Work (Scotland) Act 1968, s 94(1).
16 See para 8.12.

under the Chronically Sick and Disabled Persons Act 1970 are provided under the specific umbrella of that Act rather than under section 12. Also excluded from the definition of community care services are any services for children. In addition, local authorities are not permitted to provide community care services to certain categories of adult who are subject to immigration control.[17]

ASSESSMENT

6.4 Provision of community care services, as well as of services under the Chronically Sick and Disabled Persons Act 1970, will normally follow on from an assessment.[18] This assessment will be triggered 'where it appears to a local authority that any person for whom they are under a duty or have a power to provide, or to secure the provision of, community care services may be in need of any such services.'[19] In other words, there is no need for an assessment to be requested before a duty to assess arises, though clearly such a request might alert the authority to the potential need for community care services. There is additional provision for triggering an assessment provided by the Mental Health (Care and Treatment)(Scotland) Act 2003 which does not appear to be entirely consistent with this.[20]

In the case of services provided under the Chronically Sick and Disabled Persons Act 1970 the assessment can be triggered by a request for an assessment made by a disabled person or someone who provides a substantial amount of care to him or her on a regular basis.[21] The assessment will be limited to assessing the needs of the disabled person and whether these needs call for the provision of services from a specific menu set out in section 2 of the 1970 Act. These services are:

(a) provision of practical assistance in the home;
(b) provision of, or assistance in obtaining, wireless, television, library or similar recreational facilities;
(c) provision of lectures, games, outings or other recreational facilities outside the home or assistance in taking advantage of available educational facilities;

17 See para 1.72.
18 Though s 12A(5) of the Social Work (Scotland) Act 1968 provides that community care services can be provided without a prior assessment in cases of urgency, though normally if this is done an assessment will require to be carried out after provision of services has started (s 12(6)).
19 Social Work (Scotland) Act 1968, s 12A(1).
20 See para 8.12.
21 Disabled Persons (Services, Consultation and Representation) Act 1986, s 4.

(d) provision of facilities for, or assistance in, travelling to and from home for the purpose of participating in any services provided under arrangements made by the authority under section 12 of the 1968 Act or, with the approval of the authority, in any other services which are similar to services which could be provided under such arrangements;
(e) provision of assistance in arranging for the carrying out of any works of adaptation to the home or the provision of any additional facilities designed to secure greater safety, comfort or convenience;
(f) facilitating the taking of holidays;
(g) provision of meals;
(h) provision of, or assistance in obtaining, a telephone and any special equipment necessary to enable use of a telephone.

Once the duty to carry out an assessment has been triggered the local authority cannot refuse to carry out the assessment because it does not have the resources to do so or because it currently does not provide the sort of services which might be identified as being necessary for the person being assessed.[22]

Any assessment must be carried out in accordance with guidance and must be carried out by, or under the final control of, the local authority, in other words it is not possible to rely purely on a self-assessment carried out by the (prospective) service user.[23] The assessment process can involve two separate types of assessment – an assessment of the (potential) service user and an assessment of his or her carer.

(1) Assessment of the (potential) service user

6.5 Little is said in the relevant legislation about the process of assessment. By implication an assessment of the need for services under the Chronically Sick and Disabled Persons Act 1970 will need to con-

22 *R v Bristol City Council ex p Penfold* (1997–98) 1 CCLR 315; *R v Royal County of Berkshire ex p P* 1997 33 BMLR 71.

23 *R(B) v Cornwall County Council* [2009] EWHC 491 (Admin), noting that: 'the authority cannot avoid its obligation to assess needs etc by failing to make an appropriate assessment themselves, in favour of simply requiring the service user himself to provide evidence of his needs.' (para [68]) See also Law Commission, *Adult Social Care – a Consultation Paper* (Law com 192, 2010), paras 4.38–4.40. This does not prevent a self-assessment contributing to and forming part of the assessment carried out by the local authority.

sider whether the person being assessed falls within the definition of 'chronically sick and disabled' and whether he or she has any needs. In community care assessments the local authority can request information from the health board and a housing authority outside the authority undertaking the assessment about what services they might provide for the service user, at least in cases where it appears that he or she may need the provision of services which these bodies can provide. Where the person being assessed appears to the local authority to be disabled then, as part of the community care assessment, it must also assess need for services under the Chronically Sick and Disabled Persons Act 1970 and inform the person that it is doing so.[24]

In addition to this statutory framework, the process of assessment is fleshed out by a variety of pieces of guidance.[25] Assessment for community care services will normally take the form of a Single Shared Assessment. This assessment involves differing degrees of complexity depending on the needs of the individual being assessed and guidance identifies four forms of assessment which might be appropriate to different circumstances:[26]

- Simple assessment applies where indicated needs or requests for services are straightforward and can be dealt with by low level response. As it may involve one or more than one agency, some co-ordination of contributions to the assessment may be needed.
- Comprehensive assessment applies where a wider range and complexity of needs are indicated. It is likely to involve more than one agency in contributing to a holistic assessment of needs. Specialist

24 Social Work (Scotland) Act 1968, s 12A(4).

25 The main pieces of guidance are *Community Care in Scotland: Assessment and Care Management*, Scottish Office Circular SWSG11/91 (this is a much briefer version of Department of Health, *Caring for People, Community Care in the Next Decade and Beyond: Policy Guidance* (1990)), Department of Health, *Care Management and Assessment: Practitioner's Guide* (1991), Department of Health, *Care Management and Assessment: Manager's Guide* (1991), *Community Care Needs of Frail Elderly People – Integrating Professional Assessment and Care Management*, Scottish Office Circular SWSG10/98, *Guidance on Single Shared Assessment of Community Care Needs* Scottish Executive Circular CCD8/2001, *Guidance on Care Management in Community Care*, Scottish Executive Circular CCD8/2004, *National Minimum Standards for Assessment and Care Planning for Adults*, Scottish Executive Circular CCD3/2008.

26 *Guidance on Single Shared Assessment of Community Care Needs* Scottish Executive Circular CCD8/2001, para 19; this is a significant reduction in the seven levels of assessment set out in Department of Health, *Care Management and Assessment: Practitioner's Guide* (1991), the intelligibility of which was doubted in *R v Gloucestershire County Council, ex parte RADAR* (1997–98) 1CCLR 476.

input may be necessary to specific areas of need. In comprehensive assessment effort needs to focus on co-ordination of contributions to the assessment. People who are at risk of admission to residential care or nursing homes should receive a comprehensive assessment with specialist input, if necessary, and intensive care management to explore fully the options for rehabilitation and care at home.

- Specialist assessment may apply to simple needs of a particular nature or particularly complex needs requiring more in-depth investigation by a professional with recognised expertise.
- Self-assessment[27] is where people identify their own needs and propose solutions to meet them, as the sole assessment or in conjunction with other assessments. They may receive professional advice or the support of an advocate.

Judgement is required as to the level and type of assessment required in each case, but a core principle of any form of assessment is the need to ensure that the person being assessed is able to make as full a contribution as possible to the assessment process,[28] which may involve taking steps to assist that person in communicating his or her wishes. This need for involvement is clearly indicated in the principles[29] underlying Single Shared Assessment which are set out in the box below.

Key Principles in Single Shared Assessment

- People who use services and their carers should be actively involved and enabled to participate.
- The type(s) of assessment should be appropriate to the person's indicated needs.
- Assessment should be undertaken by the most appropriate lead professional.
- The assessor should be appropriately skilled and qualified to deal with the type and level of assessment.

27 Though see the comments above about self-assessment.

28 Various pieces of guidance emphasise this need and failure to involve the prospective service user has led to successful challenge of local authority plans or decisions, eg *R v London Borough of Islington, ex parte Rixon* (1997) 1CCLR 119.

29 *Guidance on Single Shared Assessment of Community Care Needs* Scottish Executive Circular CCD8/2001, para 4.

- Appropriate information should be shared by informed consent of the person or the person's representative.
- Single, Shared Assessment must facilitate access to all community care services.
- Other professionals and agencies must accept the results.

These principles also underline two other key features of the Single Shared Assessment: the need for joint working across organisations, particularly between social work and health services, and the need to have a lead professional responsible for coordinating the assessment process.[30]

There is mixed case law on whether the resources of the local authority are relevant in assessing the needs of an individual. In one case it almost seemed to be suggested that if the local authority had no resources then there could be no needs, though even there it was still recognised that there would be some cases of need which were so extreme that they could not be denied.[31] It is likely that, at most, this only applies to cases in which an assessment of need for services provided under section 2 of the Chronically Sick and Disabled Persons Act 1970 is being undertaken.[32] In addition, there is clear Scottish authority that resources are not relevant in assessing need.[33]

(2) Assessment of a carer

6.6 In this context a carer is anyone who provides (or who intends to provide) a substantial amount of care on a regular basis to someone else who is aged 18 or over. There is no restriction on the age of a carer, so that a child can be treated as a carer for these purposes and has the same rights to assessment as any other carer. There is no statutory definition of what is meant by 'substantial' or 'regular basis' in this context, though guidance does suggest some factors which should be considered, for example the impact of caring on the carer, the amount of time spent caring for the other

30 Two recent consultations have highlighted comments on the need for changes in the assessment process: Scottish Government, *Proposals for a Self-directed Support Strategy: Analysis of Consultation Responses* (2010), para 3.4.2; Scottish Government, *Proposals for a Self-Directed Support (Scotland) Bill: Analysis of Consultation Responses* (2010), para 11.10.

31 *R v Gloucestershire County Council, ex parte Barry* [1997] AC 584.

32 See some of the comments in *Barry* and *R v East Sussex, ex parte Tandy* [1998] AC 714.

33 *MacGregor v South Lanarkshire Council* 2001 SC 502.

person, the nature of the care involved and the age of the carer.[34] Carers who provide care either as part of their employment (or under contract) or as a volunteer are not entitled to have an assessment.

A local authority may have to carry out an assessment of a carer in a variety of different circumstances. Where it is carrying out a community care assessment of the person cared for the carer must be informed of his or her right to have an assessment carried out which will look at the carer's ability to provide or to continue to provide care to the person to whom he/she provides care. It is not necessary, however, for a community care assessment to be carried out in respect of the person who is being cared for, it is enough to trigger entitlement to a carer's assessment that the person whom he/she cares for is someone to whom the authority may provide community care services. The local authority has a general obligation to provide information about carer assessments to any carer for someone to whom the local authority may have a duty or a power to provide community care services.[35] Any such carer can then request an assessment.

Finally, some assessment of the carer will still be needed where the assessment of an adult which is being carried out by the local authority is not a community care assessment[36] or where a community care assessment is being carried out, but the carer does not request an assessment of his/her ability to provide care. This is because in taking a decision about provision of services the authority has to have regard to the ability of a carer (as defined above) to continue to provide care.[37]

PROVISION OF SERVICES

(1) The initial decision

6.7 Once the assessment has been completed a decision has to be made about provision of services. The precise statutory wording which governs this process depends on the services being provided. In the case of services provided under the Chronically Sick and Disabled Persons

34 *Community Care and Health (Scotland) Act 2002: New Statutory Rights for Carers: Guidance*, Scottish Executive Circular CCD2/2003, para 9.3. See this guidance generally on assessment of carers.

35 Social Work (Scotland) Act 1968, s 12AB.

36 Eg, though this is unlikely in practice, it is purely about services under the Chronically Sick and Disabled Persons Act 1970, in such cases the carer has no right to an assessment.

37 Disabled Persons (Services, Consultation and Representation) Act 1986, s 8.

Act 1970 the statute requires a decision to be taken as to whether the needs of the person assessed call for the provision of any of the services listed in section 2 of that Act.[38] In reaching this decision account will need to be taken of any assessment made of a carer,[39] or, if no such assessment has been carried out, of the ability of the carer to continue to provide care.

The decision to be made following a community care assessment is whether, having regard to the assessment, the needs of the person assessed call for the provision of community care services.[40] In reaching any decision any assessment of a carer has to be taken into account,[41] even if no assessment of the carer has been carried out her/his ability to continue to provide care still has to be considered.[42] Other factors which have to be considered in reaching a decision about provision of services are:

(a) the views of the service user and of any carer;
(b) consultation with a medical practitioner if it is likely that the service user will require nursing care;
(c) the care which is currently being provided by the carer.

Guidance also stresses the need to involve the service user and carer(s) in the decision making process, and the outcome of this process should be a written care plan which should be agreed with the service user,[43] who should be provided with a copy of the plan. Where the service user has complex needs she/he will come under the guidance related to care management.[44] Where care management applies:[45]

38 Chronically Sick and Disabled Persons Act 1970, s 2.

39 Though this does not appear to be a statutory requirement where only services under s 2 of the 1970 Act are being considered, any failure to do this, however, would be likely to lead to successful challenge to the decision of the local authority. The statutory position is explained in detail in Note 4 and the associated text in para 203 of the *Stair Memorial Encyclopaedia* title 'Social Work'.

40 Social Work (Scotland) Act 1968, s12A(1)(b).

41 Social Work (Scotland) Act 1968, s 12AA(2)(b).

42 Disabled Persons (Services, Consultation and Representation) Act 1986, s 8.

43 The position of service users who cannot consent is considered below. It is not in itself a ground for challenging a decision on service provision that it does not meet the service user's preferences for addressing his/her needs, *R (Macdonald) v Royal Borough of Kensington and Chelsea* [2010] EWCA Civ 1109.

44 Which is contrasted with care coordination which applies to more straightforward cases. See *Guidance on Care Management in Community Care*, Scottish Executive Circular CCD8/2004.

45 *Guidance on Care Management in Community Care*, Scottish Executive Circular CCD8/2004, annex 1, para 11. See also Scottish Government, *National Training Framework for Care Management: Practitioner's Guide*: March 2006, especially part 4 on care planning.

> Care managers should support the person to make informed choices and should agree the expected outcomes with the individual, carers and other relevant professionals or agencies. The result should be an individual care plan to meet agreed needs. Matching needs and resources will highlight areas of need which are likely to remain unmet once the care arrangements are put in place. They should be recorded. The care plan should be in a format suitable to the person's circumstances and able to be shared as appropriate. It should state the arrangements and timescale for reviewing care. The person should receive a copy of the care plan

If the services which are agreed include the provision of accommodation the service user has some choice as regards the accommodation which is provided (directly or indirectly). This is subject to the person's preferred accommodation being suitable, being available, the person providing the accommodation being prepared to provide it on the local authority's normal terms and conditions, and the preferred accommodation costing no more than the authority would normally be expected to pay for accommodation for someone with the service user's needs.[46] If the preferred accommodation is not currently available it is possible to agree that an interim placement will be made pending transfer to the preferred accommodation, though if the service user does not agree to this, or to be provided with any other accommodation, the local authority cannot provide accommodation.[47]

(2) Resources

6.8 The issue of relevance of resources in taking decisions about provision of community care services has been raised in a number of challenges to local authority decisions over the years. It seems clear that resources can be taken into account in taking the decision as to provision of services, although where the need for services is acute it may be unreasonable to refuse to provide them. At the very least this is recognised through the acceptance that it is appropriate for eligibility criteria for access to certain services to be set and applied in the deci-

46 Social Work (Scotland) Act 1968 (Choice of Accommodation) Directions 1993, para 3. See generally the Directions and the accompanying circular, Scottish Office Circular SWSG5/93.

47 There is additional provision relating to choice of accommodation on discharge from hospital, see *Choice of Accommodation – Discharge from Hospital*, Scottish Executive Circular CCD8/2003/.

sion making process.[48] Recent guidance notes that in setting eligibility criteria, local authorities:

> will have regard to a range of factors including the overall level of resources available to meet need, the cost of service provision and ensuring equity in their service decisions. Eligibility criteria are a method for deploying limited resources in a way that ensures that those resources are targeted to those in greatest need, while also recognising the types of low level intervention that can be made to halt the deterioration of people in less urgent need of services.[49]

This guidance sets out four levels of risk which define the bands of a national eligibility framework[50] and provides some guidance as to the factors to be considered in classifying service users as being at critical risk, substantial risk, moderate risk or low risk. Although this framework was originally described in the context of older service users it has subsequently been indicated that it should be applied to all community care service users.[51]

This means that a decision as to whether a service should be provided to a service user may take account of resource availability either indirectly (through the way in which eligibility criteria are set) or directly.

What now seems clear is that once it has decided that a service ought to be provided a local authority cannot use lack of available resources as a reason to refuse to provide the service.[52] In addition, although there has been no specific discussion of this in a reported Scottish case, there must be some doubt as to the extent to which waiting lists can be used in cases where need for a service has been identified, at least to the extent to which these extend beyond a reasonable period of time to make arrangements for provision of the service with what will often be

48 See, for those aged 65 or over, the single shared assessment indicator of relative need (SSA-IoRN), *Single Shared Assessment Indicator of Relative Need*, Scottish Executive Circular CCD5/2004 and the criteria set out in *National Standard Eligibility Criteria and Waiting Times for the Personal and Nursing Care of Older People – Guidance* (October 2009).

49 *National Standard Eligibility Criteria and Waiting Times for the Personal and Nursing Care of Older People – Guidance* (October 2009), para 7.1.

50 The criteria overlap with, but the guidance does not mention, the SSA-IoRN, see footnote 49 above.

51 Scottish Government, *Self-Directed Support: A National Strategy for Scotland* (2010), para 2.3.

52 See *R v Gloucestershire County Council, ex parte Barry* [1997] AC 584 (referring particularly to section 2 of the Chronically Sick and Disabled Persons Act 1970), *MacGregor v South Lanarkshire Council* 2001 SC 502 and *Argyll and Bute Council v Scottish Public Services Ombudsman* [2007] CSOH 168. See also *R (Savva) v Royal Borough of Kensington and Chelsea* [2010] EWCA Civ 1209.

a provider external to the local authority with whom a contract may have to be agreed for provision of the service.[53] Once a need for a service has been identified, resources may, however, be relevant in deciding how the service is provided and the local authority will have some discretion in making this decision. For example, if a local authority has decided that, under the provisions of section 2 of the Chronically Sick and Disabled Persons Act 1970, meals need to be provided to a service user, there is clearly a number of ways in which this service could be provided. These range from a meals-on-wheels service to employing a chef to cater for the service user. The local authority can decide how, within that range, the service is to be provided.

The other type of resource which might be relevant is the resource available to the service user. This will clearly be a factor in determining whether services are to be paid for, and at what rate, but is not in itself, and alone, an acceptable reason for refusing to provide or arrange the provision of a service. Although the House of Lords has suggested that resources should be completely discounted in the decision as to provision of services,[54] this view seems to be inconsistent with the views expressed in England and Wales on provisions intended to have the same effect. There seems to be no reason in principle why, if an individual has considerable means, the authority should not consider whether this means that a service could be provided or arranged by another individual or organisation. In practice, however, such an approach would have a potential negative consequence for the service user. As we will see below, a person is only entitled to free personal and nursing care of this is arranged by the local authority. Were the authority to refuse to make such an arrangement because of the service user's resources the effect of this would be to debar her/him from receiving free care.

(3) Providing Services

6.9 Once a decision has been taken that services are to be provided, this provision can be made in one of three different ways. First, the service can be provided by the local authority itself. Second, the

53 See the comments of Lord Hardie in *MacGregor v South Lanarkshire Council* 2001 SC 502 at 507 and Lord Macphail in *Argyll and Bute Council v Scottish Public Services Ombudsman* [2007] CSOH 168 at [90]. For older people assessed as being at critical or substantial risk and whose assessed needs include personal or nursing care, this is to be delivered within 6 weeks, in *National Standard Eligibility Criteria and Waiting Times for the Personal and Nursing Care of Older People – Guidance* (October 2009), paras 9.4–9.5.

54 *Robertson v Fife Council* 2002 UKHL 35.

local authority may arrange for services to be provided by a third party, this could be a private or third sector organisation or could be another local authority. Finally, the services may be arranged by the service user him/herself using self-directed support, this is considered more fully below.

Any changes to service provision must follow a review of the service user and any service provision will need to be monitored and reviewed on a regular basis.[55]

(4) Self-directed support

6.10 In addition to arranging the provision of services itself the local authority can offer certain groups of adult service user the option of receiving direct payments with which they can arrange their own care.[56] Support for service users is provided by the local authority as well as by independent organisations such as Glasgow Centre for Inclusive Living and Lothian Centre for Inclusive Living. There are a number of restrictions on provision of direct payments to adult service users:[57]

(a) The local authority must have carried out a community care assessment and decided that the assessed needs call for the provision of community care services.
(b) The service user must fall into one of two groups she/he must either (i) be suffering from an illness or mental disorder or be substantially handicapped by any deformity or disability, or (ii) be aged 65 or over and be in need of care and attention as a result of age or infirmity.
(c) No payments can be made to service users who appear to be incapable of managing a direct payment, even with assistance.
(d) No payments can be made to service users subject to orders requiring compulsory detention or treatment for a mental disorder or to a variety of orders or restrictions under criminal justice legislation.

55 See *Community Care in Scotland: Assessment and Care Management*, Scottish Office Circular SWSG11/91, paras 5.8 & 22.1; *Guidance on Care Management in Community Care*, Scottish Executive Circular CCD8/2004, annex 1, paras 33–35.

56 The service user is entitled to know how the sum to be paid to enable self-directed support to be arranged was arrived at, *R (Savva) v Royal Borough of Kensington and Chelsea* [2010] EWCA Civ 1209.

57 Social Work (Scotland) Act 1968, s 12B(1) and Community Care (Direct Payments) (Scotland) Regulations 2003, SSI 2003/243, regs 2 & 3.

(e) The person who is to receive the payment must have capacity to consent to the receipt of direct payments or there must be an attorney or guardian who has the power to consent on behalf of the service user.

Self-directed support can also be made available for services provided to children aged under 16 in the fulfillment of the local authorities duties to children in need and children affected by disability.[58]

Direct payments cannot be used to pay for services other than those identified in the assessment and care plan for the recipient[59] and cannot be used to pay for periods of residential care exceeding 4 weeks in any period of 12 months.[60] A final restriction is that payments for the provision of services cannot be made to those who are related to the service user, unless provision of the service by a relative is necessary to meet the service user's need for the service.[61] The list of relatives is extensive and includes parents, children; siblings, aunts, unless and cousins; spouses and civil partners; and cohabitants.

In early 2010 the Scottish Government consulted on proposals for new legislation for self-directed support. Amongst the proposals under consideration is a set of principles for self-directed care, extending the availability of direct payments in cases where the service user is unable to consent and the introduction of an opt out system for direct payments so that service users would have to opt out of direct payments instead of, as at present, being offered the possibility of direct payments by the local authority and opting in.[62] A strategy for self-directed support was published in October 2010.[63]

Funding for some packages of care may be available through the discretionary Independent Living Fund. There are a number of conditions for eligibility to apply to this, including the requirement that the applicant is in receipt of the higher care component of Disability Living Allowance

58 See ch 4.
59 Social Work (Scotland) Act 1968, s 12B(5), if it is used for other purposes the local authority can require repayment.
60 Community Care (Direct Payments) (Scotland) Regulations 2003, SSI 2003/243, reg 6.
61 Community Care (Direct Payments) (Scotland) Regulations 2003, SSI 2003/243, reg 4.
62 Scottish Government, *Proposals for a Self-Directed Support (Scotland) Bill: Consultation* (2010).
63 Scottish Government, *Self-Directed Support: A National Strategy for Scotland* (2010).

and that he or she is in receipt of a care package the weekly value of which exceeds a certain amount.[64]

(5) Provision of services to adults with incapacity[65]

6.11 Issues of consent to provision of services (and, as we have seen, self-directed support) arise where the service user does not have capacity to agree to the care plan and service provision (or to elements of it). The position of an adult who is placed in residential accommodation where issues of restriction of liberty may arise is considered in chapter 7, paras 7.18–7.20, and the concern here is with other types of service.

Following an assessment of an adult and a decision that the adult's needs call for the provision of community care services the person carrying out the assessment may have some doubt as to whether the adult has the capacity to consent to the care plan. If the adult does not have capacity to consent it may be that there is someone else who has the power to consent on her/his behalf in the form of an attorney or guardian or of someone appointed under an Intervention Order. Where there is no one who can consent on behalf of the adult (and there is no pending application for guardianship or an intervention order[66]) the local authority is empowered by section 13ZA of the Social Work (Scotland) Act 1968 to take 'any steps which they consider would help the adult to benefit' from the services to be provided under the care plan. In doing this the authority is bound by the principles set out in the Adults with Incapacity (Scotland) Act 2000.[67] Use of the section 13ZA power is only appropriate where the adult is incapable of consenting to the services which it is intended should be provided or to the taking of a particular step, for example moving him or her to residential care. In other words, it cannot be used to force services on an adult who has capacity to agree to the particular service being provided or step being taken.

64 This is currently (November 2010) £340. For more on the Independent Living fund see: http://www.dwp.gov.uk/ilf/.

65 See also Scottish Government, *Adults with Incapacity (Scotland) Act 2000: Code of Practice for Local Authorities Exercising Functions under the 2000 Act* (2008), ch 4.

66 See paras 7.7–7.11.

67 See para 7.4.

The process[68] for providing services starts with a multidisciplinary review which should take into account the views of the adult, her/his relatives and carer(s), the GP, any independent advocate the adult may have and any attorney or guardian whose powers do not extend to taking a decision on the provision of services to the adult. A mental health officer's input may also be sought. This review process will assess whether the adult has capacity in respect of the specific issue of consent to the services which the authority is to provide (or arrange provision of) in terms of the care plan. If it is concluded that capacity is lacking then consideration will need to be given as to whether an intervention under the Adults with Incapacity (Scotland) Act 2000 is required or whether the services can be provided without this. The relevant guidance suggests that intervention under the 1968 Act might be appropriate if all concerned agree with (or at least, in the case of the adult, don't disagree with) the care plan and that intervention under the 2000 Act might be appropriate where the adult is opposed to the care plan or the carer or other relatives disagree with it.[69]

A full record should be kept of this decision-making process, and if a decision is made that services are to be provided using the powers conferred under the 1968 Act or that an order should be sought under the 2000 Act a letter setting out this decision and the reasons for it should be sent to the adult, her/his primary carer and relevant professionals. This letter should set out the outcome of the decision-making process, explain the reasons for reaching the decision and set out the arrangements for review of the decision.

CHARGING FOR SERVICES

(1) The basis of charging for services

6.12 With the exception of free personal and nursing care local authorities are permitted to charge for community care

68 This is set out in Scottish Executive: *Guidance for Local Authorities (March 2007): Provision of Community Care Services to Adults with Incapacity*, Circular CCD5/2007, this also forms Annex 1 to Scottish Government, *Adults with Incapacity (Scotland) Act 2000: Code of Practice for Local Authorities Exercising Functions under the 2000 Act* (2008).

69 Scottish Executive*: Guidance for Local Authorities (March 2007): Provision of community care services to adults with incapacity*, Circular CCD5/2007, paras 23–24. This guidance also forms Annex 1 to Scottish Government, *Adults with Incapacity (Scotland) Act 2000: Code of Practice for Local Authorities Exercising Functions under the 2000 Act* (2008).

services,[70] and are obliged to recover the costs of providing accommodation.[71] The way in which liability to pay and the amount to be paid are calculated differ as between provision of accommodation and provision of other services.

Where accommodation is provided there is a statutory scheme. This requires the authority to recover the actual cost to it of providing the accommodation. Where the adult satisfies the local authority that he/she is unable to pay the amount required then an assessment must be carried out. The basic provisions of the scheme for assessing liability and payment are:[72]

(a) Any house which the adult shares with a partner or relative aged 60 or over or 15 and under will generally be excluded from any calculation.

(b) Where the capital owned by the adult exceeds a certain limit then she/he must pay the full amount.[73] Adults who hold capital below certain amount of capital will have this ignored in calculating liability to pay.[74] Where the adult's capital falls in between these sums it is deemed to generate a certain amount of income, and this income, together with any other income which the adult has, will be taken into account in determining liability to pay. In some circumstances the local authority can treat the adult as still having capital even when he or she has disposed of it, for example by transferring her house to a relative.[75] The value of the asset disposed of can only be taken into account where it is reasonable for the local authority to conclude that the disposal took place for the purpose of reducing liability to pay for accommodation. This will involve looking at the whole circumstances surrounding the transfer, and it has been suggested that the person disposing of the asset must be aware of the possibility that she/he might have

70 Social Work (Scotland) Act 1968, s 87.

71 National Assistance Act 1948, s 22(1), applied to Scotland by the Social Work (Scotland) Act 1968, s 87(3).

72 Set out in the National Assistance (Assessment of Resources) Regulations 1992, SI 1992/2977. These regulations are regularly amended to change the sums specified in them. Regularly updated guidance is also published by the Scottish Government, the current version is *Revised Guidance on Charging for Residential Accommodation* (April 2010), this accompanied Circular CCD4/2010.

73 Currently (February 2011) £22,750.

74 Currently (February 2011) £14,000.

75 As happened in *Yule v South Lanarkshire Council* 1999 SCLR 985.

to pay for accommodation.[76] If the transfer takes place at a time when the transferor is fit and well this will indicate that the transfer was not directed at reducing liability, particularly if it took place some considerable time before the need for accommodation arose.

(c) There are no statutory rules linking income to how much is to be paid, it is up to each local authority to determine its own rules on this. In taking decisions on income the authority must take account of the need to leave a specified weekly amount to the service user.[77]

Charges for other services are calculated in accordance with guidance issued by the Convention of Scottish Local Authorities which is updated annually.[78] In addition, local authorities cannot require a service user to pay more than it appears practicable for her/him to pay.[79]

Once liability to pay for accommodation is determined the authority can limit the amount payable for the first eight weeks of provision. It is also possible for the authority to enter into an arrangement which allows the service user to defer payment of any sums due for accommodation. The preferred method of doing this is a deferred payment agreement,[80] which involves the local authority taking a security over the service user's house. It follows, by implication, that payment can only be deferred where the service user has a house over which a security can be granted and where the value of the house exceeds any amount which is likely to be due to the local authority. There are three further conditions applying to deferred payment agreements:

(a) the service user must be unwilling or unable to sell the house;
(b) excluding the house, the capital held by the service user must be less than the amount to be ignored as described above, if it exceeds this payments will have to come from this other capital until it falls below this limit; and

76 *R v Dorset County Council, ex parte Beeson* [2001] EWHC Admin 986, this point was not subject to appeal: *R v Dorset County Council, ex parte Beeson* [2002] EWCA Civ 1812.

77 Currently (February 2011) £22.30.

78 The current version (February 2011) is *Charging Guidance for Non-residential Social Care Services 09/10*.

79 Social Work (Scotland) Act 1968, s 87(1A). Assessment (and reassessment) of liability to pay should involve the service user, *R(B) v Cornwall County Council* [2009] EWHC 491 (Admin).

80 Community Care (Deferred payment of Accommodation Costs) (Scotland) Regulations 2002, SSI 2002/266; *Deferred Payments and Other Funding Arrangements which Allow Care Home Residents to Delay Selling Their Homes*, Circular CCD13/2004.

(c) the house must have been taken into account in assessing liability to pay and not excluded from the calculation (see above).

An alternative method of securing payment is to take out a charging order[81] over the service user's house, though the guidance makes it clear that deferred payment agreements are the preferred means for doing this.[82]

(2) Free Personal Care

6.13 Certain types of care do not have to be paid for, at least up to a certain value. The types of care covered are:[83]

(a) Personal care, that is, care relating to the day to day physical tasks and needs of the person being provided with care. This includes tasks such as eating or washing and extends to the mental processes associated with these tasks, for example remembering to wash or to eat.
(b) Personal support, in other words counselling and support provided as part of a planned programme of care.
(c) A variety of other types of care[84] including activities related to personal hygiene (such as shaving or cleaning teeth); preparation or assistance with the preparation of the service user's food and fulfilment of special dietary needs;[85] dealing with problems of immobility where the service user is immobile or substantially immobile; assistance with medication, for example, administration of eye drops; and, assistance related to general well being, for example, dressing, getting up and going to bed, behaviour management and psychological support.
(d) Nursing care so far as not covered above.

One difficulty in practice with these provisions is their application to so-called 'self-arrangers', that is, those people who make their own

81 Health and Social Services and Social Security Adjudications Act 1983, s 23; Charging Orders (Residential Accommodation) (Scotland) Order 1993, SI 1993/1511; *Community Care: Health and Social Services and Social Security Adjudications Act 1983 (HASSASSA): Sections 21–24: Orders and Guidance*, Circular SWSG15/93.

82 *Deferred Payments and Other Funding Arrangements which Allow Care Home Residents to Delay Selling Their Homes*, Circular CCD13/2004.

83 Community Care and Health (Scotland) Act 2002, s 1. See also *Free Personal and Nursing Care – Consolidated Guidance*, Circular CCD5/2003.

84 These are set out in the Community Care and Health (Scotland) Act 2002, sch 1.

85 This excludes meals on wheels provision.

arrangements for the provision of services without approaching the local authority and being assessed by it. It was originally assumed that such self-arrangers were covered by these provisions, but it was subsequently held that this was not the case.[86] This conclusion was based on the wording of the legislation which provides that 'a local authority are not to charge for social care provided by them (or the provision of which is secured by them).'[87] The reference to care provided by a local authority or arranged by them was held to exclude self-arrangers. In order to address this the Scottish Government issued Directions and guidance in January 2010[88] which provides for those who are currently self-arrangers to be assessed by the local authority with a view to having services either provided by or arranged by the local authority. In carrying out any assessment as to whether the person's needs call for the provision of services the currently self-arranged services are to be discounted.

There is guidance on eligibility criteria for access to personal and nursing care.[89] The eligibility criteria identify four categories of risk or priority: critical, substantial, moderate and low. These are defined by reference to risks relating to neglect or health,[90] risk relating to the home, domestic routines and personal care,[91] risks relating to participation in community life,[92] and risks relating to carers.[93] Linked to these criteria are waiting times.[94] For those assessed with critical or substantial priority the maximum period of time which should pass between confirmation of the need for services and delivery of the service is six weeks, though there is an expectation that in critical cases services will be delivered very quickly. There is, at present, no target time for completing an assessment.

86 *Argyll and Bute Council v Scottish Public Services Ombudsman* [2007] CSOH 168.

87 Community Care and Health (Scotland) Act 2002, s 1(1).

88 The Personal Care and Nursing Care (Self Arrangers) (Scotland) Directions 2009, appended to *Guidance and Directions for Self Arrangers of Free Personal and Nursing Care*, Circular CCD 1/2010.

89 *National Standard Eligibility Criteria and Waiting Times for the Personal and Nursing Care of Older People – Guidance* (October 2009).

90 For example, critical risk will be present where there are major health problems causing life threatening harm to the service user or others.

91 For example, there will be substantial risk where the service user is unable to manage many aspects of domestic routines causing significant risk to independence.

92 For example, there will be moderate risk if the service user is unable to manage several aspects of involvement in work, learning or education and this will pose a risk to independence in the future.

93 For example, there will be low risk where the carer is able to manage most aspects of his/her role, even if some difficulty is experienced with one or two aspects of this as long as these pose a low risk.

94 Though see the comments above about waiting lists.

Although, as we have seen, the statutory provision refers to a local authority not charging for the services covered by free personal and nursing care it also requires the authority to make payments to third parties to cover personal and nursing care, or, where appropriate, to make direct payments to service users to cover the costs of this.

(4) Which local authority pays?

6.14 In general, liability to make payment for community care services provided to an individual lies with the local authority for the area in which that person is ordinarily resident.[95] So, for example, if a resident in Area A was on holiday in Area B and whilst in Area B required to be assessed and provided with community care services, the local authority in Area B would generally be able to recover the costs of this provision from the local authority for Area A. In determining ordinary residence any period of in-patient hospital care is ignored, but otherwise the main factor is the individual's voluntary choice as to where he or she wishes to live. The current guidance refers to a definition of ordinary residence offered by Lord Scarman as giving guidance on applying the term:[96]

> Unless, therefore, it can be shown that the statutory framework or the legal context in which the words are used requires a different meaning, I unhesitatingly subscribe to the view that 'ordinarily resident' refers to a man's abode in a particular place or country which he has adopted voluntarily and for settled purposes as part of the regular order of his life for the time being, whether of short or long duration.

These provisions also extend to cases where local authority A makes arrangements for someone who is ordinarily resident within its area to be provided with accommodation situated in the area covered by local authority B, or where it makes an arrangement for the provision of services and facilities to enable someone to live in accommodation with support in the area of local authority B. In such cases local authority A remains responsible for the costs of the provision and the

95 Social Work (Scotland) Act 1968, s 86; The Recovery of Expenditure for the Provision of Social Care Services (Scotland) Regulations 2010, SSI 2010/72.

96 *Guidance on the Recovery of Expenditure on Accommodation and Services Under Section 86 of the Social Work (Scotland) Act 1968 – Ordinary Residence*, Circular CCD3/2010, citing *R v Barnet London Borough Council, ex parte Shah* [1983] 2AC 309 at 343. See also *R(M) v London Borough of Hammersmith and Fulham* [2010] EWHC 562 (Admin).

accommodation provided, or the placement made, in the area of local authority B does not operate to change the ordinary residence of the service user.

CHALLENGING DECISIONS[97]

6.15 Decisions taken as part of the process of providing community care or related service can be challenged by using the complaints and representations procedure of the local authority and then, if the person challenging the decision not satisfied, either pursuing the matter with the Scottish Public Services Ombudsman or seeking judicial review of the decision of the authority. Complaint may be made about and challenges made to the assessment process, the outcomes of the process, the decisions about service provision, the service provision itself, changes in service provision, decisions about charging for services and decisions to take account of capital which has been disposed of. Where a service user has a complaint about a service which is not provided directly by the local authority he or she will also be able to make use of the service provider's own complaints procedure and make a complaint to the Scottish Commission for the Regulation of Care (the Care Commission).[98]

As well as individual decisions about services for individual service users, it may be the case that service users want to challenge changes to services affecting groups of people. Where a local authority proposes to make changes to services there will, particularly where the service users are disabled, have to be adequate consultation before a final decision is taken. There will also need to be clear consideration in the decision making process of the impact of the proposed change on disabled service users in light of the specific duties imposed on local authorities to, amongst other things, take account of the disabilities of disabled people and to promote equality of opportunity.[99] Similar obligations to consult will apply prior to the closure of residential accommodation, though provided that adequate consultation has taken place and provision is made for proper assessment of and support of residents who are

97 See paras 1.59–1.60.

98 This will be replaced by Social Care and Social Work Improvement Scotland in April 2011.

99 Equality Act 2010, s 149, see, for example, *Boyejo v Barnet London Borough Council* [2009] EWHC 3261 (Admin).

being moved it is unlikely that the closure will be open to challenge.[100] Where the residents are disabled there will, in addition, be a requirement to specifically consider the specific duties of the local authority just mentioned.

100 A number of challenges had previously been made to such closures founded on either Article 2 of the European Convention on Human Rights (ECHR), the basis here being increased mortality as a result of moving, or Article 8 ECHR, based on interference with the resident's home. The initial case law established the requirements set out here. Any challenge based on Article 2 will require evidence of a real and immediate risk to the life of one of the residents being moved (*R (Emily Turner) v Southampton City Council* [2009] EWCA Civ 1290). It has been suggested that current research on the effects of relocation is inconclusive and not sufficient to establish that this threshold is reached (*R (Wilson) v Coventry City Council* [2008] EWHC 2300 (Admin)).

Chapter 7

Incapacity

BACKGROUND

7.1 This chapter is concerned largely with adults with incapacity, that is, those adults who, to at least some extent, have no legal capacity, in other words, those who, legally, cannot take at least some decisions for themselves[1]:

> A person who is mentally incapable or lacks mental capacity is incapable in the legal sense of entering into a transaction or making a decision. This is because the person, due to his or her mental state, cannot understand the nature of the transaction or decision or comprehend its consequences.[2]

Discussion is limited to adults since, as we have seen, parents are able to take decisions on behalf of their children.[3]

Historically, there were a number of different means which could be used to enable decisions to be taken on behalf of an adult with incapacity. These means included:

(a) A *curator bonis* to manage the financial affairs of the adult.[4] This required application to court and was only really appropriate if the adult had a significant estate.
(b) Guardianship under the Mental Health (Scotland) Act 1984. The powers of such guardians were, however, very limited.
(c) Tutor-at-law. Appointment, by the Court of Session, was made under the Curators Act 1585 and conferred on the tutor the same powers in respect of an adult as a parent had in respect of a child.

1 As we will see in para 7.3 below, incapacity is not necessarily all or nothing.
2 Scottish Law Commission Discussion Paper No 94 (1991). A similar definition is: 'Capacity is the ability to understand information relevant to a decision or action and to appreciate the reasonably foreseeable consequences of taking or not taking that decision', Scottish Government, *Adults with Incapacity (Scotland) Act 2000: Communication and Assessing Capacity: A Guide for Social Work and Healthcare Staff* (2008), ch1, para 3.
3 See para 3.5.
4 Though in one case a curator was granted an order requiring delivery of the adult and authorising the curator to place the adult in an asylum, *Gardiner* (1869) 7 M 1130.

In the only relatively recent case seeking such an appointment the court took the view that the terminology of the 1585 Act, which referred to 'naturall foulis Ideottis and furious', should be interpreted as referring to an adult who was incapable of managing his or her affairs or of giving directions for the management of these.[5]

(d) Tutor-dative. This again required application to the Court of Session. The tutor was given only those powers specifically conferred by the court and, in more recent practice, the appointment was made for a limited time. In one case appointment was made with power to consent to sterilization of the adult.[6]

These various means (as well as some of the others mentioned below which are still available) were considered by the Scottish Law Commission, which concluded that 'Each existing method … suffers from various defects and is in need of reform. There are however more general criticisms, that the present law is fragmented, archaic and fails to provide an adequate remedy in many common situations.'[7] The Commission proposed significant change in the law, which was put into effect in the Adults with Incapacity (Scotland) Act 2000.

Some types of provision survived the implementation of the 2000, although some, such as powers of attorney, are now subject to different requirements. The main provisions of the 2000 Act are considered below, but provision not derived from this includes:

(a) Benefits appointees. It is possible for someone aged 18 or over to be appointed to receive any benefits to which the adult is entitled and to deal with them. Appointment is made following application to the Department of Work and Pensions.[8] No one can be appointed as an appointee where a financial guardian with power to receive benefits has been appointed to the adult.

(b) Setting up a trust. A trust can be set up to manage property or money for the benefit of an adult. The trust must be set up by someone with legal capacity to do so, so it will be too late to consider this once an adult no longer has capacity. One way of using a trust might be the setting up of a trust by parents to benefit a child who will have no, or limited, capacity as an adult. The setting up of a trust involves the transfer of ownership of property and/or money to trustees who

5 *Britton v Britton's Curator Bonis* 1992 SCLR 947.

6 *L, Petitioner* 1996 SCLR 538.

7 Scottish Law Commission, *Report on Incapable Adults*, Cm 2962 (1995), para 1.15.

8 Social Security (Claims and Payments) Regulations 1987, SI 1987/1968, reg 33, as amended.

will then administer the property/money in line with the purposes set out in the document setting up the trust. Trusts will only have effect in relation to property and trustees will have no power to take decisions about the welfare of the adult.

(c) *Negotiorum gestio*. This is a legal principle which allows someone to act on your behalf when you are incapable of acting for yourself, and where, were you able to, you would have authorised the other person to act on your behalf. The relevance here is that the inability to act may be due to mental disability and this principle may, for example, allow a friend or relative to act on behalf of someone who is unable to do so him/herself. It is likely that the power to act under this doctrine is now very limited. The author is aware of one case in which it was suggested that this doctrine could be used to authorise a local authority to sign a tenancy agreement on behalf of an adult. It is very unlikely that this is the case, not least because the relevant Code of Practice implies that signing a tenancy agreement (or opening a bank account on behalf of the adult) should be authorised by an intervention order made under the 2000 Act.[9] In addition, the use of *negotiorum gestio* seems inconsistent with fundamental elements of the 2000 Act, in particular, the provision of scrutiny over those acting on behalf of an adult and the principle of maximum involvement considered below.

(d) The *parens patriae* jurisdiction of the Court of Session. This is an inherent jurisdiction held by the Court of Session to do what is for the benefit of an incompetent adult. Its limits are undefined and it appears to be the case that it has not been displaced by the passage of legislation. The only recent case where this jurisdiction was invoked involved seeking a decision to turn off the life support being provided to a patient in a Persistent Vegetative State.[10]

Finally, interventions on behalf of an adult with incapacity may engage various articles of the European Convention on Human Rights. The

9 *Adults with Incapacity (Scotland) Act 2000: Revised Code of Practice for Persons Authorised under Intervention Orders and Guardians* (2008) para 2.13.

10 *Law Hospital NHS Trust v Lord Advocate* 1996 SC 301. It has been held in England that the inherent jurisdiction extends beyond adults who are incapable to vulnerable adults who are either '(i) under constraint; or (ii) subject to coercion or undue influence; or (iii) for some other reason deprived of the capacity to make the relevant decision, or disabled from making a free choice, or incapacitated or disabled from giving or expressing a real and genuine consent.' *Per* Munby, J in *Re SA (Vulnerable Adult with capacity: Marriage* [2005] EWHC 2942 at para 77, see also *A Local Authority v DL, RL & ML* [2010] EWHC 2675 (Fam).

main articles involved are: Article 5 which requires certain procedures to be followed before an individual is deprived of his/her liberty,[11] Article 6 requiring access to due process, and Article 8, the right to respect for private and family life.

LOCAL AUTHORITY FUNCTIONS AND RELEVANT ORGANISATIONS

7.2 Local authorities have a variety of obligations and functions under the 2000 Act, which are closely related to duties and functions under the legislation on mental health, vulnerable adults and community care. The principal duties are:

(a) To investigate complaints about how guardians, attorneys or persons authorised under an intervention order have carried out their functions in relation to the personal welfare of an adult.
(b) To investigate cases in which the authority become aware that the personal welfare of an adult appears to be at risk.[12] Following an investigation the authority has the power to take any action that seems to be necessary to safeguard the welfare of the adult. This might include seeking an order under the 2000 Act or taking steps under other legislation. Although there is a duty to investigate, the 2000 Act does not confer any additional powers on the local authority which might assist it to carry out such an investigation, so it may, for example, if the circumstances are appropriate, be necessary to invoke powers set out in the Adult Support and Protection (Scotland) Act 2007.[13]
(c) To supervise welfare guardians, and, where this has been ordered by the sheriff, welfare attorneys or someone authorised under an intervention order.[14]
(d) Finally, and this will be discussed more fully below, the local authority must apply for an intervention order or the appointment of a guardian in certain circumstances.

Local authorities will also provide reports in connection with applications for the appointment of a guardian or for an intervention order and will be notified when someone resigns as a welfare attorney.

11 Discussed in paras 7.18–7.20 below.
12 *Scottish Government, Adults with Incapacity (Scotland) Act 2000: Code of Practice for Local Authorities Exercising Functions under the 2000 Act* (2008), ch 9.
13 See ch 9.
14 *Scottish Government, Adults with Incapacity (Scotland) Act 2000: Code of Practice for Local Authorities Exercising Functions under the 2000 Act* (2008), ch 8.

Most, but not all, local authority functions under the 2000 Act will be carried out by a Mental Health Officer (MHO).[15] The Mental Welfare Commission[16] has some powers of investigation related to substitute decision making in the field of personal welfare, as well as investigating complaints about the conduct of investigations carried out by the local authority. A final regulatory body is the Public Guardian.[17] This body maintains a register of interventions, supervises guardians and interveners who have powers in respect of an adult's property or financial affairs, investigates complaints about the management of adult's property and financial affairs and provides information and advice.

THE MEANING OF 'INCAPACITY'

7.3 An adult will be incapable if he or she is incapable of acting, making decisions, communicating decisions, understanding decisions or retaining the memory of decisions. The incapacity must arise either from mental disorder or an inability to communicate because of physical disability. A mental disorder can be either a mental illness, personality disorder or learning disability, though a person is not to be considered to have a mental disorder by reason only of certain attributes, for example, dependence on, or use of, alcohol or drugs, acting as no prudent person would act, or behaviour that causes, or is likely to cause, harassment, alarm or distress to any other person.[18] Mental disorder may not lead directly to incapacity, but may mean that the adult is susceptible to pressure or influence from others to decide in a particular way, with the consequence that they are effectively unable to take their own decisions.[19] An adult will not be incapable because of physical disability if human (for example, an interpreter) or mechanical (for example a voice synthesiser) aids can overcome the difficulty which he or she has in communicating decisions.[20] The definition of incapable and of incapacity is slightly extended in relation to the appointment of a guardian which can

15 See para 8.2.

16 See para 8.5.

17 http://www.publicguardian-scotland.gov.uk/.

18 The 2000 Act refers to the definition of 'mental disorder' contained in s 328 of the Mental Health (Care and Treatment)(Scotland) Act 2003, Adults with Incapacity (Scotland) Act 2000, s 87(1). See para 8.8. In *Fife Council v X*, Kirkcaldy Sh Ct, 22 December 2005, the adult was incapable of safeguarding and promoting his interests, but this was not the basis for the diagnosis of mental disorder.

19 *A Local Authority v A* [2010] EWHC 1549 (Civ).

20 Adults with Incapacity (Scotland) Act 2000, s 1(6).

be based either on the adult being incapable of taking or communicating decisions in the sense discussed above, or on the adult's being incapable of acting to safeguard or promote her or his interests whether in property/financial affairs or in respect of personal welfare.[21] Therefore, for the purposes of appointing a guardian only, an adult may have the capacity to take decisions, but be incapable of safeguarding or promoting her/his interests.[22] For the purpose of determining this second type of incapacity it has been suggested that the dictionary definition of incapacity should be applied as fitting the definition set out above into the statutory terms 'incapable of … acting to safeguard or promote' leads to a formulation which is difficult to follow.[23]

Regardless of the type of incapacity involved, incapacity is context specific – an adult who is incapable of taking some decisions is likely, unless the incapacity arises from an inability to communicate, to have the capacity to take other decisions:

> … capacity is not merely issue specific in relation to different types of transaction; capacity is also issue specific in relation to different transactions of the same type. Thus a vulnerable adult may have capacity to consent to a simple medical procedure but lack capacity to consent to a more complex medical procedure.[24]

Capacity, then, will often not be completely lost and incapacity to take decisions in one area should not be assumed to imply loss of capacity in all areas. Even where an adult is incapable of taking particular decisions, the principles set out below make it clear that, as far as possible, she/he is to be involved in the decision making process.

Unlike England and Wales,[25] there is no statutory presumption in Scotland that an adult has capacity. However, in practice, the Scottish position is the same – there will need to be clear evidence that an adult lacks capacity before any court order in respect of the adult will be made or other action requiring authorisation will be permitted, as well as before

21 Adults with Incapacity (Scotland) Act 2000, s 58(1).

22 *Fife Council v X*, Kirkcaldy Sh Ct, 22 December 2005. See also *City of Edinburgh Council v D*, Edinburgh Sheriff Court, 30 September 2010.

23 *Fife Council v X*, Kirkcaldy Sh Ct, 22 December 2005. If the definition was inserted the provision would read 'incapable of acting or making decisions or communicating decisions or understanding decisions or retaining the memory of decisions, by reason of mental disorder or of inability to communicate because of physical disability acting to safeguard or promote'.

24 *Re MM (an adult); Local Authority X v MM* [2007] EWHC 2003 at [65], per Munby J.

25 Mental Capacity Act 2005, s 1(1).

decisions can be taken on behalf of an adult by a welfare attorney. This is captured in Scottish Government Guidance as follows:[26]

> The starting point for assessing someone's capacity to make a particular decision is always the assumption that the individual has capacity. In legal proceedings the burden of proof will fall on the person who asserts that capacity is lacking. A court must be satisfied that on the balance of probabilities, capacity has been shown to be lacking.

PRINCIPLES GOVERNING INTERVENTION IN THE LIVES OF ADULTS WITH INCAPACITY

7.4 Interventions in the lives of adults with incapacity under the 2000 Act must be undertaken in accordance with the principles set out in the Act. These principles govern not only courts as they take decisions on applications for orders, but also local authorities exercising functions under the Act, for example acting as welfare guardians to adults, and individuals acting as guardians, as attorneys or who are authorised under intervention orders. The principles as set out in the Act[27] are set out in the Box 1.

Any benefit provided to the adult under Principle 1 need not be financial or physical[28] and can be intangible, for example in the form of a psychological benefit[29] or a benefit in ensuring that the adult's wishes expressed while he or she had capacity are given effect to.[30] As long as the intervention confers some benefit on the adult it doesn't matter that it also confers a benefit on someone else. In one case for example, an intervention order was sought to discharge the adult's claims on the estate of his recently deceased wife in order to ensure that the couple's children would get the whole of the wife's estate, as had been their intention.[31] The adult benefited by having his previous wishes given effect to and the order could be made even though the children of the couple also benefited.

26 Scottish Government, *Adults with Incapacity (Scotland) Act 2000: Communication and Assessing Capacity: A Guide for Social Work and Healthcare Staff* (2008), ch1, para 4.
27 Adults with Incapacity (Scotland) Act 2000, s 1(2)–(5).
28 Though it can be, for example in *FB, Applicant*, Glasgow Sh Ct, 17 May 2005, an intervention order was sought to allow a compensation payment to the adult to be negotiated.
29 For example in having her son continue living with the adult, *A's Guardian, Applicant* 2007 SLT (Sh Ct) 24.
30 *M, Applicant* 2007 SLT (Sh Ct) 207; *G, Applicant* 2009 SLT (Sh Ct) 122.
31 *M, Applicant* 2007 SLT (Sh Ct) 207.

Principle 2 seems to include a number of aspects:

i. The intervention must be likely to achieve its purpose, if it won't it can't be undertaken or authorised by the court.
ii. There is a trade off between achievement of the purpose and the freedom which is left to the adult, a restriction may be justified if it is the only way to achieve a specific objective which provides benefit to the adult. In reaching the conclusion that the restriction is justified, it may be necessary to weigh up different possible courses of action and decide which is most likely to achieve the purpose of the intervention.[32]
iii. The option selected, if there is a choice, must be the least restrictive way of achieving the purpose and impose the least limitation on the adult compatible with this

All of these factors will be relevant in deciding whether any intervention is necessary; for example, it may be possible to achieve the purpose without any intervention,[33] and, if an intervention is needed, what form this should take. For example, can the matter be resolved by way of an intervention order rather than guardianship, and, if there is to be an application for guardianship, what powers should be sought for the guardian?

Box 1

The 2000 Act Principles

1 There shall be no intervention in the affairs of an adult unless the person responsible for authorising or effecting the intervention is satisfied that the intervention will benefit the adult and that such benefit cannot reasonably be achieved without the intervention.

2 Where it is determined that an intervention as mentioned in subsection (1) is to be made, such intervention shall be the least restrictive option in relation to the freedom of the adult, consistent with the purpose of the intervention.

3 In determining if an intervention is to be made and, if so, what intervention is to be made, account shall be taken of:

(a) the present and past wishes and feelings of the adult so far as they can be ascertained by any means of commu-

32 See, for example, *Fife Council v X*, Kirkcaldy Sh Ct, 22 December 2005; *City of Edinburgh Council v Z* 2005 SLT (Sh Ct) 7.

33 This point was argued unsuccessfully in *Muldoon, Applicant* 2005 SCLR.

> nication, whether human or by mechanical aid (whether of an interpretative nature or otherwise) appropriate to the adult;
>
> (b) the views of the nearest relative, named person and the primary carer of the adult, in so far as it is reasonable and practicable to do so;
>
> (c) the views of:
>
> (i) any guardian, continuing attorney or welfare attorney of the adult who has powers relating to the proposed intervention; and
>
> (ii) any person whom the sheriff has directed to be consulted,
>
> in so far as it is reasonable and practicable to do so; and
>
> (d) the views of any other person appearing to the person responsible for authorising or effecting the intervention to have an interest in the welfare of the adult or in the proposed intervention, where these views have been made known to the person responsible, in so far as it is reasonable and practicable to do so.
>
> 4 Any guardian, continuing attorney, welfare attorney or manager of an establishment exercising functions under this Act or under any order of the sheriff in relation to an adult shall, in so far as it is reasonable and practicable to do so, encourage the adult to exercise whatever skills he has concerning his property, financial affairs or personal welfare, as the case may be, and to develop new such skills.

In seeking the views of the adult under Principle 3 'strenuous efforts must be made to assist and facilitate communication' before it is concluded that the adult cannot communicate her/his views.[34] It may be, of course, that there is some written record of the adult's wishes, for example in one case where the adult had given instructions as to his will which had not been carried out properly.[35] There is no provision, as there is in England and Wales, for an adult to make an advance decision refusing treatment which will normally have to be given effect to[36], but

34 Scottish Government, *Adults with Incapacity (Scotland) Act 2000: Code of Practice For Local Authorities Exercising Functions under the 2000 Act*, (2008), p 8. This guidance refers to (a) in Principle 3 as being Principle 3, with the remaining requirements to consult being Principle 4.

35 *G, Applicant* 2009 SLT (Sh Ct) 122.

36 Mental Capacity Act 2005, ss 24–26. The only exception is the possibility of an advance statement relating to treatment for a mental disorder, see para 8.24.

there is no reason why an adult couldn't express his or her wishes on any subject against the day when capacity might be lost and any such wishes would have to be taken into account. Principle 3 only requires that views are taken into account and not that they are given effect to, and in some cases there will be a conflict of views which makes it impossible to give effect to all of them.[37] Views cannot simply be dismissed out of hand, they must be considered, and where there is a conflict a clear reason will need to be set out for preferring one view over another. The limitation to doing what is reasonable and practicable will extend beyond the taking account of views and will also cover the process of obtaining views – it will not be necessary to obtain views from anyone with an interest in the adult listed in the Act where this would not be reasonable or practicable.

Principle 4 is of more limited scope than the other principles, applying only to specific types of person, it does not, for example apply to someone authorised under an intervention order.

Missing from the principles is any reference to decisions being taken in the best interests of the adult, which plays a significant role in England and Wales.[38] Instead the emphasis is more on seeking a benefit for the adult and on substitute decision making to reach a decision reflecting what it is considered that the adult would have decided based on her/his wishes and views. The notion that an adult benefits from the intervention does not mean that any intervention must be entirely risk free:

> The fact is that all life involves risk, and the young, the elderly and the vulnerable, are exposed to additional risks and to risks they are less well equipped than others to cope with. But just as wise parents resist the temptation to keep their children metaphorically wrapped up in cotton wool, so too we must avoid the temptation always to put the physical health and safety of the elderly and the vulnerable before everything else. Often it will be appropriate to do so, but not always. Physical health and safety can sometimes be bought at too high a price in happiness and emotional welfare. The emphasis must be on sensible risk appraisal, not striving to avoid all risk, whatever the price, but instead seeking a proper balance and being willing to tolerate manageable or acceptable risks as the price appropriately to be paid in order to achieve some other good – in particular to achieve

37 For example *Cooke v Telford* 2005 SCLR 367.

38 Mental Capacity Act 2005, s 1(5), though Stevenson, G *et al* in 'Principles, Patient Welfare and the Adults with Incapacity (Scotland) Act 2000', (2009) 32 *International Journal of Law and Psychiatry* 120 argue that some courts in Scotland have effectively applied a best interests test in their decision making.

the vital good of the elderly or vulnerable person's *happiness*. What good is it making someone safer if it merely makes them miserable?[39]

MECHANISMS FOR TAKING DECISIONS ON BEHALF OF AN ADULT PROVIDED BY THE 2000 ACT

7.5 It should be clear from what has been said above that many adults who are incapable of taking some decisions will retain capacity in other areas – in such areas there is no need for anyone else to take decisions or make choices on behalf of the adult – indeed, unless a person can take advantage of the doctrine of *negotiorum gestio* there is no legal basis for them taking such decisions or making such choices. Where, however, decisions and choices do have to be made on behalf of an adult the 2000 Act provides, in addition to the powers derived from other sources discussed above, a number of different routes for doing this: appointment of an attorney, guardianship, an intervention order, withdrawal certificates, management of funds in a residential setting and decisions on medical treatment.

(1) Attorneys[40]

7.6 An attorney is someone who is appointed by the adult to take decisions on her/his behalf. The appointment must be made while the adult still has the legal capacity to do so and appointment is made by the adult granting a deed appointing the attorney to which must be added a certificate that the adult has capacity at the date of granting the deed.[41] Two types of attorney may be appointed and it is possible to appoint joint attorneys or for the person granting the power of attorney to appoint a substitute who will take over if the attorney is unable to act. First, an attorney may be appointed to look after the financial affairs or property of the adult. It has always been possible to grant a power of attorney to authorise someone manage your affairs and prior to the coming into effect of the 2000 Act such a power of attorney

39 *Re MM (an adult); Local Authority X v MM* [2007] EWHC 2003 at [120], per Munby J.

40 See *Scottish Government, Adults with Incapacity (Scotland) Act 2000: Code of Practice for Continuing and Welfare Attorneys* (2008).

41 See also below. Guidance on appointing an attorney and forms for doing this can be found on the Office of the Public Guardian website: http://www.publicguardian-scotland.gov.uk.

would continue in effect after the adult lost capacity *unless* the adult specifically stated in the appointment of the attorney that it was not to continue following her/his incapacity.[42] The 2000 Act now provides for the appointment of continuing attorneys, but for the power of attorney to continue after the adult loses capacity the document appointing the attorney must specifically state that the power granted is to be a continuing one.[43] Any such power of attorney will take effect immediately, ie while the adult still has capacity, though it may be specifically provided that it is not to take effect until the adult loses capacity. If this is provided for, the deed appointing the attorney must also state that the adult has considered how her/his capacity is to be determined and if he or she has decided on a particular means for doing this it should also be set out in the deed.

The second type of attorney is a welfare attorney, someone who is entitled to take decisions about the adult's personal welfare.[44] A welfare attorney will not have any power to act on behalf of an adult until the adult has lost capacity, and the deed appointing the attorney must also state that the adult has considered how her/his incapacity in respect of decisions covered by the power of attorney is to be determined and if a particular process has been chosen it should also be set out in the deed. The welfare attorney's power is limited – he or she only has the power to take decisions[45] in respect of which either the adult is incapable or in respect of which the attorney reasonably believes that the adult is incapable. In addition, there are restrictions on the ability of an attorney to consent to certain types of medical procedure or treatment, these are considered below.

Regardless of the type of welfare attorney appointed, the deed granting the power must contain a certificate signed by a solicitor[46] to the effect that she/he has interviewed the adult; that he/she is satisfied, either through direct knowledge of the adult or through information from a person with such knowledge, that the adult understands the nature and the extent of the powers being granted; and, that he/she has no reason to believe that the adult was acting under undue influence or that there was any other factor which would invalidate the deed granting the power of attorney. It is important that the solicitor carries out adequate enquiries

42 Law Reform (Miscellaneous Provisions) (Scotland) Act 1990, s 7(1).
43 Adults with Incapacity (Scotland) Act 2000, s 15(3)(b).
44 Adults with Incapacity (Scotland) Act 2000, s 16.
45 In other words the incapacity must affect the specific decision which the attorney is taking, it will not be enough if the adult is incapable in some areas if she/he still has capacity in respect of the decision being contemplated by the attorney.
46 Who must not be the person appointed as attorney.

into these matters before signing this certificate. Where it was established that this had not been done, the sheriff authorised the Public Guardian to refuse to register a power of attorney.[47] The consequence of this was that the attorney appointed had no power to act on behalf of the adult, since registration of the power of attorney with the Public Guardian is required as an additional step to give the attorney power to act.[48] The Public Guardian must[49] register any power of attorney provided it has the required certificate and provided that the attorney is prepared to act.[50] When a welfare power of attorney is registered, the Public Guardian must send a copy to the Mental Welfare Commission and to the local authority for the area in which the adult resides.[51]

A power of attorney can be revoked by the adult, provided that he or she still has capacity to do this.[52] Appointment of a guardian will also terminate a power of attorney, at least to the extent that the powers conferred on the guardian overlap with the powers of the attorney, so that, for example, if a welfare guardian was appointed this would have no effect on the powers conferred by a continuing power of attorney. Where the person appointed as attorney is the wife or civil partner of the adult, the power of attorney may provide that it is to continue even if the marriage or civil partnership comes to an end, otherwise this will bring the power to an end.

A power of attorney can also be brought to an end by resignation of the attorney,[53] and the sheriff may revoke either the appointment of an attorney or any of the powers conferred on an attorney following an application by anyone claiming an interest.[54] The sheriff also has extensive powers to order production of accounts and reports and to require supervision of a continuing attorney by the Public Guardian and a welfare guardian by the local authority.[55]

47 *Application by Public Guardian for Directions*, Glasgow Sheriff Court, 30 June 2010.

48 Adults with Incapacity (Scotland) Act 2000, s 19(1).

49 Hence the need for the application to the sheriff for directions in the case cited in footnote 47.

50 Though it is possible for the deed granting the power of attorney to contain a term providing that it will not be registered until the happening of a specified event, Adults with Incapacity (Scotland) Act 2000, s 19(3).

51 Adults with Incapacity (Scotland) Act 2000, s 19(2)(c).

52 Adults with Incapacity (Scotland) Act 2000, s 22.

53 Adults with Incapacity (Scotland) Act 2000, s 23, though if there is a joint attorney or a substitute attorney, they may continue to exercise the power.

54 Adults with Incapacity (Scotland) Act 2000, s 2091) &(2)(e); see *M v M*, 2 November 2006, Glasgow Sheriff Court.

55 Adults with Incapacity (Scotland) Act 2000, s 20(1) & (2)(a)–(d).

(2) Guardianship

(1) Background

7.7 Guardians are appointed by the sheriff court and can be given powers to take decisions on behalf of the adult either in relation to the adult's finances and property (a financial guardian) or in relation to the adult's personal welfare (a welfare guardian), or can be given the power to take both sorts of decision. Two guardians may be appointed (who will not be joint guardians) one as a financial guardian and the other as welfare guardian. Joint guardians can also be appointed,[56] though it has been held that this can only be done where the initial application for appointment of a guardian is for appointment of joint guardians or where there is an existing guardian and an application is made for appointment of an additional, joint, guardian.[57] In general, joint guardians must be related to the adult, either as parents, siblings or children, though the sheriff does have power, if it is considered appropriate, to appoint as joint guardians people who are not so related to the adult. Joint guardians can each exercise the powers conferred on them but must normally consult each other before doing this.[58] The other restrictions on who can be a guardian are that the guardian must be an individual (rather than, for example, a company or a charity) and that the chief social work officer cannot be appointed as a financial guardian.[59]

(2) Making the application

7.8 An application for the appointment of a guardian can be made either by the local authority (this happens in around one third of cases) or by anyone else who claims to have an interest either in the financial affairs or personal welfare of the adult, or both.[60] The most common

56 Adults with Incapacity (Scotland) Act 2000, s 62.
57 *Cooke v Telford* 2005 SCLR 367, *M, Applicant* 2009 GWD 24–394. See also below para 7.9.
58 Adults with Incapacity (Scotland) Act 2000, s 62(6), consultation is not required if it is impracticable in the circumstances (eg if a decision has to be taken very quickly), or where the joint guardians agree that it is unnecessary.
59 Adults with Incapacity (Scotland) Act 2000, s 58(5).
60 Adults with Incapacity (Scotland) Act 2000, s 57(1). See also *Scottish Government, Adults with Incapacity (Scotland) Act 2000: Revised Code of Practice for persons authorised under intervention orders and guardians* (2008), ch 4.

applicants in this category are the adult's children or siblings. Where an individual intends to apply to be appointed as a welfare guardian he or she must notify the local authority (though in practice this is likely to be done by their solicitor). The reason for this is that the application made by the individual must be accompanied by a report from the local authority (a suitability report). This report must be produced within twenty-one days of the local authority being notified of the intention to apply for appointment as guardian.[61] Legal aid is available to assist individuals in making applications for appointment as a guardian.

Unlike individuals, who may decide whether or not to apply for appointment as a guardian, the local authority has a duty to apply to court for appointment of a guardian if certain conditions are fulfilled:

(a) the adult meets the incapacity threshold[62] for the making of a guardianship order;
(b) a guardianship order is necessary to protect the property, financial affairs or personal welfare of the adult; and
(c) no one else has made or is likely to make an application for an order.[63]

The application made by the local authority may be for appointment of a financial guardian or a welfare guardian or both. In an application by the local authority is not possible for a local authority officer to be appointed as a financial guardian, though it is usual (but need not be the case) that where welfare guardianship is applied for the appointee will be the Chief Social Work Officer for the authority.

In considering whether to apply for the appointment of a guardian and in formulating the powers which are to be sought for the guardian it will be necessary to consider and apply the principles set out above, especially the requirement for the least restrictive option to be taken and the need to seek the views of a variety of people, including the adult.

Applications take the form of a summary application to the sheriff court. The application will, amongst other things, identify the person(s) whose appointment as guardian is sought and set out both the powers to be conferred on the guardian if appointed and the desired duration of the order.

61 Adults with Incapacity (Scotland) Act 2000, s 57(4).
62 See below.
63 Adults with Incapacity (Scotland) Act 2000, s 57(2). It doesn't matter that there are others who *could* apply for an order if they are not going to do so.

The default duration of a guardianship order is three years, though the sheriff can fix a different period, including an indefinite period.[64]

The application must be accompanied by a number of reports:[65]

(a) Two medical reports. These must be based on an examination and assessment of the adult carried out within 30 days before the application was lodged, though, in considering the application, the sheriff can consider an older report if satisfied that the adult's condition hasn't changed in any relevant respect since the examination and assessment was carried out. If the adult's incapacity is the result of a mental disorder[66] one of the reports must be from an 'relevant medical practitioner', that is someone who has special experience of the diagnosis and treatment of mental disorder and, because of this, appears on a list of approved practitioners maintained by the Health Board.[67]

(b) A 'suitability report'[68] will be needed where the application is for the appointment of a welfare guardian. The report will normally be prepared by a mental health officer[69] and be based on an interview with and assessment of the adult carried out within 30 days of the application being made. It will give the views of the reporter on the general appropriateness of the order being sought and, if the applicant is not the Chief Social Work Officer, an opinion on the suitability of the person(s) seeking appointment. The guidance suggests that the report should be clear about how the writer has reached his or her conclusions and should also include

64 Adults with Incapacity (Scotland) Act 2000, s 58(4). In 2009–10 only 2% of orders granted were for less than three years and 70% of orders were indefinite, Mental Welfare Commission, *Annual Monitoring Report 2009–2010*, p 73. This also notes differences of approach between local authorities in the duration of order which they seek.

65 Adults with Incapacity (Scotland) Act 2000, s 57(3).

66 99% of cases in 2009/10, Mental Welfare Commission, *Annual Monitoring Report 2009–2010*, p 73.

67 Though some doctors seem to be uncertain as to whether they are on this list, see *TH, HH & AI*, Glasgow Sheriff Court, 8 February 2008. The report may be from a doctor outside Scotland with equivalent qualifications, but he/she must also consult the Mental Welfare Commission about the report.

68 See Scottish Government, *Adults with Incapacity (Scotland) Act 2000: Code of Practice For Local Authorities Exercising Functions under the 2000 Act*, (2008), paras 6.30 to 6.42 & 7.15 to 7.42.

69 Though in the rare cases where incapacity arises solely because of inability to communicate (ie the inability to communicate is not the result of a mental disorder) the report may be prepared by a social worker who is not an MHO. The form of report by an MHO is set out in the Adults with Incapacity (Reports in Relation to Guardianship and Intervention Orders) (Scotland) Regulations 2002, SSI 2002/96, sch 2.

consideration of possible conflicts of interests, eg between the local authority and the adult or between the local authority and the adult's relatives.

(c) Where the application is for appointment of a financial guardian, the 'suitability report' must be produced by someone who has 'sufficient knowledge.' This report will cover both the suitability of the order and the suitability of the proposed guardian and must be based in part on an interview with and assessment of the adult within 30 days before the application is made.

(3) Procedure after making application

7.9 Once the application has been lodged with the court a number of people and bodies must be notified of the application. These are the adult (though see below), the adult's nearest relative, named person and primary carer, the Public Guardian, any attorney with powers affected by the application along with anyone else whom the sheriff directs to be notified, and, where the application is to appoint a welfare guardian, the Mental Welfare Commission and the local authority. It is possible to apply to the sheriff to dispense with the need to notify the adult. This can only be done if informing the adult would be likely to pose a serious threat to the health of the applicant. The application to dispense with notification to the adult must be supported by two medical certificates which confirm that notification would pose a risk to him/her, and these certificates should also explain the basis for reaching that conclusion so that the sheriff has some basis for deciding whether the criterion for dispensing with notification is met.[70]

The application may also seek appointment of an interim guardian pending the final decision on the application. An interim guardian can be appointed for up to 6 months,[71] though at the end of the appointment, if no final decision has been taken, the appointment cannot be extended and a fresh appointment of an interim guardian would be required. In any case, the interim guardian's appointment will come to an end on the appointment of a guardian.

A hearing will be fixed to take place no more than 28 days after the application, though this hearing will not necessarily decide on the application, and there is a number of reported cases where a consider-

70 *TH, HH & AI*, Glasgow Sheriff Court, 8 February 2008, *Mrs LC*, Glasgow Sheriff Court, 19 May 2005, *Application in relation to DC*, Glasgow Sheriff Court, 22 October 2010.

71 Adults with Incapacity (Scotland) Act 2000, s 57(5) & (6).

able period of time elapsed between the making of the application and the final decision on it. Anyone who has been notified of the application can lodge answers opposing the application or challenging some of the statements made in the application, for example the need for guardianship or the suitability of the proposed guardian. It is also possible to lodge a minute, for example applying for appointment of an alternative guardian. Appointment as a guardian cannot be sought by simply by lodging answers as the procedural rules for applications require any application to be made in the form of a minute.[72] A minute cannot, however, be used to seek appointment as a joint guardian, it has been held that joint guardians can only be appointed either where the initial application is for the appointment of joint guardians or where there is already an existing guardian and a fresh application is made for the appointment of an additional, joint, guardian.[73] This, perhaps unfortunate conclusion,[74] means, for example, that if an adult's partner applies for appointment as guardian to an adult, the adult's daughter cannot, as part of the same application process, seek appointment as a joint guardian with the partner. The only options open to the daughter if she wishes to be appointed as guardian would be either to oppose the partner's application and seek appointment as sole guardian or, alternatively, to not oppose the partner's application and then, after the partner has been appointed guardian, to make a fresh application to be appointed as joint guardian.

After a hearing, the sheriff must then decide how to dispose of the application. The sheriff can only appoint a guardian to the adult if certain requirements are met:

(a) The sheriff must consider the principles underlying intervention set out above (at para 7.4) and will need, for example, to be satisfied that appointment will provide a benefit to the adult and be the least restrictive course of action which achieves the desired result.
(b) The adult must be incapable and it must be likely that this incapacity will continue. In this context incapacity covers both the adult being incapable in relation to decision making and being incapable of acting to safeguard or promote her/his interests and welfare.[75]

72 *Cooke v Telford* 2005 SCLR 367; Act of Sederunt (Summary Applications, Statutory Applications and Appeals etc Rules) 1999, SI 1999/929, r 3.16.8.
73 *Cooke v Telford* 2005 SCLR 367, *M, Applicant* 2009 GWD 24–394.
74 Based on the wording of the statute which refers to '*An* application being made to the sheriff by two or more individuals…', Adults with Incapacity (Scotland) Act 2000, s 62(1)(a). In cases such as the example there is no such joint application.
75 Adults with Incapacity (Scotland) Act 2000, s 58(1)(a).

(c) No other available measures are sufficient to safeguard and promote the adult's interests.[76] If the sheriff considers that the result could be achieved by the less restrictive option of making an intervention order, then he/she has the power to make such an order instead of a guardianship order.[77]

(d) The person(s) appointed as guardian(s) must agree to the appointment(s) and must be suitable, though the sheriff doesn't have to be satisfied as to suitability where the Chief Social Work Officer is seeking appointment. At least some of the evidence for taking the decision on suitability will come from the suitability report lodged along with the applications. The factors which the sheriff has to consider in deciding on suitability are:[78]
   (i) how accessible the person is to the adult and the adult's primary carer;
   (ii) the ability of the person to carry out the functions of a guardian;
   (iii) whether the person is likely to have any conflict of interest with the adult, though such a conflict is not to be presumed only because the person is a relative of, or resides with the adult;[79]
   (iv) if any undue concentration of power over the adult will arise because of the person's appointment as guardian;
   (v) any adverse effects which appointment of the person would have on the interests of the adult; and
   (vi) any other matters which appear to the sheriff to be appropriate.

(e) the person appointed must be aware of the functions of a guardian as well as of the adults circumstances and condition and of the needs arising from these.

76 Adults with Incapacity (Scotland) Act 2000, s 58(1)(b).

77 Adults with Incapacity (Scotland) Act 2000, s 58(3).

78 Adults with Incapacity (Scotland) Act 2000, s 59(4).

79 Adults with Incapacity (Scotland) Act 2000, s 59(5). In *North Ayrshire Council v M* 2004 SCLR 956, it was argued that because there might be financial strain between the local authority and the adult there could be a conflict of interest between the Chief Social Work Officer and the adult. This, it was argued, made the appointment of someone other than the Chief Social Work Officer appropriate. The relevant guidance indicates that the suitability report should consider potential conflicts of interest, See Scottish Government, *Adults with Incapacity (Scotland) Act 2000: Code of Practice For Local Authorities Exercising Functions under the 2000 Act*, (2008), paras 6.33 to 6.37 & 7.23 to 7.33. It clearly cannot be the case that the possibility of disputes between the adult and the local authority over, for example, service provision, automatically mean that there is a conflict of interest making the Chief Social Work Officer's appointment inappropriate.

More than one person may be appointed. This will be the case where joint guardians are appointed or where one person is appointed as financial guardian and another as welfare guardian. It is also possible, however, for the sheriff to appoint both a guardian (the original guardian) and a substitute guardian who will take over the role of the original guardian if he or she becomes unable to act. It is also possible to apply for appointment of a substitute guardian after a guardian has been appointed.

In deciding who to appoint as guardian the sheriff is not limited to appointing the original applicant, anyone who has lodged a minute seeking appointment may be appointed.[80] Minuters are not required to lodge medical reports relating to the adult's incapacity or to lodge a suitability report. The sheriff will still, however, need to be satisfied as to the minuter's suitability and may order that a report on her/his suitability be prepared. It has been suggested that it is best practice for this report to be prepared by the same MHO who produced the suitability report lodged with the application.[81]

The sheriff will have to fix the duration of the appointment. The default duration of a guardianship order is three years, though the sheriff can fix a different period, including an indefinite period,[82] but this can only be done on cause shown, that is, the person seeking the appointment must set out reasons for the longer duration.

The sheriff will also have to specify the powers to be granted to the guardian, these will have to be set out in the application for the appointment of a guardian and the 2000 Act sets out the broad categories of powers which may be granted,[83] the powers applied for will normally be expressed more specifically:

(a) Power to deal with matters related to the adult's property, financial affairs or welfare specified in the guardianship order. This might include, for example, a specific power to determine where the adult stays.
(b) Power to deal with all aspects of the adult's personal welfare or with those aspects which are set out in the guardianship order.

80 Deriving from the sheriff's power to appoint '*any* individual' considered suitable and who has agreed to act, Adults with Incapacity (Scotland) Act 2000, s 59(1)(a).
81 Who will, obviously, be familiar with the case. See *M, Applicant* 2009 GWD 24–394.
82 Adults with Incapacity (Scotland) Act 2000, s 58(4). Some detail on the length of orders granted is set out in note 64 above.
83 Adults with Incapacity (Scotland) Act 2000, s 64(1).

(c) Power to manage the adult's property and financial affairs, or those parts of them which are set out in the guardianship order.
(d) Power to authorise the adult to carry out either specific transactions or categories of transactions, this power should be considered in the context of Principle 4 set out above.
(e) Power to act as the adult's legal representative in any matter which is within the guardian's powers.

In considering which powers to grant, the sheriff will have to consider the Principles set out above (at para 7.4) and may, for example, refuse to grant some powers because they are considered to be too restrictive.[84] There are also certain restrictions on the power of the guardian to consent to certain types of medical treatment or procedure, these are considered more fully below.

One final matter which has to be considered in appointing a financial guardian is whether the guardian should be required to find caution (pronounced 'kayshun'). In practice this takes the form of requiring insurance in case the guardian mismanages the adult's estate. Initially the 2000 Act required caution in every case, though it gave the sheriff discretion in fixing the amount of caution. Because of the difficulty experience by some family member financial guardians in finding caution the amount was in some cases fixed at zero, though sheriffs did express concern about the possible dangers of this. The 2000 Act has since been amended and the sheriff now has discretion as to whether to require caution. Arrangements have also been made by the Public Guardian which make it easier for guardians who are not solicitors or accountants to get caution.[85]

(4) After the order is granted[86]

7.10 Once a guardianship order has been granted, the sheriff clerk must notify the Public Guardian, who maintains a register of guardianship orders. The Public Guardian will then notify the adult, the local authority for the area in which the adult resides, and, where the incapacity arises from mental disorder, the Mental Welfare Commission. Where

84 *Application in respect of EB*, Glasgow Sheriff Court, 1 December 2005.

85 Details can be found on the Office of The Public Guardian website: www.publicguardian-scotland.gov.uk.

86 Scottish Government, *Adults with Incapacity (Scotland) Act 2000: Revised Code of Practice for Persons Authorised under Intervention Orders and Guardians* (2008), chs 5 & 6; Scottish Government, *Adults with Incapacity (Scotland) Act 2000: Code of Practice For Local Authorities Exercising Functions under the 2000 Act* (2008), paras 6.52–6.66.

the Chief Social Work Office has been appointed as a welfare guardian then he/she must, within 7 days, identify the named individual who will, in fact, carry out the duties of guardian. The person appointed will normally have been involved with the adult prior to the application being made for a guardianship order. The Code of Practice makes it clear that in considering the appointment of this individual any possible conflict of interest must be considered, for example if the same person would be acting as guardian and also as care manager for a care package for the adult.[87]

Welfare guardians must be supervised by the local authority,[88] the precise content of the supervision duty in terms of visits to the adult and the guardian depends on the length of the guardianship order. If the order is for less than one year[89] visits must take place around the mid-point of the order and then again within fourteen days of the end of the order. For longer orders an initial visit must take place within three months of the making of the order and then at least every six months.[90] In order to assist with this supervision the guardian must provide the local authority, on request, with information about the adult's welfare or the guardian's exercise of her/his power. Where a local authority worker is acting as guardian the required supervision should be carried out by the worker's line manager. Financial guardians are supervised by the Public Guardian.

During the period of guardianship it may be felt that it is necessary to change the powers which have been given to the guardian and this can be done by application to the sheriff. Where the Chief Social Work Officer is guardian then the guardianship should be reviewed annually. If the guardianship is coming to the end of the period fixed as its duration it can be renewed, but this requires an application to the sheriff. The reports required to renew are slightly different from those required for

87 Scottish Government, *Adults with Incapacity (Scotland) Act 2000: Code of Practice For Local Authorities Exercising Functions under the 2000 Act* (2008), para 6.50.

88 Scottish Government, *Adults with Incapacity (Scotland) Act 2000: Code of Practice For Local Authorities Exercising Functions under the 2000 Act* (2008), ch 8.

89 Extremely rare in practice.

90 Though it appears that these frequencies are not always complied with in practice, Mental Welfare Commission, *Support and Supervision of Private Welfare Guardians* (2010). This also notes that 'a significant numbers or adults on guardianship will not be getting the scrutiny from a local authority supervisor that was envisaged when the legislation came into force.' (p 23). An earlier MWC report, *Guardianship and Young Adults* (2008), had concluded that: 'Many social work supervising officers seem to be unaware of their duty to visit both the guardian and the adult on guardianship.' (p 22).

initial appointment. For example, only one medical report is required and the MHO's report will cover the general appropriateness of continuing the guardianship and, in cases where the Chief Social Work Officer is not the guardian, the suitability of the guardian. If the original guardian is unable or unwilling to continue to act (this, of course, could happen at any time, not just at the end of an order) a substitute or replacement guardian may be appointed. Such appointments (when not involving renewal of the order) don't require a medical or suitability report, though some evidence as to the suitability of the proposed guardian will have to be provided to the sheriff.

If the adult, or someone else, refuses to comply with a welfare guardian's decision it is possible for the guardian to seek a court order requiring compliance.[91] In the 2000 Act as originally passed the person against whom the order was sought had to be given the opportunity to make representations before such an order could be made. This made the value of this provision doubtful.[92] It is now possible for the sheriff to dispense with this requirement, though, as the Code of Practice notes:[93]

> It is anticipated that the section 70 procedure will be used only occasionally by welfare guardians, for example to remove the person from an unsuitable place to one where the guardian has decided he/she should live. It represents a potentially substantial encroachment on the personal autonomy of an individual. Before making an order or granting a warrant, the sheriff would have to be satisfied that the principles in the 2000 Act were being met. There would have to be a positive benefit to the adult and the order or warrant would have to be the only reasonable way of achieving that benefit. In dealing with a habitual absconder a new warrant would be needed for each incident.

Aside from the expiry of the period of the guardianship order without the order being renewed, guardianship, or the appointment of an individual guardian, can be terminated in a variety of different ways:

(a) The guardian may resign, though if there is no joint guardian or substitute guardian she/he can't resign until a replacement guardian has been appointed.
(b) A financial guardianship may be recalled by the Public Guardian and a welfare guardianship by the Mental Welfare Commission or the local authority. Recall of welfare guardianship may

91 Adults with Incapacity (Scotland) Act 2000, s 70.
92 See *Anne Docherty*, Glasgow Sheriff Court, 8 February 2005.
93 Scottish Government, *Adults with Incapacity (Scotland) Act 2000: Code of Practice For Local Authorities Exercising Functions under the 2000 Act* (2008), para 6.62.

be requested by someone claiming an interest in the welfare of the adult (including the adult) or, for example, the local authority may, following a review, decide to recall a guardianship.[94] Recall can only take place either if the grounds for appointing the guardian no longer exist or if there are other means of safeguarding and promoting the interests of the adult.

(c) The guardianship can be recalled by the sheriff, the grounds for this are the same as those set in (b) out above.

(d) A guardian can be removed from his/her position as guardian by the sheriff provided that there is another guardian prepared to act. Removal can be sought by anyone claiming an interest and might be appropriate if a local authority had significant concerns about a guardian.

(e) Death of the adult or of the guardian.

(3) Intervention Orders[95]

7.11 Intervention orders are appropriate where the intervention is likely to be time-limited or where a single action or decision is involved, for example, signing a tenancy agreement for the adult[96] or agreeing settlement of a compensation claim.[97] Intervention orders can relate either to the financial or to the personal welfare of the adult, though in practice a very small number of orders is concerned with personal welfare. Where it will be necessary to take decisions on behalf of an adult over a period of time on a continuing basis the appropriate form of intervention is to seek a guardianship order.

As with guardianship orders, anyone claiming an interest may seek an order, and the procedure and reports required are similar, though the reports will refer to an intervention order rather than guardianship. The local authority has duty to apply for an intervention order where

94 Adults with Incapacity (Scotland) Act 2000, s 73(3) &(4). In the case of financial guardianship the decision may be made by the Public Guardian to recall the guardianship or an application may be made by anyone having an interest in the property or financial affairs of the adult, s 73(1) & (2).

95 Scottish Government, *Adults with Incapacity (Scotland) Act 2000: Revised Code of Practice for Persons Authorised under Intervention Orders and Guardians* (2008), chs 2 & 3; Scottish Government, *Adults with Incapacity (Scotland) Act 2000: Code of Practice For Local Authorities Exercising Functions under the 2000 Act*, (2008), paras 6.1–6.16.

96 Scottish Government, *Adults with Incapacity (Scotland) Act 2000: Code of Practice For Local Authorities Exercising Functions under the 2000 Act* (2008), paras 6.1–6.16.

97 *B, Applicant* 2005 SLT (Sh Ct) 95.

it appears that an application is necessary and no application has been made or is likely to be made by anyone else.

As well as these procedural similarities, there are some important differences between guardianship and intervention orders:

(a) Although a local authority cannot apply for appointment as a financial guardian, it can apply for an intervention order in relation to the adult's finances or property.
(b) The sheriff can make an intervention order when guardianship is applied for, but can't do the opposite.
(c) Persons authorised under an intervention order will not be under the supervision of the local authority or the Public Guardian, except that the latter will have to agree to the purchase/sale price where the intervention authorised involves buying or selling a house.

(4) Withdrawal of funds[98]

7.12 The withdrawal of funds procedure allows an individual or a body to apply to the Public Guardian to be allowed to deal with the adult's money. If the application is granted the Public Guardian will issue a withdrawal certificate. One example of use of this provision is the case of a local authority which sought authority to deal with an adult's benefits. The adult spent money freely on her children to the extent that she often did not have enough to pay accommodation, food and utilities costs. The local authority (which was also the adult's welfare guardian) obtained a withdrawal certificate from the Public Guardian which allowed it to control as much of the adult's benefits as were required to pay her basic living expenses, leaving an amount over for her discretionary spending.[99]

The application can be made either by an individual or by a body, for example, the local authority, and the purposes for which the authorisation can be granted are limited to payment of taxes; payment of basic expenses for food, accommodation, clothing and fuel; payment for other services for looking after or caring for the adult; payment of debts owed by the adult; and, payment for other items authorised by the Public Guardian. If an application is made by a body other than the local

98 Scottish Government, *Adults with Incapacity (Scotland) Act 2000 Code of Practice – Access to Funds* (2008).
99 *YW v Office of the Public Guardian*, Peterhead Sheriff Court, 25 June 2010.

authority or is made by someone who is both the adult's nearest relative and her/his primary carer then it must be notified to the local authority, which must then, if it wishes to oppose the application, be given an opportunity to make representations before a decision is made by the Public Guardian.

(5) Management of resident's funds

7.13 One option for the management of the finances of an adult who is staying in a residential establishment is for these to be managed by a manager in that establishment. This is only possible in what are described as 'authorised establishments', and these include hospitals (whether independent or NHS), private psychiatric hospitals, care home services registered with the Scottish Commission for the Regulation of Care,[100] and the State Hospital. The first step in obtaining an authorisation to manage the funds of a resident is the issue of a medical certificate in to the effect that the adult is unable to manage her/his finances her/himself.[101] Once such a certificate has been issued notification must be made to the adult (unless this is likely to pose a serious risk to the health of the adult) and to the supervisory body for the establishment. In the case of NHS hospitals the supervisory body will be the Health Board, for others it will be the Scottish Commission for the Regulation of Care.[102] The supervisory body will then inform the nearest relative. The manager must also notify the adult and the supervisory body of the intention to manage the affairs of the adult. Following this the manager must apply to the supervisory body for a Certificate of Authority to withdraw the resident's funds, and only after this Certificate has been issued by the supervisory authority can the manager manage these funds.

Once the Certificate is issued the manager can claim, hold and spend pensions and benefits and hold and dispose of moveable property belonging to the adult. The manager must act for the benefit of the resident and take account of the sentimental value of any item, must keep proper records and must only spend the funds on items which are not provided by the establishment as part of its normal service. There is an upper limit of £10,000 on the amount that can be managed, though

100 Or, from April 2011, Social Care and Social Work Improvement Scotland.

101 Adults with Incapacity (Scotland) Act 2000, s 37(1); Adults with Incapacity (Management of Residents' Finances) (No. 2) (Scotland) Regulations 2003, SSI 2003/266; *Adults with Incapacity (Scotland) Act 2000: Code of Practice for Managers of Authorised Establishments under Part 4 of the Act* (SE/2003/177).

102 From April 2011, Social Care and Social Work Improvement Scotland.

agreement can be obtained from the supervisory body to manage larger amounts.

It is only possible to manage an adult's funds under an authorisation to the extent that there is no guardian, attorney or other person with powers to do this and there is no intervention order regulating a particular use of or action in relation to the adult's funds.

(6) Medical Treatment[103]

7.14 Consent to medical treatment for adults can, subject to certain restrictions described below, be given by a welfare guardian or a welfare attorney, provided that the powers conferred on them are wide enough to cover the specific treatment or may be the subject of an application for an intervention order. In addition, a decision can only be taken about medical treatment if the adult is her/himself incapable of giving or refusing consent and, as with other areas, the capacity of the adult may vary between different types of treatment. Medical practitioners and others also have powers under the 2000 Act to give treatment, both in cases where there is no attorney or guardian and where there is such an appointee.

(1) Treatment by medical practitioners

7.15 Medical practitioners (and certain others[104]) can certify that an adult is incapable in relation to specific medical treatment and, subject to what is said later, medical treatment can be given to the adult on the basis of that certification.[105] The treatment may be provided by someone other than the person issuing the certificate. There is a specific form for the certificate (a Medical Treatment Certificate)[106] and it will need to specify how long the authority to treat will last, though this is

103 Scottish Government, *Adults with Incapacity (Scotland) Act 2000: Code of Practice (Second Edition) for practitioners authorised to carry out medical treatment or research under part 5 of the Act* (2007).

104 Including dentists and registered nurses, Adults with Incapacity (Scotland) Act 2000, s 47(1A).

105 Though the MWC has continuing concerns that medical treatment is widely provided without proper certification being in place, see MWC, *Annual Overview 2008–2009*; SCRC & MWC, *Remember I'm Still Me* (2009), pp 62–64.

106 Adults with Incapacity (Medical Treatment Certificates) (Scotland) Regulations 2007, SSI 2007/104.

normally a maximum of one year.[107] If the adult's condition or circumstances change the certificate can be revoked and, if that is done, a new certificate may be issued. The authority to treat conferred by a certificate does not extend to:

(a) the use of force or detention, unless this is immediately necessary and then only for as long as necessary;
(b) any action inconsistent with a court decision; or
(c) placing an adult in hospital for treatment of a mental disorder against her/his will.

In addition, some types of treatment (see Box 2) can only be given after permission has been given by the Court of Session or after approval by a medical practitioner appointed by the Mental Welfare Commission.[108]

Box 2

Treatments requiring permission of the Court of Session:

- sterilisation in cases where there is no serious malformation or disease of the reproductive organs; and
- hormonal implants to reduce sex drive.

Treatments requiring approval by MWC appointee:

- drug treatment to reduce sex drive;
- ECT;
- abortion; or
- treatment which is likely to cause sterilisation.

Treatment can't be given if the authority to provide treatment is the subject of court proceedings or where the power to consent to treatment is the subject of an application for a guardianship order or intervention order currently before the court, unless the treatment is otherwise legally authorised to preserve the life of the adult or to prevent serious deterioration in her/his condition. If there is a proxy[109] who has power

107 This is extended to three years where the adult is incapable of consenting because of a severe or profound learning disability, dementia or a severe neurological disorder and is unlikely to improve, Adults with Incapacity (Conditions and Circumstances Applicable to Three Year Medical Treatment Certificates) (Scotland) Regulations 2005, SSI 2005/100.

108 Adults with Incapacity (Scotland) Act 2000, s 48, Adults with Incapacity (Specified Medical Treatments) (Scotland) Regulations 2002, SSI 2001/275.

109 A welfare guardian or attorney or a person authorised by an intervention order.

in relation to a particular form of treatment, and the person giving that treatment is aware of this, he/she cannot give treatment unless he/she has obtained the consent of that proxy, provided that it would be reasonable and practicable to get the proxy's consent. If consent is obtained then the treatment can go ahead, though anyone having an interest (or the person who issued the certificate if he/she is not providing the treatment) can appeal the decision about treatment to the Court of Session.

(2) Disagreements about medical treatment

7.16 If the person providing treatment and the person with power to take decisions about that treatment on behalf of the adult[110] (the proxy) disagree about medical treatment, a request can be made to the Mental Welfare Commission to nominate someone (a nominated practitioner)[111] to give an opinion on whether or not the treatment should be given. If the opinion of the nominated practitioner is that treatment should be given then it can be provided, though, regardless of the opinion of the nominated practitioner, it is possible to seek a determination from the Court of Session as to whether the treatment should be given or not.[112]

(3) Restriction on powers of proxy to consent to treatment

7.17 There are restrictions on the powers of attorneys,[113] welfare guardians[114] and persons authorised under an intervention order[115] to consent to medical treatment. In particular, leaving aside any restriction deriving from the scope of the powers conferred on them, they cannot:

(a) place the adult in hospital against her/his will for treatment of a mental disorder;[116]
(b) consent to any of the treatments set out in Box 2 above;

110 Ie a welfare guardian or attorney or someone authorised under an intervention order.
111 This happens rarely, two occasions were recorded in 2009–10, see Mental Welfare Commission, *Annual Monitoring Report 2009–2010*, none were recorded in 2007–2008.
112 Adults with Incapacity (Scotland) Act 2000, s 50(5)–(8).
113 Adults with Incapacity (Scotland) Act 2000, s 16(6).
114 Adults with Incapacity (Scotland) Act 2000, s 64(2).
115 Adults with Incapacity (Scotland) Act 2000, s 53(14).
116 Which suggests that such a placement can be made if the adult is compliant and does not attempt to leave.

(c) make a request that the adult's body be used, after death, for anatomical examination;

(d) give authorisation:

    (i) for the removal and use of part of the adult's body after death for transplant, research, education or training or audit;

    (ii) for use of an organ for live transplant;

    (iii) for a post-mortem examination; or

    (iv) for use of a tissue sample or organ for providing information about or confirming the cause of death; investigating the effect and efficacy of any medical or surgical intervention carried out on the person; obtaining information which may be relevant to the health of any other person (including a future person); or audit;

(e) nominate someone who can authorise a post-mortem examination.

PROVISION OF SERVICES TO ADULTS WITH INCAPACITY

7.18 This has been considered in part in chapter 6, para 6.11 which discussed the ability of local authorities to provide services to adults by virtue of section 13ZA of the Social Work (Scotland) Act 1968. Provision of services which do not involve the provision of accommodation may be made under this section without any difficulty, but in relation to the provision of accommodation an additional factor comes into play, that is, does the placement of an adult in residential accommodation amount to or involve a deprivation of her/his liberty? This issue will arise even in cases where the adult is compliant with the placement, in that he or she does not resist it or try to leave, and it also arises where an adult has capacity when the placement is made and agrees to it but subsequently loses capacity.[117] In this latter case the question is whether continuation of the placement involves a deprivation of liberty.

The 'deprivation of liberty' wording derives from Article 5 of the European Convention on Human Rights, which is in the following terms:

> 1. Everyone has the right to liberty and security of person. No one shall be deprived of his liberty save in the following cases and in accordance with a procedure prescribed by law:
>
> …

117 See *Anne Docherty*, Glasgow Sheriff Court, 8 February 2005.

(e) the lawful detention of persons for the prevention of the spreading of infectious diseases, of persons of unsound mind, alcoholics or drug addicts or vagrants;

...

4. Everyone who is deprived of his liberty by arrest or detention shall be entitled to take proceedings by which the lawfulness of his detention shall be decided speedily by a court and his release ordered if the detention is not lawful.

In the context of adults with incapacity this raises three questions: when is there a deprivation of liberty, can a proxy consent to deprivation of liberty, and, are the processes of review adequate?

(1) Deprivation of liberty

7.19 In *Guzzardi v Italy* it was said that:[118]

In order to determine whether someone has been 'deprived of his liberty' within the meaning of Article 5 ..., the starting point must be his concrete situation and account must be taken of a whole range of criteria such as the type, duration, effects and manner of implementation of the measure in question ....

The difference between deprivation of and restriction upon liberty is nonetheless merely one of degree or intensity, and not one of nature or substance. Although the process of classification into one or other of these categories sometimes proves to be no easy task in that some borderline cases are a matter of pure opinion, the Court cannot avoid making the selection upon which the applicability or inapplicability of Article 5...

It is therefore difficult to provide a concise description of the cases where there will be deprivation of liberty or an exhaustive set of criteria which can be applied to reach a decision. A variety of criteria are suggested in guidance, for example:[119]

(a) the person's past and present wishes;
(b) access to resources to support physical and social autonomy and interests as far as possible;

118 (1981) 3 EHRR 333, paras 92–93; see also *Austin v Commissioner of Police of the Metropolis* [2009] UKHL 5.

119 Scottish Executive: *Guidance for Local Authorities (March 2007): Provision of Community Care Services to Adults with Incapacity*, Circular CCD5/2007; see also Mental Welfare Commission, *Rights, Risks and Limits to Freedom* (2006).

(c) the extent/nature of limitations on contact with the outside world;
(d) whether the person is prevented from leaving the facility, whether by locked doors or restraint;
(e) internal design of physical environment and accessibility;
(f) external physical environment and access eg safe garden;
(g) the use of restraints.

The difficulty in practice, aside from applying this guidance in concrete cases and working out the relationship between the different factors, is that there is some authority in Scotland to the effect that any placement of an adult with incapacity in a residential setting will amount to a deprivation of liberty and infringe her/his rights under Article 5 unless this placement is made by a guardian appointed with powers to make the placement.[120] It is not clear that the reasoning underlying these decisions is sound, but it is likely that the conclusions in themselves will be correct. There is English case law which suggests that the key issue in determining deprivation of liberty is whether the person is free to leave and to choose to live elsewhere, regardless of the fact that they are permitted to take trips out of the accommodation, in other words the focus is on factor (d) above.[121] In most cases where an adult with incapacity is placed in residential accommodation he or she will not realistically have the option of leaving to live elsewhere and it is likely that were he or she to seek to leave then he or she would be prevented from doing so. In such cases it is likely that there will be deprivation of liberty. Since this is the case it must, according to Article 5, take place following a procedure prescribed by law, the most likely candidate for which in Scotland is applying for appointment of a guardian with power to determine the residence of the adult. Further support for his position can be derived from a case in which it was held that placement of a 19 year old man in a residential unit without proper authority amounted to a deprivation of liberty[122] and a case where it seems to have been regarded as self-evident that placement of a woman with Alzheimer's disease in a residential home involved deprivation of her liberty.[123]

120 *Muldoon, Applicant* 2005 SCLR 611; *M, Applicant* 2009 SLT (Sh Ct) 185.
121 *JE v DE* [2006] EWHC 3459 (Fam); see also *HL v United Kingdom* 92005) 40 EHRR 32 and *Storck v Germany* (2006) 43 EHRR 96.
122 *G v E, A Local Authority, F* [2010] EWHC 621 (Fam).
123 *A County Council v MB, JB, A Residential Home* [2010] EWHC 2508 (COP). See also *Dorset CC v EH* [2009] EWHC 784 (fam).

There will, in general be no deprivation of liberty where this is consented to on behalf of the adult[124] or where the restrictions are imposed in a domestic setting.[125]

(2) Can a proxy consent to deprivation of liberty?

7.20 The view that this is possible is implicit in the Scottish court decisions referred to above and also seems to be contemplated by the European Court of Human Rights.[126] However, it has been suggested that there is some doubt about whether a guardian or attorney can give such consent. In relation to guardians this is based on the absence of consideration of this specific power in either the 2000 Act or in the Code of Practice.[127] However, it should be borne in mind that the powers over the life of the adult which the 2000 Act contemplates conferring on guardians are extensive and without any specific limitation which would prevent guardians giving such consent. In addition, it is likely that the power given to guardians to determine the place of residence of the adult will involve deprivation of liberty in a substantial proportion of cases. Since this is the case, the Act would be failing to promote the welfare of adults. If such (appropriate) placements could not be made there is no other means for making such placements other than detention under the Mental Health (Care and Treatment)(Scotland) Act 2003 or an application to the inherent jurisdiction of the Court of Session.

(3) The adequacy of review

7.21 The requirement set out in Article 5 is for a person deprived of his/her liberty to be able to bring the matter before a court for review. In the case of an adult with incapacity who is placed in a setting which involves deprivation of liberty by a guardian or attorney, the only methods of doing this are to take action in one of the ways set out above (in para 7.10), for example, by seeking recall of the guardianship or removal of the guardian. Such action, of course, depends on the initiative being taken by a person with incapacity, and there is no automatic

124 Though such consent will not always have this effect: *Shtukaturov v Russia* [2008] MHLR 238.

125 *Re MIG and MEG* [2010] EWHC 785 (Fam), *A Local Authority v A* [2010] EWHC 978 (Fam).

126 *Shtukaturov v Russia* [2008] MHLR 238.

127 Mental Welfare Commission, *Adults with Incapacity Act: When to Invoke the Act* (2005), pp 11 & 12, referring to Ward, A, *Adult Incapacity* (2003), para 10–21.

process for review of deprivation of liberty which does not rely on the adult or another interested party taking the initiative. In the circumstances, it might be asked how realistic is this possibility and therefore how real is the right to bring the matter before the court. Despite this, a similar procedure has been held to be compliant with Article 5 and that remains the current position.[128]

(4) Conclusion

7.22 The current state of the law is rather unsatisfactory, particularly the lack of clarity as the circumstances in which guardianship is required for placements of adults with incapacity to be made and whether guardianship is necessary for *all* such placements. This has led to differences in practice between local authorities, depending on which view they take of this matter. In addition, it is not clear that the processes for review of cases which do involve deprivation of liberty are adequate and do comply with Article 5. These topics (and others relating to guardianship) are currently being considered by the Scottish Law Commission as part of its 8th Programme of Law Reform, though it does not expect to report until 2014.

128 *R (on the application of H v Secretary of State for Health)* [2005] UKHL 60; see also *Lothian Health Board v M* 2007 SCLR 478.

Chapter 8

Mental health

INTRODUCTION

8.1 Current law on mental health in Scotland is contained in the Mental Health (Care and Treatment) (Scotland) Act 2003, though there has recently been a limited review of this which may result in some changes being made in the course of 2011.[1] The Act is supplemented by a Code of Practice[2] and by good practice guidance issued by the Mental Welfare Commission. The two areas to be covered in this chapter are local authority duties under the 2003 Act and the procedures for compulsory treatment of those with a mental disorder.[3] Before going on to consider these, however, it is necessary to explain who those involved in implementing the legislation are and to define some of the terms used.

(1) Mental Health Officers

8.2 Mental Health Officers (MHOs) play an essential role in the administration of the 2003 Act. To become a MHO a social worker must have at least two years of full-time experience after qualifying[4] and must now complete a Mental Health Officer Award or have an equivalent qualification.[5] Once appointed, MHOs must complete a number of reports under the 2003 Act and other legislation to retain that status.[6] In practice MHOs will work closely with colleagues from the health service and many will be share an office with such colleagues as part of a joint service.

1 See ch 12.
2 Scottish Executive, *Mental Health (Care and Treatment) (Scotland) Act 2003: Code of Practice* (2005).
3 Mentally disordered offenders are considered in ch 10.
4 Or an equivalent part-time length of experience.
5 The Mental Health (Care and Treatment) (Scotland) Act 2003 (Requirements for appointment as mental health officers) Direction 2009.
6 Mental Health (Care and Treatment) (Scotland) Act 2003 (Requirements for continuing appointment as mental health officers) Direction 2006.

(2) Approved medical practitioner

8.3 An approved medical practitioner is a doctor who appears on a list maintained by the health board and who has special experience in the diagnosis and treatment of mental disorder.[7] Some types of authorisation can only be given, and some reports must be made, by an approved medical practitioner.

(3) Responsible medical officer (RMO)

8.4 The responsible medical officer is the doctor who is responsible for the care and treatment of a patient who is subject to compulsory treatment measures. The RMO must be an approved medical practitioner. If a patient is made subject any compulsory measures a RMO must be appointed to her/him.

(4) Mental Welfare Commission for Scotland

8.5 The Mental Welfare Commission has a variety of functions under the 2003 Act and under the Adults with Incapacity (Scotland) Act 2000. Under the 2003 Act these functions include carrying out investigations, giving advice, visiting patients, dealing with complaints from patients and publishing guidance. In addition, the commission has the power to revoke certain compulsory treatment measures.

(5) Named person[8]

8.6 The named person has an important role to play in relation to compulsory treatment, for example he or she must be sent a copy of an application for a compulsory treatment order and is entitled to take part in the proceedings following application for such an order. A patient aged 16 or over can nominate someone as her/his named person (or declare that a particular person is not to be her/his named person). If there is no nomination (or the person nominated refuses to act as named person) the 2003 Act sets out a procedure for identifying the named person, with slight differences depending on whether the patient is aged

7 The Mental Health (Care and Treatment) (Scotland) Act 2003 (Qualifications, experience and training of approved medical practitioners) Directions 2005. These require the equivalent of at least four years full-time experience in psychiatric services in order to qualify.

8 Mental Health (Care and Treatment) (Scotland) Act 2003, ss 250–253, 257.

under 16 or is 16 or older. The table below sets out these provisions, if no-one in the first row is available or prepared to act then the person in the next row will be named person. If there is no-one in any of these categories an application can be made to the Mental Health Tribunal for appointment of a named person. An application can also be made for a declaration that it is inappropriate for a named person to continue to act and for the appointment of a substitute.

16 or over	**Under 16**
Primary carer[9] (must be 16+)	Holder of parental responsibilities/rights
Any other carer (must be 16+)	Primary carer
Nearest relative	

It is likely that there will be some changes in respect of named persons.[10] At present the named person may be in that position by default and may have no, or a fractured, relationship, with the patient. Despite this the named person is, as we will see, a full participant in the processes involved in detention of patients, and has full access to medical and other reports produced during these processes.

(6) Nearest relative

8.7 The patient's nearest relative will be the person who comes highest up the following list of those related to the patient:

- Spouse or civil partner, though not if legally separated or the patient or the spouse/civil partner has left the other
- Someone who has been living with the patient as spouse/civil partner for at least 6 months
- Child
- Parent
- Sibling
- Grandparent
- Grandchild
- Uncle/Aunt
- Niece/Nephew
- Someone who has been living with the patient for at least 5 years

9 A primary carer is the person who provides all, or most, care and support for the patient, though the definition does not include someone who provides care either because they are employed to do so or because they volunteer to do so.

10 *Scottish Government Response to the 'Limited Review of the Mental Health (Care and Treatment) (Scotland) Act 2003 Report'* (2010), pp 2–3. See ch 12.

(7) Mental disorder

8.8 A mental disorder is defined as any mental illness, personality disorder or learning disability, however this is caused or manifested.[11] None of these terms are further defined in the 2003 Act, though it does specifically provide that someone is not mentally disordered only because of:

(a) sexual orientation;
(b) sexual deviancy;
(c) transsexualism;
(d) transvestism;
(e) dependence on, or use of, alcohol or drugs;
(f) behaviour that causes, or is likely to cause, harassment, alarm or distress to any other person;
(g) acting as no prudent person would act.

(8) Medical treatment

8.9 Medical treatment is defined widely in the 2003 Act. It is restricted to treatment for mental disorder, but includes nursing, care, psychological intervention, 'habilitation' (this includes education and training in work, social and independent living skills) and rehabilitation.[12] We will see below that there are some restrictions on the type of treatment that can be provided to a patient without her/his consent.[13] Although treatment is restricted to treatment of the mental disorder, it can include treatment for the symptoms or physical consequences of a mental disorder, for example naso-gastric tube feeding of a patient who is severely malnourished as a consequence of an eating disorder.[14]

(9) The Principles

8.10 The 2003 Act sets out a number of principles to which some of those discharging functions under it must have regard. Discharge includes taking decisions and actions in relation to the patient, but also extends to taking no action when there is power to act. Certain categories of actor are not required to have regard to the principles, and these include the patient and her/his named person and primary carer,

11 Mental Health (Care and Treatment) (Scotland) Act 2003, s 328(1).
12 Mental Health (Care and Treatment) (Scotland) Act 2003, s 329(1).
13 See para 8.24 below.
14 *B v Croydon HA* [1995] 2 WLR 294; *B v Croydon HA* [1995] 1 FCR 332.

the patient's solicitor or advocate, a curator *ad litem* appointed by the Mental Health Tribunal and any guardian or welfare attorney of the patient.[15] For those aged 18 or over the principles are:

(a) Regard is to be had (as far as relevant) to the following:[16]
   (i) the present and past wishes of the patient; these can be set out in the form of an advance statement, though if this is done the patient's wishes as set out there can still be overridden by the Mental Health Tribunal and by those providing treatment;[17]
   (ii) the views of the named person, carer and any guardian or welfare attorney;
   (iii) the importance of the patient participating as fully as possible and the importance of providing the patient with information and support to enable this participation;
   (iv) the range of options available in the patient's case;
   (v) the importance of providing maximum benefit to the patient;
   (vi) the need to ensure that the patient is not treated less favourably than someone who is not a patient would be treated in comparable circumstances, unless any less favourable treatment is justified by the circumstances;
   (vii) the abilities, background and characteristics of the patient, including religious background, cultural and linguistic background, sexual orientation, age, sex, racial origin and membership of any ethnic group.

(b) Functions are to be discharged in the way which 'appears', to the person discharging the function, to involve the minimum restriction on the patient's freedom that is necessary in the circumstances.[18]

(c) As far as reasonable and practicable regard is to be had to the importance of providing information to anyone who is carer to the patient which will help them to care for the patient and to the needs and circumstance of any carer, at least to the extent that the person discharging the function is aware of these and they are relevant to the discharge of the function. This principle does not apply to decisions about medical treatment.[19]

15 Mental Health (Care and Treatment) (Scotland) Act 2003, s 1(7).
16 Mental Health (Care and Treatment) (Scotland) Act 2003, s 1(3).
17 Mental Health (Care and Treatment) (Scotland) Act 2003, ss 275 & 276. See para 8.24 below.
18 Mental Health (Care and Treatment) (Scotland) Act 2003, s 1(4).
19 Mental Health (Care and Treatment) (Scotland) Act 2003, s 1(5).

(d) The importance of providing appropriate services to a patient who is or has been the subject of compulsory treatment[20] must be considered. This includes consideration of the provision of continuing care once the compulsory order is at an end.[21]

For patients under the age of 18 there is an overall requirement to discharge any function[22] or exercise any power under the 2003 Act in the way which appears to the person carrying out the function or exercising the power to best secure the welfare of the patient.[23] In deciding what course of action best secures the welfare of the patient regard is to be had to factors (a) to (d) above.[24]

(10) Links to other areas

8.11 There is clearly a close relationship between the legislation on adults with incapacity and the mental health legislation, and in some cases there may be an issue about which of these pieces of legislation is the most appropriate to take action under – for example an adult with Alzheimer's Disease may be at a stage where this qualifies as a mental disorder. The question may then be whether to proceed by seeking compulsory treatment, bearing in mind that 'treatment' includes nursing care or by establishing an alternative decision maker to take decisions about the adult's welfare by seeking welfare guardianship. There is also a link to the legislation on vulnerable adults, some adults with a mental disorder will, by virtue of that disorder, be vulnerable and may be at risk. A further link is with community care through the local authority obligation to provide services to people with mental disorders discussed below. All of these are, of course, services for adults, however there is also a link to the provision of services for children as there is no lower age limit for the application of the 2003 Act, so it is quite possible for children under 16 to be the subject of compulsory treatment. It may also be the case, of course, that the mental disorder of adults gives rise to concerns about their children, even if the children are not at risk they may very well be children affected by disability giving rise to local authority duties, which can include the provision of services and assistance to other members of the child's family.

20 Ie an Emergency Detention Certificate, a Short Term Detention Certificate, a Compulsory Treatment Order or a Compulsion Order.
21 Mental Health (Care and Treatment) (Scotland) Act 2003, s 1(6).
22 Unless there is only one way in which the function can be discharged.
23 Mental Health (Care and Treatment) (Scotland) Act 2003, s 2(4).
24 Mental Health (Care and Treatment) (Scotland) Act 2003, s 2.

LOCAL AUTHORITY DUTIES

(1) Provision of services and support

8.12 Local authorities have a duty to appoint a 'sufficient number' of MHOs to carry out the functions reserved to MHOs under the 2003 Act, the Adults with Incapacity (Scotland) Act 2000 and the Criminal Procedure (Scotland) Act 1995. It is not entirely clear what number is sufficient and there are considerable variations between local authorities in the number of MHOs per head of population and in the proportions of MHOs within qualified social work staff.[25]

Duties to provide, or to secure provision by others of, various services are also imposed on local authorities, these are without prejudice to the duty to provide services under certain other legislation.[26] The services covered by the 2003 Act, which are explicitly defined as community care services, are services for people who have or who have had a mental disorder which:

(a) provide care and support, this includes providing residential accommodation, personal care and personal support[27], but excludes nursing care;[28]
(b) are designed to promote the well-being and social development of the service users, this includes social, cultural and recreational activities, training for service users over school age and assistance in finding employment;[29]
(c) assist with travel to access the services described in (a) and (b).[30]

As these are community care services, decisions on provision will be made following an assessment in the same way as for other community care services. In the normal course of events it would be expected that an assessment would need to be carried out, as is the case in relation to other community care services, once it appeared to a local authority that an individual for whom it was under a duty or had a power to provide, or to secure the provision of, community care services may be in need

25 Scottish Government, *Mental Health Officers Survey, Scotland, 2009–10*, (2010).
26 Specifically services under ss 12(1), 13A, 13B & 14 of the Social Work (Scotland) Act 1968 and s 22(1) of the Children (Scotland) Act 1995.
27 As these are defined in the Regulation of Care (Scotland) Act 2001, s 2(28).
28 Mental Health (Care and Treatment) (Scotland) Act 2003, s 25.
29 Mental Health (Care and Treatment) (Scotland) Act 2003, s 26.
30 Mental Health (Care and Treatment) (Scotland) Act 2003, s 27.

of any such services.[31] Despite this, the 2003 Act provides for two triggers of a community care assessment for the services described above:

(a) Notification of the local authority by a MHO that an individual may be in need of such services, this must follow on from the MHOs assessment that the patient should be assessed for such services.[32] This seems over-elaborate since by virtue of the MHOs assessment the authority must be aware that the person may be in need of such services and therefore a duty to assess would seem to arise automatically.
(b) A request from a mentally disordered person or her/his primary carer or named person for an assessment. The local authority receiving such a request must respond within fourteen days to say whether it intends to carry out an assessment or not.[33] It is not clear what the basis for refusing to carry out an assessment would be as the scope for an authority to refuse to carry out a community care assessment is very limited.[34]

Local authorities can seek assistance from health boards and NHS trusts in providing services,[35] and these bodies, together with voluntary organisations are required to cooperate in the provision of services.[36] Charges can be made for these services, in the same way as for other community care services.

(2) Duty to inquire

8.13 A duty to make inquiries can arise in respect of someone aged 16 or over who appears to have a mental disorder where one of the following also applies:[37]

(a) the person may, or may have been, subject or exposed to ill-treatment, neglect, or some other deficiency of care or treatment, though only if this has not happened in a hospital;
(b) loss or damage may be or have been caused to the person's property, or there is a risk of this, though the loss or damage or the risk

31 Social Work (Scotland) Act 1968, s 12A(1).
32 Mental Health (Care and Treatment) (Scotland) Act 2003, s 227(1).
33 Mental Health (Care and Treatment) (Scotland) Act 2003, s 228.
34 See para 6.4.
35 Mental Health (Care and Treatment) (Scotland) Act 2003, s 31.
36 Mental Health (Care and Treatment) (Scotland) Act 2003, s 30.
37 Mental Health (Care and Treatment) (Scotland) Act 2003, s 33. See also ch 9 and the discussion of the powers contained in the Adult Support and Protection (Scotland) Act 2007.

must arise because of the person's mental disorder, for example because they are unable to care for their property or are likely to have it taken from them because of their disorder;

(c) the person may be living alone or without care and unable to look after her/himself or her/his property;

(d) there is a risk to the safety of some other person because of the disorder and the person with the disorder is not in hospital.

In order to complete these inquiries the local authority can ask for assistance from a variety of other bodies, including the Mental Welfare Commission, the Public Guardian, the Scottish Commission for the Regulation of Care, NHS trusts and health boards. Various warrants can also be obtained from a sheriff or a justice of the peace to help the authority to carry out its inquiries.[38] A warrant may be sought allowing entry to premises, authorising detention of the person who is the subject of the inquiries for a medical examination and requiring the production of medical records. The sheriff or justice of the peace must be satisfied, on the basis of evidence on oath from a MHO, that granting the warrant is necessary. The MHO seeking the warrant will normally work for the authority carrying out the investigation. However, where the premises to which entry is sought are outside that local authority's area, the application must be made by a MHO working for the local authority for the area where the premises are situated.

Once the inquiries are complete, a decision will need to be taken about what happens next. It may be that it is considered that nothing further need be done, for example because the concerns which prompted the investigation are unfounded. Where action is needed the sort of action which can be taken at the initiative of the local authority includes seeking appointment of a guardian (either financial or welfare or both) and the provision of community care services, as well as limited powers under the Adult Support and Protection (Scotland) Act 2007.[39]

(3) Removal Order

8.14 A removal order authorises entry to premises and the removal of a person aged over 16 who has a mental disorder to a place of safety for up to 7 days.[40] The order must usually be obtained from a sheriff,

38 Mental Health (Care and Treatment) (Scotland) Act 2003, s 35.

39 See ch 9.

40 Mental Health (Care and Treatment) (Scotland) Act 2003, s 293. See also ch 9 and the discussion of the powers contained in the Adult Support and Protection (Scotland) Act 2007.

though where any delay in applying to a sheriff would be likely to be prejudicial to the person who is to be removed, an application can be made to a justice of the peace.[41] Before making the order the sheriff (or JP) must be satisfied that one of the first three grounds ((a)–(c)) set out above in (2) above apply and that the person is likely to suffer significant harm if not removed to a place of safety. The sheriff must also give the person who is the subject of the warrant and a number of others, including her/his nearest relative and any welfare attorney, guardian or primary carer, the opportunity to make representations before a warrant is granted, but this can be dispensed with if the sheriff considers that the delay which it would cause would be likely to be prejudicial to the person.

If a warrant is granted it must be executed within 72 hours. If the person will have to remain in alternative accommodation for more that the 7 days authorised by the warrant alternative arrangements will have to be made, either by compulsory treatment measures or by securing the person's consent to staying in alternative accommodation. An application can be made for variation or recall of the warrant.[42]

COMPULSORY TREATMENT

8.15 The measures considered here, together with compulsion orders for mentally disordered offenders, are the only ways in which legal authority can be provided for the detention or for the detention and treatment of patients who do not (or cannot) consent.[43] Despite this, it appears to be the case that vaguely worded instructions are often left that patients should be detained if they try to leave a hospital ward, without it being clear what the legal authority for this is or if there is such authority.[44] It may be that the nurses power to detain[45] could be used in such circumstances, but aside from that an Emergency or Short Term Detention Certificate would be required.

41 Mental Health (Care and Treatment) (Scotland) Act 2003, s 294.

42 Mental Health (Care and Treatment) (Scotland) Act 2003, s 295.

43 See Mental Health (Care and Treatment) (Scotland) Act 2003, s 291 which provides for an application to be made to the Mental Health Tribunal to secure the release of a patient who is unlawfully detained. See also *LM v Mental Health Tribunal for Scotland*, Glasgow Sheriff Court, 31 August 2010.

44 See Mental Welfare Commission, *Short Term Detention* (2010), p 18; Mental Welfare Commission, *Report from our visits to people admitted to adult acute mental health wards* (2010), pp 10–11.

45 See para 8.23 below.

(1) Emergency Detention Certificates and Short Term Detention Certificates

8.16 Both of these measures provide for detention of an individual for a short period of time and are granted by a medical practitioner. Other means of detaining or removing an individual not involving a medical practitioner are considered below, but these generally do not provide for any treatment or assessment. The main characteristics of Emergency Detention Certificates (EDC)[46] and Short Term Detention Certificates (STDC)[47] are set out in Table 1. Both require that, if practicable, a MHO should be consulted before either of these certificates is granted. The Code of Practice makes it clear that if the MHO who is consulted does not consent to the granting of the certificate the doctor should only in exceptional circumstances approach a second MHO. If this happens the second MHO should be told that the MHO initially involved had not consented.[48]

The Code of Practice indicates that the STDC is the preferred gateway order to compulsory treatment because of the involvement of the MHO and the greater rights conferred on the patient and on the named person.[49] This preference seems to be reflected in practice with around two thirds of initial orders for detention taking the form of a STDC.[50]

In relation to STDCs the duties of the Mental Health Officer include informing the patient about the availability of independent advocacy and taking steps to ensure that the patient has the opportunity to use this service.[51] The duty explained in the table to produce a social circumstances report[52] when there is an STDC in place or to notify the Mental Welfare Commission of the reasons for not completing a report seems to be complied with only in a minority of cases.[53]

46 Mental Health (Care and Treatment) (Scotland) Act 2003, Pt 5.

47 Mental Health (Care and Treatment) (Scotland) Act 2003, Pt 6.

48 Scottish Executive, *Mental Health (Care and Treatment) (Scotland) Act 2003: Code of Practice* (2005), vol 2, ch 2, para 30 and ch 7, para 36. The latter notes that 'it would be expected that a medical practitioner could not "shop around" for an MHO who will consent . . .'

49 Scottish Executive, *Mental Health (Care and Treatment) (Scotland) Act 2003: Code of Practice* (2005), vol 2, ch 1, para 16.

50 Mental Welfare Commission, *Annual Monitoring Report 2009–2010*, p 6.

51 Mental Health (Care and Treatment) (Scotland) Act 2003, s 45.

52 See part (3)(2)(i) below.

53 Mental Welfare Commission, *Annual Monitoring Report 2009–2010*, pp 63–64. Glasgow City Council, for example, neither provided a report nor an explanation for the absence of a report in around 70% of cases.

	EDC	*STDC*
Who makes?	*a* medical practitioner	an *approved* medical practitioner
Basis for certificate	• mental disorder • ability to make treatment decisions significantly impaired[53] • urgently necessary to detain to determine need for treatment • risk to patient or third party if not detained • STDC would involve undesirable delay	• mental disorder • ability to make treatment decisions significantly impaired • urgently necessary to detain to determine what medical treatment should be given or to give treatment • risk to patient or third party if not detained • granting STDC is necessary
MHO involved?	Yes, if practicable MHO must be consulted and, if consulted, consent	• Yes, if practicable MHO must be consulted and, if consulted, consent • Specific provision requiring that patient be interviewed if practicable and for recording of any reasons why this was not practicable
Duration	72 hours (starts from admission to hospital if not already in-patient)	28 days (starts from admission to hospital if not already in-patient)
Can application for revocation be made?	No, but can be/must be (if conditions no longer satisfied) revoked by RMO.	• Yes, to Mental Health Tribunal (MHT)[54] • Can also be revoked by MWC and RMO

53 See Shek, E, *et al*, 'Understanding 'significant impaired decision-making ability' with regard to treatment for mental disorder: an empirical analysis', (2010) 34 *The Psychiatrist*, 239.

54 There is no appeal against the decision of the Tribunal to revoke the STDC, Mental Health (Care and Treatment) (Scotland) Act 2003, ss 50 & 320.

	EDC	*STDC*
Can it be extended/ renewed?	No, an STDC is required to continue detention	• Yes, by extension certificate for 3 days to allow application for CTO • If application made detention continued for further 5 days.
MHO responsibility after Certificate granted	Nil	Must prepare Social Circumstances Report (SCR) unless this would serve little or no practical purpose.
Restrictions on making (ie certificate cannot be made if one of these circumstances applies)[55]	• Existing EDC • Existing STDC or extension certificate • Detention pending review by, or further procedure before, MHT • During 5 day extension after application for CTO	• Existing STDC or extension certificate • Detention pending review by, or further procedure before, MHT • During 5 day extension after application for CTO

Table 1

55 See *LM v Mental Health Tribunal for Scotland*, Glasgow Sheriff Court, 31 August 2010.

(2) Compulsory Treatment Orders

(a) Applying for and making the Order

8.17

<table>
<tr><td rowspan="2">BOX A</td><td rowspan="2">FIVE DAYS</td><td>Examination leading to Mental Health Report 1
By approved medical practitioner</td><td rowspan="2">Reports based on examination, doctors must be satisfied of:
• Existence of disorder
• Availability of treatment
• Risk to patient or some other person if patient not treated
• Incapacity of patient to decide on treatment
• Need for compulsory treatment</td><td rowspan="2">Both reports must agree on at least one type of mental disorder and on the same measures of treatment.
One report must state views on notification of patient and patient's capacity to arrange representation</td></tr>
<tr><td>Examination leading to Mental Health Report 2
By approved medical practitioner or patient's GP</td></tr>
<tr><td rowspan="2">BOX B</td><td rowspan="2">FOURTEEN DAYS</td><td>MHO to prepare application for CTO</td><td colspan="2">MHO must:
• Identify named person
• Notify: named person; patient; MWC
• Interview patient, inform of rights and about advocacy services
• Prepare Report and Proposed Care Plan
• Advise MHT if patient likely to need curator</td></tr>
<tr><td>Apply to MHT for CTO</td><td colspan="2">Standard form completed</td></tr>
</table>

BOX C	No statutory notice period, may be influenced by duration of authorisation for detention, eg extension of period authorised by STDC for 5 days	Tribunal Hearing • No notice period	Possible outcomes Application refused Interim Order • Eg for further medical report, to allow legal representative time to prepare • Maximum 56 days Order made

Table 2

Table 2 sets out the key requirements and processes involved in applying for a compulsory treatment order, which are discussed in more detail below. The time limits set out in the second column are the maximum periods permitted by the 2003 Act, for example, the second medical examination must take place within five days of the first. (These reports are submitted to the Mental Health Officer). As discussed below, however, the period of time which may be available in practice for the Mental Health Officer to carry out his/her various duties and prepare an application for a CTO are likely to be considerably less than the statutory maximum of fourteen days.

BOX A

The process of applying for a Compulsory Treatment Order (CTO) is triggered by the completion of two reports based on examination of the patient by two doctors. Unless the patient agrees to both doctors examining her/him at the same time the examinations must be separate and there must be no conflict of interest in respect of the examinations.[57] If more than one type of mental disorder is identified it is enough that

57 On examinations see Mental Health (Care and Treatment) (Scotland) Act 2003, ss 57 & 58. Mental Health (Conflict of Interest) (No 2) Regulations 2005, SSI 2005/380.

the reports agree on one as well as on the measures which should be authorised by a CTO.[58] The view on notification of the patient is on whether notification of the proposal to apply for a CTO would be likely to cause significant harm to the patient or to someone else. There is a non-statutory form which is used in practice for these reports,[59] which, it has been held, need not be completed faultlessly, as long as, on a fair reading, it contains the required information.[60]

BOX B

If the reports comply with the requirements set out in the final column of BOX A the MHO has a duty to make an application for a CTO to the Mental Health Tribunal (MHT). The terms of the 2003 Act suggest that tasks to be carried out by the MHO, for example the identification of the named person,[61] should be carried out after this duty arises.[62] It appears that in some cases the MHT has refused to grant a CTO on the procedural grounds that the named person has been identified and contacted by the MHO before the second of the Mental Health Report has been received. This conclusion is based on the wording of the 2003 Act which is that identification and notification should take place 'as soon as practicable after the duty to make the application arises'.[63] The duty to make an application only arises, of course, after the second report is received. This seems an over literal approach to the process. The time which a MHO has to make application is often very short and, in practice, the MHO will know that a second examination has taken place, even though the report has not actually been received. Despite the criticism of named persons, they represent an important safeguard in the process and early identification is necessary, not only because of the need to notify them of the application, but also because the guidance suggests that they should be notified of, and if possible, attend the interview which the MHO has with the patient.[64] This suggests that a

58 See below for the measures which can be authorised by a CTO.

59 http://www.scotland.gov.uk/Topics/Health/health/mental-health/mhlaw/CTO2v6.

60 *Beattie v Dunbar* 2006 SCLR 777.

61 If the MHO establishes that here is no named person or cannot establish if there is one the MHO *may* apply to the Tribunal for appointment of a named person, Mental Health (Care and Treatment) (Scotland) Act 2003, s 255(1)–(4). If the MHO considers that the named person is inappropriate an application *must* be made to the Tribunal for a declaration that this person is not the named person, s 255(6).

62 Mental Health (Care and Treatment) (Scotland) Act 2003, ss 57, 59–61.

63 Mental Health (Care and Treatment) (Scotland) Act 2003, s 59, 60(1).

64 Mental Health (Care and Treatment) (Scotland) Act 2003, *Code of Practice, vol 2*, ch 3, para 55. See also para 50 noting the desirability of allowing the named person as much time as possible to prepare for the tribunal hearing.

CTO should not be refused purely on the basis that the MHO seems to have approached the nearest relative before the second report has been received. Support for this conclusion can be derived from the position taken in relation to another obligation which is imposed on MHOs after a duty to apply for a CTO arises, that is the duty to notify the patient that application for a CTO is to be made. Where the MHO had notified the patient before receiving the second report this was held[65] not to have prejudiced the patient and not to amount to a substantial deviation from the procedure set out in the 2003 Act. It was noted that there was nothing in the 2003 Act to prevent an MHO making early notification and that early notification would assist in complying with the principle of providing the patient with information to allow him/her to participate as fully as possible[66] and the Code of Practice, which emphasises the need to give the patient as much time as possible to prepare for the tribunal hearing.[67] In light of this early notification seems to be entirely consistent with the 2003 Act.

Despite any recommendation expressed in one of the medical reports about whether the patient should be notified of the application, the MHO has the final decision on whether notification is made,[68] though where the recommendation is overridden this should be discussed with the medical practitioner making the recommendation.[69]

The information on rights and advocacy services needs to be communicated effectively to the patient in such a way that she/he has as full an understanding as possible about these. The patient must not only be given information about advocacy services, but the MHO must also take steps to ensure that he/she has the opportunity to make use of the services.

Interviewing the patient is to be done unless it is impracticable and the *Code of Practice* notes that '[i]t is unlikely to ever be completely impracticable for an MHO to comply with the duty to interview the patient.'[70]

65 *JG v Mental Health Tribunal for Scotland*, Glasgow Sheriff Court, 14 October 2010.
66 Mental Health (Care and Treatment) (Scotland) Act 2003, s 1(3)(d).
67 Scottish Executive, *Mental Health (Care and Treatment) (Scotland) Act 2003: Code of Practice* (2005), vol 2, ch 3, para 50.
68 Mental Health (Care and Treatment) (Scotland) Act 2003, s 60(2)(b) – the MHO 'may, if the mental health officer considers it appropriate to do so, give … notice.'
69 Mental Health (Care and Treatment) (Scotland) Act 2003, *Code of Practice, vol 2*, ch 3, para 49.
70 Mental Health (Care and Treatment) (Scotland) Act 2003, *Code of Practice, vol 2*, ch 3, para 56, see also para 57 for practice points related to the interview.

The matters to be covered in the Report and the Proposed Care plan are set out in Boxes 1 and 2. In the report the MHO should express a view on the medical reports, though if the MHO disagrees with them, for example about the need for compulsory measures or the measures specified in the reports, this should be discussed with the medical practitioners. The MHO should also consider whether the measures proposed are the least restrictive possible.[71] In practice the report and the proposed care plan will not be separate documents, but will be incorporated into the *pro forma* CTO Application pack which prompts the MHO to address the necessary topics.[72]

Box 1

Required contents of MHO Report

(a) the name and address of the patient;
(b) if known by the mental health officer, the name and address of:
  (i) the patient's named person; and
  (ii) the patient's primary carer;
(c) the steps that the mental health officer has taken to interview the patient and inform her/him about her/his rights and about advocacy services;
(d) if it was impracticable for the mental health officer to comply with the requirement to interview the patient, the reason for that being the case;
(e) in so far as relevant for the purposes of the application, details of the personal circumstances of the patient;
(f) the mental health officer's views on the mental health reports relating to the patient;
(g) if known by the mental health officer, details of any advance statement that the patient has made (and not withdrawn); and
(h) any other information that the mental health officer considers relevant to the determination by the Tribunal of the application.

71 Mental Health (Care and Treatment) (Scotland) Act 2003, *Code of Practice, vol 2*, ch 3, paras 61–63.
72 The pack (CTO1) can be found here: http://www.scotland.gov.uk/Topics/Health/health/mental-health/mhlaw/mha-Forms/cto1v6.

The MHO should inform the MHT as to whether the patient is likely to need to have a curator (whose function is to protect and safeguard the interests of the patient) appointed for the purposes of the Tribunal proceedings. This will arise if the view is stated in one of the medical reports that the patient does not have capacity to represent him/herself at the tribunal. The need for appointment of a curator should be identified clearly in a letter accompanying the CTO Application,[73] but may, in practice, be the subject of informal discussion with the MHT before the application is lodged.

Early notification of the patient and named person has been discussed above, but one practical reason for this, and for the MHO starting to complete her/his report and the CTO application form before receipt of the second medical report, is the time constraint which arises in practice. Although there is a statutory maximum of 14 days, MHOs are unlikely to have anything like this time to prepare the application and to fulfil their other duties. The reason for this is that most CTOs follow on from a Short Term Detention Certificate[74] and in many cases a decision that a CTO is necessary is not made until late in the period of authorised detention under the STDC[75] which leaves limited time for the application to be lodged before authority to detain lapses (and also leaves limited time for a hearing to be convened to deal with the application).

Box 2

Required contents of Proposed Care Plan

(a) the type (or types) of mental disorder which the patient has;
(b) the needs of the patient for medical treatment that have been assessed by the medical practitioners who submitted the mental health reports relating to the patient;
(c) in so far as relevant for the purposes of the application:
  (i) where the patient is a child, the needs of the patient that have been assessed under the provisions of the Children (Scotland) Act 1995 applying to children affected by disability;

73 See letter from President of MHT Scotland, dated 6th November 2008, available here: http://www.mhtscotland.gov.uk/mhts/files/appointment_of_curator_ad_litem-Letter_-_Health_Boards_Nov08.pdf.

74 Only 2% of detentions in 2009/10 started with a CTO, Mental Welfare Commission, *Annual Monitoring Report 2009–2010*, p 6.

75 See, for example, Mental Welfare Commission, *Short Term Detention* (2010), pp 7–8.

(ii) where the patient is not a child, a community care assessment has been carried out;

(d) the medical treatment which it is proposed to give to the patient (including the names of the persons who would give the treatment and the addresses at which the treatment would be given);

(e) any community care services or relevant services which it is proposed to provide to the patient in relation to each of the needs specified by virtue of paragraph (c) above (including the names of the persons who would provide such services and the addresses at which such services would be provided);

(f) in so far as relevant for the purposes of the application:

(i) any treatment or care (other than treatment or care already specified in the proposed care plan); or

(ii) any service (other than a service already specified in the proposed care plan),

which it is proposed to provide to the patient (including the names of the persons who would provide such treatment, care or service and the addresses at which such treatment, care or service would be provided);

(g) which measures it is proposed that the compulsory treatment order should authorise;

(h) where it is proposed that the compulsory treatment order should authorise the detention of the patient in hospital, the name and address of the hospital;

(i) where it is proposed that the compulsory treatment order should authorise measures other than detention and the giving of treatment, details of the measure (or measures);

(j) where it is proposed that the compulsory treatment order should specify:

(i) any medical treatment specified, by virtue of paragraph (d) above, in the proposed care plan;

(ii) any community care services, or relevant services, specified, by virtue of paragraph (e) above, in the proposed care plan; or

(iii) any treatment, care or service specified, by virtue of paragraph (f) above, in the proposed care plan, that medical treatment, those services or that treatment, care, or service, as the case may be;

(k) where it is proposed that the compulsory treatment order should authorise measures other than the detention of the patient in hospital, the name of the hospital the managers of which should have responsibility for appointing the patient's responsible medical officer; and

(l) the objectives of:

(i) the medical treatment which it is proposed, by virtue of paragraph (d) above, to give to the patient;

(ii) any community care services or relevant services which it is proposed, by virtue of paragraph (e) above, to provide to the patient;

(iii) any treatment, care or service which, by virtue of paragraph (f) above, it is proposed to provide to the patient; and

(iv) the measures (other than detention of the patient in hospital) that it is proposed that the compulsory treatment order should authorise.

BOX C

Once the application for a CTO is lodged by the MHO a date for the Tribunal hearing will be set. Because of the tight timescales the amount of notice received by the patient may be short. Legal representation is available to the patient through the Assistance by Way of Representation Scheme.[76] The hearing itself will involve three members of the tribunal, a legally qualified chair, a member who is qualified as a psychiatrist and a member with experience of mental disorder or of caring for people with such a disorder. Since the application is in the name of the MHO it will be for him/her to introduce the application and set out the grounds for the application and the measures which are sought. After this, contributions will be sought from others, for example the RMO, the patient and named person, and the patient's legal representative may ask questions. The tribunal members will also ask questions and the members have a much more active role in proceedings than a judge would normally have in court proceedings, and tribunal proceedings have been described as semi-inquisitorial.[77] Tribunal proceedings are intended to

76 Though there are issues about availability in practice due to the limited amount of expertise within the legal profession in this area of law, see Dawson, A, *et al*, *An Assessment of the Operation of the Named Person Role and its Interaction with Other Firms of Patient Representation* (2009), pp 55–57; Scottish Government, *Limited Review of the Mental Health (Care and Treatment) (Scotland) Act 2003 Report* (2010), pp 57–59.

77 *Laurie v Mental Health Tribunal for Scotland*, Paisley Sheriff Court, 30 August 2007.

be conducted in a more informal setting and manner than court proceedings, the intention being to make it easier for individuals to participate in the proceedings, in practice, however, different tribunals operate in different ways and there have been complaints that some operate in a way which is too formal and legalistic.[78]

After the hearing the tribunal has a number of options. It can refuse the application. It can make an interim order, initially for up to 28 days, although the interim order can be renewed as long as the renewal does not extend the total length of the interim order beyond 56 days. The interim order might be renewed more than once, as long as the total period is not exceeded. Interim orders are widely used,[79] around 50% of applications result in such an order,[80] and can authorise any measures which can be authorised on a full order. Such an order might be used, for example, to allow time to obtain an independent medical report. Finally, the MHT might make a full CTO, which will last initially for a period of 6 months.

Before the MHT makes a CTO or an interim CTO it must be satisfied that a number of criteria are satisfied, though even if the MHT concludes that all the criteria are satisfied it still has discretion about whether to make an order and the terms of any order. The criteria are:[81]

(a) the patient has a mental disorder;
(b) medical treatment is available for the patient and this treatment would be likely to prevent the disorder from getting worse or would alleviate the symptoms or effects of the disorder;
(c) there would be a significant risk to the health or safety of the patient or to the safety of some other person if the treatment was not provided;
(d) the ability of the patient to take decisions about the medical treatment is significantly impaired by her/his disorder;
(e) making the order is necessary, for example because the patient will not voluntarily accept treatment.

78 Scottish Government, *Limited Review of the Mental Health (Care and Treatment) (Scotland) Act 2003 Report* (2010), pp 52–56.

79 Some of the reasons for this are discussed in Scottish Government, *Limited Review of the Mental Health (Care and Treatment) (Scotland) Act 2003 Report* (2010), pp 43–45. One factor is that referred to above, ie making the application for the CTO late in the period of detention authorised by a STDC which means that a hearing has to be convened at very short notice, with the consequence that there may not be enough time for the patient and her/his legal representative to prepare for the hearing properly.

80 Mental Welfare Commission, *Annual Monitoring Report 2009–2010*, pp 22–23, this is significantly less than in previous years.

81 Mental Health (Care and Treatment) (Scotland) Act 2003, s 64(5).

If a full order is made after a hearing this will usually authorise the measures set out in the application, which will derive, in turn, from the initial medical reports and the application for a CTO, though the MHT can add to these, modify them or remove particular measures. If the MHT does intend to specify measures not set out in the application[82] it must give notice of this and allow representations to be made and evidence to be produced before a decision is made.[83] In considering whether to make a CTO and what measures to authorise, the Tribunal must take account of the principles set out in 8.10 above. The measures which can be authorised in a CTO are set out in Box 3 below.

Box 3

(a) detention of the patient in the specified hospital (which may be the State Hospital);
(b) giving medical treatment to the patient;
(c) a requirement to attend for medical treatment at a place and times, these may be set out in the CTO or the requirement may be to attend for treatment as directed;
(d) a requirement on the patient to attend to receive community care services, relevant services or any treatment, care or service, as in (c) these can be set out in the CTO or to be as directed;
(e) a requirement on the patient to reside at a specified place;
(f) a requirement on the patient to allow the MHO, the RMO, or anyone responsible for providing medical treatment, community care services, relevant services or any treatment, care or service to the patient who is authorised by the RMO to visit her/him in the place where she/he resides;
(g) a requirement on the patient to obtain the approval of the MHO to any proposed change of address; and
(h) a requirement on the patient to inform the MHO of any proposed change of address.

In addition to the measures requested in the application and selected from the list above, the MHT will also set out the treatment to be pro-

82 As it did, for example in *Di Mascio v MHTS* (Glasgow Sh Ct, 4 August 2008), where the Tribunal made a community CTO when the application specified a hospital-based CTO.

83 Mental Health (Care and Treatment) (Scotland) Act 2003, s 64(7) & (8).

vided and any other services which it considers appropriate, the treatment and other services are defined as 'recorded matters'.[84] The CTO must also identify the types of mental disorder affecting the patient, and if the order is a Community CTO (ie the patient is not to be detained in hospital) it must identify the hospital whose managers are responsible for appointing the patient's RMO.

The Tribunal must set out the fact found by it, the decision reached and the reasons for reaching that decision and notice of the decision must be given to those involved in the application. It has been said that:

> The reasons for a decision must be intelligible and they must be adequate. They must enable the reader to understand why the matter was decided as it was and what conclusions were reached on the 'principal, important controversial issues' … reasons need refer only to the main issues in the dispute, not every material consideration … decision letters must be read in a straightforward manner, recognising they are addressed to parties well aware of the issues involved and the arguments advanced. A reasons challenge will only succeed if the parties aggrieved can satisfy the court that he has genuinely been substantially prejudiced by the failure to provide an adequately reasoned decision.[85]

(b) After the Order is made

8.18 After a CTO is made the hospital managers identified in the Order will have to identify an RMO for the patient and the local authority will have to designate an MHO who will be responsible for the patient. The MHO must then, within 21 days of the making of the

84 The full list of matters which can be recorded leaves considerable scope for the Tribunal: 'such medical treatment, community care services, relevant services, other treatment, care or service as the Tribunal considers appropriate,' Mental Health (Care and Treatment) (Scotland) Act 2003, s 64(4)(a)(i), though there is no satisfactory way of ensuring that the recorded matters are put into effect. The RMO does have an obligation to make a reference to the MHT it appears that a recorded matter is not being provided, Mental Health (Care and Treatment) (Scotland) Act 2003, s 96. The matter might also be referred to the MHT by the MWC under s 98 of the 2003 Act, which gives the MWC power make a reference where it appears to the MWC to be appropriate to do so. The lack of implementation of recorded matters and of any action by RMOs and the MWC are discussed in Royal College of Psychiatrists, *Recorded Matters Working Group Final Report* (Sept 2009), available here: http://www.rcpsych.ac.uk/docs/Recorded%20Matters%20FINAL%20REPORT.doc.

85 *Koca v Secretary of State for the Home Department* 2005 SC 487, *per* Lord Carloway at 499, cited in *Robbins v Mitchell* (Airdrie Sh Ct, 14 May 2007). See also *Scottish Ministers v MHTS* [2009] CSIH 9, referring to the need to give clear and intelligible reasons for rejecting expert evidence (at para [52]).

CTO (or the making of an interim CTO) prepare a Social Circumstances Report (SCR) in respect of the patient.[86] The RMO must prepare a care plan for the patient.

(c) Review of the Order

8.19 The RMO has a duty to keep the CTO under review and to revoke the order if the conditions for making a CTO have ceased to exist or to make an application to the MHT to vary the terms of the order if this is appropriate. There is a formal duty to consult the MHO in cases where the RMO decides that the terms of a CTO need to be varied, and in the absence of such a formal requirement in relation to determinations to revoke a CTO, the *Code of Practice* makes it clear that it is best practice for there to be continuing close consultation both with the MHO and with the patient's carers.[87]

A more specific duty to carry out a mandatory review arises in the period before the CTO, as initially made, or as subsequently extended, is due to expire. As we have seen, a CTO will initially expire in 6 months. Within 2 months of the expiry date the RMO must review the order and this review will include consulting the MHO. The outcome of this review can be that the order is revoked if the grounds for making a CTO no longer exist. Alternatively the order can be continued unchanged, and this is done simply by a determination made by the RMO[88] which extends the order initially for a further 6 months, at the end of which period it can be extended for further periods of 12 months. If the RMO proposes to extend the order the MHO must be notified and the MHO must then carry out the various actions set out in Box 4.[89] In light of the views of the MHO and of others consulted, the RMO must decide whether to make a determination extending the CTO. This is then recorded and submitted to the MHT.[90] The extension will only come before the Tribunal for a hearing if the MHO disagrees with the decision to extend, if the order has not been reviewed by the Tribunal in the preceding two years, or where the patient or the patient's named person applies for revocation of the extended order.

86 See para 8.25.

87 *Mental Health (Care and Treatment) (Scotland) Act 2003, Code of Practice, vol 2*, p 123, para 13.

88 The form used can be found here: http://www.scotland.gov.uk/Topics/Health/health/mental-health/mhlaw/CTO3av6.

89 See Scottish Executive, *Mental Health (Care and Treatment) (Scotland) Act 2003: Code of Practice* (2005), vol 2, ch 5, paras 33 & 55.

90 In practice this will be accompanied by a care plan for future care as well as the previous care plan.

Box 4

MHO tasks on notification by RMO

(a) interview the patient (if practicable);
(b) tell the patient that the RMO is intending to extend the order (or extend and vary the order) and what the patient's rights are in connection with this extension (and variation);
(c) make the patient aware of the availability of advocacy services and do anything necessary to ensure the patient has an opportunity to use these;
(d) inform the RMO whether she/he agrees with the proposed extension and, if the MHO disagrees, what the reasons for this are and pass on any other information the MHO considers relevant. In the process of reaching her/his conclusions, the MHO should evaluate the effectiveness of the patient's care plan and the extent to which its objectives are being fulfilled as well as assessing the continued effectiveness of the order and the extent to which the patient would accept voluntary treatment.

A final outcome of a mandatory review may be that the RMO considers that the CTO should be both extended and varied. Variation may be either in respect of the measures authorised by the CTO (eg varying from a hospital based CTO to a community CTO), the treatment offered or other recorded matters. If this conclusion is reached the RMO will need to apply to the MHT. The RMO must notify the MHO of the intention to apply for extension and variation and the MHO then must carry out the tasks set out in Box 4. After consultation the RMO then has to decide whether or not to apply to the MHT. Unlike the initial application for a CTO which is made by the MHO, it is the RMO who is responsible for applying for an extension and variation of the order (or for a variation following a time to time review).

Where a Tribunal is considering a case where the CTO is being extended and/or varied, it can request a report from the MHO, though it is good practice to provide such a report as a matter of course. This report should set out:

(a) the steps taken by the MHO to fulfil her/his obligations after being notified by the RMO;
(b) the views of the MHO on the extension and/or variation and the reasons for these views;

(c) the views of the patient and the patient's named person to the extent that there are known;
(d) any relevant details of the patient's personal circumstances;
(e) details of any advance statements made by the patient;
(f) any other information which the MHO thinks will assist the Tribunal.

(d) Appeals and revocation

8.20 As we have seen a CTO can be revoked by the RMO following a review of the order. The MWC also has the power to revoke a CTO. In addition the patient and the patient's named person can apply to the MHT for revocation of a CTO or of a determination extending a CTO or for variation of any measures or recorded matters contained in the order. Applications by the patient or the patient's named person can only be made after three months have passed since the last consideration of the order by the MHT.

A patient who is detained in the State Hospital can apply to the MHT for it to determine that he/she does not need to be detained under the security conditions which can only be provided in that hospital and ordering his/her transfer to another hospital.

Finally, there is a right of appeal against final decisions and orders of the MHT.[91] Appeal is, in the first instance, to the sheriff principal, with further appeal to the Inner House of the Court of Session. The right to appeal is conferred on the patient, the patient's named person, the patient's guardian or welfare attorney (if there is one), the MHO and the RMO. Any curator appointed for the purposes of proceedings before the MHT cannot appeal a Tribunal decision.[92] The grounds of appeal are that:

(a) the Tribunal's decision was based on an error of law;
(b) there was a procedural impropriety in the conduct of the Tribunal hearing;
(c) the Tribunal has acted unreasonably in the exercise of its discretion;
(d) that the Tribunal's decision was not supported by the facts found to be established by the Tribunal.

91 Subject to very limited exceptions, see Mental Health (Care and Treatment) (Scotland) Act 2003, s 320.
92 *Henderson v MHTS* (Edinburgh Sh Ct, 23 July 2010).

(e) Non-compliance with a CTO[93]

8.21 The 2003 Act provides certain procedures which allow the RMO to take action if a patient fails to comply with a CTO or an interim CTO. If the patient fails to attend for treatment or to comply with any other measure set out in the CTO the RMO can give authority for the patient to be taken into custody. Where the non-compliance relates to attendance for treatment, the patient can be taken to the place where she/he is supposed to receive treatment or to a hospital, though if the latter, he/she can only be kept there for up to six hours unless the CTO authorises detention in the hospital.[94] If the non-compliance relates to other measures the patient can to be taken to a hospital where she/he can initially be detained for up to 72 hours.[95] Once in hospital the patient must be examined. If the RMO is considering whether to apply to the MHT for variation of the CTO or has decided that the CTO should be varied and has then to apply to the MHT, the period of detention can be extended by 28 days from the time when the certificate authorising the further detention is granted. Before an extension is authorised the MHO must be consulted and must consent.[96] Where the patient is subject to an interim CTO the RMO can, with the consent of the MHO, grant a certificate authorising detention for the remainder of the interim CTO.[97] The patient or the patient's named person can apply to the MHT for revocation of the certificate authorising the extended detention.[98]

SUSPENSION OF DETENTION[99]

8.22 Where a patient is detained by virtue of an EDC[100] or a STDC,[101] the RMO may grant a certificate specifying that detention of the patient is not to be authorised for a specific period. This power may be used to allow the patient to leave the hospital for specific event or for a longer period and may be subject to conditions, for example that the patient remains in the charge of a specific person. The certificate may

93 *Mental Health (Care and Treatment) (Scotland) Act 2003, Code of Practice, vol 2,* ch 6.
94 Mental Health (Care and Treatment) (Scotland) Act 2003, s 112.
95 Mental Health (Care and Treatment) (Scotland) Act 2003, s 113.
96 Mental Health (Care and Treatment) (Scotland) Act 2003, s 114.
97 Mental Health (Care and Treatment) (Scotland) Act 2003, s 115.
98 Mental Health (Care and Treatment) (Scotland) Act 2003, s 120.
99 Mental Welfare Commission, *Suspension of detention* (2008).
100 Mental Health (Care and Treatment) (Scotland) Act, s 41.
101 Mental Health (Care and Treatment) (Scotland) Act 2003, s 53.

be revoked by the RMO if she/he is satisfied that this is necessary in the interests of the patient or to protect another person.[102]

In the case of a patient subject to a CTO it is possible for the RMO both to suspend the authorisation for detention[103] and to suspend other measures authorised by the CTO.[104] A certificate suspending the authorisation of detention can, at any one time, be for a period of up to 6 months, but combined periods cannot exceed 9 months in a period of 12 months. Any suspension can be made subject to conditions. A certificate authorising suspension of other measures can last for up to 3 months. Other measure can be suspended for a number of shorter periods, subject to all periods not exceeding three months. Suspensions of other measures and suspensions of detention for a period exceeding 28 days must be notified to the MWC. Either type of certificate can be revoked by the RMO[105] where she/he is satisfied that this is necessary in the interests of the patient or to protect another person.

NURSE'S POWER TO DETAIN

8.23 A patient who is not detained under any order under the 2003 Act but is in hospital and receiving medical treatment may be detained for up to two hours by a nurse.[106] This detention can only take place where it is not practicable to have the patient examined immediately by a medical practitioner and where the following additional conditions exist:

(a) the patient has a mental disorder;
(b) it is necessary to restrain the patient from leaving the hospital either to protect her/his health safety and welfare or to protect the safety of another person;
(c) a medical examination is necessary to determine whether the making of an EDC or a STDC is warranted.

MEDICAL TREATMENT

8.24 As we have seen, the medical treatment which can be given to a patient is widely defined. It is possible that the patient may have made

102 Mental Health (Care and Treatment) (Scotland) Act 2003, ss 42 & 54.
103 Mental Health (Care and Treatment) (Scotland) Act 2003, s 127.
104 Mental Health (Care and Treatment) (Scotland) Act 2003, s 128.
105 Mental Health (Care and Treatment) (Scotland) Act 2003, s 129.
106 Mental Health (Care and Treatment) (Scotland) Act, s 299. The nurse must be a mental health or learning disabilities nurse registered in Sub part 1 of the register maintained by the Nursing and Midwifery Council, Mental Health (Class of Nurse) (Scotland) Regulations, 2005, SSI 2005/996, reg 2.

an advance statement setting out either the form of treatment which he/she wishes to receive for mental disorder or setting out the ways in which he/she does not want to be treated.[107] The advance statement must be in writing and must be witnessed by someone who is a member of a class prescribed for the purpose of witnessing advance statements, these include solicitors, social workers, registered nurses, medical practitioners and people who provide, or who work in, care services.[108] As well as witnessing the signature the witness must also certify that in her/his opinion the person making the statement had capacity to do this. Once an advance statement has been made regard must be had to it by anyone providing treatment to the patient and by a tribunal in considering measures to be authorised by a CTO. The advance statement can, however, be overridden, but if this is done the reasons for this must be recorded in writing and notified to the patient making the statement, the named person, the patient's proxy (if any) and the Mental Welfare Commission.[109]

There are certain types of treatment which are subject to additional procedures and or authorisations before they can be given, though some of these are rare in practice. The first group involves brain surgery involving destruction of part of the brain or its functions as well as deep brain stimulation and can only be carried out either if the patient consents or if the patient is incapable of consent and does not resist the treatment (ie there is no power to treat a patient with capacity who refuses consent). Where the patient consents, a designated medical practitioner (DMP) appointed by the MWC must certify that the treatment is in the best interests of the patient, in addition, the DMP and two others also appointed by the MWC (and who are not medical practitioners) must certify both that the patient has capacity to consent and that he/she consents to the treatment. If the patient cannot consent, this type of treatment can only be given with the consent of the Court of Session.[110] A second set of treatments involves Electro Convulsive Therapy (ECT)

107 Mental Health (Care and Treatment) (Scotland) Act 2003, s 275(1); Scottish Executive, *Mental Health (Care and Treatment) (Scotland) Act 2003: Code of Practice* (2005), vol 1, ch 6, paras 44–89.

108 Mental Health (Care and Treatment) (Scotland) Act 2003, s 275(2); The Mental Health (Advance Statements) (Prescribed Class of Persons) (Scotland) (No 2) Regulations 2004, SSI 2004/429.

109 Mental Health (Care and Treatment) (Scotland) Act 2003, s 276(7) & (8). Such overrides are rare in practice. There were 29 in total in 2009–10, Mental Welfare Commission, *Annual Monitoring Report 2009–2010*, p 43.

110 Mental Health (Care and Treatment) (Scotland) Act 2003, s 234, Mental Health (Medical treatment subject to safeguards) (Section 234) (Scotland) Regulations 2005, SSI 2005/291.

and some rare treatments.[111] These can only be given to a patient who cannot consent if a certificate is issued by a DMP which indicates, *inter alia*, that the treatment is in the patient's best interests, or, if the patient resists or objects to the treatment, that the treatment is necessary to save the patient's life, to prevent serious deterioration in her/his condition or to alleviate serious suffering.[112] Where the patient consents to this type of treatment and this is certified by the RMO or by a DMP it can be given.[113] The same certification requirement applies to giving certain other types of treatment to consenting patients. These are medication for reducing sex drive, the giving of any medication for a period in excess of two months and artificial feeding (for example by way of a nasogastric tube).[114] If the patient is incapable of consenting to such treatments, or is capable but refuses consent, it can only be given if a certificate is issued by a DMP, which indicates, amongst other things, that it is in the patient's best interests to give the treatment.[115] If the patient refuses treatment then the DMP must have regard to the reasons for that refusal and must state the reason(s) for being of the opinion that the treatment should be given.

Aside from these special cases, treatment can be given where the patient, if capable of consent, consents in writing to the treatment. If the patient is incapable of consenting or, being capable, refuses consent, the RMO must determine that giving treatment is in the best interests of the patient. In doing this the RMO must consider the reason for not consenting, the views of the patient and her/his named person; any advance statement made by the patient and the likelihood of the treatment alleviating, or preventing deterioration in, the patient's condition. If the patient is in hospital, but not otherwise, treatment can be given by force.[116]

Urgent treatment can be given to detained patients in hospital regardless of consent.[117] Urgent treatment is treatment necessary to save the patient's life, to prevent serious deterioration in her/his condition, to alleviate serious suffering or to prevent the patient either behaving violently or being a danger to her/himself or others. There are limits on

111 Transcranial magnetic stimulation and vagus nerve stimulation, Mental Health (Care and Treatment) (Scotland) Act 2003, s 234, Mental Health (Medical treatment subject to safeguards) (Section 237) (Scotland) Regulations 2005, SSI 2005/292.

112 Mental Health (Care and Treatment) (Scotland) Act 2003, ss 237 & 239.

113 Mental Health (Care and Treatment) (Scotland) Act 2003, ss 237 & 238.

114 Mental Health (Care and Treatment) (Scotland) Act 2003, ss 240 & 238, there is provision for regulations to be made adding other types of treatment to this list, but no such regulations have been made.

115 Mental Health (Care and Treatment) (Scotland) Act 2003, s 241.

116 Mental Health (Care and Treatment) (Scotland) Act 2003, s 242.

117 Mental Health (Care and Treatment) (Scotland) Act 2003, s 243.

the treatment that can be given – ECT cannot be given if the patient can consent but refuses to; treatment for purposes other than saving the patient's life must not be likely to entail unfavourable and irreversible consequences; and treatment to alleviate suffering or to prevent violent behaviour or danger must not entail significant physical hazard to the patient.

SOCIAL CIRCUMSTANCES REPORTS

8.25 A social circumstances report[118] (SCR) must be prepared by a MHO in certain circumstances. The three events which trigger the duty to complete a SCR are the making of a STDC, the making of an interim CTO or the making of a CTO. No report is required if the MHO is of the view that preparing such a report would serve little or no practical purpose. The SCR is distinct from the report which the mental health officer has to prepare in connection with an application for a compulsory treatment order[119]:

> The MHO's report for the CTO application should focus on the assessed needs of the individual and whether the MHO believes the criteria for compulsory powers are satisfied. A proposed care plan, while commenting on assessed needs, focuses almost exclusively on future care plans. Together these documents will contain much, but not all, the information included in an SCR. It should be possible to use much of the information from an SCR to help complete an MHO's report and a proposed care plan so that there should not be any wasted effort if the decision is taken to proceed with a CTO application well after an MHO has begun the process of completing an SCR. The main added value of the SCR is that it summarises information on the personal and social circumstances of the individual, as well as the care and treatment history of the patient and places this in the context of the current admission and future care planning.

If no social circumstances report is prepared the reasons for this must be recorded and sent to the responsible medical officer and the Mental Wel-

118 See *Mental Health (Care and Treatment) (Scotland) Act 2003 Code of Practice* (Scottish Executive, 2005) vol 1, ch 11; Mental Welfare Commission, *Social Circumstances Reports* (2009).

119 *Mental Health (Care and Treatment) (Scotland) Act 2003 Code of Practice* (Scottish Executive, 2005) vol 1, ch 11, para 16.

fare Commission[120]. Examples of situations where preparation would serve little or no practical purpose given in the Code of Practice involve cases where the obligation to prepare a report arises because one event has taken place (for example short-term detention) following which a report has been prepared and this is followed shortly afterwards by the happening of another event triggering the obligation to compile a report (for example making a compulsory treatment order). Where no social circumstances report is prepared the Commission has indicated that its view is that, unless there are compelling reasons not to do so, the patient should be informed of the reason for this.[121]

The report is to contain, as far as it is relevant to their care, the following information about the patient:[122]

(a) state of physical and mental health and mental health history;
(b) personal history, including details of employment, finances and accommodation prior to the use of compulsory powers;
(c) family situation, including information about children and dependents;
(d) regular social contacts;
(e) ability to care for himself;
(f) any history of offending (including consideration of victims and those affected) and any history of substance misuse.

In addition the report must set out, again as far as is relevant to the care of the patient:

(a) Why compulsory powers were used and the views of the patient regarding their use. If the patient is unable to give a view, then, if these are available to the mental health officer the views of the patient's named person, carer, guardian and welfare attorney regarding the use of compulsory powers should be included.
(b) An assessment of the risk of harm to the patient and to others.

120 Mental Health (Care and Treatment) (Scotland) Act 2003, s 232(2). However, the Commission has consistently noted that this actually happens in a very small proportion of cases in which the duty to inform it arises: *Our Overview of Mental Welfare in Scotland* 2007–08 (Mental Welfare Commission) p 41; Mental Welfare Commission, *Annual Monitoring Report 2009–2010*, pp 64–65. See also the concerns noted by the Commission about the reasons which it receives: *Social Circumstances Reports,* pp 6–8. It notes, eg, that the fact that the patient is 'well-known to services' is not an acceptable reason for not producing a report.

121 *Social Circumstances Reports* p 11.

122 Mental Health (Social Circumstances Reports) (Scotland) Regulations 2005, SSI2005/310, reg 2. There is also a non-statutory pro forma (SCR 1) which should be used for the report available at via www.scotland.gov.uk.

(c) The care being provided to the patient prior to the use of compulsory powers.
(d) Any matters which would trigger the local authority's duty to inquire.
(e) Any alternatives to the use of compulsory powers which were considered and ruled out.
(f) Ethnic, cultural and religious factors.
(g) Whether the patient has difficulty in communicating.
(h) Any plan which has been put in place to deal with any of the matters referred to in the report.

Chapter 9

Adult support and protection

INTRODUCTION

9.1 Much of the law considered in the last three chapters is concerned with the protection of and the provision of support to adults who might be described as vulnerable. In addition, as we have seen there are duties to investigate, and some powers to assist with such investigations, conferred by the Mental Health (Care and Treatment)(Scotland) Act 2003[1] and the Adults with Incapacity (Scotland) Act 2000.[2] In addition to these there is specific provision in the Adult Support and Protection (Scotland) Act 2007.[3] The 2007 Act does a number of things. It establishes a duty of cooperation between agencies, it creates multidisciplinary Adult Protection Committees, it sets out certain principles to be followed in carrying out any functions under it, it imposes a duty to investigate on local authorities and it confers on them certain powers which can be used in carrying out these functions. As we will see, it does not provide for any long term support or provision for an adult, so this will have to be undertaken under other legislation, eg appointment of a welfare guardian.

Adult Protection Committees[4] involve the local authority, the health board, the police, the Scottish Commission for the Regulation of Care and others. The main functions of the Committee are to keep policies and procedures relating to safeguarding adults at risk under review and to provide information and advice. The Mental Welfare Commission, health board, police and Office of the Public Guardian have an obligation to cooperate with investigations and inquiries relating to adults at risk which are being carried out by a local authority.[5] Each of these

1 See ch 8, paras 8.13 and 8.14.
2 See ch 7, para 7.2.
3 Which followed on rather belatedly from the Scottish Law Commission Report on Vulnerable Adults (published in 1997).
4 Adult Support and Protection (Scotland) Act 2007, ss 42 & 43. See Scottish Government, *Code of Practice For Local Authorities and Practitioners Exercising Functions Under Part 1 of the Act* (revised 2009), ch 13, Scottish Government, *Guidance to Adult Protection Committees* (2009).
5 Adult Support and Protection (Scotland) Act 2007, s 5.

organisations also as a duty to report to the local authority any cases in which it believes that an adult is at risk and that action needs to be taken to protect the adult from harm.

THE PRINCIPLES

9.2 The principles in the 2007 Act include a number of principles as well as a series of factors to which regard must be had in carrying out any functions under the Act. As a general principle any intervention must provide a benefit to the adult which could not reasonably be provided without that intervention. In addition, where there is a range of options for action, the option which is least restrictive of the freedom of the adult must be chosen.[6]

Factors which must be considered in carrying out functions are:[7]

(a) the wishes of the adult, past and present;
(b) the views of the adult's nearest relative, primary carer, proxy,[8] and any other person with an interest in the welfare of the adult, in practice active steps should be taken to get the views of these people;
(c) the importance of the adult participating, and being enabled to participate (for example by the provision of appropriate support), as fully as possible in decisions and actions;
(d) the importance of ensuring that the adult does not receive less favourable treatment than someone who is not an adult at risk would receive in the same circumstances;
(e) the ability, background and character of the adult.

THE DUTY TO INVESTIGATE[9]

9.3 A duty on the local authority will arise where two conditions are satisfied.[10] The first is that an adult is at risk. The second is that the local authority may need to intervene to protect the adult's well-being, property or financial affairs. These conditions of course, raise the ques-

6 Adult Support and Protection (Scotland) Act 2007, s 1.
7 Adult Support and Protection (Scotland) Act 2007, s 2. See also Scottish Government, *Code of Practice For Local Authorities and Practitioners Exercising Functions Under Part 1 of the Act* (revised 2009), ch 1, paras 2–7.
8 Eg an attorney or guardian.
9 Scottish Government, *Code of Practice For Local Authorities and Practitioners Exercising Functions Under Part 1 of the Act* (revised 2009), ch 4.
10 Adult Support and Protection (Scotland) Act 2007, s 4

tion of when an adult is at risk, this will be the case if three requirements are *all* met:[11]

(a) the adult is unable to safeguard his/her own welfare, rights or other interests; *and*
(b) the adult is at risk of harm (harm is defined below), all that is required is that there is a risk of harm, it is not essential that the adult is being, or has been, harmed; *and*
(c) the adult is more likely to be harmed because he/she is affected by disability, mental disorder, illness or physical or mental infirmity; the harm may be caused by the conduct of others or may involve self-harm.

Harm includes all harmful conduct and, in particular, includes:[12]

(a) conduct which causes physical harm;
(b) conduct which causes psychological harm (for example: by causing fear, alarm or distress);
(c) unlawful conduct which appropriates or adversely affects property, rights or interests (for example: theft, fraud, embezzlement or extortion);
(d) conduct which causes self-harm.

Once the investigation has been completed the local authority will need to decide what action to take. If it decides that no action is required a report on the enquiries undertaken and the reasons for reaching the conclusion that no action is needed should be added to the adult's case file. Alternatively, the decision may be that some action needs to be taken. This may involve use of a removal order or a banning order, or it may involve use of other legislation, for example provision of community care services or an application for guardianship under the Adults with Incapacity (Scotland) Act 2000. Where the local authority decides that it needs to intervene it must have regard to the importance of providing appropriate services to the adult, including independent advocacy services.[13] A report must be made to the police if the enquiries indicate that a criminal offence has been committed against the adult.

11 Adult Support and Protection (Scotland) act 2007, s 3; Scottish Government, *Code of Practice For Local Authorities and Practitioners Exercising Functions Under Part 1 of the Act* (revised 2009), ch 1, Paras 8–12.
12 Adult Support and Protection (Scotland) Act 2007, s 53(1).
13 Adult Support and Protection (Scotland) Act 2007, s 6; Scottish Government, *Code of Practice For Local Authorities and Practitioners Exercising Functions Under Part 1 of the Act* (revised 2009), ch 3, paras 2–8.

LOCAL AUTHORITY POWERS

9.4 Local authorities have a number of powers under the 2007 Act, some of which can only be exercised after application to court, these orders are generally described as protection orders. The powers must be exercised by someone authorised by the local authority and there are restrictions in the council officers who can be authorised – they must have at least 12 months post-qualifying experience and be either:[14]

(a) registered as a social worker;
(b) registered as a social service worker;[15]
(c) registered as an occupational therapist; or
(d) registered as a nurse.

(a) Visits[16]

9.5 The local authority has the right of entry to premises to enable it to carry out enquires or to assist it with those enquiries. There are no limits on the places that can be entered, it extends not just to where the adult lives, but also to anywhere else, for example somewhere the adult spends time during the day or the home of a person who is involved with the adult. Any visit must take place at a reasonable time, and although there is a right to examine the place entered and to use any equipment required to fulfil the purpose of the visit, there is no right to force entry to premises or to any part of them. In order to force entry, for example to have a locked door opened, a warrant will be needed. This is usually obtained by application to the sheriff, though in cases of urgency a warrant can be issued by a JP. In implementing the warrant the council officer must be accompanied by a police officer, who has the power to use reasonable force to fulfil the objectives of the visit.

During any visit any adult can be interviewed, though there is no obligation to answer any questions. There is no limit to who can be interviewed during a visit, so that the council officer is empowered to interview not only the adult, but also any other adults, for example a relative or carer. The aim in interviewing the adult is to establish whether he or she has

14 Adult Support and Protection (Scotland) Act 2007, (Restriction on the Authorisation of Council Officers) Order 2008, SSI 2008/306.

15 Though such workers cannot exercise powers to apply for and implement protection orders.

16 Adult Support and Protection (Scotland) Act 2007, ss 7–9, Scottish Government, *Code of Practice For Local Authorities and Practitioners Exercising Functions Under Part 1 of the Act* (revised 2009), chs 5–7.

been subjected to harm, whether he or she feels that his/her safety is at risk and to discuss what action the adult wishes to take. In securing the consent of the adult to the interview the adult's rights should be carefully explained rather than simply informing her/him that she is not obliged to reply to any questions.[17]

A medical examination can be carried out if the adult consents to it, and this will, unless the council officer carrying out the visit is a nurse, require that a health professional accompanies the council officer on the visit. Consent of the adult is required for such an examination.

(b) Access to documents[18]

9.6 A council officer can require production of health, financial or other records relating to the adult, and it is an offence to refuse to comply with a request or to fail to comply with it unless these is a reasonable excuse for this. Records can be required during a visit or at any other time. Any health records which are accessed can only be inspected by a health professional (aside from initial scrutiny to identify them as health records). The purpose of looking at the records about the adult is restricted to enabling or assisting the local authority to decide whether it needs to take any action to protect the adult. The adult's consent is not required before access to documents is sought, though the Code of Practice suggests that consent should be obtained whenever practicable and that the right of the adult to confidentiality should be considered before information is requested.[19]

(c) Protection Orders

9.7 Three types of order, collectively described as protection orders, can be sought by a local authority. Before deciding to apply for any of these the authority must consider the principles set out in para 9.2 above. The Code of Practice also suggests that consideration be given

17 Scottish Government, *Code of Practice For Local Authorities and Practitioners Exercising Functions Under Part 1 of the Act* (revised 2009), ch 6, para 8 notes that: 'The point is to ensure that the adult is given a reasonable opportunity to answer questions whilst respecting their right not to,' and that 'the council … has to promote the adult's participation in the interview.'

18 Adult Support and Protection (Scotland) Act 2007, s 10, Scottish Government, *Code of Practice For Local Authorities and Practitioners Exercising Functions Under Part 1 of the Act* (revised 2009), ch 8.

19 Ch 8, para 14.

as to whether the adult should be referred to an independent advocacy service or provided with other services.[20]

The first of these is an assessment order[21] which allows the authority to take the adult away from any place which is being visited to another place in order to interview or carry out a medical examination of the adult. There is no need for the authority to have sought to interview or examine the adult before applying for the order. Before the order can be granted the adult must have consented to the order being made, unless any refusal of consent can be ignored.[22] The sheriff must consider the principles set out in para 9.2 above and must be satisfied:[23]

(a) that the local authority has reasonable cause to suspect that adult in respect of whom the order is sought is an adult at risk who is being, or is likely to be seriously harmed;
(b) the assessment is needed to establish whether the adult in fact falls into this category; and
(c) the place where the adult is to be interviewed or examined is both available and suitable.

The order is valid for 7 days, and only authorises removal of the adult from the place being visited if it is impracticable to interview or examine him or her there, for example because of a lack of privacy. The adult must, in spite of the order, consent to any interview or examination unless their refusal of consent can be ignored.

As well as granting the assessment order the sheriff must also grant a warrant for entry to the place where the adult is to be visited.

The second type of order is a removal order[24] which authorises removal of the adult for up to seven days and authorises the local authority to take steps to protect the adult who has been removed. The order is normally granted by the sheriff, though in urgent cases it can be granted by a JP (though this will only authorise removal for 24 hours). Before making an order the sheriff must consider the principles set out in para 9.2 above and can only grant the order:[25]

20 Ch 9, para 7; ch 10, para 10; ch 11, para 9.
21 Adult Support and Protection (Scotland) Act 2007, ss 11–13; Scottish Government, *Code of Practice For Local Authorities and Practitioners Exercising Functions Under Part 1 of the Act* (revised 2009), ch 9.
22 See below.
23 Adult Support and Protection (Scotland) Act 2007, s 12.
24 Adult Support and Protection (Scotland) Act 2007, ss 14–18; Scottish Government, *Code of Practice For Local Authorities and Practitioners Exercising Functions Under Part 1 of the Act* (revised 2009), ch 10.
25 Adult Support and Protection (Scotland) Act 2007, s 15.

(a) if the adult consents, unless the refusal of consent can be ignored;
(b) if he/she is satisfied that that adult in respect of whom the order is sought is an adult at risk who is likely to be seriously harmed if not moved to another place; and
(c) the place where the adult is to be moved to is both available and suitable.

The order can regulate contact between the adult and another person and the sheriff must also grant a warrant for entry. Implementation must take place within 72 hours (12 hours if the order is granted by a JP), and cannot take place unless the adult consents, unless any refusal of consent can be ignored. Where the order is made by a sheriff it is possible to apply for variation or recall of the order.

The final type of protection order is a banning order.[26] This bans the person[27] who is the subject of the order from being in any place specified in the order and can have further conditions attached to it, for example banning the person concerned from being in the vicinity of this place or authorising their ejection from the place. The order will last for a specified period of up to six months, or, if no period is specified, for six months. No provision is made for extension of a banning order so if it is still required a fresh application would have to be made for a new banning order.

The application for the order can be made either by the adult who would be protected by the order or anyone else who lives in the place[28] which will be covered by the order or by the local authority. Indeed the local authority has an obligation to apply for an order where it is satisfied that the criteria for granting an order exist, that nobody else is likely to apply for an order and that no other proceedings are before the courts which would have the effect of ejecting or banning the person who is to be the subject of the order from the place which is to be covered by the order.[29] Before making the application, however, the authority must consider the principles set out in para 9.2 above. When an application is made for a banning order it can be accompanied by an application for a temporary banning order. While a banning order cannot be made unless the affected person has been given an opportunity to be heard or repre-

26 Adult Support and Protection (Scotland) Act 2007, ss 19–34; Scottish Government, *Code of Practice For Local Authorities and Practitioners Exercising Functions Under Part 1 of the Act* (revised 2009), ch 11.
27 Who need not be an adult.
28 For example, if the place covered by the banning order was the adult's home, anyone else who lived there.
29 For example an action for interdict to keep the person away from a certain area.

sented in court, a temporary order can be granted before such a hearing has taken place. The temporary banning order will last:

(a) for any period specified in the order; or
(b) until the related application for a banning order is decided on; or
(c) until recalled; or
(d) for a period of 6 months from the date on which the application for the related banning order was lodged.

An order can be made by the sheriff after considering the principles set out in part (2) above, if the adult consents (or their failure to consents can be ignored) and if the sheriff is satisfied that:[30]

(a) an adult at risk is being, or is likely to be, seriously harmed by another person;
(b) his/her well-being or property would be better satisfied by banning the person who is the subject of the order from a place occupied by the adult than it would be by removing the adult from that place; and
(c) either the adult has a right[31] to occupy the place covered by the banning order or is permitted[32] to occupy it by a third party (and the subject of the order has no such right or permission) or neither the adult or the subject of the order have such a right or permission.

Once an order has been made it is possible to apply for recall or variation of the order. An order (and a temporary order) can have a power of arrest attached to it which allows for the person who is the subject of the order to be arrested for breach of the order.

(d) Consent

9.8 Granting a protection order and taking any action to implement or enforce a protection order is not permitted if the sheriff granting the order or the person taking action knows that the adult has refused to consent to it. Refusal of consent implies that the adult has capacity to consent or to refuse consent to the action which is being taken. Where the adult has no capacity (or at least has no capacity in respect of the specific action) then there can be no refusal of consent for the purposes of the 2007 Act. In cases where the adult has no capacity there may be

30 Adult Support and Protection (Scotland) Act 2007, s 20.
31 For example under a tenancy agreement or as owner of a home.
32 For example if they are staying with a relative in the relative's home.

an attorney or guardian who can consent on behalf of the adult. If not, then the Code of Practice suggests that the local authority should consider whether to make use of its powers under the Mental Health (Care and Treatment)(Scotland) Act 2003 or under the Adults with Incapacity (Scotland) Act 2000 (or, indeed, whether the authority may have a duty to apply for an order under the latter).

In cases where there is a refusal of consent this can be ignored where the person ignoring the refusal believes that the following two conditions apply:[33]

(a) The adult who has refused consent has been unduly pressurised to do so. One example of this given in the 2007 Act is the case where the action to which consent is refused is being taken to prevent harm being cause to the adult by someone in whom he or she has confidence and trust and where the adult would consent if they did not have confidence and trust in that person. Other examples might be refusal of consent because the adult has been threatened.

(b) There are no steps which could reasonably be taken with the adult's consent which would protect the adult from the harm which the action is intended to prevent.

33 Adult Support and Protection (Scotland) Act 2007, s 35(3) & (4).

Chapter 10

Offenders

LAW AND CRIME

10.1 As we noted in chapter 1, one of the principal functions of law is the maintenance of order in society. In turn, one of the main ways in which this is done is through the criminal law and the police, prosecution, courts and other associated organisations. This chapter will look in more detail at the sentences available to courts and the roles that social workers play in the criminal justice system. Before doing this, however, we want to provide a context for the rest of the chapter.

Traditionally, a link was made between crime and moral repugnance. Hume, for example, defined crime as 'a doleful or wilful offence against society in the matter of violence, dishonesty, falsehood, irreligion'. With the passing of time and the growth in the number of offences this link has become weaker. It is difficult to imagine that a substantial level of moral outrage is generated by the behaviour of someone who is drunk and incapable or of someone convicted of a minor breach of the peace. This is even clearer in the case of a large number of statutory offences. It is common, for example, for motoring offenders not to regard themselves as 'real' criminals.

The majority of criminal offences in Scotland are the product of the common law: that is, their scope is determined by judicial decision rather than being defined in statute. This has important consequences. First, aside from the limits set on the sentencing powers of particular courts, there is no limit on the sentence that can be imposed for common law crimes and offences. This is in contrast to statutory offences where, usually, the statute creating the offence will set a maximum penalty. Secondly, following from this, all common law crimes are potentially punishable by imprisonment. Thirdly, these crimes are subject to redefinition and refinement by the courts, with possible extension to cover novel circumstances. Examples of this include the extension of breach of the peace to cover a man dressed as a woman walking about in a red-light district[1] and the view of the High Court that selling what were

1 *Stewart v Lockhart* 1991 SLT 835.

effectively glue-sniffing kits amounted to 'a modern example of conduct which our law has for long regarded as criminal … [that is,] actions of any kind which cause or are a cause of real injury to the person.'[2]

Furthermore, a distinction is sometimes drawn between crimes and offences (for example, in the presentation of criminal statistics) with the implication that crimes are more serious than offences. It is not clear that there is a sound legal basis for this.

Moreover, some indication should be given of the balance of crime. In terms of reports of crime in 2009–10[3], the largest proportion are offences involving dishonesty, particularly theft, and motoring offences, which accounted for about 17% and 36% of reports respectively. Other significant contributors are miscellaneous offences, for example, drunkenness, minor assault or breach of the peace (accounting for about 25%) and wilful fire-raising and vandalism (10%). Non-sexual violent crimes are less than 2% of the total. Looking at convictions in 2008–9[4], the largest contributor is motoring offences (around 35%), followed by miscellaneous offences (about 30%) and dishonesty (about 14%). Non-sexual crimes of violence accounted for about 2% of cases.

Social work functions

10.2 In Scotland, work specified by statute with offenders and ex-offenders is principally the responsibility of local authority social workers. Also unlike the current arrangements in England and Wales, these functions are mainly carried out by professionally qualified social workers.[5]

At the time of writing (February 2011) significant changes are in the process of being made which will affect the social work role in practice in the criminal justice system. The first of these is the introduction of a new community penalty, the community payback order, which will replace probation, community service and supervised attendance orders.[6] The new community penalty is only available for crimes committed after 1st February 2011 and for crimes committed before then probation etc will still be available as a disposal. In addition, the change to the new pen-

2 *Khaliq v HMA* 1984 SLT 137 at 142–143.

3 Scottish Government, *Statistical Bulletin: Recorded Crime in Scotland 2009–10.*

4 Scottish Government, *Statistical Bulletin: Criminal Proceedings in Scottish Courts, 2008–9.*

5 For background see McNeill, F & Whyte, B, *Reducing Reoffending: Social work and community justice in Scotland* (2007), ch 1.

6 It will also replace community reparation orders which were piloted but never made widely available.

alties will not affect any disposals made before 1st February 2011, so that, for example, a community service order in place on that date will continue until it comes to an end. Because of this transitional period the new disposal is considered in chapter 12 and this chapter sets out the law which will be in place until 1 February (and beyond for offences committed before that date and orders in existence at that date).

The second main change is the replacement of the *National Objectives for Social Work Services in the Criminal Justice System* which derive, in their current form, from 2004. These standards were originally introduced in 1991 associated with a change in the funding arrangements for financing social work services. Services in the areas covered are now 100% funded by central government. The *National Standards* covered the provision of social enquiry reports and court based services, probation, throughcare, and community service and often provided detailed guidance on the performance of social work functions, for example preparation of social enquiry reports and supervision of offenders subject to a probation order. They are replaced by *National Outcomes and Standards for Social Work Services in the Criminal Justice System*[7] supplemented by more detailed practice guidance covering particular areas. The overall aims suggested in the *National Outcomes* for criminal justice social work services are to:

(a) work to contribute to the protection of the public by seeking to reduce the risks of reoffending and serious harm;
(b) help individuals to change their behaviour and become contributing members of society;
(c) deliver effective supervision that is seen as credible by the courts and the public.

These are seen as contributing to three key outcomes for social work services in this context:

(a) Community safety and public protection.
(b) The reduction of re-offending.
(c) Social inclusion to support desistance from offending.

Services are now primarily provided by specialist staff, some of whom will work full-time in this area. In practice, working with offenders and ex-offenders has proved a relatively attractive prospect to social workers

7 Scottish Government (2010), noting (at p 5) that: 'Changing Lives (the 21st Century Social Work Review) sought to build upon the professional autonomy of social work practitioners and this reinforced the need to revise the prescriptive objectives and standards originally published in 1991.' The Practice Guidance will, however, provide detailed guidance on the performance of certain functions.

who welcome the opportunity to work in a fairly prescribed and planned manner. The use of social workers' legally defined powers is an especially prominent feature of the work.[8]

The social worker performing any of the functions noted above is accountable not only to the court but also to his/her own employer. The differing value bases, policies and procedures often produce tensions which can sometimes escalate into conflicting demands being made upon the social worker. Involvement with the criminal justice system is likely to be stressful for everyone, but especially so for the accused, offender or ex-offender who may be at risk of losing liberty, money or other valued things. The structures and procedures of the criminal justice system are complex and can be particularly difficult to navigate for a person who is possibly in a state of crisis. In this situation, the social worker may contribute toward the alleviation of excessive anxiety and unclarity on the part of the accused, offender, or ex-offender by taking on both a supportive and an educative role. As in many settings which are not primarily defined by social work values and knowledge, the social worker's most notable offering may be to help to broaden the perspective of all the players to include social factors.

(1) Court-based social workers

10.3 There are social work staff permanently based in larger, busier courts, while in other courts the provision may be part-time. The main functions of these court-based social workers are dealing with requests for social enquiry reports and ensuring that they are timeously provided; monitoring the standard of reports; conducting stand-down interviews (in which the social worker interviews the offender during a brief court recess); and providing oral reports to the court; interviewing offenders immediately following a request for a report; interviewing offenders after custodial remand or sentence; interviewing offenders following sentences involving a social work contribution; and liaison with the others involved in the operation of the court.[9]

8 See M Payne *What is Professional Social Work?* (2nd edn, 2006), ch 6 for a detailed presentation about power, authority and social work.

9 See Scottish Government, *National Outcomes and Standards For Social Work Services in the Criminal Justice System: Criminal Justice Social Work Reports and Court-based Services Practice Guidance* (2010), section 4.

Court-based social workers not only perform a range of services for the court but may also be able to provide assistance to the families of those on trial or who have been sentenced, particularly those who have been sentenced to custody, and to victims of crime and to witnesses. This duality of purpose once more provides the potential for social workers to experience conflicts in relation to the various demands being made and their professional orientation. The social worker may be in a position to support and provide clarification about what is happening for the families of those appearing in court. In court when the disposal is pronounced, the offender may well be anxious and suffering from situational deafness, and unable to hear and process what is heard. In many courts there is the added practical difficulty of physically hearing the disposal when there is no sound amplification or the crucial information is not clearly announced. Moreover, some of the non-custodial disposals are not very widely used or known and so it may be necessary and appropriate for social workers to assume an educative and interpretative role with the offender in clarifying what the meaning and implications of various disposals are likely to be. In addition, the court-based social worker may be providing an intake and referral service for those at the court who are in need.

(2) Reports[10]

10.4 Most reports are prepared following a plea of guilty or a finding of guilt while the court adjourns the case[11] and prior to the decision regarding sentence or disposal of the case. Section 27(l)(a) of the Social Work (Scotland) Act 1968 (the 1968 Act) imposes a duty on local authority social work departments to 'provide reports relating to persons appearing before the court which the court may require for the disposal of the case'. Although the 1968 Act refers to social background reports, in the context of the criminal court system these reports were known as social enquiry reports (SER). However, the guidance issued as part of the *National Outcomes* process refers to a Criminal Justice Social Work Report (CJSWR), and this terminology is used in the text. A detailed discussion of the contents of such reports and the methodology for preparing them is beyond the scope of this text and detailed guidelines

10 See McNeill, F & Whyte, B, *Reducing Reoffending: Social work and community justice in Scotland* (2007), ch 4. See also para 12.19.

11 Under section 201 of the Criminal Procedure (Scotland) Act 1995.

and standards can be found in the Practice Guidance.[12] Particularly in reports written about active or known social work department service users, it is hoped that there will be a strong element of a shared understanding of the problem areas with a commitment to the empowerment of the service user.

Reports, which, in practice will be prepared by a local authority social worker, though this is not always a statutory requirement, must be obtained in certain circumstances:

(a) Before making a probation order.[13] A report must be obtained before any probation order is made. The principal purposes of the report, as set in the legislation, are to provide information on the character and circumstances of the offender and information as to arrangements for supervision if a probation order is made. Before a requirement for unpaid work can be made the report must address the suitability of the offender for such a condition.

(b) Before making a community service order[14]. Here the report is to contain information regarding the offender and his circumstances, and confirmation that arrangements can be made for the offender to perform community service.

(c) Before imposing a sentence of detention on an offender between 16 and 20.[15] The court is required to obtain (either from a local authority officer or otherwise) information about the offender's circumstances, and to take into account any information before it concerning the offender's character and physical and mental condition.

(d) Before passing a sentence of imprisonment on someone aged 21 or over who has not previously served a sentence of imprisonment.[16] The court is required to obtain (either from a local authority officer or otherwise) information about the offender's circumstances, and to take into account any information before it concerning the offender's character and physical and mental condition.

12 Scottish Government, *National Outcomes and Standards for Social Work Services in the Criminal Justice System: Criminal Justice Social Work Reports and Court-based Service Practice Guidance* (2010).

13 Criminal Procedure (Scotland) Act 1995, s 228(1)(b).

14 Criminal Procedure (Scotland) Act 1995, s 238(2)(c).

15 Criminal Procedure (Scotland) Act 1995, s 207(4).

16 Criminal Procedure (Scotland) Act 1995, s 204(2).

(e) Before sentencing a person specified in section 27(1)(b)(i)-(vi) of the Social Work (Scotland) Act 1968 a court other than a JP court must obtain a report.[17] Those specified in the 1968 Act are those under supervision because of a court order (eg on probation); those on supervision following release from prison/detention; those subject to a Community Service Order, supervised attendance order or supervision and treatment order; 16 and 17 year olds subject to a supervision requirement imposed because of commission of an offence; and, people charged but not prosecuted and referred to the local authority by the Procurator-Fiscal or Lord Advocate. The report is to be on the character of the individual, including his/her behaviour while under supervision or subject to the order.
(f) Before making a supervised release order.[18]
(g) Before passing an extended sentence.[19]
(h) Before making a drug treatment and testing order.[20]
(i) Where a summary court is dealing with an offender who has been convicted of a sexual offence or an offence involving a significant sexual element to their behaviour in committing it.[21]
(j) Before making a restriction of liberty order in respect of someone aged under 16.[22]
(k) A report must be provided for any probation review hearing.[23]
(l) Before sentencing someone convicted of incest or intercourse with a step child.[24]

In providing these reports social workers have an opportunity to provide a concise but comprehensive systemic assessment which emphasises the social functioning equation for the court. It is crucial for the court to have access to information about the offender's normal coping capacities as well as the unusual environmental demands being made on the offender.

Normally, the period available for preparation of the report is 4 weeks or 8 weeks on cause shown.[25] These periods are reduced by the time

17 Criminal Procedure (Scotland) Act 1995, s 203. The references to probation, Community Service Orders and supervised attendance orders will be replaced from February 2011 by a reference to community payback orders, but will continue to apply to these other orders until they are all completed.
18 Criminal Procedure (Scotland) Act 1995, s 209(2).
19 Criminal Procedure (Scotland) Act 1995, s 210A.
20 Criminal Procedure (Scotland) Act 1995, s 234B(3)(b).
21 Criminal Justice (Scotland) Act 2003, s 21.
22 Criminal Procedure (Scotland) Act 1995, s 254A(11A).
23 Criminal Procedure (Scotland) Act 1995, s 229A.
24 Criminal Law (Consolidation) (Scotland) Act 1995, s 4(6).
25 Criminal Procedure (Scotland) Act 1995, s 201(3).

taken to process the request and the need to complete the report in time to have it submitted to the clerk of court by midday on the day preceding the court hearing which will consider it. If the report has not been completed or further inquiries must be made, then, when the case is called, an explanation must be made to the court and the case can be continued for a further period equal to the original one. Where the offender is remanded on bail, it is a condition of the bail that the offender makes him/herself available for the purpose of preparation of any reports. Failure to co-operate should be reported to the court and failure of the offender to make him/herself available is an offence.[26] What is not so clear is what happens when the offender is available to meet the social worker, but refuses to co-operate. Moore and Wood suggest that failure to cooperate may amount to contempt of court and while this may be a possibility, there is no legal authority on the issue.[27]

A copy of the report is made available to the offender or his/her solicitor by the clerk of court. It will also be seen by the prosecutor and the judge, and some comment may be made on its contents in open court. Because of this, problems about confidentiality may arise.[28] Sensitive information may need to be noted as such in the report with a request that it is not disclosed in court.[29]

The court may request that the writer is present at the hearing where the report will be presented in the court. Additionally, the *National Standards* suggested that attendance was advisable where an unusual or complex recommendation is being made; where the writer's presence may tip the balance in favour of a non-custodial disposal; and where a report is being considered in connection with breach of a statutory order. In such cases the presence of the report writer may have a direct influence on the sentence passed. Where the writer is not present, a court-based social worker may be able to assist the court on behalf of the writer.

26 Criminal Procedure (Scotland) Act 1995, s 24(5)(d).

27 G Moore and B Whyte, *Moore and Wood's Social Work and Criminal Law in Scotland* (3rd edn, 1998), pp 66–67.

28 Though, of course, all information in the report will be disclosed to the offender.

29 See the discussion in Scottish Government, *National Outcomes and Standards for Social Work Services in the Criminal Justice System: Criminal Justice Social Work Reports and Court-based Services Practice Guidance* (2010), section 3. In *X v BBC* [2005] CSOH 80 it was suggested (at para 44) that the 'contents of social enquiry report ought to be publicly available to allow contemporaneous reporting to take place.' It was also suggested that any information contained in the SER which was not reported at the time was later to be regarded as confidential.

Finally, it is worth noting that one of the objectives of social enquiry reports is variously stated to be '[t]o provide information and advice which may make it possible to increase the use of community-based disposals where custody is likely', and 'assisting the court's consideration of community-based options'. Part of the social worker's considerations are about the potential risk of the offender to him/herself and others in prison or in the community. In Scotland, where there is an acceptance that a sizeable proportion of persons currently in prison are no such risk to themselves or others, it is a rare and priceless opportunity for social workers to provide information to influence the sentencers to ends which are more compatible with social work values.

There has in the past been some discussion about the appropriateness and/or advisability of social workers making recommendations highlighting preferred disposals in their reports. Moore and Whyte[30] quote various statements from the bench and a government White Paper which forcefully express the view that recommendations are unwelcome and outwith the social work remit. *National Objectives* (in a change from the original guidance) indicated that:[31]

> The matter of selection of sentence is one for the court in the light of all the circumstances of the case. Whilst reports must not include a recommendation as such, report writers may indicate, on the basis of their review and assessment, which non-custodial option is in their opinion most likely to prevent or reduce future offending in the event of the court deciding it not necessary to impose a custodial sentence. The feasibility of a disposal may depend critically on what it involves. This means spelling out as clearly as possible any suggested plan for supervision if the court was to make a Probation Order and, for a Community Service Order, making clear that the offender has been assessed as suitable and that a place is available

A considerably smaller number of reports are ordered prior to the alleged offender going to trial. Examples of when a pre-trial report might be requested include when the person is under the age of 21 or is an adult who has not previously been in custody and has been committed to the High Court for trial. Here, the alleged offender is not required to co-operate in the preparation of the report. A recommendation to abandon

30 G Moore and B Whyte, Moore and Wood's *Social Work and Criminal Law in Scotland* (3rd edn, 1998), pp 105–108.

31 Scottish Executive, National *Objectives for Social Work Services in the Criminal Justice System: Standards – Social Enquiry Reports and associated Court Services* (2004) para 5.6. For current guidance see para 12.18.

pre-trial reports, except in cases where there was a plea of guilty in advance, was made by the Social Work Services Inspectorate in 1996.[32]

(3) Supervision

10.5 Social work departments are expected to provide supervision in a variety of situations. The main examples are probation, community service, fine supervision orders, supervised attendance orders and supervision after release from custody. These are all considered more fully below. Social workers may also be involved in diversion schemes, where alleged offenders are diverted into some form of social work intervention rather man being prosecuted, and this is also considered below.

(4) Appearing in court

10.6 Social workers are occasionally called as witnesses in civil or criminal proceedings where they may be seen as experts on social concerns. They may also be the applicant in situations where there has been a breach of an order. In each of these situations, social workers may be cross-examined and must take an oath or affirm. It is important that the social worker prepare thoroughly, bringing notes and copies of the relevant material to court. This last can be important, since witnesses are allowed to refer to contemporaneous notes, that is, notes made at the time of or shortly after the events to which they refer, while they are giving evidence.

Suggestions for social workers from Colin Fishwick in *Court Work*[33] include accommodating to the formal codes and norms of the court situation; being prepared to have one's practice exposed; preparing 'authoritative statements rather than interpretative remarks'; direct and clear communication; and appropriate style of dress. As this list suggests, court proceedings generally take place in a very formal atmosphere subject to detailed rules as to procedure and as to how evidence may be given, and indeed what counts as evidence.[34] This formality is reflected

32 *Helping the Court Decide*, para 9.10. At the time of writing this recommendation has not been implemented. One obvious difficulty is that if the accused is maintaining his/her innocence the report cannot contain a discussion of his/her attitude to the offence.

33 C Fishwick *Court Work* (2nd edn, 1989).

34 See paras 1.39–1.56.

in the forms of address: magistrates are referred to as 'your honour', sheriffs and High Court judges as 'your lordship' or 'your ladyship'.

(5) Court reports concerning children

10.7 When a child is charged with an offence which requires a court appearance, there is a requirement for the local authority to be notified. The social work department must then provide the court with a pre-conviction report detailing the home background and social circumstances of the child to facilitate disposal of the case.[35] Useful research findings suggest that significant predictors of children's offending behaviour are more focused on the 'closeness of parental supervision and levels of parental expectation of behaviour regarding offending' than on 'social hardship'.

SENTENCING: OBJECTIVES AND CRITERIA

10.8 The objectives of sentencing and punishment have produced a substantial literature. The main objectives canvassed in the past have included individual and general deterrence; rehabilitation; reform or, more recently, supporting desistance;[36] retribution; denunciation; and containment or protection of the public. The extent to which the sentences available to the courts can meet any of these objectives is increasingly open to doubt. For example, it is debatable whether the element of calculation required for deterrence to operate is present in most crimes; the possibility of reforming someone and preparing him/her for a life integrated in society by isolating them in prison is equally debatable. The only objectives that the system can be said to attain are retribution and denunciation with, in some cases, compensation for the victim of crime, and in other cases, the possibility of some reformation. This, indeed, was recognised in the White Paper *Crime, Justice and Protecting the Public*,[37] which also contained the novel suggestion that the objective of sentencing was ensuring that criminals received their just desserts.

On a more practical level there are factors which clearly have an influence on the sentence imposed in particular cases. These include the severity of the offence; the offender's previous record; the offender's

35 Criminal Procedure (Scotland) Act 1995, s 42(7) and (8).

36 See, for example, McNeill, F & Whyte, B, *Reducing Reoffending: Social work and community justice in Scotland* (2007), ch 3.

37 Cm 965 (1990).

attitude towards the offence; the offender's culpability; the existence of any provocation; and background information about the offender. In contrast to the position in England, however, there is no discount on sentence for a plea of guilty. On the other hand, if the accused pleads guilty the court can take into account when and in what circumstances it was indicated that a guilty plea would be made in fixing the sentence.[38] On the basis of these factors experienced practitioners, on both sides of the law, can often predict the likely outcome of a particular case. The High Court also has the power when hearing appeals against sentence to give its opinion on appropriate sentences in similar cases.[39] The Criminal Justice and Licensing (Scotland) Act 2010 provides for the creation of a Scottish Sentencing Council, part of the remit of which would be to prepare sentencing guidelines to be approved by the High Court.[40]

Although these factors exist, and have to some extent been given judicial recognition, there is some evidence of disparities in sentencing between different courts and between different judges.[41]

In practice the vast majority of sentences are non-custodial. In 2008–9, for example, just over 13% of those sentenced were sentenced to custody. It should be noted, however, that the use of custody is increasing; in 1979 this figure was just over 4%.

NON-CUSTODIAL DISPOSALS

(1) Absolute discharge

10.9 An absolute discharge is appropriate where in view of the circumstances, including the nature of the offence and the character of the offender, the court decides that it is inexpedient to inflict punishment and that a probation order is not appropriate.[42] It is used very rarely and in 2008–9 was used in only 0.3% of cases. This disposal will count as a previous conviction if a further offence is committed subsequently.

38 Criminal Procedure (Scotland) Act 1995, s 196.

39 Criminal Procedure (Scotland) Act 1995, ss 118(7), 189(7) & 197.

40 Criminal Justice and Licensing (Scotland) Act 2010, s 3. As originally tabled the Bill which became the Act set out in its first two sections the purposes and principles of sentencing. The purposes were stated to be: (a) the punishment of offenders, (b) the reduction of crime (including its reduction by deterrence), (c) the reform and rehabilitation of offenders, (d) the protection of the public, and (e) the making of reparation by offenders to persons affected by their offences.

41 See, for example, N Hutton and C Tata *Patterns of Custodial Sentencing in the Sheriff Court* (1995).

42 Criminal Procedure (Scotland) Act 1995, s 246(2) & (3).

(2) Admonition

10.10 An offender may be admonished where it appears to meet the justice of the case.[43] The court may simply announce that the offender is admonished and leave it at that, or the court may add some well-chosen words of warning. This disposal counts as a conviction.

(3) Caution[44]

10.11 An offender may be required, but only following conviction on indictment, to find caution for good behaviour. This involves lodging a sum of money in court. The period of good behaviour may be up to 12 months. If the offender is of good behaviour during this period, then the caution is returned with interest. If the offender is not of good behaviour during the period, in particular, if he/she commits a further offence, then the caution is forfeited. A requirement to find caution can be imposed in addition to a fine or custodial sentence.[45]

(4) Fines

10.12 This disposal takes the form of a financial penalty paid by the offender. Fines are by far the commonest form of disposal, though their use is declining. It is, therefore, vital for social workers to appreciate how they are levied and collected. Social workers also play a central role in the preparation of means enquiry reports for the court.[46] Non-payment of a fine places the offender at risk of imprisonment or a supervised attendance order.[47]

(a) Levels of fine

10.13 In fixing the level of fine for a particular offender the court must, amongst other considerations, take the means of the offender into account; there is clearly little point in levying a fine which the offender has no practical prospect of paying. If a fine is excessive in relation to the means of the offender this will be a ground for appealing against

43 Criminal Procedure (Scotland) Act 1995, s 246(1).
44 Pronounced 'kayshun'.
45 Criminal Procedure (Scotland) Act 1995, s 227.
46 See para 10.17 below.
47 After February 2011 the supervised attendance order will be replaced by a community payback order, see paras 12.20–12.34.

the fine imposed.[48] Here, the social worker who is asked to prepare a CJSWR social enquiry report is ideally placed to help to minimise the prospect of an unpayable fine being levied by providing the sentencer with comprehensive and accurate information about the financial incomings and outgoings of the offender.

In the case of both common law and statutory offences tried on indictment, there is no maximum limit on the fine which can be imposed. In summary courts there are limits. For common law offences these are currently £5,000 in the sheriff court and for stipendiary magistrates, and £2,500 for lay magistrates in the JP court. In the case of statutory offences the statute creating the offence will normally fix the maximum fine, and this will be done by reference to one of five levels, rather than by reference to an amount of money. The reason for this is simple; it is much easier to change the values attached to the levels than to amend the amounts stated in a large, and growing, number of Acts of Parliament. Currently the levels are as follows:

Level 1	£ 200
Level 2	£ 500
Level 3	£1,000
Level 4	£2,500
Level 5	£5,000

It should be noted that the maximum fine that can be levied by lay magistrates in the JP court is stated to be level 4 and the money value will therefore change automatically when the levels change.

(b) Time for payment

10.14 The offender must be allowed at least 7 days to pay the fine, or if it is to be paid in instalments, the first instalment of the fine. The only exceptions to this, when the fine is payable immediately, are where the offender has no fixed abode; where the offender appears to have sufficient means to pay the fine forthwith; where the offender indicates that time to pay is not wanted; and where the court is satisfied that other special reasons exist for not allowing time to pay. If the court decides that no time will be allowed to pay the fine, then it must state the reasons for this decision. A summary court may order the offender to be searched and any money found to be applied to payment of the fine unless the court is satisfied that the money belongs to someone else or that the loss of the money would be more injurious to the offender's family than his/her imprisonment or detention.

48 *Hamilton v Scott* 1987 SCCR 188.

The offender may, either when the fine is imposed or subsequently, apply for more time to pay or to be allowed to pay by instalments. Further time to pay must be allowed following an application unless it appears that the offender's failure to pay is wilful or that there is no reasonable prospect of paying the fine. Social workers may find that the role of advocate on behalf of service users in negotiating for a feasible instalment schedule would be appropriate, since offenders often experience difficulty in overcoming their inhibitions in the courtroom or with the clerk of the relevant court to make such arrangements.

(c) Alternative of imprisonment[49]

10.15 An alternative sentence of imprisonment may be imposed at the same time as the fine and will become operational without the need for a means enquiry court (see (e) below) in the event of default in payment. Such an alternative is not to be imposed unless the court considers it expedient having regard to the gravity of the offence, the character of the offender or other special circumstances. The offender must be present in this instance.

(d) Fine supervision

10.16 Where time to pay a fine is allowed then an enforcement order must be made unless the court considers that such an order would not be appropriate in the circumstances.[50] (This is additional to the power to make a supervision order or to impose an alternative of imprisonment.) Once such an order is made a fines enforcement officer[51] can vary the time for payment on application by the offender. Fines enforcement officer also have extensive enforcement powers. The enforcement order authorises them to arrest the offender's income or other funds and they can ask the court to make an application for deduction from benefits being paid to the offender. In addition they have the power to seize and dispose of a motor vehicle belonging to the offender. Finally the fines enforcement officer can refer the case of the offender back to the court if he/she believes that payment is unlikely or for other reasons (eg failure to co-operate).

In addition to an enforcement order, an offender who is given time to pay or who is to make payment by instalments, may be made subject to

49 Criminal Procedure (Scotland) Act 1995, ss 214(4), 219(l)(b).

50 Criminal Procedure (Scotland) Act 1995, s 226B.

51 Fines enforcement officers have the responsibility for collecting fines.

a fine supervision order and be placed under the supervision of a social worker or other social work department employee. The offender does not need to consent to such an order being made and the order remains in force until the fine is paid in full, the offender is imprisoned for fine default, another order is made concerning the fine, or the order is transferred to another court area. An offender under 21 cannot be detained in the event of non-payment unless placed on supervision or unless it was not reasonably practicable to do this. In the event of non-payment the supervising social worker should provide a report to the court hearing called to enquire as to the reasons for non-payment (the means enquiry court: see below). There have been arguments advanced over the years that supervising the payment of fines places social workers in an unacceptable position as debt collectors for the courts, but compulsory contact between the offender and the social worker does offer the potential opportunity for more substantive and negotiated work to be undertaken together.

(e) Enforcement: imprisonment on default

10.17 Generally speaking, fines are payable to the courts which imposed them.[52] The exceptions to this are High Court fines, which are collected by the appropriate sheriff court, and cases where the offender has moved. In the latter case the fine will normally be transferred to the appropriate court covering the offender's new place of residence.

If the offender fails to pay the fine he/she may, provided that the amount outstanding on the fine is £500 or more, be imprisoned or detained instead. Where time to pay has been allowed and no alternative imposed at the time of the fine, imprisonment can take place only after enquiry by the court as to the reasons for non-payment. The hearing at which this enquiry is made is usually referred to as a means enquiry court. At this hearing the offender may be imprisoned or given further time to pay. There is statutory provision for the period of imprisonment in the event of non-payment. The relevant amount for the purpose of calculating the period of imprisonment is the amount of the fine which remains outstanding. The same provisions apply, subject to the proviso noted above, for the imposition of an alternative of detention on a young offender.

Where no time to pay is allowed and immediate payment is not made, the offender may, subject to the exception noted below, be committed

52 Though it is also possible to pay online.

to prison or to a young offenders institution forthwith. The exception arises in the case of an offender who has not previously served a term of imprisonment or detention and who is not legally represented. Such an offender cannot be immediately imprisoned unless legal aid has been refused on financial grounds or, knowing of the possibility of applying for legal aid, the offender has chosen not to apply for it.

Imprisonment for non-payment of a fine means that a person can be imprisoned for an offence which did not originally carry imprisonment as a possible penalty and for an offence for which prison had not been envisioned as a possible penalty. The number of people sentenced to imprisonment for non-payment has declined dramatically both in number and as a proportion of receptions (less than 4% in 2009/10 compared to around 25% of all receptions in 1994).

If the fine is paid while the offender is in prison or young offenders institution for fine default, then release can be secured.

(f) Supervised attendance orders[53]

10.18 Anyone who owes an amount less that £500 cannot be sent to custody/detention but must, provided the requirements noted below are met, instead be made subject to a supervised attendance order.[54] A supervised attendance order cannot be made if the amount owed by the offender exceeds £500.

Criminal justice social work services are responsible for organising schemes to implement supervised attendance orders. Orders require the offender to attend at a specified place for between 10 and 100 hours and, during that time, to comply with the instructions of his/her supervising officer (who is appointed or assigned by the local authority). The maximum number of hours depends on the amount of the fine which is outstanding. Where this does not exceed level 1 it is 50 hours, where more is outstanding but the outstanding amount is less than level 2 (the maximum outstanding amount for which supervised attendance orders are available) it is 100 hours. Supervised attendance orders can only be used in respect of offenders over 16 in cases where the offender would otherwise have been imprisoned. The offender does not have to consent to such an order being made which may have serious repercussions for its implementation. The order can be made either at the time of the fine

53 Criminal Procedure (Scotland) Act 1995, ss 235–237 and Sch 7. For offences committed after 1 February 2011 supervised attendance orders will not be available, the alternative will be a community payback order, see paras 12.20–12.34.

54 Criminal Procedure (Scotland) Act 1995, s 235(4).

as an alternative in the same way as imprisonment, or at a later stage on default by the offender. Once a supervised attendance order is made, the fine it replaces is discharged.

Before the order is made the court must explain, in ordinary language:

(a) the purpose and effect of the order;
(b) the obligations of the offender, in particular to report to the supervising officer and advise him/her of any change of address or working hours, and to comply with the instructions of the supervising officer which, so far as practicable, should not conflict with the offender's religious beliefs, normal working hours, attendance at school or other educational institution;
(c) the consequences of failure to comply: these are possible revocation of the order and imposition of imprisonment or a variation of the number of hours specified in the order, subject to the statutory maxima;
(d) the court's power to review the order on the application of the offender or a local authority officer.

The supervised attendance order remains in force, unless revoked, until the specified number of hours are completed although these should normally be completed during a twelve month period.

Supervised attendance orders can also be used by summary courts in respect of 16 and 17 year olds as an alternative to a fine rather than as an alternative to custody.[55] If the court considers that the appropriate sentence is a fine it must decide how much the fine should be and then consider whether the offender is likely to pay any fine within 28 days. If they conclude that he/she is likely to pay, the fine is imposed and an order may be imposed in case of default. If the view is taken that the offender is not likely to pay within 28 days, then the order is made in place of the fine.

Failure by the offender to comply with his/her obligations will lead to breach of the order. Proceedings for breach will normally be initiated by the supervising officer. The court can cite the offender to appear in court or can issue an arrest warrant. If the court is satisfied that the offender has failed to comply with the order without reasonable cause it may revoke the order and impose the alternative of imprisonment dictated by the outstanding amount of fine or it may vary the number of hours, provided the total does not exceed 60. The maximum custodial sentences which can be imposed are sixty days in the JP Court and three months

55 Though this is only available in some courts.

in the Sheriff Court. Only one witness is necessary to provide evidence for breach proceedings.

The offender or supervisor may apply to court for the order to be extended beyond the normal 12 months, for the number of hours to be varied, for revocation, and for revocation and the imposition of imprisonment. The court should grant such an application if it appears to them that 'it would be in the interests of justice to do so having regard to circumstances which have risen since the order was made.'

(5) Probation[56]

(a) Introduction

10.19 Probation is a disposal that requires the offender to be under the supervision of a professionally qualified social worker who is appointed as supervisor for a period between 6 months and 3 years. The offender must comply with the instructions of the supervisor and with any conditions attached to the supervision order. A court may deal with an offender by way of probation if 'it is of the opinion … having regard to the circumstances, including the nature of the offence and the character of the offender'[57] that it is expedient to do so. *National Objectives* suggested that priority should be given in recommending probation to two groups: (i) offenders whose current offending places them at risk of custody, who have significant underlying problems and who seem likely to re-offend; and (ii) repeat offenders with significant underlying problems who are at risk of custody, even if the current offence is trivial. It also suggested some priority for offenders who may be likely to receive a custodial disposal if their offending behaviour continues unchecked.

Before a probation order is made the court must obtain a report on the circumstances and character of the offender, which will usually be in the form of a CJSWR. In addition, if a requirement as to performance of unpaid work is to be made (see below) the court must consider a report from the local authority about the offender and his/her circumstances and suitability for such an order.[58] If the writer of the report is recommending probation, the report should also detail the action plan to be followed during the probation period and any special conditions which should be attached to the order. The offender must consent to the making of a probation order, and part of the social work function in

56 Replaced for offences committed after 1 February 2011 by community payback order, see paras 12.20–12.34.

57 Criminal Procedure (Scotland) Act 1995, s 228(1).

58 Criminal Procedure (Scotland) Act 1995, s 229(4)(a).

preparing the report involves explaining the consequences of a probation order to the offender and obtaining the offender's consent to the order. The court must also explain the meaning and effect of the order and the consequences of breach of conditions of the order or commission of a further offence. Copies of the order must be supplied to the offender and to the supervising social worker.

When making an order the court may set a date for a hearing to review the order. A report on progress must be prepared by the supervisor for the hearing, and the probationer must attend the hearing. At a hearing the order can be amended and a further review hearing fixed.

(b) Social work contribution

10.20 Once the order has been made the probationer should be seen as soon as possible after the order is made to serve the order and to explain its terms and conditions. The probationer should sign and date a copy of the order. The signing is taken to be the evidence that the probationer understands the meaning and conditions of the order. In the event of subsequent breach proceedings, failure to complete this procedure might provide the probationer with grounds to contest the proceedings. Research findings[59] provide clear evidence that the central tenets of social work feature prominently in effective work with offenders. The core conditions of genuineness, non-possessive warmth and accurate empathy provide the basis for trusting relationships within which the probation order can be used to confront the offender with the consequences of his/her offending behaviour. Various restrictions on the probationer's activities can be made: as the basis for identifying and resolving some of the problems which led into offending behaviour; as a means of working with the offender towards a clearer and more acceptable understanding of his/her place in society; and as a credible alternative to the court in controlling and providing an opportunity for self-help. There is a large amount of research evidence[60] documenting the complex inter-relationships amongst offending behaviour, poverty, employment, housing and health. Each of these areas may become the basis for conditions attached to probation orders and each of them generates concerns which are well known to social work practitioners and may well form the basis for effective intervention.

59 See G Boswell 'The Essential Skills of Probation Work' in T May and A Vass (eds) *Working with Offenders* (1996).

60 See M Drakeford and M Vanstone (eds) *Beyond Offending Behaviour* (1996).

It is also clear from a world-wide body of research that 'some things do work' with persistent offenders. In her review of this literature, Gill Mclvor cites the following factors which augur well for successful social work involvement:[61]

(a) a focus on the offence and on problem solving;
(b) targeting high-risk offenders rather than net widening;
(c) using a range of interventions which are based on thorough assessments of the offender, the situation and the environment;
(d) the offering of appropriate, specific and concrete services.

Further to these factors, Mclvor also cites a set of conditions which are prerequisites for effective probation project work:

(a) clear purpose;
(b) organisational support and encouragement;
(c) (targeting relatively straightforward change;
(d) stable and committed leadership;
(e) 'practitioner ownership'.[62]

The care/control dichotomy/dilemma is probably nowhere more evident than in the relationship between probationer and social worker. A detailed discussion of the contradictory demands made of supervisors of probation orders can be found elsewhere.[63] Detailed guidelines for the frequency and the content of contact through the initial, middle and final phases of the probation are available in the *National Objectives.*[64]

(c) Conditions

10.21 There are certain standard or core conditions which apply to all probation orders. These are that the offender is to be of good behaviour; is to comply with instructions given by the supervising officer; and must inform the supervisor at once of any change of address or employment. There are also specified requirements for the social worker to confront the offender with his/her responsibility to abide by the rule of law, to

61 G Mclvor *Sanctions for Serious or Persistent Offenders: A Review of the Literature* (1990).
62 See P Raynor, D Smith and M Vanstone *Effective Probation Practice* (1994), pp 75–77.
63 See eg Tim May in *Probation: Politics, Policy and Practice* (1990) and John Rodger in *Family Life and Social Control* (1996).
64 Scottish Executive, *National Objectives for Social Work Services in the Criminal Justice System: Standards Probation* (2004).

oversee the offender's compliance with the probation order and to provide the offender with advice, guidance and assistance.[65]

In addition to these core conditions there are others envisaged and provided for in the legislation. These are residence (the home surroundings of the offender must be considered before imposing such a condition); performance of unpaid work; requiring the payment of compensation to the victim of the offence; and requiring medical treatment for mental illness. Each of these will be considered in turn in the following paragraphs.

A requirement regarding residence can take two forms: it can require the offender to reside at a named place or in a named institution, or it can require that the offender's place of residence be approved by the supervisor. In the former case the requirement can last for up to 12 months from the making of the order.

The performance of unpaid work can be made a condition of a probation order. This requirement can impose between 40 and 240 hours unpaid work on the offender. The option is only available if the offender is 16 or over, arrangements exist in the appropriate area for the performance of unpaid work, and provision can be made for the offender within these arrangements.

Although a compensation order (see below) cannot be made at the same time as a probation order, it is possible to make payment of compensation a condition of a probation order. The supervisor has responsibility for supervising me payment of compensation into court.

Treatment for mental disorder can be made a condition of a probation order where the court is satisfied that the offender suffers from a mental disorder which requires and may be susceptible to treatment, but that the mental condition is not such as to justify the detention of the offender.[66] The court can make this decision on the basis of the evidence in the form of a report from a registered medical practitioner. The requirement will specify either in-patient treatment, out-patient treatment at a particular place, or treatment by a particular doctor or chartered psychologist. Where a change in the method or location of treatment from that specified in the order is necessary it can normally be achieved without resort to court. The initiative for the change comes from the doctor or psychologist treating the offender, and if it is agreed by the offender and his/her supervising officer, then it can be carried into effect. It is then the responsibility of the supervising officer to notify the court as to these

65 Criminal Procedure (Scotland) Act 1995, s 228.
66 By way of either a compulsory treatment order or a compulsion order.

changes, which are then regarded as having been incorporated into the order. Where agreement cannot be obtained to a change of treatment, or where the doctor/psychologist considers that treatment for a period longer than that contained in the order is necessary he/she will report to the supervising officer and the supervising officer will then apply to court for variation of the order.

Restrictions on the movement of the offender for up to 12 months can be imposed. Where such a condition is made it will be supervised by remote monitoring.

Finally, as well as these conditions which the legislation specifically provides for, the social worker may recommend and the court may impose any other condition which it considers to be conducive to securing the good conduct of the offender and preventing re-offending. Examples of such conditions include refraining from association with known offenders or ex-offenders, refraining from specified behaviours like drinking, or participating in identified therapeutic or other programmes, such as motoring projects.

(d) Amendment, discharge or transfer of order

10.22 The order may be amended on the application of the offender or the supervisor. Any amendment cannot reduce the period of probation or extend it beyond the 3-year maximum and cannot extend the period of residence in a named place or of medical treatment beyond 12 months from the date the order was originally made.

If the offender moves, application may be made for transfer of the order to the new area either by the offender or by the supervisor. If the application is made by the supervisor the court must grant the application.

Either the probationer or the supervisor may apply for discharge of the order. Such an application may be considered after a review of the progress made by the probationer.

(e) Breach of order: failure to comply with conditions

10.23 Where the offender breaches any of the requirements of the order, for example, by unsatisfactory performance of work or failure to comply with instructions of the supervisor, breach proceedings before the court may be initiated. In deciding whether or not to initiate proceedings the supervisor should consider the seriousness of the breach and the reasonableness of the explanation for it offered by the offender. Less serious cases can be dealt with by way of a formal written warning, with the proviso that after two warnings the breach procedure should be initiated. Since there is some discretion in this process, it is imperative that social workers and their managers have considered and agreed criteria for the decisions taken. Clearly, these decisions are not taken lightly since the liberty of an individual is in jeopardy and so it is imperative that there be internal logic and consistency. This is unfortunately also necessary in view of a history of some social worker's therapeutic optimism and/or over-identification with the service user.

Breach proceedings are initiated by the supervisor applying to the court for a breach of probation. It is then up to the court to decide whether to take action against the offender. The court may then issue a warrant for the arrest of the offender or cite him/her to attend court. As in the case of the breach of supervised attendance orders, the evidence of one witness is sufficient in these proceedings. The precise details as to how breach proceedings are initiated are the subject of local agreements.

If the breach is proved or admitted the court may simply continue the order as it is, it may also: impose a fine up to level 3 (currently £1,000); revoke the order and sentence the offender for the original offence; vary the conditions attached to the order, providing that this does not extend the order beyond 3 years; or continue the order and impose, in addition, a community service order (CSO). Before this last option can be used the preconditions for imposing a CSO must be fulfilled (see below).

(f) Breach of order: commission of further offence

10.24 When an offender on probation commits a further offence during the life of the order, breach proceedings should always be initiated. In this case the powers of the court are to continue the probation order or to impose sentence for the original offence.

(6) Community service[67]

(a) Introduction

10.25 A community service order requires the offender to perform between 80 and 300 hours (240 in a summary court) of unpaid work (the average number of hours is around 140). The sentence should normally be completed within 12 months, though the order remains in force until the number of hours specified has been worked. If the hours are not

67 Community service orders are not available for offences committed after 1st February 2011. See paras 12.20–12.34.

completed within 12 months, application to extend that period will need to be made.[68] Before a CSO is used in a particular case, the court must have obtained a social enquiry report which includes an assessment of the offender's suitability for the community service scheme and of the suitability of the available work. In producing this report the community service scheme (that is, the body which administers community service, providing and supervising placements) must be consulted. The writer of the report should explain to the offender what a CSO involves so that he/she is in a position to consent to it.

Community service orders are seen by the relevant legislation explicitly as an alternative to imprisonment or detention;[69] in other words, they should be used only where the alternative is a custodial disposal and never as a net widener. They are available only to offenders over the age of 16 and count as a conviction.

(b) The order

10.26 In making the order the court must explain the purpose and effect of the order, the consequences of failure to comply with it, and the court's power to revoke and amend the order at the instance either of the offender or the supervisor. The consent of the offender to the order must be obtained and the order must specify the number of hours to be worked.

Following sentence the offender will be seen by a community service officer who will be employed by a social work department but may not be a qualified social worker. The community service officer will allocate a work placement and be responsible for supervision during the life of the order. There is a statutory requirement to avoid conflict as far as practicable with the offender's religious beliefs and employment or education. In addition, other factors are clearly relevant, for example any skills or impairment. Typically, the work will be in painting and decorating, gardening, cleaning and kitchen work or in sports and youth clubs and the beneficiaries will be people who are elderly or frail or community neighbourhood charities. Occasionally, the work will provide opportunities for the offender to learn new skills. Appropriate performance and behaviour standards will be set at the outset and work placements must be closely monitored to ensure that these are met. The offender must notify the supervisor at once of any chance of address or change in the times of work.

68 See *HMA v Hood* 1987 SCCR 63.
69 Criminal Procedure (Scotland) Act 1995, s 238(1).

(c) Breach

10.27 The procedures to be followed in the event of breach are considered in detail in Guidance. These envisage, in serious cases, a three-stage process of formal warning, final warning and breach proceedings. At the final stage an application is made to court to institute breach proceedings. The application must be accompanied by a report from the community service officer and then it is up to the court to decide on the institution of proceedings. As in the cases of breach of a probation order or a supervised attendance order, the evidence of one witness is sufficient. If the breach is admitted or established the court may continue the order with the possible addition of a fine up to level 3 (currently £1,000); vary the number of hours, provided that the total does not exceed 300 (240 for summary courts); or revoke the order and sentence the offender for the original offence. Since a CSO is to be used only in cases where otherwise a custodial disposal would be used, it will almost certainly be the case that the alternative sentence will be custodial.

(d) Revocation, amendment and transfer

10.28 Either the supervisor or the offender may apply for revocation or amendment of the order, and the court must grant the application if it appears to be in the interests of justice to do so having regard to changes in circumstances since the order was made. Examples would include prolonged illness or change in the offender's employment situation. The amendment may be to alter the number of hours or to extend the 12-month period in which the work is to be completed. In the case of revocation the court may simply revoke the order, or may revoke the order and substitute another sentence. Where the offender moves and there are facilities for community service in the new area, the offender or the supervisor may apply for a transfer of the order to the new area. If the application is made by the supervisor the court must grant the application.

(7) Compensation order[70]

10.29 A Compensation Order is designed to provide compensation to the victim of an offence for the loss caused to him/her. It can be imposed

70 Criminal Procedure (Scotland) Act 1995, ss 249–253.

in addition to or in place of any other penalty, except that no order can be made in conjunction with a probation order or an absolute discharge, and no order can be made when sentence is deferred. In assessing the amount of compensation to order the court must consider not only the victim's loss but also the offender's means, and in particular if it considers that it would be appropriate to impose a fine and a compensation order but the offender only has the means for the latter, a compensation order alone should be imposed. The sheriff court can award compensation up to £5,000, the JP Court up to £2,500 (level 4) and solemn courts an unlimited amount.

Payments made by an offender who is both fined and ordered to pay compensation will be applied first to the compensation order. The provisions as to enforcement and application for time to pay etc applying to fines are applied to Compensation Orders. In addition the offender can seek a review of the order if the victim's loss turns out to be less than that on which the award of the compensation order was calculated.

The award of a compensation order does not prevent the victim raising a civil action for damages against the offender. However, any award in the civil case will be reduced by the amount paid under the compensation order. Payment of the sum ordered is made to the clerk of the court who passes it on to the victim. Payments made by the offender will be counted towards a compensation order before any fine made at the same time.

(8) Deferred sentence

10.30 This is not strictly a disposal, but amounts to the court deferring sentence for a period of time. Adjournments to obtain reports are not deferments of sentence and the deferred sentence provisions cannot be used to avoid the time limits on such adjournments. Sentence is usually deferred for a longer period of 3, 6 or 12 months. A court may defer sentence, for example, for the offender to be of good behaviour during the period of deferment or to allow the offender to make reparation to the victim. In such cases the expectation is that if the condition attached to the deferment is fulfilled a lesser sentence will be imposed than otherwise. In addition, in some areas of Scotland structured deferred sentence schemes are available which involve a programme to be completed by the offender during the period of deferment. Where sentence is deferred in a case where a report has been prepared, the court will often ask for a supplementary report to be prepared for the deferred hearing and such a report will be required if the offender has participated in a structured deferred sentence scheme.

If the offender commits another offence during the period of deferment he/she may be brought before the court for sentence without waiting for the deferred date.

The time of deferral can be used constructively by the social worker and offender to identify and explore problem areas and evaluate the potential effectiveness of various disposals. Although sentence can be deferred, there is no provision such as exists in England and Wales for sentences to be suspended. Unlike a deferred sentence a suspended sentence involves the imposition of a sentence of detention, the effect of which is suspended for a fixed period and will be served only if the offender commits a further offence punishable by imprisonment during that period.

(9) Restriction of Liberty Orders

10.31 These can be imposed on anyone convicted of an offence punishable by imprisonment and require them either to be at a particular place at a particular time or not to be at a particular place at a particular time. The legislation has recently been amended to make it clear that this type of order is to be imposed as an alternative to a custodial sentence.[71]

Orders cannot impose requirements covering more than 12 hours per day and can last for up to 12 months. Remote monitoring of compliance is permitted. There are provisions allowing application to court for variation or amendment of the order. On breach of the order the court has the power to impose a fine up to level 3, amend the order or revoke the order and sentence for the original offence. It is clear from the background to this provision that there will be little or no social work involvement unless the offender is, concurrently with the order, subject to a probation order. The exception to this is where the Order is made in respect of someone under the age of 16. In this case the order cannot be made unless the court is satisfied as to the support and rehabilitation services the offender will receive from the local authority for the duration of the order.

71 Criminal Procedure (Scotland) Act 1995, s 245A, as amended by the Criminal Justice (Scotland) act 2003, s 50.

(10) Drug Treatment and Testing Orders[72]

10.32 The order can be made if the offender is dependent on, or has a propensity to misuse, drugs, if this dependency is treatable and if the offender is a suitable person to be made subject to this type of order.

The order requires the offender to submit to treatment for their drug addiction and to testing for a period between 6 months and three years. The court will appoint both a treatment provider and a supervising officer, the latter being a local authority social worker. The role of the supervisor is to keep track of the offender, provide court reports for the periodic reviews of the order, to liaise with the treatment provider and to take decisions on breaching or applying for revocation of the order. The offender must be tested at periods set by the court (though this cannot be more than once every month). The order must also be reviewed periodically by the court and, at least initially, the attendance of the offender is necessary. If the court is satisfied that satisfactory progress is being made then the offender's attendance can be dispensed with. Reviews have the power to vary or revoke the order. The order can be revoked on application of the supervisor or of the offender, and can be used in combination with a probation order and/or a restriction of liberty order. In addition movements of the subject of the order can be restricted for up to 12 months and the offender can be tagged to monitor this. Courts also have the power to impose a short custodial sentence (up to 28 days) or period of community service (up to 40 hours) for failure to comply with the requirements of a DTTO. In both cases the DTTO can be kept in force.

(11) Non-Harassment Order

10.33 'Where a person is convicted of an offence involving harassment of a person ('the victim'), the prosecutor may apply to the court to make a non-harassment order against the offender requiring him to refrain from such conduct in relation to the victim as may be specified in the order for such period (which includes an indeterminate period) as may be so specified, in addition to any other disposal which may be made in relation to the offence.'[73] Before a non-harassment order can be made, it must follow on from a conviction for an offence or offences involving harassment, this in turn requires a course of conduct, that is, conduct on at least two occasions. In order to set up this course of conduct it is not

72 Criminal Procedure (Scotland) Act 1995, ss 234A-234K.
73 Criminal Procedure (Scotland) Act 1995, s 234A.

permissible to look back over previous convictions.[74] The consequence of this appears to be that in order for a non-harassment order to be obtained the prosecutor will have to draw the charge(s) carefully to make it clear that the offences were directed against the person being harassed and that there were at least two incidents. Where a non-harassment order is not available the victim may have a remedy under the civil provisions of the 1997 Act or by way of interdict at common law.

(12) Antisocial Behaviour Order

10.34 Criminal courts have the power to make an antisocial behaviour order either instead of or in addition to any other sentence imposed on conviction. Before the power can be exercised the offence must have involved the offender engaging in antisocial behaviour and the order must be necessary to protect others from antisocial behaviour. The standard of proof to be satisfied in establishing the necessity for the order is the balance of probabilities. Once an order has been made it can be varied or discharged on the application of the offender made to the court which made the order. The only restriction on the powers of variation is that the order cannot be extended, though in the case of indefinite orders this will not be an issue. The case for variation or discharge has to be established on the balance of probabilities. Notification of the order has to be made not only to the offender, but also to the authority which the court considers most relevant. This need not be the authority of the offender's residence, but may be the authority for the area where it is likely that future antisocial behaviour will take place.

ALTERNATIVES TO PROSECUTION

(1) Procurator Fiscal Warnings

10.35 These are warnings given by the Procurator Fiscal. They can only be given when there is enough evidence to prosecute the recipient and where the offence is not so trivial that it should simply be ignored.

(2) Fiscal Fines

10.36 These allow a fiscal to make an offer of a fixed penalty in any case triable in the JP Court, subject to the exclusion in general of motor-

74 *McGlennan v McKinnon* 1998 SCCR 285.

ing offences. The limits on the jurisdiction of the JP Court are relatively generous, and about half of all prosecutions take place there. The level of fixed penalty which could be offered was originally £25, but this was altered in 2008. The fiscal can now offer a fixed penalty of £50, £75, £100, £150, £200, £250 or £300. A survey of the use of fines showed the main types of case to be (in descending frequency) breach of the peace, urinating to public annoyance, theft (usually shoplifting), trespass on railway lines, assaults, drunkenness at sports grounds and drunk and incapable[75]. If the offer is accepted then no conviction will be recorded against the individual. If the offer is not accepted, the individual will be prosecuted in respect of the offence, though acceptance of an offer within the previous two years will be disclosed if the individual appears in court charged with an offence.[76] Once accepted, a fiscal fine is similar to a fine imposed by a court as regards enforcement in the case of non-payment.

(3) Compensation Offer

10.37 The fiscal can make the offender an offer of paying compensation up to £5,000 to the offender.[77] If the offer is accepted within 28 days then liability to conviction is discharged. The offences where such an offer can be made are all offences which are triable summarily and where a court could make a compensation order.

(4) Setting aside of fixed penalties and compensation offer

10.38 The fiscal can set aside an offer of a fixed penalty or a compensation offer, even if the offer has been accepted. This can be done where new information comes to the attention of the fiscal and the fiscal considers that in light of this the offer should not have been made.[78]

(5) Conditional Offers of Fixed Penalty

10.39 These relate to certain motoring offences, and operate in the same way as fiscal fines except that the offer is made by the police.

75 P. Duff, *Fiscal Fines*, Scottish Office Central Research Unit, 1996.
76 Criminal Procedure (Scotland) Act 1995, ss 69(6)-(7), 101(9)-(11) & 116 (9)-(11).
77 Criminal Procedure (Scotland) Act 1995 s 302A, Criminal Procedure (Scotland) Act 1995 Compensation Offer (Maximum Amount) Order 2008, SSI 2008/7.
78 Criminal Procedure (Scotland) Act 1995, s 303ZB.

(6) Social work diversion

10.40 There are a large number of diversion schemes operating in Scotland which involve social work input. They generally involve diversion before prosecution. In other words, the person involved accepts some appropriate form of social work intervention, for example, to tackle an alcohol problem, as an alternative to prosecution. In some schemes the acceptance of social work intervention means that no prosecution will take place, while in others the decision not to prosecute is taken after assessing the outcome of the diversion. Questions abound concerning the difficulty of getting informed consent by the person either threatened with prosecution or having already begun the process of being prosecuted.

Individuals will normally be assessed by the social work department before being accepted for diversion. The role of the social worker is complex and contradictory with respect to this task, in that the worker is responsible for data collection and analysis under what are probably very stressful circumstances; for explaining the procedure to the service user; and for offering other appropriate social work services in supporting the service user and the family through what may well be a crisis. The existence of these schemes raises a number of important issues including concerns about net widening. In other words, there is the possibility that the existence of the scheme leads to intervention where previously there would have been no prosecution, or a warning letter would have been sent; and there are concerns about the types of case where diversion is appropriate, the most contentious being violent assault in the family.

COMPENSATION FOR CRIMINAL INJURIES

10.41 People who suffer personal injury as a result of violent crimes and are considered to be 'blameless' victims are entitled to claim compensation under the criminal injuries compensation scheme, which is administered by the Criminal Injuries Compensation Authority (CICA).[79] In considering applications the character of the applicant and any previous convictions are taken into account and this may result in a reduced award or no award being made. The crime which forms the basis for the claim need not have been established in a criminal court by a prior conviction. Awards are made on the basis of a tariff which sets a value against particular types of injury. Claims which would result in an

79 www.cica.gov.uk.

award of less than £1,000 will not be entertained. Claims must normally be made within 2 years of the event causing the injury, though claims outside the time limit may be permitted where it is still possible to investigate the claim and where it was not reasonable to expect an application to be made within the two year period, for example where the application relates to child abuse and the child could not report it until he/she became an adult.[80]

One specific area is the possibility of claiming compensation for child abuse. In some cases, where the child concerned is being looked after by the local authority, the social work department may be directly involved in assisting a child to make a claim under the scheme or may in fact be the object of the claim if the child was abused while being looked after by the local authority. In child abuse cases no award will be made in certain circumstances. First, in cases where the injury happened before October 2 1979 and the victim and person responsible for the injury were living in the same household. Second, if the guilty party would benefit from the award (as might happen if victim and perpetrator were once again in the same household). Substantial awards made to children will generally be placed in an interest bearing bank account until the child is 18, though payments from the account can be made for the sole benefit of the child or for her/his education or welfare. Young people aged 16 or 17 who are living independently may be paid any award directly.

CUSTODIAL DISPOSALS

(1) Imprisonment

10.42 Imprisonment is a disposal available only for those aged 21 or over. Where an offender has not previously been sentenced to imprisonment or detention the court cannot impose a sentence of imprisonment (except the mandatory life sentence for murder) without first considering information regarding the offender's character, circumstances and physical and mental condition (usually provided in a CJSWR). In addition, the court must consider that no other disposal is appropriate and, if it is a summary court, must state and record the reason for this opinion. Someone who has not previously been imprisoned must have had legal representation, unless legal aid was refused on financial grounds or, having been informed of the right to legal aid, the offender has not applied for it.

80 Though in such cases a report must be made as soon as is reasonably possible.

The maximum length of sentence may be restricted in the case of a statutory offence by the statute creating it. In other cases the limit will be the maximum sentence the court can impose. In the case of lay magistrates this is 60 days. For stipendiary magistrates and the sheriff summary court the limit is 12 months. The sheriff solemn court can imprison for up to 5 years, and has the power, rarely used, to remit a case to the High Court for sentence where its powers are inadequate. There is no limit on the period of imprisonment that can be imposed by the High Court.

Where an offender is convicted of two or more offences, sentences of imprisonment may be imposed which are concurrent or consecutive; if the latter, the terms of imprisonment follow on from each other. Courts' powers to impose consecutive sentences may be limited by their maximum sentencing powers: for example, a sheriff sitting in a summary court could not normally impose consecutive sentences which, when added together, exceeded 12 months. This limitation will not apply where the convictions are on separate complaints or indictments and arise from distinct incidents. When imposing a sentence of imprisonment or detention, the court must take into account any period of time which the offender has already spent in custody or on remand awaiting trial or sentence.

There are restrictions on the minimum length of a custodial sentence. Summary courts cannot impose a sentence of imprisonment less than fifteen days.[81]

It is generally agreed that it is hard to justify the present extent of the use of custodial measures in Scotland. The effectiveness of custodial sentences is questionable,[82] they are frequently for very short periods, and custody is very expensive compared to any other alternative. Social workers have a special opportunity, particularly in the current climate, to develop credible alternatives and to publicise these options to sentencers.

The law relating to release is dealt with in paras 10.46–10.52 below.

(2) Detention of young offenders

10.43 Offenders between 16 and 20 may be sentenced to detention in a young offenders institution. Young offenders are incarcerated in sepa-

81 Criminal Procedure (Scotland) Act 1995, s 206. See para 12.35 for the introduction of a presumption against custodial sentences of less than 3 months.

82 Scottish Prisons Commission, *Scotland's Choice* (2008).

rate institutions from adult offenders and there is a greater emphasis, where possible, on high standards of discipline and training. Reconviction rates and recidivism remain very high. Before sentencing an offender to detention the court must consider the same information as is appropriate in the case of an offender of 21 and over who is sentenced to a first term of imprisonment. The court must also be of the opinion, based on this information, that no other way of dealing with the offender is appropriate and, except for the High Court, must record the reason for this opinion. Offenders aged between 18 and 21 who are convicted of murder will be sentenced to detention for life rather than a period of imprisonment and will be transferred from a young offenders institution to a prison at some time between their 21st and 23rd birthdays. Other young offenders will also be transferred in the same way. Release is subject to the same rules as release from prison.

(3) Detention of children[83]

10.44 Custody may be used by the court either before trial or after a finding of guilt. Before trial or sentence a child under 16 will generally be remanded to a local authority and the court has the power to require detention in secure accommodation. For children of 16 or over the options are a remand centre, young offenders institution or, where the child is still subject to a supervision requirement from a hearing, committal to a local authority.

A child under the age of 18 who is convicted of murder is to be detained without limit of time in a place and on conditions specified by the Scottish Ministers with transfer to prison at the age of 21. Children under 16 convicted in a solemn court may be sentenced to detention, again in a place and on conditions determined by the Scottish Ministers.[84] Initially this is likely to be local authority accommodation with transfer then into a young offenders institution and then to adult prison. The sheriff summary court may impose sentences of detention in residential care for up to 12 months on offenders under 16 and in this case the care is provided by the relevant local authority, and it is up to it, not the court, to select the appropriate accommodation.[85] Children sentenced in this way are looked after children.

83 See also ch 5, pt 5. The numbers of children sentenced to detention are small: in 2008/9 only 21 were dealt with in this way.

84 Criminal Procedure (Scotland) Act 1995, s 208.

85 Criminal Procedure (Scotland) Act 1995, s 44; *B, Petitioner* 1992 SCCR 596.

The rules for release of children sentenced to a determinate sentence are similar to those applying to adult determinate sentence prisoners. Where a child is sentenced to detention at her majesty's pleasure release provisions are similar to those for life sentence prisoners.

Where a person under the age of 17½ and not subject to a supervision requirement is found or pleads guilty the court may refer his/her case to the reporter for advice. On receipt of this advice the court can then either dispose of the case itself or refer it back to the reporter for disposal.[86] Where a child is subject to a supervision requirement and is appearing in the sheriff court his/her case must be referred to the reporter for advice if under 16. The same requirement does not apply to the High Court, though this court has the power to make such a referral. Referral to the reporter will not be appropriate where the sentence for the crime the child has been found guilty of is fixed by law, this would include murder and certain penalties for road traffic offences.

(4) Social work in prison[87]

10.45 There are local authority social workers based in the prisons in Scotland with the general remit of providing a social work service to prisoners in need. The overwhelming fact of life for this work is that security is the primary objective of the host institution and all other considerations are subject to directives arising out of that factor. This manifests itself in practical problems, including arranging to interview prisoners; arranging for 'welfare visits' for prisoners with their families; communicating information to prisoners and receiving information from prisoners; and prison regimes restricting the time, timing and place for interviews. Other problems include working with the possibly very different value base, attitudes and assumptions of prison staff; working within an extremely hierarchically organised institution; and, possibly, working with one member of a family system which has been broken apart. Social workers should be familiar with the rules contained in the Prisons and Young Offenders Institutions (Scotland) Rules 2006.[88] These include rules about the reception of prisoners, health and welfare, communications and visits, work, education, recreation, discipline, requests and complaints, female prisoners, discharge and temporary release.

86 The court cannot partly dispose of the case itself, for example by imposing a disqualification from driving, and also remit the case back to the hearing for disposal, *McCulloch v HMA* 2005 SCCR 775.

87 See McNeill, F & Whyte, B, *Reducing Reoffending: Social Work and Community Justice in Scotland* (2007), ch 6.

88 SSI 2004/96.

Integrated Case Management will apply to offenders serving a custodial sentence.[89] This will involve prison based social workers and, in cases where the offender will be subject to supervision after release, a community based criminal justice social worker and will involve the exchange of relevant information between prison and community based workers as well as joint involvement in planning for release.

RELEASE FROM PRISON AND DETENTION

10.46 The provisions below in general apply only to prisoners convicted after 1 October 1993. Prisoners convicted prior to then will be subject to the previous regime of remission and parole. Treatment depends on whether the prisoner is a short-term prisoner (serving between 5 days and 4 years), a long-term prisoner (serving 4 years or more) or a life prisoner.

(1) Short-term prisoners

10.47 Short-term prisoners are to be released automatically on serving half of their sentence. This release may be subject to a supervised release order, but even if it is not if the offender may be returned to prison if he/she commits an offence before the term of imprisonment has expired. This can happen if he/she appears before a court which has at least the same level of sentencing power as the one which levied the original sentence and is convicted of an offence which is punishable by imprisonment. The court can order the balance of the sentence[90] still outstanding to be served, in addition to whatever other sentence is imposed. Special provisions apply in the case of prisoners who are sentenced to 6 months or more and who will be subject to the notification requirements of the Sexual Offences Act 2003. Such prisoners will not be released unconditionally, but will be released on licence after serving half of their sentence. The licence will last until the end of the sentence. Despite the lack, in most cases, of a licence requiring social work involvement, the ex-offender may, for the period of 12 months after release, request that the local authority provide advice, guidance

89 Scottish Executive/SPS/ADSW, *ICM Practice Guidance Manual 2007*.

90 Ie the period between the commission of the offence and the date on which the original sentence would have been completed if served in full. In most cases it will only be appropriate to return the offender to prison for part of this period.

and support and the local authority has a duty to do this.[91] In practice, this supervision would be provided by a social worker.

(2) Long-term prisoners

10.48 These prisoners are to be released on licence after completion of two-thirds of their sentence. Once half of the sentence has been served the prisoner is eligible to be considered for release on parole. Before the half way point the cases of prisoners eligible for parole are automatically referred to the Parole Board for Scotland, though prisoners can opt out of having their cases considered. The prisoner will be interviewed and a dossier is then prepared by the Scottish Prison Service, including a home background report prepared by a social worker in the area where the prisoner intends to live on release and a report from a prison based social worker which will include an action plan for work with the prisoner in the period leading up to and immediately after release.

The ideal model for the compiling of these reports would be if the field social worker who wrote the original social enquiry report for the court, if one was required, or who has been working with the family of the prisoner and has maintained a through-care contact with the prisoner is the person who now completes the home circumstances report. Difficulties typically arise when there has been a break in the contact between the prisoner and the person(s) with whom the prisoner proposes to live and/or misunderstandings have arisen between these panics. After all, families have learned to live without the prisoner and may appreciate the contribution of a social worker in helping them to clarify their thoughts and feelings about the prisoner's impending return to the community.

Most of the information in the dossier is disclosed to the prisoner who may comment on it. Information classified as 'dangerous information' may be excluded, but the prisoner must be told if information is not disclosed and must be given an account of the substance of this information. An example of 'dangerous information' is information which is likely to adversely affect someone's health, welfare or safety. The dossier then goes to the Parole Board which makes a recommendation to the Scottish Ministers as to whether the prisoner should be released on parole. A prisoner must be released if the Board recommends this. A prisoner released on parole is subject to a licence lasting until the end of the sentence.

91 Social Work (Scotland) Act 1968, s 27(1)(c).

Social work with a prisoner released on licence should always be based on a comprehensive systemic assessment of the individual and situation. There are, however, several special areas which must be considered. These include helping the individual to make sense of the new living environment which may have altered considerably in the absence of the prisoner. Practical problems usually take centre stage initially, such as arranging for the payment of benefits and finding accommodation. Relationships with others may have been strained beyond reparation while others may require much effort and understanding to rejuvenate. Finding work may be especially difficult. Former prisoners are generally very vulnerable to the problems associated with mass unemployment and deprivation and unless some of the problems which resulted in offending behaviour have been outgrown or resolved, they are likely to resurface relatively quickly. Here the support and guidance of a social worker can be invaluable.

(3) Life prisoners

10.49 All life prisoners must have a period of time specified as the 'punishment period' when they are sentenced.[92] Only after serving this period will the prisoner be eligible to be considered for release on licence, and this consideration (by the Parole Board) must take place as soon as possible after the expiry of the punishment period. Where the Parole Board recommends release the prisoner must be released.

(4) Compassionate release[93]

10.50 This provision is as it sounds and allows the Scottish Ministers to release any prisoner on compassionate grounds. These grounds are not defined in the relevant legislation but would include a serious long-term or terminal illness. Any prisoner released on compassionate grounds will be subject licence conditions.

(5) Release on licence

10.51 Where a prisoner is released on licence, the licence lasts until the expiry of the sentence imposed by the court (for life prisoners, until

92 Any life prisoner who did not have such a period fixed when originally sentenced has now had one fixed.

93 Prisoners and Criminal Proceedings (Scotland) Act 1993, s 3.

death). The licence will include standard conditions to the effect that the licensee must:

(a) report forthwith to the officer in charge of a named social work office;
(b) be under the supervision of an officer assigned by the local authority, in the case of life prisoners, this requirement for supervision can be removed 10 years after their release;
(c) comply with such requirements as that officer may specify for the purposes of the supervision;
(d) keep in touch with the supervising officer in accordance with that officer's instructions;
(e) inform the supervising officer of any change in residence or employment;
(f) be of good behaviour and keep the peace;
(g) not travel outside Great Britain without the prior permission of the supervising officer.

Further conditions[94] may be added to the licence on the recommendation of, or following consultation with, the Parole Board. The terms of the licence may be varied on application to the Parole and Life Sentences Division of the Scottish Government's Criminal Justice Directorate. Life prisoners remain on licence for life (though eventually all of the conditions attaching to the licence may have been cancelled), other prisoners are on licence until the date on which their determinate sentence would have been served in full, though the licence can be cancelled early. If the released prisoner breaches the licence conditions the licence can be revoked and he/she is returned to prison/detention. Revocation of the licence and recall to prison is initiated by the supervisor making a report to the Parole and Life Sentences Division. The supervisor has some discretion in deciding whether or not to initiate this process and in some cases the case will be dealt with by way of a warning letter.

Once a report has been made a decision will then be taken about whether or not to revoke the licence. In some cases a decision can be made by the Scottish Ministers to revoke the licence without consulting the Parole Board,[95] but normally the Parole Board must be consulted and must recommend revocation before the licence can be revoked. Where a licence has been revoked prior to consultation with the Board the case must be referred to the Board which has the power to order release.

94 Including a condition requiring remote monitoring, Criminal Justice (Scotland) Act 2003, s 40.

95 Where it is considered to be expedient in the public interest to do so and it is not practicable to await a recommendation from the Parole Board.

(6) Home Detention Curfew

10.52 This system allows a prisoner to be released home early on a number of conditions,[96] the most important of which is that they are subject to a curfew for at least 9 hours per day.[97] This curfew condition will be remotely monitored.

In order to qualify for release on Home Detention Curfew the prisoner must either be a short-term prisoner serving three months or more (and who has served at least four weeks of his/her sentence) or a long term prisoner whom the Parole Board has recommended be released on licence after serving half of his/her sentence. In both cases the prisoner must have served at least one quarter of their sentence before they can be released. In addition, release cannot take place more than 166 days[98] before the day which is 14 days before the half way point of the sentence, meaning that the effective maximum period on Home Detention Curfew is 180 days, with a minimum period of 14 days (as release cannot be in the 14 days before the half way stage of the sentence is reached).

Before release on Home Detention Curfew a risk assessment will be carried out, which will involve the social work department. The final decision on release will be taken by a Prison Governor on the basis of this risk assessment and taking account of the following factors:

(a) protecting the public at large;
(b) preventing re-offending by the prisoner; and
(c) securing the successful re-integration of the prisoner into the community.

(7) Commission of a further offence by released prisoner

10.53 A prisoner who commits a further offence before the date on which the sentence, if served in full, would have expired may be returned to detention for a period not exceeding the length of time between the date of commission of the offence and the date on which the sentence would have been served in full. Note that this applies whether or not

96 Mainly set out in the Home Detention Curfew Licence (Prescribed Standard Conditions) (Scotland) (No 2) Order 2008, SSI 2008/125, different conditions apply to the different categories of prisoner released on HDC.

97 Prisoners and Criminal Proceedings (Scotland) Act 1993, s 12AB.

98 Home Detention Curfew (Amendment of Specified Days) (Scotland) Order 2008, SSI 2008/126.

the released prisoner is on licence. Thus, a released short-term prisoner could be returned to serve the rest of the sentence under this provision.

(8) Supervised release orders

10.54 This is available to courts in respect of prisoners who are sentenced to between 12 months and 4 years imprisonment. In other words, it provides supervision on release of such prisoners who, as short-term prisoners, would normally be released unconditionally. Before an order can be made the court must be satisfied that it is necessary to protect the public from serious harm from the offender on release, a report must be obtained from the local authority, and the effect and consequences of the order must be explained to the offender by the court. The order requires local authority supervision and compliance with the requirements set out in the order and those reasonably specified by the supervising officer. The object of these requirements is to secure the good conduct of the offender or to prevent or lessen the possibility of further offending. The order can be for up to 12 months, provided that it cannot extend beyond the expiry of the period of imprisonment fixed by the court. The conditions in the order can be varied by the court on application by the offender or by the supervising officer.
On breach of a supervised release order, the court can order return to prison for a period equal to the period between the date of the breach and the end of the order or vary the order. The initiative for starting breach proceedings comes from the supervising officer and the evidence of one witness is sufficient to prove the breach.

(9) Orders for lifelong restriction

10.55 These are essentially indeterminate sentences. They can be made only if specified risk criteria are considered to be met after a risk assessment report has been produced in respect of the offender. The risk criteria are that the nature of, or the circumstances of the commission of, the offence of which the convicted person has been found guilty either in themselves or as part of a pattern of behaviour are such as to demonstrate that there is a likelihood that he, if at liberty, will seriously endanger the lives, or physical or psychological well-being, of members of the public at large.[99] Once such an order has been made a risk management plan must be made up for the offender which will cover work with the offender both in prison and following release. The Risk

99 Criminal Procedure (Scotland) Act 1995, s 210E.

Management Authority[100] was set up to provide accreditation for those who have to produce the risk assessment reports and to participate in the formulation of the plans. This type of order can only be made where a sexual offence, a violent offence or an offence endangering life has been committed or where the offender has committed an offence the nature of which, or circumstances of the commission of which, are such that it appears to the court that the person has a propensity to commit one of these offences.[101]

(10) Extended sentences

10.56 Extended sentences[102] can be passed if a number of conditions are fulfilled:

(a) the offender has been convicted of a sexual offence and the court intends to impose a custodial sentence; or
(b) the offender has been convicted of a crime of violence and the court intends to impose a sentence of more than 4 years imprisonment; and
(c) the court is of the opinion, after considering a report from a local authority officer, that an extended sentence is necessary to protect the public from serious harm.

An extended sentence is designed to provide for an extended period of supervision after release, and consists of two components. The first of these is the custodial term, that is a period of imprisonment or detention. The length of this will determine the date of release from this part of the sentence. Once the prisoner is released the further period of supervision (the 'extension period') begins. The beginning of this extension period depends on whether the offender was a short term or long term prisoner in terms of their custodial term. For short term prisoners the extension period begins on release, though it should be noted that they remain liable to be returned to prison until the date on which the whole of the original custody plus the extension period expires.

The maximum extension period for both crimes of violence and sexual offences is 10 years. The maximum extension period in a sheriff court is five years.

100 http://www.rmascotland.gov.uk/.
101 Criminal Procedure (Scotland) Act 1995, s 210 B.
102 Criminal Procedure (Scotland) Act 1995, ss 210A & 210B.

(11) Home Leave

10.57 Prisoners can be permitted periods of home leave, either in the course of their sentence or in the period running up to their release from prison.[103]

(12) Early release of children

(a) Children detained after sentence on indictment

10.58 Such children can be released on licence at any time on the recommendation of the Parole Board. A child sentenced to less than 4 years detention must be released on licence after serving half of the sentence; those serving 4 years or more must be released on licence after serving two-thirds of the sentence. A child who has been released on licence may be returned to detention on the commission of a further offence or have the licence revoked for breach of the licence conditions. Children sentenced to be detained without limit of time can be released on the recommendation of the Parole Board. The number of children involved is small.

(b) Children detained after sentence on complaint[104]

10.59 Such children are kept at a place determined by the local authority. The local authority has the same powers and duties in respect of the child as it does towards a child subject to a supervision requirement. The child may be released, either conditionally or unconditionally, at any time provided that a review has been carried out and after having regard to the best interests of the child and the need to protect members of the public. In any event, the child is entitled to be released after serving half of the period of detention, but the local authority may require the child to submit to supervision for the outstanding period of the sentence. Once released, the child may be returned to detention if a further offence is committed before the end of the originally imposed period of detention. As stressful as the arrangements for release are likely to be for adults and young adults, that pressure is likely to be considerably worse for the child and family going through similar processes. Social workers will already be involved in most of these situations and

103 See Scottish Executive Circular JD 1/2007, *Integrated Practice Guidance for Staff Involved in the Home Leave Process*.

104 Criminal Procedure (Scotland) Act 1995, s 44.

so can hopefully build upon established relationships to use this period constructively. Here again, the developmental stage and tasks and the particular influence of the child's peer group are liable to be relevant in the social worker's involvement as well as the re-establishment of viable familial relationships.

MANAGEMENT OF OFFENDERS

(1) Community Justice Authorities

10.60 The Management of Offenders (Scotland) Act 2005 introduced the community justice authority, to co-ordinate the provision of services to offenders across a number of local authority areas.

There are eight authorities covering Scotland, including a large authority covering the North of Scotland and the three Islands authorities. Each will have, at least, a chief officer and a small number of administrative staff. Their functions are both strategic, in terms of preparing a plan for services, and operational, they have the power to require action by individual authorities and may also take over directly the provision of certain services, both on behalf of local authorities and on behalf of the Scottish Ministers.

More specifically, their powers and duties are:

(a) Preparation of an area plan 'for reducing re-offending' by those to whom or in respect of whom criminal justice services are being provided. Local authorities are then under an obligation to carry out their functions in accordance with this plan.
(b) Monitoring the actions of the Scottish Ministers and local authorities in implementation of the plan.
(c) The power to give directions to a local authority where it considers that the performance of the authority in implementing the plan or in co-operating with others to implement the plan. Unlike the provisions noted below for the giving of directions by the Scottish Ministers to the community justice authority, there is no right of appeal by local authorities against directions made by the community justice authority. Where the same failings are observed on the part of the Scottish Ministers, recommendations can be made to them.
(d) Promotion of good practice.
(e) Allocation of certain grants and the ability to impose conditions on the use of these.
(f) To make arrangements for information sharing.

(g) To provide an annual report.
(h) To undertake any functions of a local authority or the Scottish Ministers which have been transferred it.

The authority also has powers of enforcement against individual local authorities. In addition to the criminal justice authorities there is also a specific duty on local authorities to cooperate, included within this is an obligation to share information.

(2) Sex Offender Notification

10.61 The Sexual Offences Act 2003 requires certain sex offenders to register with their local police force. There are fairly tight time limits for this registration. The duration of the requirement for registration will depend on the sentence imposed by the court for the offence. Once the offender has been registered, guidance indicates that he/she should be the subject of a risk assessment on the basis of which it may be necessary to develop a plan for managing that risk. The guidance indicates that such a risk management plan will be appropriate even if the offender is not subject to other forms of supervision, eg probation or a parole or non parole licence.

(3) Multi Agency Public Protection Arrangements

10.62 These arrangements currently apply to a limited range of individuals, in particular:[105]

(a) those subject to notification requirements as a sex offender;
(b) those who were prosecuted on indictment for an offence inferring violence, have been acquitted on the ground of insanity and have been made subject to a hospital order with a restriction order;
(c) those who have been prosecuted for an offence inferring violence but have been found to be insane in bar of trial; and
(d) those convicted of any offence who, by reason of that conviction are considered to be a person who may cause serious harm to the public at large.

In time this will be extended to those convicted on indictment of an offence involving violence and sentenced to probation or who will be subject to supervision on release from a custodial sentence.

105 Management of Offenders etc (Scotland) Act 2005, s 10(1).

In respect of these categories, what are described as the 'responsible authorities' in an area have the duty to establish arrangements for the assessment and management of the risks posed by someone who falls into one of these categories. The 'responsible authorities' are the Scottish Ministers, the chief constable, the local authority and the Health Board or Special Health Board. In establishing and implementing such arrangements duties of co-operation are placed on these authorities and on others, including social landlords, the Principal Reporter and remote monitoring providers. These statutory provisions are supplemented by extensive guidance.[106]

The arrangements made by the responsible authorities must be reported on annually. The arrangements will include the appointment of a MAPPA Co-ordinator or Co-ordinators in each criminal justice authority area, and the holding of regular meetings to manage cases which are to be managed either through MAPPA arrangements or through a Multi Agency Public Protection Partnership (MAPPP). Within these arrangements the authority which will be the lead authority for a particular offender will depend on that offender's status. If he or she is only subject to sex offender notification requirements it will be the police, if subject to local authority supervision it will be the local authority, for restricted patients it will be the health authority. Where an offender is subject to more than one requirement, for example being under supervision and subject to the notification requirement the responsibility will be shared between the relevant agencies.

A first stage in respect of any individual is to carry out an assessment[107] to determine the level of risk which he or she presents and to determine the level of management which he or she requires. There are three levels of risk management envisaged under the guidance and any decision as to the placement of an offender into one or other of these levels must be defensible.[108]

Level 1 is for those assessed as being of low to medium risk and who can be managed by one of the responsible authorities without significantly or actively involving others. Most offenders will fall into this category and will therefore be managed either by the policed or the local authority (or, as noted above, both together). The assessment of an offender as falling into this level must be notified to the MAPPA Co-ordinator

106 6 Scottish Government, *MAPPA Guidance* (version 4, April 2008), Circular CEL 19(2008), *Multi Agency Public Protection Arrangements: Extension of Management of Offenders (Scotland) Act 2005 to Restricted Patients: Health Service Guidance*.

107 See Scottish Government, *MAPPA Guidance* (version 4, April 2008), Annex E.

108 Scottish Government, *MAPPA Guidance* (version 4, April 2008), Part 3, para 3.

for the area. Offenders who fall into the last category of those currently covered by MAPPA arrangements cannot fall into this level because, by definition, they pose a significant risk to the public.

Those offenders assessed as requiring management at level 2 will require active involvement from a number of different agencies. The case must be referred to the MAPPA Co-ordinator who will then have to arrange the first of a series of meetings to manage the case within 20 days of the referral. These will involve representatives from all of the agencies with an active role to play in the management of the offender's case.

High risk offenders will be managed at level 3 through a Multi Agency Public Protection Partnership. Offenders will fall into this category if they either present a high or very high risk of serious harm and there is a need for close co-operation between agencies at a senior level in order to manage this risk or where there is a likelihood that there will be a high level of media scrutiny of, or public interest in, the management of a particular case. Level 3 is distinguished from level 2 largely by the seniority of the representatives of the various agencies involved. As with the other two levels, the case is referred to the MAPPA Co-ordinator, who must arrange an initial meeting within five days of the referral.

Offenders will be subject to these arrangements for a period determined by their reason for qualifying for such arrangements. This means that when qualification derives from being subject to sex offender notification requirements the arrangements will cease to apply when the offender is no longer subject to these requirements. Where the offender is subject to the arrangements because of a restriction order or because he or she is subject to local authority supervision, the arrangements will cease to apply when the order or supervision comes to an end. Those offenders who fall into the last category, ie category (d) above, will continue to be subject to these management arrangements for as long as they are assessed to meet the qualifying conditions.

MENTALLY DISORDERED OFFENDERS

(1) Assessment and Treatment Orders

10.63 An assessment order[109] can be made in respect of an offender who appears to have a mental disorder.[110] Such an order and can only be made once an accused has been charged and before the case has been

109 Criminal Procedure (Scotland) Act 1995, ss 52B–52J.
110 See para 8.8.

disposed of (eg by conviction or acquittal). The order may be applied for by the prosecution or can be made on the court's own initiative. The order must be supported by the evidence of one doctor and authorises detention and treatment for a period of 21 days. After an order is made a mental health officer (MHO) must be designated for the patient and the MHO must produce a social circumstances report unless this would serve little or no practical purpose.[111]

In the same circumstances as it is possible to make an assessment order it is also possible to make a treatment order,[112] though this requires two medical reports. The order authorises detention and treatment of the patient and will come to an end on the happening of a variety of events, for example passing sentence on the accused or making a compulsion or interim compulsion order. After an order is made a MHO must be designated for the patient and the MHO must produce a social circumstances report unless this would serve little or no practical purpose.[113]

(2) Post-conviction powers

(a) Compulsion and interim compulsion orders[114]

10.64 A compulsion order can be made following conviction of an offence other than murder which is punishable by imprisonment The grounds for making an order are similar to those for making a compulsory treatment order,[115] except that there is no requirement that the ability of the patient to take decisions is significantly impaired. Before making the order the court must consider a report from a MHO[116] and the order can authorise the same type of measure as a compulsory treatment order. Initially the order will last for six months, but it can be renewed for a further six months and then for further periods of twelve months. The processes involved in extension are similar to those which apply in the case of compulsory treatment orders except that the first continuation requires an application to be made to the mental health tribunal. A compulsion order cannot be combined with an interim compulsion order, a guardianship order, a sentence of imprisonment, a pro-

111 Mental Health (Care and Treatment) (Scotland) Act 2003, ss 231(1) & 232(b)(iii).
112 Criminal Procedure (Scotland) Act 1995, ss 52K–52S.
113 Mental Health (Care and Treatment) (Scotland) Act 2003, ss 231(1) & 232(b)(iii).
114 Criminal Procedure (Scotland) Act 1995, ss 57A–57D.
115 See para 8.17.
116 Scottish Executive, *Mental Health (Care and Treatment) (Scotland) Act 2003: Code of Practice*,(2005), vol 3, pt 1, ch 5, paras 32–44.

bation order, a community service order, a community payback order, a drug treatment and testing order; or a restriction of liberty order.

Where, following conviction, a compulsion order with a restriction order or a hospital direction would be an appropriate disposal for an offender the court may make an interim compulsion order. This order can be made if an assessment is needed to establish the availability of medical treatment for the patient and the likelihood of risk to him/her or to others without treatment.[117]

(b) Restriction order

10.65 A restriction order can be combined with a compulsion order where the court considers that this is necessary to protect the public from serious harm.[118] In deciding this it must consider the nature of the offence, the past history of the offender and the risk of reoffending related to the offender's mental disorder. If a restriction order is made the detention authorised continues indefinitely, with special procedures for review. When a review takes place the MHO must be consulted, the report following the review is sent to the Scottish Ministers and will be considered by the mental health tribunal, which in such cases will normally be chaired by a sheriff.

(c) Hospital directions and transfer and treatment directions

10.66 A hospital direction[119] is combined with a sentence of imprisonment where the offender is convicted on indictment. It means that the offender will initially be treated in hospital and then, when discharged from hospital, transferred to prison. Before a direction can be made the court must consider a report from a MHO. The direction is reviewed annually and making a direction triggers an obligation to produce a social circumstances report unless this would not serve any, or would serve little, practical purpose. If the offender is still in hospital at the end of the sentence of imprisonment he or she will be discharged unless other measures are taken to authorise continued detention.

117 Criminal Procedure (Scotland) Act 1995, ss 53–53D.
118 Criminal Procedure (Scotland) Act 1995, s 59, see also Scottish Government, *Memorandum of Procedure on Restricted Patients* (2010).
119 Criminal Procedure (Scotland) Act 1995, ss 59A–60A.

(d) Guardianship or intervention order

10.67 In cases other than those involving a conviction for murder a criminal court can make a guardianship[120] or intervention order.[121] The grounds for making such an order are the same as those set out in chapter 7.

(d) Remand for medical examination

10.68 Where a court requires further information regarding the physical or mental health of an offender, it has the power to order a remand for up to 3 weeks for medical examination. A condition of a remand for inquiry into the offender's mental condition will be that the offender must be examined by two doctors. If the remand is not in custody a condition as to residence may be imposed.

(3) Insanity in bar of trial or as a ground for acquittal[122]

10.69 If a court is satisfied that a person appearing before it charged with a crime or offence is insane so that the trial of that person cannot proceed or continue, then it must make a finding that this is the case; order an 'examination of facts'; and remand the accused to appear at that examination. The remand may be to a hospital (by way of a temporary compulsion order) if the accused is suffering from a disorder, there is treatment available that would prevent the disorder from worsening or alleviate the symptoms or effect of the disorder, and there would be a significant risk to health and safety if treatment was not provided. Evidence both of the disorder and the degree of disorder must be provided by two doctors.

The 'examination of facts' is a further court hearing, which can take the form of a continuation of the trial diet if that is the stage at which the order for it to take place is made. At this hearing the court has to decide two things. First, it must decide if it is satisfied, beyond a reasonable doubt, that the accused committed the offence. Secondly it must be satisfied, on the balance of probabilities, that there are no grounds for acquitting the accused. If the court decides that it is satisfied on both of

120 Criminal Procedure (Scotland) Act 1995, s 58.
121 Criminal Procedure (Scotland) Act 1995, s 60B.
122 Criminal Procedure (Scotland) Act 1995, ss 54–57.

these then it must make a finding to that effect. If it is not so satisfied the accused is to be acquitted.

Where a finding is made in these terms or where the accused is acquitted by reason of insanity at the time of the offence, the court has four options for disposal: a compulsion order with or without a restriction order; a guardianship order; a supervision and treatment order or no order.

(4) Supervision and treatment order[123]

10.70 This places the individual under social work supervision for a period of up to 3 years and requires the individual to comply with the instructions of the supervisor and to submit to treatment for the improvement of his/her mental condition. Before an order can be made the court must be satisfied that it is the most suitable way of dealing with the individual; that the person's mental condition is treatable and not such as to warrant the equivalent of a hospital or guardianship order; that the supervisor is willing to supervise; and that arrangements have been made for the treatment specified in the order. Before the order is made the effect of the order and the powers of the courts to review the order must be explained to the individual in ordinary language. There are provisions for amending and revoking the order, but no specific provision for alternative action in the case of breach of its terms.

(5) Detention of those acquitted

10.71 Where someone charged with an offence is acquitted (other than on the grounds of insanity at the time of the offence) the court can order their detention in a place of safety for up to 6 hours. Before this can happen the court must be satisfied, on the evidence of two doctors, that the person is suffering from a disorder, there is treatment available that would prevent the disorder from worsening or alleviate the symptoms or effect of the disorder, and there would be a significant risk to health and safety if treatment was not provided. Detention beyond the 6 hours would have to be authorised by an Emergency Detention Certificate or a Short Term Detention Certificate.

123 Criminal Procedure (Scotland) Act 1995, sch 4.

REHABILITATION OF OFFENDERS

10.72 All ex-offenders including parolees are subject to the stipulations of the Rehabilitation of Offenders Act 1974 which is a legislative attempt to enable ex-offenders to put their histories behind them. The main exceptions to the law are life imprisonment and sentences of more than 30 months. Once the period of rehabilitation is over, and this involves complex calculations for various sentences but is generally a period of 3, 5, 7 or 10 years which is halved if the offender was under 17 at the time of the offence, then the person is to be treated as if the offence had not been committed. 'Spent' convictions need not be disclosed in applying for jobs, making agreements for credit or insurance, or giving evidence in civil proceedings. There are certain exceptions to this which include the disclosure of an offence relating to children or of violence when applying to work for a social work department; when a fine for the conviction is outstanding; when a prohibition or disqualification (as in driving) is in effect for a period longer than the period during which the conviction is spent; and in circumstances where there has been royal intervention.

VICTIMS

(1) Victim statements[124]

10.73 These give victims of certain crimes the right to submit a statement to a court setting out the impact of the crime on them. The crimes involved include crimes of violence, sexual offences, crimes of indecency, housebreaking and racial motivated crimes.[125] The court will have to take the statement into account in sentencing. The statement must be disclosed to the accused and the victim may be questioned about it. The opportunity to make such statements is available in all solemn courts.

(2) Victim notification[126]

10.74 Victims of certain crimes,[127] particularly those involving violence or racial hatred and sexual offences are entitled to be notified of

124 Criminal Justice (Scotland) Act 2003, s 14.
125 Victim Statements (Prescribed Offences) (No. 2) (Scotland) Order 2009, SSI 2009/71.
126 Criminal Justice (Scotland) Act 2003, ss 16–17.
127 Victim Notification (Prescribed Offences) (Scotland) Order 2004, SSI 2004/411.

certain events involving the person found guilty of the offence. These rights only arise where the offender was sentenced to imprisonment for 18 months or more or for life. The victim is to be informed when the prisoner is released, dies, is transferred outside Scotland, is eligible for temporary release or has escaped. In addition the victim must be given the opportunity to make representations before a decision is taken to release the offender on licence. If release is recommended the victim must be notified of this.

Chapter 11

Professional regulation, responsibility and accountability

INTRODUCTION

11.1 There is a recognition that social workers are unique in the extent to which they are expected to be legally, organisationally and ethically responsible and accountable. These expectations do not sit neatly together, are often confusing or vague and may even be contradictory. Social workers also have a special set of responsibilities arising from the nature of the work undertaken and by virtue of the vulnerability of many service users. Legal responsibilities are generally concerned with minimum acceptable standards and will be dealt with below. Organisational responsibilities are context-dependent but often relate to the managerial requirements of large bureaucratic structures which are reliant upon conformity to policy and regulations. Ethical responsibilities complicate this picture further. Social workers have a commitment to service user empowerment and all that entails and yet remain accountable to both service user and employer while continuing to fulfil legal responsibilities.[1]

Nearly every day reports appear in the press about the activities of social workers and upon closer reading, it is clear that the term social worker is being used interchangeably with anyone working in the welfare and caring fields. This is confusing and reflects poorly on qualified social workers. Since the previous edition of this text was published the length of educational preparation for social workers has been increased and the Scottish Social Services Council established to accredit and register qualified workers as well as impose sanctions for unacceptable practice. Most social workers are employed by local authorities which are bureaucratic hierarchies with command structures which can be less than amenable to the requirements of relatively autonomous pro-

1 See BASW, *Code of Ethics for Social Work*, Scottish Social Services Council, *Code of Practice for Social Service Workers*. The latter requires that: 'As a social service worker you must be accountable for the quality of your work and take responsibility for maintaining and improving your knowledge and skills'.

fessional workers and within which individual workers must be provided with appropriate support and supervision in order to encourage and ensure good practice.

Most social workers would agree that financial gain was certainly not amongst their motivations for embarking upon a career in social work. In fact, most would argue that social work salaries are no reflection of the level of responsibility inherent in the work and the disparity is even more striking in residential social work. In spite of all of these factors, it has been suggested that social workers are unique in accepting a professional responsibility which is more in tune with their sense of moral responsibility than with the responsibility imposed on them by the law. We look below at the legal position regarding registration, accountability and liability.

REGISTRATION AND REGULATION

(1) Professional Regulation

11.2 All social workers,[2] as well as most others employed in social work and in the provision of care services, including those who work in (adult) care homes and residential child care workers, must be registered with the Scottish Social Services Council.[3] The requirement to register (and meet any required criteria) already applies to all social workers and certain other groups (for example, residential child care workers), but is in the process of introduction for some other groups, for example, support workers in care home services for adults.[4] In order to register, an applicant must satisfy requirements as to competence and qualifications, as well as being of good character.[5] Once granted, registration lasts for a fixed period at the end of which registration must be renewed. The fixed period is three years for social workers and for most other categories of registered worker it is five years. During this period of registration anyone who is registered must comply with the *Code of Practice for Social Service Workers* and must comply with requirements for continuing professional development.[6]

2 And student social workers.

3 Which also accredits educational provision leading to qualification as a social worker.

4 See http://www.sssc.uk.com/sssc/all-about-registration/what-are-the-timescales-for-registration.html.

5 Scottish Social Services Council, Registration Rules 2009B, supplemented by additional requirements specified for groups of workers other than social workers available via the Council's website, www.sssc.uk.com.

6 For established social workers this requires completion of 15 days of continuing professional development in every registration period.

Complaints about registered workers can be made to the Scottish Social Services Council. The Council has the power, ultimately, to remove a worker from the register following a conviction or following misconduct, which is defined as:

> conduct, whether by act or omission, which falls short of the standard of conduct expected of a person registered with the Scottish Social Services Council, having particular regard to the Code of Practice for Social Service Workers ...and the Scottish Social Services Council (Registration) Rules 2009B.[7]

Following a conviction or a complaint the Council must investigate and the person concerned will have a right to be heard and make representations. If misconduct is established the possible penalties include removal from the register, suspension from the register for a period of time, imposing conditions which must be fulfilled for the person's registration to continue,[8] and issuing a warning.

(2) Registration of Care Services

11.3 Before certain types of care services can be provided, the provider must register with the Scottish Commission for the Regulation of Care (SCRC) or, from 1 April 2011, with Social Care and Social Work Improvement Scotland (SCSWIS). Services which must be registered include child minders, support services, care homes, housing support services and adoption and fostering services.[9] It is also possible for a service provider which provides accommodation but would not otherwise need to be registered to apply for limited registration in order to allow the provider to make use of the provisions of the Adults with Incapacity (Scotland) Act 2000 relating to management of residents finances.[10] The requirement to register adoption and fostering services, and other services aside from field social work services extends to local authorities as well as to other providers. There are however some slightly different procedures applying to local authority adoption and fostering services and to other services which authorities are required to provide by a statutory duty and these cover both the process of application and

7 Scottish Social Services Council (Registration) Rules 2009B, r 2(1).

8 For example a requirement to undertake further training.

9 Regulation of Care (Scotland) Act 2001, ss 7 (requirement for registration) and 2 (definitions). From 1 April 2011 these will be replaced respectively by Public Services Reform (Scotland) Act 2010, s 59 and s 47 & sch 12.

10 See para 7.13.

enforcement action.[11] There are some exceptions to the requirement to register specific services, these apply where the service is provided informally (for example care within a family) or by the National Health Service.

Applicants to register a service must satisfy the SCRC (or SCSWIS) as to their fitness to run the service and as to the fitness of the premises from which the service is to be provided. In considering the application SCRC (or SCSWIS) will take into account the applicable National Care Standards[12] and any other regulations relevant to the provision of the service. An application may be granted as applied for, it may be refused or it may be granted subject to conditions. In the last two cases the applicant must be notified of the proposed decision and given an opportunity to make representations before a final decision is made.

If an application for registration is granted the registered service provider must comply with a variety of regulations.[13] These cover matters such as the fitness, qualifications and registration of staff employed to provide the service and as to staffing levels and record keeping. Services must also be provided in accordance with any applicable National Care Standards. Registered services are subject to periodic inspection, with the period between inspections being different for different types of service. Inspection is currently based on a self-assessment prepared by the service provider followed by a visit from a member of SCRC staff. After the inspection a report will be prepared which will also contain a grading for the service. The report may impose requirements on the service provider, which can lead to the imposition by SCRC of conditions (or additional conditions) on the service provider.

Deficiencies in service can be addressed in a variety of ways. As we have seen, if these come to light in an inspection it is possible to impose conditions on the service provider, a similar possibility exists, as will be noted below, if investigation of a complaint brings deficiencies to light. A further step which can be taken is the service of an improvement notice on the provider, which requires the provider to make a significant improvement in the service, the nature of this improvement is set out in the notice. The consequences of failure to comply with an improvement notice

11 See Regulation of Care (Scotland) Act 2001, part 2. From 1 April 2011 this will be replaced by Public Services Reform (Scotland) Act 2010, part 5, ch 4.

12 There are 23 of these standards and they cover, for example, care homes, care provided at home, adoption services and fostering services. They can be accessed here: http://www.scotland.gov.uk/Topics/Health/care/17652/National-Care-Standards-1-1.

13 Regulation of Care (Requirements as to Care Services) (Scotland) Regulations 2002, SSI 2002/114.

depend on the type of service involved. Where a notice is served on a local authority in respect of an adoption or fostering service or another service which the authority is required by statute[14] to provide and the authority fails to make the required improvements, a report can be sent to the Scottish Ministers who have the power to require the authority to take corrective action. In other cases failure to make improvements can lead to a proposal being made to cancel the registration of the service, though there is no clear alignment between the grounds for serving an improvement notice, failure to comply with a notice and the grounds for cancellation of registration.[15] A proposal to cancel registration can be made where someone has been convicted of one of a number of offences in relation to the service[16] or the service is being or has been carried out in a way which is not in accordance with any requirements made by SCRC (or SCSWIS) or with a condition of the registration or the requirements of any regulations applying to the registered service. After a proposal to cancel registration has been made, the service provider must be given an opportunity to make representations in writing before the SCRC (or SCSWIS) decides whether or not to implement the proposal. Where no representations are made the registration must be cancelled unless SCRC (or SCSWIS) consider that it is not appropriate to do so.

In emergencies SCRC (or SCSWIS) can apply to the sheriff for cancellation of the registration of a service. Such an application may only be granted if it appears to the sheriff that there is a serious risk to life, health or well-being unless the order is made.

Registration may also be cancelled by the service provider applying for such cancellation, but any application for cancellation must set out what arrangements are being made to ensure that services continue to be provided to current users of the registered service.

Finally, it is a condition of registration that a registered service provider has in place a complaints procedure for dealing with complaints about their services. Complaints about registered services can also be made directly to SCRC (or SCSWIS) (and will trigger a fast track process in some cases[17]) and the SCRC (or SCSWIS) has a complaints procedure for dealing with complaints about its own operation. Follow-

14 But not other services which the authority may provide, but which there is no statutory duty to provide.

15 *Hastie v SCRC* 2006 SLT (Sh Ct) 14.

16 That is any offence under the legislation governing registration or any other offence which the SCRC considers makes it appropriate to cancel registration.

17 This will be used where the complaint involves (a) allegations of abuse or neglect; (b) conduct which may be a criminal offence; (c) serious malpractice; or (d) present or potential risk to service users.

ing investigation of a complaint about a service provider, a number of options are available if the complaint is upheld. Recommendations can be made for improving the service, conditions can be imposed on the provider (or existing conditions varied), the provider can be required to prepare an action plan for improvement, or an improvement notice can be served. If a complaint about a service not provided by a local authority is upheld there is no requirement that the authority is notified of this, though SCRC has undertaken to notify authorities of the outcome of any compliant made by the authority and of any complaints triggering the fast track procedure.

(3) Inspection of Social Work Services

11.4 Inspection of Social Work Services is currently undertaken partly by the Social Work Inspection Agency (SWIA) which carries out reviews of local authority social work services every three years, and which may also be asked to investigate specific events or issues and has, in the past produced themed reports, for example on social work services in the criminal justice system. SWIA has also produced some practice guidance.[18] Children's services are inspected by the Services for Children Unit HM Inspectorate of Education. This body and the SWIA become part of Social Care and Social Work Improvement Scotland on 1st April 2011.

(4) Protection of Vulnerable Groups

11.5 A new scheme is introduced in 2011 designed to protect particular groups from those who are not suitable to work with them. It derives from the Bichard Inquiry[19] and replaces the existing provision for those working with children.[20] From the end of February 2011 anyone undertaking regulated work with children or with protected adults must be a member of the Protection of Vulnerable Groups Scheme which will be administered by Disclosure Scotland.[21] This requirement will only apply when the normal duties of the person involve this type of work (see Box 1[22]). 'Work' includes unpaid work

18 For example, *On the Record – Getting it Right: Effective Management of Social Work Recording* (2010).

19 Bichard Inquiry Report, HC 653 (2004).

20 Protection of Children (Scotland) Act 2003.

21 These requirements do not mean that disclosure or enhanced disclosure may not be required for other types of work.

22 Derived from Disclosure Scotland, *Protecting Vulnerable Groups Scheme Guidance for Individuals, Organisations and Personal Employers* (June 2010), ch 2, paras 79–83.

and the provision of foster care, though work done for an individual in a family setting or in the course of a personal relationship is not covered.[23] 'Regulated' work is defined separately for children and adults[24] by reference to activities, e.g. caring for adults or children, establishments, e.g. a children's home or a care home for adults and by reference to positions, e.g. being a foster carer of the chief social work officer. A child is anyone under the age of 18[25] and protected adults are individuals over the age of 16[26] who are being provided with a range of services, including community care services and welfare services (i.e. services which provide support, assistance, advice or counselling top individuals with particular needs) which fulfil a number of additional requirements, the effect of which is that almost all social work with adults will be with protected adults.[27]

Box 1: Normal duties

The concept of normal duties is extremely important in limiting the scope of regulated work. For an activity or work in an establishment to be regulated work, the carrying out of the activity or the work in the establishment must be part of the individual's normal duties.

Normal duties can be considered as something the individual might be expected to do as part of their post on an ongoing basis, for example appearing in a job description. Normal duties exclude one-off occurrences and unforeseeable events.

No particular frequency for undertaking the work or duration of work are specified in the Act as these will depend on the context.

23 Protection of Vulnerable Groups (Scotland) Act 2007, s 95.

24 Protection of Vulnerable Groups (Scotland) Act 2007, schs 2 & 3. A self-assessment tool is available here: http://www.disclosurescotland.co.uk/pvg_training/self-assessment/.

25 Protection of Vulnerable Groups (Scotland) Act 2007, s 97(1).

26 So that a 17 year old may be both a child and a protected adult.

27 The additional requirements are that the service (a) is provided in the course of work to one or more persons over the age of 16; (b) is delivered on behalf of an organisation; (c) requires training to be undertaken by the person delivering the service; (d) has a frequency and formality attached to the service; and (e) either, (i) requires a contract to be agreed between the service provider and the recipient of the service prior to the services being carried out; or (ii) is personalised to an individual's needs. (The Protection of Vulnerable Groups (Scotland) Act 2007 (Prescribed Services) (Protected Adults) Regulations 2010, SSI 2010/161, reg 5).

An activity or work is likely to be 'normal duties' when:

- it appears in an individual's job description, task description or contract (but these should not be manipulated to stretch the boundary of the PVG Scheme);
- it can reasonably be anticipated; or
- it occurs regularly.

An activity or work is unlikely to be 'normal duties' when:

- done in response to an emergency (unless by an emergency worker);
- arranged at the last minute to stand in for sickness or other unexpected absence of another worker; or
- done as a one-off activity of short duration which is not part of the individual's normal routine or occupation.

The new statutory framework also provides for the keeping of two lists, one for adults and one for children, of people who are unsuitable to work with that group. People who appear on these lists will be barred from undertaking regulated work with children (if they are on the children's list) or protected adults (if they are on the adults list) or both (if they are on both lists). Listing will take place after a referral to Disclosure Scotland by a court following either a conviction for a relevant offence[28] or a conviction for another offence where the court considers that it would be appropriate for the person to be listed.[29] Referrals must also be made by employers where disciplinary action is taken against an individual (or would have been taken if the person had not left employment) on the basis of causing harm to a child or protected adult, putting such a person at risk of harm or engaging in inappropriate sexual conduct with such a person.[30] In addition, referrals can also be made by professional bodies including the Scottish Social Services Council.[31] Where a referral is made Disclosure Scotland must consider whether to list the individual concerned if the referral is from a court following conviction of a relevant offence, in other cases it must consider whether to list in cases where the referral was not made for vexatious or frivolous

28 These are set out in sch 1 of the 2007 Act and are all offences involving children, including sexual offences, cruelty and neglect.
29 Protection of Vulnerable Groups (Scotland) Act 2007, s 7.
30 Protection of Vulnerable Groups (Scotland) Act 2007, ss 2 & 3.
31 Protection of Vulnerable Groups (Scotland) Act 2007, s 8.

purposes and where the information in the referral indicates that listing may be appropriate.[32] Information obtained as a result of routine vetting of a Scheme member may also suggest that listing should be considered. Where listing is being considered, the individual involved has a right to make representations (and consideration for listing does not in itself prevent them continuing to work) and there is a right of appeal against a decision to list and a right to seek removal from the list.

THE LEGAL FRAMEWORK FOR LIABILITY AND ACCOUNTABILITY

11.6 People who are unhappy about social work decisions or actions may seek either to claim compensation for any harm they claim to have suffered as a result[33] or to challenge the decision or course of action. If they are seeking compensation, the normal way of doing this is by claiming breach of a legal duty. If they are seeking to challenge the decision, there are a variety of avenues open to them: complaints procedures; a complaint to the Scottish Public Services Ombudsman; or judicial review.

(1) Breach of duty

11.7 The breach claimed may be breach of a statutory duty by an authority. Success in such a claim is difficult. The claimant has to establish that the statute was designed to protect a limited group of people of which the claimant is a member and, more importantly, that the terms of the Act in question indicate a clear intention to create a right to claim compensation for breach of a duty. The existence of other forms of redress and the wide discretion usually conferred on authorities make proving this second element difficult. In the context of child care there is an especial reluctance to interfere with the performance of authorities' statutory duties.

Breach of a common law duty of care may also be claimed. It may be argued that the authority itself owes a duty of care to the affected individual or it may be argued that the individual worker owes the duty. Where the worker owes a duty and is doing what he/she is employed to

32 Protection of Vulnerable Groups (Scotland) Act 2007, s 10.
33 The harm may involve physical harm, damage to property or psychological harm.

do,[34] the doctrine of vicarious liability makes the employer liable for any damage caused by an employee's breach of duty.

In general terms, you will owe a common law duty of care if:

(i) loss to the injured person is a foreseeable consequence of your actions (this may include inaction or giving advice);
(ii) the relationship between you and the person suffering the loss is close enough to give rise to a duty of care; and
(iii) it is just and reasonable to impose a duty of care in all the circumstances of the case.[35]

Once the existence of a duty of care is established, it is fulfilled by taking reasonable care in the circumstances and liability is restricted to those harmful consequences which are foreseeable if this standard is not achieved and which can be clearly said to follow from the breach of duty.[36] For professionals, the standard will be the standard of a reasonably competent member of the profession.[37] Following common practice will usually be enough to meet the standard of care required, but it should not be assumed that it will automatically do so, nor should it be assumed that departing from common practice will, in itself, amount to negligence. Departures will be acceptable where they are reasonable in the circumstances. Breach of this common law duty has formed the basis of a number of cases that we will look at below.

One potential difficulty is that claims for personal injury (physical or psychiatric) must in general be brought within three years of the injury occurring, though in the case of children this period does not start until after the child reaches the age of 16.[38] This has been an issue in cases involving historic child abuse, which may have occurred years, if not decades, before any legal action is raised. Such cases may be able to go

34 Though the vicarious liability of the employer can extend beyond any reasonable description of what the employee's role might involve, particularly in cases involving abuse in residential care, *Lister v Hesley Hall Ltd* [2001] UKHL 22, *Gorrie v Marist Brothers* 2002 SCLR 436, *J v Fife Council* 2007 SLT 85.

35 *Caparo Industries plc v Dickman* [1990] 1 All ER 568. See also *Mitchell v Glasgow City Council* [2009] UKHL 11.

36 See, for example, *Lambert v Cardiff City Council* [2007] EWHC 869 (QB). Various breaches of duty were established but were held not to have caused the loss suffered.

37 Though various inquiries into cases of child abuse reveal recurring failures of the same, or a similar, type, see for example, Laming, *The Protection of Children in England: A Progress Report* (2009), 2008–9 HC 330, ch 1. Another way of looking at this requirement is to say that practice must be evidence based and must learn from research, experience and the findings and proposals of various inquiries.

38 Prescription and Limitation (Scotland) Act 1973, s 17.

ahead as the court has the power to allow a claim made outwith the three year period to proceed if it would be equitable to do so.[39]

There is almost no Scottish case law in this area; most of the cases referred to are therefore English. It is likely, however, that Scottish courts would reach similar conclusions.

Finally, a claim may be made that a local authority has failed in its duty to act compatibly with those rights set out in the European Convention on Human Rights which were incorporated into UK law by the Human Rights Act 1998.[40] Fulfilment of this duty is unlikely to require a standard of performance different to that required by the common law duty of care. Claims under the Human Rights Act must be made within one year of the date on which the act of the local authority which is complained about took place, though the court has the power to allow a claim made outwith the one year period to proceed if it would be equitable to do so.[41]

(2) Judicial review[42]

11.8 As we have already seen, judicial review offers a means of challenging decisions made by local authorities. Sometimes the consequence of a successful application for review will be that a local authority is directed to act in a particular way. On other occasions the decision of the authority will be set aside and will have to be taken again, often with a strong hint from the court about what the new decision should be. It is not, in general, possible to claim compensation in judicial review proceedings and applications may be refused where there are other remedies available, most notably, in this context, the complaints and representations procedure.[43]

An applicant for judicial review must argue that there has been a defect in the decision-making process rather than simply arguing that the decision is wrong, and the grounds for such arguments are relatively restricted. They can be categorised in a variety of ways. One common approach sets out three categories:

39 Prescription and Limitation (Scotland) Act 1973, s 19A, *B v Murray (No 2)* [2008] UKHL 32.
40 Human Rights Act 1998, s 6(1).
41 Human Rights Act 1998, s 7(5).
42 See para 1.59.
43 See *R v Birmingham City Council, ex parte A* [1997] 2 FLR 841.

(i) The authority has acted *ultra vires;* it has, in other words, done something which it has no power to do. This may involve exercising a power which it is not entitled to or reaching a decision in a way in which it is not entitled to.
(ii) There has been a breach of the requirements of natural justice. Briefly, these require decision-makers to be impartial and to give people likely to be affected by a decision the right to put their point of view before the decision is taken.
(iii) The authority has acted unreasonably. Examples of this might include taking into account things which were irrelevant to the decision or failing to take into account something which they were required by law or by guidance to take account of.

Following the implementation of the Human Rights Act 1998, the court may take into account human rights considerations in determining an application for judicial review and an application for judicial review may be based on a claimed human rights infringement.[44]

(c) Other remedies

11.9 Aside from court action, there are two other remedies which can be used by people unhappy with social work services. One is to use one of the variety of complaints procedures which exists. Each local authority is required to have and which deals with complaints about all types of social work services.[45] In addition, complaints about social workers (and others employed in providing social care who are registered) can be made to the Scottish Social Services Council. Registered providers of care service must have own complaints procedures and complaints about them can also be made to the Scottish Council for the Regulation of Care. The other is the Scottish Public Services Ombudsman.[46] The Ombudsman can deal with complaints about decision-making or administration[47] by the authority or about the failure to provide a service or the quality of any service provided. Investigations can only take place, however, when the person making the complaint has sustained injustice or hardship as a result of the authority's performance. Complaints about a local authority can be made direct to the Ombudsman, though in general complaints cannot be investigated if the

44 Human Rights Act 1998, s 7.
45 See para 1.60.
46 http://www.spso.org.uk/.
47 A number of complaints about social work involve failure to follow correct procedures in transferring files where a service user moves to a new area and failure to do this in a reasonable time, see, for example *Case 200701327: Renfrewshire Council.*

person complaining has not used the council's complaints procedure or some right of recourse through an appeals procedure. Once a complaint is accepted, it will be investigated. Initially this may take the form of an informal approach to the local authority and many complaints are resolved informally. If there is no resolution an investigation will be carried out and a report produced a copy of which is given to Scottish Ministers and laid before the Scottish Parliament. This may recommend action on the pan of the authority and may recommend the payment of compensation to someone who has suffered as a result of what the authority did. Councils are not bound to follow the recommendation of the Ombudsman, though in practice most do, and the Ombudsman has no power to force them to comply.

BREACH OF DUTY

(a) Child Care and Child Protection

11.10 It is clear that local authorities have certain statutory duties in respect of child protection and certain duties towards children who are being looked after by them. If they fail in these duties, what remedy does the injured party have?

In the context of child protection there are two possible types of failure. The authority may have failed to intervene appropriately with the result that a child was harmed, or the authority may have intervened inappropriately, also causing harm to a child and to his/her parents. Both of these possibilities came before the House of Lords when they dealt at the same time with the cases of *X (minors) v Bedfordshire County Council* and *M (a minor) v Newham London Borough Council* (the X and M cases).[48] In these cases, children who claimed to have been harmed respectively by under and over intervention sought to claim damages from the authorities responsible. They set out three grounds for their claim.

First, they argued that there had been a breach of the duties imposed by statute on the authorities. This argument was rejected on the grounds that the statute involved did not confer a clear right on children to claim damages if duties were not complied with. All of the statutory provisions concerned were in general terms and conferred considerable discretion on local authorities.

48 [1995] 2 AC 633.

Secondly, they claimed that the local authority owed them a common law duty of care. Although it was accepted that the first two requirements for such a duty which were noted above applied, the claimed duty was rejected on the grounds that it was not just and reasonable to impose a duty on the authority. A variety of policy reasons were put forward for this, most of them, it must be said, highly contentious and speculative.[49] Amongst these were the arguments that allowing liability would give rise to defensive practice; that resources would be diverted from child care to fighting compensation claims; that the decisions involved were very difficult and delicate (since they involved interfering between parent and child) and the courts should not intrude; that there were other remedies available by way of judicial review and the complaints process; and that imposing liability only on the local authority would be unfair because of the multidisciplinary approach taken to children at risk.

Finally, it was argued that the authorities were vicariously liable for the actions of their employees. For this to be the case it would have to be established that the workers owed the children a duty of care. It was held that they did not; the children were not clients of the workers; and that the workers' job was to provide a report for the local authority. The position of the worker was likened to that of a doctor who carries out an examination to provide a report for an insurance company. Such a doctor owes a duty of care to the company, but not to the person examined.

The outcome of this case was quite clear: social workers and local authorities could not be liable for decisions they take in child protection; they could not be liable because they owe children no legal duty of care.

Following the decision of the House of Lords, the children who had claimed that the local authority had a duty to remove them from home applied to the European Commission on Human Rights claiming that their human rights as set out in the European Convention on Human Rights (ECHR) had been infringed by the failure to remove them. The outcome was a finding that the conditions in which the children were living amounted to inhuman and degrading treatment and that the local authority was in breach of its duty under Article 3 of ECHR in failing to remove them.[50] In light of this the position of the courts in the UK has changed and it is now recognised that there is a common law duty of

49 T Guthrie, 'Legal Liability and Accountability for Child-care decisions', (1998) 28 BJSW 403.

50 *Z v United Kingdom* (2001) EHRR 97.

care owed to children in respect of decisions to remove them from their parents[51] as well as in respect of decisions and actions after removal and while the child is being looked after by the local authority, for example decisions about placement and about return to the child's family.[52] This common law duty runs alongside the possibility of a claim being made that a local authority has not acted consistently with the child's human rights.

Although the position has changed in respect of children, there is no duty of care owed to the parents of a child (or anyone else) who is suspected of child abuse. This issue has arisen in cases where a local authority (often acting on medical advice) has taken action on the basis that a child has been abused only for it to be found subsequently that there has been no such abuse.[53] In such cases it has been held that no duty is owed by the local authority to the parent or other alleged abuser on policy grounds.[54] These are said to arise from a conflict of interest between the child and the suspected parent (or other abuser). Based on this it is considered that imposing a duty to the suspected parent, for example a duty to avoid causing psychiatric harm by concluding that he or she had abused the child, would have an impact on the duty owed to the child:

> If the doctor[55] is to be held liable in law for any injury to the parent occasioned by the taking of his child into care, that can only be because the doctor, in fulfilling his primary duty to safeguard the child against abuse, also owed the parent a separate duty to take account of his, the parent's interest, in not being unreasonably suspected of child abuse. I find it impossible to see how such a duty could fail to impact upon the doctor's approach to his task and create a conflict of interest. Of course, if he acts within the bounds of proper professional skill and care he is liable to no one. But if he were to act negligently he would know that whereas a negligent non-diagnosis of child abuse would expose him to liability only to the child, a neg-

51 See, for example, *NXS v London Borough of Camden* [2009] EWHC 1786.

52 *Barrett v Enfield London Borough Council* [2001] 2 AC 550; *Pierce v Doncaster Metropolitan Council* [2007] EWHC 2968 (QB).

53 For example where broken bones appear initially to be the result of a non-accidental injury but subsequently it is established that they result from brittle bone disease.

54 *J D v East Berkshire Community Health NHS Trust* [2005] UKHL 23, *Fairlie v Perth and Kinross Healthcare NHS Trust* 2004 SLT 1200, *AD & OH v Bury Metropolitan Borough Council* [2006] EWCA Civ 1, *Lawrence v Pembrokeshire County Council* [2007] EWCA Civ 446, and, *B Reading Borough Council & Ors* [2007] EWCA Civ 1313.

55 It is accepted by the courts that the same principles apply to social workers.

> ligent diagnosis based on suspicions unreasonably held would render him liable also to the parent.[56]

It has also, however, been noted (though without altering the application of the rule) that:

> The fact that there is such a conflict in this context does not mean that social workers cannot have regard to both conflicting interests and yet behave professionally. But it does not follow that, in acting professionally they owe a duty of care to each interest....[57]

The lack of a remedy by way of a common law duty of care does not, however, mean that parents (in particular) may not have a claim against the local authority under either Article 6 or Article 8 of the ECHR, based either on defective procedures or on an unwarranted interference with the enjoyment of family life.[58] In two cases the European Court of Human Rights has upheld claims that parents' Art 8 rights were infringed, though it has noted that:[59]

> The Court would reiterate that mistaken judgments or assessments by professionals do not per se render child-care measures incompatible with the requirements of art.8 . The authorities, medical and social, have duties to protect children and cannot be held liable every time genuine and reasonably-held concerns about the safety of children vis-à-vis members of their families are proved, retrospectively, to have been misguided.

In one case the infringement resulted from a failure to carry out a fuller investigation recommended by a review of the case[60] and in the second from a failure to carry out a proper assessment and to intervene in a less intrusive way.[61] Both cases also involved a finding by the Court that there was a breach of the Convention because the parents had no effective remedy as a result of the policy exclusion of such claims. This

56 *J D v East Berkshire Community Health NHS Trust* [2005] UKHL 23, *per* Lord Brown at para. 129.

57 *Lawrence v Pembrokeshire County Council* [2007] EWCA Civ 446, *per* Auld LJ at par 52.

58 The potential for this was recognised in *RK & AK v United Kingdom* (2009) 48 EHRR 29, though the claim that Art 8 had been breached was not upheld. The applicants in this case were the claimants in *J D v East Berkshire Community Health NHS Trust*. The claim arises because if Article 8 has been infringed the local authority will be in breach of its duty under s 6 of the Human Rights Act 1998 not to act in a way which is incompatible with a Convention right.

59 *RK & AK v United Kingdom* (2009) 48 EHRR 29, para 36.

60 *MAK & RK v United Kingdom* (2010) 51 EHRR 14.

61 *AD & OD v United Kingdom* (2010) 51 EHRR 8 following on from *AD & OH v Bury Metropolitan Borough Council* [2006] EWCA Civ 1.

is no longer likely to be the case since, as noted, the parents will have a claim under, most commonly, Article 8, though such a claim will only be possible where the events giving rise to it took place after the Human Rights Act 1998 came into force in October 2000.[62]

The duties under Article 8 do not require any higher standard of care than would be required by a common law duty of care, nor do they require that no harm or distress on the parents of the child. A recent judgement on a claim for breach of Article 8 in connection with a child protection investigation noted that:[63]

> Sadly the experiences of the appellant simply illustrate the truth that viable child protection procedures in any society will sometimes inflict what turns out to have been unnecessary distress on families. That does not make them or the exercise of them thereby unlawful.

(b) Liability in other Cases

11.11 Outwith the area of child protection, there is no reason why individual social workers and social work departments should not owe a duty of care to service users and to members of the public. In the M case, for example, the point was made in the Court of Appeal 'that the social worker owes some duty to the person in his care; for example, he should not advise or encourage a child to engage in some activity which has a hidden danger, such as taking drugs or running across the road'.[64] Equally, a social worker having the care or supervision of a child, or indeed anyone else, will be under a duty to take reasonable care for their safety, for example, by ensuring adequate supervision or ensuring that they are not avoidably placed in a position where they risk coming to harm. In this respect the social worker is in the same position as everyone else.[65]

It is clear, however, that the duty may extend beyond this to cases where those under a social worker's charge cause damage to the property of another person. The best known instance of this is a case where the Home Office was held liable for inadequate supervision of a group

62 See also the cases discussed in paras 5.33–5.36.

63 *A v East Sussex County Council* [2010] EHCA Civ 743.

64 *M (a minor) v Newham London Borough Council* [1994] 4 All ER 602 at 629i, per Staughton LJ.

65 See *Kirkham v Chief Constable of the Greater Manchester Police* [1990] 3 All ER 246 for an example of duties owed by the police to people in their care suffering from mental illness.

of borstal trainees which resulted in damage to property.[66] There are illustrations of this in the context of social work. A court social worker did not inform those responsible for placing a child remanded into the care of a social services department of the child's suspected involvement in arson. He was placed in a community home under light supervision, left the home, and set a fire in a church causing considerable damage. It was held that the authority was in breach of its duty of supervision of the child, though this case also involved negligence by the court social worker in failing to pass on all the relevant information.[67] That the duty of supervision involves only a requirement to take reasonable care is illustrated by another example where a person under supervision set a fire. There had been an earlier fire, but it was not clear that it had been started by the person setting the second fire. Therefore there was no obligation to exercise close supervision over her, since there were no reasonable grounds for suspecting that she would do what she did.[68] In that case the point was made that 'a balance has to be struck between the risk of damage to others and the risk of impairing the treatment being given' through excessively rigorous control and supervision.

Aside from cases where the person causing damage is under the control of the local authority or where the authority has assumed responsibility for the protection of an individual, a local authority will not be liable for damage caused by third parties.[69] In *X v Hounslow London Borough Council*[70] the local authority was providing services to two adults with learning difficulties, as well as providing services to their children. The local authority was aware of the threat posed to the couple by a number of younger people living in the area and was seeking to arrange a change of accommodation for the couple and their children. Before this could happen they were seriously injured and harmed by the young people. It was held that the council was not liable for failing to protect the couple. It had no duty to do so and the provision of services to the couple under statutory powers was not enough to create a duty of care or to amount to an assumption of a duty of care. On the way to reaching this conclusion a distinction was made between vulnerable adults and children because of the existence of the specific statutory duties which local authorities have towards children. If a similar case were to arise in Scotland this

66 *Dorset Yacht Co Ltd v Home Office* [1970] AC 1004.

67 *Vicar of Writtle v Essex County Council* (1979) 77 LGR 656.

68 *Swift v Westham Central Mission* (6 June 1984, unreported) QB.

69 Though see *Merthyr Tydfil CBC v C* [2010] EWHC 62 (QB) where it was considered that (following the hearing of evidence) it might be fair, just and reasonable to impose a duty owed to a mother in relation to the actions of the child of a neighbour who had abused her children.

70 [2009] EWCA Civ 286.

argument would not be as relevant because of the existence of specific statutory duties involving vulnerable adults.[71]

Liability can arise not only for damage caused by an action on the part of a social worker, or indeed inaction on his/her part, but also for negligent advice. Where advice is offered in the knowledge that the person receiving the advice is likely to rely on it in deciding what to do the person giving the advice will usually, provided the advice is given in a professional capacity, be regarded as undertaking a duty of care towards the person advised. Most reported cases of this concern other professions, but there is one case illustrating this in the context of social work. A mother wanted to place her son, T, with a child minder. She identified one possibility and phoned the social worker who co-ordinated child minding for the local authority to check on her suitability. The advice given was that there was no reason why the child should not be placed with the particular child minder. This advice was given despite the fact that the worker giving it knew that a child had previously suffered a non-accidental injury while in the care of the child minder and that the minder had voluntarily agreed not to accept any young children into her care. T suffered a non-accidental injury while in the care of the minder and sued the authority. He was successful in a claim based on negligent advice given by the worker. The worker had undertaken to give advice to T's mother and in doing so had undertaken a duty not to give negligent advice.[72] Potential liability for negligent advice could cover a wide range of advice given by social workers, but it should be stressed again that the worker's duty, in law, is to take reasonable care, not to guarantee the accuracy of the advice.

Another example of potential liability is a case where a child is placed for adoption but is then discovered to have a serious medical condition. This question arose in *M and M v Glasgow Corporation*[73] where a child placed with the pursuers was later diagnosed as being severely mentally subnormal to the extent that she would always be dependent on them. They sued arguing that the local authority (acting as adoption agency) had a duty of care to ensure that a child medically unfit in this way was not placed for adoption. They were unsuccessful as the adoption agency did not have, and could not be expected to have, the medical skill needed to foresee the problems that arose in this case. The sheriff did, however, canvass the possibility of action

71 Adult Support and Protection (Scotland) Act 2007. See ch 9.

72 *T (a minor) v Surrey County Council* [1994] 4 All ER 577.

73 1976 SLT (Sh Ct) 45. See also *P v Tayside Regional Council* 1989 SCLR 165.

if the agency had failed to carry through the correct procedures, for example, by failing to obtain a medical report and concluded that:

'If a local authority negligently ignored some medical warning in the statutory medical report that a child was medically unsuitable for placing for adoption they might well be required to answer for it…'.[74]

Subsequent to this decision the duty of local authorities in respect of provision of information to adopters (and foster carers) has been considered in the English courts. In relation to adopters, it has been held that the authority has a duty to make sure that it does in fact pass on any information which it has decided is to be communicated to the adopter (either as an explicit decision about information to be communicated in an individual case or as a matter of policy). Beyond this there is no duty to pass on other information about the child unless the decision not to communicate any specific information was one which no reasonable authority would have taken.[75] The same approach has been taken to duties towards foster carers,[76] though there is authority to the effect that there is a potentially broader duty towards foster carers.[77] That case involved a placement with foster carers of a child who had previously sexually abused another child. The parents had made it clear that they did not want to have a sexual abuser placed with them, and after the placement was made the placed child abused the children of the foster carers. At an earlier stage in the court proceedings it was held that the authority owed a duty of care to the children of the foster carers.[78]

JUDICIAL REVIEW: FURTHER EXAMPLES

(1) Fostering cases

11.12 Under this broad heading are cases dealing with decisions to remove a child from a foster placement; decisions to remove a person from a list of approved foster carers; and decisions to inform other foster carers of allegations of sexual abuse against a foster parent.

74 *M and M v Glasgow Corporation* 1976 SLT (Sh Ct) 45 at 49.
75 *A v Essex County Council* [2003] EWCA Civ 1848.
76 *Lambert v Cardiff City Council* [2007] EWHC 869 (QB).
77 *W v Essex County Council* [2001] 2 AC 592.
78 *W v Essex County Council* [1999] Fam. 90

In the last category is *R v Lewisham London Borough Council, ex parte P.*[79] The applicant had been a foster carer. Allegations of sexual abuse had been made against him by one former foster child and the authority decided, following its policy, to advise people having care of children who had previously been fostered by P of the allegations of abuse and the identity of the alleged abuser. P successfully challenged the decision to identify him. The court took the view that the authority had simply carried out its policy without properly weighing up all the relevant factors in the case, for example, the reliability of the accusations, and had therefore acted unreasonably.

Where removal from the list of foster carers takes place, the prospects of success in an action for judicial review will depend on the reasons behind the removal. If they relate to the character or temperament of the foster carer they will not be reviewable. On the other hand, if they arise from allegations about the conduct of the foster carer that individual has a right to be informed of the allegations and to be heard in reply. Where a foster carer was not told the substance of the case against her and given the chance to make a case to challenge them, her removal from the list was quashed on review.[80] The ground for this decision was that the requirements of natural justice had not been complied with. This case also makes the point that the decisions that have to be made about reputation, character, etc in approving a foster carer are not open to challenge.

If foster carers are closely involved in the decision as to placement of a child, especially when the placement is to be a long-term one, they have a legitimate expectation that they will be consulted before the child is taken out of their care. Failure to consult and to allow them to make representations will be a breach of natural justice.[81] This requirement to consult would not arise in cases where serious allegations were made about the foster carers which required urgent action on the part of the local authority to protect the interests of a child. In such cases the local authority would have a statutory obligation to take action.[82] Removal of a child from foster carers may also give rise to arguments about

79 [1991] 3 All ER 529.

80 *R v London Borough of Wandsworth, ex parte P* [1989] 1 FLR 387. Contrast *R v Avon County Council, ex parte Crabtree* (22 March 1994, unreported) QB, where a foster carer was given the opportunity to be heard and his removal from the list was not challengeable by judicial review.

81 *R v Hereford and Worcester County Council, ex parte D* [1992] 1 FLR 448.

82 See eg the Looked After Children (Scotland) Regulations 2009, SI 2009/210, reg 47.

breach of rights under Art 8 of the European Convention on Human Rights as part of the judicial review claim.[83]

(2) Child protection cases

11.13 In *R v Harrow London Borough Council, ex parte D*[84] the applicant for judicial review was a woman whose children had been placed on the child protection register after a case conference which the applicant was not allowed to attend, though she was allowed to make written submissions. The decision of the authority was not regarded as unreasonable. There was medical and other evidence suggesting that the applicant was responsible for injuries to the children and there was no breach of the requirements of natural justice because she had been given the opportunity to put her version of events before the case conference.

One notable point to come out of the *Harrow* case is that it will be very difficult in cases involving child protection to succeed in a case based on judicial review. The view was expressed by the Court of Appeal that review would succeed only in an exceptional case raising an important point of principle and that the decision of the local authority would have to be utterly unreasonable. The reason for this is that in the child protection system the interests of the adults involved come second to those of the children. The point was made as follows by Butler-Sloss LJ:

> 'In balancing adequate protection for the child and fairness to the adult, the interests of an adult may have to be placed second to the needs of a child. All concerned in this difficult and delicate area should be allowed to perform their task without looking over their shoulder all the time for possible intervention of the court. The important power of the court to intervene should be kept very much in reserve, perhaps confined to the exceptional case which involves a point of principle which needs to be resolved, not only for the individual case but in general, so as to establish that registration is not being conducted in an unsatisfactory manner … In this area unbridled resort to judicial review could frustrate the ability of those involved in their effort to protect the victim of abuse.'[85]

83 See paras 5.33–5.36.

84 [1990] 3 All ER 12. See also *A v Surrey County Council* [2008] EWHC 1886 (Admin).

85 *R v Harrow London Borough Council, ex parte D* [1990] 3 All ER 12 at 17b-e. This point is reflected in one of the policy reasons given in the X and M cases for refusing to recognise the existence of a duty of care.

(3) Removal from parents while on home placement

11.14 Social work departments have a statutory duty to seek to have the care of a child who is being looked after by them taken over by that child's parent(s). What happens when additionally the authority has parental rights or responsibilities and placement with the parents is not working? Can the parents seek review of a decision to remove the children from their care, and in what circumstances is such a review likely to succeed? The only reported cases on this issue suggest that a parent will succeed in an application for review only if the reason for removal was an unsubstantiated allegation and the parent was not given an opportunity to respond to it before the decision to remove was made.[86] On the other hand, where a decision is based on a number of factors, such as the knowledge of social workers, assessments of the parent(s), reports from school and the views of doctors, the decision will not be challengeable. Such a decision is well within the scope of parental discretion allowed to an authority which has parental rights or responsibilities.[87]

What all of these cases indicate is that, as suggested in *Harrow,* the courts will be prepared to intervene only where a decision is based on an allegation which the complainer has not had the opportunity to challenge: in other words, where there has been a failure to comply with the requirements of natural justice. In the absence of a case based on natural justice, the courts are reluctant to overturn a local authority decision on the grounds that it is unreasonable. Courts often refer to the words of Lord Diplock in defining what criteria have to be met before a decision can be regarded as unreasonable. He said of unreasonableness that:

> 'It applies to a decision which is so outrageous in its defiance of logic or of accepted moral standards that no sensible person who had applied his mind to the question to be decided could have arrived at it.'[88]

This standard is so exacting that it is very difficult to meet.

It would also be possible to argue that removal of the child had infringed rights under Art 8 of the European Convention on Human Rights.[89]

86 *R v Bedfordshire County Council, ex parte C* [1987] 1 FLR 239.
87 *R v Hertfordshire County Council, ex parte B* [1987] 1 FLR 239.
88 *Council of Civil Service Unions v Minister for the Civil Service* [1985] AC 374 at 410D.
89 See paras 5.33–5.36.

(4) Other cases

11.15 Although judicial review may be difficult to use in the context of child protection, there is no reason why it should not be used successfully in other areas of social work provision. For example, in *R v London Borough of Ealing, ex parte Leaman*[90] Mr Leaman applied for assistance towards the cost of a holiday under the Chronically Sick and Disabled Persons Act 1970. The council, without considering the merits of the application, responded that because of financial constraints no grants were available for private holidays. It was held that they had acted improperly in declining to consider the application and simply applying a blanket policy without consideration of the merits of the application.

In *R v Avon County Council, ex parte M*[91] the placement of M, an adult with Down's Syndrome, was the subject of a dispute between the local authority and M's parents. It was agreed that M's needs would be assessed by the review panel set up under the council's complaints procedure. This panel heard evidence and reported, recommending a placement at an establishment called Milton Heights. The recommendation went to the social services committee who overturned it and substituted an alternative placement. That decision was overturned on application to the court, partly because the committee had failed to take M's psychological needs into account as required by the relevant legislation, and partly because the committee had failed to give proper weight to the panel's recommendation.

EMPLOYERS' LIABILITY FOR AND TO SOCIAL WORKERS

11.16 The contracts of employment which affect most social workers imply the acceptance of some degree of liability by the employer for the social worker. There are obligations for the social worker to be accountable to the employer and abide by the employer's policies and procedures and in turn the employer agrees to accept responsibility for the actions of the social worker undertaken on its behalf. Most of the major employers are covered by insurance for these areas and with respect to their employees suffering accidental injury or death, though most employers require social workers to take out their own

90 (1984) Times, 10 February.
91 [1994] 2 FCR 259.

insurance coverage for personal effects and for using their cars for business purposes. In practice, when there is public scrutiny of the actions of a social worker and the implication that malpractice may have occurred, the moral panic which ensues occasionally results in the employers jettisoning responsibility for the social worker and the direct line manager either in the short term or the long term. In light of the frequency of this experience, the major professional association, the British Association of Social Workers, has established an advice and representation service and additional insurance coverage for members who find themselves in this situation.

The nature of social work is such that sometimes it requires close contact by isolated workers with very vulnerable and needy people in situations which can be extremely stressful. An almost inevitable consequence is that occasionally a service user will resort to the use of violence directed at the social worker. Whether a social worker uses self-defence or retreats will depend on the particular circumstances and what is reasonably necessary to stop the violence, but a social worker choosing the former is as liable as any other individual to prosecution if the worker's actions are considered unreasonable by the procurator fiscal.

Anecdotal and research evidence[92] suggests that assaults on social workers are relatively frequent and reported to senior managers usually when there is no alternative. Many social workers hold the ill-founded belief that being assaulted reflects badly on their professional competence and many are confirmed in this belief by management practices. It is very important to report any assault to senior managers and many organisations have instituted policies which require the reporting of any incident which is beneficial in relieving the possibly traumatised worker from the decision.

Like any other employer, the employer of a social worker owes employees certain duties of care. Some of these will be under the Health and Safety at Work etc Act 1974, but the employer also owes common law duties to the employee. One of these is the duty to provide a safe system of work. Breach of this obligation was the basis for a successful action by a social worker who claimed that stress at work had caused him a nervous breakdown.[93] The social worker had suffered one nervous breakdown, for which the authority was not liable because it was not reasonably foreseeable. He then returned to work. He raised con-

92 S Balloch 'Working in the social services: How staff cope with violence and stress' *Research Policy and Harming* (1996) 14(1), pp 74–76.
93 *Walker v Northumberland County Council* [1995] 1 All ER 737.

cerns about his workload with his employers and they knew of his previous breakdown. In the circumstances it was foreseeable that he might suffer another breakdown if overworked. The employers' failure to take steps to reduce his workload was held to be in breach of their duty to provide a safe system of work. The duty they owed him was formulated as follows:

> 'It is clear law that the employer has a duty to provide his employee with a reasonably safe system of work and to take reasonable steps to protect him from risks which are reasonably foreseeable. Whereas the law on the extent of this duty has developed almost exclusively in cases involving physical injury to the employee as distinct from injury to his mental health, there is no logical reason why risk of psychiatric damage should be excluded from the scope of an employer's duty of care ...'[94]

The broad scope of this duty should be noted. It is arguable that it extends to circumstances where a social worker is being sent into a situation that is known to be dangerous, for example, to interview someone who is known to be violent, has a history of attacking workers or has a history of sexual assault. In such cases it would appear likely that the employer owes the worker a duty to guard against such risks and that an injured worker could sue the employer.

Later reported claims by social workers have been less successful. In these cases the worker was unable to establish foreseeability because the effect of their workload on their health was not drawn specifically to the attention of their employer.[95] It is clear that if a worker has concerns about the impact of workload on his/her health this should be drawn clearly to the attention of their employer, for example through supervision sessions, and supported by appropriate evidence. It has been suggested that:[96]

> Unless he knows of some particular problem or vulnerability, an employer is usually entitled to assume that his employee is up to the normal pressures of the job.

94 At 749c-e, per Colman J.

95 *Green v Argyll & Bute Council*, unreported, Outer House, 28 February 2002, *Patley v Surrey County Council* [2003] EWCA Civ 1067.

96 *Hatton v Sutherland* [2002] EWCA Civ 76, para 29.

CONCLUSION

11.17 This survey indicates that there are a number of areas where social workers and their employers will clearly be legally liable for what is done in the course of their work. The precise contours of this liability are not always entirely clear, and as we have seen the law is subject to development, in recent years this has been particularly under the influence of the European Convention on Human Rights. There has been some discussion in the case law about the impact of imposing liability on the creation of defensive practice and, in relation to the possible existence of a duty to suspected abusers, of trying to manage inconsistent interests. There are also pressures from the media (and the public) which often seems to assume that there is clear evidence available to social workers and that it is possible to minimise risk (for example to children) to a vanishingly low level, although this is not the approach adopted in the courts. What should not be lost sight of in all of this is that what the law requires, whether in a negligence claim or in a claim under the Human Rights Act 1998, is that the social worker practices competently. In this it is at one with the ethics and standards of the profession in emphasising the fundamental importance of good, accountable practice. Employers have a part to play in this process in ensuring that the structures, resources and supervision are in place to encourage and support good practice.

Chapter 12

Changes

12.1 This chapter sets out some of the changes in law which have either been implemented, are imminent or which are being discussed for the longer term by the Scottish Government. Coverage is set out by chapter of the text.

CHAPTER 5

12.2 The Children's Hearing's (Scotland) Act 2011, which is to be implemented in the course of 2011 makes changes to the administration of the children's hearings system. It sets up a new body, Children's Hearings Scotland, provides for a new post of National Convener of Children's Hearings Scotland and sets up a national children's panel rather than the current 32 local panels. It also makes a number of other changes to the law regarding the operation of hearings.

(1) Local authority duty to investigate

12.3 The duty of the local authority to investigate is recast and under the 2011 Act will arise where the authority considers it likely that a child is in need of protection, guidance, treatment or control, and that it might be necessary for a compulsory supervision order to be made in relation to the child.[1] Where the authority considers it likely that a child is in need of protection, guidance, treatment or control, and that it might be necessary for a compulsory supervision order to be made in relation to the child then it must pass on any information it has to the Reporter.[2]

(2) Child Protection Orders

12.4 A child protection order which authorises removal of a child to a place of safety will cease to have effect after six days if the child

1 Children's Hearings (Scotland) Act 2011, s 60.
2 Children's Hearings (Scotland) Act 2011, s 60(3). A similar requirement applies to police officers, s 61.

has not been removed in that period.[3] Where the order has been implemented it will expire after eight days either from the date on which the order was made or, if the order authorises removal of the child, from the date of removal.[4] There will still be a hearing on the second working day after implementation. There is no specific requirement in the 2011 for the eighth day hearing, though the provisions as to expiry of the order require that, if the case is going to a hearing for consideration of grounds of referral, this happens before the order expires. The order will also cease to have effect at the beginning of a hearing held to consider the child's case and it is made clear that the order will expire if the Reporter decides that there is no need to refer the case to a hearing.[5]

(3) Child Assessment Orders

12.5 The 2011 Act clarifies the position regarding the child's consent to any medical examination authorised by a child assessment order, making it clear that such consent is required.[6]

(4) Children's Hearings

12.6 The 2011 Act will make number of procedural changes to the operation of children's hearings, the main changes are set out below. In relation to aspects of procedure not considered below, these will remain as set out in chapter 5. One change in terminology should be noted, the orders made by hearings will, after implementation, be known as compulsory supervision orders.

(a) Grounds for referral

12.7 The 2011 Act contains a revised list of grounds on which a child may be in need of compulsory supervision. Some of these essentially replicate the grounds which apply under the Children (Scotland)

3 Children's Hearings (Scotland) Act 2011, s 52. The requirement to attempt to implement the order within 24 hours (or 12 hours in the case of a JP authorisation) will still apply.
4 Children's Hearings (Scotland) Act 2011, s 54.
5 Children's Hearings (Scotland) Act 2011, s 54(b).
6 See para 5.7, Children's Hearings (Scotland) Act 2011, s 186.

Act 1995 others are new, for example grounds (c), (m) and (p). The grounds are:[7]

(a) the child is likely to suffer unnecessarily, or the health or development of the child is likely to be seriously impaired, due to a lack of parental care;
(b) a schedule 1 offence has been committed in respect of the child;
(c) the child has, or is likely to have, a close connection with a person who has committed a schedule 1 offence;
(d) the child is, or is likely to become, a member of the same household as a child in respect of whom a schedule 1 offence has been committed;
(e) the child is being, or is likely to be, exposed to persons whose conduct is (or has been) such that it is likely that—
    (i) the child will be abused or harmed; or
    (ii) the child's health, safety or development will be seriously adversely affected;
(f) the child has, or is likely to have, a close connection with a person who has carried out domestic abuse;
(g) the child has, or is likely to have, a close connection with a person who has committed an offence under Part 1, 4 or 5 of the Sexual Offences (Scotland) Act 2009;
(h) the child is being provided with accommodation by a local authority under section 25 of the 1995 Act and special measures are needed to support the child;
(i) a permanence order is in force in respect of the child and special measures are needed to support the child;
(j) the child has committed an offence;
(k) the child has misused alcohol;
(l) the child has misused a drug (whether or not a controlled drug);
(m) the child's conduct has had, or is likely to have, a serious adverse effect on the health, safety or development of the child or another person;
(n) the child is beyond the control of a relevant person;
(o) the child has failed without reasonable excuse to attend regularly at school;
(p) the child:
    (i) is being, or is likely to be, subjected to physical, emotional or other pressure to enter into a marriage or civil partnership; or

7 Children's Hearings (Scotland) Act 2011, s 67.

(ii) is, or is likely to become, a member of the same household as such a child.

(b) Excusing the child's attendance

12.8 The child's attendance either at all or part of a hearing can be excused if:[8]

(a) her/his attendance would place his/her physical, mental or moral welfare at risk;
(b) the grounds being considered are grounds (b), (c), (d) or (g) set out above and the attendance of the child is not necessary for a fair hearing; or
(c) the child is not capable of understanding what happens at the hearing or that part of it.

It is also made clear that a child can be excused attendance at the hearing where the grounds of referral are explained.[9]

(c) Pre-hearing panels

12.9 These will replace business meetings, but have a slightly different remit. The 2011 Act provides that such meetings (rather than the courts) can determine whether or not a person is a relevant person. This issue must be referred to a pre-hearing panel if the Reporter is requested to do this by the person seeking to be recognised as a relevant person, the child or a relevant person.[10] In other cases the Reporter may refer the question to a pre-hearing panel. After considering such a referral, the panel must deem the individual in question to be a relevant person if it considers that he/she has (or has recently had) significant involvement in the upbringing of the child.[11] The individual concerned has a right of appeal against the panel's decision if it decides that he/she is not a relevant person.[12] The Reporter can also refer other issues to the panel: whether the child or relevant person should be excused attendance, whether it is likely that any compulsory supervision order (cso) is likely to include a secure accommodation authorisation and any other matter set out in rules (which have not yet been made). A pre-hearing panel can also appoint a safeguarder to the child.

8 Children's Hearings (Scotland) Act 2011, s 73(3).
9 Children's Hearings (Scotland) Act 2011, s 73(4).
10 Children's Hearings (Scotland) Act 2011, s 79(2)(a).
11 Children's Hearings (Scotland) Act 2011, s 81(3).
12 Children's Hearings (Scotland) Act 2011, s 160.

(d) Secure accommodation authorisation and movement restriction condition[13]

12.10 The grounds for these are slightly reformulated. A hearing must be satisfied either that:

(a) that the child has previously absconded and is likely to abscond again and, if the child were to abscond, it is likely that the child's physical, mental or moral welfare would be at risk; or
(b) that the child is likely to engage in self-harming conduct; or
(c) that the child is likely to cause injury to another person.

In addition, the hearing must be satisfied that the condition is necessary, and before reaching a conclusion that a secure accommodation authorisation is necessary it must have considered the other options available, including a movement restriction condition.

(f) Procedure at the hearing

12.11 As at present a hearing will start with an explanation of the grounds of referral, with the hearing at which the grounds are explained being referred to as a grounds hearing.[14] This hearing may, if it considers it appropriate, defer a decision on whether to make a cso. If it does defer the case it can make an interim compulsory supervision order. An interim cso can include any requirement which can be included in a cso and will last initially for 22 days, though it can be extended.[15] When a case is deferred the hearing may also make a medical examination order requiring, for example, that the child attends a clinic or hospital or that the local authority arrange a specified medical examination of the child.[16] The consent of the child is required for any examination or treatment.[17]

If there is no deferment the hearing must make a cso if it satisfied that it is necessary to do so for the protection, guidance, treatment or control of the child, otherwise the referral will be discharged.

13 Children's Hearings (Scotland) Act 2011, s 83(4)–(6).
14 Children's Hearings (Scotland) Act 2011, s 90.
15 For example where a proof hearing has not taken place by the time the interim cso would expire Children's Hearings (Scotland) Act 2011, s 86.
16 Children's Hearings (Scotland) Act 2011, s 87.
17 Children's Hearings (Scotland) Act 2011, s 186.

(g) Review of finding that grounds of referral established

12.12 The 2011 Act makes slight changes on the grounds on which a sheriff can review a previous finding that grounds of referral were established (a grounds determination).[18] Such a determination can be reviewed where:[19]

(a) evidence was not considered by the sheriff in making the determination;
(b) the evidence would have been admissible;
(c) there is a reasonable explanation for the failure to lead evidence at the proof hearing; and
(d) the evidence is significant and relevant to whether the grounds should have been held to be established.

A sheriff considering a review of a grounds determination may be satisfied that there is another possible ground for referral not considered in the hearing which led to the grounds determination, if so he/she must determine that ground is established and refer the matter to the Reporter.[20]

(h) Procedural matters

12.13 The hearing must confirm that the child has had an opportunity to express his/her views before the hearing,[21] must tell him/her about the availability of the (yet to be set up) children's advocacy service unless this is inappropriate having regard to the age and maturity of the child,[22] and must establish the age of the child.[23]

(i) Reviews

12.14 A date before which a review must be carried out has to be fixed by the hearing making a cso where it contains a movement restriction condition, and may be fixed in other cases.[24] A review hearing can,

18 See para 5.19.
19 Children's Hearings (Scotland) Act 2011, s 111(3).
20 Children's Hearings (Scotland) Act 2011, s 117.
21 Children's Hearings (Scotland) Act 2011, s 121.
22 Children's Hearings (Scotland) Act 2011, s 123.
23 Children's Hearings (Scotland) Act 2011, s 124.
24 Children's Hearings (Scotland) Act 2011, s 125.

if the hearing is deferred, make an interim variation of any condition attached to the cso.[25]

It is also possible for a person who has contact with a child under the terms of a contact or permanence order (and who fulfils certain other requirements to be set out in regulations[26]) to request a review of a cso[27] which contains a direction relating to contact which affects him/her. On receiving such a request the Reporter must arrange a hearing which can confirm the cso or vary it.[28] There is a right of appeal to the sheriff against the decision of the hearing.[29]

(j) Local authority non-compliance

12.15 Under the 2011 Act the process of enforcing the obligations of a local authority to give effect to a cso or to any requirements forming part of it is modified.[30] The main change is that instead of instructing the Reporter to take this action, it will instruct the National Convener to take enforcement action.[31]

(k) Appeals

12.16 Where the 1995 Act simply provides for an appeal against any decision of a hearing,[32] the 2011 Act lists the decisions of a hearing against which the child, a relevant person, or the child's safeguarder can appeal. These are:[33]

(a) a decision to make, vary or continue a compulsory supervision order;
(b) a decision to discharge a referral by the Principal Reporter;
(c) a decision to terminate a compulsory supervision order;
(d) a decision to make an interim compulsory supervision order;
(e) a decision to make an interim variation of a compulsory supervision order;

25 Children's Hearings (Scotland) Act 2011, s 140.
26 And who would not be relevant person by virtue solely of the contact order.
27 Or an interim cso, interim variation of a cso or medical examination order having effect for more than 5 days.
28 Children's Hearings (Scotland) Act 2011, s 126.
29 Children's Hearings (Scotland) Act 2011, s 161.
30 See para 5.16.
31 Children's Hearings (Scotland) Act 2011, ss 144–148.
32 Children (Scotland) Act 1995, s 51(1)(a).
33 Children's Hearings (Scotland) Act 2011, s 154.

(f) a decision to make a medical examination order; or
(g) a decision to grant a warrant to secure attendance.

The 2011 Act also provides that some appeals must be heard and disposed of within three days, these are decisions to:[34]

(a) make a compulsory supervision order including a secure accommodation authorisation or movement restriction condition;
(b) make an interim compulsory supervision order;
(c) make an interim variation of a compulsory supervision order;
(d) make a medical examination order; or
(e) grant a warrant to secure attendance.

Where a secure accommodation authorisation is made there is a right of appeal held by the child and her/his relevant person(s) against a decision of the chief social work officer to implement the authorisation, not to implement it or to remove the child from secure accommodation.[35]

(5) Relevant person

12.17 As noted in (4)(i) above, a person whose only connection with a child is because of a right to contact under a contact or permanence order has a right to have decisions made by a hearing which affect their contact with the child reviewed. This means that a new mechanism is provided to allow for a proper determination of his/her civil right to contact. The effect of this is that once the 2011 Act comes into effect it will no longer be necessary to read the definition of relevant person as including individuals contact rights.[36]

CHAPTER 8

12.18 Following from the Limited Review of the Mental Health (Care and Treatment)(Scotland) Act 2003 the Scottish Government has produced its response. The principal changes proposed in this are:[37]

(a) Making it clear it is good practice to discuss making an advance statement with a patient who is recovering.

34 Children's Hearings (Scotland) Act 2011, s 157.
35 Children's Hearings (Scotland) Act 2011, s 162.
36 See para 5.8. This requirement was set out in *Knox v S* [2010] CSIH 45 because of the absence under the 1995 Act of any other way for a person holding only a right to contact to participate in hearing decisions which might be made affecting his/her contact rights.
37 *Scottish Government Response to the 'Limited Review of the Mental Health (Care and Treatment) (Scotland) Act 2003: Report'* (2010).

(b) The current default identification of named persons will be retained – the more extensive proposals made by the Review for reform have been rejected. The main change which is proposed is that patients will be able to opt out of having a named person altogether, currently the only opt out is to specify that a particular individual is not to be the patient's named person.

(c) Two medical reports will continue to be required for application for a CTO in most cases, but in it is proposed that one should be obtained from an approved medical practitioner and that he other should consist of information from the patient's GP commenting on the first report. However, where no GP could be identified there would be no requirement for this second report, though in such a case an independent medical report would be required, and if his was not instructed by the patient it would be up to the Tribunal to instruct it.

(d) The maximum limit on suspension of detention where a CTO authorises detention will be removed (it is currently set at 9 months in each 12 month period).

(e) The period of authorisation of continued detention when a patient is detained under a short term detention certificate would be extended from 5 to 10 days, though this additional 5 days would count towards the maximum period for which an interim compulsory treatment order can authorise detention. The purpose behind extending this period is to allow more time for preparation for the initial Tribunal hearing and avoid the use of interim orders.

(f) A copy of an application for a compulsory treatment order will be given to the patient and/or his/her solicitor by the MHO at the same time as the MHO sends this to the Tribunal.

(g) Time limits would be set for disposing of appeals. In the case of appeals against short term detention certificates the limit would be 3 days. In other cases it would be 28 days.

CHAPTER 10

(1) Criminal Justice Social Work Reports

12.19 As noted in the chapter, Social Enquiry Reports are replaced from 1 February 2011 by Criminal Justice Social Work Reports which follow a fixed template. Detailed guidance on these is contained in *National Outcomes and Standards for Social Work Services in the Criminal Justice System: CRIMINAL JUSTICE SOCIAL WORK REPORTS and COURT-BASED SERVICES PRACTICE GUIDANCE* (2010). They will be required in any cases in which, prior to 1 February, a social enquiry report was required.

The report should be prepared on a nationally agreed reporting template and must include a risk assessment and a review of the sentencing options which are relevant for the offender, in all cases this assessment must consider a community payback order and, where there is a significant drug problem, a drug treatment and testing order.

The Practice Guidance concludes that:[38]

> The report should highlight the worker's professional analysis. Language is important in the report and never more so than in this area, as some Sentencers may regard it as inappropriate for the report to offer any recommendation as to what the court might impose as a disposal. On the other hand, in some courts, such suggestions, when they form part of the overall professional analysis, are regarded as good practice. It is important to bear in mind that the decision on what disposal to apply is entirely for the court. The author of the report requires to be discerning in his/her choice of words, but can however, offer their professional assessment of which relevant sentencing options may maximise the opportunity for the individual to reduce reoffending and change their behaviour.

(2) Community Payback Orders

12.20 Community Payback Orders will replace a variety of community sentences for *offences* which are committed *after* 1 February 2011. In the case of offences committed before this date the former community sentences will be available, regardless of the date on which the offender is sentenced. The existing orders which are replaced are probation, community service, supervised attendance and community reparation orders.[39] There are substantial similarities between the provisions applying to the community payback order and those applying to these orders. The community payback order can be used either as an initial sentence or following default in payment of a fine and can be combined with another penalty other than imprisonment. Detailed guidance on the implementation of community payback orders is contained in *National Outcomes and Standards for Social Work Services in the Criminal Justice System: COMMUNITY PAYBACK ORDERS PRACTICE GUIDANCE* (2010).

38 Para 6.36.
39 Though these last were only ever piloted.

(a) Making the order

12.21 Before a community payback order is made a number of requirements must be met:

(a) A Criminal Justice Social Work Report must normally have been obtained and must be considered by the court before any order is made. A Report is not needed when he court is only imposing a level 1 unpaid work or other activity requirement or where he order is being made on a fine defaulter.
(b) The effect of the order and the consequences of breaching it must be explained to the offender, who must indicate that he/she understands the explanation and that he/she is willing to comply with each of the requirements that are to be imposed as part of the order. Willingness to comply is not required where an order is made in respect of a fine defaulter.
(c) The offence must be punishable by imprisonment and the power is given to the court to make a payback order 'instead of' imposing a sentence of imprisonment.[40] It is also possible to make a payback order as well as or instead of a fine, though the conditions which such an order can contain are limited.
(d) The court must consider that the offence(s) of which the offender has been convicted is (are) serious enough to warrant imposing an order.

(b) Requirements in an order

12.22 The community payback order can contain a variety of requirements:

(a) an offender supervision requirement;
(b) a compensation requirement;
(c) an unpaid work or other activity requirement;
(d) a programme requirement;
(e) a residence requirement;
(f) a mental health treatment requirement;
(g) a drug treatment requirement;
(h) an alcohol treatment requirement;
(i) a conduct requirement.

Each of these is considered briefly below. The order can contain a number of different requirements, though if any of requirements other

40 Criminal Procedure (Scotland) Act 1995, s 227a(1).

than an unpaid work or other activity requirement is made then an offender supervision requirement must also be made. A JP court can only impose requirements (a), (b), (c) (though there is a limit on the hours that can be specified), (e) or (i). Where a payback order is being made as well as or instead of a fine it can only contain requirements (a), (c) (though limited to a level 1 requirement, see below) or (i). Finally, where an order is made in respect of a fine defaulter only requirement (c) can be imposed, though where the offender is aged 16 or 17 an offender supervision requirement must also be made.

(c) Offender supervision requirement

12.23 This requires that the offender is supervised for a period of between 6 months and three years, with the purpose of 'promoting the offender's rehabilitation.' It is, effectively, the equivalent of a probation order without any additional conditions.

(d) Compensation requirement

12.24 This is a requirement to pay compensation either in a lump sum or by instalments. Payment has to be made by the earlier of either 18 months from the making of the requirement or two months before the end of the offender supervision requirement which has to be made along with the compensation requirement.

(e) Unpaid work or other activity requirement

12.25 This is broadly equivalent to a community service order. The requirement can relate either to unpaid work or to the performance of unpaid work and the completion of or attendance at other activities. Examples of other activities given in the guidance include training in literacy or numeracy, opportunities to address anger management issues and addressing issues related to employment. It is for the person supervising the offender (the responsible officer) to allocate time between unpaid work and other activity, but time spent on other activity must not exceed the lower of 30 hours or 30% of the hours specified in the requirement. The number of hours which may be specified is between 20 and 300. A requirement to undertake 100 hours or less is described as a level 1 requirement with a requirement for more than 100 hours being a level 2 requirement.

This type of requirement cannot be made in respect of an offender aged 15 or under. Before making the order, the court must be satisfied that the offender is a suitable person to undertake unpaid work, though this is not required in the case of a level 1 requirement or where the requirement is being imposed on a fine defaulter. The hours set out in the requirement must be completed within 3 months for a level 1 requirement and 6 months for a level 2 requirement, though the court can specify a longer period in the requirement.

(f) Unpaid work/other activity for fine defaulters

12.26 Instead of imprisoning a fine defaulter the court:[41]

(a) must impose a community payback order imposing a level 1 unpaid work or other activity requirement where the amount of the fine or of any missed instalment is not more than level 2; and
(b) in other cases may impose such an order.

If an order is imposed on someone aged 16 or 17 an offender supervision requirement must be made and where the amount of the fine or instalment is less than level 1 the maximum number of hours that can be imposed is 50.

(g) Programme requirement

12.27 A programme requirement can only be made if the programme specified in the requirement has been recommended in the Criminal Justice Social Work Report as being suitable for the offender to participate in.[42] A programme is:[43]

> …a course or other planned set of activities, taking place over a period of time, and provided to individuals or groups of individuals for the purpose of addressing offending behavioural needs.

The programme requirement cannot extend beyond the end of the supervision requirement imposed as part of the same community payback order and if compliance with the requirement would involve the cooperation of someone other than the offender (eg the manager or provider of the programme) that person must consent before the requirement can be imposed.

41 Criminal Procedure (Scotland) Act 1995, s 227M(2).
42 Criminal Procedure (Scotland) Act 1995, s 227P(3).
43 Criminal Procedure (Scotland) Act 1995, s 227P(2).

(h) Residence requirement

12.28 A requirement that the offender resides at a specified place can be imposed, but can only last as long as the offender supervision requirement which must be made at the same time. The specified place can be a hostel or other institution only if it has been recommended as suitable for the offender in the Criminal Justice Social Work Report.[44]

(i) Mental health treatment requirement

12.29 This effectively reproduces the provisions for a requirement for medical treatment which can be made as a condition of a probation order.[45]

(j) Drug treatment requirement

12.30 This type of requirement can be made if the offender is dependent on, or has a propensity to misuse, controlled drugs. Additional requirements are that the dependency or propensity must require, and may be susceptible to, treatment and that arrangements have been, or can be, made for treatment to be provided.[46] The requirement will require the offender to undergo treatment, though it cannot last for longer than the offender supervision requirement which must be made at the same time.

(k) Alcohol treatment requirement

12.31 This type of requirement can be made when the offender is dependent on alcohol. Some guidance on this is given in the Practice Guidance which lists factors which, if a number of them are present over a period of time suggest dependency. These include a desire or sense of compulsion to consume alcohol, impaired capacity to control drinking, withdrawal symptoms when alcohol use is reduced or terminated and preoccupation with alcohol.[47] Additional requirements are that the dependency requires and may be susceptible to treatment and that

44 Criminal Procedure (Scotland) Act 1995, s 227Q(3).
45 Criminal Procedure (Scotland) Act 1995, ss 227R–227T, see para 10.21.
46 Criminal Procedure (Scotland) Act 1995, s 227U(6).
47 *National Outcomes and Standards for Social Work Services in the Criminal Justice System: COMMUNITY PAYBACK ORDERS PRACTICE GUIDANCE* (2010), para 11.8.

arrangements have been, or can be, made for treatment.[48] The requirement will require the offender to undergo treatment, though it cannot last for longer than the offender supervision requirement which must be made at the same time.

(l) Conduct requirement

12.32 This is a requirement that the offender does, or refrains from doing, certain things for the period specified in the order and effectively replicates he power to impose additional conditions to a probation order. Any requirement must be directed at securing or promoting good behaviour or preventing further offending.[49] There is no provision, as there was in relation to probation orders, for the court making a payback order to attach restrictions on the offender's movements which would be remotely monitored.

(m) Implementing the order

12.33 As with probation orders, the court making the order may set a date for review. In respect of giving effect to the order, detailed guidelines are set out in the Practice Guidance, and the provisions for dealing with breach of the order, both in terms of guidance and law are similar to those which apply to probation orders.[50] Similar provisions also apply to variation and discharge of the order.

(n) Powers of the court on breach

12.34 If an order is breached by breaching one of the requirements of the order and this is established in breach proceedings, the court has a variety of options, though these depend on whether the payback order was imposed on a fine defaulter or not. Where the order was made following non-payment of a fine the court can:[51]

(a) Revoke the order and impose a limited period of imprisonment.
(b) Vary the number of hours of work or other activity imposed under the order.
(c) Leave the original order in place.

48 Criminal Procedure (Scotland) Act 1995, s 227V(6).
49 Criminal Procedure (Scotland) Act 1995, s 227W(2).
50 *National Outcomes and Standards for Social Work Services in the Criminal Justice System: COMMUNITY PAYBACK ORDERS PRACTICE GUIDANCE* (2010), ch 14.
51 Criminal Procedure (Scotland) Act 1995, s 227ZC(8).

In other cases the court has the power to:[52]

(a) Leave the original order in place.
(b) Impose a fine up to level 3.
(c) Revoke the order and:
   (i) where the order was imposed as an alternative to imprisonment, sentence the offender as if the payback order had not been made; or
   (ii) where the order was made as an alternative to a fine, sentence to imprisonment for up to 60 days in the JP court, or 3 months in other courts.
(d) Vary the order or any requirement in it.
(e) Impose a fine and vary the order or any requirement.
(f) Impose a restricted movement requirement which will impose restrictions on the movement of the offender which will be remotely monitored.[53]

(3) Custodial Sentences

12.35 For offences committed after 1 February 2011 there is a presumption against custodial sentences of 3 months or less.[54] Such a sentence can only be passed if the court considers that no other method of dealing with the offender is appropriate. The reasons for reaching such a conclusion must be recorded.

The Criminal Justice and Licensing (Scotland) Act 2010, through amendments to the Custodial Sentences and Weapons (Scotland) Act 2007, also contains provisions altering the system of release from custodial sentences, though these will not be introduced until at least 2012.[55] Custodial sentences would be custody and community sentences. Where these were short-term the prisoner would be released after half of the sentence, but all released short-term prisoners would be subject to a licence. For other prisoners the court would set an overall sentence consisting of a custody part of the sentence (at least one half) and a licence part. Prisoners will be released on licence only after completing this part of the sentence, though if the prisoner would be likely to cause serious harm to the public if released, he/she could be kept in custody.

52 Criminal Procedure (Scotland) Act 1995, s 227ZC(7).
53 Criminal Procedure (Scotland) Act 1995, ss 227ZE–227 ZK.
54 Criminal Justice and Licensing (Scotland) Act 2010, s 17.
55 See Answer by Kenny McAskill to question S3W-38289 from James Kelly MSP, 14 January 2011.

Index

[*references are to paragraph number*]

A

Abuse, *see also* Child; Domestic violence, measures against; Harm
- risk of
  - child protection order, *see* Emergency protection
  - referral to reporter, 5.6

Accommodation, *see* Housing; Local authority accommodation; Residential accommodation; Secure accommodation
- incapacitated adult, 7.18–7.21

Accountability, *see* Liability and accountability

Adoption, 3.17–3.28
- agency, placement by, 3.17–3.20
  - approval of applicants, 3.19
  - child subject to supervision requirements, referral of, 3.22
  - liability, 11.11
- allowances, 3.26
- child's right as to consent, 3.2, 3.20
- confidentiality, 3.25
- parents' rights, 3.21
  - dispensing with consent, 3.21
- permanence order, 3.23
- placement for, 3.17–3.20, 3.24
  - liability issues, 11.11
- procedure, 3.25
- records, access rights, 3.27
- support services, 3.28
- welfare of child, 3.18
- who can adopt, 3.19
- who can be adopted, 3.20
- wishes of child, 3.25

Adult support and protection
- adult protection committees, 9.1
- document production, 9.6
- factors to be considered in carrying out functions, 9.2
- 'harm', 9.3
- investigation duty, pre-conditions for, 9.3
- powers, 9.5, 9.6
  - exercise of, personnel for, 9.4
- principles for, 9.2, 9.7
- protection orders, 9.7
  - assessment order, 9.7
  - banning order, 9.7
  - consent, issues, 9.8
  - removal order, 9.7
- visits to premises, 9.5

Advance statement
- medical treatment, as to, 8.24

Advocates, 1.11

Age, *see* Child; Elderly person

Alcohol problem
- community payback order, treatment requirement in, 12.31
- intervention to tackle, 10.40

Antisocial behaviour order, 10.34

Assault
- social worker, on, 11.16

Assessment
- assessment order (adult), 9.7
- child, *see* Assessment of child
- community care services, *see* Community care
- lifelong restriction order, prior to, 10.55
- mentally disordered offenders, assessment and treatment orders, 10.63

Assessment of child
child assessment order when harm likely, 5.7
child in need, 4.5, 4.6
looked after child, 4.13, 4.15
pathway assessment, 4.44
secure accommodation placement, prior to, 5.16
Attorneys, 7.6

B

Banning order/temporary banning order, 9.7
Benefits, 2.1
Breach of duty, 2.1, 11.7
adoption, failure to carry out correct procedures, 11.11
child minder, negligent advice on, 11.11
child protection/child care, 11.10
common law duty of care, 11.7, 11.10, 11.11
service users and members of public, duty, 11.11
statutory duty, 11.7, 11.10
Business meeting, 5.12, 5.13
replacement by pre-hearing panel, 12.9

C

Capacity, legal
adult without, *see* Incapacity
child, of, 3.1, 3.2
Care plan
child, 4.8, 4.15, 4.16
mental health patient, 8.18
services, *see* Services provision
Care services, 11.3
Carer
adult, assessment of, 6.6
child, of, responsibilities, 3.6
Challenge to decision, *see also* Complaints procedure
community care provision, 6.15
looked after child/family or provision of services, 4.46
methods, 11.6–11.9

Changes to law
child assessment order, 12.5
child protection order, 12.4
children's hearings, procedural changes, 12.6–12.16
community payback order, introduction of, *see* Community payback order
custodial sentences, 12.35
investigation duty of local authority, 12.3
mental health provisions, 12.18
social enquiry report, renaming and guidance, 12.19
Charge for services, 6.12
Child
abuse or harm, risk of
assessment order, 5.7
compensation for abuse, 10.41
disclosure of information, 2.31
duty of social work department, 5.7
interdict restraining, 3.36
local authority services provision, 4.1
protection from, factor for court order, 3.7
accommodation provision for, *see* Housing; Looked after child
court order for local authority accommodation, 5.21
adoption, *see* Adoption
age of, relevance, 3.4, 4.1
legal consequences, 3.1, 3.2
assessment of, *see* Assessment of child
attendance at hearing, 5.11, 12.8
capacity, legal, 3.1, 3.2
care plan, 4.8, 4.15, 4.16
carer with no parental responsibilities, powers, 3.6
contact with family
promotion of, 4.19, 5.36
relevant person, and review, changes, 12.14, 12.17
court order, 3.7, 3.13
principles applying, 5.2–5.5

Child – *contd*
criminal offence against under 17-year-old, 5.37
criminal prosecution, 3.2, 5.20, 5.21, *see also* Criminal offence
custodial sentence, 5.21, 10.44
social worker report, 10.7
detention of, 5.21, 10.44
early release from detention, 10.58, 10.59
disabled, 4.4, 4.6
divorce of parents, arrangements on, 3.13
emergency protection of, *see* Emergency protection
evidence from, 1.56
financial support by parent, 3.3
hearings, 1.18, 1.57, 3.3
child's power to conduct proceedings, 3.2
overriding principles, 5.2–5.5
parent as legal representative, 3.5
procedure, changes to, 12.6–12.16, *see also* Changes to law
solicitor, child instructing, 3.2
supervision measures, *see* Supervision measures for child
human rights, 5.33–5.36
legal representation, 5.13
parent, 3.5, 5.13
'relevant person', 5.13
safeguarder, 5.13
solicitor, 3.2
legislation, 1.9, 1.70, 1.71
local authority services, 4.1 *et seq*
children in need, 4.1, 4.3–4.12
Getting it Right for Every Child (GIRFEC), approach under, 4.1, 4.2
see also Services provision
looked after, 4.1, 4.13–4.20
placement, 4.21–4.33
see also Looked after child
minors, 3.1

Child – *contd*
need, child in, 4.1, 4.3–4.12, *see also* Services provision
parents' responsibilities and rights, *see* Parents
person with, priority need for housing, 2.8
powers, 3.1, 3.2
protection, 5.1 *et seq*, *see also* Emergency protection
complaint about intervention/under-intervention, 11.10
judicial review, 11.13
pupils, 3.1
removal from home, 5.23, *see also* Emergency protection
placement with parents, from, judicial review issues, 11.14
rights, 3.3
siblings, 4.15, 4.19
supervision, *see* Supervision measures for child
unsuitability to work with, list, 11.5
views, 3.3, 3.7, 4.8, 4.10
'right to be heard' principle, 5.4
supervision measures hearing, 5.14
welfare of
adoption, and, 3.18
paramount in application for court order, 3.7, 5.3
promotion by local authority, 4.3, 5.23
promotion by parents, 3.4
services provision, 4.8
will, power to make, 3.2
work with, regulation of, 11.5
Child assessment order, 5.7
change to law, 12.5
Child minder
advice on use, social worker liability, 11.11
complaints, 11.9
registration and inspection, 11.3
Child protection order, *see* Emergency protection

Child support, 3.16
Children's panel, 5.10
Civil courts, *see* Court system
Civil partnership, 3.14
  discrimination, protected characteristic, 2.21, 3.14
  dissolution, 3.14
Code of Practice
  Adults with Incapacity, 7.10
  Social Workers, 2.28
Cohabitation, 3.8, 3.15, 3.31
Community care, 6.1 *et seq*
  assessment, 6.1, 6.4–6.7
    carer, of, 6.6
    decision after, 6.7
    judicial review of, 1.59
    mental disorder, 8.12
    types, 6.5
  change to, consultation on, 6.15
  challenge to decision on, 6.15
  charge for services, 6.12
  consent to care plan, 6.11
    procedure where no one to consent, 6.11
  disabled person, services for, 6.4
    information from other departments, 6.5
  eligibility criteria, setting, 6.8
  financial help, 6.10
  guidance, 6.2
  legal framework, 6.2
  medical disorder, person with, 8.12, *see also* Mental health
  nursing care, 6.12
  objectives, 6.1
  payment for, 6.12–6.14
  personal care, 6.13
  resources, guidance on, 6.8
  self-directed support, 6.10
  services, 6.3
    assessment for, 6.1, 6.4–6.7, 8.12
    methods of providing, 6.9
    monitoring, 6.9
Community justice authority, 10.60
Community payback order, 12.20–12.34
  breach, court powers, 12.34
Community payback order – *contd*
  implementation and review, 12.33
  introduction of, 10.2, 12.20
  requirements with, 12.22–12.32
Community service order, 10.25–10.28
  breach, 10.27
  community payback order, replacement as, 10.2, 12.20
  nature and procedure, 10.25, 10.26
  report prior to, 10.4
  revocation or amendment, 10.28
  transfer, 10.28
  unpaid work, 10.25, 10.26
Compensation
  breach of legal duty, for, client claiming, 11.6
  community payback order requirement, 12.24
Compensation offer, 10.37
Compensation order, 10.29
  fine with, application of payments, 10.29
  probation order, incompatible with, 10.21, 10.29
Complaints procedure, 1.60, 6.12
  see also Breach of duty; Judicial review
  care services, 11.3, 11.9
  Ombudsman, to, 11.9
  registered social worker, complaint about, 11.2, 11.9
Compulsion order, 10.64
Compulsory supervision order
  change in name to, 12.6
  investigation, changes to law, 12.3
Compulsory treatment order, 8.15–8.19, *see also* Mental health
Conduct
  community payback order, requirement as to, 12.32
Confidentiality, 2.28–2.32
  breach, 2.29
  Code provision, and importance of, 2.28
  data protection, 2.30, 2.31
    child's right to personal information, 3.3

Confidentiality – *contd*
disclosure of information, 2.30–2.32
consent issues, 2.30, 2.31
interdict preventing, 2.29
legal duty, 2.31
public interest, in, 2.29
risk of harm or abuse, 2.31, 2.32
warning, duty, 2.31
guidance on, 2.32
sharing confidential information, 2.29
Consent
care plan and community care services, 6.11
deprivation of liberty, by proxy, 7.20
medical treatment
child, 3.1, 3.2
incapacitated adult, for, 7.14, 7.15, 7.17
protection order, 9.8
Contact, *see* Child
Contract
child entering, 3.2, 3.4
Court order
parental responsibilities and rights, relating to, 3.7
Court system
see also Evidence; Sheriff court; Solicitors
civil, 1.17–1.25
children's hearing, 3.2, 5.2, *see also* Child
Court of Session, 1.19
procedures, 1.21–1.24
sheriff court, 1.18, 1.48
standard of proof, 1.25
Supreme Court, 1.20
criminal, 1.26–1.38
accelerated diets, 1.38
appeals, 1.37
bail, 1.36
hearsay evidence, 1.53
High Court, 1.30, 1.31
Justice of the Peace courts, 1.27
procedures, solemn and summary, 1.26, 1.32–1.34
Court system – *contd*
criminal – *contd*
sheriff courts, 1.28, 1.29
trial, 1.34–1.36
see also Criminal offence; Offender
evidence, *see* EVIDENCE
personnel, 1.11–1.16
Clerks of court, 1.14
judges, 1.13
prosecution, 1.12
Sheriff officers and messengers-at-arms, 1.15
solicitors and advocates, 1.11
Criminal courts, *see* Court system
Criminal injuries compensation, 10.41
Criminal offence
see also Offender
child, by, 3.2, 5.20
local authority accommodation, order for, 5.21
referral of, 5.20
report requirement, 10.7
supervision, *see* Supervision measures for child
child, against (Schedule 1 offences), 5.8, 5.15, 5.37
reference of child to reporter, 5.20
common law, 10.1
compensation for criminal injury, 10.41
mentally disordered offender, 10.63–10.71
insanity, finding of, 10.62, 10.69
prosecution alternatives, 10.35–10.40
compensation offer
fiscal fine, 10.36
sentencing, *see* Sentence
social work involvement, 10.2–10.4
appearance in court, 10.6
child, report on, 10.7
conflict, potential for, 10.3
court-based social workers, 10.3
pre-trial etc reports, 10.4

Criminal offence – *contd*
social work involvement – *contd*
social enquiry reports, 10.3, 10.4, 12.19
supervision, 10.5
statistics, 10.1
Custodial disposal, *see* Prison; Sentence

D

Data protection, *see* Confidentiality
Debt recovery, 2.14–2.19
court for, 2.14
procedure, 2.14
remedies
arrestment, 2.16
arrestment of earnings, 2.17
attachment, 2.15
debt arrangement scheme (DAS), 2.18
social worker role, 2.19
Deferred sentence, 10.30
Deprivation of liberty, *see* Human rights
Detention
see also Prison
child
court order for, 5.21, 10.44
early release of, 10.58, 10.59
deprivation of liberty aspects, *see* Human rights
mental health legislation, under, 8.15–8.22
release, 10.46–10.59
young person sentenced to, report requirement, 10.4
Disability, person with
alterations by tenant/adaptation help, 2.3
child, disabled/affected by disability in family, 4.4, 4.6, 6.2
community care services, 6.4, 6.5
change to, local authority duties, 6.15
discrimination law, *see* Discrimination
legislation for, 1.9
Disability, person with – *contd*
local authority duties to, 4.6, *see also* Community care
person in need, 1.67
service provision, 1.10, 4.4–4.6
Disclosure of information, 2.28–2.32, *see also* Confidentiality
Discretion
application of law in social work, 1.1, 1.10
Discrimination, 2.20–2.27
disabled persons, 2.21, 2.27
more favourable treatment, 2.25
reasonable adjustments duty, 2.23
enforcement of rights, 2.26
direct or indirect, 2.22
justification, 2.25
legislation and implementation bodies, 2.20
local authority elimination duty, 2.27
meaning, 2.22
protected characteristics, 2.21
services provision, 2.24
Diversion schemes, 10.40
Divorce
child(ren), arrangements for, 3.13
financial provision, 3.12
grounds, 3.10
procedure, 3.11
Domestic violence, measures against, 3.32–3.38
'abuse', meaning, 3.38
exclusion order, 3.33–3.35
need for, relevant questions for court, 3.34
unjustified or unreasonable, 3.33, 3.35
harassment, protection from, 3.37
interdict, 3.36–3.38
power of arrest, 3.36
application for attachment of, 3.38
scope, 3.32, 3.36

Drug treatment and testing order, 10.32
community payback order, drug treatment requirement in, 12.30
report prior to, 10.4
Duties
powers compared, 1.10
Duty of care
employer owing to social worker, 11.16
social worker owing, and breach of, *see* Breach of duty

E

Education
18–25 year-old in, 3.2, 3.3
looked after child, 4.17
parents' rights and duties, 2.33
Elderly person, *see also* Vulnerable person
accommodation provision, 6.3
discrimination, 'age' as protected characteristic, 2.21
homes/housing, 1.69, 2.1, 2.8
legislation, 1.71
Emergency protection, 5.22 *et seq*
child protection committees/ register, 5.1
child protection order (CPO), 5.22–5.27
applicant, 5.23
change to law, 12.4
discharge/variation, 5.26
duration, 5.26
effect of/authorisations in, 5.24
grounds, 5.23
implementation, 5.25
lapse, 5.26
notification of reporter, 5.24
'significant' harm, 5.23
subsequent routes, 5.26
complaint about, 11.10
judicial review of authority's decision, 11.13
see also Breach of duty; Complaints procedure
Emergency protection – *contd*
exclusion order, 5.28–5.31
conditions for, 5.29
duration, 5.31
effect, 5.30
guidance, 5.1
legislation, 5.1
mental disorder, emergency detention certificate, 8.16
placement, 4.29, 4.30
home placement, 4.22, 4.23
removal of child on home placement, judicial review case, 11.14
reform under consideration, 5.1
refuge, short-term, 5.32
removal authorisation where no time to apply to sheriff, 5.27
Employer's liability
social worker, for, 11.16
Entry to premises
adult at risk
visit, for, 9.5
warrant, for assessment order, 9.7
Evidence, 1.39–1.56
admissible, 1.41–1.45, 1.49
competent witness, 1.46
confessions, 1.50
corroboration, 1.54
decision on, 1.55
hearsay, 1.42, 1.47–1.53
civil proceedings, 1.48
criminal proceedings, 1.53
rule, 1.47
improperly obtained, 1.43
opinion, 1.45
privilege, protected by, 1.44
relevant, 1.40
Exclusion order, 3.33–3.35
protection of child, for, 5.28–5.31
Exclusions from services, 1.72

F

Family
child to be brought up with, 4.1
home, *see* Occupancy rights
meaning, 4.1

Family – *contd*
placement of looked after child with, 4.22, 4.23
removal of child, judicial review issues, 11.14
Father, *see* Parents
Financial assistance, *see* Payments
Financial guardian, *see* Guardian (incapacity)
Fine, *see* Sentence
Fostering, 4.24–4.27
judicial review, 11.12
notifications duty, 4.31
private, 4.34
Framework, 1.1 *et seq*

G

Gender reassignment
discrimination, protected characteristic, 2.21
Gender recognition certificate, 3.14
General law, 2.1 *et seq*
Getting it Right for Every Child (GIRFEC), 4.1, 4.2, 5.1
core components, 4.2
Guardian, parental appointment, 3.6
Guardian (incapacity), 7.2, 7.7–7.10
see also Incapacity; Mental health
appointment of, 7.7–7.9
application procedure, 7.8
conditions requiring local authority to apply, 7.8
court for, 7.7, 7.8
duration, 7.9, 7.10
notification and hearing, 7.9
requirements to be met, 7.9
attorney's appointment, effect on, 7.6
caution against mismanagement, 7.9
decision enforcement, 7.10
deprivation of liberty, consent to, 7.20
financial, 7.8, 7.9
supervision, 7.10
interim, 7.9

Guardian (incapacity) – *contd*
joint, 7.7
order appointing
action after, 7.10
court power after conviction for offence, 10.67
powers, 7.9
change to, 7.10
consent to medical treatment, 7.14, 7.17
money management, 7.12, 7.13
resignation, 7.10
termination, 7.10
welfare, 7.8, 7.9
supervision, 7.10
views of, regard to, 8.10
Guidance, 2.32, 4.4, 4.15, 5.1, *see also Getting it Right for Every Child* (GIRFEC)
resources and community care provision, 6.8
Working Together to Safeguard Children, 5.23

H

Harassment,
homelessness, and, 2.8
living in accommodation unreasonable because of, 2.6
landlord of tenant, offence, 2.4
local authority elimination duty, 2.27
non-harassment order, 3.37, 10.33
breach, offence, 3.37
services provision, prohibition in, 2.24
Harm
adult at risk of, 9.3, *see also* Adult support and protection
child suffering/likely to suffer
assessment order, 5.7
child protection order, 5.23
exclusion order, 5.29
supervision measures, duty, 5.7, *see also* Supervision measures for child
see also Emergency protection

Health
see also Medical treatment; Mental health
social worker, employer liability issues, 11.16
Hearing
see also Court system
child needing special supervision measures, *see* Supervision measures for child
child, relating to, *see* Child
Home, family, *see* Occupancy rights
Homeless person, 2.5–2.13
Code for, 2.5–2.7
local authority duties, 2.10, 2.11, 2.13
local connection, 2.9
priority need, persons with, 2.8
abolition of category, 2.8
social worker role, 2.12
Hospital
mental disorder treatment
detention in mental health legislation, *see* Mental health
direction for, criminal offender, 10.66
probation order condition, 10.21
Housing, 2.2–2.13
child, accommodation provision for, 3.2, 4.10
remedies against sudden removal, 4.11
right to object, 4.11
eviction and protection from, 2.4
landlords' maintenance and repair duties, 2.3
priority need for, *see* Homeless person
private, 2.3, 2.4
public, 2.3, 2.4
social worker involvement, 2.2–2.4, 2.12
Human rights, 1.65
child, of, 3.3, 5.33–5.36
confidentiality law, effect on, 2.28, 2.32
Human rights – *contd*
degrading treatment or torture prohibition (Art 3), 5.34, 11.10
deprivation of liberty (Art 5), 7.19
consent by proxy, 7.20
review adequacy, 7.21
fair trial (Art 6), 5.35, 11.10
incapacitated adult, considerations, 7.1
infringement
claim for, 11.7
judicial review ground, 11.8
private and family life (Art 8), 5.36, 11.10
infringed by state of housing, 2.2

I

Incapacity, 7.1–7.22
see also Consent
advance statement as to medical treatment, 8.24
attorney, 7.6
consent to deprivation of liberty, 7.20
consent to medical treatment, 7.17
continuing after loss of capacity, 7.6
revocation and termination of power, 7.6
types, 7.6
care plan and services, procedure, 6.11
decision-taking, 7.4, 7.5, *see also* Guardian (incapacity)
deprivation of liberty, 7.19, 7.20
review, 7.21
evidence of, 7.3
financial affairs, attorney for, 7.6
guardian, *see* Guardian (incapacity)
historical overview, 7.1
intervention order, 7.4, 10.67
local authority duties and functions, 7.2, 7.4

Incapacity – *contd*
medical treatment, 7.14–7.17
consent by proxy, 7.14, 7.17
dispute resolution, 7.16
meaning, 7.3
mental disorder, treatment and services, *see* Mental health
mental health officer, *see* Mental health
money, management of
residential establishment, person in, 7.13
withdrawal of funds procedure, 7.12
placement of incapacitated adult, 7.19, 7.20, 7.22
principles for intervention , 7.4
protection order, and, 9.8
services provision, 7.18, *see also* Community care
welfare attorney, 7.6
Information
see also Confidentiality
access and sharing of, 2.28–2.32
adoption records, child's access to, 3.27
document production powers, 9.6
Insanity, finding of, 10.69
protection arrangements, multi agency, 10.62
Inspection
care services, 11.3
social work services, 11.4
Intervention order, 7.4, 10.67
Investigations
see also Assessment; Report; Supervision measures for child
child reporter, by, 5.9
duty, *see* Local authority
vulnerable adults, 7.2, 8.5, 8.13, 9.1, 9.3

J

Judges, 1.13
Judicial review, 11.12–11.15
application, 11.8
child protection cases, 11.13, 11.14
Judicial review – *contd*
drawbacks, 1.59
fostering cases, 11.12
grounds, 11.8
use outside child protection, 11.15
Jury, 1.34

L

Landlord, *see* Housing
Law in society
changes to law, *see* Changes to law
functions of, 1.2–1.7
Legal aid, 1.61–1.64
civil, 1.63
debt recovery, 2.14
criminal, 1.64
guardianship application, for, 7.8
Legal context, 1.1 *et seq*
statutory basis, 1.1, 1.10, 5.1
Legal personnel, *see* Court system; Prosecution; Solicitor
Legal representation of child, *see* Child
Legislation, 1.9, 1.66–1.70
changes affecting social work practice, 1.71
Liability and accountability, 11.6 *et seq*
see also Complaints procedure
breach of duty, for, *see* Breach of duty
conclusion, 11.17
decision challenge, *see* Challenge to decision
employer's liability for social worker, 11.16
judicial review, *see* Judicial review
Liberty
deprivation of, human rights issues, *see* Human rights
restriction of liberty order, 10.31
Local authority
accommodation, *see* Housing; Local authority accommodation; Residential accommodation; Secure accommodation

Local authority – *contd*
adoption
notification to, and report preparation, 3.25
support services, 3.28
adult support and protection, *see* Adult support and protection
challenge to decision of, 1.59
complaints procedure, 1.60
homeless person, 2.11
judicial review, 1.59
community care provision, *see* Community care
discrimination, duties as to
elimination duty, 2.27
equality scheme implementation, 2.27
services provision, no discrimination in, 2.24
guardianship application, when duty arises, 7.8
homeless person, duties to, 2.10, 2.11, 2.13
incapacity, duties in case of, *see* Incapacity
investigations and enquiries, 7.2, 8.5, 8.13, 9.1
duty, law change, 12.3
reporter, as to child needing supervision, 5.9
see also Assessment; Supervision measures for child
legal obligations, 1.10, *see also* specific headings
looked after children, *see* Looked after child
services
children in need, 4.1, 4.3–4.12
discrimination in provision prohibited, 2.24
generally, 4.8
see also Services provision
social workers employed by, 1.1, 1.6, 1.10
statutory basis of, 1.10
Local authority accommodation
order sending child to, 5.21

Looked after child, 4.13–4.20
challenge to local authority decision, 4.46
duties to
after-care, 4.42–4.45
assessment, 4.13, 4.15, 4.44
child's plan, 4.15, 4.16
contact, 4.19
education, 4.17
health care, 4.16
information to be obtained on, 4.15
records, 4.20
regulations and guidance, 4.15
statutory, 4.14
meaning, 4.13
pathway assessment, 4.45
pathway plan, 4.45
placement, 4.21–4.24
emergency, not residential establishment, 4.29
emergency, residential establishment, 4.30
foster care, 4.24–4.27
health care, 4.16
kinship care, 4.23
notifications duty, 4.31
parents, with, 4.22
private fostering, 4.34
records, 4.33
residential care, 4.28
reviews, 4.32
secure accommodation, *see* Secure accommodation
visits, 4.32
respite care, within, 4.18
supervision requirement, duties, 5.16

M

Marriage, 3.8
age, minimum, 3.1, 3.2, 3.8
discrimination, protected characteristic, 2.21
family home, *see* Occupancy rights
irretrievable breakdown, grounds, 3.10

Maternity, *see* Pregnancy
Matrimonial home, *see* Occupancy rights
Means
charge for community care services, and, 6.12
Medical examination
remand for, 10.68
Medical practitioner
mental disorder, responsible medical officer, 8.3, 8.4
Medical treatment
consent or refusal by child, 3.1, 3.2
incapacitated adult, 7.14–7.17
looked after child, 4.16
mental disorder, for, *see* Mental health
Mental health, 8.1 *et seq*
see also Incapacity
accommodation for people with mental disorder, 6.3
assessment order, criminal offender, 10.63
compulsory treatment, 8.4, 8.15 *et seq*
additional authorisations, treatment requiring, 8.24
care plan, 8.17, 8.18
changes to law, 12.18
community payback order requirement, 12.29
detention for, powers, 8.15–8.22
duration of CTO, 8.17, 12.18
examination and assessment, 8.17
emergency detention certificate, 8.16, 8.22
extension of CTO, 8.18, 8.19
interim CTO, 8.17
medical reports, 7.8, 7.9, 8.25, 12.18
medical treatment, 8.9, 8.24
named person, and role, 8.6, 12.18
nurse's power to detain patient in hospital, 8.23
order (CTO) and enforcement of, 8.17–8.22

Mental health – *contd*
compulsory treatment – *contd*
probation order condition, 10.21
revocation, 8.5, 8.19, 8.20, 8.22
services to person subject to/ following, 8.10
short term detention certificate, 8.16, 8.22, 12.18
social circumstances report, circumstances for, 8.25
suspension of detention, 8.22
treatment, scope of, 8.9, 8.24
trigger for, 8.17
consent to care plan and services, incapacitated adult, 6.11
criminal offender, mentally disordered person, *see* Offender
guidance and advice, 8.5
legislation, 1.71, 8.1
incapacity legislation, interaction with, 8.11
local authority duties and powers, 8.12–8.14
detention measures, 8.15
inquiries duty, 8.13
removal order, 8.14
services provision, 8.12
medical examination, remand of offender for, 10.68
medical officer, responsible (RMO), 8.3, 8.4, 8.16 *et seq*
social circumstances report, circumstances for, 8.25
medical treatment, 8.9, 8.24
advance statement as to, 8.24
compulsory, *see above*
'mental disorder', 8.8
mentally disordered offender, *see* Offender
mental health officer, 8.2, 8.12
designation for CTO, 8.18
functions, 7.2, 7.9, 7.10, 8.19
qualification, 8.2
report by, 7.8, 7.9, 8.25
named person, 8.6, 8.9
nearest relative, 8.7

Mental health – *contd*
offender with mental disorder, court powers, 10.63–10.71
place of safety, removal for, 8.14
primary carer, 8.6, 8.9
principles, 8.10
sensitive personal data, 2.30
services provision, 8.10, 8.12
community care services, 8.12
social circumstances report, 8.25
treatment for mental disorder
compulsory, *see* above
order for, criminal offender, 10.63
Mental health officer, *see* Mental health
Mental Health Tribunal, 8.6, 8.10
compulsory treatment order
application for, 8.17
revocation application, 8.16
Mental Welfare Commission, 7.2, 8.5, 9.1
Movement restriction
condition of probation order, 10.21
order, 5.16
Multidisciplinary action
adult protection committees, *see* Adult support and protection
child protection, 5.1
protection arrangements, sex offenders/violent offenders found insane, 10.62
review, 6.11

N

Need, person in, 1.67
community care provision, 6.3
court-based social worker, and, 10.3
Negligence, *see* Breach of duty; Complaints procedure
Non-custodial disposal, 10.9–10.41
Nurse
detention of mental health patient, power, 8.23

O

Occupancy rights, 3.29–3.31
cohabitants, 3.31
spouses
enforcement, 3.29
entitled spouse, of, 3.29
non-entitled spouse losing, 3.29
transfer of tenancy, order for, 3.30
Offender
insanity, finding of, 10.69
management, 10.60–10.62
community justice authorities, powers and duties, 10.60
disclosure of information, 2.31
legislation, 1.71
mentally disordered, 10.63–10.71
assessment and treatment order, 10.63
compulsion order/interim compulsion order, 10.64
guardianship order, 10.67
hospital direction/treatment direction, 10.66
intervention order, 10.67
restriction order, 10.65
supervision and treatment order, 10.70
rehabilitation, 10.72
sex offenders
disclosure pilot scheme, 2.32
notification, 10.61, 10.62
social worker responsibility, 10.2, 10.3
supervision/reports, 1.68
Ombudsman, complaint to, 11.9

P

Parenting order, 5.17
Parents
see also Child; Cohabitation; Divorce; Marriage
accommodation provision for child, objection right, 4.11
decision for child, 3.2–3.4
deprivation of rights, 3.7
education rights and duties, 2.33

Parents – *contd*
father, biological
child's right to support from biological, 3.3
parental responsibilities, position as to, 3.6, 3.8
guardian, appointing, 3.6
legal representative for child, 3.5, 5.13
placement of looked after child with, 4.22
removal of child, judicial review issues, 11.14
responsibilities for child, 3.3, 3.4
court order as to, 3.7, 3.13
parental responsibilities orders, 4.41
rights to enable fulfilment of, 3.5
who holds, 3.6, 3.8
separated, 3.5, 3.16
Pathway assessment, 4.44
Pathway plan, 4.45
Payments
independent Living Fund, 6.10
local authority
child/young person, to or for, 4.12, 4.45, 6.10
community care provision services, for, 6.10, 6.12, 6.14
visits to child etc, community care provisions, 6.3
Permanence order, 3.23
Personal care/support
free, 6.12
Personal injury
time-limit for claim, 11.7
Placement
adoption, *see* Adoption
family, 4.23
fostering, *see* Fostering
looked after child, *see* Looked after child
parents, with, 4.22
removal of child, judicial review issues, 11.14
Plan, child's, 4.8, 4.15, 4.16
Police
adult protection, involvement with, 9.1, 9.3
conditional offer, motoring offence, 10.39
Powers, 1.10
Pregnancy
community care provision, 6.3
discrimination
protected characteristic, 2.21
special treatment justified, 2.25
homelessness, priority need, 2.8
Prison
fine default, on, 10.15, 10.17
release from, 10.46–10.59
changes to law, 12.35
child, early release of, 10.58, 10.59
compassionate release, 10.50
extended sentence, supervision under, 10.56
further offence committed, 10.53
home detention curfew, 10.52
home leave, 10.57
licence, on, 10.51
life prisoner, 10.49
lifelong restriction order, 10.55
long-term prisoner, 10.48
pre-1 Oct 1993 regime, 10.46
short-term prisoner, 10.47
supervised release order, 10.54
sentence, custodial, *see* Prison; Sentence
social worker based in, 10.45
Privilege, 1.44
Probation order, 10.19–10.24
action plan, 10.19
amendment or discharge, 10.22
breach, 10.23, 10.24
community payback order, replacement by, 12.20
conditions, 10.21
non-compliance, 10.23
court power, 10.19
report prior to, 10.4, 10.19
review hearing, 10.19

Probation order – *contd*
social worker role, 10.20
transfer, 10.22
Probation services, 1.1, 1.8
supervision, 10.5
Procurator fiscal, *see* Prosecution
Professional regulation, 11.1 *et seq*
work with vulnerable groups, 11.5
Programme requirement, 12.27
Prosecution
see also Criminal offence
alternatives to, 10.35–10.40
compensation offer, 10.37
conditional offer, motoring offence, 10.39
fiscal fine, 10.36
social work diversion schemes, 10.40
procurator fiscal, 1.12, 10.35–10.40
setting aside penalty or offer, power, 10.38
system, 1.12
Protection of Vulnerable Groups Scheme, 11.5
Protection orders
adult, *see* Adult support and protection
child, emergency, *see* Emergency protection
Public Guardian
guardianship, role in, 7.2, 7.6, 7.11, 7.12
notification of appointment of guardian/register, 7.9, 7.10
supervision of financial guardian, 7.10
withdrawal of funds procedure, 7.12

R

Race discrimination, *see* Discrimination
Records, access to, *see* Confidentiality; Information
Reform of law, see Changes to law
Refuge
child, for, 5.32
Registration
care services, 11.3
professional, 11.2
complaints and removal from, 11.2
Rehabilitation of offenders, 10.72
Relative, *see also* Family; Parents; Spouse
nearest, named person for person with mental disorder, 8.7
Release from prison, *see* Prison
Religion
child's
adoption, relevance to, 3.18, 3.23
looked after child, information on, 4.15
discrimination prohibition, *see* Discrimination
Removal
see also Safety, place of
child, from home, *see* Emergency protection
placement with parents, from, judicial review issues, 11.14
removal order, 9.7
mentally disordered person, relating to, 8.14
Report
adult at risk, bodies with duty as to, 9.1
disclosure and confidentiality aspects, *see* Confidentiality
means enquiry report, 10.12
mental health social circumstances report, 8.25
pre-sentence reports, circumstances and procedure, 10.4
pre-trial etc, 10.4
probation order, prior to, 10.4, 10.19
referral of child at risk, social worker duty on, 5.7
social enquiry, on offender, 10.3, 10.4
circumstances for, 10.4
objectives, 10.4

Report – *contd*
social enquiry, on offender – *contd*
replacement with Criminal Justice Social Work Report, 12.19
Reporter
child protection order, discharge of, 5.26
investigation by, 5.9
notification of emergency protection, 5.26, 5.27
reference of child's case to, 3.7, 3.13, 5.6
child subject to supervision requirements, agency adoption placement, 3.22
parenting order, consideration of, 5.17
person under the age of 17½, advice on, 10.44
who may refer, 5.6
Residence
community payback order requirement, 12.28
probation order condition, 10.21
Residential accommodation
community care legislation, provision under, 6.3
incapacitated adult, for, 7.18–7.21
money management, 7.13
registration of, 1.69
Resources, relevance of, 2.27, 6.8
Restriction order, 10.65
Rights
general or specific, 1.10
Risk
adult at, *see* Adult support and protection
child at, *see* Emergency protection
community care provision, and resources, 6.8
released prisoner, lifelong restriction order, 10.55

S

Safeguarder, *see* Supervision measures for child
Safety, place of
child protection order, under, 5.23, 5.24
circumstances for, general, 5.11, 5.19, 5.27
detained child, 5.21
detention in, after acquittal, 10.71
mentally disordered person, removal order, 8.14
warrant for child, 5.14
Schedule 1 offence, 5.8, 5.15, 5.37
reference of child to reporter, 5.20
Schools
punishment in, 2.33
Scots law
see also Sources of law
distinctive character of, 1.8
Secure accommodation, 4.35–4.40
change to law, 12.10
placement in, supervision requirement, 5.16
Sentence
absolute discharge, 10.9
admonition, 10.10
caution, 10.11
criteria, 10.8
custodial, 10.42–10.45
detention (child), 10.44
detention (young offender), 10.43
imprisonment, 10.42
presumption, change to law, 12.35
social work with person serving, 10.45
deferred, 10.30
extended sentence, supervision under, 10.56
fine, 10.12–10.17
imprisonment sentence alternative, 10.15, 10.17
level of, 10.13
means enquiry report, 10.12
non-payment, 10.12, 10.15, 10.17
supervision order, 10.16
time for payment, 10.14
non-custodial, 10.9–10.41

Sentence – *contd*
objectives, 10.8
pre-sentence reports, 10.4
release, *see* Prison
supervised attendance order, 10.18
replacement of, 12.20
Separation, 3.9
legal consequences, 3.9
separated parents
child support, 3.16
decisions about child, 3.5
Services provision
assessment of need prior to, 6.1, 6.4, 6.5
care plan, 4.8, 4.13, 6.11
challenge to local authority decision, 4.46
child in need, for, 4.1, 4.3–4.12
accommodation provision, 4.10, 4.11
assessment, 4.5, 4.6
assistance from other authority, 4.7
cash or kind, assistance in, 4.12
day care/after school care, 4.9
disabled child/child affected by disability in family, 4.4, 4.6
duty owed to, guidance on, 4.4
meaning, 4.4
relationship with other service provision, 4.8
community care, *see* Community care
discrimination prohibition, 2.24
duty owed by social worker to user, and liability issues, 11.11
GIRFEC, approach under, 4.1, 4.2
core components, 4.2
incapacitated adult, 7.18
judicial review of, 1.59
looked after children, *see* Looked after child
mental disorder, for person with, 8.10, 8.12
Sex offender
disclosure pilot scheme, 2.32
notification, 10.61, 10.62
Sex/sexual orientation
discrimination, protected characteristics for, 2.21
Sheriff court
appeal from, 1.19
civil, 1.18, 1.48
debt recovery, 2.14
eviction proceedings, 2.4
guardian's appointment, 7.7–7.9
suitability decision, 7.9
procurator fiscal, 1.12
proof hearing (children), 1.56, 1.63, 5.15
Sheriff officers and messengers-at-arms, 1.15
solemn, 1.29, 1.33–1.35
summary, 1.27, 1.28
supervision measures hearing, *see* Supervision measures for child
Social Care and Social Work Improvement Scotland, 11.3, 11.4
Social welfare
legal solutions to problems, amenability to, 1.7
promotion of, law as tool for, 1.6
Solicitors, 1.11
child's capacity to instruct, 3.2
Sources of Scots law
Acts of Parliament and delegated legislation, 1.9, 1.66–1.70
changes affecting social work practice, 1.71
English and Welsh law compared, 1.8, 1.9
Spouse
nearest relative for person with mental disorder, 8.7
Supervised attendance order, 10.18
replacement of, 12.20
Supervision
see also Probation order
child, *see* Supervision measures for child
community payback order requirement, 12.23
extended sentence, under, 10.56

Supervision – *contd*
fine supervision order, 10.16
social work department, by, circumstances, 10.5
supervised attendance order, 10.18, 12.20
supervised release order, 10.54
supervision and treatment order, 10.70
Supervision measures for child, 5.6–5.19
appeal rights, 5.19
change to law, 12.16
assessment order, 5.7
changes to law, 12.6–12.16
child in need of, circumstances, 5.8
children's panel, 5.10
compulsory supervision order, name change to, 12.6
investigation duty changes, 12.3
conditions, 5.14
grounds, 5.8
changes to, 12.7
hearing
attendance, 5.11, 12.8
business meeting without child, 5.12, 5.13
changes to law, 12.6–12.16
decision that required, 5.9
legal representation, 5.13
pre-hearing panel, introduction of, 12.9
procedure and outcomes, 5.14, 12.11
views of child, 5.14, 12.13
investigation, 5.1, 5.6
changes to law, 12.3
reporter, by, 5.9
overriding principles, 5.2–5.5. 5.7
parenting order, 5.17
proof hearing, 1.56, 1.63, 5.15
outcomes, 5.15
relevant person, 5.7, 5.8, 5.11 *et seq*
change to law, 12.17
report and reviews, 5.7, 12.12, 12.14

Supervision measures for child – *contd*
reporter, referral to and investigation by, *see* Reporter
review hearing, 5.18
safeguarder
appointment of, 5.13
report, 5.15
Schedule 1 offence, child victim of/in household, 5.8, 5.15, 5.37
reference of child to reporter, 5.20
social work department duties, 5.7
supervision requirement, 5.16
duration and review, 5.18
local authority accommodation order, 5.21
local authority duty and enforcement of, 5.16

T

Tenancy
see also Housing
transfer of, 3.30
Tribunals, 1.58

V

Vicarious liability, 11.16
Victim of crime, 10.73, 10.74
criminal injuries compensation, 10.41
victim notification, 10.74
victim statement, 10.73
Victimisation, *see* Discrimination; Harassment
Views of child, *see* Child
Violence, domestic, *see* Domestic violence
Visits
adult at risk, to, 9.5
Vulnerable person
see also Child; Community care
evidence, 1.56
incapacitated person, *see* Incapacity
legislation for, 1.71

Vulnerable person – *contd*
mental disorder, with, *see* Mental disorder
priority need for housing, 2.8
support and protection for, 9.1 *et seq*
unsuitability to work with, list, 11.5
work with, membership of PVG Scheme requirement, 11.5
'regulated work' and normal duties, 11.5

W

Welfare attorney, 7.6
Welfare benefits, 2.1
Welfare guardian, *see* Guardian (incapacity)
Welfare of child, *see* Child
Welfare, personal
incapacitated adult, *see* Incapacity
Witness, 1.58
see also Evidence
competent, 1.46
vulnerable/child, 1.56
Work, unpaid
community payback order requirement, 12.25
community service order, under, 10.25, 10.26
probation order condition, 10.21
***Working Together to Safeguard Children*,** 5.23

Y

Young offenders institution, 5.21
Young person
detention, 10.43
non-payment of fine, 10.17
report prior to sentence of, 10.4
priority need for housing, 2.8